The New
Guide to

Restaurants in New York City 2004

William Grimes
Eric Asimov

The New York Times
New York, New York

Please send all comments to:

The New York Times Restaurant Guide
122 E. 42nd St., 14th Floor
New York, NY 10168

Published by:
The New York Times
229 W. 43rd St.
New York, NY 10036

ISBN 1-930881-07-X
Printed in the United States of America
First Printing 2003
10 9 8 7 6 5 4 3 2 1

For the New York Times: Susan Chira, Editorial Director, Book
Development; Thomas K. Carley, President, News Services Division;
Nancy Lee, Director of Business Development; Mitchel Levitas, Book
Development.

Prepared by Elizabeth Publishing: *General Editor:* John W. Wright.
Senior Editors: Alice Finer and Alan Joyce. *Editor:* Jerold Kappes.
Researchers: James Garver and Laura Stickney.

Design and Production: G&H SoHo, Hoboken, N.J.; Jim Harris, Gerry
Burstein.

Cover Design: Barbara Chilenskas.

Distributed by St. Martin's Press

Preface

The reviews in this guide are derived, for the most part, from the original ones written by William Grimes and Eric Asimov for *The New York Times*. A number of reviews written by former *Times* reviewer Ruth Reichl remain but many of the most popular restaurants have been updated by Mr. Grimes and Mr. Asimov. All of these are noted. Other reviews by Ms. Reichl have been updated in various sections of the newspaper and on the *Times'* Web site (*www.nytimes.com/dining*). Almost all of the reviews designated "$25 & Under" were written by Mr. Asimov, and several were written by Amanda Hesser or Sam Sifton of the *Times*.

Using This Book

What the Stars Mean:

✩✩✩✩	Extraordinary
✩✩✩	Excellent
✩✩	Very Good
✩	Good

Price Range: The dollar signs that appear at the top of each review are based on the cost of a three-course dinner and a 15 percent tip (but *not* drinks).

$	$25 and under
$$	$25 to $40
$$$	$40 to $55
$$$$	$55 and over

$25 & Under: A restaurant where you can get a complete meal, exclusive of drinks and tip, for $25 or less; recently, as a concession to inflation, some restaurants have been included where only an appetizer and main course total $25.

Abbreviations: Meals: B = Breakfast, Br = Brunch, L = Lunch, D = Dinner. LN = Late Night (restaurants open till midnight or later). **Credit cards**: AE = American Express; DC = Diner's Club; D = Discover; MC = Master Card; V = Visa; "All major" means at least three of these cards are accepted.

Table of Contents

The Best New Restaurants in New York

by William Grimes

A bitterly cold winter and a wet, dismal spring seemed to set the tone for the dining year in New York. The lingering effects of the World Trade Center attacks, combined with a sluggish economy and a dip in tourism, spelled misery for restaurant owners, who scrambled to retool and reinvent in order to keep their customers happy. All over town, chefs worked overtime to simplify their menus and hold down their prices. They discovered the beauty of the bistro-brasserie formula, and the low-budget allure of tapas, a small-bites format that lets diners experience big flavors at a small price.

Guastavino, a palatial two-level restaurant at the base of the Queensboro Bridge, transformed its first floor into an American brasserie and closed its elegant second floor, which is now for private parties only. **The Tonic** transformed itself into **Amuse,** with a menu devoted entirely to appetizer-style dishes. **Bolo,** Bobby Flay's Spanish-inspired restaurant, rewrote its menu to place the spotlight on tapas, an inspired move for a restaurant that had been looking a little tired in recent years. The reworked Bolo now seems as fresh as the day it opened a decade ago.

Smart restaurateurs managed to make a niche for themselves despite the bleak economic picture. Jimmy Bradley, who has won an enormous following at the **Red Cat** and **Harrison,** is no stranger to making the best of a bad situation. Harrison, a stone's throw from the World Trade Center, had been scheduled to open in fall 2001. Events altered those plans. But Harrison, when it did open, prospered despite the long shadow cast by 9/11. This year, Mr. Bradley ventured to the East Village and opened the **Mermaid Inn,** with a low-price fish-shack menu devoted to classic American shore dishes like clam fritters and fried oysters. The wine list, priced at just a few dollars over retail, was calculated to ravish Manhattan's grape-heads.

Tom Collichio, who has already spun off a low-budget alternative to **Craft** in **Craftbar,** went downmarket another notch with the fancifully named **'Wichcraft,** a tiny cafe specializing in sandwiches like anchovy with eggs.

At **Tuscan Steak,** a clamorous Italian food trough in Midtown, Rocco DiSpirito of **Union Pacific** was drafted to revise and simplify a menu that had focused on lobsters the size of attack dogs, yard-long slices of garlic bread and steaks that hung over the side of the plate. A new, much improved restaurant, renamed **Tuscan,** emerged, with an attention-getting list of homey Italian-American dishes that included meatballs made by Mr. DiSpirito's mother.

They immediately became the most celebrated New York dish of the year, although not nearly as celebrated as Mr. DiSpirito's next move, which was to let NBC film the opening of **Rocco's on 22nd** and shape it into a six-part reality soap opera called *The Restaurant*.

Tuscan was not the only surprise turnaround. **Domingo's,** Placido Domingo's less than enthralling Spanish restaurant, had been struggling to find a new identity for several years. Enter Richard Sandoval, the chef and owner of **Maya,** unleashed by Mr. Domingo to work a little magic on 49th Street. Mr. Sandoval obliged, devising a Mexican seafood menu that was impressive for its range and sophistication. It amounted to a tutorial on Mexican flavors, textures and spices, with special emphasis on chiles, from the mild anchos, anaheims and guajillos to the fiery habañero and jalapeños. **Pampano's** new look, with a white-on-white color scheme and rotating palm fans, summoned up images of bright blue water and blazing white sand. You could almost hear the waves breaking outside.

Mario Batali and Joseph Bastianich, the potent team behind **Esca, Babbo** and **Lupa,** also showed they had not lost their touch. Their Village pizzeria, **Otto,** started off the year with a bang, drawing hordes with its shrewdly conceived menu of house-cured meats, little antipasto dishes, and small thin-crust pizza with unusual toppings, notably the signature pizza with thin slices of lardo, or cured salt pork.

Two other eagerly awaited openings also seemed to hark back to the boom years of the late 1990's. Wylie Dufresne, whose **71 Clinton Fresh Food** transformed him overnight into a major culinary star, rang up the curtain on act two of his brief but brilliant career. Located just across the street from his first restaurant, **WD-50** had the food press and the critics in a tizzy months before serving its first meal. Mr. Dufresne is an unpredictable, thoroughly original artist, and daring too, as he proved at WD-50, an amalgam of his initials and the restaurant's address on Clinton Street. He almost disdainfully refused to take the easy route and replicate the elegant, instantly pleasing food that had drawn diners to 71 Clinton. Instead, he challenged even the most adventurous foodies with dishes like a terrine of foie gras layered with anchovies, and a visually stunning dish of oysters pureed and pressed into a flat, thin square that looked like polished marble.

Jean Georges Vongerichten opened **66,** a Chinese restaurant with Shanghai leanings and a twist or two. The restaurant, with a cool, drop-dead elegant interior by Richard Meier, immediately found its way into *Sex and the City*. The waiters, clad in Vivienne Tam, and the designer fish, posing like fashion models in huge tanks just outside the kitchen, made for an environment that thin, beautiful Manhattanites could not resist. The food swung erratically from sheer genius to Chinese take-out, but as a dining environment and a beautifully realized concept, 66 gave a few lessons in how to create a restaurant and make a little news. Even the fortune cookies, in chocolate and green-tea, got people talking.

The owners of **Marseilles,** the stylish theater-district brasserie, extended their reach to the Upper West Side, a neighborhood that cannot seem to get enough French food after decades of deprivation. The restaurant, named after the Riviera's biggest daily newspaper, forced local residents to take a deep breath and try to pronounce pissaladiere and pan bagnat, just two of the specialties dear to the Niçois, and now firmly entrenched on West 79th Street.

The biggest restaurant news of the year was bad. **Lespinasse,** a resplendent four stars under both Gray Kunz and his successor, Christian Delouvrier, closed its doors, a victim of the lean economy and a dwindling tourist base. The idea that a four-star restaurant could fail was hard to absorb. If that was possible, anything could happen. And it did. All over town, restaurants that had received glowing notices suddenly found that could not make a go of it. Some were small, like **Kloe** on West 14th Street.

Others, like **Chicama,** were large and bustling, but not bustling enough. **Pico,** John Villa's romantic Portuguese restaurant in TriBeCa, closed and then reopened in August as **Dominic Restaurant/Social Club**, with a simple Italian-American menu. The restaurant had earned a three-star review from the *Times* and the accolades of every food writer in town. It wasn't enough. **Pazo**, a sharp experimental fusion restaurant, also folded. Matthew Kenney, one of the brighter talents of recent years, continued his slide into Chapter 11, closing down **Commissary** on Third Avenue after closing **Commune** at the end of last year.

As the year wore on, the economy seemed to be sending out faint, hopeful signals. Would the gradually rising tide come in fast enough, though. to float the mammoth project on Columbus Circle, the twin towers of AOL and Time Warner? For restaurant goers, the fate of the two companies, and their soaring new corporate cathedral, had more to do with food than stock price. Plans for the AOL Time Warner Center called for a mall-like retail area with space set aside for some very ambitious restaurants, a kind of vertical food court where the tenants, instead of Wendy's and Sbarro's, would be America's most eminent chefs. Jean Georges Vongertichen planned to open **Prime,** a New York counterpart of his phenomenally successful Las Vegas steakhouse. Thomas Keller was on board to open a branch of the **French Laundry,** perhaps the most venerated restaurant in the United States, and Gray Kunz, at loose ends ever since leaving Lespinasse in 1998, was scheduled to create a brasserie. And Masa Takayama planned a Manhattan version of his brutally expensive Los Angeles sushi restaurant, **Ginza Sushi-Ko.**

Would New Yorkers ride an escalator to eat dinner? Would the building be finished in time to let the chefs make their late-year opening deadlines? And would Columbus Circle, of all places, become New York's newest, most exciting restaurant neighborhood? The city that has bounced back from adversity time and again seemed to be taking on a tall order. But diners were crossing their fingers and getting ready for what promised to be the most exciting series of restaurant openings in years. After a steady diet of somber news, New York has worked up quite an appetite.

Eric Asimov's Inside Tips

Below are lists of restaurants organized by type of food or special feature that well-known food critic, Eric Asimov, has singled out for recommendation to readers of this guide.

WHERE TO GO WITH CHILDREN

Chickenbone Café in Williamsburg, Brooklyn, a quirky little place with a small menu of excellent little sandwiches, bites and salads, plus a homemade ice cream sandwich that children will love. (177 S. 4th St. near Driggs Ave.)

Churrascaria Plataforma in the theater district, an all-you-can-eat Brazilian rodizio, where children will love the ritual of the endless procession of meats. (316 W. 49th St.)

Havana Central, a lively Cuban fantasy where children can gorge on fried yucca, rice and beans, and pork ribs. (22 E. 17th St.)

Otto in Greenwich Village, for excellent griddled pizzas and great gelato in unusual flavors. (1 Fifth Ave. at 8th St.)

Pig Heaven on the Upper East Side, a Cantonese-American restaurant where pork—what else?—is the specialty. (1540 Second Ave. near 80th St.)

P.J. Clarke's, the historic bar on the East Side, where kids can indulge in burgers and fries, and enjoy the not-so-forbidden pleasures of saloon dining. (915 Third Ave. at 55th St.)

REALLY CHEAP PLACES

38th Street Restaurant and Bakery, for barbecued pork, chicken and duck for almost nothing. (273 W. 38th St.)

Charles's Southern-Style Kitchen in Harlem, for an all-you-can-eat buffet with great fried chicken and other top-notch southern specialties. (2841 Frederick Douglass Blvd. near 151st St.)

El Rincón Boricua in East Harlem for great roast suckling pig and other Puerto Rican specialties. (158 East 119th St.)

Krik Krak, a bright little Haitian restaurant on the Upper West Side, for griot limbe, small chunks of mellow pork marinated in garlic, lemon and spices, boiled and then fried until crisp. (844 Amsterdam Ave. near 101st St.)

Mama's Food Shop in the East Village, for excellent homey American dishes like roast chicken and meatloaf, and superb vegetables. (200 E. 3rd St. at Ave. B)

East Buffet and Restaurant in Flushing, a huge Hong Kong-style dining hall that is a little more expensive, but the $20 price buys all you can eat from an enormous selection. (42-07 Main St.)

CHINATOWN RESTAURANTS

Congee, for fresh, vivid food with clear spicing and pure flavors. Highlights include salt-baked squid with cashews and peppers, and deep fried chicken topped with plenty of garlic and chopped scallions. (98 Bowery, between Grand and Hester Sts.)

Funky Broome, on the edge of Chinatown, for excellent razor clams in black bean sauce and unusual dishes like dried beef mixed with rice and shrimp paste. (176 Mott St. at Broome St.)

Great New York Noodletown, for terrific shrimp and pork dishes, and noodles, too, of course. (28 Bowery near Bayard St.)

Ping's, for all manner of Hong Kong-style seafood, like impeccably fresh shrimp, steamed scallops and bean curd stuffed with shrimp paste. (22 Mott St.)

Sunrise 27, a Hong Kong banquet hall, for great sautéed clams with seasonal greens, and a stunningly good whole striped bass, steamed with ginger, soy and rice wine. (27 Division St.)

GRAND CENTRAL TERMINAL FOOD COURT

Nem offers excellent Vietnamese specialties like cool grilled beef salad that sparkles with flavor and well-constructed bahn mi, or Vietnamese hero sandwiches.

Café Spice, for good Indian dishes, from tandoori chicken to vegetarian dosas.

Knodel, for American-style sausages with European veneration, like smoky, spicy andouille or sweet and smoky chicken-and-apple sausage, served on fresh potato rolls with assorted toppings.

Zocalo, for Mexican food and margaritas, which you can get with deli sandwiches and the famous cheesecake at **Junior's.**

EASTERN EUROPEAN FARE

Djerdan Burek, in the Garment District, for "Balkanian" specialties, like bureks, delicious phyllo-encased savory pastries, and excellent stuffed cabbage. (221 W. 38th St.)

Edison Café (known as the Polish Tearoom) near Times Square, for matzo brei, a mixture of eggs, crumbled matzo and butter. It's chewy, rich and utterly satisfying. (Hotel Edison, 228 W. 47th St.)

Lomzynianka in Greenpoint, Brooklyn, for three varieties of borscht, including a dill-scented beet broth with chunks of potato and fat white beans. (646 Manhattan Ave., near Nassau Ave.)

Milan's in Greenwood Heights, Brooklyn, for fabulous goulash, including one variety in which the meat is blended with a rich, creamy sauce and sauerkraut. (710 Fifth Ave. near 22nd St.)

Veselka in the East Village, for thick potato pancakes, classic blintzes and delicious borscht. (144 Second Ave. at 9th St.)

CUBAN

Café con Leche on the Upper West Side, for hearty breakfasts with rice, beans, eggs, roasted pork, and the wonderful namesake coffee with steamed milk. (424 Amsterdam Ave. near 80th St.)

El Sitio, a luncheonette in Woodside, Queens, for the classic Cubano, a sandwich in which each element — cheese, mustard, mayonnaise, pickles, garlic-and-lime and the rich, garlic-imbued roasted pork — is exactly as it should be. (68-28 Roosevelt Ave.)

Havana Chelsea, for wonderful octopus salad and tender shredded pork. (188 Eighth Ave., near 20th St.)

Havana NY in the Garment district, for an excellent grilled skirt steak, beefy and charred crisp around the edges, and more delicate fare, like a fine octopus salad. (27 W. 38th St.)

La Rosita, an old Columbia University hangout, for white bean soup and shrimp creole. (2809 Broadway, near 108th St.)

National Café, a tiny place in the East Village, for terrific roast pork sandwiches and mofungo. (210 First Ave., near 13th St.)

INDIAN

Amma on the East Side, where the precise seasoning and spicing bring some of the old standby dishes alive. (246 E. 51st St.)

Bread Bar near Madison Square Park, for superb bread and larger dishes like gingery, peppery chicken tikka and wonderful lamb and mashed potato sandwiches. (11 Madison Ave. at 25th St.)

Bukhara Grill, for superb northern Indian cooking, with the sort of resonant yet subtle spicing that is all too rare in Indian restaurants, and a great wine list. (230 E. 58th St. and 217 E. 49th St.)

Dakshin, for excellent south Indian dishes like stir-fried chicken with chilies, ginger and garlic. (741 Ninth Ave. at 50th Street, and 1713 First Ave. near 88th St.)

Diwan in midtown, for extraordinary tandoori dishes, fine lamb chops and even venison. (148 East 48th St.)

Mirchi in Greenwich Village, for excellent Indian street foods and specialties like jaipuri lal maas, a spicy yet subtle lamb dish made with 30 red chilies. (29 Seventh Ave. S. near Morton St.)

KOREATOWN

Gam Mee Ok has a tiny menu. The specialty is sul long tang, a milky soup with rice, noodles and beef, made from long-simmered oxtails. (43 W. 32nd St.)

Han Bat, open 24 hours, for excellent pajun, a scallion pancake studded with shrimp and squid, and bindae duk, a savory pancake of ground mung beans with bits of pork. (53 W. 35th St.)

Mandoo Bar, for dumplings, or mandoo, which chefs prepare in the glass-enclosed kitchen up front. Flower-shaped meat-and-cabbage dumplings are especially good. (2 W. 32nd St.)

New York Kom Tang, a cook-it-yourself restaurant, with excellent beef and pork grilled at the table over coals, and especially good soups. (32 W. 32nd St.)

Yang Pyong Seoul, for wonderful soups, especially gom tang, a long-simmered bone marrow broth, and earthy dishes like stir-fried squid and savory mung bean pancakes. (43 W. 33rd St.)

OYSTER BARS

Aquagrill in SoHo, where the selection of oysters is always excellent and you can always order a good Muscadet or Chablis to go with them. Lunch is an especially good deal. (210 Spring Street at Sixth Ave.)

Bongo in Chelsea, which always has a half dozen exquisitely fresh oysters, along with a small menu of other specialties, like a delicious lobster roll. (299 10th Ave., near 28th St.)

Fish in Greenwich Village, a boisterous storefront with a small selection of fine oysters and a good small fish house menu. (280 Bleecker St.)

The Oyster Bar at Grand Central, where the wide selection changes daily. (Grand Central Terminal dining concourse)

Shaffer City Oyster Bar and Grill, a quietly popular restaurant in the Flatiron district, with excellent oysters and an enticing wine list. (5 W. 21st St.)

Svenningsen's, which looks like a Midwestern airport restaurant thrust in near the Empire State Building, for a superb selection of oysters and good crab cakes. (292 Fifth Ave. near 31st St.)

NEIGHBORHOOD SUSHI BARS

Ajisai on the Upper East Side, for a small but superb sushi menu and equally good nonsushi dishes. (1466 First Ave. near 76th St.)

Esashi in the East Village, for a small but exceptionally fresh and beautifully presented sushi selection. (32 Ave. A, near 3rd St.)

Marumi near NYU, for casual Japanese dining, from a superb selection of sushi and sashimi to noodle dishes to one-pot meals to bento-boxes. (546 La Guardia Pl. near W. 3rd St.)

Miyagi in the West Village, for sushi with the cool distant flavor of the ocean, as well as other specialties, like ground salmon, asparagus and mint wrapped in seaweed and expertly deep-fried, then served with a miso dressing. (220 W. 13th St.)

Taka in the West Village, for artistic sushi, like tuna decorated with leaves of edible gold, or squid stuffed with spiced cod roe and shiso, cut into pinwheels and stacked like sculpture. (61 Grove St.)

Tsuki on the Upper East Side, for an extensive list of unusual dishes, like little crabs, fried until they just turn red, and eaten shell and all, and baby eels, slender, white and about an inch long, with the faint impression of an eye at one end. (1410 First Ave. near 75th St.)

The Burger Takes Center Stage

by Ed Levine

New York is a hamburger heaven. All are represented here: the bar burgers, diner burgers, white-tablecloth loaves and fast-food pucks, flame-broiled, pan-seared and roasted. They were on the menu at Delmonico's as early as 1833; at 10 cents a plate, or a shade more than $2 today, a burger was about the best deal in the restaurant. The classic New York burger is encased in American or cheddar cheese, with lettuce and tomato and a few slices of onion on the side. Fries, of course, should be on the plate as well. And to drink? Have a shake, or a chocolate malt. That way you get your beverage and your dessert simultaneously.

Steakhouse Burger

The burger served at **Peter Luger** in Williamsburg, Brooklyn combines fresh-ground chuck with trimmings from dry-aged porterhouse steaks to create a burger of incredible tangy perfection, served only at lunch. $5.95 ($7.95 with cheese and a side of fries). At 178 Broadway (Driggs Avenue); (718) 387-7400.

The burger at **Keens Steakhouse** is a two-fisted wonder, best consumed at the restaurant's beautiful old bar, built in 1884. (It isn't even served in the formal dining room next door.) At 72 West 36th Street; (212) 947-3636.

Restaurant Burger

Bill Telepan, the chef at **Judson Grill**, grinds wet-aged chuck steak and serves the result (at lunchtime and at the bar only) as a 10-ounce burger with homemade bread and butter pickles on a brioche roll. At 152 West 52nd Street; (212) 582-5252.

Daniel Boulud's DB Burger, served at his **DB Bistro Moderne** in Midtown, is a delicious, if expensive, specimen of ground and braised meats, served with wonderful fries. At 55 West 44th Street; (212) 391-2400.

Bar Burger

A burger tastes better when it's eaten in the proper setting. Eating the solid, clean-tasting burger and good fries at **Old Town**, after you've slid into one of the century-old brown wooden booths up front, is a quintessential New York eating experience. At 45 East 18th Street; (212) 529-6732.

At **Donovan's** in Woodside, Queens, a classic Irish pub, the substantial buttery-rich burger is accompanied by the best and sweetest sautéed onions in the city. 57-24 Roosevelt Avenue (at 58th Street), Queens; (718) 429-9339.

Coffee Shop Burger

The $4.50 cheeseburger served at **Prime Burger** is made from four ounces of prime beef, making it both the right size for me and the right price. You must specify that the burger be cooked to order, though. When the restaurant is busy, the staff parbroils the meat. At 5 East 51st Street; (212) 759-4729.

The chairs are profoundly uncomfortable, and it takes forever to get your food, but the burgers at the **Fairway Cafe**, cooked by the idiosyncratic Mitchel London, are great. At 2127 Broadway (74th Street); (212) 595-1888.

Quick Burger

The people behind **Blue 9** are clearly gearing up to create an East Coast rival to California's In-N-Out chain. The freshly grilled thin patties taste beefy enough, and the ratio of meat to bun to toppings is close to the inexpensive burger Platonic ideal. At 92 Third Avenue (12th Street); (212) 979-0053.

The Parker Meridien Hotel is about the most unlikely place to find a decent burger in the city. But tucked away in a corner of the lobby, the **Burger Joint** meticulously char-grills to order a terrific five-ounce hamburger made of freshly ground top sirloin and shoulder. At 119 West 56th Street; (212) 708-7414.

Pizza: The State Of the Slice

by Ed Levine

What's the best way to set New Yorkers to bickering? Ask where to find the best slice of pizza in the city. Pizza, introduced to New York in 1905 by Gennaro Lombardi, has long been the food of choice for peripatetic New Yorkers of every age, sex, race and class. Today, the pizza slice is ubiquitous on New York streets. Slices are cheap, almost always $2 or less. They are convenient, with a pizzeria seemingly on every block. And they are often filling, thanks to the thick blanket of cheese that covers most pizza-by-the-slice. Here are six places that make Neapolitan-style slices worth going out of your way for:

DiFara Pizza, 1424 Avenue J (East 15th Street), Midwood, Brooklyn; (718) 258-1367. Domenico DeMarco uses a blend of mozzarellas, freshly grated grana padana, and a combination of tomatoes to create a supremely flavorful and tangy slice.

Joe & Pat's, 1758 Victory Boulevard (Manor Road), Staten Island; (718) 981-0887. Giuseppe Pappalardo, an owner, makes slices distinguished by a superthin crispy crust.

Joe's Pizza, 233 Bleecker Street (Carmine Street), (212) 366-1182, and 7 Carmine Street (Avenue of the Americas) in the Village, (212) 255-3946. Giuseppi Vitale is a slice purist: his motto is "pride, knowledge and ingredients." The regular slice and fresh mozzarella slice both have superbly crisp crusts.

Louie & Ernie's, 1300 Crosby Avenue (Waterbury Avenue), Bronx; (718) 829-6230. A Louie & Ernie's slice is a diminutive triangle of pizza pleasure in which grated cheese and full-cream mozzarella sparingly cover a thin-enough crust. A word to the wise, however: don't arrive too late. The pizzeria ends its day when all the dough is used up.

Nunzio's, 2155 Hylan Boulevard (Midland Avenue), Staten Island; (718) 667-9647. A slice from Nunzio's is a pristine exercise in elegant pizza minimalism. Everything about it is right: the ratio of sauce to cheese, the crisp yet pliant crust and the tangy sauce enlivened by fresh basil.

Patsy's, 2291 First Avenue (118th Street), East Harlem; (212) 534-9783. Patsy's is the only pizzeria left in a century-old Italian neighborhood that once was a hotbed of pizza activity. The slices are small; they have just enough cheese and the great crust that can come only from a coal-fired brick oven.

Pastrami: An Ageless Pleasure

by Ed Levine

Pastrami is a touchstone of the New York experience, and a comfort to all New Yorkers, at least all those who relish the luscious, fatty pleasures of cured, smoked and steamed beef navel on rye. The number of sources for real pastrami in New York may be small, but the variations in pastrami quality found in the delis that buy from them affirm that how the meat is treated once it arrives at the delicatessen is paramount.

Top Restaurants for Pastrami

Katz's Deli, 205 East Houston Street, at Ludlow Street; (212) 254-2246. The experience of eating Katz's juicy and flavorful pastrami is rivaled only by the ritual of its order and preparation. The counterman will offer you a taste. If the pastrami seems understeamed or a little tough, don't be afraid to ask for another pastrami that has been steaming longer. Sandwich, $10.50.

Ben's Best, 96-40 Queens Boulevard, at 53rd Drive, Rego Park, Queens; (718) 897-1700. Jay Parker, the owner, is a throwback, a man who believes that pastrami is all about taste and texture. His sandwiches provide both, and are fabulous. $8.75.

Second Avenue Deli, 156 Second Avenue, at 10th Street; (212) 677-0606. When asked about the Pastrami at this East Village landmark, Jack Lebewohl, the owner, answers without hesitation. "Empire makes it for me," he says. "I tell them I want it fatty." It's very tasty, and large. $9.95.

Mill Basin Deli, 5823 Avenue T at East 58th Street, Mill Basin, Brooklyn; (718) 241-4910. Made from Hebrew National meat, this pastrami is juicy and tender, but not too assertively spiced or flavored. It's pastrami for a tender tummy. $8.75.

Carnegie Deli, 854 Seventh Avenue, at 55th Street; (212) 757-2245. The Carnegie is the deli New Yorkers love to hate, mostly because they get annoyed by the incessant shtick of the place. But the pastrami can be extremely good, tender and juicy and suffused with flavor. One sandwich is enough for at least four people. $11.95.

Artie's, 2290 Broadway, at 83rd Street; (212) 579-5959. When they have it right, Artie's pastrami is very fine, indeed, lush and dark red with a nice garlicky, coriander-laden spice rub. When it's not right, though, it is pale pink and understeamed. So ask for the most heavily steamed pastrami in the place. $8.25.

The New Cellar Set

by Ed Levine

New York has become awash in neighborhood wine bars, from Williamsburg to Woodside, Queens, and in seemingly every part of Manhattan. Most are humble places that appeal mostly to local crowds more interested in enjoyment than in connoisseurship, people who most likely wouldn't know a Côte de Beaune from a Côtes du Rhône, but nonetheless like to drink wine with food. The wine bars also attract many solo diners, but the allure goes far beyond wine. The typically casual, unpressured, drop-in atmosphere is also a big draw. These are just a few of the wine bars pouring tastes around New York.

The Bar @ Etats-Unis, 247 East 81st Street, (212) 396-9928. Smart global list; restaurant menu available.

Bar Demi, 125 1/2 East 17th Street, near Irving Place, (212) 260-0900. Excellent list with many half bottles.

Bar Veloce, 17 Cleveland Place, near Kenmare Street, (212) 966-7334; 175 Second Avenue, near East 11th Street, (212) 260-3200. Slender, sleek and alluring, with all-Italian list.

Belly, 155 Rivington Street, near Clinton Street, (212) 533-1810. Modest and convivial, with snacks and 14 wines by the glass; not for purists.

D.O.C. Wine Bar, 83 North Seventh Street, Brooklyn, (718) 963-1925. Like a farmhouse, with a lively Sardinian bent.

Enoteca I Trulli, 124 East 27th Street, (212) 481-7372. Small university for Italian wines, excellent Apulian food.

Il Posto Accanto, 190 East Second Street, near Avenue B, (212) 228-3562. Rustic, dim and friendly. Fine Italian wines and simple foods.

Le Bateau Ivre, 230 East 51st Street, (212) 583-0579. Entirely French list, dozens by the glass.

Morrell Wine Bar and Cafe, 1 Rockefeller Plaza (West 49th Street between Fifth Avenue and Avenue of the Americas), (212) 262-7700. An extraordinary list and good food.

Punch & Judy, 26 Clinton Street, (212) 982-1116. Lounge milieu with global wines and small plates of food.

Rhône, 63 Gansevoort Street, near Greenwich Street, (212) 367-8440. Big and loud; all-Rhone list, bar crowd takes over late.

Quick Guide to the Best Restaurants

☆☆☆☆ — **Extraordinary**

Alain Ducasse	Bouley	Daniel
Jean Georges	Le Bernardin	

☆☆☆ — **Excellent**

Aquavit	Gotham Bar and Grill	Next Door Nobu
Atelier	Gramercy Tavern	Nobu
AZ	Honmura An	Oceana
Babbo	Ilo	Olica
Bolo	Jo Jo	Park Bistro
Café Boulud	Judson Grill	Patria
Chanterelle	Kurumazushi	Peter Luger
Craft	La Caravelle	Picholine
Danube	La Côte Basque	RM
Felidia	La Grenouille	Sushi Yasuda
Fiamma Osteria	Le Cirque 2000	Tabla
Fifty Seven Fifty	L'Impero	Town
Seven	March	Union Pacific
The Four Seasons	Montrachet	Veritas

☆☆ — **Very Good**

Ada	Cho Dang Gol	Il Gattopardo
Aix	Churrascaria	Il Valentino
Amuse	Plataforma	I Trulli
Annissa	Circus	Jefferson
Aquagrill	Citarella	Joe's Shanghai
Arqua	City Hall	Kai
Artisanal	Compass	Layla
Aureole	D'Artagnan	Le Colonial
Balthazar	DB Bistro	Le Madri
Bambou	Diwan	Le Perigord
Bayard's	Dumonet at the	Lutèce
Beacon	Carlyle	Manhattan Ocean
Beppe	Eight Mile Creek	Club
Bice	Eleven Madison Park	Marseille
Blue Fin	Esca	Maya
Blue Hill	Estiatorio Milos	Mercer Kitchen
Blue Ribbon Sushi	Etats-Unis	Mesa Grill
Bolo	Firebird	Mi Cocina
Brasserie	Fleur de Sel	Michael Jordan's
Brasserie 360	Fresh	Michael's
Cafe Centro	Gabriel's	Moda
Café Sabarsky	Guastivino's	Molyvos
Capitale	Hangawi	Nadaman Hakubai
Centolire	The Harrison	Nice Matin
Chelsea Bistro & Bar	Heartbeat	Nick & Toni's Cafe
Chez Josephine	Icon	Nicole's

Odeon
Orsay
Otabe
Otto
Ouest
Pampano
Paola's
Park Avenue Cafe
Park View at the
   Boathouse
Payard Patisserie
Petrossian
Ping's
Ping's Seafood
Remi

River Cafe
Ruby Foo's
Salaam Bombay
San Domenico
Screening Room
Sea Grill
71 Clinton Fresh Food
66
Shaan of India
Shun Lee Palace
Smith & Wollensky
Solera
Surya
Sushi Seki
Tamarind

Terrance Brennan's
Tocqueville
Tribeca Grill
Triomphe
Tuscan
"21" Club
Union Square Café
Upstairs at "21"
Wallsé
Washington Park
Water Club
WD-50
Zarela

☆ — Good

Agave
Alfama
American Park
Angelo & Maxie's
Arabelle
Arezzo
Asia de Cuba
Avra
Azafron
Baldoria
Barbalùc
Barrio
The Basil
Ben Benson's
Blue Ribbon Sushi
   (Brooklyn)
Blue Smoke
Blue Water Grill
Bobby Van's
Bouterin
Branzini
Brasserie 8 $^1/_2$
Butter
Calle Ocho
Candela
Coup
Cucina
Dawat
Delmonico's
Dim Sum Go Go
District
Django
Dock's Oyster Bar
Dos Caminos
Downtown
14 Wall Street

Frank's
Goody's
Grand Sichuan
The Grocery
Hacienda de
   Argentina
Ida Mae Kitchen
industry(food)
Jack Rose
Jane
Jarnac
Jean-Luc
La Grolla
Lamu
La Nonna
Lentini
Les Halles
   Downtown
Le Zinc
Lotus
Lozoo
Maloney & Porcelli
Man Ray
MarkJoseph
Meet
Morrells
Nicholson
92
NL
Noche
Novitá
Ocean Grill
Ola
Olives
One If By Land, Two
   If By Sea

Onieal's Grand Street
Osteria del Circo
Parish & Company
Pastis
Patroon
Peasant
Pop
Primavera
Provence
Red Bar Restaurant
The Red Cat
Redeye Grill
Salón Mexico
Scalini Fedeli
Sciuscia
Sparks
Strip House
Suba
Tappo
The Tasting Room
Tavern on the Green
Teodora
36 Bar and Barbecue
Thom
Verbena
Viceversa
Village
Vine
Vox
Voyage
Yujin
Zipangu
Zitoune
Zocalo

Quick Guide to the Best Inexpensive Restaurants

Selected by Eric Asimov

Ajisai
aKa Café
Al Di La
Alias
Anh
Bar Pitti
Bistro St. Mark's
Bread Bar at Tabla
Bukhara Grill
Cabo Rojo
Celeste
Charles's Southern-
    Style Kitchen
Chickenbone Café
Churrascaria Girassol
Congee
Congee Village
Cooke's Corner
Craftbar
Da Andrea
Dakshin
DiFara Pizza
Diner
East Buffet and
    Restaurant
El Rincón Boricua

Ferdinando's
    Focacceria
Funky Broome
Garden Café
Grand Sichuan
    Eastern
Holy Basil
'ino
Kabab King Diner
Katsu-Hama
Katz's Deli
Kori
La Esquina Criolla
La Palapa
Le Zie 2000
Locanda Vini & Olii
Lombardi's
Luca
Lunchbox Food
    Company
Lupa
Mama's Food Shop
Mermaid Inn
Mexicana Mama
Mirchi
Moustache

Nam
National Cafe
Nha Trang
O Mai
Our Place Shanghai
    Tea Garden
Pam Real Thai Food
Pearl Oyster Bar
Pearson's Texas
    Barbecue
Petrosino
Po
Pongal
Prune
Rocking Horse Café
Snack
Soba-Ya
Sripraphai
Supper
Taco Taco
Tournesol
Tsuki
Turkuaz
Vatan
Wu Liang Ye
Yang Pyung Seoul

Restaurants of New York, A to Z

Acquario
$25 & Under — MEDITERRANEAN
5 Bleecker St. (near Bowery)   (212) 260-4666
Credit cards: Cash only   Meals: D   Closed Sun.

With its candles, brick walls and casual service, Acquario is a small, warm place straight out of the Village's bohemian past. The menu starts with salads and flows seamlessly through large appetizers — a couple of which can easily make a light meal — into main courses. Fennel salad is wonderful, though it's hard to find a more alluring dish than Portuguese fish stew.

Other recommended dishes: Boquerones (Spanish anchovies), grilled chipilones (squid), grilled gambas (big shrimp), penne with bacalao (salted cod), warm chocolate cupcake. **Wine list:** Includes some unusual choices and terrific values. **Price range:** Apps., $5–$10; entrees, $12–$18.

Ada   ☆☆ $$$$ INDIAN
208 E. 58th St. (at Second Ave.)   (212) 371-6060
Credit cards: All major   Meals: L, D   Closed Sun.

Ada aims to elevate the status of Indian cuisine in New York. The name, in Urdu, means something done with style or flair, and the owner has definite ideas about what style can do for Indian food. The décor, for one thing, steers clear of Indian fabrics, ornate brass plates and beaded curtains. The food gets an upgrade as well. The results, for the most part, disarm criticism.

Spices are used with great delicacy. Tandoori usually means desiccated, artificially reddened meat. At Ada, the spices and marinades penetrate every fiber of the meats, which arrive in a state of melting tenderness. The syrupy, sour-sweet tamarind sauce makes the ideal foil for chicken suffused with the flavors of saffron, garam masala and chilies. The dessert menu uses a few Indian ingredients strategically, with some success. Coconut panna cotta, covered with ice-wine gelee and tiny apple dice, has a perfect sweet-tart balance.

Wine list: A spare list of 20 wines that have little to do with the food. **Price range:** Lunch: apps., $10; entrees, $16; desserts, $9; three-course prix fixe, $28. Dinner: three-course prix fixe, $55 or $65. **Wheelchair access:** Not accessible.

Aesop's Tables $$ NEW AMERICAN
1233 Bay St., Staten Island   (718) 720-2005
Credit cards: All major   Meals: L, D

From the bountiful garden at this warm little country restaurant, you can actually see stars. The menu features contemporary American items like asparagus, fennel and grapefruit salad, and seared chicken glazed with lingonberries and balsamic vinegar.

Price range: Avg. lunch, $4–$8. Dinner: apps., $4–$9; entrees, $14–$20; desserts, $5. **Wheelchair access:** Fully accessible. **Features:** Outdoor dining.

Agave ☆ $$ SOUTHWESTERN

140 Seventh Ave. S. (near Charles St.) (212) 989-2100
Credit cards: All major Meals: D

The cuisine at Agave is billed as New Southwestern, and it comes in handsome surroundings. The prevailing mood of calm and restraint ends with the menu, which makes eating here an impetuous, slightly mad adventure, a blur of spices, colors and textures. The cuisine at Agave, by design, has a large trash element to it. One of the best things on the menu is a sloppy bowl of three melted cheeses poured over pieces of spicy chorizo. Short ribs are a mountain of rich, tender beef braised in mole colorado. There comes a time when the wisest course of action is to pile on, and the chef understands this. The flops at Agave are unmistakable. Most of the salsas seem tired, as does the ceviche of red snapper. Desserts fall short. A modest Key lime meringue tart turns out to be the winner of the bunch.

Other recommended dishes: Roadhouse chili, corn-crusted calamari, pepita-crusted salmon, snapper in rice-paper skin. **Wine list:** A so-so list of about 40 wines, mostly from California, Australia and New Zealand. **Price range:** Apps., $7–$12; entrees, $14–$23; desserts, $7–$8. **Wheelchair access:** Not accessible.

Aix ☆☆ $$$ FRENCH

2398 Broadway (near 88th St.) (212) 874-7400
Credit cards: All major Meals: D

Aix's chef treats Provence as a repository of images and taste sensations, which he freely reinterprets, sometimes ingeniously, sometimes not. Pistou, one of the triumphs, is a riff on the region's traditional vegetable and pesto soup, with a lightly pressed cake of sardine tartare in the middle. Main courses, like broiled squab and venison, are robust. Aix has the kind of wine list you hope for in a restaurant celebrating the South of France. The dessert menu reflects the avant-garde school of dessert making, whose adherents believe that diners should be challenged, not coddled. The Provence salad, a layering of candied green tomatoes, thin-sliced fennel and melon topped with mint sorbet, really does grow on you, gradually; it's a pastry chef's version of tough love. Aix has a bustling, cheery atmosphere and an interior, with three dining levels, that looks as if it were designed by Piranesi.

Other recommended dishes: Tomato tart, chicken with star anise and honey, chocolate banana tart with banana flan. **Wine list:** An appealing, modestly priced list of about 225 wines emphasizing the Rhone, Provence and the Southwest. **Price range:** Apps., $8–$14; entrees, $22–$29; desserts, $7–$16; five-course tasting menu, $78. **Wheelchair access:** Two steps up to dining room.

Ajisai
$25 & Under   Japanese/Sushi

1466 First Ave. (near 76th St.)   (212) 717-5464
Credit cards: All major   Meals: L, D   Closed Mon.

Ajisai's pleasant dining room, with cross-hatched burgundy walls and comfortable red banquettes, conveys a feeling of warmth and ease. The sushi and sashimi selection is not extensive, but the quality is superb. Amaebi, or sweet shrimp, have a sweet flavor and a soft, gelatinous texture. Buttery chutoro tuna, not as rich as the fatty toro, still melts in the mouth. As a finale, if it's available, the sea urchin is wonderful, soft and custardlike with a lingering flavor that tastes like the musky sea.

Ajisai is the rare Japanese restaurant that serves equally good non-sushi dishes. Chunks of tofu in a light broth have a nutty, almost pretzel-like flavor. Butakakuni, or stewed pork belly, is soft and tender enough to cut with chopsticks, and absolutely delicious.

Price range: Apps., $3.75–$9.50; entrees, $14–$20; sushi and sashimi dinners, $12–$27. **Wheelchair access:** Not accessible.

aKa Café
$25 & Under   Fusion

49 Clinton St. (near Rivington St.)   (212) 979-6096
Credit cards: All major   Meals: Br, L, D

A storefront offshoot of 71 Clinton Fresh Food on the Lower East Side, aKa Café offers food that takes the familiar downtown sandwich-and-wine bar into a stratosphere of unexpected flavor combinations. The signature lamb tongue sandwich is the oddest offering, but it's one of the most successful, a balance of savory, sweet and rich on spongy Italian bread.

The cafe, which seats about 30, could easily be as much about drinking as eating. The back-lighted bar is the central feature of an otherwise minimally decorated room. Yet the menu grabs the attention right away.

Other recommended dishes: Ceviche, soups, hanger steak sandwich. **Price range:** Everything is $7–$13. **Wheelchair access:** One level.

Alain Ducasse at the Essex House
☆☆☆☆   **$$$$**   French

155 W. 58th St. (bet. Sixth & Seventh Aves.)   (212) 265-7300
Credit cards: All major   Meals: L (Thu. & Fri.), D   Closed Sun.

When it opened a few years ago, Alain Ducasse at the Essex House was set out to ravish. It was more expensive, more sumptuous, more ritualized — more everything — than any other restaurant in Manhattan. Ducasse would be the restaurant that made the others also-rans.

It did not work out that way at first. As the city's attention drifted, Alain Ducasse and his rock-steady chef de cuisine, Didier Elena, got down to work. The payoff is evident every night at the Essex House, where Mr. Ducasse now offers, with much less fanfare, the kind of food that brings diners to their knees. Mr. Ducasse, a chef in the classic French tradition, promised New York a great restaurant. Now he has delivered it.

The kinks have been worked out of the service, which now has a polish and grace befitting the jewel box of a dining room. The easier, happier atmosphere emanates, ultimately, from the kitchen. Mr. Ducasse has always sworn allegiance to the philosophy that ingredients should rule the kitchen and his menu abounds in simple classic preparations.

Wine list: An inventive, adventurous list of 150 wines that changes monthly, supplemented by a very expensive reserve list, mostly French wines from major houses, but also Spanish, Italian and Portuguese wines. **Price range:** Lunch: two-course "menu salad," $65; three-course prix fixe, $145; four-course prix fixe, $160. Dinner: three-course prix fixe, $145; four-course prix fixe and five-course seasonal tasting menu, $160; six-course truffle menu, $300. **Wheelchair access:** Enter on Central Park South.

Al Di La $25 & Under ITALIAN

248 Fifth Ave. (at Carroll St.), Park Slope, Brooklyn (718) 783-4555
Credit cards: Cash only   Meals: D   Closed Tue.

The food at Al Di La is soulful and gutsy, with profound flavors. This neighborhood restaurant serves on bare wooden tables, but hints at a more sensual attitude with such luxurious touches as velvet drapes and chandeliers. The chef coaxes deep flavors out of simple dishes, and all the pastas are wonderful.

Recommended dishes: Braised rabbit with olives, steamed pork shoulder, sautéed liver, grilled hanger steak, casunziei ravioli, bigoli in salsa, malfatti, tagliatelle with meat sauce, apple crisp, poached pear. **Price range:** Apps., $6–$8; entrees, $8–$16. **Wheelchair access:** Small step in front; narrow entrance to restroom.

Alfama ☆ $$$ PORTUGUESE

551 Hudson St. (near Perry St.)   (212) 645-2500
Credit cards: All major   Meals: L, D

The food at Alfama, a warm and inviting little Portuguese restaurant in the West Village, can be robust and blunt, but it can also reach a level of elegance that nonetheless manages to retain the forceful flavors that are so characteristic of Portuguese cuisine. The sautéed fresh cod with broa, the Portuguese corn-and-wheat bread, is lively and delicious. Prawns with a lemon-shellfish bread pudding is another superb dish. The selection of more than 100 Portuguese wines may be the best in the city. Desserts are a high point, particularly the disco voador, a wonderful sweet tart of ground walnuts and almonds. *(Eric Asimov)*

Other recommended dishes: Octopus carpaccio, steamed clams with chorizo, sautéed pork with clams and potatoes, filet mignon with chorizo and garlic sauce, mango mousse, crème brûlée. **Wine list:** Long and almost entirely Portuguese. **Price range:** Apps., $5–$15; entrees, $16–$25; desserts, $5–$8; prix fixe regional menu, $45. **Wheelchair access:** Small ramp at entrance; hallway and entrance to restrooms are narrow.

The Algonquin $$$ AMERICAN
59 W. 44th St. (bet. Fifth & Sixth Aves.)   (212) 840-6800
Credit cards: All major   Meals: B, Br, L, D, LN

The lobby and restaurant of the famous hotel were redecorated a few years back to the tune of several million dollars. Even so, the ghost of Dorothy Parker will probably not take up residence. Now a lobby more than a restaurant, it offers modern dishes like grilled shrimp in a roasted garlic salsa, as well as hamburgers, lobster hash and Caesar salad. As long as you're not looking for a real meal, it's fine for a nibble before or after the theater.

Price range: Apps., $11–$16; entrees, $18–$29; desserts, $9.
Wheelchair access: Fully accessible.

Alias $25 & Under   NEW AMERICAN
76 Clinton St. (at Rivington St.)   (212) 505-5011
Credit cards: All major   Meals: D   Closed Sun.

Alias serves conventional appetizer-main course meals but in jaunty bistro style. The small, boxy dining room shows a clean, modern design. Tables are close together but it's comfortable unless you are stuck in the low-ceilinged alcove near the restroom, which is loud and claustrophobic. The menu is small and predictably eccentric, but you'll love the silken-textured, melt-in-your-mouth house-cured sable. As with the other restaurants, the inventive wine list offers many choices by the glass. The bottle values here are in the $30 to $40 range.

Price range: Apps., $5–$9; entrees, $15–$18. **Wheelchair access:** Not accessible.

Alice's Tea Cup $25 & Under   AMERICAN
102 W. 73rd St. (near Columbus Ave.)   (212) 799-3006
Credit cards: All Major   Meals: Br, L, D   Closed Mon.

Just as steakhouses are largely masculine domains, tearooms like Alice's Tea Cup are perceived as feminine, full of lacy trappings and curlicues. Lunch one day included a triple-tiered tray of two sandwiches, two scones, cake and cookies ($25 with tea). There's is fine smoked chicken breast sandwich, served with juicy apple slices and goat cheese, or the loosely knit egg salad with tea-infused mayonnaise. Salads are generous, like Belgian endive with pear, Stilton, watercress and caramelized onions.

Price range: Afternoon tea, $20–$30; soups, salads and sandwiches, $5–$13. **Wheelchair access:** Steps to entrance.

Alma $25 & Under   MEXICAN
187 Columbia St., Carroll Gardens, Brooklyn   (718) 643-5400
Credit cards: All major   Meals: D

From Alma, Lower Manhattan appears like a stage backdrop. It is there for your pleasure, to take in during lulls in the meal, nothing more, it seems, than a facade. This is because it is difficult to grasp how such a good restaurant could be in such an odd place, amid a strip that includes a shipyard, car lots and a live poultry market on the edge of Carroll Gardens in Brooklyn.

There is nothing on the menu you shouldn't order. The cooking is thoughtful and precise, with distinctive splashes of spice and heat and brilliant sauces. Chicken with mole is a beautiful dish. Key lime pie is made with a fine, crumbly graham cracker crust filled with an herbal lime curd. Take in the spectacular view and, when you get the bill, feel superior to everyone at the River Café. (*Amanda Hesser*)

Other recommended dishes: Tamales del dia, chilaquiles ranchero, ancho relleno, arroz con queso, coconut cheesecake. **Price range:** Apps., $5–$8; entrees, $10–$18. **Wheelchair access:** Not accessible.

Alouette $25 & Under BISTRO/FRENCH
2588 Broadway (near 97th St.) (212) 222-6808
Credit cards: All major Meals: Br, D

Early crowds seemed to overwhelm the kitchen, but Alouette seems to have gotten both the food and the quality of service under control. Dishes are cleverly conceived, beautifully presented and moderately priced; each item promises excitement. Service has its ups and downs, and the second-floor dining room is warm and stuffy.

Recommended dishes: Roasted flounder, seafood pot-au-feu, hanger steak, vacherin (vanilla ice cream sandwiched between airy meringues). **Price range:** Apps., $6–$8; entrees, $15–$19. **Wheelchair access:** Two steps in front; restrooms are narrow.

Amarone $25 & Under ITALIAN
686 Ninth Ave. (near 47th St.) (212) 245-6060
Credit cards: All major Meals: L, D

The rectangular dining room at this friendly restaurant, named after the powerful red wine from northeastern Italy, is bright and happy, suffused with the appetizing aromas of bread, herbs and olive oil. The centerpiece of the menu is a selection of fresh pastas with an ever-changing choice of sauces like strangolapreti ("priest stranglers"), fluffy twists of pasta served in a marinara sauce given a pleasantly bitter kick by broccoli rabe.

Other recommended dishes: Pappardelle with shiitake mushrooms; agnolotti stuffed with veal, beef and Parmesan; broiled calamari; apple tart; hazelnut gelato. **Wine list:** Includes a dozen Amarones, mostly from excellent producers, but the list as a whole is too expensive. **Price range:** Apps., $5–$9; entrees, $8–$20. **Wheelchair access:** Step up at entrance. **Features:** Outdoor dining.

American Park ☆ $$$ NEW AMERICAN
Battery Park (near State St.) (212) 809-5508
Credit cards: All major Meals: Br, L, D

This restaurant may offer Manhattan's most spectacular view: from the big-windowed room you look right out at the ferries chugging toward the Statue of Liberty. The mostly seafood menu is inventive and beautifully presented. The restaurant is so earnest and hard-working that you really want to admire it. So why is it so hard to appreciate? It is mainly a matter of excess. The chef seldom uses a single ingredient when he can use two. Black sea bass, simply roasted in the wood-burning oven and topped with cracked coriander, red onions and capers, is almost always excellent. At the end of the meal, the impulse to excess suddenly becomes an asset: the pastry chef has terrific fun turning chocolate mousse cake into the Statue of Liberty, scooping green tea ice cream onto coconut cake and serving a plum tart with white peaches and a perfectly restrained basil ice cream.

Wine list: Large, interesting, all-American and oddly chosen for the food. **Price range:** Apps., $9–$17; entrees, $18–$32; desserts, $8. Outdoor grill salads, sandwiches and snacks, $7–$11. **Wheelchair access:** Everything at ground level. **Features:** Good view, outdoor dining (patio).

Amuse ☆☆ $$ NEW AMERICAN
108 W.18th St. (near Sixth Ave.) (212) 929-9755
Credit cards: All major   Meals: L, D, LN   Closed Sun.

Generally, it's not a good sign when a restaurant starts fiddling and fussing with its format. But Amuse, formerly the Tonic, somehow beats the odds. Amuse is short for amuse-bouche, the French term for the bite-size preappetizers intended to titillate the palate. Here the entire menu is designed around small tastes, doing away with the appetizer-entree dichotomy. There are a half dozen choices in four price categories, $5, $10, $15, and $20. With each increase in price, the preparations become more complex. Cheap can be good, like the golden puff-pastry gougères, filled with melted Gruyère and tiny nuggets of smoked ham. At the $10 level, slivers of piquillo pepper and spicy ginger cracklings give citrus-marinated fluke the complexity and interest of an entree. Lacquered squab, a $15 dish, seems more like a superappetizer than an entree, with one succulent, brick-red squab surrounded by curried couscous. Butter-poached lobster, at $20, seems in its own way rather modest, despite the deluxe main ingredient. The desserts, all $5, come through with distinction.

Other recommended dishes: Mushroom velouté with peanut sabayon, cod cakes, vanilla crème brûlée, chocolate napoleon. **Wine list:** A fairly conservative international list of about 80 wines. **Price range:** Dishes in four categories: $5, $10, $15 and $20; desserts, $5. Tasting menus, $35, $45 and $55. **Wheelchair access:** Restrooms are on dining level.

Amy Ruth's $25 & Under SOUTHERN
113 W. 116th St. (bet. Lenox & Seventh Aves.) (212) 280-8779
Credit cards: All major   Meals: B, L, D

Amy Ruth's succeeds in presenting Southern food that manages to be up-to-date without sacrificing time-honored traditions. The waffles are wonderful, crisp yet fluffy. The real stars of the menu include short ribs that are falling-off-the-bone tender, deliciously spicy shrimp and baked spareribs served in a sweet barbecue sauce. Each main course comes with two side dishes, and many of Amy Ruth's shine, like buttery string beans served almost al dente. Pineapple-coconut cake is big and terrific.

Other recommended dishes: Salmon croquettes, smothered pork chops, black-eyed peas, collard greens, peach cobbler, sweet-potato pie. **Price range:** Breakfast, $4–$10; lunch and dinner, $8–$18. **Wheelchair access:** All one level.

Anh $25 & Under   VIETNAMESE
363 Third Ave. (near 27th St.)   (212) 532-2858
Credit Cards: All major   Meals: L, D

Few cuisines can match the light, refreshing qualities of Vietnamese with its blend of raw and cooked, fresh herbs and piquant dipping sauces. The dining room at Anh is dim and stylish. One wall of fieldstones and polished wooden louvers looks as if it came from a Frank Lloyd Wright catalog.

Many of the dishes on the menu may seem familiar. Yet the kitchen renders them expertly, capturing the cuisine's low-key delicacy with just the right light touch. One of the best things about Vietnamese food is the custom of wrapping small snacks in a lettuce leaf and dipping it in nuoc cham, a sweet and tangy sauce. This method especially enhanced banh xeo, a crepe made with coconut and rice flour and stuffed with chicken, shrimp and bean sprouts. Main courses exhibit a winning subtlety.

Other recommended dishes: Grilled Asian eggplant, green papaya salad, wok-seared swordfish with sesame rice crackers, spring rolls, grilled beef in sesame leaves, sautéed marinated duck, lemongrass chicken, steamed sea bass, crisp red snapper, pork chop with rice noodles. **Price range:** Apps., $4–7; entrees, $7–$14. **Wheelchair access:** All one level.

Angelo & Maxie's   ☆ $$ STEAKHOUSE
233 Park Ave. S. (at 19th St.)   (212) 220-9200
Credit cards: All major   Meals: L, D

Angelo & Maxie's celebrates a long-gone America where people smoked and drank and ate huge hunks of red meat. Order a salad and a whole garden of greens appears in a big wooden bowl. Meat comes big and bigger. Cocktails are served in glasses that could double as hummingbird baths. The porterhouse steak for two is the best of the beef, but Peter Luger certainly has no cause for concern. *(Ruth Reichl)*

Wine list: The selection is excellent, the prices are reasonable, and if you want to splurge on a great Bordeaux, this is the place to do it. **Price range:** Apps., $5–$13; entrees, $10–$21; desserts, $4–$6. **Wheelchair access:** Fully accessible.

Annisa   ☆☆ $$$ NEW AMERICAN
13 Barrow St. (bet. W. 4th St. & Seventh Ave.)   (212) 741-6699
Credit cards: All major   Meals: D

Annisa is a restaurant with a small room, a small staff and a small menu. But with disarming ease, it manages to make a big impression. Annisa, whose name means "women" in Arabic, is a two-woman show. Anita Lo turns out the food; her partner, Jennifer Scism, runs the front of the house. Both of them seem to be very clear-eyed about the kind of restaurant they want, a place with clean lines, a welcoming, inclusive atmosphere and a quietly persuasive menu, filled with arresting ingredient and flavor combinations.

Ms. Lo reaches far and wide for ideas and influences, without strain. Throughout, her cooking is defined by good taste and good judgment. Fish is infallible at Annisa. For dessert, there's no resisting the attractive fluted carrot cake. The apple tart, surrounded by a sticky pool of caramel sauce, ranks very high, a beautifully executed classic with a textbook crust and ideally tart apples.

Wine list: An eclectic list of about 100 wines. About a third are under $40, and 20 are sold by the glass. **Price range:** Apps., $8–$16; entrees, $23–$29; desserts, $8. **Wheelchair access:** Steps to entrance; restrooms not accessible.

A.O.C. Bedford $$ SPANISH
14 Bedford St. (near Downing St.)   (212) 414-4764
Credit cards: All major   Meals: D

Restaurants like A.O.C. Bedford have defined Greenwich Village for generations. It's a tiny place with heavy beams and a few tables and chairs. In warm weather the floor-to-ceiling windows open onto the sidewalk. A.O.C. refers to a government label applied to certain products, especially wine, that meet strict standards governing where and how they are made. It's a roundabout way of emphasizing the restaurant's commitment to good raw ingredients on its mostly Spanish menu. The zeal for authentic ingredients runs even to dry red pepper from Spain, the seasoning for a carpaccio of octopus dressed with olive oil and fleur de sel. The big production numbers on the very simple, straightforward menu are the paella for two, a faithful rendition, and a slow-cooked leg of suckling pig with Bosc pear and braised endive. A.O.C is quirky, which means it fits the neighborhood like glove.

Price range: Apps., $6–$11; entrees, $14–$29; desserts, $8. **Wheelchair access:** One step up to restaurant.

Aquagrill   ☆☆ $$$ SEAFOOD
210 Spring St. (at Sixth Ave.)   (212) 274-0505
Credit cards: All major   Meals: Br, L, D   Closed Mon.

Aquagrill has the comfortable air of a neighborhood place, the sort of restaurant that ought to be serving burgers and beer. Instead there's an oyster bar in front and the menu is refreshingly original. Devoted almost entirely to fish, it offers unusual dishes like "snail-snaps" (bite-size popovers holding a single snail) and salmon in falafel crust. All the fish is well prepared and some with imagination. Yellow potato hash is, deservedly, a beloved signature dish. Desserts are homey and occasionally too sweet, but save room for the apple tart with cinnamon ice cream and caramel sauce.

A recent visit suggests strongly, however, that Aquagrill is slipping. Service is indifferent, the cooking pallid, and the dining room cramped and noisy. The oyster list still impresses, but this very popular restaurant is riding on its reputation.

Wine list: Excellent, out-of-the-ordinary wines at reasonable prices. **Price range:** Lunch: prix fixe "shucker special," $15. Dinner: apps., $9–$15; entrees, $19–$26; desserts, $6–$10. **Wheelchair access:** One step into dining room; restrooms not accessible.

Aquavit ☆ ☆ ☆ $$$$ SWEDISH

13 W. 54th St. (bet. Fifth & Sixth Aves.) (212) 307-7311
Credit cards: All major Meals: Br, L, D

Aquavit serves inventive Swedish-inspired cuisine in a former town house divided into a ground-floor cafe and a two-part downstairs dining room decorated with contemporary Swedish art. Marcus Samuelsson, Aquavit's restlessly inventive executive chef, is a fully mature artist with a distinctive style, the culinary version of counterpoint, in which precisely defined flavors talk back and forth to each other rather than blending into a single smooth harmonic effect. He keeps your palate on edge.

The menu sparkles with bright thoughts. Aquavit's herring plate, served with an icy shot of aquavit and a Carlsberg beer, amounts to a dazzling showcase for the national fish. If the food is Swedish, it often looks Japanese. Mr. Samuelsson likes big plates, spare arrangements and bright colors. His pièce de résistance is his pellucid arctic char, pinkish orange and delicately smoked.

For dessert, cheesecake here looks like no other cheesecake on earth. It comes in three taco-like pastry shells arranged like a fan and surrounded by a mint syrup and cracked black pepper.

Wine list: A solid international list of about 250 wines, with 15 wines by the glass and a large selection of aquavits, many of them flavored at the restaurant. **Price range:** Lunch: apps., $9–$14; entrees, $24–$26; desserts, $8; five-course tasting menu, $48 ($73 with wines); three-course prix fixe, $30; four-course vegetarian menu, $35. Dinner: three-course pre-theater menu, served from 5:30 to 6:15 P.M., $39; three-course prix fixe, $69; seven-course tasting menu, $90 ($115 with wine); seven-course vegetarian menu, $58 ($93 with wine); 16-course "bite" menu, $110 ($170 with wines). **Wheelchair access:** Steps to the cafe; flight down to the dining room and restrooms.

Arabelle ☆ $$$$ FRENCH

Hôtel Plaza Athénée, 37 E. 64th St. (bet. Madison & Park Aves.)
(212) 606-4647
Credit cards: All major Meals: B, L, D

Arabelle has a subtly luxurious feel, with pale pink wall panels, wispy gold curtains and a gold-domed ceiling. The moodily lighted lounge and bar just outside the restaurant's entrance should be on everyone's list of romantic meeting spots. The food is another matter, proving that the restaurant world, too, has its fashion victims. There's a little too much of everything here. As a result, ingredients often wage war on one another, or sit superfluously on the plate, awaiting instructions. There are wonderful appetizers, however.

Among the desserts, the cheesecake is closer to a sideways napoleon, with paper-thin rounds of roasted pineapple sandwiching dollops of cheese filling that brilliantly evokes Philadelphia cream cheese. This is a compliment.

Price range: Apps., $11–$19; entrees, $27–$39; desserts, $13.
Wheelchair access: Entrance with ramp; small step into lounge.

Arezzo ☆ $$$ ITALIAN

46 W. 22nd St. (bet. Fifth & Sixth Aves.)   (212) 206-0555
Credit cards: All major   Meals: L, D   Closed Sun.

Arrezo, a modest low-ceilinged dining room with a coal-burning oven, is the setting for Tuscan and Piedmontese cuisine, with some modernizing. The oven, source of the more traditional dishes, produces what may be the best appetizer on the menu, focaccina split in half and spread with a mixture of robiola cheese, potato and spinach, then drizzled with truffle oil.

The pastas are good, not great. Pea-flavored cavatelli with a sauce of hot and sweet sausages is one of the best. The pastry chef, outdoes himself with a very dense, intensely flavored bitter-chocolate panna cotta.

Wine list: An adventurous list of 65 wines covering all Italy, with 10 wines by the glass and five half bottles. **Price range:** Lunch: apps., $7–$12; entrees, $14–$22. Dinner: apps., $9–$18; entrees, $17–$35; desserts, $8.50. **Wheelchair access:** Step at entrance.

Arharn Thai $25 & Under THAI

32-05 36th Ave., Astoria, Queens   (718) 728-5563
Credit cards: All major   Meals: L, D

Thai cooking depends above all on maintaining a subtle interplay between hot, sour, sweet and salty flavors, and this balancing act is almost always played out in the salads, or yums. At this small and nondescript neighborhood place near the border of Astoria and Long Island City, the salads offer a wonderful and largely accurate sign of things to come. Yum woonsen, for example, is a salad of chewy glass noodles, and tossed with red onions and ground pork. Lime juice adds sweet and sour elements, while chili produces a heat that builds in the mouth, stopping just short of searing, and nam pla, the Thai fermented fish sauce, adds a salty pungency.

Main courses follow through on the promise of the salads. Crisp duck is savory and delicious, bathed in a spicy red curry sauce. Moo ka prow, sautéed pork with basil leaves and chili is especially good. As in many of Arharn's dishes, the chili heat is gripping.

Other recommended dishes: Fried whole fish with red chili sauce, chicken with masaman curry, pad thai, banana steamed in coconut milk. **Price range:** Apps., $4–$8; entrees, $7–$16. **Wheelchair access:** Entrances to restrooms are narrow.

Arqua ☆☆ $$$ ITALIAN

281 Church St. (at White St.)   (212) 334-1888
Credit cards: All major   Meals: L, D

The setting of this restaurant named for Arqua Petrarca, a village in northern Italy, is alluring, but the noise can be deafening when all the chairs are occupied at night. Lunch is a more tranquil time, and the rustic fare is unfailingly good. Main dishes include pan-seared tuna loin with ginger sauce; duck breast with a sauce of black currant and cassis, and braised rabbit with white wine and herbs.

Price range: Apps., $8–$10; entrees, $16–$22; desserts, $8. Prix–fixe lunch, $20; prix–fixe dinner, $25. **Wheelchair access:** Not accessible.

Artie's New York Delicatessen

$25 & Under   DELI

2290 Broadway (bet. 82nd & 83rd Sts.)   (212) 579-5959
Credit cards: All major   Meals: L, D

Artie's may not be ready to take its place among the deli elite, but it shows promise. And it already makes a fine egg cream. Artie's pastrami has potential, and the hot dogs are excellent. Potato pancakes are exceptionally crisp, with a solid center trailing crunchy slivers of potato. The dining room is bright and functional, and it's clear that Artie's has also been working on the deli atmosphere.

Other recommended dishes: Chicken soup, flanken in a pot. **Price range:** Sandwiches, $5–$11; entrees, $8–$18. **Wheelchair access:** All one level.

Artisanal ☆☆ $$$ BISTRO

2 Park Ave. (at 32nd St.)   (212) 725-8585
Credit cards: All major   Meals: L, D, LN

Artisanal is a big, very good-looking brasserie with more varieties of cheese than most human beings will encounter in a lifetime. It is an easy restaurant to like. The interior, designed by Adam Tihany, is bold, cheery and inviting, with lots of banquettes and a retail cheese counter with a tilted overhead mirror that lets everyone in the room admire the merchandise. Fondue can be ordered in a small pot or a big one, filled with plain Swiss or combinations like cheddar-bacon.

About half the menu at Artisanal is honest bistro cooking. The frites are just fine, the steaks respectable. The other half shows some genuinely inspired flashes like rabbit in riesling sauce. A half chicken pressed under a brick comes out crisp and moist. After the entrees comes the moment of truth. You will have cheese. That's not open to debate. Of the nearly 200 cheeses the restaurant handles, about 80 are ripe at one particular moment.

Wine list: A very good, modestly priced international list of about 140 wines, all available by the glass. **Price range:** Lunch entrees, $13.50–$38. Dinner: apps., $6.50–$18.50; entrees, $17.50–$38; desserts, $6–$10. **Wheelchair access:** One level.

Asia de Cuba ☆ $$$ ASIAN/LATIN AMERICAN

237 Madison Ave. (near 37th St.)   (212) 726-7755
Credit cards: All major   Meals: L, D, LN

You won't eat very well at Asia de Cuba. But you will have so much fun being there that you may not notice. The manic energy of the place makes every night feel like a party. Try sitting at the long communal table (if you can get a reservation). The most successful invention is the oxtail spring roll, a wonderful combination of rich, fatty meat with crisp pastry and forceful flavors. But who can think about all that when desserts are exploding all over the room? Guava Dynamite is the life of this party; it is just guava mousse wrapped in a chocolate tuile, but the sparkler on top is seductive.

Wine list: Pleasant, but this is very hard food to match with wine; rum seems more appropriate. **Price range:** Apps., $15–$24; entrees,

$22–$34; desserts, $8–$10. Prix fixe, $65–$85 per person. **Wheelchair access:** Fully accessible.

Assenzio $25 & Under ITALIAN

205 E. 4th St. (near Ave. A) (212) 677-9466
Credit cards: Cash only Meals: L, D, LN

Assenzio, a pleasant osteria with hearty Sardinian cuisine and an emphasis on suckling pig and wild boar, is calm and rustic, with big windows, flickering candles, sturdy wooden chairs and tables, and dish-towel napkins. Artichokes show up frequently, and lightly fried leaves add a deliciously woodsy touch to fried calamari. Pastas win points for avoiding the obvious. Assenzio offers unusual winners like gnocchetti in a piquant tomato and wild boar ragù. Assenzio's wild boar, braised and served in a red wine sauce with juniper berries, is juicy and full of mildly gamy flavor. The suckling pig is gently flavored with myrtle, and includes tender ribs, both light and dark meat and plenty of crisp skin. Desserts also offer relief from the usual. Try a tart yogurt mousse topped with strawberries or vanilla gelato drizzled with myrtle berry liqueur.

Other recommended dishes: Fregola with clams, polenta with artichoke hearts, Ligurian salad, Sardinian suckling pig carpaccio, trenette with sardines and oranges. **Price range:** Apps., $6.95–$10.95; entrees, $8.95–$15.95. **Wheelchair access:** Ramp at entrance; narrow doors to restrooms.

Atelier ☆☆☆ $$$ FRENCH

Ritz-Carlton Hotel, 50 Central Park S. (at Sixth Ave.) (212) 521-6125
Credit cards: All major Meals: L, D

Atelier has firmly established itself as one of the city's finest French restaurants. Executive chef Gabriel Kreuther continues to come up with dazzling ideas, achieving exciting flavor effects through unexpected means. He excels at lighter-than-air, herb-based sauces that shine a new, flattering light on the main ingredients of a dish, and his range is impressive. His menu embraces minimalist spa dishes like steamed black sea bass in a lemon verbena jus and a punchy, explosively flavorful oxtail crepinette stuffed with wild mushrooms and coated, almost like a candy apple, in a sticky, syrupy reduction. It's a profound meat experience, as though a 20-ounce ribeye has been compressed into a container the size of a squash ball. Perhaps most impressive is the featherweight fine-herb jus pooled around slices of pink muscovy duck, baked in a clay papillote. The restaurant has a new pastry chef, Eric Hubert, who delivers fireworks and a sense of fun: his cherry sampler is a whirlwind tour of cherry flavors expressed in gradations from tart to very sweet, in a vacherin, a terrific clafoutis, a savarin, and, amusingly, a little scoop of chopped-up relish billed as a tartare. It's perfect for Atelier, whose refined aesthetic places a premium on pure pleasure and the shock of the unexpected.

Wine list: An impressive thousand-bottle list strong in Australian and Spanish reds and boutique Calfornia wineries. **Price range:** Lunch: apps., $12–$22; entrees, $22–$34; three-course prix fixe, $32; four-course prix fixe, $42. Dinner: apps., $20–$32; entrees,

$26–$40; dessert, $9; three-course prix fixe, $68; six-course tasting menu, $95. **Wheelchair access:** Elevator to restrooms.

Aureole ☆☆ $$$$ NEW AMERICAN

34 E. 61st St. (bet. Madison & Park Aves.) (212) 319-1660
Credit cards: All major Meals: L, D Closed Sun.

Aureole is one of the city's most popular and revered restaurants. The reasons are perfectly understandable. Aureole serves appealing food in stylish surroundings. The service is polished, the atmosphere warm. Manhattan has no shortage of restaurants that could be described in the same way, but very few of them have achieved Aureole's invincible appeal. After 13 years as the executive chef at Aureole, Charlie Palmer, the owner, passed the baton. The menu is lighter and more international, with hidden pockets of unabashed richness here and there. So Aureole continues to be what it has always been, a very civilized dining spot on the edge of a very tony Upper East Side. If diners tend to inflate the Aureole experience, it's not hard to see why.

Wine list: A solid, reasonably priced 325-bottle list, mostly French and American, with 21 half bottles and 20 wines by the glass. **Price range:** Lunch: apps., $8–$42; entrees, $20–$29; desserts, $9–$10; three-course "market lunch," $35. Dinner, three-course prix fixe, $69; tasting menu, $85 ($125 with wines). **Wheelchair access:** Not accessible.

Avenue $25 & Under BISTRO/FRENCH

520 Columbus Ave. (at 85th St.) (212) 579-3194
Credit cards: All major Meals: B, Br, L, D, LN

This informal corner restaurant (with an unexpectedly French atmosphere and efficient service) serves breakfasts and light meals by day and full dinners at night. Avenue has toyed with the traditional menu, dividing appetizers into small, medium and large plates — which has nothing to do with size, but rather with the costliness of the ingredients. Smoked pork loin, sliced lamb and sliced steak are excellent. At brunch, try the hot chocolate, which is thick as pudding and rich as a chocolate truffle. From the terrific food to the daylong service and the good values, Avenue is a formula that works.

Other recommended dishes: Fried calamari; leek and Gruyere tartlet; risotto with morels, asparagus and peas; lobster bisque; walnut tart; chocolate cake; berry cobbler. **Price range:** Apps, $6–$14; entrees, $14–$17. **Wheelchair access:** Restrooms are narrow. **Features:** Outdoor dining.

Avra ☆ $$$ GREEK/SEAFOOD

141 E. 48th St. (bet. Third & Lexington Aves.) (212) 759-8550
Credit cards: All major Meals: L, D

This restaurant has a spacious, easy feeling to it, and just enough decorative pieces to suggest a country taverna without belaboring the point. It is a soothing place.

Greek cuisine is a modest thing, and Avra gives it honest, honorable representation. Fresh fish, barely touched, is the selling point here. In the open kitchen, a ball of fire blasts each side of a sea bass or red snapper imprisoned in a grilling basket; the fish gets a squirt of lemon, a drizzling of olive oil and a sprinkling of herbs, then heads to the table. It's an appealing formula, to which Avra brings its own brand of charm. For those who insist on meat, lamb loin chops are tender and flavorful. Avra's spanakopita is a flawless layering of good feta cheese, firm spinach and leeks, with crackling-fresh leaves of phyllo dough.

Wine list: About 130 wines, most moderately priced, with 23 Greek wines. **Price range:** Lunch: apps., $7–$13; entrees, $10–$27; three-course prix fixe, $20. Dinner: apps., $7–$15; entrees, $19–$26; desserts, $7. **Wheelchair access:** Street-level restroom.

AZ ☆☆☆ $$$ FUSION
21 W. 17th St. (bet. Fifth & Sixth Aves.) (212) 691-8888
Credit cards: All major Meals: Br, L, D

AZ is gorgeous, an improbable but enchanting blend of strict Asian geometry, Western Art Nouveau and turn-of-the century Viennese craft influences. The décor, in other words, matches the menu. The sultry bar and lounge on the ground floor attracts the young and the beautiful. But the lucky ones step into the silver steel elevator and head for the third-floor dining room. Tilted glass panels open up to the sky in clear weather, and a thin sheet of water flows down a stone slab near the entrance. It's a room to dream in. When the food arrives, however, the stargazing stops and Patricia Yeo's wildly successful brand of fusion cooking holds center stage. She shows a rare combination of audacity and refinement, sustained with admirable consistency over the entire menu.

Wine list: A far-ranging, very original list of about 350 wines, with nearly 60 half bottles and 24 wines by the glass. **Price range:** Dinner: three-course prix fixe, $52; six-course tasting menu, $75. **Features:** Outdoor dining.

Azafrón ☆ $$$ SPANISH/TAPAS
77 Warren St. (near W. Broadway) (212) 284-0577
Credit cards: All major Meals: L, D Closed Mon.

Azafrón, an unassuming neighborhood spot, aims to do the right thing by tapas. Despite its austere setting and punishing acoustics, Azafrón succeeds where many have failed. Almost anything involving shrimp steps immediately to the head of the class, whether it's shrimp sautéed in olive oil, garlic and red pepper; heads-on shrimp grilled with rock salt; or a brochette of shrimp marinated in spices and skewered with date. Close rivals are the croquettes, stuffed with a rich béchamel sauce and nuggets of Spanish ham, Manchego cheese or mushrooms. The paella, alas, fails to rise above its station. For dessert, the crema catalana is dense and satisfying.

Other recommended dishes: Sautéed piquillo peppers; grilled eggplant with mint, garlic and chili; apple tart. **Wine list:** An all-Spanish list of about 60 wines. **Price range:** Apps., $5–$14; entrees, $11–$22; desserts, $7–$8. **Wheelchair access:** Ramp to dining room.

Babbo ☆☆☆ $$$$ ITALIAN

110 Waverly Pl. (at Sixth Ave.) (212) 777-0303
Credit cards: All major Meals: D

Mario Batali and Joseph Bastianich took one of the city's most
beloved old restaurants, the Coach House, gutted its interior, and
created a small, spare, intimate room with warm golden light. The
menu is loaded with dishes Americans are not supposed to like:
Fresh anchovies and warm testa (head cheese) are among the appetizers, and pastas include bucatini with octopus, and ravioli filled
with beef cheeks. Lamb's tongues and calf's brains are frequent
specials. There is also spicy, robust calamari, and a pasta tasting
menu. And all this comes at a relatively moderate price.

The entirely Italian wine list is filled with names unfamiliar to
most Americans, and wine is not served by the glass but by quarti-
nos (250 ml, or a third of a bottle). Try one. If you don't like it, the
kitchen will take it back. If you leave room for dessert, ice creams
are creamy and concentrated. But the best ending is saffron panna
cotta with poached peaches. (Ruth Reichl)

Wine list: Focused on Italy; unusual and fairly priced. **Price range:**
Apps., $9–$15; entrees, $15–$35; desserts, $8; seven–course pasta
tasting menu, $59; seven–course traditional tasting menu, $65.
Wheelchair access: Fully accessible.

Bahia $25 & Under SALVADORAN

690 Grand St., Williamsburg, Brooklyn (718) 218-9592
Credit cards: All major Meals: B, L, D

Corn is the keystone of the Central American culinary universe, as
is clear if you visit a Salvadoran restaurant like this bright and airy
place. Although the extensive menu includes hamburgers and
spaghetti puttanesca, the specialties are typical Salvadoran dishes
like pupusas, corn pancakes that serve primarily as a vehicle for
conveying the satisfying flavors of small amounts of meats and vegetables, which are stuffed into the center of the pancake. Corn
shows up in many other dishes, like Salvadoran chicken tamales.
Other dishes, even those without corn, can be fabulous, like a mess
of fried yuca with chunks of fried pork. Bahia does not serve alcohol, but don't pass up horchata, a sweet iced rice drink with cinnamon and cocoa that has a wonderful, almost malty flavor.

Other recommended dishes: Sopa de res, empanada de leche.
Price range: Apps., $2–$10; entrees, $7–$15. **Wheelchair access:**
All one level.

Bajo el Puente $25 & Under PERUVIAN

45-02 Junction Blvd., Corona, Queens (718) 592-1916
Credit cards: All major Meals: Br, L, D, LN Closed Wed.

At Bajo, an unpretentious Peruvian restaurant, ceviches are treated
as a delicacy rather than an adornment. Ceviche de mariscos, a hill
of supremely fresh shrimp, octopus, squid and conch, arrives under
a plateau of pickled red onions, sliced thin. The excellent tamale is

stuffed not only with pork but with hard-cooked eggs, olives and peanuts. Papa a la huancaina, a classic dish, is no more than boiled potatoes, sliced and covered in a winning sauce of queso blanco, a white cheese made pale yellow and just spicy enough to notice by aji amarillo, a mild chili pepper.

Other recommended dishes: Pig's feet in peanut sauce, chicken and potatoes in cream sauce, papa rellena, fried fish topped with seafood. **Alcohol:** Beer and wine. **Price range:** Apps., $4–$13; entrees, $6–$14. **Wheelchair access:** Not accessible.

Baldoria ☆ $$$ ITALIAN

249 W. 49th St. (bet. Seventh & Eighth Aves.) (212) 582-0460
Credit cards: All major Meals: D Closed Sun.

Baldoria (pronounced bal-DOR-ia, meaning "rollicking good time") is a big slice of neighborhood Italian, New York style, transferred, in a slicker format, to the theater district. It serves feel-good food in a feel-good atmosphere. In restaurants like these, Frank Sinatra is more important than the chef.

Baldoria is authentic, even naïve, and in an ironic, cynical age, that makes it tremendously appealing. It is possible to eat very well at Baldoria, or not. When it's good, Baldoria is quite good. Pastas perform strongly, especially trenette with prosciutto, peas and onions in a light cream sauce. Get the costata di manzo, a thuggish-looking hunk of rib chop, weighing in at 54 ounces; it's an incredibly flavorful piece of beef, juicy, tender and perfectly cooked.

Wine list: A work in progress, with about 100 wines, mostly Italian, with enough interesting selections to suggest a good list in the making. **Price range:** Apps., $8–$18; entrees, $18–$32; desserts, $8. **Wheelchair access:** Street-level restroom.

Bali Nusa Indah $25 & Under INDONESIAN

651 Ninth Ave. (near 45th St.) (212) 265-2200
Credit cards: All major Meals: L, D

Indonesian restaurants are rare in New York, but this is a good one, offering fresh and lively Indonesian dishes in a tranquil and pretty setting. Most of the food is forcefully spiced, yet respectful of the flavors of each dish. Among the dishes worth trying are Javanese fisherman's soup; corn fritters gently flavored with shrimp; nasi goreng, the wonderful Indonesian version of fried rice, and sea bass broiled in a banana leaf. Most Asian restaurants are not known for their desserts, but there are exceptional ones here.

Other recommended dishes: Stuffed squid; spring rolls; fish mousse; pan–fried whole red snapper; beef with green chilies; chicken in chili sauce; pisang goreng (fried banana); lapis legit (mellow cinnamon cake with vanilla ice cream). **Alcohol:** Bring your own. **Price range:** Apps., $3–$4; entrees, $6–$14; daily specials, $13–$15; prix fixe, $12–$20. **Wheelchair access:** Restrooms are narrow. **Features:** Good view, outdoor dining.

Balkh Shish Kebab House

$25 & Under

AFGHAN/MIDDLE EASTERN

23-10 31st St., Astoria, Queens
Credit cards: Cash only

(718) 721-5020
Meals: Br, L, D, LN

Balkh, named after a town north of Kabul, is a simple restaurant with a breezy garden in the rear. The waitresses are friendly and helpful, and the owners make it a point to stop by your table to make sure everything is all right. The highlight of the menu is the dumplings — either ashak, a lacy ravioli stuffed with scallions and served in a wonderful sauce of yogurt and grilled onions, or manto, stuffed with ground beef and served in the same sauce. Main course portions are enormous.

Other recommended dishes: Bolani (flat bread stuffed with potato purée), kabli kofta (brown rice blended with carrots, raisins and lamb), sabzey chalow (mild lamb and spinach curry), lassi (yogurt drink), rice pudding. **Alcohol:** Bring your own. **Price range:** Apps., $2–$6; entrees, $5–$8.

Balthazar ☆☆ $$$

BRASSERIE/FRENCH

80 Spring St. (bet. Lafayette St. & Broadway)
Credit cards: All major

(212) 965-1785
Meals: B, L, D, LN

The bold-faced names have largely moved on, but this SoHo French brasserie continues to draw crowds for its affordable and delicious food. Try going for lunch, when tables are easier to come by and the food is just as good. The Balthazar salad is a fine mix of asparagus, haricots verts, fennel and ricotta salata in a truffle vinaigrette. Sautéed foie gras is excellent, as is an appetizer of grilled mackerel with a warm potato salad. The short ribs are awesome: rich and meaty, they are accompanied by fat-soaked carrots and buttery mashed potatoes. Lighter dishes are also attractive, like seared salmon served over polenta. (*Ruth Reichl, updated by Eric Asimov*)

Wine list: Well chosen and fairly priced. **Price range:** Brunch: $13–$22. Lunch: apps., $7–$14; entrees, $11–$19. Dinner: apps., $8–$14; entrees, $16–$32; desserts, $7–$9. **Wheelchair access:** Fully accessible.

Bambou ☆☆ $$$

CARIBBEAN

243 E. 14th St. (bet. Second & Third Aves.)
Credit cards: All major

(212) 505-1180
Meals: D

Some of the best Caribbean food in New York City is served in this cozy, elegant room. There is no better way to begin a meal here than with the eggplant soup, a thick dark liquid with the scent of curry and the deep, intoxicating taste of coconut. Bambou shrimp, each encrusted in coconut, are sweet and tasty, an appetizer that could almost be a dessert. Grilled marlin, a dense, meaty fish steak, comes on a buttery bed of mashed plantain that is the perfect foil for the subtle flavor of the fish. The tropical fruit plate glows with color and the coconut crème brûlée is fabulous.

Wine list: Small but reasonable. **Price range:** Apps., $8–$13; entrees, $18–$26; desserts, $8. **Wheelchair access:** Fully accessible.

Banania Café $25 & Under   BISTRO/FRENCH

241 Smith St. (near Butler St.), Brooklyn   (718) 237-9100
Credit cards: Cash only   Meals: L, D

Banania, named for a French children's drink, has an enticing
menu of reasonably priced bistro dishes. There are Asian and Middle Eastern touches, so that though it feels French, it falls into that
catchall international category that might be called contemporary.
Among main courses, braised lamb shank is delicious — tender
shreds of rosemary-flavored meat framed by chicory and a purée of
white beans. Moist roasted cod is served with luscious potatoes
mashed with black olives and roasted tomatoes. Desserts range
from a classical tarte Tatin to crisp little wontons stuffed with
puréed banana in a white-chocolate and ginger sauce.

Other recommended dishes: Sautéed foie gras; escargots; steak
frites; poached chicken breast; Key lime tart; chocolate mousse.
Price range: Apps., $5–$8; entrees, $12–$15. **Wheelchair access:**
All one level.

Bandol $25 & Under   FRENCH

181 E. 78th St. (bet. Third & Lexington Aves.)   (212) 744-1800
Credit cards: AE   Meals: D   Closed Sun.

Bandol, named for a fine Provençal wine, offers dreamy Mediterranean flavors. The food is very good, the atmosphere warm and
neighborly. Even the overly familiar dishes like lamb shank, salmon
and scallops have clear, direct flavors that convey their appeal
rather than their popularity. Among the appetizers, the pissaladiére
is so good that you could eat two and call it a meal. Fish soup is
also traditional and excellent. The tender lamb shank offers primal
enjoyment. The atmosphere is right and the food delicious, but
what about the wine? Here, Bandol falls short of the ideal. The
mostly French list is long but not very exciting.

Other recommended dishes: Coq au vin, grilled steak, chocolate
cake, apple tart, profiteroles. **Price range:** Apps., $6–$10; entrees,
$14–$18. **Wheelchair access:** Not accessible.

Barbalùc   ☆ $$$ ITALIAN

135 E. 65th St. (near Lexington Ave.)   (212) 774-1999
Credit cards: All major   Meals: L, D

Barbalùc serves the cuisine of Friuli, fitfully presented and occasionally reinterpreted, in a smart town house. Friuli is one of Italy's
richest culinary regions with the country's best white wines. After
an initial fear of genuine commitment to Friulian cuisine, Barbalùc
has become less timid and its menu has begun to catch up with its
wine list. The ravioli filled with branzino and fennel, and served
with roasted sardine and fennel, fried to a golden crisp, is stunning.
It faces stiff competition from puffy potato gnocchi smothered in a
rich rabbit ragù. Veal, sautéed and then braised, also ascends to the
astral plane. For dessert, a small polenta cake dotted with bits of
melted chocolate is a sweet and clever homage to Friuli's staple

food. The service is solicitous and warm, but the acoustics of the cramped and windowless dining room are atrocious.

Other recommended dishes: Roasted red snapper with seasonal vegetables, blancmange with asparagus foam. **Wine list:** A heavily Italian list of about 150 wines. **Price range:** Lunch: apps., $8–$19; entrees, $18–$22; desserts, $7–$12. Dinner: apps., $11–$20; entrees, $24–$29; desserts, $7–$12. **Wheelchair access:** Fully accessible.

Barbetta $$$

ITALIAN

321 W. 46th St. (bet. Eighth & Ninth Aves.)

(212) 246-9171

Credit cards: All major

Meals; L, D

Dappled sunlight filters through the branches of ancient trees and a fountain creates cool music. Waiters move lazily across a stone floor, pouring wine for impossibly elegant people. Can this be Midtown Manhattan? On an afternoon in late spring, there is no nicer place for lunch than the garden at Barbetta; it is the most beautiful in Midtown. The menu in this restaurant, open since 1906, is so old it seems new. The best dishes are the handmade pastas.

Price range: Avg. app., $10; entree, $29; dessert, $10. **Wheelchair access:** Restrooms not accessible.

Barking Dog Luncheonette $25 & Under

DINER

1678 Third Ave. (at 94th St.)

(212) 831-1800

1453 York Ave. (bet. E. 77th & 78th Sts.)

(212) 861-3600

Credit cards: Cash only

Meals: B, Br, L, D, LN

With its dark wood paneling, comfortable booths, bookshelves and low-key lighting, the Barking Dog looks more like a library than a luncheonette. That, in part, explains its appeal to adults, along with its up-to-date American menu, which ranges from hamburgers, fried chicken and meatloaf to leg of lamb and roasted trout. If the children begin to fidget while waiting for the rich, bountiful desserts, distract them with the restaurant's dog tchotchkes, which can be a parent's best friend.

Alcohol: Beer and wine. **Price range:** Avg. entree, $11; dessert, $5. **Wheelchair access:** Fully accessible. **Features:** Outdoor dining.

Barney Greengrass $$

DELI

541 Amsterdam Ave. (bet. 86th & 87th Sts.)

(212) 724-4707

Credit cards: MC/V   Meals: B, Br, L

Closed Mon.

Why are all those people standing in line for such a dreary-looking establishment? For three reasons. In the first place, the restaurant sells truly great smoked and cured fish. Second, the kitchen makes awesome omelets and all manner of terrific deli dishes. Third, it's a true New York City institution, and for many people the weekend just wouldn't count without a visit to Barney Greengrass. (Note: Accepts cash only on weekends.)

Alcohol: Beer. **Price range:** Apps., $6–$14; entrees, $8–$35; desserts, $3–$5. **Wheelchair access:** Restrooms not accessible.

Bar Pitti

$25 & Under   ITALIAN

268 Sixth Ave. (near Houston St.)   (212) 982-3300
Credit cards: Cash only   Meals: L, D, LN

This casual cafe offers superbly simple Tuscan fare and draws an
arty, fashion-conscious crowd. Bar Pitti's ease with people and with
food is what makes it seem so Italian; its atmosphere of jangly controlled frenzy makes it a wonderful New York experience. Outdoor
seating on Sixth Avenue is remarkably pleasant. The menu is small
and familiar, and almost all the main courses are superb. Peak
hours are not times for a quiet meal here, but even just before closing time, you will receive the same beautifully cooked food and off-
hand service.

Recommended dishes: Eggplant Parmesan; veal meatballs;
taglierini with leeks and artichokes; osso buco; lemon torte. **Alcohol:** Beer and wine. **Price range:** Apps., $5–$9; entrees, $11–$19.
Wheelchair access: Steps to restrooms. **Features:** Outdoor dining.

Barrio   ☆ $$ BISTRO

99 Stanton St. (at Ludlow St.)   (212) 533-9212
Credit cards: All major   Meals: Open 24 hours

Barrio lives up to the neighborhood in carrying on the melting-pot
tradition. The name suggests Latino, but the menu speaks
Esperanto. It abounds in small flourishes and flavor detours that
add interest to fundamentally simple food that stresses fresh,
organic ingredients. The strategy seems sensible. Barrio's round-
the-clock, seven-day schedule makes it a cross between a diner and
a bistro. That means the food needs to be sharp and hip, but not so
clever that it scares away local residents hankering for a quick bite.
    The lunch menu is mostly given over to soup, sandwiches and
salads. But the soup could be a thick, silken blend of rutabaga and
parsley root, sneakily spiced with cayenne and ginger, and the
sandwiches outperform their bargain price of about $6. The prix-
fixe makes it possible to enjoy lunch with substantial main courses
like braised veal cheeks on a sweet-sour bed of marinated beet
greens. Plenty of dishes play it straight, however, like the very basic
pearl-onion tart. Desserts could be better.

Wine list: An acceptable list of about 50 wines, with eight wines by
the glass and four by the half bottle. **Price range:** Lunch entrees,
$6–$9; two-course prix fixe, $15; three courses, $18. Dinner: apps.,
$6–$11; entrees, $13–$27; desserts, $6–$8. **Wheelchair access:**
Ramp to restrooms.

Bar Veloce   **$25 & Under**   ITALIAN/SANDWICHES

175 Second Ave. (near E. 11th St.)   (212) 260-3200
Credit cards: All major   Meals: D, LN

The sleek metallic style of this small Italian wine and sandwich bar
masks a warm and passionate establishment. The bartenders wax
enthusiastic over the list of fine Italian wines, many available by
the glass, which go well with the precisely made sandwiches, like a
Sicilian tuna tramezzino, a triple-decker of soft crustless white
bread with marinated tuna, arugula, tomatoes and a minty pesto
that brings the flavors together.

Other recommended dishes: Smoked prosciutto with apple and taleggio. **Price range:** Avg. sandwich, $7. **Wheelchair access:** Restrooms not accessible.

The Basil ☆ $$ THAI
206 W. 23rd St. (near Seventh Ave.)   (212) 242-1014
Credit cards: All major   Meals: D

With silk walls, a slate floor and abstract, cocoon-shaped objects set into wall niches, the Basil has the cool, minimalist air of a Zen conference center. The young, good-looking waitstaff eagerly steers you to a list of colorful cocktails, none of which seem to be particularly well conceived. But the wine list is another matter. It is ambitious, full of good values, and the Basil makes a compelling case that the right wine can enhance even piquant Thai cuisine.

Some of the dishes are quite wonderful. Basil chicken rolls is actually a combination of several Thai dishes in one. Simpler combinations succeed, too. Thick, beautifully textured lamb chops, rubbed with chili and basil, come with a spicy eggplant salad. Stewed pork belly is full of tender rich flavor, served over delicate glass noodles with sautéed greens.

Desserts are tropical and refreshing. Thin slices of mango come with a scoop of intensely flavored mango ice cream and small mounds of sticky rice and coconut ice cream surrounded by dots of tapioca in a light coconut sauce. *(Eric Asimov)*

Other recommended dishes: Striped bass with red curry, duck with curry and coconut milk, rack of lamb, stewed pork belly, green papaya salad, stuffed chicken wings, mixed grilled seafood with Thai sausage, curry puffs. **Wine list:** Ambitious and exceptionally well chosen, offering a chance to taste how well wine can pair with Thai food. **Price range:** Apps., $6–$12; entrees, $12–$25; desserts, $7. **Wheelchair access:** One level.

Bayard's ☆☆ $$$ FRENCH
1 Hanover Sq. (bet. Pearl & Stone Sts.)   (212) 514-9454
Credit cards: All major   Meals: D   Closed Sun.

Bayard's may be the most distinctive, romantic dining room in Manhattan, its Federal-style interior and maritime paintings more Boston or Philadelphia than New York. It's a stage set within the stage set of Hanover Square, eerily hushed at night and nearly deserted. In an appropriately quiet way, Eberhard Müller, formerly of Le Bernardin and Lutèce, has refashioned the food to suit the surroundings.

It pays to remember that Mr. Müller is a farmer as well as a chef. He grows his own produce, and it features prominently on the menu. A restaurant like Bayard's, so distinguished-looking that you feel you should be drafting the Federalist Papers there, demands Dover sole, and it is excellent. Mr. Müller loves duck, and he expresses his love in many different ways. The solid dessert list offers classics as well as highly inventive desserts.

Wine list: An outstanding list, mostly French and American, with many older wines at bargain prices. **Price range:** Apps., $9–$16; entrees, $29–$38; desserts, $9–$10. **Wheelchair access:** Lift at side entrance on Stone Street. Elevator serves all levels.

Bayou $25 & Under

308 Lenox Ave. (bet. 125th & 126th Sts.)
(212) 426-3800
Credit cards: All major
Meals: L, D

Bayou, a handsome Creole restaurant in Harlem, would do any New Orleans native proud. With its brick walls, retro brass lamps and woody touches, Bayou looks like countless other neighborhood bars and grills, but its big picture windows and second-floor setting offer an unusual New York panorama, unimpeded by tall buildings that might elsewhere blot out the sun setting over the Hudson.

The menu is short, but includes standout appetizers like earthy chicken livers in a rich port wine sauce. The rich turtle soup is thick with bits of turtle meat and smoky andouille sausage, spiked with sherry and lemon. Fried oysters and spinach topped with melted Brie were exceptional. The sautéed fish was moist and altogether delicious. Bayou has two excellent desserts, a bread pudding with vanilla-whiskey sauce and a fudgy, wedge-shaped pecan brownie topped with peppermint ice cream and chocolate sauce. Both were passed around a table of five and nobody got seconds.

Other recommended dishes: Shrimp rémoulade; crawfish étouffée; shrimp Creole; deep-fried catfish. **Price range:** Apps., $5–$9; entrees, $13–$22. **Wheelchair access:** Restaurant up one flight.

Beacon ☆☆ $$$$

NEW AMERICAN

25 W. 56th St. (bet. Fifth & Sixth Aves.)
(212) 332-0500
Credit cards: All major   Meals: L, D
Closed Sun.

This classy-looking new Midtown restaurant knows exactly what it's about. It offers civilized dining in a beautiful setting. Organized around an open kitchen and a huge wood-burning oven, it delivers uncomplicated big-flavored food emphasizing fresh, seasonal ingredients. The chef, Waldy Malouf, has a good thing going with this oven and he makes the most of it. Two of the best entrees are triple lamb chops, rubbed with cumin and puréed picholine olives, and a plain trout roasted over high heat with a bright vinaigrette of chervil, parsley, cilantro and shallots. For dessert soufflés are a point of pride but it's the carmelized apple pancake that grabs the brass ring.

Wine list: Reasonably priced, touches all the bases without showing a strong personality. **Price range:** Apps., $8–$14; entrees, $19–$32; desserts, $7–$11; pre-theater prix fixe, 5:30– 6:30 P.M., $35. **Wheelchair access:** Main dining room and bar are on street level; kitchen dining room is down several steps.

Becco $$

ITALIAN

355 W. 46th St. (bet. Eighth & Ninth Aves.)
(212) 397-7597
Credit cards: All major
Meals: B, L, D

With a menu and a wine list that are decidedly unusual, Becco is one of the more intriguing restaurants in New York. Its dependable Italian food is served two ways. You choose a Caesar salad or antipasto plate and then either unlimited servings of the three pastas of the day, or any of a dozen enticing main courses, like roasted rabbit with prosciutto, osso buco or whole roasted fish of the day. The wine list is a fabulous value, with dozens of interesting, inexpensive, primarily Italian wines. If you have an ingrained need to spend more money, Becco also has a reserve list, ranging from $22 to $180.

Price range: Apps., $5–$10; entrees, $18–$30; desserts, $7. Prix–fixe lunch, $17; prix–fixe dinner, $22. **Wheelchair access:** Restrooms not accessible.

Bella Via $$ ITALIAN
47-46 Vernon Blvd., Long Island City, Queens   (718) 361-7510
Credit cards: All major   Meals: L, D

Bella Via is a small neighborhood restaurant, but fresh, grilled dishes and imaginative thin-crust pizzas make it a large presence on Vernon Boulevard, which, if it is the "beautiful street" of the restaurant's name, proves that the owners have a rich sense of humor. The heart and soul of Bella Via is its coal-fired brick oven that turns out a half-dozen styles of pizza, all built on a proper foundation of thin, crisp flaky dough. Two of the best are an arugula and prosciutto pie, and a white pie of mozzarella, ham and Parmesan cheese. Grilled dishes are pretty much infallible. Baby calamari are lifted from the heat at just the right moment. Good ingredients and correctly cooked pasta seem like revolutionary ideas, given the level of competition in the area. Ricotta-spinach gnocchi with tomato and olives may be the standout here. About half the main courses are competently done warhorses like chicken marsala. Interest picks up with dishes like grilled salmon with mustard sauce and grilled pork chops in a caper and Barolo sauce.

Price range: Apps., $6.50–$9.95; entrees, $8.95–$17.95; desserts, $4–$5.50. **Wheelchair access:** Fully accessible.

Ben Benson's   ☆ $$$$ STEAKHOUSE
123 W. 52nd St. (bet. Sixth & Seventh Aves.)   (212) 581-8888
Credit cards: All major   Meals: L, D, LN

In a city full of quirky steakhouses, Ben Benson's stands out for its relative normality. Lacking Peter Luger's oddball traditions and passionate devotion to dry-aged steak, for example, or Sparks' weighty wine list and crusty sirloins, or even Smith & Wollensky's frat-room masculinity, Ben Benson's offers a wholesome blandness. If it lacks personality, it at least means well, with big, thick steaks, good broiled lamb chops, a solid wine list and a pleasant terrace. *(Review by Eric Asimov; stars previously awarded by Ruth Reichl.)*

Wine list: Fair selection of mid-priced to expensive California red wines and chardonnays, weak on inexpensive wines. **Price range:** Apps., $6–$16; entrees, $17–$33; desserts, $6–$8. **Wheelchair access:** Restrooms not accessible. **Features:** Outdoor dining.

Bennie's Thai Café $25 & Under   THAI
88 Fulton St. (at Gold St.)   (212) 587-8930
Credit cards: AE   Meals: L, D

Bennie's Thai Café, sits at the basement corner of Fulton and Gold Streets. At lunch, it serves as a kind of cafeteria for office workers spooning down curries, at dinner as a kind of kitchen table for college students and neighborhood singles eating pad Thai. Very good pad Thai, at that. The salads display a rare talent. Try the sweet sausage and the grilled beef with Thai chili sauce. Entrees include curries made with a far thinner sauce than what's become standard at most Thai places, but with no less flavor. There's also a triumphant house special of grilled Thai-style chicken, served with a Thai take on plum sauce. For dessert, a slice of baked acorn squash filled with squash custard, hits a pleasant note. And like everything else at Bennie's, it has the feeling and flavor of food cooked to a different standard than that of a restaurant: the home. *(Sam Sifton)*

Other recommended dishes: Shrimp fritters, soups, fried tofu in chile sauce, spicy duck, deep-fried bass, eggplant with basil. **Price range:** Starters, $4–$8; entrees, $7–$16. **Wheelchair access:** Restaurant is down a steep flight of stairs.

Beppe ☆☆ $$$ ITALIAN
45 E. 22nd St. (bet. Park Ave. S. & Broadway)   (212) 982-8422
Credit cards: All major   Meals: L, D   Closed Sun.

The comfortable rustic Tuscan room at Beppe has exposed brick walls, wood beams, wooden floors and a wood-burning fireplace that is damped down in the summer. But is this really Tuscan food?

We'll settle for the chef's description — free-range Tuscan. But he is at his very best with the Tuscan dishes. Order anything made with farro, the nutty whole grain, which is served in soup and as farrotto, a risotto-style dish that changes ingredients with the season. The fried chicken would make a cook of the Deep South proud. The spareribs are spicy, meaty and tender. The 11-herb pasta is perfectly cooked, and filled with flavor. The desserts also play with Italian tradition to produce sweets appealing to the American palate. The cannoli are really rolled lace cookies. An all-American plum and cherry cobbler is a must. *(Marian Burros)*

Wine list: Interesting variety of Tuscan wines, well priced. **Price range:** Antipasti and soup, $7–$12; pasta, $16–$20; secondi, $23–$29; dessert, $7–$8. **Wheelchair access:** Fully accessible.

Beyoglu $25 & Under TURKISH
1431 Third Ave. (at 81st St.) `   (212) 570-5666
Credit cards: All major   Meals: D

The owner is adamant: Beyoglu (pronounced BAY-oh-loo) is not a Turkish restaurant, he insists. It is a meze house, a meyhane. The menu consists of 20 or so mezes, or little tastes — the rough equivalent of Spanish tapas — in Turkey, Greece, the Balkans and parts of the Middle East and North Africa. Many of the selections are familiar, yet deliciously executed, like creamy hummus and exceptional tabbouleh. As good as these dishes are, the highlights are a lovely, pastoral soup of creamy yogurt, rice and mint, and crisp little cubes of pan-fried calf's liver, served with red onions dusted with cumin. Pride of place on the menu is reserved for doner kebab; it is a full plate of food. For dessert try the beautifully textured halvah. Beyoglu may not be a Turkish restaurant, but it's no doubt a Turkish delight

Other recommended dishes: Shepherd's salad, eggplant salad, tossed eggplant and tomato, cacik, taramasalata, marinated octopus, marinated sardines. **Price range:** Mezes, $3.50–$14.50. **Wheelchair access:** Up a flight of stairs.

Bice ☆ ☆ $$$ ITALIAN

7 E. 54th St. (bet. Fifth & Madison Aves.) (212) 688-1999
Credit cards: All major Meals: L, D, LN

With a main dining room done in beige and wood with brass sconces and indirect lighting, Bice is the handsomest Italian restaurant in town. If you have lots of money, good ears and a desire to see the fast and the fashionable, this offshoot of a Milanese restaurant is for you. The food is predictable but good. Fresh pastas, risotto, and the essentially uncomplicated main courses — veal chop, chicken paillard and duck breast with mango — are all recommended. The mostly Italian wine list is well chosen. Desserts include a napoleon with strawberry sorbet, ricotta cheesecake, hazelnut parfait and caramelized banana tart with apricot compote. (*Ruth Reichl*)

Price range: Avg. app., $15; entree, $24; dessert, $9. **Wheelchair access:** Restrooms not accessible. **Features:** Outdoor dining.

Billy's Restaurant $$ AMERICAN

948 First Ave. (bet. 52nd & 53rd Sts.) (212) 753-1870
Credit cards: All major Meals: Br, L, D, LN

Billy's may have changed since it opened in March of 1870, but not so you'd notice. It's still the archetypal family restaurant, and it may be New York City's lowest-key celebrity-laden restaurant. A dish of cole slaw appears the moment you sit down, and the menu includes old favorites like Salisbury steak, lamb stew and shepherd's pie. Billy's also serves a well-aged rib steak, crisp roast chicken, calf's liver, pork chops and the like. The straight-ahead American fare is old-fashioned and fine, the atmosphere is casual and the waiters could not be nicer.

Price range: Apps., $7–$13; entrees, $14–$30; desserts, $4–$8. Brunch, $16. **Wheelchair access:** Fully accessible.

Biricchino $25 & Under ITALIAN

260 W. 29th St. (at Eighth Ave.) (212) 695-6690
Credit cards: All major Meals: L, D Closed Sun.

This unusual Italian restaurant is one of the better choices near Madison Square Garden. It offers a special feature: wonderful homemade sausages from its neighbor, Salumeria Biellese. The selection changes daily, but may include chicken and apricot or lemongrass; duck with Grand Marnier; or plump garlic sausages.

Price range: Avg. app., $7; entree, $16; dessert, $5. **Wheelchair access:** Restrooms are downstairs.

Biscuit
$25 & Under   SOUTHERN/BARBECUE

367 Flatbush Ave. (near Sterling Pl.), Prospect Heights, Brooklyn
(718) 398-2227

Credit cards: Cash only   Meals: B, L, D

Biscuit, a no-nonsense barbecue storefront, serves fried chicken, ribs and pulled-meat sandwiches to a mostly takeout crowd. There's the scent of smoke and grease in the air, squeeze bottles of hot sauce, plastic utensils, and a few tables. The double-fried chicken is a golden, shining mess of a thing, with the soft meat falling off the bone. And say what you like about what the rack of ribs lacks in flavor precision, but Biscuit makes up for some of it with very slow smoke-box cooking. Two sides come free with every entree. Biscuit does a fine cole slaw, good porky collards, tangy red beans and rice, and a creamy mac-and-cheese. Skip the potato salad. But Biscuit's biscuits are the real thing. *(Sam Sifton)*

Other recommended dish: Pulled pork. **Price range:** Breakfast, $1.25–$3.50; sandwiches, $3–$5.50; entrees, $6–13. **Wheelchair access:** Restaurant is one step up.

Bistro le Steak
$25 & Under   BISTRO/STEAK

1309 Third Ave. (at 75th St.)   (212) 517-3800
Credit cards: All major   Meals: L, D

It's tempting to pass off Bistro le Steak as a too-obvious marketing scheme. The surprise is that Bistro le Steak hardly strikes a false note. It does look Parisian. The friendly staff conveys warmth and informality, and the food is both good and an excellent value. Steak is the specialty, but other simple bistro specialties are consistently satisfying. Wines are not as good a value, but desserts are terrific.

Other recommended dishes: Country paté, mussels, shrimp St. Tropez, house salad, Parisian cut sirloin, filet mignon, chocolate cake, lemon tart. **Alcohol:** Beer and wine. **Price range:** Apps., $4–$20; entrees, $15–$30; desserts, $10. **Wheelchair access:** Entrance is one step up; restrooms are downstairs.

Bistro St. Mark's
$25 & Under   BISTRO

76 St. Mark's Ave. (near Flatbush Ave.), Park Slope, Brooklyn
(718) 857-8600

Credit cards: All major   Meals: L, D

The subtle blue storefront of Bistro St. Mark's blends so inconspicuously with the surroundings that you might walk right by. A look at the menu provokes a double take, because this is no simple bistro fare. Bistro St. Mark's uses the guise of neighborhood conviviality to cloak serious and creative cooking. Even traditional dishes are far from standard fare, like the crisp Provençal tomato tart with anchovies and caramelized onions, and fresh, briny grilled sardines in a lemon vinaigrette. Halibut, served over a buttery potato purée, has a meaty depth, and richly flavorful braised beef cheeks, tinged with horseradish, arrive atop the same purée, surrounded by carrots and caramelized garlic cloves.

The loftlike dining room is spare and handsome, but with its soaring ceiling and hard surfaces, it tends to be loud.

Other recommended dishes: Scallop carpaccio, caramelized sea scallops, lemon cake. **Price range:** Apps., $5–$9; entrees, $14–$19. **Wheelchair access:** All one level.

Bistrot Margot $25 & Under   BISTRO/FRENCH

26 Prince St. (near Mott St.)   (212) 274-1027
Credit cards: Cash and check only   Meals: Br, L, D

With its brick-red Parisian exterior, a French spelling of "bistro" and the inward-opening entrance that requires one to "poussez," Bistrot Margot is a Francophile's dream. By day, it is more like a cafe, serving light breakfasts, sandwiches and salads to patrons who feel free to while away the time with cafe au lait. At lunch and dinner, the bistro menu offers a small selection of simple, filling dishes, like marvelous Provençal lamb stew, lusty roast pork and beef stewed in red wine. While many things about Margot are delightful, there is a novice quality to the restaurant, expressed more as good-natured disorganization than anything else.

Other recommended dishes: Mesclun salad, charcuterie platter, tapenade, duck confit, shrimp with rice, raspberry tart, apple tart. **Alcohol:** Beer and wine. **Price range:** Apps., $5–$13; entrees, $9–$16; desserts, $7. **Wheelchair access:** One step up to dining room; restroom is large. **Features:** Outdoor dining.

Blue Fin   ☆☆ $$$ SEAFOOD

W Times Square Hotel, 1567 Broadway (at 47th St.)   (212) 918-1400
Credit cards: All major   Meals: L, D, LN

At Blue Fin, a very good restaurant, the theme is fish. And because it's part of an empire that buys a lot of fish, Blue Fin gets first dibs. The quality is unmistakable. One way to test the waters is simply to order sushi or sashimi by the piece, from a list of 20 varieties. The main menu, where the fin fish swim, is where Blue Fin impresses the most. The chef does not overload the plate or step on the fish. The most impressive entree is a crisply sautéed fillet of Atlantic black bass served on a creamy shrimp and asparagus risotto. The genius touch is a shallow pool of chive nage. Desserts are first-class, especially the coconut-milk panna cotta and the sour-cherry toasted almond cake.

Wine list: An eclectic global list, with about 300 wines at every price range, nearly 30 wines by the glass and 25 half bottles. **Price range:** Lunch: apps., $6; entrees, $11–$22; desserts, $8. Dinner: apps., $7–$12; entrees, $19–$38; desserts, $8–$9. **Wheelchair access:** Elevator to restrooms.

Blue Hill   ☆☆ $$ FRENCH

75 Washington Pl. (at Sixth Ave.)   (212) 539-1776
Credit cards: All major   Meals: D

A few steps below sidewalk level in an old Greenwich Village town house, Blue Hill almost shrinks from notice. The décor barely exists, just enough to give off a vaguely pleasant impression. The menu is small, with tiny print. Prices are astoundingly low. This quiet, adult setting admirably suits a style of cooking that is both inventive and highly assured. The overall standard is high, high enough to make up for the excruciating banquette seating, where diners are pressed so close to one another that conversation becomes a survival exercise. Poached duck, an entree that deserves to be the restaurant's signature, shows the Blue Hill style to advantage. Two of the four desserts are puddings. They are also clearly the best in this little pack. Chocolate bread pudding is a conversation-stopper.

Wine list: A modestly priced, highly international list of 80 wines, with 10 wines and 2 sherries by the glass. **Price range:** Apps., $9–$14; entrees, $23–$28; desserts, $7–$8. **Wheelchair access:** Entrance is three steps down. **Features:** Outdoor dining.

Blue Ribbon $$$ NEW AMERICAN
97 Sullivan St. (bet. Prince & Spring Sts.)   (212) 274-0404
Credit cards: All major   Meals: D, LN   Closed Mon.

A favorite hangout for chefs, who like the late hours. Blue Ribbon offers a full menu until 4 A.M., and by then the sound level may have descended to a roar. The eclectic food is terrific.

Price range: Apps., $8–$19; entrees, $10–$30; desserts, $7–$9.
Wheelchair access: Fully accessible.

Blue Ribbon Bakery $$ BISTRO
33 Downing St. (at Bedford St.)   (212) 337-0404
Credit cards: All major   Meals: B, L, D, LN   Closed Mon.

Going downstairs at Blue Ribbon Bakery is a little like descending into the catacombs, a dark and mysterious space. In this clamorous place, people sit at small tables having serious discussions as they eat just about anything you can imagine. Blue Ribbon Bakery seems to want to be all things to all people. So you can have a hamburger, a sandwich, a bowl of hummus or a heap of beluga caviar. You can have less: just a plate of olives, a dish of french fries, a piece of cheese or a hot fudge sundae. And you can have more: sweetbreads in red wine sauce, breast of duck in raspberry sauce, New Orleans barbecue shrimp. The food can be delicious.

Price range: Apps., $4–$19; entrees, $8–$28; desserts, $6–$9.
Prix–fixe menus, $35–$100. **Wheelchair access:** Fully accessible.

Blue Ribbon Brooklyn $$$ NEW AMERICAN
280 Fifth Ave. (at 1st St.)   (718) 840-0404
Credit cards: All major   Meals: D, LN

The Brooklyn outpost of the Blue Ribbon empire feels like many things at once. It's part saloon, part oyster bar, part bistro, part diner and part Jewish deli, if matzo ball soup is anything to go by. The extensive menu hops and skips from herring to clam stew to hummus to a fried catfish hero. The menu includes a special fruits de mer section with oysters, clams, crayfish, crabs and lobster sold by the piece or offered as plateaux de fruits de mer. Seafood, however, is less than the half of it. It shares space with just about anything else: pirogies, steak tartare, cream of tomato soup, tofu ravioli and pork barbecue. There are almost no wimpy desserts at Blue

Ribbon. Fresh berries and sorbets are simply engulfed by a caloric tide of soda-fountain and diner favorites, like hot fudge sundae and banana walnut bread pudding in a banana caramel sauce.

Price range: Apps., $5–$14; entrees, $8–$30 (more for some specials); desserts, $6–$11. **Wheelchair access:** Steps to entrance.

Blue Ribbon Sushi ☆☆ $$$ JAPANESE/SUSHI

119 Sullivan St. (bet. Prince & Spring Sts.) (212) 343-0404
Credit cards: All major   Meals: D, LN   Closed Mon.

Blue Ribbon Sushi has good fish and an awesome list of sakes, but beyond that it has very little in common with a classic Japanese sushi bar. If you have ever felt like a clumsy foreigner and worried about doing the wrong thing, this is the sushi bar for you. The menu is enormous, but the high point of the meal is always sushi and sashimi. The sushi chefs are at their best when inventing interesting specials like an appealing roll filled with fried oysters. And unfettered by tradition, they create unusual special platters filled with whatever happens to be best that day. Just name the price you are willing to pay and let them amaze you. (*Ruth Reichl*)

Wine list: Minimal, but 11 sakes are nicely described and sold by the glass, cedar box or bottle. **Price range:** Apps., $4–$16; entrees, $12–$28. **Wheelchair access:** Steps to dining room.

Blue Ribbon Sushi (Brooklyn)
☆ $$ JAPANESE/SUSHI

278 Fifth Ave. (near 1st St.), Park Slope, Brooklyn   (718) 840-0408
Credit cards: All major   Meals: D

Blue Ribbon Sushi, an offshoot of the hugely popular Blue Ribbon restaurants in Manhattan, brings a hip, downtown sensibility from Manhattan but tones it down and loosens it up for local consumption. The dining room, with its beamed ceilings and dark wooden window slats, is visually soothing. The menu is extensive and varied, supplemented by a daily list of specials. One could live happily on the specials and the sushi. Blue Ribbon has come up with some good rolls, led by the flagship Blue Ribbon roll — half a lobster perfumed with shiso leaf and topped off with dollops of caviar. The kitchen excels in flash-frying fish to a feather-light crunch. For dessert, try the strange, puck-shaped artifact called the chocolate bruno.

Other recommended dishes: Spicy lobster roll, spicy tuna and tempura flake roll, fried flounder with ponzu sauce, monkfish liver. **Wine list:** A minimal list supplemented by 12 to 15 sakes. **Price range:** Apps., $3.75–$14; sushi and sashimi, $2.50–$5 a piece; sushi rolls, $3.50–$16.75; entrees, $14.50–$27.50; desserts, $5–$7.50. **Wheelchair access:** All one level.

Blue Smoke ☆ $$ BARBECUE

116 E. 27th St. (bet. Park & Lexington Aves.) (212) 447-7733
Credit cards: All major   Meals: D, LN

In this rustic dining room with rough-hewn maple wainscoting and a suitably boisterous atmosphere, Danny Meyer has taken on the quixotic quest of building a fine barbecue emporium in Manhattan. Others have tried and they have been turned back by a complex web of environmental regulations. But if anyone could give New York great barbecue, it would be Danny Meyer. Unfortunately, for all the money and engineering put into the big metal smokers, the barbecue is inconsistent. Although the beef ribs are among the best you'll find anywhere, the brisket, the staple dish of Texas barbecue, is texturally more reminiscent of corned beef than fine Texas brisket. Desserts are the proper stuff of barbecue joints: direct, uncomplicated, huge. *(Eric Asimov)*

Wine list: Extensive selection of reds and an equally extensive beer list. **Price range:** Apps., $5–$13; entrees, $12–$23; desserts, $6–$7. **Wheelchair access:** One level.

Blue Velvet 1929 $25 & Under   VIETNAMESE

227 First Ave. (near 14th St.)   (212) 260-9808
Credit cards: All major   Meals: L

Despite the suggestive name, this is in fact a low-key Vietnamese restaurant with a focus on the French. The kitchen presents each dish simply but beautifully, graced with banana leaves, stalks of lemon grass and other modest adornments, with food carefully calibrated to intrigue but not intimidate. Blue Velvet excels at delicate and fresh Vietnamese appetizers. Spring rolls are crisp and narrow, stuffed with minced chicken and herbs. They are delicious when wrapped in fresh lettuce leaves and dipped in nuoc cham, the invigorating sweet-and-sour Vietnamese condiment of fish sauce, lime juice and vinegar. Banh cuon are even better: chicken, shrimp, bean sprouts and shallots are wrapped in almost transparent crepes and steamed just enough.

Other recommended dishes: Seafood soup, gui cuon, baby back ribs, roast duck with ginger, stuffed whole prawns, lemon tart. **Price range:** Apps., $5–$9; entrees, $9–$14. **Wheelchair access:** Restrooms are narrow.

Blue Water Grill   ☆ $$ SEAFOOD

31 Union Sq. W. (at 16th St.)   (212) 675-9500
Credit cards: All major   Meals: Br, L, D, LN

Built as a bank in 1904, this is a big, breezy room with a sidewalk cafe and a casual air. Along with pleasant service, large portions and reasonable prices can come large crowds and long waits. While it's not the most creative menu in the world, the food is well prepared and very good. Shrimp and oysters are good choices; so is the grilled fish. Desserts are not among Blue Water Grill's happy surprises, but the brownie sundae would make most people very happy. *(Ruth Reichl, updated by Eric Asimov)*

Wine list: The wine list has both pitfalls and happy surprises. Avoid the Sancerre; try the Bandol rose. Prices are fair. **Price range:** Lunch entrees, $10–$25; Dinner: apps., $6–$11; entrees, $18–$28; desserts, $6–$7. **Wheelchair access:** Restrooms not accessible. **Features:** Outdoor dining (street-side patio).

Bobby Van's   ☆ $$$$ STEAKHOUSE

230 Park Ave. (at 46th St.)   (212) 867-5490
Credit cards: All major   Meals: L, D   Closed Sun.

Bobby Van's is a classic two-fisted steakhouse. With white table-cloths and lots of wood, this is a meat eater's paradise where most of the waiters are old pros who make you feel lucky to be in their hands. The Harry salad, a hearty mixture of green beans, chopped shrimp, bacon and tomatoes, is curiously tasty, and shrimp broiled with lemon and pepper are very appealing. Even the shrimp cocktail is good. The lobster is gorgeously cooked and so tasty that the big dishes of butter are completely unnecessary. The tenderloin is funky, rich and delicious. Desserts are so large they are almost obscene. There's a serious wine list and a bar in front filled with men drinking martinis. They look as if they have been sitting there forever. (*Ruth Reichl*)

Wine list: Many big red wines that go well with meat, at average prices. **Price range:** Apps., $7–$15; entrees, $23–$35; desserts, $5–$9. **Wheelchair access:** Fully accessible.

Boca Chica $25 & Under   PAN-LATIN

13 First Ave. (at 1st St.)   (212) 473-0108
Credit cards: All major   Meals: L, D

Brazil, Bolivia, Argentina, Mexico, Cuba and the Dominican Republic are just some of the countries whose cuisines are juxtaposed on the enticing menu of this little pan-Latin restaurant. Top choices include camarones chipotle — shrimp in a tomato, chili and cilantro sauce; crisp, tangy chicharrones de pollo — the classic Dominican dish of chicken pieces marinated in lime, soy and spices; and pinones — sweet plantains stuffed with ground beef and pork. Service is sometimes slow when the boisterous dining room is filled.

Other recommended dishes: Shrimp, cheese, avocado and green chili quesadillas; vegetable burrito. **Price range:** Apps., $4–$7; entrees, $7–$16; desserts, $4. **Wheelchair access:** Restrooms not accessible.

Bolo   ☆ ☆ ☆ $$$$ SPANISH

23 E. 22nd St. (bet. Broadway & Park Ave. S.)   (212) 228-2200
Credit cards: All major   Meals: L (Mon.–Fri.), D

After showing some slippage over the decade since it opened, Bolo is newly energized. The Spanish-influenced menu has been updated. The wine list has been improved and more tightly focused. And the new tapas menu shows star chef Bobby Flay at his best. It forces him to work in miniature, a format that shows off his talent for expressing simple flavors clearly, with precise seasoning. Sour orange dressing and small orange segments cut the unctuousness and salt in marinated white anchovies. A chunk of seared duck liver gets treated as a serious cut of meat, with a sweet-sharp jolt of sherry vinegar tempered by honey and black pepper. Appetizers on the new menu seem like a midway stage between tapas and entree, a little larger and just a little more complex.

Mr. Flay has managed to develop distinctive dishes that draw on Spanish flavors and spices in a disciplined way. The humble fig in Mr. Flay's hands becomes an opulent sauce that doubles the richness of the walnut romesco stuffing in an entree of pork tenderloin. A garlicky potato gratin makes this dish one of the true heavyweights on the menu, along with a fiercely concentrated squid-ink risotto packed with prawn and lobster meat, surrounded by a pungent green-onion vinaigrette.

The restaurant looks like a glorified cafe and feels like a chummy saloon. The food says it's more than that. Moving into its second decade, Bolo has rediscovered its youth, and, improbably, become fresher and more vibrant than the day it opened.

Wine list: A well-edited list of 150 wines, with about 25 sherries and dessert wines. **Price range:** Lunch entrees, $13–$18.50. Dinner: tapas, four for $15; apps., $8–$13.50; entrees, $26–$31; desserts, $9. **Wheelchair access:** All one level.

Bongo $25 & Under SEAFOOD
299 10th Ave. (near 28th St.) (212) 947-3654
Credit cards: MC/V Meals: D, LN

On any given day, Bongo serves half a dozen kinds of oysters, from Fanny Bays, which have a flavor shockingly like cucumbers, to Pemaquids, which are impressively salty, to Wellfleets, which have a pronounced mineral tang. With no more than a squirt of lemon, they are always impeccably fresh and gloriously sensual. The decadent allure of the oysters makes an amusing contrast to the suburban 20th-century modern style of the room, a quirky replica of 1950's living rooms. Aside from the oysters, the limited menu has a few other highlights, like wonderful, meaty lobster rolls and an excellent smoked trout salad

Price range: Oysters, $2–$2.25 each (minimum order, half-dozen); salads, shrimp and lobster rolls, $6–$16; chilled lobster, $20. **Wheelchair access:** Step to entrance; step to restrooms.

Bottino $$ ITALIAN
246 10th Ave. (bet. 24th & 25th Sts.) (212) 206-6766
Credit cards: All major Meals: D

Set in the midst of the West Chelsea gallery scene, this restaurant and wine bar has a delightful outdoor garden. Fifteen wines are offered by the glass to accompany items like bocconcini of fresh mozzarella, tuna carpaccio and bresaola with arugula. For more than a quick bite, Bottino offers grilled fish and pastas. There is an adjacent takeout section.

Price range: Apps., $7–$14; entrees, $15–$27; desserts, $7. **Wheelchair access:** One step into dining room. **Features:** Outdoor dining.

Boughalem $25 & Under BISTRO
14 Bedford St. (bet. Houston & Downing Sts.) (212) 414-4764
Credit cards: AE Meals: D

This is one of the most charming of the city's small, moderately priced bistros, with a stylish dining room that appeals to both uptown and downtown crowds, professional service and terrific food. Highlights include a circle of couscous that conceals a pungent array of grilled shrimp and roasted tomatoes embedded within; crisp little oval potato dumplings stuffed with minced shrimp, and terrific seared sea scallops.

Other recommended dishes: Grilled chicken; seared tuna steak; pan–roasted monkfish. **Price range:** Apps., $6–$9; entrees, $13–$20; desserts, $8.

Bouley ☆☆☆☆ $$$$ FRENCH
120 W. Broadway (at Duane St.) (212) 964-2525
Credit cards: All major Meals: L, D

The events of Sept. 11, 2001 played havoc with Bouley Bakery, which had risen to new heights after an expansion and slick renovation. Forced to close for months, owner-chef David Bouley lost many staff members. He closed down the bakery half of the operation, dropped his plans to expand, and began the painful task of bringing the restaurant back to its former level. Mr. Bouley was soon turning out food that was nothing less than inspired.

As a chef, Mr. Bouley has it all—elegance, finesse and flair. His flavors are extraordinarily clear and exquisitely balanced; his use of seasoning is so deft as to be insidious. Even his most complex creations have a classical simplicity to them. Mr. Bouley cooks the way Racine wrote and Descartes thought. Rack of lamb with glazed salsify and chanterelles is potent, with an intoxicating overlay of sage. Even roast chicken takes flight in his hands. It comes with an opulent Madeira sauce that enfolds nicoise olives and organic tomatoes like a silken cloak.

Diners who demand the full monty when it come to desserts will not be disappointed by "sweet pleasure," a multilayer affair of thin milk chocolate leaves separating layers of milk-chocolate ganache and chantilly cream, all of it sitting on a toasted hazelnut dacquoise.

Bouley retains the feel of a neighborhood restaurant where diners feel comfortable showing up in shirtsleeves. But the staff shrewdly maintains a delicate balance between informality and a more disciplined level of service implicit in the food and décor. The waiters seem passionate about the food and deeply concerned that diners enjoy it to the full.

Wine list: An imaginative bistro list of about 90 wines, with a dozen wines by the glass and a reserve list of 30 wines. **Price range:** Lunch: apps., $8–$12; entrees, $24–$32; desserts, $7–$10; five-course prix fixe, $35; six courses, $45. Dinner: apps., $10–$18; entrees, $27–$38; desserts, $9–$14; six-course tasting menu, $75. **Wheelchair access:** All one level.

Bouterin ☆ $$$$ FRENCH
420 E. 59th St. (bet. First Ave. & Sutton Pl.) (212) 758-0323
Credit cards: All major Meals: D

Serving Provençal food in a Provençal atmosphere, this restaurant can be charming. The room has a casual cluttered feeling, and it is all so sweet that it is easy to be indulgent. The best dishes are the chef's old family recipes, like the hearty vegetable soupe au pistou, which tastes the way it might if had been made on a wood-burning oven on a Provençal farm. The tarte a la Provençale is a solid, savory wedge that seems like a snack that might be sold on the streets of Marseille. The rack of lamb wrapped in a herbal crust and sea bass in a bold bouillabaisse sauce each give a purely Provençal impression. The daube of beef, too, is delicious, the beef slowly stewed in red wine and garlic. (*Ruth Reichl*)

Other recommended dishes: Floating island; soufflés. **Wine list:** Little imagination has gone into the list, but the prices are fair. **Prices:** Apps., $8–$11; entrees, $20–$32; desserts, $5–$8. **Wheelchair access:** Entrance is four steps down.

Branzini ☆ $$ ITALIAN/MEDITERRANEAN

299 Madison Ave. (near 41st St.) (212) 557-3340
Credit cards: All major   Meals: L, D   Closed Sun.

Branzini is a modest trattoria with a no-frills setting that took a while to find its footing. But the restaurant has evolved into an honest trattoria, with a few atypical dishes and a strong emphasis on single-estate olive oils from Oliviers & Company. Truth to tell, the branzino, or sea bass, a mainstay of northern Italy for which the restaurant is named, is not the star of the show. That prize goes to the Portuguese sardines. Over all, appetizers and pastas make the best showing.

Other recommended dishes: Crab cake with chipotle mayonnaise; mushroom penne with rosemary and truffle oil; hanger steak with spinach salad; salmon with white beans and preserved lemon; almond and golden raisin bread pudding; caramelized banana tart. **Wine list:** A small international list of about 30 wines. **Price range:** Lunch: apps., $9–$14; entrees, $16–$23; desserts, $9. Dinner: apps., $8–$15; entrees, $16–$23; desserts, $9. **Wheelchair access:** Elevator to restrooms.

Brasserie ☆☆ $$$ BRASSERIE/FRENCH

100 E. 53rd St. (at Lexington Ave.) (212) 751-4840
Credit cards: All major   Meals: B, Br, L, D, LN

The old Brasserie, which opened in 1959 and closed in 1995 after a kitchen fire, was so much a part of the city's fabric that the temptation must have been strong to reconstruct it. But when patrons of the old Brasserie enter now, their jaws drop. The interior has been sheathed in a thin perforated pearwood veneer, arranged in overlapping panels that suggest airplane flaps with futuristic booths along the side of the room. For nostalgia, look to the menu. The onion soup is still there. It's only so-so, a pallid artifact. The goujonettes of sole are there, too — firm, expertly fried fingers of breaded fish with a thick, sharp mustard rémoulade for dipping. The short rib pot-au-feu, another of the Brasserie classics indicated on the menu in boldface, have a startling freshness. For dessert try the chocolate beignets.

Wine list: An intelligently selected bistro list of about 260 mostly French wines; 30 half bottles, 20 by the glass. **Price range:** Apps., $8–$14; entrees, $15–$29; desserts, $8. **Wheelchair access:** Wheelchair lift to the right of the entrance.

Brasserie 8 ½ ☆ $$$ BRASSERIE/FRENCH

9 W. 57th St. (bet. Fifth & Sixth Aves.) (212) 829-0812
Credit cards: All major Meals: B, Br, L, D, LN

Visually, Brasserie 8 ½ is a knockout. Diners descend a circular staircase in thick salmon carpeting that winds down through an enormous hole in the floor to a low-slung illuminated onyx bar and lounge, where cushioned black leather chairs cluster. The anteroom feels like the departure lounge for the space shuttle. The dining room could be a galactic mess hall, with a white terrazzo tile floor and black leather booths.

The traditional brasserie menu can be seen in a weekly rotation of specials like bouillabaisse, confit of suckling pig and an excellent Muscovy duck breast. For dessert try the arresting milk–chocolate crème brûlée, iced with a rose marmalade.

There is a design flaw. The booths in the center of the room are so deep that often the staff cannot reach the diners on the inside. It makes "pardon my reach" the mantra for the evening.

Wine list: An eclectic international list of about 150 wines, with a dozen half bottles and wines by the glass. **Price range:** Apps., $8–$16; entrees, $18–$30; desserts, $8. **Wheelchair access:** Elevators to dining room; restrooms via corridor.

Brasserie 360 ☆ ☆ $$$ FRENCH/SUSHI

200 E. 60th St. (near Third Ave.) (212) 688-8688
Credit cards: All major Meals: L, D

A three-building complex across from Bloomingdale's has been transformed into a bright, bustling brasserie. Downstairs, diners enter a brasserie so French it could be installed in a museum. Upstairs, in a quiet, intimate room, is a smart-looking sushi bar. Diners, both upstairs and down, get two menus, one for the brasserie kitchen, the other for the sushi.

The brasserie offers small surprises. The Flemish carbonade, a potent, slowly simmered beef casserole, is a stellar cold-weather entree. Coq au vin, a sad old warhorse at too many restaurants, is a real star. Even the bouillabaisse comes through with flying colors. Upstairs, the sushi bar offers dependably fresh fish of about 20 species, including one or two less common fry, like spotted sardine. The finest example of cross-cultural pollination is found among the desserts — an unctuous, rich pudding made from sushi rice and coconut cream, with a bright accent provided by crunchy mango croquettes.

Other recommended dishes: Chicken mushroom croquette, braised pig's feet, toro tartare, fried oyster roll. **Wine list:** A fairly well-chosen list of 150 wines, mostly French. **Price range:** Lunch: apps., $7–$12; entrees, $12–$29; desserts, $7–$8. Dinner: apps., $7–$16; entrees, $19–$29; desserts, $7–$8. Sushi, $3–$6 apiece; sushi rolls, $4–$8. **Wheelchair access:** Downstairs dining room is on street level; restrooms upstairs.

Bread

$25 & Under

20 Spring St. (near Elizabeth St.)
Credit cards: All major

(212) 334-1015
Meals: L, D

It's hard to imagine a simpler place than Bread, where the most complex piece of equipment is probably the espresso maker. Like countless SoHo cafes, it has intimate little tables. When a restaurant specializes in sandwiches and salads, ingredients are the most important thing. There, Bread succeeds marvelously, whether it's the fruitiness of the olive oil, the pungency of the preserved tuna or, of course, the bread. Crusty, irresistible slices of rustic peasant bread, from the Balthazar Bakery a few blocks west, arrive with the menus. Sandwiches are carefully constructed and manageable, each a well-designed combination of complementary flavors and textures, like Gorgonzola with apple slices and honey on dense cranberry-raisin bread. Heartier pressed sandwiches include speck, an Alpine ham, with sharp Brie and asparagus on ciabatta.

Other recommended dishes: Mozzarella and tomato salad, bresaola with fennel, shrimp salad, cheesecake, chocolate mousses, sweetened ricotta. **Price range:** Sandwiches, $7–$9; other dishes, $4–$16. **Wheelchair access:** Not accessible.

Bread Bar at Tabla

$25 & Under
NEW AMERICAN/FUSION

11 Madison Ave. (at 25th St.)
Credit cards: All major

(212) 889-0667
Meals: L (Mon.–Fri.), D

Bread Bar, Tabla's less formal, less expensive cousin, is finally radiating a beauty of its own that shines right through its dim and noisy dining room. Bread Bar serves home-style dishes and street snacks full of authentic flavors, with the occasional Western element thrown in.

Bread Bar operates family style, with dishes arriving as they are ready. If you've got a larger group, dishes begin to arrive rapidly in a crescendo of bites and flavors, delicious and stimulating. The parade slows as the bigger dishes arrive. For dessert, doughnut holes, glazed with sugar and orange-blossom water, are delicious, and the coffee kulfi pop is a triumph.

Other recommended dishes: Onion rings, potato-apple chat, beet salad, breads, pakoras, lamb sandwich. **Price range:** Small dishes, $6–$12; large dishes, $10–$18. **Wheelchair access:** One level.

Bricco

$25 & Under

304 W. 56th St. (bet. Eighth & Ninth Aves.)
Credit cards: All major   Meals: L, D

ITALIAN
(212) 245-7160
Closed Sun.

This inventive trattoria offers enough twists on the basic Italian formula to keep you intrigued, such as an appetizer of fresh anchovies the size of sardines, marinated but still firm and briny. Other excellent appetizers include tiny tender clams in a white wine and garlic broth and broiled rings of calamari, still smoky from the wood fire. Don't count on tranquility; when crowded, the dining room is loud.

Other recommended dishes: Octopus, fennel and arugula salad; steamed clams; veal chop; filet mignon in creamy peppercorn–brandy sauce. **Price range:** Apps., $6–$7; entrees, $10–$20; desserts, $6. **Wheelchair access:** Fully accessible.

Brick Lane Curry House $25 & Under INDIAN
342 E. 6th St. (First Ave.) (212) 979-2900
Credit cards: All major Meals: Br, D

At Brick Lane, a spare and casual place, the food is powerfully spiced, distinctively flavored, extremely fresh. Sitting in the tiny front dining room, listening to the world-beat soundtrack beneath walls stained to a soft-focus sunset red, it is possible to feel transported — if not to Bombay, then at least to England. Brick Lane takes its name from a stretch of Indian restaurants in East London — and it serves the standard fare of modern England: chicken tikka masala, curries, lamb vindaloo. The difference is that this Brick Lane prepares its food with unusual care and ability. The flavorful lamb jalfrezi is heated with green chilies and balanced by ginger, and the mustardy, ever-so-slightly-sweet shrimp Madras. A splendid vegan dish called peeli dal and dal makhani, a creamy, gently spiced stew of smoky black lentils, may be the restaurant's finest creation. For dessert try the mango lassi. *(Sam Sifton)*

Price range: Apps., $5; kebabs and rolls, $8–$14; entrees, $9–$17. **Wheelchair access:** Entrance is a step up; bathrooms are small.

Bright Food Shop $25 & Under ASIAN FUSION
216 Eighth Ave. (at 21st St.) (212) 243-4433
Credit cards: Cash only Meals: Br, D

This spare, minimalist former luncheonette serves an exciting blend of Asian and Southwestern ingredients. Scallop ceviche is a terrific appetizer. Green chili pozole is tart, vinegary and thick with chorizo and hominy, while the smoked trout and red peppers, wrapped in rice and seaweed, is a post-modern sushi roll. Bluefish salpicon, in which the fish is chopped and pickled with vinegar and chilies and served in corn tortillas, stands out among the main courses.

Other recommended dishes: Chips and salsa; tomato and shrimp soup; mushroom enchiladas; salmon with black sesame seeds; blackberry–and–nectarine crisp; chocolate pudding. **Alcohol:** Beer and wine. **Price range:** Apps., $5–$8; entrees, $13–$16; desserts, $5. **Wheelchair access:** Restrooms not accessible.

Brother Jimmy's BBQ $$ BARBECUE
1644 Third Ave. (at 92nd St.) (212) 426-2020
428 Amsterdam Ave. (bet. 80th & 81st Sts.) (212) 501-7515
1485 Second Ave. (bet. 77th & 78th Sts.) (212) 288-0999
Credit cards: All major Meals: D, LN

These restaurants are loud, continuous frat parties, but the Southern food and barbecue are pretty good, especially the excellent spareribs, available with sauce or with a dry spice rub. Is it worth braving the crowd? Takeout is a good option.

Price range: Avg. app., $7; entree, $15; dessert, $4.

Bukhara Grill $25 & Under   INDIAN

230 E. 58th St. (bet. Second & Third Aves.)   (212) 339-0090
217 E. 49th St. (bet. Second & Third Aves.)   (212) 888-2839
Credit cards: All major   Meals: L, D

Bukhara Grill's small dining room (58th St.), with slate-tile walls
and glossy pine tables, is restful in a rustic way. The northern
Indian cooking is mostly superb, with the sort of precise, resonant,
yet subtle spicing that is all too rare in Indian restaurants.
Bukhara's extensive, fairly priced wine list also stands out.

Try the slender, lively kebabs made entirely of minced vegetables, and dahi aloo papri, a blend of potatoes and chickpeas in
wonton skins with a tangy tamarind sauce. Highlights among the
excellent curries include pepper chicken, a rich dish with distinct
layers of black pepper, ginger and chili flavors, and gazob ki boti,
chunks of tender lamb in a creamy yet surprisingly sour and gingery sauce.

Other recommended dishes: Pickled mushrooms. **Price range:**
Apps., $6–$11; entrees, $12–$28. **Wheelchair access:** Steps at the
entrance.

Bulgin' Waffles $25 & Under   WAFFLES

49 1/2 First Ave. (near Third St.)   (212) 477-6555
Credit cards: All major   Meals: B, L, D

This spare corner restaurant, which most resembles an American
college-town coffeehouse, serves wonderful waffles. The namesake
Bulgin' Waffle, the kind you might find in Belgium, is indeed big
and thick, yet it's airy and fluffy. Even better are the smaller buckwheat wafflettes, exquisitely light and crisp, with more flavor than
the big, white-flour waffles. You won't find those in Belgium, which
is Belgium's loss. The biggest drawbacks at Bulgin' are that the
waffles are served on paper plates with flimsy plastic cutlery and
that you have to pay $.85 for pure maple syrup or any of the excel-
lent fruit syrups.

Alcohol: Beer only. **Price range:** Entrees, $4–$5. **Wheelchair
access:** Fully accessible.

Butter   ☆ $$$ NEW AMERICAN

415 Lafayette St. (near Astor Pl.)   (212) 253-2828
Credit cards: All major   Meals: D, LN   Closed Sun.

In many ways, Butter epitomizes the conflicted priorities of certain
downtown restaurants that teeter between dining room and club.
Upstairs is a professionally run vaulted dining room that looks like
a cross between a chalet and a sauna. Downstairs is a dim lounge.
The chef has put together a serious contemporary American menu
with all the requisite high-end ingredients and global touches.
Appetizers struggle, but main courses, especially fish dishes, are
more sure-footed. The delicate grilled turbot has an Asian character,
perhaps because of the sake in the beurre blanc. A tapenade coating enlivened a rosy piece of tuna. A lamb chop and loin are juicy
enough, and a beef fillet will do the job of placating beef lovers.
The amiable list of desserts does not break new ground, though
some offer appealing architecture. Dense and creamy chocolate-

mocha cake comes with coffee gelato, the two linked by a spiral bridge of crisp cocoa pastry. (Eric Asimov)

Wine list: Well-chosen list of about 100 bottles, with many attractive choices in the $40 to $50 range. **Price range:** Apps., $10–$16; entrees, $27–$30; desserts, $8–$10. **Wheelchair access:** Steps to main dining room.

Cabo Rojo $25 & Under   PUERTO RICAN
254 10th Ave. (near 25th St.)   (212) 242-1202
Credit cards: Cash only   Meals: B, L, D   Closed Sun.

Cabo Rojo offers stellar variations on Puerto Rico's favorite themes: sweet, salt, sour, fire. Baked pork chops are tender and fragrant with sofrito. Fried in bacon fat, with achiote added for color, it is the island's national seasoning. There's a touch of it beneath in picadillo con maduros (ground meat with plantains), in the gravy that adorns the beef stew and in the sauce that floods a thick slice of meatloaf. Generous servings of rice and beans (some days pigeon peas) come with every order. For those eating fish, try anything made with the restaurant's ropy, delectable bacalao — salty, savory salt cod. An achiote-tinged flan makes for a delightful capper. (Sam Sifton)

Other recommended dishes: Oxtail stew, roast pork, baked chicken, coconut custard, bread pudding. **Price range:** Lunch and dinner, $3–$9.25. **Wheelchair access:** Step to entrance.

Cafe Asean $25 & Under   PAN-ASIAN
117 W. 10th St. (bet. Greenwich & Sixth Aves.)   (212) 633-0348
Credit cards: Cash only   Meals: L, D

The dining room looks like a stylized New England farmhouse, but the menu is pan-Asian, with Vietnamese dishes being the best bets. A friendly, welcoming atmosphere and pleasant garden make Cafe Asean quite the civilized place to eat.

Recommended dishes: Bun tom (rice vermicelli with grilled shrimp), salads, goi cuon (shrimp and rice noodles). **Alcohol:** Beer and wine. **Price range:** Apps., $5–$6; entrees, $9–$13; desserts, $3–$5. **Wheelchair access:** Restrooms not accessible. **Features:** Outdoor dining.

Café Boulud   ☆☆☆ $$$$ FRENCH
20 E. 76th St. (near Madison Ave.)   (212) 772-2600
Credit cards: All major   Meals: L (Tue.–Sat.), D

Café Boulud is sleek and easy. In the crowded, sometimes noisy dining room, cheerful waiters walk around wearing grins and shirt-sleeves. In the kitchen, Mr. Boulud and his chef are playing with food. This is your opportunity to find out what happens when a great chef at the top of his form stretches out and takes chances.

The menu, which changes frequently, is divided into four sections: La Tradition (classic country cooking), La Saison (seasonal dishes), Le Potager (vegetarian choices), and Le Voyage (world cuisine). What that really means is, anything goes. Most days there are

30 or more dishes, and none are ordinary. They are all completely delicious.

Wine list: Exciting, with many selections at reasonable prices. The sommelier offer very intelligent advice. **Price range:** Lunch: apps., $10–$18; entrees, $18–$38; two-course prix fixe, $29; three-course prix fixe, $36. Dinner: apps., $10–$18; entrees, $26–$38; desserts, $9–$13. **Wheelchair access:** Fully accessible. **Features:** Outdoor dining (sidewalk).

Cafe Centro ☆☆ $$$ FRENCH/MEDITERRANEAN
200 Park Ave. (at 45th St.)   (212) 818-1222
Credit cards: All major   Meals: L, D   Closed Sun.

Cafe Centro feeds throngs of businessmen in and around Grand Central, yet it manages to maintain respectable standards. It is not a destination restaurant, but it is a surprisingly sharp operation given the numbers its serves. Green asparagus soup, although oversea-soned, swims with toothsome slices of firm asparagus, and marinated shrimp with red mustard greens have an assertive heat that contrasts nicely with a sweet citrus vinaigrette. The lunch menu concentrates on dishes like lobster salad with chickpea vinaigrette or seared scallops with tabbouleh salad. The big steaks and seafood platters come out at night. The wine program is imaginative, and the service obliging. *(Review by William Grimes; stars previously awarded by Ruth Reichl.)*

Wine list: Well thought out and well priced with good wines by the glass and a fine selection of beers. **Price range:** Apps., $9–$13.50; entrees, $19.50–$28.50; desserts, $6.50–$8. **Wheelchair access:** All one level. **Features:** Outdoor dining.

Cafe Colonial $25 & Under BRAZILIAN
73 E. Houston St. (at Elizabeth St.)   (212) 274-0044
Credit cards: All major   Meals: B, Br, L, D, LN

Perched on the edge of a trendy neighborhood, Cafe Colonial could easily be a cliché of bad food and worse attitude. The surprise is that the food is so good and the service so sweet. The restaurant has no culinary point to make. Top dishes include a terrific fried soft-shell crab sandwich; tilapia, sautéed until crisp around the edges yet still moist and flavorful within; and grilled squid, served in a cool salad with slices of excellent baguette.

Other recommended dishes: Mussels in spicy tomato sauce; pan-roasted sea bass fillet; Bahian shrimp in coconut sauce; chocolate bread pudding. **Alcohol:** Beer and wine. **Price range:** Apps., $3–$9; entrees, $8–$17. **Features:** Outdoor dining.

Cafe Con Leche $ LATIN AMERICAN
424 Amsterdam Ave. (bet. 80th & 81st Sts.)   (212) 595-7000
726 Amsterdam Ave. (bet. 95th & 96th Sts.)   (212) 678-7000
Credit cards: All major   Meals: B, L, D

These colorful, modern Hispanic restaurants specialize in robust Cuban and Dominican dishes. Portions are huge, prices are low, and while the newer uptown branch may be friendlier, the food is not yet up to the standard of the further downtown branch, where the roasted pork is a specialty.

Price range: Apps., $3–$6; entrees, $7–$14; desserts, $3–$4.
Wheelchair access: Restrooms not accessible. **Features:** Outdoor dining.

Café de Bruxelles $$ BELGIAN
118 Greenwich Ave. (bet. Seventh & Eighth Aves.)   (212) 206-1830
Credit cards: All major   Meals: Br, L, D

The little zinc-topped bar at this cozy Belgian cafe is a warm and welcoming stop. The frites, served in silver cones with dishes of mayonnaise, go beautifully with the unusual Belgian beers, while mussel dishes and heartier Belgian stews are all very good. The small tables near the battered zinc bar are good for solo diners.

Price range: Lunch: apps., $5; entrees, $8–$13; desserts, $6. Dinner: apps., $4–$8; entrees, $14–$20; desserts, $7. **Wheelchair access:** Not accessible.

Café des Artistes $$$ CONTINENTAL
1 W. 67th St. (bet. Central Park W. & Columbus Ave.) (212) 877-3500
Credit cards: All major   Meals: Br, L, D

Its signature murals, leaded-glass windows and paneled wood walls contribute to the genteel impression at this grand cafe. The main room is more friendly and louder than the intimate tables around the bar on the second level. The continental food, though, is surprisingly old-fashioned. Best for grazing before or after a concert.

Price range: Lunch: Apps., $8–$30; entrees, $22–$40; desserts, $8–$25.

Café Frida $25 & Under   MEXICAN
368 Columbus Ave. (bet. 77th & 78th Sts.)   (212) 712-2929
Credit cards: All major   Meals: Br, D

No serapes in the dining room, no mariachi music in the background and no burritos on the menu. Café Frida is one of the new wave of Mexican restaurants in New York, presenting dishes like marinated lamb shank with avocado leaves and chiles en nogada, poblano chilies stuffed with meat and walnuts and draped in ethereal walnut cream. The food's not always consistent but when it hits, it can be superb.

Price range: Brunch: prix fixe, $10. Apps, $8–$12; entrees, $13–$17. **Wheelchair access:** Not accessible.

Cafe Habana $25 & Under   LATIN AMERICAN
17 Prince St. (at Elizabeth St.)   (212) 625-2001
Credit cards: All major   Meals: B, L, D, LN

Much of the food here is hearty and enjoyable, certainly not fussy or pretentious: great roast pork, terrific grilled steak and good hamburgers. Its design is sleek and minimalist but true to the look of the old luncheonette. Café Habana imitates its models with love and respect, not irony, preserving the diner's cheap prices and function as a local hangout. Still, not all of the dishes work as well as they should, particularly those with a Mexican touch to them, and some of the basics need work, like making rice properly and improving the cafe con leche.

Other recommended dishes: Shrimp in garlic sauce; mushrooms in garlic, lemon and olive oil; shrimp and crab croquettes; coconut flan; grilled corn. **Price range:** Apps., $3–$7; entrees, $5–$13. **Wheelchair access:** Narrow way to restrooms.

Cafe La Grolla $25 & Under ITALIAN
411A Amsterdam Ave. (near 80th St.) (212) 579-9200
Credit cards: All major Meals: D

This cafe is tiny, holding no more than 30 people. The lighting is a little too bright, the brick and yellow walls a little too plain, but almost everything on the menu is delicious, and it is anything but generic Italian. Salads are excellent and individual pizzas are superb. Agnolotti is rich and warming. Fish are treated with the utmost respect. Even desserts are very good. About all that is missing is a well-chosen Italian wine list.

Other recommended dishes: Panzanella, artichoke hearts with almond pesto, pappardelle with veal ragu, monkfish. **Price range:** Apps., $7–$10; entrees, $9–$20. **Wheelchair access:** All one level.

Café Lebowitz $25 & Under NEW AMERICAN
14 Spring St. (near Elizabeth St.) (212) 219-2399
Credit cards: All major Meals: B, L, D, LN

Café Lebowitz is just a couple of blocks east of Balthazar on Spring Street, but it comes off a bit like a country-mouse relative in comparison which behaves a bit like Fran Lebowitz, the humorist, who suggested the name to the owner. It sits back and takes a long drag on its cigarette before acknowledging your presence. So does the staff. But being a country mouse has its advantages. Like open tables. You can saunter into Café Lebowitz at 8 on a Saturday night without a worry. You get the dim bistro lighting and tile floors — along with duck confit and croque-monsieur for less. Be careful with the menu. As one dining partner put it, you would be wise to order the charcuterie platter (enough for an entree), the cheesecake for dessert and cappuccino. That is, it's best to order things French and Italian, which Café Lebowitz excels at. *(Amanda Hesser)*

Other recommended dishes: Smoked trout frisée salad; artichoke vinaigrette; perciatelli with chicken and potatoes; steak frites; cheesecake. **Price range:** Apps., $5–$9; entrees, $7–$23. **Wheelchair access:** Step to entrance.

Cafe Luxembourg $$$ BISTRO
200 W. 70th St. (bet. West End & Amsterdam Aves.) (212) 873-7411
Credit cards: All major Meals: Br, L, D

The Art Deco room here has a timeless appeal, with cream-colored tile walls, a black-and-white terrazzo floor, sconces and cafe

tables. Patrons cluster at the long zinc-topped bar in the early
evening. The dining room is a tightly arranged maze of red banquettes and rattan-style chairs. At night the room is soft and seductive. The seasonal menu is orchestrated to offer everything from
simple salads and steaks to more refined creations.

Price range: Lunch: apps., $7–$9; entrees, $11–$22; desserts,
$5–$8. Dinner: apps., $8–$10; entrees, $17–$32; desserts, $5–$8.
Wheelchair access: Restrooms are narrow.

Cafe Riazor　　　$25 & Under　　　SPANISH
245 W. 16th St. (bet. Seventh & Eighth Aves.)　　(212) 727-2132
Credit cards: AE　　　　　　　　　　　　　Meals: L, D

At this wonderful old-style subterranean Spanish restaurant in the
middle of a residential block in Chelsea, stick with the classics —
shrimp, chorizo, octopus, pork — and the sangria. The décor is
strictly 1950's bohemian.

Price range: Lunch: apps., $4–$7; entrees, $6–$19; desserts, $2–$4.
Dinner: apps., $5–$8; entrees, $10–$19; desserts, $2–$4. **Wheelchair access:** Not accessible.

Cafe Sabarsky　☆☆　$$　AUSTRO-HUNGARIAN
Neue Gallerie, 1048 Fifth Ave. (near 86th St.)　　(212) 288-0665
Credit cards: All major　　　Meals: L, D　　　Closed Tue.

When Ronald S. Lauder decided to create a museum to house the
collection of Austrian and German art assembled by Serge Sabarsky,
he wanted a cafe to go with it. It would be a real Viennese cafe,
with marble tabletops, chairs designed by Adolf Loos and an
authentic Viennese menu. The end of the meal is the beginning,
really. The rest of the menu presents some tried and true Austro-
Hungarian staples, but the goulash, herring sandwiches and boiled
beef are merely a warm-up to the desserts. The house specialty is a
Klimt torte, neatly stacked layers of hazelnut cake alternating with
firm, bittersweet chocolate. It deserves classic status, along with the
linzer torte and the Sacher torte, both flawless. Two other desserts
deserve special mention: a visually striking multilayer dobosch
torte and the apple strudel, which, when it is good, somehow manages to rise above the rest, not easy for an apple strudel to do.

The coffee at Cafe Sabarsky comes from Meinl's in Vienna, and
it may be the best coffee in the city: rich, robust and deep.

Wine list: A well-chosen list of two dozen Austrian wines, four by
the glass. **Price range:** Apps., $10–$16; sandwiches, $11–$13;
entrees, $10–$25; desserts, $6. **Wheelchair access:** Elevator access.

Cafe Topsy　　　$25 & Under　　　ENGLISH
575 Hudson St. (near Bank St.)　　　　　(646) 638-2900
Credit cards: All major　　　Meals: B, L, D　　　Closed Mon.

As soon as the subject of eating in England comes up, the jokes
about the food begin. Cafe Topsy serves just that sort of English
food, full of soft textures, potatoes and funny names. But eat as you
laugh, because you just might find yourself enjoying more of the
food than you could imagine. The dim, warm dining room is a

hodgepodge of rustic farmhouse tables and flea market chairs. Antique mirrors and prints of donkeys adorn the walls. It's a suitably Python-esque derivation for a place that is thoroughly but not kitschily English.

The best dishes are gutsy and unrefined. Beef brisket braised in Guinness stout is a big and flavorful stew, tender and slightly vinegary. Of the English classics, try the fish and chips. Chicken and chips was a surprisingly good variation. Desserts are the most consistent course. Chocolate ganache tart is delicate and delicious. It was not at all funny, but it sure was good.

Other recommended dishes: Topsy coddler; beet, goat cheese and walnut salad; Scottish salmon with celery root rémoulade; Bakewell tart; crème brûlée. **Price range:** Apps., $7–$9; entrees, $10–$22. **Wheelchair access:** Restrooms are downstairs.

Caffe Bella Sera $25 & Under   PIZZA

1606 First Ave. (near 84th St.)   (212) 396-9401
Credit cards: Cash only   Meals: L, D, LN   Closed Mon.

This is a classic New York City pizzeria with a coal oven. The crust is light, thin, unusually smooth, crisp and blackened on the bottom, and the toppings are all top quality. Caffe Bella Sera offers the time-honored pizzeria trappings, like a high pressed-tin ceiling and, of course, Frank Sinatra and Tony Bennett in the background. Service is charming, draft beer is served at the right temperature with adequate carbonation, and there is a small selection of decent pasta dishes. It's hard to imagine coming here for anything but pizza.

Alcohol: Beer and wine. **Price range:** Apps., $5–$9; entrees, $7–$14. **Wheelchair access:** Fully accessible. **Features:** Outdoor dining.

Calle Ocho   ☆ $$ PAN-LATIN

446 Columbus Ave. (bet. 81st & 82nd Sts.)   (212) 873-5025
Credit cards: All major   Meals: Br, D

Lively and casual with a busy bar and lounge scene, Calle Ocho has a cavernous main dining room seating nearly 200 people. The cooking is as hectic as the nonstop high volume Latin soundtrack. Start with the lobster ceviche, which keeps the taste buds on full alert with a subtly insistent chili flare. For the main course the Argentine hanger steak is a meat lover's delight. Thick, moist slabs of pork loin pick up a spicy piquancy after being rubbed with adobo, a paste made from ground chilies, and they find just the right surroundings in a big dollop of chipotle mashed potatoes and roasted corn salsa. Latin desserts are not for the meek. Sweet on top of sweet is only half-sweet enough, so be prepared when you order banana fritters with mamey ice cream and banana caramel sauce, or the coffee-soaked sponge cake with caramel cream.

Wine list: Budget-priced bistro list, with emphasis on the wines of Spain, Argentina and Chile, and some interesting sherries and Spanish brandies. **Price range:** Apps., $8–$14; entrees, $16–$24; dessert, $5–$8. Brunch, $20. **Wheelchair access:** Enter through 100 W. 81st St.; three steps to restroom.

Cal's $$ CONTINENTAL/MEDITERRANEAN

55 W. 21st St. (bet. Fifth & Sixth Aves.)   (212) 929-0740
Credit cards: All major   Meals: L, D, LN

This is a neighborhood restaurant worth leaving your neighborhood for, combining the warmth of a local hangout with the cool creativity of the Flatiron district's advertising firms and photographers. The food is a lively blend of Continental and Mediterranean cuisines, with a nice wine list and terrific hamburgers. Service is friendly, the interior is airy and inviting, and the long, handsome bar can be a treat for solo diners.

Wine list: Modest list, mostly $25–$40. **Price range:** Apps., $6–$9; entrees, $16–$22; desserts, $7. **Wheelchair access:** All one level. **Features:** Outdoor dining.

Cambodian Cuisine $25 & Under CAMBODIAN

87 S. Elliott Pl., Fort Greene, Brooklyn   (718) 858-3262
Credit cards: MC/V   Meals: L, D

This may be the only Cambodian restaurant in New York City and is worth checking out for that reason alone. Most dishes are similar to Thai and Vietnamese foods — where lemongrass, galangal, basil, lime juice and peanuts as well as various fish sauces are characteristic — but some of the preparations are unusual. In the signature dish, chicken ahmok, chicken breast is marinated in coconut milk, lemongrass, galangal and kaffir lime and steamed until it achieves a soft, puddinglike texture. The voluminous menu also includes quite a few dishes that seem more Chinese than Cambodian, and a list of interesting-sounding desserts.

Other recommended dishes: Tchrok spey kdaob (sweet, pickled vegetables); hot-and-spicy ground beef appetizer; samlor mchookrong (shrimp, tomato, and pineapple soup); nhioem salad (rice noodles and vegetables with lime-and-peanut sauce). **Price range:** Apps., $.95–$6; entrees, $4–$15; desserts, $3. **Wheelchair access:** Several steps down from sidewalk; restroom is narrow.

Candela ☆ $$ NEW AMERICAN

116 E. 16th St. (near Union Sq.)   (212) 254-1600
Credit cards: All major   Meals: Br, D

When the dishes click, the food is very exciting. But Candela is maddeningly inconsistent. The candle-lit dining room has a rustic, medieval air but it is vast, dark and clamorous (perfect for a Halloween date). What makes this especially disappointing is that the menu is so enticing. Every dish sounds delicious, and the menu is varied enough to offer something for almost anyone. The braised lamb shank is satisfying and flavorful; so is the monkfish. The angel food cake with balsamic-splashed strawberries is good, as is a wonderful apple tart, with its Calvados and dried cranberries.

Wine list: Well chosen and fairly priced. **Price range:** Apps., $5–$10; entrees, $12–$23; desserts, $7; three-course pre-theater prix fixe, 5:30–6:30 P.M., $20. **Wheelchair access:** Fully accessible. **Features:** Good view, outdoor dining (sidewalk).

Candle Cafe $25 & Under

VEGETARIAN

1307 Third Ave. (bet. 74th & 75th Sts.)

(212) 472-0970

Credit cards: MC/V

Meals: Br, L, D

This inviting little restaurant serves food fit not just for vegetarians but also for vegans, meaning no food of animal origins — no milk, no eggs, no cheese. Sometimes this works, but look out for familiar dishes that replace an essential ingredient with a nonanimal substitute. Cows would volunteer their services if they tasted cappuccino with soy milk.

Recommended dishes: French toast; tempeh and mushroom burger. **Alcohol:** Beer and wine. **Price range:** Apps., $7–$9; entrees, $11–$15. **Wheelchair access:** Restrooms not accessible.

Canteen $$$

NEW AMERICAN

142 Mercer St. (at Prince St.)

(212) 431-7676

Credit cards: All major

Meals: Br, L, D

Canteen does make an impression. In an homage to the Lamborghini of the 1970's, half its circular booths and swivel chairs are upholstered in Day-Glo orange, the other half in deep chocolate. The chairs themselves, in a tall, body-hugging design, look as if they were engineered for Warp Speed 9. And the kitchen turns out extroverted food, updated diner and fanciful bistro dishes with an imaginative twist here and there. Chicken pot pie, a big one, comes with an herbed crust, and porcini mushrooms mingle with the chicken, carrot and potato chunks. One dish has no wrinkles. The "classic shrimp cocktail" is just that. It's served in a martini glass, of course, but the shrimp hanging over the rim are full of flavor, and the rough-textured cocktail sauce is vibrant.

Wine List: $24–$350. By the glass, $6–$12. **Price range:** Apps., $8–$14; entrees, $16–$26. **Wheelchair access:** Separate wheelchair entrance.

Capitale ☆☆ $$$

NEW AMERICAN

130 Bowery (near Grand St.)

(212) 334-5500

Credit cards: All major

Meals: D

Closed Sun.

In a city with no shortage of grand dining rooms, Capitale takes the cake. Formerly the Bowery Savings Bank, it is almost preposterously opulent, a gilt-encrusted temple with 45-foot-high coffered ceilings. The chef turns out to be a good match for the room. Roasted carabineros in the shell, nearly the size of langoustines, draw attention away from the ceiling and back to the plate. Braised cabbage, a low-rent interloper at sumptuous Capitale, adds a little crunch and mild flavor to a potent entree of roasted sea scallops and smoked pork belly. The menu wanders hither and yon in a sometimes disorienting way. How did linguine and foie gras find themselves side by side on the same list of appetizers? Sometimes the gambles pay off. Slivers of pickled beets bring a small electrical charge to slow-cooked salmon with a Moroccan-spiced gremolata and a subtle carrot broth. For dessert, chilled Meyer-lemon custard, radiantly lemony and unflinchingly tart, manages to be solid yet voluptuous.

Other recommended dishes: Ginger-accented borscht; grilled bison with chocolate oil and mustard greens; crème Catalan and sonhos. **Wine list:** A self-consciously deluxe list, not very adventurous, with high prices. **Price range:** Apps., $10–$19; entrees, $24–$45; desserts, $10–$12. **Wheelchair access:** Ramp to entrance available.

Caracas Arepa Bar $25 & Under   VENEZUELAN

91 E. 7th St. (near First Ave.)   (212) 228-5062
Credit cards: Cash only   Meals: L, D   Closed Mon.

New York's fascination with sandwiches embraces many variations. Venezuela's entry is the arepa, which combines the virtues of the soft corn tortilla and the pita into what is essentially a pouched corn cake. Enter Caracas Arepa Bar, a tiny spot that may finally win for Venezuelan arepas the recognition they deserve. The colorful dining room is little more than a large vestibule, with barely enough room to squeeze in 20 seats. The arepas are offered with 17 different fillings, and the appetizing aroma of the grilling corn dough makes patience difficult. Finally the steaming arepas come — two are a full meal. Almost all the combinations are excellent, like reina pepiada, a chicken-and-avocado salad, a Venezuelan classic, and the domino, earthy black beans and shredded cheese.

Other recommended dishes: Mixed plate, papelón con limón. **Price range:** $2.50–$6.50. **Wheelchair access:** Step at entrance; narrow restroom.

Caravan of Dreams $25 & Under
KOSHER/VEGETARIAN

405 E. 6th St. (bet. First Ave. & Ave. A)   (212) 254-1613
Credit cards: All major   Meals: Br, L, D, LN

The food at this vegetarian restaurant, which looks more like a college hangout than a health-food spot, is nothing to sneer at. Caravan is more concerned about making food that tastes good than about prescribing food that is good for you; as a result, a dish like nachos, made with fresh organic blue corn chips, spicy salsa and black beans, is wonderful, better than at most Mexican restaurants. At lunch, Caravan serves several egg dishes and pancakes, like pear pancakes made of oat and wheat flours. One area in which Caravan stints with dairy products is, sadly, dessert, but you can get a very good cappuccino with real milk.

Other recommended dishes: Hummus; peanut sesame noodles; vegetable burger. **Alcohol:** Beer and wine. **Price range:** Apps., $5–$7; entrees, $9–$13; desserts, $4–$7. **Wheelchair access:** Dining room only. **Features:** Outdoor dining.

Caribbean Spice $25 & Under   CARIBBEAN

402 W. 44th St. (bet. Ninth & 10th Aves.)   (212) 765-1737
Credit cards: All major   Meals: L, D

This little storefront, almost hidden behind metal gates that always seem to be closed, offers refined Caribbean cooking to a steady stream of show business types. Little beef patties, gently spiced bits of ground beef encased in half-moons of flaky dough, are a savory way to begin, and earthy red bean soup has a long, lingering, slightly smoky flavor. Caribbean Spice's jerk barbecue (pork or chicken) is excellent. Caribbean Spice serves beer and wine as well as Caribbean concoctions like sorrell, a tart, refreshing deep-red beverage made from hibiscus. Desserts are somewhat limited.

Price range: Apps., $3–$13; entrees, $9–$22; desserts, $4–$5.
Wheelchair access: Not accessible.

Carmine's $$ ITALIAN

200 W. 44th St. (at Seventh Ave.) (212) 221-3800
2450 Broadway (bet. 90th & 91st Sts.) (212) 362-2200
Credit cards: All major Meals: L, D, LN

This duo of restaurants has been a hit from the day they opened and has inspired many imitators, serving garlic-laden family-style platters of old-fashioned Italian-American classics. With a big, noisy group, Carmine's is fine fun (and you can share), but don't expect subtlety. Do expect long waits.

Price range: Apps., $6–$19; entrees, $17–$47; desserts, $5–$12. All designed to share.

Carnegie Deli $$ DELI

854 Seventh Ave. (at 55th St.) (212) 757-2245
Credit cards: Cash only Meals: B, L, D, LN

Carnegie's sandwiches are legendarily enormous, big enough to feed you and a friend and still provide lunch for tomorrow. That doesn't stop people from trying to eat the whole thing, a sight that must gratify the deli's notoriously crabby waiters. The pastrami is wonderful, of course, but so are the cheese blintzes with sour cream, which are only slightly more modest. A raucous, quintessential New York City experience, from pickles to pastrami. Whatsamatter, you don't want no cheesecake?

Alcohol: Beer only. **Price range:** Apps., $6–$8; entrees, $10–$20; desserts, $5–$7. **Wheelchair access:** Restrooms not accessible.

Carne $25 & Under STEAKHOUSE

2737 Broadway (at 105th St.) (212) 663-7010
Credit cards: MC/V Meals: Br, D

Carne, a small steakhouse-style restaurant near Columbia University, draws a steady stream of diners from the neighborhood. The appeal is clear. In an area with plenty of inexpensive restaurants, one option was lacking: a grown-up place for a well-made cocktail, a thick steak and a good bottle of wine.

The appetizers are plain but satisfying. Fried oysters need no more than a squeeze of lemon juice. It's all a prelude to the main courses, like strip steak, a thick, charred cut of meat. If it doesn't quite have the tang of aged prime beef, it still beats most other similarly priced steaks out there. Same with a buttery filet mignon and a broiled skirt steak, with its deliciously crusty edges.

For dessert, rich bourbon bread pudding fits the menu perfectly. It's unusual to find a thoughtful wine list at a neighborhood restaurant like Carne, but the small list, heavy on wines of the Northwest, includes some gems.

Price range: Apps., $4–$12; entrees, $9–$19. **Wheelchair access:** Ramp at entrance.

Casa Adela $

CARIBBEAN

66 Ave. C (at 5th St.)
Credit cards: Cash only

(212) 473-1882
Meals: B, L, D

Adela specializes in Puerto Rican dishes that are both powerful enough to awaken the most jaded taste buds and filling enough to make you want to take a nap when you're done. Garlic is the key ingredient in dishes like pernil asado, moist chunks of roast pork occasionally adorned with crisp bits of skin, and mofongo, a potent blend of mashed plantains and crisp pork cracklings.

Price range: Entrees, $6–$8; desserts, $2. **Wheelchair access:** Fully accessible.

Casimir $25 & Under

BISTRO/FRENCH

103 Ave. B (bet. 6th & 7th Sts.)
Credit cards: AE

(212) 358-9683
Meals: D, LN

The food at Casimir is uncomplicated, easy to enjoy, occasionally inspiring and several dollars cheaper than at comparable spots. All very appealing, unless you mind inattentive service, a long wait for food and a crowd shoehorned into cramped quarters. Eating there feels more like a test of endurance than a pleasure. The menu includes a few surprises like excellent pigs' feet, rich with marrow and dense with flavor, served off the bone in a crisp-topped cake over mashed potatoes.

Other recommended dishes: Filet mignon; sautéed chicken liver, green salad with beets, celery and tomatoes. **Price range:** Apps., $5–$7; entrees, $13–$17; desserts, $5.

Caviar Russe $$$$

RUSSIAN

538 Madison Ave. (bet. 54th & 55th Sts.)
Credit cards: All major

(212) 980-5908
Meals: L, D

Caviar is naturally romantic, and Caviar Russe, with its blue and white walls and fanciful murals, seems to belong more in a fairy tale than in Midtown Manhattan. In the old-fashioned rooms, brimming with tiny mother-of-pearl spoons and antique silver caviar dispensers, caviar is served in tiny tastes, nice if you want to deliberate about your indulgence, as well as in serious portions. While caviar unadorned is the main feature, the menu also has small, delicate dishes in which caviar is a supporting player, like chilled oysters topped with beluga, and a lobster claw set in cream-puff dough with caviar on top.

Price range: Apps., $7–$26; entrees, $16–$47; desserts, $9–$12. Tasting menus: five-course, $55; seven-course, $75.

Caviarteria $$$$

502 Park Ave. (at 59th St.)
310 W. Broadway (at Canal St.)
Grand Central Terminal (at 42nd St.)
Credit cards: All major

EAST EUROPEAN
(212) 759-7410
(212) 925-5515
(212) 682-5355
Meals: B, L, D

Good caviar at very fair prices. Caviarteria intends to put a caviar
bar in every community, but in the meantime we have a sort of
caviar coffee shop on the Upper East Side, a far more substantial
shop in SoHo and a new branch at Grand Central. If you yearn to
learn about caviar, this is the perfect place to discover the differences between beluga, osetra and sevruga. Other options include a
club du roi sandwich, made with an ounce of beluga and smoked
salmon, and a beluga crepe made with an ounce of broken beluga
eggs. The champagne selection tends toward the very expensive.

Alcohol: Beer and wine. **Price range:** Apps., $8–$25; entrees,
$14–$125; desserts, $3–$8. **Wheelchair access:** Fully accessible.

Cavo $$

42-18 31st Ave., Astoria, Queens
Credit cards: All major

GREEK
(718) 721-1001
Meals: Br, D

Astoria ranks near the top when it comes to sheer numbers of
Greek restaurants and sidewalk cafes. Cavo combines both, in a setting straight out of Club Med. The place is enormous, with a bar
and lounge up front and a vast dining room whose front section,
called the Paradiso Lounge, is dominated by a living bamboo tree.
A large sunken patio equipped with its own bar, takes care of the
outdoor-cafe function. Cavo aims higher than steam-table Greek.
The menu includes a good list of mezedes, or Greek tapas. Main
courses do an end run around pastitsio and moussaka in favor of
dishes like herb-crusted lamb chops. One of the best entrees features the largest shrimp you've ever laid eyes on, skewered on a
sprig of rosemary and served in a deeply concentrated tomato
sauce with giant cannelini beans and olives. The best dessert is
dense Greek yogurt sprinkled with berries.

Price range: Apps., $8–$12; entrees, $14–$26; desserts, $6–$9.
Wheelchair access: Fully accessible.

Celeste $25 & Under

502 Amsterdam Ave. (near 85th St.)
Credit cards: Cash only

PIZZA/ITALIAN
(212) 874-4559
Meals: Br, D

Celeste is that rare bird: a true neighborhood restaurant. The
atmosphere is convivial. The staff is pleasant and efficient. And the
food is sublime. Start with a pizza from the wood oven at the back,
though it is worth it to ask for a well-done crust. Other starters
include a wonderful fried buffalo ricotta, and exquisite crostini with
marinated white anchovies. Entrees are a weak spot. Far better are
salads — on the one hand, a stunningly good bread salad with marinated tuna, and on the other, a mound of fresh baby spinach, with
apples, walnuts and a bright, lemony vinaigrette. Pastas are good as
well. The best of these is the raviolini — pillowy little ravioli stuffed
with ricotta and spinach in a butter-sage sauce. Desserts bring

gelato and sorbet from Gino Cammarata and an enjoyable tartuffo stuffed with lemon ice cream. *(Sam Sifton)*

Other recommended dishes: Fritto misto de pesce, chicken livers.
Price range: Apps., $6–$8.50; pizzas, $9–$12; entrees, $8–$15.
Wheelchair access: Restaurant is up one high step.

Centolire ☆☆ $$$ ITALIAN

1167 Madison Ave. (near 86th St.) (212) 734-7711
Credit cards: All major Meals: Br, L, D

Centolire is a large, good-looking trattoria with a warm, beating heart. The food, doled out in substantial portions, is honest, well executed and deeply satisfying. One of Centolire's gimmicks is the coccio, or crock, that appears as a little symbol next to dishes like baked calamari, chicken scarpariello and stinco, a whopping veal shank braised with rigatoni that is intended for four diners. The crock symbol is shorthand for rustic, and most of the dishes cooked in the coccio are also covered in a thick bread dough, crosta di pane, that transforms them into an Italian potpie.

Centolire's second gimmick is the way the menu divides appetizers, pastas and entrees into two categories, Old World and New World. The pastas, old or new, have a rough-hewn integrity that makes them impossible not to order. All are served in appetizer or entree portions, which helps matters.

Wine list: A not very adventurous list of 55 mostly Italian wines, with 11 wines by the glass. **Price range:** Lunch: apps., $7–$15; entrees, $12–$18. Dinner: apps., $8–$14; entrees, $21–$34; desserts, $9–$14. **Wheelchair access:** Elevator access to upstairs.

Chanterelle ☆☆☆ $$$$ FRENCH

2 Harrison St. (at Hudson St.) (212) 966-6960
Credit cards: All major Meals: L, D Closed Sun.

Some restaurants win admiration. Others inspire love. Chanterelle does both. It's not hard to understand why New Yorkers keep a warm spot in their hearts for Chanterelle. Few restaurants are as welcoming or comfortable to enter. There's a soft, casual edge to the atmosphere and the service. It is unquestionably a fine restaurant, but the once fresh face in TriBeCa is well into middle age now. Admittedly, it's a Catherine Deneuve sort of middle age, but Chanterelle is not quite the ravishing young thing that turned TriBeCa into a glamour neighborhood.

David Waltuck, the chef and (with his wife, Karen) owner of the restaurant, favors an opulent style. His strong suits are depth and intensity of flavor, and he doesn't shy away from thick, rich sauces in his quest to ravish the palate. The menu changes every four weeks and includes splendid dishes like a simple, pristine beef fillet, drenched in a red wine and shallot sauce with more layers of flavor than a complex Burgundy.

The service at Chanterelle is gracious but perplexing, especially during the settling-in phase. The room itself looks as though it should be serene and hushed, but in fact the acoustics are poor, and when the place fills up, it takes some real lung power to carry on a conversation.

Wine list: Impressive but pricey. About 600 mostly French wines; two dozen in half-bottles and a dozen by the glass. **Price range:** Lunch: apps., $8–$15; entrees, $20–$24; desserts, $9–$11; three-course prix fixe, $38. Dinner: three-course prix fixe, $84; six-course tasting menu, $94 or $154 with matching wines. **Wheelchair access:** Restrooms, with stalls for the disabled, on street level.

Charles' Southern-Style Kitchen
$25 & Under   SOUTHERN
2841 Frederick Douglass Blvd. (near 151st St.)   (212) 926-4313
Credit cards: All major   Meals: D, LN

Charles Gabriel, the chef and owner of this small restaurant (25 seats) and takeout spot in Harlem, is an artist at work. This is the sort of food you don't think about so much as feel, and the soulful feeling it provokes makes the term apt. The fried chicken may be the peak of Mr. Gabriel's artistry, but it is by no means all he does. Pork ribs are sweet and meaty, and falling-off-the-bone tender. Oxtails in an oniony brown gravy provoke sighs of contentment, while salmon cakes are light but forcefully flavored, a real treat if you can get them. Not everything is available all the time.

Alcohol: None. **Price range:** Buffet: $7 from 1–4 P.M., $10 after 4 P.M. Lunch and dinner: Entrees, $7–$8, desserts, $2. **Wheelchair access:** Fully accessible.

Chat 'n Chew $25 & Under   AMERICAN
10 E. 16th St. (bet. Fifth Ave. & Union Sq. W.)   (212) 243-1616
Credit cards: All major   Meals: Br, L, D

Middle American farm dishes and homespun décor set the tone at this restaurant, which could lead you to believe it was off a small-town courthouse square rather than off Union Square. Portions are huge, desserts are luscious and the place is particularly appealing to children.

Price range: Apps., $4–$6; entrees, $7–$14; desserts, $4–$5. **Features:** Outdoor dining.

Chelsea Bistro & Bar ☆☆ $$$ BISTRO/FRENCH
358 W. 23rd St. (bet. Eighth & Ninth Aves.)   (212) 727-2026
Credit cards: All major   Meals: D, LN

With a cozy fireplace, a great wine list and really good French bistro food, this is a find in the neighborhood. While the wines seem rather fancy for a bistro, the menu itself has fewer pretensions. Some of the dishes are superb. If the first thing you eat at Chelsea Bistro is the fabulous mussel and clam soup, you will be hooked forever. Most of the food is the satisfying fare you expect in a bistro. The hanger steak is fine and rare, with a dense red-wine sauce. The restaurant serves predictable and good classic New York bistro desserts. (*Ruth Reichl*)

Wine list: Large, well chosen and fairly priced. **Price range:** Apps., $7–$9; entrees, $18–$27; desserts, $8–$9; pre-theater prix fixe, $29. **Wheelchair access:** Dining room is down two small steps.

Chez Josephine ☆☆ $$$ BISTRO/FRENCH

414 W. 42nd St. (bet. Ninth & 10th Aves.) (212) 594-1925
Credit cards: All major Meals: D, LN Closed Sun.

This Theater Row pioneer has been entertaining us with its colorful parade of musicians, singers and dancers for more than a decade and is still going strong. Its reliably pleasing bistro fare and attentive service add to the charm. Favorites among entrees include lobster cassoulet replete with scallops, shrimp, lobster, seafood sausage and black beans; and sautéed calf's liver with honey mustard sauce and grilled onions. *(Ruth Reichl)*

Price range: Avg. app., $7; entree, $19; dessert, $7. **Wheelchair access:** Restrooms not accessible.

Chickenbone Café $25 & Under NEW AMERICAN

177 S. 4th St. (near Driggs Ave.), Williamsburg, Brooklyn
(718) 302-2663
Credit cards: MC/V Meals: D, LN Closed Mon.

Chickenbone's inexpensive menu — largely bruschettas, salads, sandwiches and soups — is intriguing. The handcrafted look of the room with walls of cedar and brick, a hickory floor, a sheet-metal bar and tables constructed of barn timbers, is entirely distinctive. It makes no sense at all, yet perfect sense, to have on the same table delicious starters like tartiflette, a hearty casserole of thin-sliced potatoes layered with smoky bacon and reblochon cheese, and bruschetta of kielbasa with mustard and minced pickles. The excellent sandwiches make admirable use of pork in several distinctive forms. A soft, savory confit is served with a tangy gribiche sauce in one, and matches prosciutto with creamy, nutlike mozzarella and roasted tomato on another. Departing from pork, try the sandwich of salmon with wasabi and watercress on a pumpernickel roll.

Other recommended dishes: Vietnamese sausage sandwich, cannellini bruschetta, garlic soup, braised goat, ricotta with maple syrup and pine nuts. **Price range:** $3–$15. **Wheelchair access:** Small step at entrance.

Chimichurri Grill $$ LATIN AMERICAN/ARGENTINE

606 Ninth Ave. (bet. 43rd & 44th St.) (212) 586-8655
Credit cards: All major Meals: L, D Closed Mon.

If you're looking for a casual place for a good dinner before or after the theater, you can hardly do better than this minuscule Argentine restaurant. Simultaneously sophisticated and homelike, it combines all the elements that make the food of Argentina so appealing: great grilled beef, a few Italian pasta dishes and some pure home cooking, like the tortilla, a frittata filled with potatoes, chorizo and onions. You could easily eat the empanadas every day, crisp little turnovers filled with a mixture of ground beef and olives.

Alcohol: Wine and beer. **Price range:** Lunch: apps., $5–$7; entrees, $8–$17; desserts, $6–$7. Dinner: apps., $6–$9; entrees, $14–$24; desserts, $6–$7. **Wheelchair access:** One step up to restaurant; narrow restrooms.

China Fun $ CHINESE

1653 Broadway (bet. 51st & 52nd Sts.)   (212) 333-2622
246 Columbus Ave. (bet. 71st & 72nd Sts.)   (212) 580-1516
Credit cards: All major   Meals: Br, L, D, LN

The food in these quirky restaurants is sometimes good but more
often mediocre, always fast and always cheap. Décor is appealingly
industrial but tends to amplify the noise when crowds are heavy.
Try the dim sum, like the crisp pan-fried radish cake, or the delicate
shrimp dumplings, as well as the noodle dishes and the roast pork.

Price range: Dumplings, $5; entrees, $10–$13. **Wheelchair access:**
Fully accessible.

Chip Shop $25 & Under   ENGLISH

383 Fifth Ave. (at 6th St.), Park Slope, Brooklyn   (718) 832-7701
Credit cards: Cash only   Meals: L, D

Bad English food is an old joke. At this small, extremely English
fish and chips restaurant, some items on the menu may sound
funny — mushy peas (they are supposed to be mushy) — but
much of the food is honest and forthright, filling and satisfying. Not
that the Chip Shop is your basic blue-collar fish and chippery. With
the beat of acid jazz and trance music at high volume, the pitch is
clearly toward a younger crowd. Still, the yellow dining room is
cheerful and pleasant. Fish here can be excellent, especially the
moist cod. The Chip Shop offers some of England's greatest pub
hits, like fine bangers and mash, plump pork-and-cereal sausages
over mashed potatoes. For dessert, the deep-fried Mars bar, with its
crisp coating and gooey chocolate and caramel filling, is delicious.

Price range: Apps., $3–$6; entrees, $6–$11. **Wheelchair access:**
Small step at entrance; aisle in dining room is narrow.

The Chipper $ ENGLISH

41-28 Queens Boulevard, Sunnyside, Queens   (718) 729-2148
Credit cards: Cash only   Meals: L, D

In the Irish heart of Sunnyside, comes the ultimate in downmarket
no-frills fried food, the Chipper. The décor is stark. There are no
tables or chairs, just counters and some huge frying vats, where the
magic takes place. The Chipper does two fish, cod and haddock.
The cod comes two ways, smoked or unsmoked. The smoked is
well and truly smoked, and much better than it has a right to be.
Portions are very large, and the Chipper sells some appropriately
brutish dips and sauces, the best being a thick curry gravy ideal for
slopping over the fries. The Chipper sells the mandatory side dishes
from hell, like mushy peas and Heinz beans, along with surprisingly upscale portobello mushrooms coated in batter and fried.
They are excellent, especially when dipped in curry sauce. This is
the home of the fried fruit pie.

Price range: Apps., $2–$3; entrees, $3.50–$7.95; desserts, $1–$2.
Wheelchair access: One step up to restaurant.

Cho Dang Gol ☆☆ $$$ KOREAN

55 W. 35th St. (bet. Fifth & Sixth Aves.) (212) 695-8222
Credit cards: All major Meals: L, D

Cho Dang Gol serves uniquely rustic food that is very different from
what is available at other Korean restaurants in the surrounding
blocks. The specialty here is fresh soybean curd, made daily at the
restaurant. The kitchen makes each dish with extreme care. Even
the panchan, the little saladlike appetizers, are of remarkably high
quality. For the uninitiated, searching out the best dishes is not
easy. Cho-dang-gol jung-sik arrives in three bowls: one with rice
dotted with beans, another with "bean-curd dregs" (which hardly
conveys its utter deliciousness) and the third with a pungent soup-
stew containing pork, seafood, onions and chilies. Also try chung-
kook-jang, too, soybean-paste stew with an elemental flavor, and
doo-boo doo-roo-chi-gi, a combination of pork, pan-fried kimchi,
clear vermicelli and big triangles of bean curd.

Wine list: Try beer, so ju (Korean sweet-potato vodka) or makkolli
(the rough, milky rice liquor). **Price range:** Apps., $7–$19; entrees,
$11–$30. **Wheelchair access:** All one level.

Christos Hasapo-Taverna $25 & Under
GREEK/STEAKHOUSE

41-08 23rd Ave., Astoria, Queens (718) 726-5195
Credit cards: All major   Meals: L, D, LN Closed Tue.

This cheerful, handsome Greek steakhouse recreates the traditional
Greek pairing of a butcher shop and a restaurant. Meals begin with
fresh tzatziki, a combination of yogurt, garlic and cucumber, and
tarama, the wonderful fish roe purée. Appetizer portions are big
and easily shared, and there is a large selection of grilled offal if
you like to precede your meat with more meat. Richly flavored
steaks and chops dominate the menu, and some nights more traditional fare, like piglet and baby lamb, is turned on the rotisserie.
Best desserts include baklava, a wonderful apple cake, and a plate
of prunes and figs marinated in sweet wine.

Price range: Apps., $5–$15; entrees, $20–$25; desserts, $4. **Wheel-
chair access:** Steps to dining room. **Features:** Parking available.

Churrascaria Girassol $25 & Under BRAZILIAN
33-18 28th Ave., Astoria, Queens (718) 545-8250
Credit cards: All major Meals: L, D, LN

Girassol is a plain room with half a dozen tables and a small
counter. During televised Brazilian soccer matches, diners leap out
of their seats and scream with each goal and near miss. That's part
of the charm. No other churrascaria in New York is as truly Brazilian as Girassol, where everybody speaks Portuguese. The chef and
owner, Lilian Fagundes, prepares almost everything from scratch.
Her touch is evident in classic dishes like an excellent feijoada, a
flavorful black bean stew thick with all manner of pork. If it's steak
you want, the medalhão, a thick marinated tenderloin, is superb.
Portions are large enough for two. As good as these dishes are,

most people seem to come for the rodìzio. Compared with banquet-hall rodìzios, which may serve as many as 20 cuts of meat, Girassol's selection of a half-dozen may seem paltry, but it is satisfying.

Other recommended dishes: Fish stew, dulce de leche with coconut, passion fruit pudding. **Alcohol:** Beer and wine. **Price range:** Apps., $1–$4; entrees, $9–$16. **Wheelchair access:** The entrances to the dining room and restroom are narrow.

Churrascaria Plataforma ☆☆ $$$

BRAZILIAN

316 W. 49th St. (bet. Eighth & Ninth Aves.)   (212) 245-0505
Credit cards: All major   Meals: L, D, LN

Two things are required to truly appreciate Churrascaria Plataforma: a large appetite to keep you eating and a large group to cheer you on. A caipirinha or two, the potent Brazilian drink, doesn't hurt either. This rodizio (all-you-can-eat Brazilian restaurant) is distinguished from the others by the high quality of the food and the charming attitude of the waiters. The waiters will entice you with ham, sausage, lamb, wonderfully crisp and juicy chicken legs, pork ribs, even the occasional side of salmon, which is delicious in its caper sauce. But it is beef that has pride of place: sirloin, baby beef, top round, skirt steak, brisket, short ribs, special top round. If the desserts are more interesting than wonderful, that is all to the good. The only reason to eat dessert after so much meat is to prove that you can. (*Ruth Reichl*)

Wine list: Small and not particularly interesting; besides, everybody's drinking caipirinhas. **Price range:** All-you-can-eat rodizio meal, $39; children under 10, $20. **Wheelchair access:** Ramp to dining room; restrooms down a flight of stairs.

Circus Restaurant ☆☆ $$$ BRAZILIAN

808 Lexington Ave. (near 62nd St.)   (212) 223-2965
Credit cards: All major   Meals: L, D, LN

An upscale Brazilian restaurant that turns into a party every night. While churrascarias faithfully reproduce a form of restaurant popular in Brazil, Circus serves the food your mother might cook if you were raised in São Paulo or Bahia. It is a warm and cozy place, usually packed with Brazilians eager for a taste of home. Try picadinho, beef sautéed with wine and thyme, topped with a poached egg and accompanied by rice, beans and cooked bananas. Another particularly satisfying dish is an appetizer, bolo de milho e rabada, little polenta cakes baked with Manchego cheese and served with a robust oxtail sauce. Desserts are sweet and tropical. (*Ruth Reichl*)

Wine list: Mostly Iberian and Latin American with some United States labels, often overpriced in low-end wines, some bargains among the older Spanish wines. **Price range:** Lunch: apps., $5–$10; entrees, $11–$19; prix fixe, $18. Dinner: apps., $6–$13; entrees, $16–$24. **Wheelchair access:** Steps down to dining room and restroom. **Features:** Outdoor dining.

Citarella the Restaurant ☆☆ $$$

1240 Sixth Ave. (near 49th St.) (212) 332-1515
Credit cards: All major   Meals: L, D   Closed Sun.

Citarella the Restaurant, an offshoot of the famous food store, has a
quiet sense of style. The theme here is fish, fresh from the market,
and David Rockwell, the designer, has embraced it warmly and wit-
tily. In the cozy second-floor dining room, with wraparound views
of 49th Street and the Exxon Building fountain across the avenue,
he has dotted the subtly sparkling wall panels with little underwa-
ter dioramas.

Joseph Gurrera, the owner of the Citarella stores, has obviously
made a deal with his kitchen team: I'll give you the finest fish that
swim, and you give me a fish restaurant worth talking about. On
balance, dishes are fresh, exciting and in every way worthy of the
top-quality ingredients. At lunch, Citarella offers a full sushi menu
downstairs, and the upstairs lunch menu includes a five-piece sushi
appetizer and a 12-piece sushi entree. The presentation is simple,
the fish pristine.

Citarella's dessert menu ratchets the entire operation up at least
one notch. The warm vanilla cake with vanilla ice cream is already
gaining cult status.

Wine list: An appealing international list of about 180 wines, many
very modestly priced, with 21 wines by the glass. **Price range:**
Lunch entrees, $21–$28. Dinner: apps., $9–$18; entrees, $25–$37;
desserts, $9–$12. **Wheelchair access:** Elevator access.

Cité $$$ STEAKHOUSE

120 W. 51st St. (bet. Sixth & Seventh Aves.) (212) 956-7100
Credit cards: All major   Meals: Br, L, D

If you visit this large, boisterous Art Deco restaurant and you see
the wine flowing like water, it must be after 8 P.M., when one of
New York's great wine deals goes into effect. From 8 to midnight,
Cité — one of Alan Stillman's stable of restaurants, which also
includes the Post House, Smith & Wollensky and the Park Avenue
Cafe, among others — will pour as much as you want of four different wines, which usually include champagne, a decent white and a
couple of decent reds. Along with the wine, Cité serves fine sirloin
and other steakhouse staples.

Price range: Apps., $6–$13; entrees, $19–$30; desserts, $9. Three-
course pre-theater prix fixe, $43; three-course prix-fixe grill, $40;
wine dinner, $60. **Wheelchair access:** Fully accessible.

City Hall ☆☆ $$$ AMERICAN

131 Duane St. (near Church St.) (212) 227-7777
Credit cards: All major   Meals: L, D, LN   Closed Sun.

The cavernous dining room has the spare quality of an old steakhouse, but the clean details, loud music and hip clientele give it an
up-to-date air. The menu includes all the old classics, from iceberg
lettuce to baked Alaska. Just as you are relaxing into this retro

mode, however, you realize there is more to City Hall than old-fashioned fare. Among the meat dishes try the huge double steak, still on the bone and served for two. For dessert, the apple bread pudding made with brioche is very, very good.

Time has begun to expose City Hall's weaknesses. It now seems like an unusually handsome restaurant serving very average food. The three-herring appetizer packs a punch, and the exuberantly presented all-American steaks, chops and seafoods have razzle-dazzle, but there's nothing much going on. You could do worse. You could do better. (*Ruth Reichl, updated by William Grimes*)

Wine list: Interesting and offbeat; try the New Zealand sauvignon blancs with the oysters, the Rhones with the steaks. **Price range:** Apps., $7–$16; entrees, $18–$32; side dishes, $7; desserts, $6–$8. **Wheelchair access:** Accesssible.

Cocina Cuzco $25 & Under   PERUVIAN
55 Ave. A (at 4th St.)   (212) 529-3469
Credit cards: Cash only   Meals: L, D, LN

Peruvian cuisine is a melting pot of Asian, European, African and ancient American influences. The chef has had long restaurant experience in Peru, and his main courses demonstrate many sides of Peruvian cuisine. Lomo saltado, stir-fried beef flavored with soy and onions and served over rice and French fries, shows the influence of the Chinese laborers who came to Peru a century ago. The influence of former African slaves can be seen in red snapper, crusted in thin slices of sweet potatoes, making it crisp on the outside and moist within. Desserts are delicious, like bread pudding flavored with dulce de leche, and mazamorra morada, a kind of sweet and fruity gelatin.

Other recommended dishes: Ceviches, octopus with rosemary, papas a la huancaina, roasted pork, roasted chicken, skirt steak. **Price range:** Apps., $3–$9; entrees, $9–$14. **Wheelchair access:** All one level.

Coco Roco $25 & Under   PERUVIAN
392 Fifth Ave., Park Slope, Brooklyn   (718) 965-3376
Credit cards: All major   Meals: L, D

This bright, pleasant restaurant offers some of the best Peruvian food in New York. The menu ranges from tender, delicious ceviches from Peru's coast to Andean dishes that have been enjoyed since the days of the Incan empire. Cancha, simply roasted, salted corn kernels, is served in a bowl before the meal and also shows up in several dishes, like tamalitos verdes, a tamale topped with roast pork and cilantro sauce. Roast chicken is excellent, and desserts like rice pudding and lucuma ice cream, made with a Peruvian fruit, are wonderful.

Other recommended dishes: Chicharrón, mixed seafood ceviche, clam ceviche, octopus in rosemary sauce, red snapper crusted in sweet potato, skirt steak, bread pudding. **Alcohol:** Beer and a modest list of inexpensive Argentine wines. **Price range:** Apps., $5–$8; entrees, $9–$17.

Cocotte
$25 & Under   FRENCH/BISTRO
337 Fifth Ave. (at 4th St.), Park Slope, Brooklyn   (718) 832-6848
Credit cards: All major   Meals: D   Closed Tue.

At Cocotte you'll find buffed brick walls and rough-hewn artificial beams; dark wood is everywhere. Ingredients run to foie gras, lobster, peekytoe crab meat and New Zealand rib-eye prepared in ways that are regionally French or at any rate French-ish. There is great value to be found in a plate of delicious oven-roasted chicken served with smoky garlic mashed potatoes and vegetables cooked in the juice of the bird, as well as in an excellent frisée salad with shredded duck confit, apples and spicy baked walnuts. Or try a fillet of black cod, served over lobster mashed potatoes with grilled asparagus and a merlot demi-glace. For dessert, the best option is a pithiviers with caramelized apple, its soft almondy flavor a glove-like fit for the taste of the warm fruit. *(Sam Sifton)*

Price range: Apps., $7–$12; entrees, $13–$21; desserts, $7. **Wheelchair access:** Small step to entrance.

Coffee Shop
$$ BRAZILIAN
29 Union Square W. (at 16th St.)   (212) 243-7969
Credit cards: All major   Meals: B, Br, L, D, LN

Big attitude, big crowd, very trendy. Great late at night when it's filled with models or people who should be. Casual, inexpensive, open until 5:30 A.M. except Sundays.

Price range: Apps., $6–$8; entrees, $8–$20; desserts, $5–$7. **Wheelchair access:** Fully accessible. **Features:** Outdoor dining.

Col Legno
$25 & Under   ITALIAN
231 E. 9th St. (bet. Second & Third Aves.)   (212) 777-4650
Credit cards: AE   Meals: D   Closed Mon.

This sedate Tuscan trattoria (whose name means "with wood," a musical term for playing a violin with the back of a bow) offers simple, lusty yet delicate dishes invigorated by just a touch of wood, achieved by a chef who plays the wood fire like a musical instrument. Pastas are unusual and superb, while pizzas and grilled dishes, prepared in a big wood-burning oven, are all top-notch. Col Legno's desserts are simple but just right: a huge glass of rich hazelnut gelato, or a tiramisu that actually tastes of rum, espresso, chocolate and cream.

Alcohol: Beer and a brief list of inexpensive wines that go perfectly with the food. **Price range:** Apps., $4–$7; entrees, $8–$17; desserts, $5. **Wheelchair access:** Not accessible.

Compass
☆☆ **$$$**   NEW AMERICAN
208 W. 70th St. (bet. Amsterdam & West End Aves.)   (212) 875-8600
Credit cards: All major   Meals: Br, D

The name could not be more appropriate, because this is a restaurant that has found its way. The main dining room is in the lobby of an apartment building, but it is striking with slate-covered pillars and a long abstract painting in red along the rear wall. While the dining room constitutes opulence for the Upper West Side, formality is not enforced. The menu is simultaneously simple yet sneakily sophisticated in the contemporary American vein. Ingredients are superb. You can virtually taste the ocean in a soft square of poached Copper River salmon. A sturdy cylinder of pork loin, juicy and full of flavor, arrives towering over a gorgeous sliced heirloom tomato and a sweet charred Vidalia onion. A three-course, $30 bistro menu is available, and in the spacious bar in front, Compass offers an attractive lounge menu. For dessert try the lemongrass-flavored panna cotta. There is also an excellent selection of about a dozen cheeses. *(Eric Asimov)*

Wine list: Mostly American, with the best selection in the $50 to $75 range. **Price range:** Apps., $9–$16; entrees, $22–$32; desserts, $8; bistro menu, $30.**Wheelchair access:** Steps at entrance.

Congee　　　　$25 & Under　　　CHINESE
98 Bowery (bet. Grand & Hester Sts.)　　　(212) 965-5028
Credit cards: All major　　　　　　　　　Meals: L, D

Congee is little more than thin rice porridge, bland as milquetoast, yet it arouses strong feelings. Perhaps it is a reaction to the ingredients typically added to the dish, which can range from humble organ meats to bits of exquisite lobster. Congee, the restaurant, is not much to look at. But the food is fresh and vivid, with clear spicing and pure flavors. Congee's congee is outstanding. Try it with slivers of savory pork and bits of pungent preserved egg, or with black mushrooms and velvety slices of chicken breast, and a shot of hot sauce. If your soul does not cry out for congee, the extensive menu includes more than 200 dishes, with none better than deep-fried golden-skinned chicken, topped with plenty of chopped garlic and scallions.

Other recommended dishes: Squab with soy sauce, sautéed razor clams, snow pea greens, sizzling eel in casserole, scallion pancake, salt-baked squid. **Price range:** Congee and apps., $2–$8; entrees, $7–$19. **Wheelchair access:** Steps at entrance.

Congee Village　　　$25 & Under　　　CHINESE
100 Allen St. (bet. Delancey & Broome Sts.)　　　(212) 941-1818
Credit cards: All major　　　　　　　　　Meals: L, D, LN

The best congee in New York is in this friendly restaurant. Congee, also known as jook, is nothing more than Chinese hot cereal, a milky rice porridge. More than two dozen versions of congee are served here, some with additions as exotic as fish maws or frog, each served steaming in a pretty ceramic crock and flavored with cilantro, scallions and slivers of pungent ginger. The congee is especially good with a side of fried bread, which comes with a thick, sweet sauce but is better dunked in the congee. The rest of the menu offers excellent Cantonese and Hong Kong dishes, like tender, delicious and beautiful razor clams in a salty black bean sauce, and specials like sweet potato greens, shiny and deeply colored, flavored with bits of dried pork and XO sauce.

Other recommended dishes: Congees, including: pork with preserved egg; fish; roast duck with meatballs; and chicken with black

mushrooms. **Price range:** Congee, $3–$5; dim sum and soup,
$1–$9. **Wheelchair access:** Narrow ramp to restroom.

Cooke's Corner $25 & Under   AMERICAN

618 Amsterdam Ave. (at 90th St.)   (212) 712-2872
Credit cards: AE   Meals: D

This charmingly subdued little restaurant, with its small, well-
designed menu and intelligent wine list, is free of what plagues so
many restaurants in the neighborhood: loud music, a bar crowd
and big-screen television sets. With its comfortable chairs, inlaid
wood tables, subtle décor and low-key service, Cooke's is a restaurant that caters to grown-ups and makes no apologies for it. It even
takes reservations.

The menu is quietly satisfying with attention to details. Main
courses include a juicy, flavorful roast chicken, and a fine piece of
maple-glazed salmon that was not overly sweet. Beef, braised for
four hours until remarkably tender, has a lively Eastern European
scent of caraway and coriander seeds and comes with buttery
spaetzle. Desserts are weak, aside from a rich German chocolate
cake with a dark chocolate sauce.

Price range: Apps., $5–$9; entrees, $12–$22 (some specials are
$25). **Wheelchair access:** All one level.

Copeland's $$ SOUTHERN

547 W. 145th St. (bet. Amsterdam Ave & Broadway) (212) 234-2357
Credit cards: All major   Meals: B, L, D

The Southern buffet at this Harlem institution offers all the traditional specialties. Among the entrees are such specialties as Southern fried chicken, chitterlings and champagne, barbecued short ribs
of beef and braised oxtails. It's not likely to surprise you, but it will
fill you up.

Price range: Lunch: avg. app., $4; entree, $11; dessert, $3. Dinner:
avg. app., $5; entree, $25; dessert, $4. **Wheelchair access:** Fully
accessible.

Corner Bistro $ BAR SNACKS

331 W. 4th St. (at Jane St.)   (212) 242-9502
Credit cards: Cash only   Meals: L, D, LN

This old bar is renowned for its hamburgers, which are big and
juicy but nowhere near the best in the city. It would be a great
place to have in your neighborhood but is not worth a trip.

Price range: Apps. and sides, $2–$3; sandwiches, $4–$6. **Wheelchair acceess:** Restrooms not accessible.

Coup   ☆ $$ NEW AMERICAN

509 E. 6th St. (bet. Aves. A & B)   (212) 979-2815
Credit cards: All major   Meals: D

Like the rest of the East Village, Coup takes an ascetic stand on
visual stimulation. The walls and the concrete floor are battleship

gray. What little light is allowed comes from translucent white wall fixtures that look like glowing pharmaceutical capsules. Somehow, this sensory deprivation induces a feeling of tranquility. Beneath the cloak of mystery lies a deceptively normal neighborhood restaurant, one that is not only in, but of, the blocks around it. It fits stylistically. The food does not aim too high, but what it aims at, it hits. It's the kind of place that always seems like a good idea. The roast Cornish hen takes some beating. Brown as a berry and pleasingly plump, it's packed with chunks of coarse-grained sourdough bread and Michigan cherries. The stuffing is beyond praise. Coup also has a deeply limey Key lime pie and an honest, homey pineapple upside-down cake.

Wine list: A budget-priced, not very exciting list of about 40 bottles. **Price range:** Apps., $5–$9; entrees, $16–$21; desserts, $7. **Wheelchair access:** All one level. **Features:** Outdoor dining.

Craft ☆☆☆ $$$$ NEW AMERICAN
43 E. 19th St. (bet. Park Ave. S. & Broadway)　　　(212) 780-0880
Credit cards: All major　　　　　　　　　Meals: L (Mon.–Fri.), D

This is a handsome restaurant, with a clean, vaguely Mission-influenced look that supports the culinary theme. Craft invites diners to take a trip. The destination is a simpler, cleaner, more honest America; it's a vision of food heaven, a land of strong, pure flavors and back-to-basics cooking techniques. But in pursuit of his vision, Tom Colicchio, the chef and an owner, has placed demands on his customers that make Craft one of the most baroque dining experiences in New York. At Craft, diners build their own meals.

The saving grace at Craft, from the beginning, has been the high quality of the ingredients and their masterly handling by Mr. Colicchio and his chef de cuisine. Nothing at the restaurant sounds like much. Lunch could start with a half-dozen Belon oysters, followed by a thick slice of stuffed veal breast with roasted spring onions and roasted bluefoot mushrooms. Every bite is a revelation. The oysters sparkle. The veal, a humble cut of meat wrapped around some simple roast vegetables, has an honesty and a depth of flavor that will stop you cold. Craft pulls off this quiet magic with deceptive ease. In a city famous for steak worship, the frighteningly large porterhouse, neatly sliced into rectangles, ranks as one of the finest large-scale hunks of beef you'll encounter.

Wine list: A rather short but carefully chosen international list of about 125 wines, with a dozen by the glass. **Price range:** Lunch: apps., $10–$14; entrees, $20–$26; three-course prix fixe, $32. Dinner: apps., $10–$20; entrees, $22–$36; side dishes, $6–$12; desserts, $4–$12; five-course tasting menu, $68. **Wheelchair access:** Restrooms on dining room level.

Craftbar $25 & Under NEW AMERICAN
47 E. 19th St. (bet. Park Ave. S. & Broadway)　　　(212) 780-0880
Credit cards: All major　　　　　　　　　Meals: L, D, LN

From the soft leather banquette, the thick linens, the flattering lighting and the vaultlike designer bathrooms, it is clear that Craftbar, the casual adjunct to Craft, is more than a knockoff of the humble Italian wine-and-sandwich shops that are its inspiration.

In looks and service alone, Craftbar sets itself leagues beyond the typical low-rent sandwich shop. And yet, its snacks, soups, salads and sandwiches, supplemented each day by a meat, a fish and a pasta dish, exude the simplicity of a wine bar, where needs are joyfully met rather than challenged.

Sandwiches are uniformly excellent. Delicate house-made mortadella, on a triple-decker of crustless white bread, is a Platonic ideal of bologna. For dessert, coconut panna cotta is unbelievably light and flavorful, while apple fritters are like glorious sugar- and cinnamon-coated doughnuts.

Other recommended dishes: Stuffed sage leaves, fried oysters, braised pork belly, braised lamb spareribs, braised rabbit, gingerbread and roasted pineapple. **Price range:** Apps., $4–$8; sandwiches and salads, $9–$11; entrees, $14–$18. **Wheelchair access:** One level.

Crispo $25 & Under   ITALIAN
240 W. 14th St. (bet. Seventh & Eighth Aves.)   (212) 229-1818
Credit cards: All major   Meals: D   Closed Sun.

Crispo's dining room — dark and cozy, with the electric-lamp glow of modernized rusticity — fills early. The fresh and unassuming menu comes as a welcome antidote to the greenhorn staff. The pastas, also available as half orders, vary in quality. The rigatoni with cherry tomatoes, spicy arugula and mozzarella is, however, a genuine pleasure. Crispo's spaghetti carbonara is an absolute model of the form, and in many ways, the restaurant's best dish. Main courses run the gamut of modern Italian-American trattoria fare. Lamb chops Milanese are terrific with their dollop of eggplant caviar on the side. And it would be a hard person who did not enjoy the smoky interplay between grilled salmon and its pancetta and savoy cabbage accompaniment. For dessert, best is an outstanding buttermilk panna cotta with roast peach. *(Sam Sifton)*

Other recommended dishes: Portobello mushroom and asparagus salad, roast peppers and anchovies, prosciutto with figs and Parmigiano. **Price range:** Apps., $6–$9; entrees, $12.50–$17. **Wheelchair access:** Several steps down from sidewalk.

Crudo $25 & Under   SPANISH
54 Clinton St. (near Rivington St.)   (646) 654-0116
Credit cards: All major   Meals: D   Closed Sun., Mon.

Crudo, where each dish revolves around raw fish, is an offshoot of 1492, a Spanish restaurant next door, and hardly bigger than a slender piece of sashimi. With flattering lighting, raw walls of brick and textured plaster and vintage Eames chairs, Crudo has all the makings of a great first-date restaurant. The menu lists only 10 dishes, in either small or large portions. Each dish is presented as a composition, offering plenty to discuss, should other talk flag. With neither oven nor stove, the food is by necessity light and fresh. The chef works in the ceviche tradition, marinating fish to flavor them. The best dishes playfully mix sweet and salty flavors and gracefully blend textures. The most complicated dish, scallops cured in verjus, wrapped in prosciutto and served with pear was a favorite.

Other recommended dishes: Oysters three-way, clam and octopus ceviche, hamachi. **Price range:** Small dishes, $6–$10; large, $9–$17. **Wheelchair access:** Not accessible.

Cucina ☆ $$ ITALIAN

256 Fifth Ave. (near Carroll St.), Park Slope, Brooklyn (718) 230-0711
Credit cards: All major   Meals: D   Closed Mon.

Cucina is beginning to feel fresher and more vigorous than it has in a long time. It retains some of the old warhorses of Italian cuisine, while newer additions to the menu, most of them big improvements, make the place much less Italian than it was. The kitchen is now more responsive to the Greenmarket and the seasons. Still one of the best dishes was spaghetti frutti di mare, a dish that disappoints nine times out of 10. At Cucina, it's a revelation: a concentrated, spicy diavolo sauce wrapped around properly cooked mussels, clams, shrimp and lobster. For dessert, the almond cannoli filled with ricotta and mascarpone are delicate and crunchy.

Wine list: A serviceable list of about 35 wines, mostly Italian, nearly all under $50, and a dozen wines by the glass. **Price range:** Apps., $6–$10; entrees, $14–$28; desserts, $8; three-course prix fixe (Tue.–Fri. until 7 P.M.), $25. **Wheelchair access:** One level.

Cupping Room Cafe $$ NEW AMERICAN

359 W. Broadway (bet. Broome & Grand Sts.)   (212) 925-2898
Credit cards: All major   Meals: B, Br, L, D

A SoHo pioneer that continues to serve good, straightforward American food, like burgers and chicken, and great coffee in a charmingly battered atmosphere.

Price range: Lunch: apps., $8–$12; entrees, $16–$23; desserts, $4–$8. **Wheelchair access:** Not accessible.

Cyclo $25 & Under VIETNAMESE

203 First Ave. (at 12th St.)   (212) 673-3957
Credit cards: All major   Meals: D, LN

This stylish little East Village restaurant serves some of the best Vietnamese food in New York City: It is inventive, impeccably fresh and meticulously prepared, while service is friendly and informative. Try cha gio, crisp and delicate spring rolls, and chao tom, grilled shrimp paste wrapped around sugar cane. Don't hesitate to order fruit for dessert, like cubes of wonderfully fresh mango that are the perfect end to a stellar meal. The only problem is the constant crowds.

Other recommended dishes: Ca bam (seared monkfish); goi du du (green papaya salad); pho (oxtail broth with rice noodles); bun thit nuong (grilled pork over rice noodle pillows). **Price range:** Apps., $5–$8; entrees, $10–$15; desserts, $4–$7. **Wheelchair access:** All one level.

Da Andrea $25 & Under   ITALIAN
557 Hudson St. (near Perry St.)   (212) 367-1979
Credit cards: MC/V   Meals: D

After a young couple from Bologna took over, Da Andrea revealed itself to be a dependably good local favorite, one with ambition. Before anything, order a plate of tigelle. It takes a while. It's a plate of thin, warm biscuits fresh from the oven. You slice a biscuit open, sprinkle grated Parmesan cheese on the steaming bread, fold some thin-sliced prosciutto onto one side, close the covers and eat the melting flavors. The pastas are made daily and worth exploring as a shared appetizer or as a supper in themselves. The entrees are less assured. The lamb shank, however, is terrific. For dessert, enjoy a plate of the kitchen's crunchy biscotti, a glass of house-made limoncello and your memories of that artful tigelle. *(Sam Sifton)*

Other recommended dishes: Octopus salad, baby squid salad.
Price range: Apps., $4.50–$8.50; pastas, $9–$10.50; entrees, $12–$18.50. **Wheelchair access:** Not accessible.

Da Antonio $$$ ITALIAN
157 E. 55th St. (bet. Third & Lexington Aves.)   (212) 588-1545
Credit cards: All major   Meals: L, D

The pastas are superb at this gracious, quietly dignified restaurant. Agnolotti stuffed with sausages and broccoli rabe is particularly good. Service is lovely; the owner hands you a large Italian menu and leaves you to peruse it. When he returns to tell you about the specials, he actually describes each dish. You can almost dine on his enthusiasm.

Price Range: Lunch: apps., $6–$10; entrees, $13–$19; desserts, $7–$10. Dinner: apps., $8–$13; entrees, $16–$30; desserts, $7–$10. **Wheelchair access:** Not accessible.

Da Ciro $25 & Under   ITALIAN
229 Lexington Ave. (near 33rd St.)   (212) 532-1636
Credit cards: All major   Meals: L, D

An excellent, often overlooked little Italian restaurant. Specialties, cooked in a wood-burning oven, include terrific pizzas like focaccia robiola, a wonderfully crisp double-crusted pizza encasing earthy, melted robiola cheese that has been drizzled with truffle oil. Also excellent is a casserole of wild mushrooms baked in a crock with arugula, goat cheese, olives, tomatoes and mozzarella. The pastas are simple but lively, and full-flavored desserts like bitter chocolate mousse cake and hazelnut semifreddo more than hold their own.

Price range: Apps., $6–$13; pastas, $13–$16; entrees, $16–$28. **Wheelchair access:** All one level.

Daily Chow $25 & Under   PAN-ASIAN
2 E. 2nd St. (at Bowery)   (212) 254-7887
Credit cards: All major   Meals: L, D, LN

Daily Chow brings together Thai and Korean dishes with Chinese, Japanese and Vietnamese preparations. It does enough things well and is so good-natured that a meal there can be thoroughly enjoyable. Korean main courses are quite successful. Bibimbop, the rice, beef and egg dish, is served with vegetables in a hot stone crock so that the bottom layer turns crisp. One of the best dishes is a dessert, mango sticky rice, sweetened with coconut milk and served with mango slices. A ginger-flavored brownie with coconut ice cream is about as Asian as a Big Mac, but delicious nonetheless.

The food can certainly seem secondary. Daily Chow focuses on a drinking crowd, offering pitchers of cocktails with names like ginger kamikaze and Thai dye, though there is a small but well-chosen list of wines.

Other recommended dishes: Thai soups, Vietnamese pork chops, bulgogi, beef massaman curry. **Price range:** Apps., $3–$9; entrees, $8–$15. **Wheelchair access:** Ramp at entrance.

Dakshin $25 & Under   INDIAN
1713 First Ave. (near 89th St.)   (212) 987-9839
741 Ninth Ave. (near 50th St.)   (212) 757-4545
Credit cards: All major   Meals: L, D

Perhaps no other cuisine pays as much attention to spices and seasonings as Indian, and yet so much Indian food in Manhattan is bland. So it is a great pleasure to find lively spicing in more than a few dishes at Dakshin. Dakshin's breads are excellent, especially mint paratha, rich with ghee and tasting powerfully and refreshingly of mint, and garlic nan, made smoky in the clay oven. Kebabs of minced lamb are especially flavorful, as are cubes of lemony boneless chicken breast. Among the meat main courses, try the chicken Chettinad, with a thick sauce made lively by black pepper and curry leaves. Dakshin's vegetable dishes excel, especially punj rattani dal. This creamy, mellow dish, made with five types of lentils and flavored with lots of garlic and ginger, is true home cooking.

Other recommended dishes: Seva batata poori, jhinga jal toori, Mangalorean stir-fried chicken, tandoori assortment, lamb vindaloo, baby eggplant with ginger and coconut, bharta. **Price range:** Apps., $3–$6; entrees, $7–$17. **Wheelchair access:** Step at entrance.

Dalia's $25 & Under   TAPAS
984 Amsterdam Ave. (near 109th St.)   (212) 865-9541
Credit cards: All major   Meals: D, LN

With its dark walls and soft lighting, Dalia's offers a warm haven on a part of Amsterdam Avenue that is as sedate as a chain saw. Portions are on the large side, closer to what the Spanish call *raciones*, or large appetizers, so three tapas can make a meal. A simple tapa like toast rubbed with garlic and olive oil and topped with ham and cheese is a fine starter, and the cold potato-and-onion omelet has a pleasant but unusual texture, courtesy of oatmeal that the chef had mixed in. Potatoes cut into cubes, fried until crisp and served with aioli are irresistible, while grilled chorizo is always a crowd-pleaser.

Other recommended dishes: Steamed clams, grilled sardines, omelets. **Price range:** Tapas, $5–$9. **Wheelchair access:** All one level.

Da Mario $$$ ITALIAN

883 First Ave. (bet. 49th & 50th Sts.)   (212) 750-1804
Credit cards: All major   Meals: L, D

It looks like dozens of other small Italian restaurants in New York City, but this one is distinguished by its Sicilian bent, its warmth and its careful cooking. Expect a fine-looking array of antipasti, a long list of fish specials and a we-can-make-anything-you-want sort of attitude. Good pastas, surprisingly good desserts and a wine list with a strong Italian emphasis.

Price range: Lunch: apps., $6–$9; entrees, $10–$19; desserts, $6; prix fixe, $17. Dinner: apps., $7–$11; entrees, $14–$24; desserts, $6; prix fixe, $27. **Wheelchair access:** Restrooms are small.

Danal $25 & Under   NEW AMERICAN

90 E. 10th St. (bet. Third & Fourth Aves.)   (212) 982-6930
Credit cards: MC/V   Meals: Br, L, D

The warm, cozy country atmosphere is one of the highlights at this enduring favorite. The reliably enticing homey American fare is the other. The menu changes daily, but typical offerings include beet salad; grilled duck breast with orange sauce; and roast monkfish with a soy-balsamic reduction. Danal also does a nice afternoon tea and a fine Sunday brunch. It's a great place for a date.

Other recommended dishes: Roast chicken, pork chops, smoked trout, beef tenderloin, banana bread pudding, chocolate macadamia tart. **Alcohol:** Beer and wine. **Price range:** Avg. lunch: $11. Dinner: avg. app., $7; entrée, $18; dessert, $6. **Wheelchair access:** Not accessible. **Features:** Outdoor dining.

Da Nico $25 & Under   ITALIAN

164 Mulberry St. (bet. Grand & Broome Sts.)   (212) 343-1212
Credit cards: All major   Meals: L, D, LN

One of the few Italian restaurants in Little Italy that is actually worth trying. Rotisserie dishes, roasts and pizzas from the wood-burning oven are the best bets. Pizzas boast thin crusts and fresh, stylish toppings but could use another minute in the oven for additional crisping. The restaurant is an invitingly informal place in brick, wood and pewter with stools at a counter, tables in the food-filled front room facing the street and an airy, more secluded dining room in back.

Price range: Prix-fixe lunch, $6–$7. Avg. dinner, $25. **Wheelchair access:** Fully accessible. **Features:** Outdoor dining.

Daniel ☆☆☆☆ $$$$ FRENCH

Mayfair Hotel, 60 E. 65th St. (bet. Park & Madison Aves.)
(212) 288-0033
Credit cards: All major   Meals: D   Closed Sun.

Located in a luxurious hotel dining room, Daniel is a top-flight French restaurant, sumptuous and rather grand, but still very much the personal expression of its chef and owner, Daniel Boulud. There's a definite tone at Daniel, a warmth usually associated with small neighborhood restaurants.

Mr. Boulud has both feet planted in the rich gastronomic soil of the Lyonnais region, an area renowned for its robust cuisine. He is ceaselessly inventive in a free and easy way. The influences come from all over the Mediterranean, and as far afield as Japan and India, pulled in and made French with total assurance. One of the more intriguing dishes on the menu is cod crusted in black truffles, served on a rustic bed of lentils.

There are lots of pleasant surprises like that at Daniel, culminating in a dessert menu remarkable for its elegance and restraint. The left side is devoted to fruit desserts, the right to chocolate, and it's understandable if eyes tend to drift rightward to the thin leaves of chocolate filled with gianduja and amaretto or the glistening, nearly black chocolate bombe.

It is highly advisable to study the cheese trolley when it rolls around. The selection is well organized, the cheeses superb.

Service, confident and expert, goes a long way to explain the neighborhood's love affair with Daniel. Diners feel well cared for. There's none of the hovering that passes for attentive service at lesser restaurants. The tone is pitch-perfect, and as a result, patrons feel at ease.

Wine list: An outstanding list, tilted toward French wines but highly international. Broad and deep, it has a good selection of half bottles and wines by the glass. **Price range:** Three courses, $85; five-course tasting menu, $120; eight-course tasting menu $160. **Wheelchair access:** Entrance near main door.

Danube ☆☆☆ $$$$ VIENNESE/GERMAN

30 Hudson St. (at Duane St.)   (212) 791-3771
Credit cards: All major   Meals: D

David Bouley does not do things in a small way. Using fin-de-siécle Vienna as a culinary source, and a repository of romantic images, he has created Danube, the most enchanting restaurant New York has seen in decades. The Vienna of Schnitzler, Freud and Musil shimmers with a seductive light, captured brilliantly in Danube's décor. This is an opium dream of lush fabrics, decadent colors and lustrous glazed surfaces, dominated by the large, unabashedly excessive Klimts on the walls. If ever a restaurant was made for a four-hour meal, Danube is it.

After anchoring the menu with a handful of classics, he has conjured up his own private Austria or, in some cases, taken leave of the country altogether. More typically, Mr. Bouley has lightened, modernized and personalized traditional dishes, or invented new ones using traditional ingredients, often with stunning results. There are two thoroughly traditional desserts, both flawless: a

Czech palacsintak, or crêpe, and a Salzburger nockerl, a mound-shaped soufflé dusted in confectioners' sugar and served with raspberries.

Wine list: A pioneering list of 300 wines, half of them Austrian.
Price range: Apps., $8–$19; entrees, $25–$35; desserts, $9–$10.
Wheelchair access: Restroom on first floor.

D'Artagnan ☆☆ $$$$ FRENCH
152 E. 46th St. (bet. Third & Lexington Aves.) (212) 687-0300
Credit cards: All major Meals: L, D Closed Sun.

D'Artagnan has so much personality it could sell it by the pound. The food is Gascon, from France's legendary region of foie gras, duck, Armagnac and prunes. In pursuit of the Gascon flavor, the owner has turned D'Artagnan into a "Three Musketeers" theme park. The waiters are even outfitted in traditional Gascon garb. This is not a restaurant for diners who pick at their food. The cuisine of the musketeers is meat in its richest forms, washed down with big sturdy reds like Cahors or Madiran. The food is authentic, robust, earthy and powerfully flavored. Cassoulet is a religion in Gascony, and the one served here is a mighty heap of garlic sausage, duck-Armagnac sausage, duck leg confit, duck gizzard confit and the pancettalike ventrèche embedded in a layer of garlicky coco beans dense enough to give the silverware a fight.

The cheese course is small but pleasing, a rustic selection of Petit Basque, Roquefort and Coach Farm goat cheese. For the most part, the desserts seem like a distraction before the important business of pouring the aged Armagnac. One Gascon speciality deserves attention: apple croustade, which relies for its effect on a thousand-layered pastry so froufrou that in French it's called a bridal veil.

Wine list: An admirably focused list of about 60 wines, most from southwestern France, 20 available by the glass. **Price range:** Lunch: apps., $7–$19; entrees, $13–$26; desserts, $7–$9; three-course prix fixe, $20. Dinner: apps., $6–$19; entrees, $19–$26; desserts, $7–$9; three-course pre-theater menu, 5:30–7 P.M., $36; seven-course foie-gras tasting menu, $75. **Wheelchair access:** Main dining room upstairs.

Da Silvano $$$ ITALIAN
260 Sixth Ave. (bet. Houston & Bleecker Sts.) (212) 982-2343
Credit cards: All major Meals: L, D, LN

In a city filled with Italian restaurants, Da Silvano is often overlooked, though not by its regulars, who on any given night still constitute a veritable gossip column full of recognizable names. Yet no matter how many other places open claiming to be Tuscan, few have been able to duplicate Da Silvano's Tuscan reverence for simplicity. For more than 20 years the restaurant has been turning out simple, authentic Italian dishes. Good pastas, an interesting wine list and one of Manhattan's best opportunities for people-watching, especially from the outdoor cafe, have made this a perennial favorite. The street-side seats are most in demand. Sitting toward the rear is a less colorful experience, though a slice of beefy, well-grilled steak with an arugula salad, or fusilli with sausage, chopped green beans and grape tomatoes, help the social medicine go down.

The newest wing, called Da Silvano Cantinetta, meaning little cellar, offers a slightly smaller menu that is slightly less expensive than the one at the main restaurant. But it is by no means slight.

Price range: Apps., $7–$13; entrees, $13–$29; desserts, $8 and up. **Wheelchair access:** Fully accessible. **Features:** Outdoor dining.

Dawat ☆ $$$ INDIAN

210 E. 58th St. (bet. Second & Third Aves.) (212) 355-7555
Credit cards: All major Meals: L, D

Once New York City's most innovative Indian restaurant, it no longer seems so cutting-edge. Most of the vegetable dishes — the small baked eggplant with tamarind sauce, the potatoes mixed with ginger and tomatoes, the homemade cheese in spinach sauce — are excellent. The set lunches are a bargain. Two dishes stand out: Cornish hen with green chilies, "a very hot specialty of Kerala's Baghdadi Jews," and sarson ka sag, a sour, spicy, buttery purée of mustard greens. Bhaja are also impressive: Whole leaves of spinach, battered so lightly that the green glows through the coating, are paired with light little potato-skin fritters. (*Ruth Reichl*)

Wine list: The wine list irritatingly does not include the vintage years, and wines could be more creatively chosen to match the food. **Price range:** Prix-fixe lunch, $13 and $14. Dinner: apps., $6–$10; entrees, $16–$24; side dishes, $4–$13; desserts, $5. **Wheelchair access:** All one level.

DB Bistro Moderne ☆ ☆ $$$$ BISTRO

55 W. 44th St. (bet. Fifth & Sixth Aves.) (212) 391-2400
Credit cards: All major Meals: L, D

Daniel Boulud's lively, even raucous restaurant tries to pass for a bistro but can't quite disguise its high-class leanings. The cooking, although simplified to suit the bistro concept and even countrified on occasion, plays to Mr. Boulud's strength, his refined rusticity. There's nothing fancy about Mr. Boulud's tarte Tatin heaped with roasted tomatoes, goat cheese, basil and black olives, but a perfect buttery crust and tomatoes brought to peak concentration of flavor make a little miracle out of this humble tart.

Years of catering to an Upper East Side clientele have given Mr. Boulud a supernatural hand with salads and spa fare. The menu also manages the trick of making very light desserts, like melon carpaccio with ginger sorbet as appealing as the clafoutis tout chocolat, a small round chocolate cake, runny in the center, that looks like no clafoutis on earth. No one will object.

Wine list: A shrewd international list of about 140 wines, with 13 wines by the glass. **Price range:** Lunch: apps., $10–$16; entrees, $24–$29; desserts, $9–$11; prix-fixe, $24–$30. Dinner: apps, $12–$17; entrees, $28–$32; desserts, $9–$11; three-course prix fixe, $39. **Wheelchair access:** Entrance through hotel lobby leads to upper dining room; restrooms on upper dining room level.

Deborah $25 & Under   NEW AMERICAN

43 Carmine St. (bet. Bedford & Bleecker Sts.)   (212) 242-2606
Credit cards: All major   Meals: L, D   Closed Mon.

In the best sense of the phrase, Deborah Stanton has been around the block a few times, cooking all over the city and beyond. Now she has settled in Greenwich Village with her own restaurant, offering modern American food that, with deceptive complexity, transcends most neighborhood restaurant clichés. While some chefs offer hamburgers only grumpily, Ms. Stanton makes the most of her challenge, serving a civilized, tasty burger topped with greens, a slice of tomato roasted to concentrate the flavor and a crisp onion ring. An open kitchen divides the narrow dining room, with its clean lines of brick, black tables and red banquettes. Loud music in the front can make it uncomfortable. The rear is more tranquil.

Other recommended dishes: Calamari, prawn cakes, grilled pizza, mushroom timbale, short ribs, chicken, banana pudding, chocolate fudge cheesecake. **Price range:** Apps., $7–$10; entrees, $13–$19. **Wheelchair access:** Not accessible.

Delhi Palace $25 & Under   INDIAN

37-33 74th St., Jackson Heights, Queens   (718) 507-0666
Credit cards: All major   Meals: L, D, LN

The menu promises the "haute cuisine of India," and the dining room has an almost stilted formality. The best dishes here are the rich, complex curries, each tailored for its particular dish. Shrimp vindaloo comes in a remarkable dark brown curry, tasting of vinegar and chocolate. Kadai gosht is another exceptional curry, with tender pieces of lamb in a tomato-and-onion sauce flavored with ginger and chilies. With the exception of reshmi kebab (tender pieces of chicken marinated in a lemon and garlic mixture), the Tandoori specialties are disappointing. Don't bother with the desserts; if you want a sweet, try the nearby bakeries.

Alcohol: Beer and wine. **Price range:** Apps., $2–$5; entrees, $10–$13. **Wheelchair access:** All one level.

Delmonico's   ☆ $$$ ITALIAN/NEW AMERICAN

56 Beaver St. (at Williams St.)   (212) 509-1144
Credit cards: All major   Meals: B, L, D

An American icon has been restored to its former glory. Opulent, old-fashioned and dignified, the huge rooms are rich with stained wood and soft upholstery, and the tables are swathed in oceans of white linen. It can be noisy in the middle of the room. The best dishes are in the section headed "Pasta, Risotti." Linguine with clams is a classic that is very well done. Ricotta and spinach ravioli may lack delicacy, but they are generous little pockets topped with clarified butter and fresh sage, and they make a satisfying meal. There is one steak to recommend: the rib-eye may not have the pedigree of a porterhouse or Delmonico, but it is big, tasty and perfectly cooked. For dessert try the baked Alaska.

Wine list: Not brilliant, but there are a few good wines at fair prices. **Price range:** Apps., $8–$16 ($32 for the cold seafood platter); pastas, $16–$22; entrees, $21–$34; desserts, $6–$10. **Wheelchair access:** Steps to dining room.

Demetris $25 & Under   GREEK
32-11 Broadway, Astoria, Queens   (718) 278-1877
Credit cards: All major   Meals: L, D, LN

With its glass ceiling, blue-and-white dining room and murals of island scenes, Demetris will look familiar to anybody who remembers the restaurant when it was known as Syros. As in many other Astoria restaurants, a musician is on hand and someone may get up to dance as the audience claps. The menu includes family-style dishes big enough to serve two, like grilled Guatemalan shrimp, four head-on monsters the size of lobsters with the rich, deep flavor of shrimp at their best. The porgy, one of the most underrated fishes, is especially good, simply grilled. Not every dish gets the porgy treatment. But the kitchen recaptures its magic with exquisite fried smelts no bigger than a pinky. Service is efficient, and when you've vowed that you can eat no more, a waiter appears with a platter of free semolina cakes and baked apples. Resisting the apples, bathed in cinnamon and spices, is a challenge.

Other recommended dishes: Whole flounder, fried red mullet, broiled scallops. **Price range:** Apps., $4.25–$10.95; entrees, $12–$25. **Wheelchair access:** Restrooms are downstairs.

DiFara Pizza $25 & Under   PIZZA
1424 Ave. J, Midwood, Brooklyn   (718) 258-1367
Credit cards: Cash only   Meals: L, D

In Midwood, Brooklyn, owner Dominic DeMarco fashions his pizzas in a glorious tribute to the way things ought to be. He is obsessed with the quality of the ingredients and one bite of the pizza will convince you. The texture of the crust is exceptional. The tomato sauce has spice and flavor, the cheese is mellow and the extra ingredients are superb, including pungent anchovies, rich fennel sausage and freshly charred peppers.

The kitchen also turns out top-notch dishes like tender chunks of veal with peppers served in a tomato sauce that is as complex and flavorful as a true gravy, with onions, garlic, herbs and pepper.

Other recommended dishes: Veal dishes, pasta with marinara sauce. **Price range:** Pizzas: pie, $11 and up; slice, $2 and up. Entrees, $7–$12. **Wheelchair access:** Not accessible.

Dim Sum Go Go   ☆ $$ CHINESE
5 E. Broadway (at Chatham Sq.)   (212) 732-0797
Credit cards: All major   Meals: L, D

Dim Sum Go Go is a bright, happy extrovert clinging to the edge of Chinatown like a goofy sidekick. The restaurant's interior design is done on the cheap but with genuine flair. It has a clean, streamlined look, with perforated steel chairs, bright red screens and a clever wall pattern taken from medieval scrolls with dining scenes.

The chef has developed a quirky, very appealing menu that plays Western variations on Chinese themes, sometimes seriously, sometimes for the sheer fun of it, as in the Go Go hamburger, a steamed bun folded over a patty made from dim sum beef and served with taro French fries. The dim sum is presented on a separate miniature menu. The better, more inventive food can be found on a larger menu of 60 dishes abounding in pleasant surprises. Bean curd skin is one of them, stuffed with bits of black mushroom and chopped spinach, then folded like a crêpe and fried.

Wine list: One white, one red, beers. **Price range:** Apps., $2–$10; entrees $9–$17; dessert, $3. **Wheelchair access:** Restrooms down one flight or up one flight.

Diner

$25 & Under   NEW AMERICAN

85 Broadway, Williamsburg, Brooklyn   (718) 486-3077
Credit cards: Cash only   Meals: Br, L, D, LN

The owners of this tattered luncheonette underneath the Williamsburg Bridge had the good sense not to create a diner-theme restaurant. Instead, Diner brings the diner idea up to date, offering the sort of everyday food that appeals to the local art crowd. The basics — roast chicken, french fries, hamburgers, etc. — are fine, and other dishes can be superb, like skirt steak, perfectly cooked whole trout, black bean soup and eggs scrambled with grilled trout. The atmosphere is bustling.

Other recommended dishes: French salad, goat cheese salad, black-eyed pea soup, mussels, roasted fresh ham, rib-eye steak, flourless chocolate cake. **Price range:** Apps., $4–$9; entrees, $7–$15. **Wheelchair access:** Two steps at entrance; restroom not accessible.

District   ☆ $$$

NEW AMERICAN

130 W. 46th St. (bet. Sixth & Seventh Aves.)   (212) 485-2999
Credit cards: All major   Meals: B, L, D

There's a theatrical aspect to dining at District. It hits you full force the moment you walk in the door and get a faceful of David Rockwell's design. The walls look like flats, and ropes behind the banquettes create the illusion that the scenery might be raised at any moment. As a stage set, District is witty, sophisticated and surprisingly cozy, especially if you land one of the wraparound booths.

The kitchen can be perplexingly erratic, but when it hits the marks, it's worth the ticket. The food is rich, florid, over the top and, when it works, irresistible in a way that makes you feel vaguely guilty. The pastry chef likes lush, very sweet desserts, but a tall, fluffy cheesecake with huckleberry compote scores a direct hit.

Wine list: An international, rather dull list of about 60 wines, with six wines by the glass and nine by the half bottle. **Price range:** Lunch: combined appetizer and entree, $13–$19; desserts, $5. Dinner: apps., $8–$15; entrees, $21–$38; desserts, $7. Three-course pre-theater menu, 5:30–6:30 P.M., $28. **Wheelchair access:** Restrooms are on street level.

Diwan ☆☆ $$ INDIAN

148 E. 48th St. (near Lexington Ave.) (212) 593-5425
Credit cards: All major Meals: L, D

Diwan has the somewhat impersonal appearance of a hotel restaurant, but it is unmistakably Indian. The chef has shaken up the menu, adding unusual fare like venison and wild boar chops. Good appetizers include shrimp bathed in a wonderfully tangy Goan sauce of onions and tomatoes, and bhajjia, perfectly fried crisp vegetable fritters. The tandoori dishes are superb, putting to shame the usual dry, orange-tinged chickens that have come to symbolize Indian cooking in New York. Diwan's tandoori halibut was a revelation. Also good are vegetable dishes like khatte aloo chole, chick peas and potatoes. Sarson ka saag, buttery mustard greens and spinach, is comforting and delicious. The standout among the desserts is a lovely chai pot de crème. (*Eric Asimov*)

Other recommended dishes: Beggar's purses, tikki chat, sabzi seekh kebabs, lamb chops, chicken potli, basil chicken. **Wine list:** Old-fashioned bistro list is being phased out for a more appropriate selection. **Price range:** Apps., $6.50–$10.50; entrees, $11–$25; desserts, $6–$7. **Wheelchair access:** Narrow hallway and two steps to restrooms.

Diwan's Curry House $25 & Under INDIAN

302 Columbus Ave. (at 74th St.) (212) 721-3400
Credit cards: All major Meals: L, D

Here are two things you almost never see in Indian restaurants: pork spareribs and a dining room decorated in a zebra-skin motif. Diwan's Curry House has them both. The zebra fabric lines the lounge area, making the dining room look like an after-hours club. But those pork ribs are something else, bathed in yogurt and grilled to crisp perfection. Of course, almost nobody in India eats pork. They don't eat nan with garlic, rosemary and olive oil either, though it's quite good here. It all seems pretty bizarre. But the ribs and other dishes are welcome rewards. The menu's more conventional items can be excellent, like katori chat, little pastry cups containing potatoes, chickpeas and yogurt with a zingy tamarind-mint sauce, and bhel poori, a Bombay favorite, made with potatoes, onions, crisp puffed rice and a similar tamarind sauce. The curries are a mixed bag. Try the rogan josh, tender lamb in a yogurt sauce flavored with fennel and the tikka makhanwala, chunks of chicken in a spicy creamy tomato sauce. Curries tend to be spicy.

Price range: Apps., $6–$8; entrees, $11–$18. **Wheelchair access:** Restrooms are one flight down.

Django ☆ $$$ FRENCH/BISTRO

480 Lexington Ave. (at 46th St.) (212) 871-6600
Credit cards: All major Meals: L, D Closed Sun.

Django is a dazzling, shimmery evocation of a brasserie in prewar Paris. Its food plays shy sideman to the design, able to keep the beat, perhaps, but adding little in the way of excitement or invention. Apart from the showy platters of raw shellfish, crabs and lobsters that trumpet brasserie service, Django's menu sticks for the most part to bistro standards. Vichyssoise emanates potato essence, while a foie gras terrine is as smooth and rich as one could ask. Charcuterie is not inspiring. Far more satisfaction can be found among the main courses. Meat courses include excellent steak au poivre and roasted rack of lamb. One of the best dishes is a simple roast chicken. For dessert, the soufflé "Arlequin," a pinwheel of six different flavors, is as playful and engaging as most everything else on the menu is not. *(Eric Asimov)*

Other recommended dishes: Frisée salad, grilled salmon, roasted whole branzino. **Wine list:** Mostly French and American; not particularly deep. **Price range:** Lunch: apps., salads and sandwiches, $7–$24; entrees, $17–$24; desserts, $7–$12. Dinner: apps., $8–$18; entrees, $15–$29; desserts, $7–$12. **Wheelchair access:** Second-floor dining room can be entered directly from 245 Park Avenue.

Djerdan Burek $25 & Under   BALKAN
221 W. 38th St. (bet. Seventh & Eighth Aves.)   (212) 921-1183
Credit cards: Cash only   Meals: B, L   Closed Sat., Sun.

Djerdan Burek, one of the newest in an ever-changing population of hole-in-the-wall eating establishments in the garment district, offers what a sandwich board in front sweetly calls "Balkanian food." The menu includes pastas, American-style sandwiches and salads, along with the small but most interesting section of Balkan specialties. If the bureks come straight from the oven, they are superb, the phyllo crust light and delicately flaky. Good as the bureks are, the stuffed cabbage is even better. Or try the goulash, with tender chunks of beef in a sauce subtly flavored with cloves and black pepper. You won't find a more typically Yugoslav dish than cevapi, a platter of thin beef sausages served with a wedge of crumbly white cheese, raw onions and a blob of sweet red sauce. For dessert, try tolumba, two stubby crullers in syrup.

Price range: $2–$10.50. **Wheelchair access:** Steps at entrance; restrooms are narrow.

Dock's Oyster Bar   ☆ $$ SEAFOOD
633 Third Ave. (at 40th St.)   (212) 986-8080
2427 Broadway (at 89th St.)   (212) 724-5588
Credit cards: All major   Meals: Br, L, D, LN

These bustling fish houses with a sparkling shellfish bar from which to choose shrimp or lobster cocktails or oysters and clams on the half shell are crowded fish emporiums that give you your money's worth. Favorites among starters are the Dock's clam chowder, Maryland crab cakes and steamers in beer broth. Steamed lobsters come in one- to two-pound sizes, and there is a New England clambake on Sunday and Monday nights. *(Ruth Reichl)*

Price range: Apps., $6–$11; entrees, $15–$22; desserts, $5–$7. **Wheelchair access:** Fully accessible.

Do Hwa $$ KOREAN

55 Carmine St. (at Bedford St.)   (212) 414-2815
Credit cards: All major   Meals: L, D   Closed Sun.

Do Hwa is one of a recent breed of Korean restaurants that are trying to win converts by making their food more understandable to curious Americans. In an imaginative step to demystify Korean food, the restaurant presents four tasting menus intended for parties of four. Three of the menus offer dishes from a specific region. The fourth is vegetarian.

The set menus remove the burden of choice, but diners who want to forage can move on to a menu of traditional dishes. Most tables do not have grills for do-it-yourself barbecuing, but the kitchen makes kalbi (grilled beef short ribs) and deji bulgogi (grilled pork slices), eaten burrito style in a leaf of red lettuce flavored with garlic, shiso and chilies. It sounds like home cooking, and it is. The executive chef is the owner's mother.

Price Range: Apps., $5–$10; entrees, $12–$22; desserts, $8. **Wheelchair access:** One step up from sidewalk.

Dok Suni $25 & Under KOREAN

119 First Ave. (bet. 7th St. & St. Marks Pl.)   (212) 477-9506
Credit cards: Cash only   Meals: D, LN

The dining room has loud music, would-be models and tame Korean food simultaneously made hip for the East Village and palatable for cautious Westerners. Potato pancakes are an unusual Korean starter, but they are delicious and go well with the soy-and-vinegar dipping sauce. Fried dumplings with a ground vegetable stuffing are tame compared with the spicy kimchee pancake. Main courses are also short on traditional Korean dishes. Bulgogi — grilled slices of marinated beef — is served with a mildly spicy sauce and large leaves of lettuce for rolling up the meat with rice. A seafood pancake, made with oysters, squid and shrimp, is mildly flavored, though the accompanying kimchee is spicy.

Price range: Apps., $4–$9; entrees, $9–$16. **Wheelchair access:** Restrooms not accessible.

Dos Caminos ☆ $$$ MEXICAN

373 Park Ave. S. (near 26th St.)   (212) 294-1000
Credit cards: All major   Meals: L, D

Dos Caminos, a recent addition to Stephen Hanson's B. R. Guest restaurant group that has already spawned a SoHo clone, attracts crowds for the usual Mexican restaurant promise of margaritas augmented by a casual, easy-to-enjoy menu. It is a highly programmed operation. With its list of more than 100 tequilas, a lot of celebrating goes on, and during prime evening hours the handsome dining room is as loud as a full-tilt party.

The guacamole is superb, but the riskiest appetizer is also the best — three little cornmeal cakes adorned with huitlacoche, a corn fungus with a rich, earthy flavor. The better options among the entrees include chicken in a complex mole poblano and pork pibil, tender braised pork in an orange and pickled onion sauce. The most enticing desserts are flan and a tres leches cake with almond mousse. *(Eric Asimov)*

Other recommended dishes: Shrimp empanada, taco asada, Chilean sea bass. **Wine list:** While tequila is the priority, the small list is well chosen and moderately priced. **Price range:** Apps., $6–$12; entrees, $16.50–$24; desserts, $5–$8. **Wheelchair access:** All one level.

Downtown ☆ $$$ ITALIAN
376 W. Broadway (at Broome St.) (212) 343-0999
Credit cards: All major Meals: L, D, LN

Uptown has invaded downtown in this restaurant where most men wear suits and all the women are gorgeous. Clearly people go to Downtown to look swell, to see and be seen. They get good Italian food at outrageous prices. Mussels and clams veneziana is a nice dish, and the thin slices of carpaccio à la cipriani are cut from a gorgeous piece of meat. And the baked tagliolini, made famous by the original Harry's Bar in Venice, is rich and creamy, elegant comfort food. The main courses are even better, including beautifully grilled chicken. The one sure thing is the prix-fixe meal, which includes a good salad, fine pasta, dessert and coffee. The service is always gracious and accommodating, and the scene is worth the voyage.

Wine list: The vintages are not listed, the choices are unimaginative and many of the wines are sold out. Prices, however, are average. **Price range:** Apps., $10–$21; entrees, $22–$36; desserts, $11. **Wheelchair access:** Everything is at ground level. **Features:** Outdoor dining (sidewalk).

Dumonet at the Carlyle ☆☆ $$$$ FRENCH
Carlyle Hotel, 35 E. 76th St. (near Madison Ave.) (212) 744-1600
Credit cards: All major Meals: L (except Sun.), D

The restaurant at the Carlyle has reopened with a new name and a much more pleasing personality. Jean-Louis Dumonet, the chef, has hit on a shrewd blend of classic haute-cuisine dishes like tournedos Rossini and equally classic bistro dishes like rabbit in mustard sauce. It is a high-low design that flatters the Carlyle's aristocratic bone structure while opening the door to a little fun. Who would ever expect to eat smoked herring fillets and warm potato salad within earshot of Bobby Short? The menu could use a few more unexpected touches, but the honed-down, simplified style that Mr. Dumonet has chosen does not always tie his hands. Plump langoustines, lightly roasted, are flattered by the sweet, buttery qualities of Parmesan, made into a transparent emulsion. The wild card on the ultraconservative dessert menu is a juicy pineapple tarte Tatin with a smooth, fruity banana coulis.

There really is no substitute for eating in a place like the Carlyle, one of the last restaurants in the city where even the most militantly casual diner recognizes instantly that it is wrong — utterly and totally — even to think of entering without a coat and tie. But the feeling is different now, more relaxed and spontaneous, and less a caricature of high-class service circa 1955. Luxury with an antic touch — that's the new tone at the Carlyle.

Other recommended dishes: Morels in cream sauce, chaudrée san-
tongeaise, tournedos Rossini, salmon in puff pastry with sorrel
sauce. Wine list: An unimaginative French-oriented list heavily
reliant on a few highly predictable names. Price range: Lunch: two
courses, $36; three courses $42. Dinner: apps., $14 or $19.50;
entrees, $32 or $42; desserts, $12 or $18 for cheese cart. Wheelchair access: Ramp available.

DuMont $25 & Under   NEW AMERICAN
432 Union Ave. (near Metropolitan Ave.)
Williamsburg, Brooklyn   (718) 486-7717
Credit cards: MC/V   Meals: L, D

DuMont, just east of the grimy shadows cast by the Brooklyn-
Queens Expressway, is a warm and pleasant refuge for young
daters, old neighborhood hands, even the occasional visitor. It
serves a simple menu of six items, accompanied by daily chalk-
board specials. Seared scallops are a frequent appetizer offering,
served sometimes with wilted frisée and sometimes with sautéed
shallots and unwilted frisée. Either will do. For entrees, there is no
sense in avoiding that fragrant "yardbird" chicken, served in its
crackling gold skin, with succulent meat tinctured with garlic and
olive oil. Smart money goes with the buttery burger, served with a
woodpile of golden French fries dusted with parsley. The kitchen is
a little less triumphant when it comes to fin fish. Desserts vary
daily, but on one visit an almost caramel-hued bread pudding was
marvelous. *(Sam Sifton)*

Other recommended dishes: Salads, filet mignon. Price range:
Apps., $5.50–$8; entrees, $8.25–$18. Wheelchair access: Restaurant is up one step.

Ear Inn $ BAR SNACKS
326 Spring St. (bet. Greenwich & Washington Sts.)   (212) 226-9060
Credit cards: All major   Meals: L, D, LN

Since 1817 the landmark James Brown House, named after a Revolutionary War–era tobacco trader, has housed some sort of tavern.
When New York was a great commercial port, it was a sailors' dive.
Since it became the Ear Inn, more than 20 years ago, it has drawn
an eclectic crowd of artists, writers, bikers and construction workers for whom the air of an unpretentious neighborhood watering
hole has an unending appeal. The food is basic and inexpensive.
Try grilled shell steak, grilled salmon, chicken pot pie and spaghetti
with shrimp and scallops.

Price range: Apps., $5–$6; entrees, $5–$10; desserts, $5. Wheel-
chair access: Fully accessible.

East Buffet & Restaurant $25 & Under CHINESE
42-07 Main St., Flushing, Queens   (718) 353-6333
Credit cards: All major   Meals: L, D

This huge, glossy Chinese eating hall seats 400 people in the buffet
hall and 350 in another room (separated by a reception area) for sit-
down service. Three islands run down the center of the narrow buf-

fet area. You will be astonished at the bounty before you: more than 30 dim sum selections, a dozen soups, 40 dishes served cold and another 40 served hot. There are stations for poaching shrimp and clams, a satay station, a great big platter of steamed crab legs, a raw bar and a sushi bar.

Where to start? Try the superb cold appetizers. Dim sum can be excellent, too. Roast suckling pig is extremely tender. For dessert, try the gelatinous puddings in flavors like green tea, red bean, lotus seed and tapioca, or black sesame gelatin, rolled into cylinders and barely sweetened.

Other recommended dishes: Tubular greens, cold noodles in hot oil, fried taro cakes, pork buns, shrimp balls, turnip cakes, steamed crab legs, congee, salt-and-pepper shrimp. **Price range:** Lunch, $9; dinner, $20–$24; brunch, $16. **Wheelchair access:** Elevator to dining room.

Edison Cafe $ DINER
Edison Hotel, 228 W. 47th St. (bet. Broadway & Eighth Ave.)
(212) 840-5000
Credit cards: Cash only   Meals: B, L, D

Known as the "Polish Tearoom," Edison Cafe is an institution and one of the last remnants of the old Times Square. Sitting in the faded glory of what was once a fancy restaurant, you eat great matzoh ball soup, potato pancakes and terrific sandwiches while waitresses straight out of Damon Runyon tell you their troubles.

Alcohol: Beer. **Price range:** Breakfast, $6. Lunch and dinner entrees, $8–$12. **Wheelchair access:** Fully accessible.

Eight Mile Creek $$$ AUSTRALIAN
240 Mulberry St. (at Prince St.)   (212) 431-4635
Credit cards: All major   Meals: Br, D, LN

When a restaurant announces that it will be serving Australian cuisine, you expect good comic material, not good food. The joke stops when the kangaroo salad arrives: large cubes of the loin languish in a marinade flavored with coriander, smoked paprika and garlic, and then seared and served on lettuce-leaf wrappers. Eight Mile Creek is cheery, outgoing and warm, with a bar scene enlivened by a scattering of Australian expats. It is also very uncomfortable. The menu is short, but the chef makes every dish count. Oyster pie, a pastry-wrapped stew of precisely cooked oysters, suspended in a cream sauce chunky with salsify and leeks, is worth trying. Australia without lamb is an impossibility. Here you get a whopping big shank surrounded by parsnips, chanterelles and roasted apple.

Wine list: An excellent, nearly all-Australian 42-bottle list, modestly priced, with some hard-to-find wines and some exciting Australian dessert wines by the glass. **Price range:** Apps., $7–$9; entrees, $14–$23; desserts, $8–$11. **Wheelchair access:** Restrooms on street level. **Features:** Outdoor dining.

EJ's Luncheonette $ DINER

447 Amsterdam Ave. (bet. 81st & 82nd Sts.)   (212) 873-3444
1271 Third Ave. (at 73rd St.)   (212) 472-0600
432 Sixth Ave. (bet. 9th & 10th Sts.)   (212) 473-5555
Credit cards: Cash only   Meals: B, Br, L, D

These reproductions of classic 1950's luncheonettes are often
packed. Despite the occasional contemporary dish, generous portions of old-fashioned recipes are what sell, along with huge
desserts and malteds. It's hard to see what all the fuss is about.

Alcohol: Beer and wine. **Price range:** Lunch: apps., $3–$5; entrees,
$7–$9; desserts, $2–$5. Dinner: apps., $3–$5; entrees, $10–$15;
desserts, $2–$5. **Wheelchair access:** Fully accessible.

Elaine's $$$ ITALIAN

1703 Second Ave. (bet. 88th & 89th Sts.)   (212) 534-8103
Credit cards: All major   Meals: D, LN

Yes, movie folks hang out here. The literati do too. The question is,
Why? It looks like an ordinary tavern and the food is mediocre.

Price range: Apps., $7–$14; entrees, $15–$39; desserts, $7. **Wheel-
chair access:** Restrooms not accessible.

El Cid $25 & Under   SPANISH

322 W. 15th St. (bet. Eighth & Ninth Aves.)   (212) 929-9332
Credit cards: AE/D   Meals: LN   Closed Mon.

El Cid is delightful, with delicious food and a professional staff that
handles any problem with élan. Tapas are a highlight, and you can
make a meal of dishes like grilled shrimp that are still freshly briny;
tiny smelt fillets marinated in vinegar and spices; and chunks of
savory marinated pork with french fries. The paella is exceptional.
This is not a restaurant for quiet heart-to-heart talks. The simple
décor features hard surfaces that amplify noise, producing a rollicking party atmosphere as the room gets crowded. And it does get
crowded.

Price range: Apps., $4–$10; entrees, $15–$28; desserts, $5–$6.
Wheelchair access: Two steps up to dining room; small restrooms.

11 Madison Park   ☆☆ $$$ CONTINENTAL

11 Madison Ave. (at 24th St.)   (212) 889-0905
Credit cards: All major   Meals: L, D

Madison Square, beautifully renovated and lanscaped, finally gives
11 Madison Park the setting it deserves. At dusk, the ghosts of Cafe
Martin and Delmonico's hover in the air, lending a wistful, romantic note to the sharp, clean New American cuisine of Kerry Heffernan. The food can be elegantly simple, with appetizers like tomato
consomme with shrimp ravioli accented by lemon verbena, or
cheekily downscale, like crisped pig's feet and sweetbreads in

champagne-mustard jus, perhaps the wittiest high-low combination in town. A low-rent ingreedient like squid can find itself elevated to unexpected heights with pea shoots and cauliflower royale in lobster sauce. Mr. Heffernan uses fresh produce to freshen his flavors. Salsify and pea shoots mediate between a dark truffle jus and pink, translucent arctic char. Coriander, with its penetrating, citric note, animates a rich beurre noisette poured over halibut. Mr. Heffernan doesn't hestitate when it's time to go for the knockout punch. His spiced duck breast with foie gras and cabbage is potent, and a liberal application of armagnac sauce pushes it right up to the edge.

Desserts have the easy assurance that seems to be the house style, expressed perfectly in a raspberry millefeuille with ice wine granite and lychee sorbet. *(Review by William Grimes; stars previously awarded by Ruth Reichl.)*

Wine list: A specialty in the second labels of the big chateaus of Bordeaux. Impressive list of Calvados. **Price range:** Lunch: apps., $8–$14; entrees, $17–$24. Dinner: apps., $8–$18; entrees, $19–$32; desserts, $8. **Wheelchair access:** All one level.

El Gauchito $25 & Under   LATIN AMERICAN/ARGENTINE

94-60 Corona Ave., Corona, Queens   (718) 271-8198
Credit cards: MC/V   Meals: L, D   Closed Wed.

This tiny storefront restaurant and butcher shop offers an authentic Argentine dining experience. Family groups crowd the few tables in the dining room, keeping up a lively banter in Spanish with the staff. The most popular dish seems to be the mixed grill, a huge plate of food that includes a plump pork sausage, a rich blood sausage and all manner of internal organs.

Alcohol: Beer and wine. **Price range:** Apps., $2–$7; entrees, $6.90–$12.90; desserts, $3–$4. **Wheelchair access:** Restrooms not accessible.

Elias Corner $25 & Under   GREEK/SEAFOOD

24-02 31st St., Astoria, Queens   (718) 932-1510
Credit cards: Cash only   Meals: D, LN

Regulars at this bright, raucous Greek seafood specialist know to check the glass display case in front before selecting the freshest-looking fish. Without a doubt, meals should start with a huge plate of delicious, pinky-size whitebait, dredged in flour and flash-fried whole. Other worthwhile starters include taramosalata, a lemony fish roe purée, and tzatziki, a blend of yogurt, mint and cucumber. The grilled fish are almost all delicious, basted with olive oil, lemon juice and herbs and cooked over charcoal until charred on the outside and juicy within. The small front room is less relaxed than the bright rear room, where big wraparound windows looking away from the overpass convey the feeling of a cruise ship. Elias is best in the off-hours, before the crowd arrives.

Alcohol: Beer and wine. **Price range:** Apps., $4–$8; entrees, $12–$17. **Wheelchair access:** One level, narrow entry to restroom. **Features:** Parking available.

El Paso Taqueria $25 & Under MEXICAN

1642 Lexington Ave. (at 104th St.)   (212) 831-9831
Credit cards: Cash only   Meals: B, L, D

One of the best restaurants in the area is this extremely plain yet
bustling little corner spot. It isn't much to look at; it doesn't even
serve alcohol. But it excels at feeding people well, and that's nothing to take for granted. Tacos are a natural starting point. The fragrant soft corn tortillas are doubled up in authentic Mexican style
to contain fillings like tangy marinated pork, spicy crumbled
chorizo sausage and grilled beef. But the highlights at El Paso are
the daily specials, all served with rice and refried beans. They
might include puerco adobo, tender, vinegary pork served on the
bone in a spicy tomato sauce, or cecina asada, a huge thin cut of
beef that has been dried, salted and spiced, with sautéed chilies
and cactus pads. On Saturdays and Sundays, El Paso serves pozole,
the satisfying soup of pork and puffed corn.

Other recommended dishes: Pork ribs with mole poblano, flautas,
meatballs in chipotle sauce, chilaquiles. **Price range:** Apps., $2–$7;
entrees, $5–$10. **Wheelchair access:** Step at entrance; restroom not
accessible.

El Presidente $25 & Under CARIBBEAN/PAN-LATIN

3938 Broadway (bet. 164th & 165th Sts.)   (212) 927-7011
Credit cards: All major   Meals: B, L, D, LN

This small, bright restaurant near Columbia-Presbyterian Medical
Center specializes in the foods of the Hispanic Caribbean — Cuba,
Puerto Rico and the Dominican Republic — where flavors are pow-
ered by garlic, bell peppers and annatto rather than the heat of
chilies. Pernil, or roast pork, is simple but wonderfully satisfying. El
Presidente also serves an excellent charcoal-broiled skirt steak, with
grilled onions and peppers, charred around the edges yet still juicy.

Alcohol: Beer and wine. **Price range:** Breakfast: $2–$5. Lunch and
dinner: apps, $2; entrees, $6–$15.

El Rincón Boricua $25 & Under PUERTO RICAN

158 E. 119th St. (bet. Third & Lexington Aves.)   (212) 534-9400
Credit cards: Cash only   Meals: L

El Rincón Boricua, is a tiny place, barely big enough to hold a half-
dozen people. Its owners, bustle back and forth behind the little
counter, hacking and snipping pork, doling out heaping portions of
rice, beans and other dishes, and keeping up a friendly patter with
the hungry customers who throng the place for takeout at prime
time, noon to 2 or 3 P.M. By late afternoon, the food is usually
gone, and at 6 P.M. the restaurant closes. The pig is rich and powerfully flavored. Portions usually include both dark, reddish meat—
savory and pungent with a definite salty quality — and paler,
moister meat — less porky and with crisp, glistening amber skin.
With a pile of sweet plantains, tender red beans and fluffy yellow
rice, this is great Puerto Rican home cooking.

Price range: Everything under $10. **Wheelchair access:** Not accessible.

El Teddy's $$ MEXICAN/TEX-MEX

219 W. Broadway (bet. White & Franklin Sts.)   (212) 941-7071
Credit cards: All major   Meals: L, D, LN

The dining rooms of this spirited Mexican restaurant and bar look like an astral collision in a science-fiction movie, but all the silliness belies some spirited and intelligently composed food. There are several burritos, quesadillas, soups and salads. Entree possibilities include pan sautéed duck breast; grilled rare tuna on a shiitake cactus salad; and shredded beef with chorizo, avocado, tomato and homemade tortillas. Sweet final notes might be tequila-soaked baba filled with lemon Chantilly cream and a cold purée of guava with tropical fruit ceviche.

Price range: Lunch: apps., $5–$9; entrees, $9–$14. Dinner: apps., $5–$9; entrees, $14–$20. **Wheelchair access:** Fully accessible. **Features:** Outdoor dining.

Elvie's Turo-Turo $25 & Under   FILIPINO

214 First Ave. (bet. 12th & 13th Sts.)   (212) 473-7785
Credit cards: Cash only   Meals: L, D

This friendly little restaurant offers a daily buffet of Filipino dishes. All you do is turo-turo, or point-point. This is not light food. Most dishes are beef or pork, with the occasional chicken and fish dish. The pork adobo, the national dish of the Philippines, is excellent. For dessert, point to sweet cassava cake.

Alcohol: Bring your own. **Price range:** Apps., $2–$4; entrees, $6–$8; desserts, $2–$4. **Wheelchair access:** Not accessible. **Features:** Outdoor dining.

Emily's $25 & Under   SOUTHERN

1325 Fifth Ave. (at 111th St.)   (212) 996-1212
Credit cards: All major   Meals: Br, L, D, LN

This pleasant but institutional restaurant offers a diverse Southern menu and draws an integrated crowd. If you go, go for the meaty, tender baby back pork ribs, subtly smoky and bathed in tangy barbecue sauce, or the big plate of chopped pork barbecue. The best sides include savory rice and peas (actually red beans) and peppery stuffing, and all dishes come with a basket of fine corn bread. Sweet potato pie is the traditional dessert, and Emily's version is nice and nutmeggy.

Other recommended dishes: Fried chicken, candied yams. **Price range:** Lunch entrees, $5–$10.65. Dinner: apps, $6–$10; entrees, $10–$25; desserts, $4. **Wheelchair access:** All one level. **Features:** Outdoor dining.

Emo's $25 & Under   KOREAN

1564 Second Ave. (near 81st St.)   (212) 628-8699
Credit cards: All major   Meals: L, D

A Korean restaurant outside the confines of Midtown is no longer
unusual. What makes Emo's especially noteworthy is that, aside
from American-style service and the addition of fresh salad greens
to several dishes, it pulls few punches, offering robust, spicy,
authentic fare that is full of flavor. The highlights are the superb
main courses, like oh jing uh gui, wonderfully tender cylinders of
barbecued squid scored to resemble pale pine cones and touched
with hot sauce to add dimension to the squid's mellow flavor. A
variation of this is jae yook gui, barbecued pork in a delectable
smoky, spicy sauce.

There is an American-style bar that lines the entryway to the
spare, narrow but airy dining room. Korean beer and barley liquor
are available, of course, but so are martinis, micro brews and California wines.

Other recommended dishes: Marinated short ribs, miso stew with
beef, codfish in soy-and-garlic sauce. **Price range:** Apps., $3–$7;
entrees, $11–$18. **Wheelchair access:** One step in front, restroom is
narrow.

Empire Diner $$ DINER

210 10th Ave. (at 22nd St.)   (212) 243-2736
Credit cards: All major   Meals: B, Br, L, D, LN

One of the early entries in the modern revival of America's love
affair with diners was this campy Art Deco gem that attracted a hip
late-night crowd in the 1980's. Nowadays, the Empire is a tourist
destination. The up-to-date diner basics with some Mediterranean
touches are not bad at all — better than at most diners, in fact —
which is reflected in the prices.

Price range: Apps., $6–$8; entrees, $10–$17; desserts, $4–$7.
Wheelchair access: Not accessible. **Features:** Outdoor dining.

Esashi $25 & Under   SUSHI

32 Ave. A (bet. 2nd & 3rd Sts.)   (212) 505-8726
Credit cards: All major   Meals: D

Esashi is a modest, informal restaurant that stands out for its sushi
and many other well-prepared Japanese dishes. The sushi selection
is not particularly large or unusual, but everything is exceptionally
fresh and beautifully presented. Gyu-tataki, paper-thin slices of beef
seared on the edges and rare in the center, are tender and delicious,
especially with a squeeze of lemon. Tiger eye, an unusually beautiful appetizer with a subtle flavor, is a strip of cooked skate wrapped
around salmon with a layer of seaweed. Esashi has a wide selection
of sakes, warm and cold.

Alcohol: Beer and wine. **Price range:** Apps., $3–$4; entrees,
$11–$18. **Wheelchair access:** Fully accessible.

Esca ☆☆ $$$ ITALIAN/SEAFOOD

402 W. 43rd St. (at Ninth Ave.)
Credit cards: All major

(212) 564-7272
Meals: L, D

At Esca — the name means "bait" — the most important word in
the Italian language is *crudo*. It means raw, and that's the way the
fish comes to the table in a dazzling array of appetizers that could
be thought of as Italian sushi. The *crudo* appetizers at Esca are the
freshest, most exciting thing to happen to Italian food in recent
memory. The menu changes daily depending on what comes out of
the sea. Half the menu consists of knockouts. Half is rather ordinary, although the surroundings at Esca can trick any diner into
believing otherwise. The lemon-yellow walls and sea-green tiles
give it a bright, cool look, and the solid wooden table in the center
of the dining room, loaded down with vegetable side dishes, strikes
a rustic note while communicating the food philosophy: fresh from
the market, and prepared without fuss.

Wine list: A connoisseur's and bargain-hunter's list of about 240
wines from all regions of Italy, with 11 wines sold in glass-and-a-
half decanters called quartini. **Price range:** Lunch: apps, $7–$12;
entrees, $16–$21; desserts, $8. Dinner: apps., $8–$14; entrees,
$17–$28; desserts, $8; six-course tasting menu, $65 ($95 with
matching wines). **Wheelchair access:** Restrooms on street level.
Features: Outdoor dining (garden).

Esperanto $25 & Under PAN-LATIN

145 Ave. C (at 9th St.)
Credit cards: AE

(212) 505-6559
Meals: D, LN

This is a warm and welcoming place with Latin food that can be
surprisingly subtle and delicate. Bolinho de peixe, deep-fried balls
of codfish, are exceptionally light, crisp and flavorful, with a terrific
dipping sauce galvanized by spicy mustard. Another good appetizer
is salpicão, a Brazilian chicken salad. Esperanto's main courses are
sturdy and hard to mess up. Steak is good and beefy, bathed in
chimichurri, the Argentine condiment of garlic and parsley; and feijoada, the Brazilian stew of black beans and smoked meats, has a
nice, gritty texture and an almost yeasty flavor. Esperanto serves
potent caipirinhas or mojitos, a sort of Cuban mint julep, and features a brief wine list with some good, rustic reds. And don't miss
the stellar coconut flan.

Price range: Apps., $4–$6; entrees, $9–$14. **Wheelchair access:**
Steps are at entrance; restrooms are narrow.

Estiatorio Milos ☆☆ $$$$ GREEK/SEAFOOD

125 W. 55th St. (bet. Sixth & Seventh Aves.)
Credit cards: All major

(212) 245-7400
Meals: L, D, LN

If you love the Greek fish places in Astoria but wish the fish were
better, try this. The room is clean, spare, blindingly white, and the
entire focus is on the display of gorgeous fish by the open kitchen.
Choose one and it is grilled simply and brought to the table. If you

like big fish, bring a crowd. Most of the fish are cooked whole. And the lamb chops, a concession to meat eaters, are excellent. Appetizers are wonderful, too. The homemade yogurt — thick, slightly sour and served with a scattering of wild blueberries and drizzles of wild honey — is the ideal way to end these meals. (*Ruth Reichl*)

Wine list: Intelligently chosen for the food and fairly priced. **Price range:** Prix-fixe lunch, $33. Apps., $10–$20; fish for main courses is sold whole and by weight, from $25–$34 a pound; lamb chops, $32; desserts, $8–$25. **Wheelchair access:** A few steps up to the main dining room, but there are a few tables near the bar, at street level. **Features:** Outdoor dining (sidewalk).

Etats-Unis ☆ ☆ $$$ NEW AMERICAN
242 E. 81st St. (bet. Second & Third Aves.) (212) 517-8826
Credit cards: All major Meals: D

The once intimate, clubby restaurant has taken on a snazzy bistro look. It is still tiny, and still a bright spot in the neighborhood, but the kitchen has lost some of the excitement of its early years. The eclectic menu, a little French and a little American (braised pork shoulder in a spicy barbecue sauce is typical), pleases well enough, but the overall average is, well, pretty average. One exception must be noted, the signature date pudding, a dessert that must never be allowed to leave the menu. (*Ruth Reichl, updated by William Grimes*)

Wine list: Small, personally selected, unusual and wide-ranging list. **Price range:** Apps., $9–$15; entrees, $24–$34; desserts, $7–$10. **Wheelchair access:** One level, but the restaurant is small and quite crowded.

Euzkadi $25 & Under BASQUE
108 E. 4th St. (bet. First & Second Aves.) (212) 982-9788
Credit cards: AE Meals: D Closed Sun.

Basque restaurants don't seem to register much on New York's culinary radar. In truth, Euzkadi reflects the East Village far more than the Pyrenees. No traditional Basque outfits or sheep-herding scenes here, just a small, brick-walled dining room with comfortable Mission-style banquettes and a young clientele. The menu is not so much unusual as subtly different, with items like an excellent appetizer of a cake of bacalao, or dried salt cod, that is puréed and deep-fried. Service is swift and attentive. Dishes served á la plancha, or sizzling on a cast-iron skillet, like shrimp, which arrive with heads still on, are first-rate. Seafood dominates the menu, but two other dishes are worth highlighting: a pork paillard, served over a delicious ragout of escarole, sausage and white beans, and tender braised rabbit in a slightly sweet wine and prune sauce.

Other recommended dishes: Green bean, fig and walnut salad; grilled sardines; lentil salad with sausage; calamari piperade; bacon-wrapped trout; braised monkfish; roasted cod; figs with rosemary; quince tarte Tatin. **Price range:** Apps., $5–$8; entrees, $13–$15. **Wheelchair access:** Not accessible.

Excellent Dumpling House $ CHINESE

111 Lafayette St. (bet. Canal & Walker Sts.)   (212) 219-0212
Credit cards: Cash only   Meals: L, D

Great dumplings and other Chinese dishes, served in a plain dining room. It's especially popular with the jury-duty crowd.

Alcohol: Beer. **Price range:** Apps., $2–$5; entrees, $8–$11. **Wheelchair access:** Fully accessible.

F&B $25 & Under   HOT DOGS/SAUSAGES

269 W. 23rd St. (bet. Seventh & Eighth Aves.)   (646) 486-4441
Credit cards: Cash only   Meals: B, L, D

F&B, a sleek storefront decorated in soothing pastels with pleasant lighting, offers a self-consciously European visage. The name stands for frites and beignets, but hot dogs are the centerpiece, including the excellent Great Dane, a slender, red Danish sausage with bright snap to it. It is eaten just as it is in Denmark, on a roll with frizzled onions, marinated cucumbers, mustard, ketchup and remoulade. It sounds like a lot, but it's an easy mouthful, especially compared with the Top Dog, a plumper German-style sausage topped with tame sauerkraut and crumbled bacon. Frites are crisp and savory, and for an extra 50 cents, they are served with toppings including aioli, blue cheese and truffle oil.

Alcohol: Beer and wine. **Price range:** Entrees, $2–$5. **Wheelchair access:** One step down from street.

Feeding Tree $25 & Under   CARIBBEAN

892 Gerard Ave. (near 161st St.), the Bronx   (718) 293-5025
Credit cards: All major   Meals: B, L, D

This casual West Indian restaurant near Yankee Stadium looks like a bright takeout place. But to the right of the counter is a closed door leading to a trim dining room, with sleek Formica tables, some green plants and a glossy bar. The touchstone of a Jamaican restaurant is its jerk, and Feeding Tree's jerk chicken is excellent. But the best dish on the menu is the magnificently mellow curried goat, tender chunks of meat in a mild green sauce. Beer goes well with this food, but so does sorrel, a sweet and spicy cold drink made from the flowers of a plant in the hibiscus family, steeped with ginger, cloves and other flavorings.

Other recommended dish: Beef stew, oxtail stew, coconut drops. **Price range:** Entrees, $6–$10. **Wheelchair access:** Entrance and restrooms are narrow.

Felidia   ☆☆☆ $$$$ ITALIAN

243 E. 58th St. (bet. Second & Third Aves.)   (212) 758-1479
Credit cards: All major   Meals: L (Mon.–Fri.), D   Closed Sun.

Felidia offers itself in the guise of an old-fashioned restaurant, comfortable and rustic, but there's a professional polish in the dining room and high ambition in the kitchen. The menu, which changes with the seasons, concentrates on the foods of Italy's northeast:

Friuli, the Veneto as well as Istria, now part of Croatia, and the home of owners Felice and Lidia Bastianich.

This is robust food served in generous portions, revolving around game, organ meats, and slow-cooked sauces. This is not to say you can't eat lightly. Felidia serves lots of seafood, including lobster and crabmeat salad, and an impressive spiced monkfish in clam broth. Roasted fish arrives at the table with its head and tail; filleted, slicked with olive oil and served with grilled tomatoes, it is simple and satisfying. Despite her expanding career as a television chef and cookbook writer, Ms. Bastianich has managed to keep standards admirably high. It would be a shame to miss Felidia's unusual specialties. Krafi, for instance, festive ravioli filled with cheese, raisins, rum and grated lemon rind. Or fuzi, little twists with broccoli rabe and sausage. Good desserts include apple strudel, and the wonderful sweet crepes called palacinke. (*Ruth Reichl, updated by William Grimes.*)

Wine list: One of the city's finest Italian lists; great wines at great prices and unusual regional specialties. The staff is knowledgeable and helpful. **Price range:** Lunch: apps, $12–$18; entrees, $20–$28; desserts, $10. Dinner: apps., $12–$18; entrees, $22–$34; desserts, $10. **Wheelchair access:** Restrooms not accessible.

Ferdinando's Focacceria $25 & Under   ITALIAN

151 Union St., Carroll Gardens, Brooklyn   (718) 855-1545
Credit cards: Cash only   Meals: L, D   Closed Sun.

They filmed *Moonstruck* on this street, and you can see why. This restaurant is a throwback to turn-of-the-century Brooklyn, before Ebbets Field had even been built. Ferdinando's serves old Sicilian dishes, like chickpea-flour fritters; vasteddi, a focaccia made with calf's spleen; and pasta topped with sardines canned by the owner. It's worth a visit.

Alcohol: Beer and wine. **Price range:** Apps., $7; entrees, $10–$13; desserts, $4. **Wheelchair access:** Fully accessible.

Fiamma Osteria ☆☆☆ $$$ ITALIAN

206 Spring St. (near Sullivan St.)   (212) 653-0100
Credit cards: All major   Meals: L (Mon.–Fri.), D

Fiamma Osteria is a beautifully realized restaurant, highly satisfying in every way. It's located in a SoHo town house with dining rooms on two levels. Upstairs, the designer Jeffrey Beers has created a subdued atmosphere with rich, saturated reds and browns. The downstairs room is lighter, brighter and louder, more brasserie than restaurant.

The food lives up to the setting. The chef stays firmly rooted in the core principles of Italian cooking, putting prime ingredients on a sparely designed stage and letting them speak with minimum interference. The Fiamma veal chop, perfumed with sage, is visually impressive, a big player on the plate, but the chef heads off veal fatigue by supplying handsomely caramelized sweet and sour cipollini onions and flavorful asparagus roasted, sliced into thin lengths and wrapped like a sheaf in a slice of prosciutto. The pastas at Fiamma are exceptional. Two deserve special mention, raviolini stuffed with braised veal shank in a potent, reduced veal sauce enriched with formaggio de fossa and broad bands of spinach pasta tossed with braised rabbit Bolognese in a Parmesan cream sauce.

The dessert rotation changes, but the showstopper is a layered hazelnut chocolate torte on a crackling pastry base, served with gianduja gelato and chocolate sauce.

Wine list: An ambitious 400-bottle list emphasizing newer regional Italian wines, with 20 wines sold by the glass in two sizes. **Price range:** Apps., $9–$14; entrees, $17–$42; desserts, $9. **Wheelchair access:** Elevator service.

Fifty Seven Fifty Seven ☆☆☆ $$$$

NEW AMERICAN

Four Seasons Hotel, 57 E. 57th St. (212) 758-5757
Credit cards: All major Meals: B, L, D

Fifty Seven Fifty Seven is a restaurant that trumpets its hotel affiliation. The diner steps into the imposing I.M. Pei lobby of the Four Seasons Hotel and begins an architectural journey through a procession of monumental spaces, up a flight of stairs and into one of the city's stateliest dining rooms. Service is solicitous and the menu offers something for absolutely every taste.

The food is decidedly American with a modern bent. The menu changes frequently with a different prix-fixe offering every day. Architectural though the entrees may be, the visually restrained desserts are rich in flavor and texture. With its solicitous service in a memorable public space, Fifty Seven Fifty Seven is setting a new standard for an old tradition. (*Ruth Reichl*)

Wine list: Many hard-to-find wines, but prices are high. **Price range:** Breakfast, $40. Lunch: apps., $10–$15; entrees, $22–$31; desserts, $10; prix fixe, $45. Dinner: apps., $12–$22; entrees, $25–$40; desserts, $10; prix fixe, $75; vegetarian prix fixe, $52. **Wheelchair access:** Fully accessible.

F.illi Ponte Satisfactory $$$ ITALIAN

39 Desbrosses St. (near West St.) (212) 226-4621
Credit cards: All major Meals: L, D Closed Sun.

F.illi Ponte, with its lovely rustic brick dining room and Hudson views, is still beautiful and evocative. But after getting a two-star rating in 1995, the restaurant no longer seems to care much about the food. What self-respecting Italian restaurant would serve sides of the sort of mushy julienned vegetables that are diner staples? Or a Caprese salad at the end of summer with pale, wan tomatoes? This is not to say that you cannot enjoy a good meal at Ponte. The big thick veal chop has an unusually fine flavor, while osso buco for two is superb. Angry lobster, Ponte's signature dish, is impressive, though the chili pepper used to incite the anger is no longer apparent. Pastas are a maddening mixed bag. For dessert, try the tiramisù or pumpkin-molasses tart. (*Eric Asimov*)

Other recommended dishes: Sausages with broccoli rabe, fried calamari, white truffle gnocchi with sausage and Napa cabbage, mint tagliolini with braised lamb, risotto. **Wine list:** Deep selection of Tuscan and Piedmont reds at fair prices. **Price range:** Apps., $9–$12; entrees, $18–$37 (lobster, $25 a pound). **Wheelchair access:** Incline at door; elevator to second floor.

Firebird ☆☆ $$$ RUSSIAN

365 W. 46th St. (bet. Eighth & Ninth Aves.)   (212) 586-0244
Credit cards: All major   Meals: L, D

With a room as ornate and luxurious as a Fabergé egg, and a staff so polished, it will seem that you have entered some more serene and lavish era. The caviar arrives with its own private waiter who turns the service into a performance. Among the first courses, the manti, hearty steamed lamb dumplings served in a dish of minted sour cream, and the herring in a blanket of potatoes, beets, onion and chopped eggs are worth ordering.

If you want to eat lightly, try the grilled sturgeon in a creamy mustard sauce. On a recent visit, Firebird continued to offer imaginatively updated Russian classics, like chicken tabaka with plum sauce, and grilled sturgeon with sorrel-potato puree. Desserts, once a weak point, have improved greatly. This is the place to try the traditional molded cheesecake, an Easter treat in Russia, called pashka. (*Ruth Reichl, updated by William Grimes*)

Wine list: Not nearly as impressive as the vodka list. **Price range:** Lunch: apps., $7–$16; entrees, $18–$22; prix fixe, $20. Dinner: apps., $8–$18; entrees, $26–$38; desserts, $9; prix fixe, $37 (Thu.–Sat.), $30 (rest of the week) **Wheelchair access:** First floor fully accessible.

First $25 & Under NEW AMERICAN

87 First Ave. (bet. 5th & 6th Sts.)   (212) 674-3823
Credit cards: All major   Meals: D, LN

Ambitious, creative contemporary American fare at relatively modest prices, served late into the night. First also offers an intelligently chosen list of wines and beers and worthwhile weekly specials, like its Sunday night pig roast.

Recommended dishes: Grilled guinea hen paillard, crisp oysters with seaweed salad, pizzas, chicken wings, sandwiches. **Price range:** Avg. app., $9; entree, $17; dessert, $6. **Wheelchair access:** Not accessible.

Fish $25 & Under SEAFOOD

280 Bleecker St. (at Jones St.)   (212) 727-2879
Credit cards: All major   Meals: L, D, LN

The simple menu at Fish focuses on chowders, an expanded raw bar, lobster rolls and grilled fish. The bar is dim, the beer is flowing, and the illusion of waterfront dissolution, which gives oyster bars such character, is intact. There are few places to find fresher or better oysters on the half shell. The East Coast oysters are especially good, like clean, saline Spinney Creeks, and meaty, minerally Blue Points. Simple dishes are the best, like a New England chowder chock full of clams, and an excellent, compact lobster roll. Shrimp cocktail is unusually flavorful, and the crab cakes are big and meaty. You'll love the casual, rakish feel of Fish, waiters in white aprons, rickety tables, the scent of horseradish in the air.

Other recommended dishes: Scallop ceviche, fried oysters, sea bream. **Price range:** Apps., $5–$12; entrees, $9–$28 (for steak). **Wheelchair access:** Not accessible.

Fleur de Sel ☆☆ $$$$ FRENCH
5 E. 20th St. (bet. Broadway and Fifth Ave.) (212) 460-9100
Credit cards: All major Meals: L, D

Who doesn't pine for that little neighborhood restaurant, tucked away on a side street, where the lighting is subdued, the chef is French and the food is terrific? Well, here it is. Cyril Renaud, the chef and owner, put in his time cooking at places like Bouley and La Caravelle. He has hung the lemon-color walls with his own paintings; the menus display his watercolors with culinary themes.

The fixed-price menu is perfectly calibrated to the small room, with five appetizers, seven main courses and five desserts, and Mr. Renaud knows in a quiet sort of way how to create excitement on the plate. With a dozen tables, Fleur de Sel barely has room for the pastries, but desserts verge on the spectacular. Try the raspberry feuilleté. Precise, minimal and drop-dead elegant. There's also a thick, chewy crepe filled with caramelized apples and smothered in Devonshire cream. It's homey, in the French way that reminds you that French homes are very different from American ones.

Wine list: About 250 wines, largely French and Californian, two ciders from Brittany. **Price range:** Lunch: three courses, $25. Dinner: six courses, $75. **Wheelchair access:** Restroom on street level.

Florent $$ FRENCH
69 Gansevoort St. (bet. Washington & Greenwich Sts.)
(212) 989-5779
Credit cards: Cash only Meals: B, Br, L, D, LN

Breakfast at 7 A.M. at this pioneer of the meat-packing district, when the transvestites are going out and the families are coming in, remains one of the quintessential New York City experiences. Otherwise, the French-American food is decent and it won't break the bank. Open 24 hours Saturday and Sunday.

Price range: Lunch: apps., $4–$6; entrees, $6–$14; desserts, $4–$5; prix fixe, $7.25 or $11. Dinner: apps., $5–$10; entrees, $8–$18; desserts, $4–$5; prix fixe, $19. **Wheelchair access:** Fully accessible. **Features:** Outdoor dining.

Flor's Kitchen $25 & Under VENEZUELAN
149 First Ave. (near 9th St.) (212) 387-8949
Credit cards: All major Meals: L, D, LN

Tiny, bright and colorful, this new Venezuelan restaurant offers many snacking foods like empanadas criollas—smooth, crisp pastries with fillings like savory shredded beef or puréed chicken. Among the arepas — corncakes with varied fillings — try the chicken and avocado salada. Two sauces — one made with avocado, lemon juice and oil; the second, a hot sauce — make dishes like chachapas (corn pancakes with ham and cheese) taste even better. Soups are superb, and desserts are rich and homespun.

Other recommended dishes: Pescado a la plancha (planked fish); arroz con pollo (chicken and rice); pabellon criollo (stewed shredded beef). **Price range:** Apps., $2–$4; entrees, $4–$9. **Wheelchair access:** Path to restroom extremely narrow.

The Four Seasons ☆☆☆ $$$$ NEW AMERICAN
99 E. 52nd St. (bet. Park & Lexington Aves.)   (212) 754-9494
Credit cards: All major   Meals L (Mon.–Fri.), D   Closed Sun.

Few restaurants occupy as honored a position in New York as the Four Seasons, now in its fifth decade as a destination for the high, the haute, and almost anybody feeling celebratory. The two rooms, designed by Philip Johnson, are as cool and elegant as ever, understated examples of the best of mid-century style. By day, the Grill Room is power central for the worlds of finance, fashion and publishing. Food is almost besides the point. By night, the shimmering Pool Room takes over.

While the kitchen under Christian Albin nods in the direction of recent trends, offering many dishes with an Asian accent, for example, it is at its best with elegant classics, like broiled Dover sole or fabulously tender rack of lamb with ethereal mashed potatoes. Occasionally a sauce will be too sweet, but such quibbles do not detract from the feeling of timeless sophistication. By the way, you can calculate the astounding number of tables celebrating birthdays and anniversaries by counting how many receive special orders of pink cotton candy. *(Review by Eric Asimov; stars previously awarded by Ruth Reichl.)*

Wine list: Big, expensive and strong in Italian wines as well as the French and American bottles. It is surprising that such an old restaurant has such a young wine list. **Price range:** Apps., $15–$25; entrees, $30–$45; desserts, $14. Prix fixe: pre-theater (Mon.–Fri.) or after-theater (Sat.), $55. **Wheelchair access:** Elevator to dining room is available.

14 Wall Street ☆ $$$ FRENCH/NEW AMERICAN
14 Wall St., 31st Fl. (bet. Broadway & Broad St.)   (212) 233-2780
Credit cards: All major   Meals: B, L, D   Closed Sat., Sun.

This is a place for power meals with a view of the financial district. Once J.P. Morgan's residence, the dining rooms have a slightly old-fashioned air, looking more like a private dining area for a big corporation than an establishment that is open to the public. The service is very professional, and the food is pleasingly straightforward. Breakfast is a bargain, and at lunchtime the restaurant overflows with diners intent on serious food; they think nothing of sitting down to a lunch of foie gras, grilled lamb chops and crème brûlée. Salads are excellent, but the best main courses are the chef's signature dishes, like beautifully cooked liver with mashed potatoes, or brook trout stuffed with fennel, lightly smoked and served on a wooden plank. The most interesting dessert is a tasting of crème brûlée, three little pots of custard flavored with vanilla, pistachio and Armagnac.

Wine list: Best choices are French; no bargains. **Price range:** Apps., $8–$15; entrees, $19–$28; desserts, $8. **Wheelchair access:** Elevators to dining rooms. **Features:** Good view.

Frank $25 & Under ITALIAN
88 Second Ave. (near 5th St.)   (212) 420-0202
Credit cards: Cash only   Meals: Br, L, D, LN

This sweet, unpretentious restaurant, with its crowded, ragtag dining room, has been packed from the moment it opened. Start with an order of insalata Caprese, ripe tomatoes and mozzarella di bufala, and you may forget the tight surroundings. Among the entrees, polpettone, a savory meatloaf, with a classic, slow-cooked gravy, and orecchiette with fennel and pecorino Toscano are excellent. If you go early, you can expect special touches, like a free plate of tiny potato croquettes, or a dish of olive oil flavored with orange rind with your bread.

Other recommended dishes: Fennel salad; mussels; green bean, potato and egg salad; roasted trout; chicken with garlic and rosemary. **Alcohol:** Beer and wine. **Price range:** Apps., $4–$8; entrees, $7–$15. **Wheelchair access:** Narrow and small, particularly the restroom.

Franklin Station Cafe $ SOUTHEAST ASIAN
222 W. Broadway (at Franklin St.)   (212) 274-8525
Credit cards: All major   Meals: B, Br, L, D

It calls itself a French-Malaysian cafe, but the French part is hard to discern. No matter: The curries and other Asian dishes are enticing, as are the salads and sandwiches, served in a pleasant if unremarkable setting.

Alcohol: None. **Price range:** Apps., $3–$7; entrees, $7–$17; desserts, $3–$5. **Wheelchair access:** Not accessible.

Frank's ☆ $$$ STEAKHOUSE
85 10th Ave. (at 15th St.)   (212) 243-1349
Credit cards: All major   Meals: L, D

A paradise for carnivores. The bare brick walls and long bar announce this as a restaurant whose only desire is to serve big portions to hungry people. Three or four shrimp in a cocktail would probably provide enough protein for an average person: they are giant creatures of the sea, and absolutely delicious. The T-bone steak is a great charred hunk with the fine, funky flavor of meat that has been dry-aged for a long time. The steak fries are long and thick, the sort of fries that give potatoes a good name. The same family has been running Frank's since 1912; they want you to feel at home, and you will. (*Ruth Reichl*)

Wine list: The list is small and seems like an afterthought; if you want great wine with your steak you'd be better off at Sparks or Smith & Wollensky. **Price range:** Lunch: apps., $6–$14; entrees, $9–$24; desserts, $4–$9. Dinner: apps., $7–$15; entrees, $18–$30; desserts, $4–$9. **Wheelchair access:** The restaurant is up five steps.

Fred's $25 & Under   AMERICAN
476 Amsterdam Ave. (at 83rd St.)   (212) 579-3076
Credit cards: All major   Meals: B, Br, L, D, LN

This subterranean bar and restaurant offers homey American fare
and relaxed, friendly service, a combination that has made it a
neighborhood hit from the night it opened. It's a simple, familiar
formula, but Fred's, named for the owner's dog, does it well. The
best main courses are meats, like an excellent, thick pork chop
cooked perfectly and served with roasted apples, potatoes roasted
with rosemary and a mixture of broccoli and zucchini. Desserts are
huge and eager to please, like an intensely fudgy brownie and a
spicy apple-berry crisp.

Other recommended dishes: Mesclun with blue cheese, apple and
roasted pecans; fried calamari; fillet of beef; beef stew; tuna steak;
salmon fillet. **Price range:** Apps., $3–$9; entrees, $9–$17. **Wheelchair access:** Dining room is five steps down from street. **Features:**
Outdoor dining.

Fresco Tortilla Grill $25 & Under   TEX-MEX
36 Lexington Ave. (bet. 23rd & 24th Sts.)   (212) 475-7380
253 Eighth Ave. (bet. 22nd & 23rd Sts.)   (212) 463-8877
769 Sixth Ave. (bet. 25th & 26th Sts.)   (212) 691-5588
215 W. 14th St. (bet. Seventh & Eighth Aves.)   (212) 352-0686
Credit cards: All major   Meals: L, D

Superb Tex-Mex fast food served in a tiny storefront. Fresco has been
so successful that it's given rise to an indecipherable number of
related branches and unrelated imitators, all with similar names. The
original branch, on Lexington Avenue, is still the best.

Recommended dishes: Taco al carbon, tacos with ground chorizo,
quesadillas, fajitas, sincronizadas. **Alcohol:** Bring your own. **Price
range:** Entrees, $5–$14. **Wheelchair access:** All one level. **Features:** Outdoor dining.

Fresh   ☆☆ $$$$ SEAFOOD
105 Reade St. (near W. Broadway)   (212) 406-1900
Credit cards: All major   Meals: D

Bold and playful shuffling of ingredients makes Fresh, an airy
seafood restaurant, so intriguing. Straightforward dishes like a mess
of fried clams are soft and full of intense clam flavor have their
moments. A steamed lobster is terrifically sweet and sumptuous.
Still, Fresh rises and falls on its more expressive dishes, like smoky,
buttery rillettes of Gaspé cod and finnan haddie blended with
shaved fennel, a delicious combination. Kobe toro, tuna that is
thick and buttery rich, tastes as babied as the legendary Kobe beef.
Conventional cuts of seafood earn a more delicate treatment. A
whole flounder is lightly fried to retain its beautiful nutlike flavor
and served in a ginger-soy broth. Crisp batter-fried haddock, served
with chunks of fried potatoes, may well be the best fish and chips
around. Desserts include clever modern tweaks, such as adding
yuzu curd to an already excellent blueberry financier.

Occasional inconsistencies in the food are a problem, and service can be surprisingly amateurish in an otherwise professional operation. (*Eric Asimov*)

Other recommended dishes: Fried halibut cheeks, New England clam chowder, gazpacho, fried cod tongues with duck breast, sea scallop and corn soup, prime rib of swordfish, tournedo of Atlantic salmon, soft-shell crabs, chocolate hazelnut cake. **Wine list:** An odd list casts a wide but not deep net. **Price range:** Apps., $9–$18; entrees, $19–$34; desserts, $7–$8. **Wheelchair access:** Steps in front (ramp available).

Funky Broome $25 & Under   CHINESE

176 Mott St. (bet. Broome & Kenmare Sts.)   (212) 941-8628
Credit cards: All major   Meals: L, D, LN

From its odd name to its brightly colored interior, Funky Broome suggests youth and energy rather than conformity. Though the menu is largely Cantonese and Hong Kong, Funky Broome has stirred it up a bit with some Thai touches and by making mini-woks centerpieces. The small woks are set over Sterno flames, which keep everything bubbling hot but can make it difficult to pass around the wok. Nonetheless, some of the dishes are unusual and good, like a delicious vegetarian casserole of nutty-tasting fried lotus roots in a gingery sauce with dried cherries. Seafood dishes are excellent. Salt and pepper seafood, a familiar Cantonese dish of fried shrimp, scallops and squid, is flawless. Funky Broome can breathe new life into hoary old dishes like crisp and tender beef with broccoli, while shredded chicken with Chinese vegetables is full of distinct and honest flavors.

Other recommended dishes: Sautéed bok choy greens, sautéed water spinach, shredded dried beef with shrimp paste and rice, steamed oysters. **Price range:** Apps., $5–$11; entrees, $8–$14. **Wheelchair access:** All one level.

Gabriela's $25 & Under   MEXICAN

685 Amsterdam Ave. (at 93rd St.)   (212) 961-0574
311 Amsterdam Ave. (at 75th St.)
Credit cards: All major   Meals: B, L, D

This place is owned by the same people who own two Carmine's, three Ollie's Noodle Shops, two Dock's Oyster Bars and one Virgil's Real BBQ, but unlike those high-volume restaurants, named after fictional characters, there really is a Gabriela, and she makes terrific, authentic Mexican dishes. Taquitos al pastor, tiny corn tortillas topped with vinegary roast pork, pineapple salsa and cilantro, are a wonderful Mexican street dish. Gabriela's pozole, the traditional Mexican soup made with hominy, is a meal in itself, served in a huge bowl with chunks of tender pork or chicken. Entrees all come with fragrant tortillas. And one last surprise: Gabriela's offers several superb desserts, including capirotada, a buttery bread pudding with lots of honey.

Other recommended dishes: Chips, guacamole, salad with nopales, tacos, tamales, carnitas, chochinta pibil, shrimp in chipotle sauce, jericalls, rice pudding. **Alcohol:** Beer, wine and tequila-based drinks. **Price range:** Apps., $3–$8; entrees, $6–$15. **Wheelchair access:** Entrance and dining room are on one level; restrooms are down one flight.

Gabriel's ☆☆ $$$ ITALIAN

11 W. 60th St. (bet. Broadway & Columbus Ave.) (212) 956-4600
Credit cards: All major   Meals: L, D   Closed Sun.

This clubby and comfortable restaurant is a great choice before or after the symphony, with its great big portions and fabulous friendly service. Although the food is called Tuscan, it is not. It is far too American for that, too original. Look around the restaurant and the dish you see on almost every table is an earthy and seductive buckwheat polenta. The salads are inventive but they work. None of the pastas are ordinary, either. The real winner here is homemade gnocchi, little dumplings so light they float into your mouth and down your throat. Among the entrees, roast kid is a big, tasty hunk of meat. Desserts, with the exception of the wonderful sorbets and gelatos, are not very exciting. (*Ruth Reichl*)

Wine list: The mostly Italian list is quirky, personal and carefully chosen. **Price range:** Lunch: apps., $7–$10; entrees, $14–$19; desserts, $8–$12. Dinner: apps., $9–$12; entrees, $18–$32; desserts, $8–$12. **Wheelchair access:** Fully accessible.

Gage & Tollner $$ SEAFOOD/SOUTHERN

372 Fulton St., Brooklyn Heights, Brooklyn (718) 875-5181
Credit cards: All major   Meals: L, D   Closed Sun.

Gage & Tollner, the bastion of seafood and Southern cooking, lives on, its dignified face blinking a little awkwardly in the tackiness of Fulton Mall. Everything has been restored at Gage & Tollner, which opened in 1879 and moved to its current downtown Brooklyn location in 1892. It is a wonderfully old-fashioned room. The beautiful old gas-fired lights have been retrofitted, and they now flicker appealingly, making everyone look beautiful, and acoustic tiles have been removed, exposing the original vaulted ceiling. Unlike the room, the menu has barely changed in a century, with old favorites like soft clam bellies, lobster Newburg, she-crab soup and "blooming onions," which are fried whole. It's not likely to be the best lobster or the best steak you'll ever eat, but at Gage & Tollner it's the history and beauty, not the food, that's really the point.

Price range: Lunch: apps., $6–$12; entrees, $12–$21; desserts, $5–$7. Dinner: apps., $7–$12; entrees, $15–$27; desserts, $5–$7. **Wheelchair access:** Restrooms not accessible. **Features:** Parking available.

Gallagher's $$$ STEAKHOUSE

228 W. 52nd St. (bet. Broadway & Eighth Ave.) (212) 245-5336
Credit cards: All major   Meals: L, D, LN

The slabs of prime beef hanging in the windows of Gallagher's are a steak lover's delight, and if you know anything about meat so much the better: you may go into the refrigerated room with its hanging meat and pick your own steak. The best bet at this shrine to long-gone prizefighters and sports stars is to stick with the sirloin steak and other basics, like the fabulous steak fries and terrific onion rings.

Price range: Lunch entrees, $13–$43. Dinner: apps., $8–$16; entrees, $17–$43; desserts, $4–$6. **Wheelchair access:** Side entrance available; restrooms not accessible.

Garden Cafe $25 & Under   NEW AMERICAN
620 Vanderbilt Ave., Prospect Heights, Brooklyn   (718) 857-8863
Credit cards: All major   Meals: D   Closed Sun., Mon.

This family-run operation serves an ever-changing menu of artful American food that is always satisfying. Standards like grilled veal chops and steaks are superb, and the chef occasionally comes up with dishes like jambalaya with Middle Eastern spicing. It's the kind of place you wish was in your neighborhood.

Other recommended dishes: Green salad with lemon vinaigrette; lemon soufflé in raspberry sauce. **Alcohol:** Beer and wine. **Price range:** Apps., $6–$7; entrees, $18–$20; desserts, $6. Weeknight three-course dinner, $25. **Wheelchair access:** Fully accessible.

Gennaro $25 & Under   ITALIAN/MEDITERRANEAN
665 Amsterdam Ave. (near 93rd St.)   (212) 665-5348
Credit cards: Cash only   Meals: D

This newly expanded, simply decorated Italian restaurant is one of the best things to happen to the Upper West Side in years, serving wonderful dishes like an awesome osso bucco and terrific pastas. Appetizer specials are satisfying, like ribbolita, the classic Tuscan vegetable and bean soup, served over thick slices of bread. Cornish hen roasted with lemon is also excellent. Gennaro serves its own pear tart, flaky and delicious, and a rich flourless chocolate cake.

Other recommended dishes: Grilled vegetables, beef carpaccio, orecchiette with broccoli and provolone, tortelloni with spinach and ricotta, braised lamb shank. **Alcohol:** Beer and wine. **Price range:** Apps., $6–$9; entrees, $9–$15; desserts, $5–$6. **Wheelchair access:** Entrance and dining room on one level; restroom is narrow.

Ghenet $25 & Under   AFRICAN/ETHIOPIAN
284 Mulberry St. (near Houston St.)   (212) 343-4888
Credit cards: All major   Meals: L, D

This friendly, enticing restaurant offers an introduction to Ethiopian food, not quite as spicy or as gamy as you might find elsewhere, but good just the same. Highlights include kategna, simply a length of injera — the smooth, brownish bread made from fermented tef toasted until crisp and painted with berbere, a fiery sauce, and kibe, a clarified butter that resembles the Indian ghee. The main courses are tasty but mildly spiced: Siga wat, cubes of tender, delicious beef, comes in a sauce milder than usual, since "wat" ordinarily means hot; doro wat is also tamer than expected, a chicken stew served, as is traditional, with a hard-boiled egg.

Alcohol: Beer and wine. **Price range:** Apps., $4–$5; entrees, $9–$14. **Wheelchair access:** Restrooms not accessible.

Gino $$ ITALIAN

780 Lexington Ave. (bet. 60th & 61st Sts.) (212) 223-9658
Credit cards: Cash only Meals: L, D

You saw it in *Mighty Aphrodite*, zebra wallpaper and all. Unless you're a regular customer, the charms of this old-time Italian restaurant might elude you.

Price range: Dinner: apps, $6–$13; entrees, $14–$27; desserts, $4. **Wheelchair access:** Restrooms not accessible.

Gonzo $25 & Under PIZZA/ITALIAN

140 W. 13th St. (bet. Sixth & Seventh Aves.) (212) 645-4606
Credit cards: All major Meals: D, LN Closed Mon.

Gonzo specializes in antipasti and pizzas, but it hedges its bets with a conventional Italian menu, too. The dining room is loud, but dim, and almost Gothic with a high, paneled ceiling and tapestries. Gonzo clearly has an audience. They come for the pizzas, which arrive irregularly shaped. The crust is thin and curled, with doughy flavor and elasticity, crisp and surprisingly light. Try the sopressata pie, topped with pungent salami and roasted red pepper purée, and the Siciliano, with sweet caponata and ricotta cheese. You can make a light meal with pizza and a few cicchetti, Italian-style tapas. Things become uncertain when you stray from the pizzas and cicchetti. A few dishes stood out: penne baked in a crock with Parmesan and pancetta, and meaty roasted quail stuffed with a mixture of ground chicken, apples and rosemary.

Price range: Cicchetti, $4.50–$7; apps., $8–$12; pizzas, $13–$15; entrees, $14–$17.50 (whole snapper, $32). **Wheelchair access:** Three steps at entrance.

Good $25 & Under NEW AMERICAN/PAN-LATIN

89 Greenwich Ave. (at Bank St.) (212) 691-8080
Credit cards: All major Meals: L, D Closed Mon.

It is possible to eat unusually, eclectically and very well here. The burger is big and meaty and sure to satisfy; even better is the grilled flank steak with parsley-garlic sauce. And definitely take the chilaquiles, a Mexican solution to the problem of what to do with leftover tortillas: grill them and toss them with other leftovers (in this case, chicken, onions, cilantro and chili sauce).

The service is warm and professional. The signature dessert, house-made doughnuts, are rather dry and tasteless, but the demitasse of Oaxacan chocolate served with them is delicious.

Other recommended dishes: Grilled calamari, arepa with scallops, Camembert crisp with pear chutney, peanut chicken, flank steak, pork sandwich, tuna glazed in molasses. **Price range:** Apps., $5–$8; entrees, $10–$17. **Wheelchair access:** All one level.

Good World Bar and Grill

$25 & Under
SCANDINAVIAN

3 Orchard St. (at Division St.)
Credit cards: All major

(212) 925-9975
Meals: D, LN

If for no other reason, Good World Bar and Grill beckons because it's a bar in an old barbershop in Chinatown that serves Scandinavian food. As a restaurant, it's unpolished. Yet, it offers a spirit of adventure, a departure from the routine. It's not entirely Scandinavian, but the lack of rigor reflects the laid-back spirit of the place, with its spacey service but appealing downtown ambiance. Skagen is shrimp with crème fraîche and dill, served on toast. It's a nice prelude to the fabulous fish soup, a bisque that tastes like the essence of the sea, made with sour cream and onions and full of shrimp and mussels. Basic dishes like Swedish meatballs and potato pancakes can be unpredictable. Good World is on far firmer ground with seafood, like an offering of three kinds of herring.

Other recommended dishes: Grilled sardines, crab cakes, three-berry pie. **Price range:** Apps , $3–$6; medium and large plates, $8–$16. **Wheelchair access:** All one level.

Goody's ☆ $

CHINESE

1 E. Broadway (at Chatham Sq.)
Credit cards: All major

(212) 577-2922
Meals: L, D

Great Shanghai food from the people who went on to open the Joe's Shanghai chain. Don't miss the soup dumplings, xiao long bao. Goody's pride is the crab meat version, tinted pink by the seafood that glows through the sheer, silky skin. But there are other unusual dishes, like fabulous turnip pastries, yellowfish fingers in seaweed batter, and braised pork shoulder, a kind of candied meat. This dish is so rich that it must be eaten in small bites. Goody's kitchen also works magic with bean curd, mixed with crab meat so it becomes rich and delicious.

Other recommended dishes: Steamed pork buns, dried bean curd with jalapeños. **Alcohol:** Beer. **Price range:** $15–$20 for a full meal. **Wheelchair access:** Restrooms are narrow.

Gotham Bar and Grill ☆ ☆ ☆ $$$$

NEW AMERICAN

12 E. 12th St. (bet. Fifth Ave. & University Pl.)
Credit cards: All major

(212) 620-4020
Meals: L (Mon. –Fri.), D

Gotham Bar and Grill is a cheerful, welcoming restaurant in an open, high-ceilinged room with a lively bar. Through some trick of design, each table offers intimacy: seated, you have the sense of watching without being watched. Starched men in suits mingle with rumpled guys in blue jeans. Gotham's service is a big part of its ambiance. Waiters anticipating diners' every wish and make them feel remarkably well cared for.

And then there's the food. The chef, famous for his vertical dishes, is working with an architecture of flavor, composing his dishes so each element contributes something vital. The food seems modern but is almost classic in its balance. The signature dish is seafood salad, a spiral of scallops, squid, octopus, lobster and avo-cado that swirls onto the plate like a mini-tornado. Desserts, like the wonderful chocolate cake, are intense and very American.

On a recent visit, the restaurant showed no signs of slowing down or slacking off. In fact, it would be hard to think of another three-star restaurant of comparable age that continues to perform, dish after dish, with such admirable consistency. The food is taller than ever, but it may be better than ever. The range of flavors and treatments is impressive. (*Ruth Reichl, updated by William Grimes*)

Wine list: The waiters are very helpful in navigating the unusual and well-chosen list. It would be nice if there were more lower-priced bottles. **Price range:** Lunch: apps., $12–$17; entrees, $16–$20; desserts, $8–$9; three-course prix fixe, $25. Dinner: apps., $12–$23; entrees, $28–$44; desserts, $8–$9. **Wheelchair access:** Ramp available to the dining room; restrooms downstairs.

Grace $$ NEW AMERICAN

114 Franklin St. (bet W. Broadway & Church St.)   (212) 343-4200
Credit cards: All major   Meals: Br, L, D, LN

It's hard to know whether Grace is a restaurant with a bar or a bar with a restaurant. Visually the bar comes first. Weighty, glossy and a mile long, it dominates the front room. The dining room, though, is more than an afterthought, with a grazing menu that's strong on bright, assertive flavors with smartly targeted Southwestern and Asian ingredients. The dishes can be as minimal as a sandwich of melted raclette and Westphalian ham, or mussels steamed in Bel-gian beer and served with a side of fries, and there's a fundamental simplicity to even the more complicated choices.

Other recommended dishes: Chipotle-marinated skirt steak, mas-carpone polenta cakes, seared tuna in pepper crust. **Wine list:** American and French wines from $20–$50; by the glass, $6–$10. **Price range:** Small plates, $8–$13. Dinner: apps, $8–$12; entrees, $9–$14, desserts, $5–$8. **Wheelchair access:** Steps to entrance.

Gradisca $25 & Under ITALIAN

126 W. 13th St. (bet. Sixth & Seventh Aves.)   (212) 691-4886
Credit cards: Cash only   Meals: D

Gradisca epitomizes the local trattoria, downtown style. The dining room is rustic: tables covered in butcher paper, walls of brick and rough-hewn wood, which are covered in officially sanctioned graf-fiti, and candles throwing so little light you can barely make out the menu. Its waiters conform to a more modern stereotype: young, hip and lanky in tight black T-shirts. Piadinas are excellent starters. These round, unleavened flatbreads from the Romagna region of northern Italy are cooked on a griddle and then stuffed with things like prosciutto and fresh mozzarella, or spinach and pecorino. Gradisca even serves spaghetti carbonara as it was intended, simply with eggs and bacon. The list of main courses is small, but includes two superb selections: sliced leg of lamb that is tender and full of flavor in its red wine sauce, and a big pork chop that holds its own under a cloud of crisp leeks.

Desserts standouts include salame di cioccolato, a deliciously dense, bittersweet chocolate torte made to resemble salami slices, and a jiggly, satisfying amaretto semifreddo.

Other recommended dishes: Carrot soup, eggplant with tomato and anchovies, pappardelle with lamb ragu, spaghetti with cuttlefish and black ink sauce, lasagna. **Price range:** Apps., $5–$8; entrees, $12–$20. **Wheelchair access:** Two steps at entrance.

Gramercy Tavern ☆☆☆ $$$$ NEW AMERICAN
42 E. 20th St. (bet. Broadway & Park Ave. S.) (212) 477-0777
Credit cards: All major Meals: L, D

When Gramercy Tavern opened in 1994 the owners, Danny Meyer and Tom Colicchio, said they intended to redefine grand dining in New York. The large and lively Tavern has fulfilled this promise. Chef Tom Colicchio cooks with extraordinary confidence, creating dishes characterized by bold flavors and unusual harmonies. Service is solicitous but unceremonial. For a less expensive alternative, the handsome bar in front offers a casual but excellent menu.

On a recent visit, the restaurant lived up to its three stars, with consistently fresh, inventive new American dishes like crab ragout with sweet-pea puree, braised veal cheek lasagna, and poached bass with cucumbers, fennel and pickled watermelon. Claudia Fleming's desserts remain a highlight, especially her honey pine-nut tart with roasted figs and honey-orange lavender ice cream. (*Ruth Reichl, updated by William Grimes*)

Wine list: Interesting, accessible and well priced. **Price range:** Lunch: three-course prix fixe, $36. Dinner: three-course prix fixe, $68; seasonal tasting menus, $80–$95. **Wheelchair access:** Fully accessible.

Grand Sichuan Eastern $25 & Under CHINESE
1049 Second Ave. (near 56th St.) (212) 355-5855
Credit cards: All major Meals: L, D

The newest of the Grand Sichuan restaurants, a bright, boxy storefront that conforms largely to the Chinatown school of interior design, has added 96 dishes to the menu under the heading "New Sichuan Food." You've probably never had anything like Chong Qing spicy and aromatic chicken, a daunting dish that looks like a mountain of slender red chili peppers embedded with cubes of chicken. The heat has been tamed in some of the new dishes, but Second Sister's diced rabbit has more bones than meat and more heat than bones, while bean curd with spicy sauce is scorching. Weaving milder dishes into the meal is imperative, like dry sautéed shrimp or slender Asian eggplants in "wonder sauce." While the new dishes are intriguing, do not let a trip to Grand Sichuan pass without checking in on old favorites. There's nothing better than paper-thin slices of cured pork with tender garlic shoots, except the tea-smoked duck — likely the best barbecue in New York.

Other recommended dishes: Crispy toothpick chicken skin, Chengdu spicy dumplings, Chong Qing sour cabbage fish, sautéed corn with spicy pepper. **Price range:** Apps., $1.50–$14.95; entrees, $7.25–$16.95. **Wheelchair access:** Step at entrance; restroom is very narrow.

Grand Sichuan International $25 & Under

229 Ninth Ave. (at 24th St.)   (212) 620-5200
745 Ninth Ave. (bet. 50th & 51st Sts.)   (212) 582-2288
Credit cards: All major   Meals: L, D

These restaurants are notable not only for their terrific Sichuan and
Hunan food, but also for a remarkable approach to their clientele.
The owner hands out a 27-page pamphlet that explains five Chinese
regional cuisines and describes dozens of dishes the restaurant
serves. The eating is as interesting as the reading, with wonderful
dishes like sour stringbeans with minced pork and tea-smoked
duck. While Sichuan food is indeed spicy, that is only part of the
story, as you see when you taste a fabulous cold dish like sliced
conch with wild pepper sauce, coated with ground Sichuan peppercorns, which are not hot but effervescent and almost refreshing.

Other recommended dishes: Sichuan wontons with red oil; cold
Sichuan noodles; broad beans in scallion sauce; prawns with garlic
sauce; red-cooked pork with chestnuts; bean curd with spicy sauce.
Alcohol: Beer and wine. **Price range:** Apps., $1–$9; entrees,
$6–$19. **Wheelchair access:** Aisle to restrooms is very narrow.

Green Field $25 & Under   LATIN AMERICAN

108-01 Northern Blvd., Corona, Queens   (718) 672-5202
Credit cards: All major   Meals: L, D, LN

With a dining room the size of a soccer field, this Brazilian barbecue restaurant does a huge business with its all-you-can-eat menu.
The best selections are the sausages and the tenderloin steak
charred on the outside and flavored with olive oil and rosemary. At
the end, a simple piece of fruit from the salad bar is just right for
dessert. The food is good, and the routine of signaling for more
from the spit-wielding waiters is fun. The key is not to fill up at the
huge salad bar.

Other recommended dishes: Pork loin; rib-eye steak; turkey
wrapped in bacon; beef ribs; chicken hearts; venison. **Price range:**
$20 all-you-can-eat. **Wheelchair access:** All one level. **Features:**
Parking available.

Green Table $25 & Under   NEW AMERICAN

Chelsea Market, 75 Ninth Ave. (at 15th St.)   (212) 741-9174
Credit cards: All major   Meals: L, D Closed Sun.

Acting on the Manhattan principle that space is precious, the
Cleaver Company, a longtime New York caterer, carved out a small
triangular dining room next to its takeout shop in the Chelsea Market, where it opened Green Table, a little cafe and wine bar devoted
to organic foods and beverages. The dining room, done up like a little bungalow with green farmhouse windows and walls the color of
an opulent sunset, seats fewer than 20, with room for six outside.

Green Table could offer no better advertisement for its catering
business than its superb mezze plate, which might include a dollop
of rich foie gras perched on a juicy apple slice or a tantalizing
brioche crouton topped with caviar and crème fraîche. Soups offer
a small window for eccentricity, and sandwiches and quiches are

117

all top-notch. The Cleaver Company is deservedly known for its chicken potpie. Even better is spicy crayfish potpie. You might be tempted to stop at Green Table just for dessert. Try the rich, dense chocolate pot de crème.

Other recommended dishes: Mezze plate, pea soup with citrus cream, panino of pork loin, meatloaf, cece bean ravioli, maple-cured salmon, ginger doughnuts, cherry cobbler. **Price range:** Apps., $2.50–$6.75; entrees, $7.50–$11.50; desserts, $4–$6. **Wheelchair access:** All one level.

The Grocery ☆ $$ NEW AMERICAN

288 Smith St. (bet. Union & Sackett Sts.) (718) 596-3335
Credit cards: MC/V Meals: D Closed Sun.

The Grocery likes to project the image of the little restaurant that could, a struggling Brooklyn storefront operation where things can and will go wrong, but in a way that makes you laugh. Don't be fooled by the act. Despite serious service problems, it is a focused, high-quality restaurant that, in fits and starts, rises to heights that make it much more than a nice neighborhood spot.

Many restaurants sell themselves as market-driven, but the Grocery follows through on the pledge. Fresh produce, good fish and flavorful meat are the foundation of the Grocery's cuisine, an internationalized style of bistro cooking with an Italian insistence on pristine ingredients. The menu finishes strong with excellent, homey desserts with an exotic touch here and there.

Wine list: A modestly priced, eclectic 35-bottle list, with nine wines by the glass. **Price range:** Dinner: apps., $6–$8; entrees, $16–$19; desserts, $6–$7. **Wheelchair access:** One step down to garden; restrooms not accessible.

Guastavino's ☆☆ $$$$ ENGLISH/FRENCH

409 E. 59th St. (bet. First & York Aves.) (212) 980-2455
Credit cards: All major Meals: L, D

Sir Terence Conran has made good on the theatrical possibilities in the tiled vaults under the Queensboro Bridge. Named after the father-and son-team that created the tiled ceilings in the bridge's vaults (as well as the ceilings in the Grand Central Oyster Bar and several other sites), the restaurant encourages the eye to linger on the powerful pillars that lead upward to cathedral-like ceilings. It's not so much a restaurant as an opportunity to live, for two or three hours, a certain mood, and a certain sense of style, that suits every time zone and speaks every language. While the food may not light up the night, at its best it is well conceived and well executed.

The restaurant is a 300-seat brasserie, clamorous and casual, with a glorious brasserie-style shellfish display in front of the kitchen. The menu sticks to straightforward brasserie fare. Prawns, oysters and lobsters from the raw bar fairly crackle with freshness. The upscale dining room upstairs is open only for private parties.

Wine list: An international bistro list of 80 modest wines, plus 12 half bottles, 10 wines by the glass. **Price range:** Apps., $8–$18; entrees, $14–$30; desserts, $7–$9. **Wheelchair access:** Fully accessible.

Gus's Figs $25 & Under   MEDITERRANEAN
250 W. 27th St. (bet. Seventh & Eighth Aves.)   (212) 352-8822
Credit cards: All major   Meals: L, D, LN

Figs captures the dreamy, generous, sun-soaked aura that makes
the Mediterranean so endlessly appealing. The chef excels at blending flavors and textures in main courses like moist, flavorful
chicken, braised in a clay pot and served over creamy polenta. Top
dishes include tender pieces of lamb served over a soft bread pudding made savory with goat cheese and pine nuts and sweetened
with figs; and pan-roasted cod with grilled leeks, orange sections
and pomegranate vinaigrette.

Other recommended dishes: Bruschetta; phyllo tasting plate;
grilled polenta cake; beet and goat cheese salad; cassoulet; kakavia;
grilled tuna; whole grilled snapper; almond cake; poached pear.
Price range: Apps., $5–$9; entrees, $13–$20. **Wheelchair access:**
Restrooms and dining room are on one level; a ramp is planned for
entrance.

Habib's Place $25 & Under
NORTH AFRICAN/MIDDLE EASTERN
130 St. Marks Pl. (near Ave. A)   (212) 979-2243
Credit cards: Cash only   Meals: L, D, LN

The new Habib's Place is colorful and commodious, and bigger
than the original a block away which closed in 2001. The menu
runs the gamut of familiar Middle Eastern and North African specialties, but couscous is the thing, served in handsome ceramic
tagines. The array of steamed carrots, squash, chickpeas, peppers
and lamb arrayed across the top almost obscures the couscous
underneath. With the tagine comes a bowl of lamb broth, complex
and delicious enough to eat by itself. Alternatives include superb
kebabs. The lamb shawarma is especially noteworthy. Falafel is so
fresh you can taste the cumin, coriander, garlic and onion in the
chickpea blend.

Other recommended dishes: Hummus, tabbouleh, baba ghanouj.
Price range: $3–$12. **Wheelchair access:** Ramp at entrance;
restroom is very narrow.

Hacienda de Argentina   ☆ $$ ARGENTINE
339 E. 75th St. (bet. First & Second Aves.)   (212) 472-5300
Credit cards: All major   Meals: D

This small dining room, enveloped in a thick layer of darkness, is
crowded with heavy Old World oak furniture, burnished cande-
labra, gilt mirrors and, inexplicably, a full suit of armor back near
the kitchen. Eating here is like sitting down to dinner with Don
Diego in an episode of *Zorro*. The restaurant aims to present a faithful rendition of Argentina's distinctive beef-crazy cuisine, an odd
mixture of grilled steaks, sausages and offal influenced by the cooking of Italian, Spanish and German immigrants. The juicy, tender,
beautifully marbled shell steak is one of two cuts, the other being
filet mignon, that are offered Argentine (grass-fed) or American
(grain-fed) style. The restaurant serves a first-rate morcilla, or blood

sausage. For dessert proceed directly to the flourless torte made with Belgian chocolate. It couldn't be any better.

It does not pay to quiz the young waiters too closely about the wine list, or anything else for that matter. The level of expertise is a notch or two above Denny's, with the same chatty, cheery attitude.

Other recommended dishes: Empanadas, veal sweetbreads, chorizo plate, Argentine fries. **Wine list:** A perfunctory list that emphasizes Spanish and Argentine wines. **Price range:** Apps., $7–$7.95; entrees, $13.50–$35.75; desserts, $7. **Wheelchair access:** Restrooms downstairs.

The Half King $25 & Under   PUB/IRISH

505 W. 23rd St. (bet. Tenth & Eleventh Aves.)   (212) 462-4300
Credit cards: All major   Meals: B, L, D

Owned by Sebastian Junger, author of *The Perfect Storm*, and named for an 18th-century American Indian leader, the Half King is unlike any conventional notion of a writers' bar. The music is so loud that conversation is hard and brooding impossible. The patrons are so young they probably wouldn't know a typewriter from a martini. One more thing sets the Half King apart from other writers' bars: food that you can actually enjoy.

The starting point is Irish pub grub, skillfully elevated from its proletarian moorings while retaining its heartiness and simplicity. Main courses include a superbly flavorful pork roast, and a surprisingly delicate fillet of sole. There is an inexpensive, serviceable wine list. Desserts are good and rustic, like a rough-hewn berry, peach and apple crumble.

By day, the bar is empty, and it's easier to notice the handsome simplicity of the woody décor, with its occasional nautical artifacts. A small garden in the rear is pleasant at lunch, or at breakfast, when you can sample the delicious house-made scones, served warm with clotted cream and jam, or the huge Irish breakfast.

Other recommended dishes: Seafood chowder, smoked salmon salad, seaweed salad, hamburger, lamb steak, shepherd's pie, lemon tart. **Price range:** Apps., $4–$10; entrees, $9–$16. **Wheelchair access:** All one level.

Hallo Berlin $25 & Under   GERMAN

402 W. 51st St. (at Ninth Ave.)   (212) 541-6248
626 10th Ave. (at 44th St.)   (212) 977-1944
Credit cards: Only at 10th Ave. location   Meals: L, D

For inexpensive German specialties, it's hard to do better than Hallo Berlin. The half dozen kinds of mildly spiced sausages are excellent; and rouladen, beef fillets sliced thin and rolled around bacon and cucumber, are almost like sausages themselves. Fat white meatballs, a mixture of pork and beef, are boiled and then bathed in a creamy caper sauce and come with mashed potatoes, peas and carrots. All this food goes perfectly with the selection of German beers, though the setting — a few rickety tables — is barely more comfortable than a bench on the sidewalk.

Other recommended dishes: Potato pancakes; rollmops; wurst; rouladen; smoked pork chops. **Alcohol:** Beer and wine. **Price**

range: Apps., $1–$3; entrees, $9–$15; desserts, $3–$4. **Wheelchair access:** 10th Ave. location fully accessible; 51st St. dining room is two steps from street. **Features:** Outdoor dining.

Han Bat
$25 & Under   KOREAN

53 W. 35th St. (bet. Fifth Ave. & Broadway)   (212) 629-5588
Credit cards: All major   Meals: L, D   Open 24 hours

This spare, clean, round-the-clock restaurant is unusual because it specializes in the country dishes of southern Korea. Typical Korean dishes, like scallion and seafood pancakes, fiery stir-fried baby octopus and bibimbab, are all excellent. Meals here are served family style and include several little appetizers; almost all dishes are served with rice, a welcome balm to the spicier fare, and crocks of the rich beef soup, which is full of noodles and scallions but needs a shot of salt.

Other recommended dishes: Binde duk; jaeyuk bokum; bul go ki; nakji bokum; gobdol bibambab. **Alcohol:** Beer and wine. **Price range:** Apps., $6–$10; entrees, $7–$16. **Wheelchair access:** All one level.

Hangawi
☆ ☆ $$$ KOREAN/VEGETARIAN

12 E. 32nd St. (bet. Fifth & Madison Aves.)   (212) 213-0077
Credit cards: All major   Meals: L, D

Eating in this calm, elegant space with its smooth wooden bowls and heavy ceramic cups is utterly peaceful. Diners remove their shoes on entering and sit at low tables with their feet dangling comfortably into the sunken space beneath them. They are surrounded by unearthly Korean music, wonderful objects and people who move with deliberate grace. Even people accustomed to eating on the far side of food may find these greens, porridges and mountain roots exotic. Much of the menu can be sampled by ordering the emperor's meal, which includes a tray of nine kinds of mountain greens surrounded by 10 side dishes: kimchi, cold spinach, sweet lotus root with sesame, chili cabbage and the like. (*Ruth Reichl*)

Price range: Apps., $6–$11; entrees, $15–$25; desserts, $4–$6; prix-fixe dinners, $30 and $35. **Wheelchair access:** Dining room and restrooms are a few steps up; see details above for seating.

The Harrison
☆ ☆ $$$ NEW AMERICAN

355 Greenwich St. (at Harrison St.)   (212) 274-9319
Credit cards: All major   Meals: L, D   Closed Sun.

Every once in a while, a restaurant comes along that matches, in style and cuisine, the mood of the moment. With a clean, all-American look for the interior, the Harrison offers a modestly priced menu poised carefully between new American and fusion cooking. The walls and the ceiling are white-painted country planks. The iron chandeliers somehow invoke the wagon-wheel aesthetic. The food may speak with an accent, but it's American food.

Shell steak gets some inspired Italian tailoring, a rich, crunchy topping of crisped pancetta with bitter radicchio and balsamic vinegar. Likewise, chicken crisped in the pan refuses to be a mere chicken dish for bland diners; its lemon-mustard sauce has the immediacy of a slap in the face. The desserts look precious for a place like this. But not the quince and apple crisp, a rip-roaring mainstream pleaser.

Wine list: A very good, adventurous international list of about 180 wines, with 16 wines by the glass, 14 half bottles and a generous selection of aperitifs, beers and after-dinner drinks. **Price range:** Lunch: apps., $6–$10; entrees, $9–$18. Dinner: apps., $8–$12; entrees, $17–$28; desserts, $6–$8. **Wheelchair access:** Restrooms downstairs.

Harry's at Hanover Square $$$ CONTINENTAL
1 Hanover Sq. (bet. Stone & Pearl Sts.)   (212) 425-3412
Credit cards: All major   Meals: L, D   Closed Sat., Sun.

This restaurant and saloon, long a landmark for Wall Street workers, is fittingly housed in the landmark India House, which was built in 1851. Harry's menu, with dishes like steak Diane, fillet of sole amandine and shrimp fra diavolo, might variously be described as classic, traditional or old-fashioned. There's nothing frumpy about Harry's wine cellar, though, which is one of the best in the city and is known for having the lowest prices for expensive wines.

Price range: Apps., $7–$14; entrees, $12–$35; desserts, $4–$7. **Wheelchair access:** Not accessible.

Havana Central $25 & Under CUBAN/PAN-LATIN
22 E. 17th St. (bet. Fifth Ave. & Union Square W.)   (212) 414-4999
Credit cards: All major   Meals: L, D

Somewhere in the imagination resides a fantasy of pre-Castro Havana. Enter Havana Central. The long, narrow room is exciting and loud, with sounds echoing off the high ceiling. The lighting is as warm as a tropical sunset. The menu takes liberties. The best dishes, though, are those that stay close to the Cuban ideal. Ropa vieja, the classic stew of shredded beef, is brightly spiced with plenty of pepper and onions, while pernil, tender pieces of roasted pork, is rightfully laden with garlic. Skip the "paella bar." Without time to meld, your selections simply taste like rice with toppings. Service is friendly but can be slow. If you have the time, wait for one of the worthy desserts, like a surprisingly light tres leches cake or slender cinnamon-scented churros, wands of fried dough, delicious dipped in caramel or chocolate sauce.

Other recommended dishes: Fried yuca, fried plantains, pork ribs, jumbo shrimp, cod fillets, arroz con pollo, flan. **Price range:** Apps., $4–$8.75; entrees, $9–$22. **Wheelchair access:** All one level.

Havana NY $25 & Under CUBAN/LATIN AMERICAN
27 W. 38th St. (bet. Fifth & Sixth Aves.)   (212) 944-0990
Credit cards: All major   Meals: L, D   Closed Sat. & Sun.

This bustling Cuban restaurant is a lunchtime hot spot, serving tasty, inexpensive food in pleasant surroundings. Walk past the bar, past the elderly patrons eating their lunches and watching the television, and you will see that Havana NY opens into a trim brick-walled dining room. The food is typically robust, flavored with lusty doses of garlic and lime, dishes like the excellent grilled skirt steak, served with a pungent chimichurri sauce. Vaca frita is thin strips of sautéed beef in a tangy sauce of lime, bitter orange juice and plenty of onions. All the main courses are enormous, served with rice, beans and sweet plantains — so appetizers are usually unnecessary.

Other recommended dishes: Masitas de cerdo; fried yuca fingers; beef empanadas. **Price range:** Apps., $3–$7; entrees, $9–$13. **Wheelchair access:** Step at entrance; steps to dining room and restrooms.

Heartbeat ☆☆ $$$ NEW AMERICAN
149 E. 49th St. (at Lexington Ave.) (212) 407-2900
Credit cards: All major Meals: B, Br, L, D

New York's hippest spa food brings models to mingle with moguls in a slick setting. You could describe Heartbeat that way, but it would be doing the restaurant a disservice; this is a very comfortable, crowded and surprisingly quiet room with good service and good food. This approach works best when the food is simply left alone, like mackerel ceviche with a lemon-chervil sauce, or whole roasted quail with a mushroom-and-fig hash. Try the simple grills, the good meats and the Japanese-accented dishes. Be prepared for the tea sommelier to show up at the end of the meal. (*Ruth Reichl*)

Wine list: Interesting and fairly priced. **Price range:** Apps., $9–$14; entrees, $18–$30; desserts, $8–$10. **Wheelchair access:** Dining room is up a few steps, but there is an elevator.

Heidelberg $25 & Under GERMAN
1648 Second Ave. (near 85th St.) (212) 628-2332.
Credit cards: All major Meals: L, D

Heidelberg is swathed in history, presenting its worn and faded face without touch-ups or apologies. With waiters in lederhosen, chandeliers made of deer antlers and sturdy oil paintings dulled by decades of smoke, Heidelberg is almost a stereotype of a German beer hall. Yet it is a friendly, laid-back place, and just right for the sort of hearty rib-sticking fare that Yorkville-ites once took for granted. Main course portions are typically enormous, so the selection of appetizers is sensibly brief. They taste like afterthoughts, too. Go directly to the entrees. The sauerbraten, a tender beef roast redolent of vinegar and cloves is superb. The light and delicious spaetzle comes as a side with the excellent roulade, thin slices of vinegary beef curled around pickles, onions and bacon.

Beer, predictably, is the preferred beverage, with good German brands on tap. Desserts, though, are woeful.

Other recommended dishes: Schweinebraten (roast pork), kassler rippchen (smoked pork chops), potato pancakes, wurst. **Price range:** Apps., $3.25–$9; entrees, $9–$25. **Wheelchair access:** Step at entrance; restrooms are narrow.

Hell's Kitchen $25 & Under MEXICAN

679 Ninth Ave. (near 47th St.) (212) 977-1588
Credit cards: All major Meals: D, LN

For almost three years, Sue Torres was the chef at Rocking Horse
Cafe in Chelsea, a showcase for the possibilities of Mexican food
beyond burritos and refried beans. If you're interested in what Ms.
Torres can do when she's inspired, head directly for the interpretations of Mexican dishes. Her appetizer of tuna tostadas is brilliant.
Her quesadillas, house-made flour tortillas layered with cheese and
other fillings are like small main courses; in spirit, they succeed
because they retain their clear Mexican identity even with creative
enhancements. The best main course is a pork loin flavored with
chili and set over steamed corn and pineapple.

In atmosphere, Hell's Kitchen is international. There is a small
wine list, with some good choices. Incidentally, the loud music and
hopping bar suggest that conversations will be difficult, but the
acoustics are surprisingly good.

Other recommended dishes: Chayote and portobello roll; fried
calamari; sirloin steak; banana empanada; artichoke and mushroom quesadilla; cold peach soup; chocolate terrine; sorbets;
coconut flan. **Price range:** Apps., $6–$8; entrees, $13–$18. **Wheelchair access:** Step to entrance.

Henry's Evergreen $25 & Under CHINESE

1288 First Ave. (near 70th St.) (212) 744-3266
Credit cards: All major Meals: L, D

This bright and appealing restaurant follows the decorating scheme
of many other Chinese restaurants, but a glance beyond the tanks
of fish and the gleaming bar reveals something else: polished wood
wine racks stuffed with bottles. The biggest part of the surprising
wine list is devoted to California reds, and includes some midlevel
zinfandels and pinot noirs as well as some whites that go brilliantly
with the food. Many of the dishes are fresh and appealing. The real
excitement, though, is discovering how good the wine and food
combinations can be.

Dim sum and appetizers tend to be the best part of Henry's
menu; main courses are much less consistent. Shredded chicken in
oyster sauce with vegetables is a plain but satisfying dish, as is lean
chicken breast cooked in a clay pot.

Other recommended dishes: Cold sesame noodles, steamed Asian
flatfish, white scallops in XO sauce. **Price range:** Apps., $3.20–$11;
entrees, $8–$28. **Wheelchair access:** One step at entrance (amp
available); restrooms downstairs.

Herban Kitchen $25 & Under HEALTH FOOD

290 Hudson St. (near Spring St.) (212) 627-2257
Credit cards: All major Meals: L, D, LN

Herban is representative of a new generation of hedonistic health-
food restaurants where good organic ingredients are made even better in the kitchen. Most people would be happy to make a meal of
appetizers here, starting with the basket of country bread that

comes with a tasty mushroom-lentil spread. A main course called un-fried free-range chicken is a complete surprise: it is baked and has the crusty, savory quality of fried chicken, while remaining moist and tender. Aside from a salmon burger on a whole-wheat bun, fish dishes are less successful. Check out the list of organic wines and beers.

Other recommended dishes: Fish cakes; red pepper soup; hummus; green salad; barbecued chicken. **Alcohol:** Beer and wine. **Price range:** Apps., $5–$8; entrees, $11–$18; desserts, $7. **Wheelchair access:** Step in front. **Features:** Outdoor dining.

Holy Basil $25 & Under THAI

149 Second Ave. (bet. 9th & 10th Sts.) (212) 460-5557
Credit cards: All major Meals: D, LN

This is one of the best Thai restaurants in the city, turning out highly spiced, beautifully balanced dishes like green papaya salad, elegant curries and delicious noodles. The dining room looks more like a beautiful church than a restaurant, jazz usually plays in the background and the wine list offers terrific choices. *(See "The Basil" for second location.)*

Other recommended dishes: Yum pla muok (spicy squid salad); chicken laab; green papaya. **Price range:** Apps., $4–$8; entrees, $8–$16; desserts, $4–$8. **Wheelchair access:** Not accessible.

Honmura An ☆☆☆ $$$ JAPANESE/NOODLES

170 Mercer St. (bet. Houston & Prince Sts.) (212) 334-5253
Credit cards: All major Meals L, D Closed Mon.

The buckwheat noodles known as soba have been eaten in Japan for 400 years. The Japanese say it takes a year to learn to mix the dough, another year to learn to roll it, a third to learn the correct cut. The soba chefs at Honmura An have clearly put in their time — the soba here is wonderful and worth the high price. The spare, soothing space will certainly put you in the mood.

Many dishes are worth trying here, but nothing is remotely on a par with the noodles. To appreciate how fine they are, you must eat them cold. The noodles are earthy and elastic, and when you dip them into the briny bowl of dashi land and sea come, briefly, together. Soba also comes with various toppings: seaweed, mushrooms, even giant fried prawns. And you can get them hot in a bowl of soup with chicken, seafood or greens floating on top.

Honmura An also makes excellent udon — the fat wheat noodles. Served cold with a sesame dipping sauce, they snap when you bite into them. Served hot, in the dish called nabeyaki (a staple of cheap noodle shops), they virtually redefine the dish.

On a recent visit, Honmura An seemed secure in its position as one of the most fascinating and distinctive Japanese restaurants in the city, with tantalizing appetizers like slices of smoked duck breast with a rich border of fat; cold pressed whitefish, with the texture of a thick pasta; and giant shrimp flown in from the Tokyo fish market and turned into tempura. (*Ruth Reichl, updated by William Grimes*)

Wine list: Try the cold sake. **Price range:** Apps., $4–$28; entrees, $9–$22; desserts, $6–$8. **Wheelchair access:** Dining room is upstairs.

Hoomoos Asli $25 & Under   MIDDLE EASTERN

100 Kenmare St. (at Lafayette St.)   (212) 966-0022
Credit cards: Cash only   Meals: B, L, D, LN

There is nightly chaos at Hoomoos Asli, which diners are willing to endure, even enjoy, because of the owner's sparkling Israeli dishes and good cheer. "Please don't pronounce it humm-us," the menu says. The "hoomoos" it calls asli is a Turkish word meaning "the real thing," and it is wonderful, simply a smooth chickpea purée with a lemony tang and a deep flavor, served with fresh puffy pita bread. The menu offers much more, including a selection of extremely fresh salads. Among the other dishes, try the mallawach, a Yemenite Jewish dish of flaky flatbread pan-fried until crisp on the bottom and topped with feta cheese, black olives, olive oil and zatar, a fragrant Middle Eastern spice.

Other recommended dishes: Baba ghanoouj; tabbouleh; carrot salad; Israeli salad. **Price range:** Apps., $4–$7; entrees, $8–$17. **Wheelchair access:** Ramp at entrance.

Hope & Anchor $25 & Under   DINER/AMERICAN

347 Van Brunt St. (near Wolcott St.), Red Hook, Brooklyn
    (718) 237-0276
Credit cards: All major   Meals: B, Br, L, D   Closed Mon.

Deep in Red Hook, Brooklyn, where you can smell the salt off New York Bay, there's the Hope & Anchor. It's a neighborhood place in a neighborhood that doesn't have a lot of people, and it needs to serve a number of purposes at once. It's a standard-issue diner breakfast spot — eggs served all day — and a purveyor of lunchtime sandwiches to local artists, homesteaders and layabouts. It's also an art-world dinner spot, serving would-be Basquiats luxe tuna steaks on the cheap, and a wings-and-burgers joint for those on their way home from work or on their way out to a bar. There is also a lot on the menu, both upscale and down, which can lead to amusing combinations. Dessert is what's available in the retro-kitsch spinning glass refrigerator in the corner: chocolate pudding to take you back to grade school, for instance, or apple pie à la mode. *(Sam Sifton)*

Other recommended dishes: Cheese steak, clam cakes, balsamic-glazed calf's liver, pirogi, seared monkfish, seared tuna steak. **Price range:** Breakfast, $3–$6.50. Lunch and dinner: apps., $4–$8; entrees, $5–$12. **Wheelchair access:** Ramp available to entrance.

Icon   ☆☆ $$ NEW AMERICAN

W Court Hotel, 130 E. 39th St. (bet. Lexington & Park Aves.)
    (212) 592-8888
Credit cards: All major   Meals: B, Br, L, D

Icon is swanky, slinky, murky. Located in the W Court Hotel, it has a mildly lurid décor and a lighting philosophy perfectly designed for illegal trysts and furtive meetings. It comes with a boutique hotel attached, ensuring a steady flow of youngish, stylish diners. Once your eyes adjust to the gloom, they behold a pleasing sight. Icon has a rich, indulgent feel, with its red-velvet chairs and banquettes, its steely gray ceiling and its fat pillars. Visually, it is soothing to the nerves. Aurally, it's touch and go. As the evening progresses, a thumping rock soundtrack forces diners to shout across the table, and the whoops of gaiety from Wet Bar across the lobby become intrusive.

The food at Icon is better than the setting might suggest. Paul Sale, the executive chef, lets his ingredients do a lot of the work, and he changes the menu frequently to take advantage of seasonal produce. Desserts are not flashy; quiet good taste is more the style.

Price range: Lunch: three-course prix fixe, $20. Dinner: apps., $9–$13; entrees, $19–$27; desserts, $8; three-course prix fixe, $30. **Wheelchair access:** Alternate wheelchair entrance. **Features:** Outdoor dining (patio).

Ida Mae Kitchen-n-Lounge ☆ $$$

NEW AMERICAN/SOUTHERN

111 W. 38th St. (near Broadway) (212) 704-0038
Credit cards: All major   Meals:L, D   Closed Sun.

The cooking at Ida Mae Kitchen-n-Lounge is pan-Southern, but the chef, Kenneth W. Collins, pushes it forward, creating an urbanized, and globalized, version of the food he grew up with in Dallas. Mr. Collins, at every turn, either invents a new role for old-fashioned ingredients, or gives time-honored dishes a French or Asian spin. Most of the time, he pulls it off, although his presentations can be mannered and froufrou. Lamb chops are treated to a gumbo makeover, with slices of red-hot andouille sausage, cala rice cakes and a smothering of gumbo vegetables. Try the mushroom napoleon, a suspiciously refined appetizer of crisp wonton sheets sandwiching grilled portobello, crimini, chanterelle, oyster and shiitake mushrooms in an intense truffled port-wine syrup. If this be Southern, then they're whistling Dixie in Paris. It happens to be just about the best appetizer on the menu. The desserts are appropriately caloric and sweet. Try the pecan torte, dense enough to require knife and fork.

The adjoining lounge encroaches. The music and the martinis may be on that side of the curtain, but the real action is on the other.

Other recommended dishes: Sweet potato ravioli, skewered shrimp with chili-peach sauce, grilled pork tostaditas, chocolate tart. **Wine list:** A rudimentary list with a small selection of wines by the glass. **Price range:** Lunch entrees, $10–$24. Dinner: apps., $6–$18; entrees, $23–$27; desserts, $7–$8. Wheelchair access: Restrooms on dining level.

Il Bagatto $$

ITALIAN

192 E. 2nd St. (bet. Aves. A & B) (212) 228-0977
Credit cards: Cash only   Meals: D   Closed Mon.

Limousines and town cars aren't usually found idling outside restaurants in the East Village, but fresh ingredients, simply prepared, have made this casual trattoria incredibly popular. Bottom line: the food is good, though over-hyped, but the low prices make Il Bagatto an exceptional value if you don't mind loud music and claustrophobic seating.

Price range: Apps., $4–$8; entrees, $8–$16; desserts, $5–$6.
Wheelchair access: With assistance.

Il Covo dell'Est $$ ITALIAN
210 Ave. A (near 13th St.)   (212) 253-0777
Credit cards: All major   Meals: L, D

The menu is Tuscan, and the atmosphere is uncompromisingly Italian. Within 30 seconds of sitting down, a friendly arm is draped around your shoulder and a booming voice is reciting what seems like the longest list of specials ever assembled. They can distract and detract from the very attractive main menu, which stays regional without lapsing into cliché. The restaurant (whose name the owner translates as "the Hangout") serves Florentine gnudi — sticky balls of spinach and ricotta — with a classic butter and sage sauce. The rest of the pasta list does what Italy does best, combining dough in a thousand formats with ingredients whose freshness jumps off the plate. Try the tagliatelli topped with a robust meat sauce contributed by the chef's grandmother. Braised rabbit with olives and tomatoes stands out among the meat entrees, although it has a rival in a centuries-old dish called peposo alla fiorentina: boneless beef shank cooked very slowly with red wine, black pepper and sauted spinach.

Wine list: All Italian, several by the glass: $6–$15. **Price range:** Lunch: prix-fixe, $13. Dinner: apps $7–$9; entrees, $13–$20.
Wheelchair access: Fully accessible.

Il Gattopardo   ☆ ☆ $$$ ITALIAN
33 W. 54th St. (bet. Fifth & Sixth Aves.)   (212) 246-0412
Credit cards: All major   Meals: L, D   Closed Sun.

There is nothing the least bit fussy about Il Gattopardo (The Leopard), a tiny, almost spartan Neapolitan restaurant where an emphasis on simplicity often translates into high satisfaction. The uncomplicated elegance of its meatballs — patties of beef and veal flavored with white wine and thyme and served tightly wrapped in silky cabbage leaves — stirs the soul. The appetizer selection includes many of the menu's highlights, including braised escarole, baby artichokes with Parmesan and smoked mozzarella, and fried cakes of buffalo milk ricotta and eggplant. Pastas succeed as well. The Genovese sauce is superb, a rich ragù of pork and onions.

With the exception of a terrifically savory meatloaf and roasted lamb chops flavored with herbs, the main courses are several notches less enticing. Moscato d'Asti is the perfect dessert, although the granular ricotta cheese cake known as pastiera comes close, as does an excellent lemon tart. *(Eric Asimov)*

Other recommended dishes: Cold zucchini soup with mint, smoked veal salad, spaghetti alla chitarra, veal-and-ricotta ravioli, rack of lamb, sea scallops in garlic sauce. **Wine list:** Well chosen.
Price range: Apps., $8–$12; pastas, $15–$20; entrees, $18–$32;

desserts, $7–$8. **Wheelchair access:** Ramp to entrance available; restrooms are narrow.

Il Mulino $$$$ ITALIAN

86 W. 3rd St. (bet. Sullivan & Thompson Sts.)   (212) 673-3783
Credit cards: All major   Meals: L, D, LN   Closed Sun.

Big portions, long waits, a halcyon atmosphere. No wonder New Yorkers are so enthralled with this garlic haven. While the portions are large, so are the prices. Dinner might begin with a dish of shrimp fricassee with garlic; bresaola of beef served over mixed greens tossed in a well-seasoned vinaigrette, or aromatic baked clams oreganato. The pasta roster includes fettuccine Alfredo; spaghettini in a robust Bolognese sauce; trenette tossed in pesto sauce; and capellini all'arrabbiata, or in a spicy tomato sauce. The menu carries a dozen veal preparations, along with beef tenderloin in a shallot, white wine and sage sauce and broiled sirloin.

Price range: Apps., from $15; entrees, from $24; desserts, $12. **Wheelchair access:** One step up to dining room; difficult access to restrooms.

Ilo   ☆☆☆ $$$$ NEW AMERICAN

Bryant Park Hotel, 40 W. 40th St. (bet. Fifth & Sixth Aves.)
(212) 642-2255
Credit cards: All major   Meals: L, D

At Ilo, a Finnish word meaning something like "bliss," Chef Rick Laakkonen creates complex dishes that seem simple. He knows how to coax pure flavors from his ingredients, and how to keep those flavors clear and distinct. Major ingredients bask in the spotlight. Ilo's rabbit shows that a dish can be rustic and rarefied at the same time. Every ingredient in the dish is as humble as a wooden shoe. Chilled apricot soup is a regular on the dessert menu. It is a blazing slick of yellow, punctuated by a bright red stack of cherry sorbet disks topped with an orange tuile. Ilo's cheese cart is a serious, well-organized but not overwhelming affair with some unusual, even quirky cheeses.

Wine list: An appealing, well-thought-out international list of about 250 wines, with attention paid to up-and-coming regions and varietals. **Price range:** Lunch entrees, $19–$29. Early dinner (5:30–6:30 P.M.): two courses, $30; three courses, $39. Dinner: apps., $10–$24; entrees $26–$38; desserts, $9–$22 (for two); three-course prix fixe, $68; beef tasting menu, $85 ($120 with wines); seven-course vegetarian tasting menu, $65; seven-course chef's tasting menu, $95. **Wheelchair access:** Fully accessible by lobby elevator.

Il Postino $$$$ ITALIAN

337 E. 49th St. (bet. First & Second Aves.)   (212) 688-0033
Credit cards: All major   Meals: L, D

One of those restaurants where the list of specials is four times as big as the menu. And four times as expensive. Although it's not worth the money, the northern Italian food is good.

Price range: Entrees, $19–29; daily specials, $35–$40. **Wheelchair access:** Restrooms not accessible.

Il Posto Accanto $25 & Under   ITALIAN/SANDWICHES

190 E. 2nd St. (near Ave. B)   (212) 228-3562
Credit cards: MC/V   Meals: D, LN   Closed Mon.

This dim, intriguing Italian sandwich and wine bar, next door to its parent, the popular though charmless trattoria Il Bagatto, has the effortless appeal of a crooked grin, a rumpled sweater and a dangling cigarette. The wine list is especially inviting, where varietals from all parts of Italy can be served in carafes containing the equivalent of a half- or quarter-bottle. Sandwiches are made to order, slowly and carefully. The best include the Boncompagni, combining the brisk bite of bresaola with the richness of goat cheese, the pungency of arugula and the warmth of truffle oil. The sandwich menu is supplemented with simple but delicious dishes like spinach sautéed in olive oil with pine nuts, an ideal combination of flavor and texture.

Other recommended dishes: Medaglione (prosciutto and mozzarella). **Price range:** Sandwiches, $6–$11. **Wheelchair access:** Restrooms not accessible.

Il Valentino   ☆☆ $$ ITALIAN

Sutton Hotel, 330 E. 56th St. (near First Ave.)   (212) 355-0001
Credit cards: All major   Meals: L, D

In a city where purely pleasant restaurants have become increasingly rare, Il Valentino feels like an oasis. It is neither a small, cramped space nor one of those noisy factories. The timbered ceiling and terra-cotta floor give the room a cool rustic feeling. But the restaurant's appeal is mostly due to its admirably limited ambitions. Il Valentino wants to feed you well, but it does not seem set on becoming a big-deal multistar establishment. Il Valentino serves simple, tasty Tuscan fare. The artichoke salad is delicious, and the Caesar salad is impressive. But it is the pastas that really shine. Try the handmade garganelli, little quills tossed in a classic white veal, prosciutto and mortadella ragu. Main courses tend to be straightforward. Grilled lamb chops and osso buco are excellent. But you don't go to Il Valentino for the best meal of your life. You go because the food is reliable, you don't have to wait for your table and you know you will be able to hear your friends when they talk. (*Ruth Reichl*)

Wine list: Small and mostly fairly priced. **Price range:** Lunch: apps., $6–$8; entrees, $11–$20; desserts, $5–$7. Dinner: apps., $6–$10; entrees, $16–$25; desserts, $6–$9. **Wheelchair access:** Through hotel lobby.

industry(food)   ☆ $$$ BISTRO

509 E. 6th St. (near Ave. A)   (212) 777-5920
Credit cards: All major   Meals: D, LN

Despite the grave pretensions of its name, despite the lapses of discipline in the kitchen, industry(food) is at base an unpretentious, likable neighborhood restaurant. It has improved considerably since its opening in spring 2002. Begin with the lobster bruschetta or roasted baby octopus. The menu features some gutsy pairings, like roast chicken with tasso ham and black-eyed peas; braised veal cheeks with celery root purée; and pan-seared scallops with purée of roasted pumpkin. Desserts require you to tread carefully. The successes include a rich chocolate hazelnut torte and a blueberry Bundt cake. *(Eric Asimov)*

Wine list: Well-chosen global list. **Price range:** Apps., $6–$15; entrees, $17–$24; desserts, $6–$8. **Wheelchair access:** All one level.

'ino $25 & Under   ITALIAN/SANDWICHES
21 Bedford St. (bet. Sixth Ave. & Downing St.)   (212) 989-5769
Credit cards: Cash only   Meals: B, Br, L, D, LN

Armed with only an Italian sandwich press and a small hot plate, this inviting little Italian sandwich shop and wine bar offers intensely satisfying variations on the sandwich theme. The menu is divided into three parts: panini, sandwiches made with crusty toasted ciabatta; tramezzini, made with untoasted white bread, crusts removed and cut into triangles; and bruschetta, in which ingredients are simply placed atop a slice of toasted bread. One dish that doesn't fall into any category but is nonetheless wonderful is truffled egg toast, a soft cooked egg served on top of toasted ciabatta with sliced asparagus and drizzled with truffle oil. It's like warm, delicious baby food.

Alcohol: Beer and wine. **Price range:** Everything is $2–$10. **Wheelchair access:** Fully accessible.

Inside $25 & Under   NEW AMERICAN
9 Jones St. (bet. 4th & Bleecker Sts.)   (212) 229-9999
Credit cards: All major   Meals: Br, D

Inside has the simplified approach of a place ready for leaner economic times. The handsome wood bar in front and the professional greeting bespeak the comfort of a more expensive restaurant, yet the almost bare white walls make the dining room feel airy and streamlined. The menu, which changes weekly, is confined to a single sheet of yellow paper. With dishes based on no more than three seasonal and simple ingredients, Inside can keep prices gentle. The best appetizer is a handful of shrimp with a light, crisp salt-and-pepper crust, topped with a tangy grapefruit confit. Main courses are similarly streamlined. Newport steak is thick and beefy. Tender braised lamb with cinnamon and olives achieves an almost Moroccan balance of savory and sweet.

The wine list is well selected, though more choices in the $25 range would be appreciated. Desserts are similarly up and down. Try the panna cotta.

Price range: Apps., $6–$9; entrees, $13–$18. **Wheelchair access:** Restroom entrances are narrow.

Ipanema $25 & Under   BRAZILIAN

13 W. 46th St. (bet. Fifth & Sixth Aves.)   (212) 730-5848
Credit cards: All major   Meals: L, D

This relaxed, gracious Brazilian restaurant offers big portions of
solid fare like shrimp in garlic-and-wine sauce, and vatapa, a silky
purée of fish, shrimp and nuts. Feijoada, the national dish of Brazil,
is both an impressive presentation and an unmanageable portion:
an iron platter full of a rich black bean stew and various types of
smoked pork and sausage, a bowl of rice, a dish of orange slices, a
plate of crunchy cassava blended with egg and a portion of collard
greens. Desserts are as robust as the rest of the fare, not exactly a
light close. The décor has a certain Midtown stiffness, but the
owner and host makes Ipanema a lighthearted pleasure.

Other recommended dishes: Linguica frita, hearts of palm salad,
broiled halibut, churrasco misto. **Price range:** Apps., $2–$9; salads,
$6–$8; entrees, $15–$20; desserts, $4. **Wheelchair access:** All one
level.

Irving on Irving $25 & Under   AMERICAN

52 Irving Pl. (at 17th St.)   (212) 358-1300
Credit cards: All major   Meals: B, L, D

By day, Irving offers counter service for breakfast and lunch, mostly
pastries, soups, salads and sandwiches. By night, waiters and waitresses come out, and it becomes a real restaurant. When crowded,
the small room becomes loud and clattery.

    The chef has put together a menu of uncomplicated ingredients,
prepared simply. Appetizers show off their humble origins, like
what the menu calls "poor man's crab cakes." These are actually
excellent codfish cakes. While the main courses are not exactly
made of humble ingredients, they are resolutely plain, with the possible exception of the peppery grilled swordfish. Irving has a decent
though small list of wines by the glass and beers. The best dessert
is the cinnamon doughnuts, more like small beignets, actually,
made to order and served hot and airy in a brown lunch bag.

Other recommended dishes: Mini-burgers, sausages, roast chicken.
Price range: Apps., $5–$13; entrees, $11–$17. **Wheelchair access:**
Restroom entrance is narrow.

Isla $$$ CUBAN/PAN-LATIN

39 Downing St. (bet Bedford & Varick Sts.)   (212) 352-2822
Credit Cards: All major   Meals: D   Closed Sun.

The place looks like a cabana, with a sleek, blue-tiled facade and a
long, louvered window facing the street. Inside, the décor blends
beach, 50's kitsch and Miami modern in one highly inviting package. The place is cool. The chef is Mexican by heritage but he has
created a Cuban fantasy, a freely improvised list of nuevo latino
dishes like smoked chicken croquettes with chorizo and a saffron
sofrito sauce and strip steak with Madeira sauce and fried yuca.
The desserts are tropical and sweet. The killer is natilla con basitos:
layers of butterscotch custard and gingerbread topped with
meringue kisses.

Wine list: Focuses on Spain and South America. Several wines by the glass for $12. **Price range:** Apps. $14–$16; entrees, $18–$26. **Wheelchair access:** Fully accessible.

Island Burgers & Shakes $25 & Under

766 Ninth Ave. (bet. 51st & 52nd Sts.)   (212) 307-7934
Credit cards: Cash only   Meals: L, D

While no more than a little aisle, stylish Island, decorated in summer pastels, turns out a huge menu of burgers (44 variations) and chicken sandwiches along with terrific sides like house-made potato chips. The burgers aren't bad, but the grilled chicken sandwiches are exceptional.

Price range: Apps., $4–$5; entrees, $5–$9. **Wheelchair access:** Fully accessible.

Island Grill $25 & Under   CARIBBEAN

2 Lafayette St. (at Centre St.)   (212) 227-9566
Credit cards: All major   Meals: L

This small Jamaican restaurant in TriBeCa offers an extensive menu of curries, rotis and jerk dishes. Try the delicious ackee and saltfish, a typical Jamaican blend of salt cod and ackee, a reddish orange fruit that is sautéed and resembles scrambled eggs. If you like spicy food, make sure to let them know. The dining room is colorful and pleasant, but the music is pounding.

Price range: Apps., $1–$4; entrees, $6–$8; desserts, $3. **Wheelchair access:** Fully accessible.

Isola $25 & Under   ITALIAN

485 Columbus Ave. (bet. 83rd & 84th Sts.)   (212) 362-7400
Credit cards: All major   Meals: Br, L, D

When Isola is crowded, its dining room, full of hard surfaces, can be unbearably loud, but the restaurant offers some of the best Italian food on the Upper West Side, with lively pastas like spaghetti in a purée of black olives and oregano, and fettuccine with crumbled sausages and porcini mushrooms. The wine list is nicely chosen.

Price range: Apps., $5–$8; entrees, $10–$18; desserts, $5. **Wheelchair access:** Fully accessible. **Features:** Outdoor dining.

I Trulli   ☆☆ $$$ ITALIAN

122 E. 27th St. (bet. Lexington Ave. & Park Ave. S.)   (212) 481-7372
Credit cards: All major   Meals: L, D   Closed Sun.

This is New York City's best and most attractive restaurant dedicated to the cooking of Apulia. It serves interesting, unusual food in an understated room, dominated by a glass-enclosed fireplace, that is both elegant and warm; there is also a beautiful garden for outdoor dining. The rustic food from Italy's heel does not have the subtle charm of northern Italian food or the tomato-and-garlic heartiness of Neapolitan cuisine. The menu relies on bitter greens (arugula, dandelions, broccoli rabe) and many foods that Americans rarely eat. The pastas have a basic earthy quality. Orechiette are made by the owner.

A recent visit showed that I Trulli remains a good bet, with well-executed Italian dishes, good service and pleasant surroundings. The menu, rustic but shrewd, avoids the obvious, with appetizers like stuffed squid with zucchini, black olives and mint, pastas like Sardinian dumplings with ground sausage and saffron, and entrees like lamb chops in herb sauce with fava bean puree and dandelions. (*Ruth Reichl, updated by William Grimes*)

Wine list: Wonderful and well-priced list with unusual wines. **Price range:** Apps., $9–$14; entrees, $18–$32; desserts, $9. **Wheelchair access:** All one level. **Features:** Outdoor dining (garden).

Jack Rose ☆ $$$ NEW AMERICAN/STEAKHOUSE
771 Eighth Ave. (at 47th St.)   (212) 247-7518.
Credit cards: All major   Meals: L, D

Jack Rose is an artful exercise in nostalgia. The smooth, dark wood floors and brown leather booths feel like the 1930's. The huge horizontal stone fireplace, the polished driftwood accents and the rec room paneling evoke postwar suburbia with a touch of lounge. It's a classic, four-square, no-punches-pulled all-American joint that specializes in seafood, steaks, chops and no funny stuff.

Scallops wrapped in bacon deliver a gutsy American flavor. Clams casino, one of the great Edsels of American cuisine, puts on a brave front. Although Jack Rose reserves a lot of room on the menu for steaks, Peter Luger has nothing to fear. The beef covers the plate, but it makes a pretty feeble impression on the palate. The kitchen can still win you over with the oysters Rockefeller or a plump, moist chicken. Aside from the bread pudding and a more than respectable crème brûlée, the desserts never quite hit the spot. Jack Rose seems about halfway there. When you hit, you hit big. When you don't — nothing.

Wine list: A reasonable if uninspiring list of about 110 mostly American and French wines, with 17 half bottles and a dozen wines by the glass. **Price range:** Lunch entrees, $11–$29. Dinner: apps., $6–$12; entrees, $16–$30; desserts $6. **Wheelchair access:** Restrooms are on street level.

Jackson Diner $ INDIAN
37-47 74th St. (bet. 37th & Roosevelt Aves.)   (718) 672-1232
Credit cards: Cash only   Meals: L, D

Good Indian food at microscopic prices has resulted in a considerable reputation for this plain restaurant in Jackson Heights. The food's not even close to being the best in the city, but the value is terrific, particularly with South Indian vegetarian dishes like rasa vada, lentil doughnuts served in a spicy broth, and masala dosai, huge, spicy crepes stuffed with potato and onions.

Alcohol: Bring your own. **Price range:** Lunch buffet: weekdays, $6; weekends, $8. Apps., $3–$7; entrees, $8–$19; desserts, $3. **Wheelchair access:** Restrooms not accessible.

Jane ☆ $$ NEW AMERICAN/BISTRO
100 W. Houston St. (at Thompson St.)   (212) 254-7000
Credit cards: All major   Meals: L, D

Jane is a restaurant with the soul of a cafe. There's an air of cool, loungy relaxation inside, the wood floors and the studiedly neutral décor massage the nerves, and the menu couldn't be more friendly. Jane sets itself modest goals. For the most part it delivers, at a fair price. The appetizer portions are so large that some diners may have second thoughts about their entrees. The tuna and salmon tartar is delicious. Shrimp and tomato flatbread, plain as it might sound, makes a big impression. Entrees do not live up to the appetizers. An exception is the dark, richly gamy hanger steak, swimming in a red wine sauce and onion marmalade. Jane knows what to do when dessert time rolls around. The bias is toward American flavors, but with a little twist here and there. Minted strawberries with Champagne cream sounds like food for the gods, and in this case, reality does not disappoint.

Wine list: A sturdy if unexciting international list of about 35 wines, most under $40, with a dozen wines by the glass. **Price range:** Lunch: apps., $5–$8; entrees, $8–$19. Dinner: apps., $8–$14; entrees, $17–$21; desserts, $7–$8. **Wheelchair access:** Restrooms downstairs.

Japonica $$$ JAPANESE/SUSHI
100 University Pl. (at 12th St.)   (212) 243-7752
Credit cards: AE   Meals: L, D

In the N.Y.U. neighborhood, this sparkling Japanese restaurant is as popular as spring break. And little wonder, for the food is pristine, beautifully presented and delectable. Japonica is larger than it appears at first glance, with a wraparound dining room done in natural wood, colorful Japanese lanterns overhead and a handsome sushi bar. Most items are appealing, including a deluxe sushi assortment, yakitori and beef dumplings.

Price range: Apps., $7–$18; entrees, $11–$30; desserts, $5–$6. **Wheelchair access:** Restrooms not accessible.

Jarnac ☆ $$$ FRENCH
328 W. 12th St. (near Greenwich St.)   (212) 924-3413
Credit cards: All major   Meals: Br, D
Closed Mon. (Sun., brunch only)

Jarnac is in many ways a dream bistro. A small and attractive restaurant, it sits on a tranquil corner of the far West Village, with windows that open out and offer prime viewing of chic couples striding briskly toward the restaurants and clubs of the meatpacking district. The menu is short, sweet and French. The wine list has personality. The owner drops by each table a couple of times during the evening to make sure the happiness level doesn't sag.

At its best, Jarnac offers nicely executed food with an original twist. The Jarnac BLT, for example, is a chewy, sloppy, delicious interpretation of the classic American sandwich, with pancetta instead of bacon, arugula instead of lettuce, and a big sourdough crouton to support it all. One of the best dishes was roasted poussin with butter walnut sauce that looks grim. Don't look, eat. The big, highly disorganized strawberry and blueberry shortcake is excellent. A very decorous round chocolate cake with espresso ice cream restores a little balance.

Wine list: A nicely chosen international list of about 100 wines, with nine wines by the glass and quarter-liter. **Price range:** Apps., $8–$10; entrees, $20–$24; desserts, $8. **Wheelchair access:** Step to dining room; restrooms downstairs.

Jean Claude $25 & Under   BISTRO/FRENCH
137 Sullivan St. (bet. Prince & Houston Sts.)   (212) 475-9232
Credit cards: Cash only   Meals: D

The bustling dining room is authentically Parisian, with the sound of French in the air. For these low prices you don't expect to find appetizers like seared sea scallops with roasted beets or main courses like roasted monkfish with savoy cabbage, olives and onions.

Other recommended dishes: Sautéed duck breast with turnips, white beans, and citrus compote. **Alcohol:** Beer and wine. **Price range:** Apps., $6–$8; entrees, $12–$16; desserts, $6. **Wheelchair access:** Fully accessible. **Features:** Outdoor dining.

Jean Georges ☆☆☆☆ $$$$ NEW AMERICAN
Trump Hotel, 1 Central Park W. (at 60th St.)   (212) 299-3900
Credit cards: All major   Meals: B, L, D

On the surface, Jean Georges looks like just another expensive restaurant. But take a deeper look: in a quiet way, chef and co-owner, Jean-Georges Vongerichten, has created an entirely new kind of four-star restaurant. He has examined all the details that make dining luxurious, and refined them for an American audience. The changes are so subtle that they are easy to miss, but nothing, from the neutral look of the dining room to the composition of the staff to the pacing of the meal, follows a classic model.

Most important, he has returned the focus to the food. Mr. Vongerichten introduced simplicity to four-star cooking years ago and here the food is essentially simple, although there are signs, recently, that his daring experiments in French Asian fusion may be becoming a bit mannered.

The austerity of the design of the restaurant also puts the focus on food. The dining room is comfortable and expensive but so low-key it is easy to ignore. While some restaurants are more concerned with who is in the room than what is on the plate, the people at Jean Georges neither fawn nor intimidate. All over the dining room, waiters bend over the food, carving or pouring, intent only on their guests' pleasure. Ask for wine advice and the excellent sommelier uncondescendingly recommends reasonably priced bottles. (*Ruth Reichl, updated by William Grimes*).

Wine list: Excellent, with many unusual wines, many affordable wines and a knowledgeable staff. **Price range:** Lunch: two courses,

$24. Dinner: three courses, $87; seven-course tasting menu, $118. Nougatine dining room: three-course prix-fixe lunch, $20; five-course prix-fixe dinner, $65. Formal dining room closed Sun. **Wheelchair access:** Separate entrance.

Jean-Luc ☆ $$ BISTRO/FRENCH
507 Columbus Ave. (near 84th St.) (212) 712-1700
Credit cards: All major Meals: D Closed Mon.

New York has lots of technically correct bistros, but they often lack a certain something — something that Jean-Luc indisputably has. Something that emanates from Edmond Kleefield, better known as Jean-Luc. It's called personality. Nightly, Mr. Kleefield meets and greets, circulates from table to table, and holds forth on any topic that comes into his head. The noise level can be deafening.

The menu includes some strange, not very successful dishes, as well as completely enthralling inventions. One bit of advertising on the menu is nothing less than the truth. The "mouthwatering" tournedos of beef really does deserve special billing. Pan-seared magret of duck carries a recommendation, as does the poussin with candied root vegetables. The desserts, by and large, make a dim impression. The excellent apple-almond tart with a scoop of pure vanilla ice cream on top stands out.

Wine list: A modest but very respectable list of about 60 wines, mostly French. **Price range:** Apps., $6–$17; entrees, $17–$25; desserts, $7–$9. **Wheelchair access:** Ramp to restroom.

Jefferson ☆☆ $$$ NEW AMERICAN/ASIAN
121 W. 10th St. (near Greenwich Ave.) (212) 255-3333
Credit cards: All major Meals: D Closed Sun.

Nowhere has fusion cuisine put down stronger roots than at Jefferson. The cuisine, served in a spacious dining room, is billed as New American. This America thrives on immigrant energies. In culinary terms, that means ravioli made from edamame, with ginkgo nuts and mascarpone cheese, or scallops crusted in rice shavings and dressed with a white miso tangerine sauce. The menu includes a gentle spin on fairly traditional dishes. The lamb chops with a spicy crust and mint sauce and the Asian surf-and-turf appetizer of tuna tartar and slices of seared duck breast are excellent. But the chef comes into his own with go-for-broke dishes like snapper with caramelized persimmon, baby leeks and enoki mushrooms. One vegetarian dish deserves praise, a robust plate of sautéed shimeji mushrooms with butternut squash, shisito peppers and truffle-accented gnocchi. On the dessert menu, banana pudding with bittersweet chocolate rum sauce is pure bliss. At a time when restaurants all over town are simplifying and, in many cases, dumbing down, Jefferson has smartened up.

Wine list: A tidy, sensible choice of 30 international wines. **Price range:** Apps., $9–$19; entrees, $20–$28; desserts, $7–$9. **Wheelchair access:** All one level.

Jewel Bako $25 & Under   SUSHI

239 E. 5th St. (bet. Second & Third Aves.)   (212) 979-1012
Credit cards: All major   Meals: D   Closed Sun.

The first taste at Jewel Bako will leave no doubt that there is great sushi here. The absolute freshness of the fish, the unusual variety of selections and the beauty of the chef's creations combine to form a sublimely sensual experience. With six seats at the sushi bar in the rear, the restaurant holds about 30 people. Jewel Bako, Japanese slang for jewel box, is aptly named. The clean lines of the small dining room, under an arched bamboo ceiling, echo the purity of the sushi. Order à la carte, allowing the chef to guide you. Don't say no if he suggests the top-of-the-line toro, as creamy and tender as melted butter. There is a refreshing dessert of stewed mission figs, served cool in a sweetened white wine and shiso broth.

Price range: Sushi and sashimi selections, $12–$29; $3–$5 a piece; some specials higher. **Wheelchair access:** All one level.

Jimmy's Downtown $$$ PAN-LATIN

400 E. 57th St. (at First Ave.)   (212) 486-6400
Credit cards: All major   Meals: D

Aside from the young women wearing little black dresses or less, the first thing you notice at Jimmy's Downtown is a long, long bar on one side of a narrow, low-slung room, and an equally long leather banquette with boxy tables on the other.

In the dining room, the crowd is one of the most ethnically diverse you'll see in any New York restaurant, with elderly residents from the neighborhood dining side by side with a table of Harlem politicians and across the way from an after-work office party. With a low ceiling and plenty of hard surfaces, the noise level makes it almost impossible for ordinary conversation. The menu, which speaks the modern pan-Latin vernacular with a slight Southern accent, is enticing. But the food, which promises bold flavors, barely whispers. Chicharons de pollo, crisp little nuggets of fried chicken on the bone, are fair enough, though at $10 for an appetizer portion, twice the price of what you could expect to pay at any decent Cuban luncheonette. (*Eric Asimov*)

Price range: Apps., $8–$14; entrees, $19–$28.

Jing Fong $ CHINESE

20 Elizabeth St. (bet. Bayard & Canal Sts.)   (212) 964-5256
Credit cards: All major   Meals: L, D

Chinatown's biggest restaurant serves awesome dim sum during the day. At night the cavernous dining room serves good Cantonese fare, but if you order ahead you can get a pretty terrific spread served in a private room. Ask for the banquet manager.

Price range: Apps., $4–$6; entrees, $9–$18; desserts, $1.90. **Wheelchair access:** Fully accessible.

Joe Allen $$ NEW AMERICAN

326 W. 46th St. (bet. Eighth & Ninth Aves.) (212) 581-6464
Credit cards: All major
Meals: Br, L, D

Chili and celebrities in the heart of Broadway. The food's not great,
but it's not expensive either. If you're looking for safe, unpretentious American food in the high-rent Restaurant Row, this is the
place.

Price range: Apps., $4–$8; entrees, $9–$20; desserts, $6. **Wheel-
chair access:** Fully accessible.

Joe's Shanghai ☆☆ $ CHINESE

24 W. 56th St. (bet. Fifth & Sixth Aves.) (212) 333-3868
9 Pell St. (bet. Bowery & Catherine St.) (212) 233-8888
136-21 37th Ave., Flushing, Queens (718) 539-3838
82-74 Broadway, Elmhurst, Queens (718) 639-6888
Credit cards: All major
Meals: L, D

In addition to hip, handsome, friendly waiters (even, shocking for
Chinatown, some women) and an exciting menu of Shanghai specialties, these spartan restaurants, serve awesome dumplings filled
with soup. The xiao lung bao are modestly listed on the menu as
"steamed buns," but they are Shanghai soup dumplings. The chef
has perfected the art of wrapping hot liquid in pastry: the filling is
rich, light and swimming in hot soup. Everybody orders steamed
dumplings, but there are many other wonderful dishes, including
smoked fish, strongly flavored with star anise, vegetarian duck,
sheets of braised tofu folded like skin over mushrooms, and
drunken crabs, raw marinated blue crabs with a musty, fruity flavor
that is powerful and unforgettable. Also try the turnip cakes, the
chewy Shanghai noodles, fried bean curd with spinach and crispy
yellow fish fingers with dry seaweed. (*Ruth Reichl*)

Alcohol: Beer; full bar in Midtown. **Price range:** Entrees, $10 and
up. **Wheelchair access:** Everything on one floor.

John's Pizzeria $25 & Under ITALIAN/PIZZA

408 E. 64th St. (bet. First & York Aves.) (212) 935-2895
278 Bleecker St. (near Seventh Ave. S.) (212) 243-1680
48 W. 65th St. (near Central Park W.) (212) 721-7001
260 W. 44th St. (bet. Seventh & Eighth Aves.) (212) 391-7560
Credit cards: All major (64th & 65th, AE only)
Meals: L, D

John's earns its reputation for great pizza every day. What sets
John's apart is the expert economy of its pizza: no waste or excess,
a thin and faintly smoky crust, just crisp enough to offer a delicate
crunch, while the other ingredients are fine: creamy mozzarella,
slightly spicy tomato sauce, crumbled fennel sausage from Faicco
Pork Store in the Village. Of the four John's locations, the best are
the original, a brusque, battered, sprawling place on Bleecker
Street, and the Times Square outlet, a huge pizzeria in a beautiful
old church.

Alcohol: Beer and wine. **Price range:** Pizzas, $6–$11. **Wheelchair
access:** Fully accessible. **Features:** Outdoor dining.

Jo Jo ☆☆☆ $$$ NEW AMERICAN

160 E. 64th St. (bet. Lexington & Third Aves.)   (212) 223-5656
Credit cards: All major   Meals: L, D

After an extensive renovation, Jo Jo has shown, with extraordinary grace, how a restaurant can age without looking old. The place looks sumptuous now. At the same time, it still has the heart of a bistro. The style of service is not overformal. The menu is a fairly short read, and the wine list, with perhaps 65 selections, makes a serious effort to please the $50 customer.

Owner Jean-Georges Vongerichten has wisely retained a few signature dishes. The menu continues to offer an appetizer of shrimp dusted in orange powder, and the renowned roast chicken with chickpea fries is still an entree. The food at Jo Jo never clamors for attention. A pristine pea soup sets itself a single goal, to express pea flavor with maximum clarity and presence, which it does. In a bold but entirely successful move, Mr. Vongerichten conjures up a light, bright and fruity sauce for black sea bass, with sweet shreds of carrot "confit" suspended in orange juice and olive oil accented with cumin.

For dessert, a dainty lemon meringue tart comes with a scoop of tingling lemon-verbena ice cream, its flavor as clear as crystal. This little shock of pure citrus is shorthand for the new Jo Jo. It's older now, but still new in all the ways that count.

Wine list: A carefully chosen international list of about 65 bottles, nearly half under $50, with eight wines by the glass. **Price range:** Lunch: apps., $9–$13; entrees, $18–$32; desserts, $8–$10; three-course prix fixe, $20. Dinner: apps., $9–$19; entrees, $18–$36; desserts, $8–$10; four-course vegetarian menu, $48; four-course tasting menu, $70. **Wheelchair access:** Steps to dining room.

Josie's $25 & Under NEW AMERICAN

300 Amsterdam Ave. (at 74th St.)   (212) 769-1212
565 Third Ave. (at 37th St.)   (212) 490-1558
Credit cards: All major   Meals: L, D, LN

Much of the food at Josie's is billed as organically raised. Many dishes are dairy-free, napkins are unbleached brown paper, and according to the menu, "water used for drinking, cooking and ice is Multi-Pure filtered." The surprise is that so much of the food is so good, with highlights like potato dumplings in a lively tomato coulis spiked with chipotle pepper, ravioli stuffed with sweet potato purée, superb grilled tuna with a wasabi glaze and wonderful gazpacho. Josie's offers about two dozen reasonably priced wines, some organic beers and freshly squeezed juices, including tart blueberry lemonade. Even the organic hot dogs are good.

Price range: Apps., $5–$8; entrees, $10–$16; desserts, $6. **Wheelchair access:** Restrooms not accessible.

Jubilee $$$ FRENCH

347 E. 54th St. (bet. First & Second Aves.)   (212) 888-3569
Credit cards: All major   Meals: L, D

Small, crowded and exuberant, this is a great Sutton Place find. It offers simple and good bistro food, like steak frites and roast chicken. The restaurant makes something of a specialty of mussels, offering them in five guises with terrific french fries or a green salad, all for reasonable prices.

Price range: Apps., $6–$14; entrees, $13–$24; desserts, $6–$9.
Wheelchair access: Not accessible.

Judson Grill ☆ ☆ ☆ $$$ NEW AMERICAN
152 W. 52nd St. (bet Sixth & Seventh Aves.) (212) 582-5252
Credit cards: All major   Meals: L,D   Closed Sun.

Now open for almost a decade, Judson Grill has taken its place in the background of midtown Manhattan, always present but as taken for granted as the constant whisper of city traffic. It's hard to imagine how a restaurant as good as Judson Grill can slip the mind so easily. Partly it's because Judson Grill is so civilized, so adult, that it would never stoop to call attention to itself. The accomplished chef, Bill Telepan, cooks in a similar vein, emphasizing pure ingredients and graceful combinations without resorting to pyrotechnics or demanding the spotlight. His menu is effortlessly seasonal and naturally harmonious, with clear, unobstructed flavors and garnishes that make each bite an unexpected pleasure. The big, bright dining room is inviting and casual in the American fashion, and the bar is a prime after-work gathering spot. *(Review by Eric Asimov; stars previously awarded by Ruth Reichl.)*

Wine list: Interesting, intelligently chosen; affordable special values and big deal wines bought at auction. **Price range:** Lunch: apps., $9–$13; entrees, $21–$29; desserts, $7–$10. Dinner: apps., $9–$16; entrees, $22–$35; desserts, $7–$10. Five-course seasonal tasting menu, $65; with wines, $85. **Wheelchair access:** Fully accessible.

Junno's $25 & Under   JAPANESE/KOREAN
64 Downing St. (bet. Bedford & Varick Sts.)   (212) 627-7995
Credit cards: All major   Meals: D   Closed Sun.

The food at this friendly Japanese-Korean fusion restaurant is not great, but it can be good if you order wisely. Appetizers are especially good, like tataki of tuna with ponzu sauce, thin-cut rectangles of tuna that are seared around the edges and rare in the middle. The best main courses are the most robust, like a delectable Korean dish, grilled short ribs, sweetened by a soy marinade and served off the bone with a nice little salad.

Other recommended dishes: Ravioli of sweet shrimp, grilled squid, sliced braised pork, udon noodle soup with braised beef, roast ginger chicken, warm chocolate cake, pear sorbet. **Price range:** Apps., $4–$6; entrees, $8–$14. **Wheelchair access:** All one level.

Kabab King Diner $25 & Under   PAKISTANI
73-01 37th Rd., Jackson Heights, Queens   (718) 457-5857
Credit cards: Cash only   Meals: 24 hours

Perhaps it's fitting that a place celebrating the humble kebab is itself as humble and unprepossessing as Kabab King Diner. A bright and cluttered Pakistani restaurant, it looks like a cabby haunt, with

141

a big steam table and communal tables set with pitchers of water, where diners eat with plastic utensils from plastic foam plates.

But behind the steam table, where assorted curries and stews sit warming, dozens of skewers hang from a rack, waiting to be inserted into one of the tandoor ovens. And from these ovens emerge kebabs as moist and succulent as you can imagine, layered in a thick yogurt marinade, well-herbed and intensely spiced. These kebabs do not fade into the dry background babble. They shock you into taking notice.

Other recommended dishes: Chicken and beef tikka, chicken and beef seekh kebabs, lamb chops, haleem. **Price range:** $7 is the upper limit. **Wheelchair access:** Not accessible.

Kabul Cafe $ AFGHAN

265 W. 54th St. (bet. Eighth Ave. & Broadway) (212) 757-2037
Credit cards: All major   Meals: L, D

This is one of several small, dim Afghan cafes that offer good value in the Midtown area. Like the others, Kabul Cafe serves huge lamb and chicken kebabs with lots of rice, and good salads and other meatless entrees.

Alcohol: Beer and wine. **Price range:** Lunch entrees, $5–$12. Dinner: apps., $4–$5; entrees, $9–$14, desserts, $3–$4. **Wheelchair access:** Not accessible.

Kai ☆☆ $$$$ JAPANESE

822 Madison Ave. (at 69th St.)   (212) 988-7277
Credit cards: All major   Meals: L, D   Closed Sun.

Kai is short for kaiseki, the traditional meal of refined little bites that grew up around the tea ceremony. The commitment to style and presentation at Kai is total. When a server explains that aged cubes of beef fillet have been sizzling on volcanic stone from Mount Fuji, it comes as no surprise. The simplest of the three prix fixe formulas begins with a cup of jasmine tea. It clears the stage for a small plate of tiny bites (*deai*) that might include rich slices of duck or sliced bamboo shoots with mayonnaiselike tama miso dressing. Soup follows, either an unctuous, luxurious version made from lily bulbs and milk, or an ethereal clear one with a strongly flavored cube of pressed mushroom, clam and cod. A small plate of sashimi follows.

The chef has grafted French ideas onto kaiseki cuisine, and he has done so with an elegant hand. Yogan yaki, small, dice-size cubes of aged prime beef, bears a resemblance to filet mignon with béarnaise sauce. A steakhouse empire could be built solely on this dish. Chilled soba noodles, made at the restaurant, always round out the meal, followed by Western-style but Japanese-accented desserts and green tea.

Wine list: Nine wines, six by the glass, supplemented by seven sakes. **Price range:** Lunch, $12–$22. Dinner, prix fixe menus for $55, $70, $85. An omakase or tasting menu can be arranged with a minimum of one day's notice (price varies). **Wheelchair access:** Elevator at rear.

Kaña $25 & Under SPANISH

324 Spring St. (near Greenwich St.)   (212) 343-8180
Credit cards: All major   Meals: L, D, LN

Tapas are satisfying and traditional at this friendly, lively bar.
Boquerones, anchovies pickled in a sweet-and-sour marinade, are
delicious; another good choice is tuna escabeche, tender, tasty
cubes of fresh tuna marinated in citrus with fennel and served cool.
Hot tapas don't stray from the traditional, but they are lively and
often prepared to order.

Other recommended dishes: Shrimp in green garlic sauce, sardines, chorizo, octopus in red wine. **Price range:** Entrees, $14–$16.
Alcohol: Beer and wine. **Wheelchair access:** All one level. **Features:** Outdoor dining.

Kapadokya $25 & Under TURKISH

142 Montague St. (near Henry St.), Brooklyn Heights (718) 875-2211
Credit cards: All major   Meals: L, D

From the flowers strewn on the stairway leading to the dining room
to the belly dancers, Kapadokya tries hard to make everybody feel
welcome. Waiters wear traditional Turkish costumes, and the dining
room is bedecked with colorful Turkish lanterns.

To anyone experienced with the grilled meats, savory stews and
pungent dips that are Turkish touchstones, Kapadokya does the
familiar well. Cold dips are the essential starters, like patlican
salatasi, a terrifically smoky eggplant salad, and acili ezme,
chopped walnuts, peppers and onions mixed with tomato sauce.
The bread, though, could be better. The hot appetizers do not
encourage further exploration. Entrees, by contrast, were cooked
with care. Lamb kebabs and kofte kebabs are moist and appealing.
Iskender, thin slices of doner kebab served over pieces of toasted
pita is a winning combination. The biggest surprise was salmon
dolma, grape leaves stuffed with cubes of salmon and then grilled.
The leaves protect the fish, keeping each piece juicy and flavorful.

Price range: Apps., $3–$8; entrees, $11.50–$20; desserts, $5.
Wheelchair access: Restaurant is a second-floor walkup.

Katsu-Hama $25 & Under JAPANESE

11 E. 47th St. (bet. Madison & Fifth Aves.)   (212) 758-5909
Credit cards: All major   Meals: L, D

Katsu-Hama doesn't offer much in the way of atmosphere or creature comforts, but it is an authentic Japanese experience. To enter
it, you need to walk through a takeout sushi restaurant (Sushi-Tei)
and pass through a curtain divider; there, you encounter an
almost entirely Japanese crowd who've come for the restaurant's
specialty: tonkatsu, or deep-fried pork cutlets. The cutlet comes
bathed in a rich, robust curry sauce, for example, or it is served
over rice with scallions and egg sauce, a cozy, oozy, Japanese
comfort food. But the best treatment is unadorned, dipped into a
special condiment that resembles freshly made Worcestershire
sauce blended with sesame seeds.

Alcohol: Beer, wine and sake. **Price range:** Platters, $9–$14.
Wheelchair access: Path to restrooms is narrow.

Katz's Deli $ DELI

205 E. Houston St. (at Ludlow St.)   (212) 254-2246
Credit cards: All major   Meals: B, Br, L, D, LN

A wonderful Lower East Side artifact and originator of the World
War II slogan, "Send a salami to your boy in the Army." It is one of
the very few New York City delis that still carves pastrami and
corned beef by hand, which makes for delicious sandwiches.

Alcohol: Beer and wine. **Price range:** Apps., $2–$5; entrees,
$5–$11; desserts, $3. **Wheelchair access:** Fully accessible.

Kazan Turkish Cuisine $25 & Under   TURKISH

95-36 Queens Blvd., Rego Park, Queens   (718) 897-1509
Credit cards: All major   Meals: L, D

Kazan is a spare, open dining room adorned with a hookah and an
old Turkish coffee urn. There is also a stone oven that produces
exceptional pide, soft football-shape loaves of bread dotted with
sesame seeds, which are just right with any of the superb cold
appetizers. Eggplant is excellent, either charcoal grilled and puréed
with garlic or left chunky and served with tomato and garlic. Don't
ignore the tangy hummus, either, or fragrant, minty grape leaves
stuffed with rice and pine nuts. Kazan's short selection of main
courses also includes some real winners like shish yogurtlu, juicy
chunks of tender grilled lamb served over a sauce of yogurt blended
with tomatoes. Kasarli kofte is another standout, made with
chopped lamb blended with mild kasseri cheese, which gives the
meat an unusual airiness. Desserts are extremely sweet.

Other recommended dishes: Yogurt with cucumber or with walnuts, white bean salad, minced vegetables, tarama. **Price range:**
Apps., $4–$5; entrees, $9–$14. **Wheelchair access:** All one level.

K.B. Garden $$ CHINESE

136-28 39th Ave., Flushing, Queens   (718) 961-9088
Credit cards: All major   Meals: L, D

Flushing's biggest Hong Kong seafood palace is a cavernous room
decorated with fish tanks. The size of a couple of football fields, it
is filled at lunchtime with women wheeling dim sum carts through
the vast space and calling out the names of their wares. You can go
for dim sum (and expect to wait for a table on weekends) or call
ahead and order a banquet for a group. There is just about anything you can imagine, from the usual har gow and shiu mai
dumplings to braised duck feet, spicy tripe and green-lipped mussels topped with mayonnaise.

Price range: Apps., $2–$14; entrees, $8–$40. **Wheelchair access:**
Fully accessible.

Keens $$$$ STEAKHOUSE

72 W. 36th St. (bet. Fifth & Sixth Aves.) (212) 947-3636
Credit cards: All major Meals: L, D

Opened in 1885, Keens looks like something out of a tale by Dickens. The scene is wonderful: big tables filled mostly with men chowing down on big platters of meat as they inhale tankards of beer and any of the more than 60 single-malt Scotches. The restaurant served its millionth mutton chop decades ago, and that continues to be the best thing on the menu. The best of the appetizers is the shrimp cocktail, with oysters on the half shell a close second. All the standard side dishes are on hand: creamed spinach, sautéed mushrooms, potatoes in any number of guises.

Price range: Lunch entrees, $14–$20. Dinner: apps., $6–$16; entrees, $19–$35; desserts, $6–$7. **Wheelchair access:** Not accessible.

Kelley & Ping $$ NOODLES/THAI

127 Greene St. (bet. Houston & Prince Sts.) (212) 228-1212
Credit cards: All major Meals: L, D

This stylish combination Thai restaurant, tearoom and retail shop is best for a quick bowl of noodles or a cup of tea. The room is pleasant and the food is thankfully not too ambitious.

Alcohol: Beer and wine. **Price range:** Lunch: apps., $4–$6; entrees, $5–$8. Dinner: apps., $5–$7; entrees, $8–$14; desserts, $6. **Wheelchair access:** Fully accessible.

Khao Sarn $25 & Under THAI

311 Bedford Ave. (at S. 2nd St.), Brooklyn (718) 963-1238
Credit cards: Cash only Meals: L, D

Khao Sarn is a sweet and simple place. Judging by its plywood benches, strewn with soft pillows, the rough-hewn counter and the paper menus that double as takeout flyers. It's a low-budget operation and that is part of its charm.

The food is low-key, spicy but not fiery, delicately balanced between hot, sour, salty and sweet, rather than overtly assertive. Soups are superb, especially the tom yum, spicy, full of shrimp and gloriously sour yet fresh, and the tom kha, made rich and soothing with coconut milk and tender chicken breast. Curries are likewise deftly prepared, full of flavors that grow slowly in the mouth. The pad Thai was supple and slightly moist. The restaurant offers the usual desserts with one exception, the unfortunately named Thai sticks. These are excellent little beignets, crisp yet billowy, served with a dipping sauce of sweet condensed milk and crushed peanuts.

Other recommended dishes: Squid salad, pork larb, massaman curry. **Alcohol:** Bring your own. **Price range:** Starters: $2.50–$7.95; entrees, $5.50–$12.95. **Wheelchair access:** One level.

Kitchen Club $$ FRENCH/JAPANESE

30 Prince St. (at Mott St.)   (212) 274-0025
Credit cards: All major   Meals: L, D   Closed Mon.

The menu is ever-changing at this creative restaurant, where the
Dutch chef and owner offers her own blend of Asian and European
dishes, like steamed shrimp served cold in a bento box and cod in
sake sauce. The tiny Zen garden in front sets a tone of serenity.

Alcohol: Beer and wine. **Price range:** Apps., $9–$11; entrees,
$15–$24; desserts, $6–$8. **Wheelchair access:** Fully accessible.

Kitchenette $ NEW AMERICAN

80 W. Broadway (at Warren St.)   (212) 267-6740
Credit cards: AE   Meals: B, Br, L, D

Breakfast is best at this small farmhouse-style restaurant in SoHo.
Dishes like orange-poppy-seed waffles, blueberry pancakes and biscuits are homey and delicious. Lunch, unfortunately, is dominated
by prepackaged sandwiches that have lost their zip by the time they
are served.

Price range: Apps., $3–$6; entrees, $11–$16; desserts, $3–$4.
Wheelchair access: Fully accessible.

Knickerbocker Bar & Grill $$ AMERICAN

33 University Pl. (at 9th St.)   (212) 228-8490
Credit cards: All major   Meals: L, D, LN

Huge portions, huge menu, great service. An old reliable restaurant
with good American food that never lets you down. No wonder it's
a neighborhood favorite.

Price range: Lunch: apps., $5; entrees, $10–$15; desserts, $5–$6.
Dinner: apps., $6–$12; entrees, $14–$18; desserts, $5–$6; prix fixe,
$17. **Wheelchair access:** Not accessible.

Knödel $25 & Under   SCANDINAVIAN/FAST FOOD

Grand Central Terminal, Lower Level   (212) 986-1230
Credit cards: All major   Meals: L, D

The restaurant is Scandinavian, but the plump and rich sausages
are American, served on fresh potato rolls with assorted toppings
like hot dogs, though derived from the European tradition of creative sausage making. The fine Knodel brat, for example, is mostly
savory pork, with puréed fig for softer texture and, surprise, pine
nuts, which fit in perfectly. Knodel also serves an excellent smoky,
spicy andouille and a sweet and smoky chicken-and-apple sausage.
Sides include sesame-scented Asian slaw, with red cabbage, carrots
and raisins.

Alcohol: Beer and wine. **Price range:** Entrees, $5–$12. **Wheelchair
access:** Fully accessible.

Kori $25 & Under KOREAN

253 Church St. (near Leonard St.) (212) 334-0908
Credit cards: All major Meals: L, D Closed Sun.

Kori seems a wholly personal expression of its owner and chef, Kori
Kim: up-to-date and appealing to Americans but tied to Korean traditions. She learned to cook in a big, traditional Korean family in
Seoul, and she said her hope was to serve her customers exactly
the same food she made for her family. It is hard to imagine Ms.
Kim serving food at home as polished as her dubu sobegi, a tofu
croquette stuffed with savory ground Asian mushrooms and beautifully presented. If it is power you want, duk bokki, soft rice-flour
cylinders with a pleasant bite to them, come in a red chili sauce
that is pure fire. Galbi jim is a wonderful stew of short ribs with
sweet dates, chestnuts and turnips.

Kori is a bar as well, and noise occasionally wafts through the
narrow dining room. There are some excellent cocktails made with
soju along with a small selection of wines.

Other recommended dishes: Bulgogi, marinated beef with Asian
pear, eel, mung-bean pancakes, octopus with noodles, bibimbop.
Price range: Apps., $5–$12; entrees, $13–$25. **Wheelchair access:**
Small steps at entrance.

Kurumazushi ☆ ☆ ☆ $$$$ SUSHI

7 E. 47th St. (bet. Madison & Fifth Aves.), 2nd Fl. (212) 317-2802
Credit cards: All major Meals: L, D Closed Sun.

Few restaurants are more welcoming to diners who do not speak
Japanese, and few chefs are better at introducing people to sushi
than Toshihiro Uezu, proprietor of Kurumazushi. One of New York
City's most venerable sushi bars, it serves only sushi and sashimi
and is, admittedly, expensive.

Increasing competition has made the restaurant seem a little less
of a standout, and service at lunch can be glacial. But the list of
seafood flown overnight from Japan is still impressive, and a recent
visit showed the restaurant to be firmly entrenched among the best
sushi parlors in Manhattan. (*Ruth Reichl, updated by William
Grimes*)

Price range: Apps., $6–$15; entrees, $25–$100; desserts, $5.
Wheelchair access: Elevator to right in front of restaurant.

L'Acajou $$ BISTRO/FRENCH

53 W. 19th St. (bet. Fifth & Sixth Aves.) (212) 645-1706
Credit cards: All major Meals: L, D, LN

Regular customers make going to this well-worn Chelsea bistro feel
like coming home. Reliable food, a terrific wine list and an ever-
changing art show add to the slightly funky atmosphere.

Price range: Lunch entrees, $9–$17. Dinner: apps., $5–$18;
entrees, $16–$26; desserts, $4–$6. **Wheelchair access:** Not
accessible.

La Caravelle ☆☆☆ $$$$ FRENCH

33 W. 55th St. (near Fifth Ave.) (212) 586-4252
Credit cards: All major   Meals: L, D   Closed Sun.

For better and for worse, formality lives on in restaurants like La
Caravelle. But unlike other Midtown French restaurants, which
seem like fusty museum pieces, La Caravelle pulses with forward
momentum and energy, even while paying respect to the past. The
chef composes each dish without excess or waste, offering food that
is eloquent rather than dazzling. An amuse bouche of meltingly
pure eggplant over spaghetti squash, imbued with Indian curry
spices, is exquisite. The chef's affinity for seafood is reflected in the
luscious soft-shell crab appetizer.

For the main course, seared yellowtail, steamed fillet of black
sea bass and roasted lobster are all excellent. The restaurant has
preserved a small selection of classic French dishes. You will find
no better Dover sole than La Caravelle's. Good desserts include passion fruit tart with a crisp cashew crust, and a white chocolate
mousse on a crunchy pecan-praline base.

Service at La Caravelle is as understated and professional as it
gets. If you need a setting for a fairy tale, one that looks good and
tastes better, La Caravelle is the place. *(Eric Asimov)*

Other recommended dishes: Soft-shell crab, langoustine with red
pepper essence, marinated tuna and gravlax, sautéed foie gras, pike
quenelles, soufflés, chocolate tart, crème brûlée. **Wine list:** Long
and deep, with a natural French concentration. **Price range:** Lunch,
$38 prix fixe. Dinner, $72 prix fixe. **Wheelchair access:** All one
level.

La Côte Basque ☆☆☆ $$$$ FRENCH

60 W. 55th St. (bet. Fifth & Sixth Aves.) (212) 688-6525
Credit cards: All major   Meals: L, D

For more than 40 years in two locations, La Côte Basque has been a
bastion of classic French haute cuisine. Time has passed this sort of
cooking by, which does not make it any less alluring or enjoyable.
Who could not delight in a rich lobster bisque, ladled out of a little
brass pot? What could be better than a crisp roasted duck with wild
rice and a sweet cherry sauce, or a light-as-air raspberry soufflé? If
the food gives La Côte Basque the feeling of a museum, the dining
room feels more like a musty antique shop. Tables are too close
together, carpets and waiters' uniforms feel a little faded, and service seems a beat off rather than crisp. Existing more in the past
than the present, La Côte Basque is a reminder of a world that soon
will no longer exist. The restaurant may no longer be among the
best, but it will always be memorable. *(Review by Eric Asimov; stars
previously awarded by Ruth Reichl.)*

Wine list: Mostly French and mostly expensive, with a few lower-
priced selections. **Price range:** Prix-fixe lunch, $38; prix-fixe dinner,
$70, with supplements. **Wheelchair access:** Dining room at street
level. Restrooms downstairs but there is an elevator.

Lady Mendl's Tea Parlour $$ ENGLISH

56 Irving Pl. (bet. 17th & 18th Sts.)   (212) 533-4466
Credit cards: All major   Meals: D   Closed Mon., Tue.

This haute Victorian parlor in the Inn at Irving Place offers a popular afternoon tea that is traditional but not slavishly so. Sandwiches might include excellent smoked salmon or thin-sliced cucumber brushed with mascarpone. Then, a scone with luxurious clotted cream and preserves, and finally desserts, like a luscious apricot tart or maybe some refreshing fruit. Teas are carefully chosen and include some unusual blends like Eros, a mixture of black tea, hibiscus and mallow flowers.

Price range: Five courses, $30 per person. **Wheelchair access:** Not accessible.

La Esquina Criolla $25 & Under
ARGENTINE/URUGUAYAN

94-67 Corona Blvd., Corona, Queens   (718) 699-5579
Credit cards: All major   Meals: L, D

Like other Argentine and Uruguayan grills in the area, La Esquina Criolla is both meat market and restaurant. While some customers may take home one of the reasonably priced steaks, almost everybody in the throng on a Saturday night is filling up right there. Certainly, some grills are prettier than La Esquina Criolla — "the Spanish corner," as one of the owners translates the name. But it's hard to imagine a sweeter restaurant, despite a language barrier. And you can't get a better steak value than La Criolla's shell steak, a thick cut with the mineral tang and charred crust that you ordinarily find only in a dry-aged steak.

Each table is set with a bowl of chimichurri, a condiment made primarily of garlic, parsley and olive oil, which goes well with the excellent entraña, a well-charred beefy skirt steak with robust flavors. All meals are supplemented with vegetables like flawless yuca frita — puffy chunks of fried yuca — or fried plantains, both sweet and green. Cap it off with an excellent flan topped with creamy dulce de leche, which is like pure caramel.

Other recommended dishes: Roast chicken, mixed grill. **Price range:** Apps., $2–$4; entrees, $6–$19. **Wheelchair access:** All one level.

La Flor $25 & Under   ECLECTIC
53-02 Roosevelt Ave., Woodside, Queens   (718) 426-8023
Credit cards: Cash only   Meals: B, L, D

The gloomy corner of Roosevelt Avenue and 53rd Street in Queens is an unlikely spot to find a lively and unusual restaurant, but La Flor has become a culinary center for the neighborhood. In an ocean of franchise duplicates, formula menus and by-the-numbers décor, La Flor stands out both for its looks and its food. The chef has assembled a menu that puts specialties from Mexico side by side with French and Italian dishes. The polyglot menu includes excellent individual pizzas. The Mexican pizza, made with queso blanco, studded with chili rounds and juicy pieces of marinated pork, and scented with cilantro, is a standout. Breakfast includes bourbon-vanilla French toast and fine huevos rancheros. Best of all, though, are the baked goods, like fabulous cheese biscuits and sticky buns. Desserts are a high point, too, from the sophisticated blueberry and walnut tart to the fudgy, spectacularly big chocolate cookie.

Other recommended dishes: Tacos with carnitas, sandwiches, spareribs, steak, house salad, corn salad. **Alcohol:** Bring your own. **Price range:** Apps., $4–$6; entrees, $6–$13. **Wheelchair access:** Not accessible.

La Fonda Boricua $25 & Under   PUERTO RICAN
169 E. 106th St. (bet. Third & Lexington Aves.)   (212) 410-7292
Credit cards: All major   Meals: L, D

This handsome little place in East Harlem offers big helpings of excellent Puerto Rican home cooking. La Fonda Boricua, which essentially means Puerto Rican Diner, is a spacious place, with brick walls, plants and comfortable seating for 75.

While that is enough to draw you in, the food makes you want to stay. Chicharrones of chicken is Caribbean fried chicken, crisp and greaseless. Pork dishes include roast pork shoulder, full of garlic and pepper, satisfying baked pork chops smothered in onions. Steak, marinated in tangy citrus juice is remarkably tender and also comes covered in onions.

Other recommended dishes: Octopus salad, arroz con pollo, green plantains, rice and beans. **Price range:** Everything $10 and under. **Wheelchair access:** Ramp at entrance.

La Grenouille   ☆ ☆ ☆ $$$$ FRENCH
3 E. 52nd St. (near Fifth Ave.)   (212) 752-1495
Credit cards: All major   Meals: L, D   Closed Sun., Mon.

Now entering its fifth decade, La Grenouille is still giving lessons in how an elegant French restaurant should be run. The scale is intimate, the floral arrangements spectacular, the cooking classic. Patrons still come for frog legs Provençal style, quenelles de brochets Lyonnaise style and grilled sole with mustard sauce. But the restaurant's menu includes more modern dishes, expertly prepared, like zucchini blossoms in a ravigote sauce, and calf's liver with almonds and sweet and sour turnips. The setting is formal but warm. The captain service is old-fashioned in the best sense. La Grenouille not only survives, it thrives, despite breathtakingly high prices. *(Review by William Grimes; stars previously awarded by Ruth Reichl.)*

Wine list: Affordable bottles have been added to the Old Bordeaux still available for the very rich. **Price range:** Lunch: prix-fixe, $45; three-course business lunch, $35. Dinner: apps., $16–$42; entrees, $29–$55; desserts, $12–$17; prix fixe, $82; tasting menu, $110. **Wheelchair access:** All one level.

La Grolla ☆ $$ ITALIAN
413 Amsterdam Ave. (near 80th St.) (212) 496-0890
Credit cards: All major Meals: Br, L, D

La Grolla is a small, cramped but friendly restaurant offering warm
if not very good service. It showcases the rustic, simple cuisine of
Val d'Aosta, a tiny region of Italy wedged tightly between the
French and Swiss Alps. The food leans heavily toward hearty fare
intended to keep shepherds moving uphill in freezing weather.

Start with fonduta, an Italian versian of fondue made with
Fontina cheese. The flavor is irresistible; nutty, with a distinct tang.
The seupa Valpellinzentsche, a peasant-simple soup thick enough
to bend a spoon, is a casserole of whole-wheat bread chunks, savoy
cabbage and fontina cheese in an oxtail stock. All the pastas are
made on the premises but they are not all that successful. The
restaurant does a fine roasted rabbit, and the chicken stew with
rosemary and chestnuts is wonderfully sweet and savory. Desserts
are straightforward and good. After dinner, try the grolla (for which
the restaurant is named), a box with a mixture of coffee, grappa,
Grand Marnier, sugar and orange zest that is set afire to burn off
the alcohol.

Wine list: Modest, but modestly priced. Poor selection of wines by
the glass, but interesting after-dinner wines and grappas. **Price
range:** Apps., $6–$11; entrees, $12–$23; desserts, $6–$8. **Wheelchair access:** All one level.

Lakruwana $25 & Under SRI LANKAN
358 W. 44th St. (bet. Eighth & Ninth Aves.) (212) 957-4480
Credit cards: All major Meals: L, D

One of the city's very few Sri Lankan restaurants, Lakruwana offers
a great opportunity to taste this spicy, unusual cuisine, close to
Indian food but with its own spicy character. Try hoppers, delicate
pancakes made of rice flour and coconut milk; masala wade, a
deep-fried disk of lentils and onions eaten with a fiery sauce, and
pittu, a rich, dry, light grain served with curries. Lentil soup is
unlike any lentil soup I've ever had, puréed lentils blended with
coconut milk to an unbelievably creamy consistency, garnished
with parsley and crisp, buttery croutons. There's even a worthwhile
dessert, watalappan, a light, creamy pudding that tastes of caramel
and nutmeg.

Other recommended dishes: Cutlet, kotthu roti, shrimp biryani,
lamb black curry. **Alcohol:** Bring your own. **Price range:** Apps.,
$4–$7; entrees, $12–$17; desserts, $3.90. **Wheelchair access:** All
one level.

La Locanda dei Vini $25 & Under ITALIAN
737 Ninth Ave. (near 50th St.) (212) 258-2900
Credit cards: All major Meals: L, D

La Locanda serves pastas and meat dishes that stand out for their
simplicity and flavor, and offers an enticing and unusually arranged
wine list. Pastas can be excellent, either as a shared appetizer or as
a main course. Penne alla Genovese is perfectly al dente, with car-

rots, celery and onions cooked until meltingly sweet and flavored with a sprinkle of herbs.

Sliced leg of lamb, served like all the main courses with roasted potatoes and sautéed broccoli rabe, is past the point of pink, but the sauce, simply lamb juices and herbs, imbues the meat with flavor. The same is true of veal shoulder. The wine list is large and worth noting, with good choices at low prices. For dessert, skip tiramisu and profiteroles, and opt instead for the rustic blueberry tart or the compact French-style strawberry tart.

Other recommended dishes: Rice salad, orechiette with broccoli rabe, linguine with tiny clams and garlic, sautéed calf's liver, roasted pork with green olive and mustard sauce. **Price range:** Apps., $8–$11; pastas and entrees, $11–$22. **Wheelchair access:** Step at entrance; restrooms are small and entrance is narrow.

La Lupe $25 & Under   MEXICAN/TEX-MEX

43-16 Greenpoint Ave., Sunnyside, Queens   (718) 784-2528
Credit cards: Cash only   Meals: L, D, LN

This neat, bright taquería has all the atmospheric hallmarks of authenticity, from the blaring jukebox to the big television tuned to Spanish soap operas to the dour men silently sipping beer. Tacos are fine, the pozole — a soulful, mild soup thick with puffed hominy and chunks of pork — is terrific, and the long list of main courses includes some unusual dishes like pierna adobada, chunks of tender pork in an extremely spicy sauce, and pollo en salsa chipotle, chicken breasts flattened, grilled and served in moderately spicy sauce with the distinctive smoky flavor of chipotle chilies.

Other recommended dishes: Enchiladas de mole poblano, chilaquiles verdes. **Price range:** Almost everything is under $10. **Wheelchair access:** Restroom is downstairs.

La Metairie $$ FRENCH

189 W. 10th St. (at W. 4th St.)   (212) 989-0343
Credit cards: All major   Meals: Br, D, LN

A Village dream, that cozy, rustic little restaurant hidden among twisting streets. Good Provençal food and dim lighting make this a romantic retreat.

Alcohol: Beer and wine. **Price range:** Lunch: apps., $6–$16; entrees, $12–$22; desserts, $8. Dinner: apps., $7–$19; entrees, $18–$26; desserts, $9. **Wheelchair access:** Fully accessible.

Lamu   ☆ $$$ GLOBAL/MEDITERRANEAN

39 E. 19th St. (bet. Broadway & Park Ave. S.)   (212) 358-7775
Credit cards: All major   Meals: L, D   Closed Sun.

Lamu is an island off the coast of Kenya, but the chef is more likely to snatch his ideas from Italy. The restaurant's reach is international, but it never stretches. Almost everything on Lamu's compact menu has an unforced air about it. Ravioli stuffed with mascarpone and radicchio, an appetizer, is a wonderful blending of sweet and bitter. Mustard cream gives the needed kick to a visually impressive terrine of salmon wrapped around braised lentils. A reduction of smoked salmon adds depth to salmon with roasted cabbage, pancetta and black trumpet mushrooms. Desserts are surprisingly fancy, with two winners: a simplified chocolate hazelnut mille-feuille and a fanciful mascarpone and white chocolate mousse.

Other recommended dishes: Butternut squash soup with quince and hazelnuts, duck breast with squash purée and fruit mostardo.
Wine list: A serviceable list of about 40 modestly priced international wines. **Price range:** Lunch: apps., $6–$10; entrees, $14–$19; two-course prix fixe, $15. Dinner: apps., $8–$13; entrees, $19–$24; desserts, $8–$9. **Wheelchair access:** All one level.

La Nonna ☆ $$ ITALIAN
133 W. 13th St. (bet. Sixth & Seventh Aves.)   (212) 741-3663
Credit cards: All major   Meals: L, D

La Nonna is a warm, inviting place that does a perfectly good job with its no-nonsense menu of thoroughly traditional Tuscan dishes. The emphasis is on meat and fish roasted or grilled in a wood-burning oven that you can see in the back of the dining room, framed by decorative Italian tiles. The dining room has a simple, inviting look, with well-spaced tables and antique engravings of Tuscan scenes on the walls. You can find better meals, but rarely in such agreeable surroundings.

Pasta turns out to be the most dependable category on the menu. The Gorgonzola gnocchi are as light as whipped cream. Anyone determined to get to the heart of the cuisine should proceed directly to the trippa alla Fiorentina. By some mysterious process, it becomes a deeply satisfying, earthy mix of sharp tomato flavor, fragrant rosemary, white wine and sweetly rich vegetables wrapped around chewy slivers of tripe.

Other recommended dishes: Pappardelle with duck ragú, Cornish hen, Italian cheesecake. **Price range:** Lunch: apps., $5–$9; entrees, $10–$22; desserts, $7. Dinner: apps., $6–$10; entrees, $17–$25; desserts, $7. **Wheelchair access:** Three steps down to entrance.

La Paella $25 & Under SPANISH
214 E. 9th St. (bet Second & Third Aves.)   (212) 598-4321
Credit cards: MC/V   Meals: D, LN

Dark, crowded and loud, La Paella is like an American's fantasy of a Spanish tapas bar and includes the basic tapas repertory, like thick wedges of Manchego cheese with apple slices, delicate rounds of cold marinated squid and a puffy potato omelet. About 20 selections — sort of an introduction to tapas — are available each day, and almost all are very good, but it's best to order a chef's selection, a plate with enough to feed three people. The paellas are rich, full of flavor and enormous. For dessert, the crema catalana is so good that the owner should consider naming the restaurant after this dish instead.

Alcohol: Beer and wine. **Price range:** Apps., $4–$9; entrees, $12–$17; desserts, $5. **Wheelchair access:** Restrooms not accessible.

La Palapa

La Palapa	$25 & Under	MEXICAN
77 St. Marks Pl.		(212) 777-2537
Credit cards: All major		Meals: L, D, LN

This bright and cheerful restaurant one in a fleet of Mexican restaurants that reveal the regional glories of Mexico rather than the familiar one-dimensional margarita-fueled Tex-Mex dishes. The fascinating menu shows off all sorts of complex flavor combinations based on traditional Mexican ingredients. Tacos are authentically Mexican and come with fillings like spicy chili-rubbed chicken. Guacamole is chunky and well spiced.

The real excitement comes with the main courses, like thin slices of duck breast, fanned out in a wonderful sesame mole. Chicken enchiladas are almost stewlike, in a soupy tomatillo sauce that is very spicy but tangy as well. For dessert, try rich Mexican chocolate ice cream and a spicy chili-laced peach sorbet. They also accompany other delicious desserts, like an empanada stuffed with cinnamon-flavored rice pudding.

Other recommended dishes: Jicama and pineapple salas, ceviche, catfish tamal, shrimp with garlic, pork chop, roast chicken. **Price range:** Apps., $5–$9; entrees, $10–$20. **Wheelchair access:** All one level.

Larry Forgione's Signature Café $

NEW AMERICAN

Lord & Taylor, 424 Fifth Ave. (at 39th St.), 6th Fl.   (212) 391-3015
Credit cards: All major   Meals: L, D

When Larry Forgione began writing the menu for his cafe in Lord & Taylor, he knew he wanted panini. He also knew he wanted lots of ice cream. The two ideas come together in his reconfigured ice cream sandwiches, which are real sandwiches, thick slices of toasted bread pressing against a generous slice of ice cream filling. They come in five flavors, although experiments continue on an extension of the basic line. The plainest is strawberry-and-vanilla ice cream between layers of butter-toasted brioche. At the far end conceptually is a sandwich of mango and coconut ice cream on lemon poppy-seed bread, a bright, tropical combination. The cafe, a cheery-looking, brightly decorated place emphasizes salads, big-bowl soups, little pizzas and the aforementioned panini, but the heavy thinking has gone into the desserts.

Price range: Entrees, $7.95–$15.95; desserts, $5.95–$7.95. **Wheelchair access:** Fully accessible.

La Sandwicherie

$25 & Under
SANDWICHES/MOROCCAN

842 Greenwich St. (near Gansevoort St.)   (212) 675-3281
Credit cards: All major   Meals: B, L   Closed Sun.

La Sandwicherie, a narrow slice of a place, carved out of a storeroom in the rear of the Moroccan restaurant Zitoune, is quite possibly the smallest restaurant in the city. But it's good to know that in the too-hip-for-you meatpacking district, somebody is remembering to provide moderately priced lunches that actually taste great. Sandwiches are not particularly Moroccan, but La Sandwicherie gives them a pronounced Moroccan accent, seasoning a big meaty hamburger, for example, with plenty of cumin, and fish and chips with mayonnaise blended with chermoula, a zesty Moroccan spice mix. The menu offers some ordinary sandwiches, but stick to the more Moroccan choices, like excellent merguez, or fresh, well-flavored sardines with a tangy tapenade. Chicken breast, sliced ultrathin and grilled, is terrific with an anise-and-curry seasoning.

As good as the sandwiches are, the best dish on the menu is harira, a deliciously tangy soup made here with chickpeas and tender chunks of beef rather than the more traditional lamb.

Price range: Soups and salads, $4–$8; sandwiches and couscous, $6–$9. **Wheelchair access:** Not accessible.

La Taza de Oro $25 & Under PUERTO RICAN
96 Eighth Ave. (bet. 14th & 15th Sts.) (212) 243-9946
Credit cards: Cash only Meals: B, L, D

This little Puerto Rican restaurant has not changed at all in decades. And why tamper with success? A cheerful waiter greets diners with "Hello, capitan," though regulars are promoted to general. The food is forceful and delicious, and the portions are huge, from garlic-suffused roast pork to tender octopus salad with marinated onions. The inexpensive café con leche is better than almost any coffee bar's cappuccino, at a third the price.

Alcohol: Bring your own. **Price range:** Apps., $2–$3; entrees, $4–$11; desserts, $2. **Wheelchair access:** Not accessible.

Lavagna $25 & Under MEDITERRANEAN
545 E. 5th St. (at Ave. B) (212) 979-1005
Credit cards: Cash only Meals: D, LN Closed Sun.

Lavagna's food is fresh and generous, with honest, straightforward flavors. The simple rectangular dining room is casual and inviting, but can get loud when it's crowded. Pastas are best, both simple dishes like rigatoni with crumbled fennel sausage, peas, tomatoes and cream, and more complicated ones like fresh pappardelle with rabbit stew. Cacciucco, the Tuscan fish soup scented with saffron and anise, and served with mussels, cockles and chunks of fish, is a great value.

Other recommended dishes: Grilled vegetables with goat cheese, grilled stuffed squid, sweetbreads with polenta and mushrooms, roasted sardines, chicken grilled under a brick, roasted sea bass, cheesecake, panna cotta. **Alcohol:** Bring your own. **Price range:** Apps., $5–$7; entrees, $11–$17. **Wheelchair access:** All one level.

La Vineria $25 & Under ITALIAN
19 W. 55th St. (at Fifth Ave.) (212) 247-3400
Credit cards: All major Meals: L, D

With its brick walls lined with wine bottles, its tile floor and its timbered ceiling, La Vineria is a warm, modestly priced oasis in a midtown neighborhood full of expensive restaurants and fast-food joints. What's best at La Vineria is what's least expensive: the salads and the fine, individual-size brick-oven pizzas. The best thing at La Vineria is a pizza with the poetic name Miseria e Nobilta, a 12-inch round of pizza topped with mozzarella and Parmesan, and covered in huge arugula leaves and footlong slices of prosciutto. It is pizza nirvana.

Other recommended dishes: Field greens, insalata caprese, prosciutto and melon, quattro stagioni and boscaiola pizzas. **Alcohol:** Beer and wine. **Price range:** Apps., $7–$13; entrees, $12–$29; desserts, $6–$7. **Wheelchair access:** Fully accessible.

Layla ☆☆ $$$ MIDDLE EASTERN/MEDITERRANEAN

211 W. Broadway (at Franklin St.) (212) 431-0700
Credit cards: All major Meals: L, D

For months after Sept. 11, 2001, Layla, the Middle Eastern restaurant that is part of the Drew Nieporent-Robert De Niro restaurant empire, remained closed. Mr. Nieporent was concerned that an angry public might reject all things Middle Eastern. He considered transforming the restaurant. "But at the end of the day," he said, "you can't condemn a whole food culture just because of what happened." So Layla finally reopened that spring with a new chef. And despite Mr. Nieporent's affection for Middle Eastern cooking, the menu has swiveled toward other parts of the Mediterranean. Now the Middle East is connoted more through spices and flavorings than through the usual repertory of regional dishes.

Among the main courses, dishes that you would have expected to find at the old Layla, like a Moroccan tagine of duck with couscous and toasted pistachios, or moist chicken kebabs marinated in the harissa, are supplemented by scallop-size cylinders of monkfish wrapped in prosciutto with pesto-flavored risotto, and a chewy but flavorful steak, imbued with garlic and served with a smoky ragout of gigante beans. Desserts have always been Middle Eastern fantasies, and so they remain, like a feathery halvah mousse over chocolate, with bits of sesame brittle strewn about. One more thing: belly dancers still shake it nightly. *(Eric Asimov)*

Price range: Dinner entrees, $15–$29. **Wheelchair access:** Four steps up to dining room. **Features:** Outdoor dining (patio).

Le Bateau Ivre $25 & Under BISTRO/FRENCH

230 E. 51st St. (bet. Second & Third Aves.) (212) 583-0579
Credit cards: All major Meals: D, LN

This little wine bar and restaurant is so wholeheartedly French that every one of the 250 wines on its list, including 150 available by the glass, is French. There are some good buys, but navigate carefully; there are just as many expensive bottles. The menu is likewise straightforwardly French, with some good choices like lobster bisque and grilled lamb. A generous portion of mussels marinières is perfectly cooked, and roast chicken is juicy and inviting.

Other recommended dishes: Grilled salmon, hamburger, lamb chops. **Price range:** Apps., $5–$9; entrees, $8–$19. **Wheelchair access:** All one level.

Le Bernardin ☆☆☆☆ $$$$ FRENCH/SEAFOOD

155 W. 51st St. (bet. Sixth & Seventh Aves.)   (212) 489-1515
Credit cards: All major   Meals: L (Mon.–Fri.), D   Closed Sun.

Most restaurants grow into their stars. Not Le Bernardin: at the ripe old age of three months, it had all four stars bestowed upon it. The restaurant has been in the spotlight ever since. The key to Le Bernardin's food has always been to coax forward the flavor of each fish. Impressive starters include the deeply flavored fish soup and the extraordinarily delicious fricassee of shellfish with sweet and delicate mussels, clams and oysters. Main courses are even more admirable. Each fish has been stripped to its basic elements and dressed up to emphasize them. Delicate halibut is simply poached in a saffron bouillon.

A subtle face-lift a few years ago freshened the dining room without changing the character of the place. As for the food, it seems only to improve. Mr. Ripert divides the menu into departments titled almost raw, barely touched and slightly cooked. The almost raw dishes include fluke done in four different ceviches, and a memorable geoduck clam sliced into slivers flavored with lemon, olive oil and chives. Barely touched might be quickly baked kumamoto oysters and littleneck clams with thyme and garlic butter, or a potent bouillabaisse with an aioli crab cake. The subtlety and finesse of Mr. Ripert's cooking is a marvel. (*Ruth Reichl, updated by William Grimes*)

Wine list: Once featuring mostly expensive wines, the list has been expanded to include a few less expensive bottles. **Price range:** Lunch prix fixe, $35 or $48. Dinner prix fixe, $83; tasting menus, $98 and $135 ($165 and $240 with wines). **Wheelchair access:** Fully accessible.

Le Cirque 2000 ☆☆☆ $$$$ FRENCH/ITALIAN

New York Palace Hotel, 455 Madison Ave. (bet. 50th & 51st Sts.)
    (212) 303-7788
Credit cards: All major   Meals: L, D

Behold Le Cirque 2000, a giddy swirl of wealth and privilege, of gilt without guilt, a glittering social pageant that cries out for a Balzac or a Wharton. As pure spectacle, there is nothing in New York like it. Diners go to Le Cirque to see and be seen. They check in, have their self-esteem validated by Sirio Maccioni and settle in for a sumptuous evening surrounded by their own kind, preferably, but not necessarily, in the smaller of the two dining rooms, with its higher ratio of moguls to mortals. More than any restaurant since Le Pavillon, Le Cirque is a one-man show. It is Mr. Maccioni, and Mr. Maccioni is it. An evening at Le Cirque without a table-side visit from him is social death.

As a social dynamo, the restaurant thrums along, but the kitchen merely equals the performance of the better two-star restaurants in town. The cuisine is hard to make sense of. Is the place French, Italian or Mediterranean? One thing is certain, no one leaves hungry. One of Le Cirque's signature dishes, black sea bass wrapped in sheets of crisp, paper-thin potato and lavished with Barolo sauce, lives up to one's blissful memory of it. Simpler dishes deliver, like beef short ribs, one of the rotating daily specials.

Le Cirque's gaudy, even silly undertone swells to a mighty wave at dessert time. All over the dining room, ridiculous sugar sculptures and chocolate trees make their way to tables where diners grin like kids at a birthday party. Adam Tihany's circus-theme décor, much ridiculed when the new Le Cirque opened in the spring of 1997, suddenly makes perfect sense. The famous chocolate stove, a Le Cirque classics, carries on. But it has been joined by newer desserts, like "Lady's Hat," a big Easter parade saucer of pastry sheet arranged over roasted fruit and sorbets.

Wine list: An outstanding list, mostly French, of 710 wines, about 100 of them priced under $50. There are 50 half bottles and 18 wines by the glass. **Price range:** Lunch: apps., $12–$35; entrees, $28–$43; desserts, $10–$12, three-course prix-fixe, $44. Dinner: apps., $12–$35; entrees, $28–$43; desserts, $10–$12. **Wheelchair access:** Accessible by elevator at the 50th Street entrance.

L'ecole $$ FRENCH
462 Broadway (at Grand St.) (212) 219-3300
Credit cards: All major Meals: L, D Closed Sun.

Eating at the practice restaurant of the French Culinary Institute is a far surer bet than, say, getting your hair cut at the local barber college. The students are well drilled in the classics and well supervised by teachers such as Jacques Pepin and Andre Soltner. Even mistakes have a certain charm, and it's hard to beat the price.

Price range: Prix fixe: lunch, $18; dinner, $26. **Wheelchair access:** Can use service entrance.

Le Colonial ☆ ☆ $$ VIETNAMESE
149 E. 57th St. (bet. Lexington & Third Aves.) (212) 752-0808
Credit cards: All major Meals: L, D

Nostalgic for the old days when the French filled Saigon and the wind whispered in the palm trees? Then this is for you. In fickle Manhattan, Le Colonial is no longer a rallying point for the chic and the beautiful, so you're left with Vietnamese food for the not terribly adventurous. Vietnamese cuisine, as interpreted here, is sedate Asian fare that is more delicate than Chinese food, less spicy than Thai and notable mostly for its abundance of vegetables and its absence of grease. Spring rolls at Le Colonial are so delicate you tend to forget that they are fried. The spicy beef salad is still a standout. Grilled spareribs were fragrant, chewy and just lightly herbal. The steamed fish has a pleasantly savory taste, and vegetable dishes like grilled eggplant in a spicy basil lime sauce, or steamed okra in ginger-lime sauce make a more vivid impression than the meat dishes. (*Ruth Reichl, updated by William Grimes*)

Wine list: Small but well priced and mostly French. **Price range:** Apps., $7–$12; entrees, $14–$23; desserts, $6–$8. Pre-theater prix fixe, $24. **Wheelchair access:** Second floor lounge not accessible.

Le Gamin $$

183 Ninth Ave. (at 21st St.)   (212) 243-8864
50 Macdougal St. (bet. Houston & Prince Sts.)   (212) 254-4678
536 E. 5th St. (bet. Aves. A & B)   (212) 254-8409
27 Bedford St. (bet. Downing & Houston Sts.)   (212) 743-2846
5 Front St. (at Old Fulton St.), Brooklyn   (718) 246-0170
Credit cards: Cash only   Meals: Br, L, D, LN

These little restaurants are like slivers of France, where the Parisian atmosphere is as thick as Gitane smoke. They offer a typical cafe menu of salads, sandwiches and omelets, but the best dishes are the crepes. With a frothy café au lait, a ham and melted cheese crepe, followed by a lemon crepe, makes a wonderful light meal.

Price range: Crepes, $4–$9; salads, $7–$11; desserts, $4–$6.
Wheelchair access: Fully accessible.

Le Gigot $25 & Under   FRENCH

18 Cornelia St. (bet. 4th & Bleecker Sts.)   (212) 627-3737
Credit cards: AE   Meals: Br, L, D   Closed Mon.

This little restaurant, with its little zinc bar and mirrored wall criss-crossed with polished wood, pulses with the welcoming spirit of a Parisian hangout. The Provence-inflected food adds to the illusion, with excellent bistro fare like leg of lamb in a red wine reduction; lamb stew; endive salad with apples, walnuts and Roquefort, and rounds of baguette smeared with goat cheese and smoky tapenade. There are disappointments, like the steak frites. The bland, beige veal stew. The wine list, too, needs rethinking. The best desserts are the sweet, moist, caramelized tarte Tatin, the excellent bananas flambé, and the great little cheese course.

Alcohol: Beer and wine. **Price range:** Apps., $7–$9; entrees, $12–$17; desserts, $7. **Wheelchair access:** Step to dining room.

Le Madeleine $$ FRENCH

403 W. 43rd St. (bet. Ninth & 10th Aves.)   (212) 246-2993
Credit cards: All major   Meals: L, D

Proust would not have been inspired here. The menu hasn't changed in years at this little restaurant, which crowds up on matinee days and before the nightly curtains. The food is competently prepared but unexciting, and the menu of familiar French dishes won't surprise.

Price range: Apps., $5–$9; entrees, $8–$23; desserts, $6–$8.
Wheelchair access: Fully accessible. **Features:** Outdoor dining.

Le Madri   ☆☆ $$$ ITALIAN

168 W. 18th St. (bet. Sixth & Seventh Aves.)   (212) 727-8022
Credit cards: All major   Meals: L, D

Le Madri opened in 1989 to a great deal of heat and fanfare. Those stylish days are long gone. And yet, Le Madri has evolved rather than ossified. The food is better than ever. The dining room is cozier and quieter. The menu combines a respect for Italian traditions with an international sensibility. This is typified by an excellent appetizer of tender pan-roasted clams, served with cubes of chorizo, cranberry beans and sawed-off tubetti pasta in a broth of tomatoes and chipotle chilies. Most of the pastas are distinct and lively, including cappelletti filled with roasted butternut squash. The best entrees are an impressive prime rib of beef, served as a mound of wide slices surrounding a bare bone, and an outstanding grilled rack of lamb. Desserts are not on a par with the rest of the meal, except for the top-notch tiramisù.

When Le Madri was hot, it promised more than it delivered. Now it's the other way around. *(Eric Asimov)*

Other recommended dishes: Rabbit confit; sautéed chicken livers; fritto misto; pizzas; chestnut soup with rice and pancetta; chestnut pasta with brussels sprouts and squash; spaghetti with oil, garlic and tomato; wood-roasted whole fish. **Wine list:** Surprisingly skimpy. **Price range:** Apps., $9–$17; entrees, $14–$38; desserts, $9. **Wheelchair access:** Not accessible.

Lentini   ☆ $$$$ ITALIAN

1562 Second Ave. (at 81st St.)   (212) 628-3131
Credit cards: All major   Meals: D

Chef Giuseppe Lentini has no revolutionary ideas. He seems to operate according to the touching precept that if you are Italian and cook the food you love, the customers will come. Location and atmosphere make this a neighborhood restaurant. Some of the dishes do, too, like spaghetti with clam sauce, fried calamari and chicken cacciatore. But look more closely at the menu, scan the ambitious wine list and its equally ambitious prices, and it becomes clear that Mr. Lentini wants to be more than a nice little local standby. Pastas are also a very good bet. For dessert, try cassata, a dense, even sludgy mass of sweetened ricotta and spongecake topped with loose marzipan.

Wine list: An unexpectedly ambitious and often pricey list of more than 200 wines, nearly half of them Italian, with 26 half bottles and a large selection of grappas. **Price range:** Apps., $8–$13; entrees, $18–$30; desserts, $8–$10. **Wheelchair access:** Steps to entrance.

Lento's $ ITALIAN

7003 Third Ave., Bay Ridge, Brooklyn   (718) 745-9197
833 Union St., Park Slope, Brooklyn   (718) 399-8782
Credit cards: Cash only   Meals: L, D, LN

It's hard to lump these sibling restaurants together. The original branch in Bay Ridge is a relic from the days of restaurants and pizzas past. It's just a simple brick corner tavern with a good-time neighborhood feel to it, but at one time Lento's had an air of formality that made restaurant-going a dignified business, traces of which still linger. The pizza, too, is a throwback, with a wafer-thin, extra crisp crust that makes up with texture what it lacks in elasticity or smoky flavor. The mozzarella is mellow, the tomato sauce is slightly spicy and the sausage is chunky and flavorful. The newer

Park Slope branch, a handsome spot in a former firehouse, makes decent pizza but is no match for the older place.

Price range: Avg. app., $7; entree, $9; dessert, $3. **Wheelchair access:** Fully accessible. **Features:** Outdoor dining.

Le Périgord ☆☆ $$$$ FRENCH
405 E. 52nd St. (east of First Ave.) (212) 755-6244
Credit cards: All major Meals: L, D

For more than 35 years Le Périgord has been a dignified presence on the dining scene. It's a French restaurant the way French restaurants used to be. The waiters, well on in years, wear white jackets. The even more senior captains wear tuxedos. On the dessert trolley you know with dead certainty that you will find floating island, chocolate mousse and tarte Tatin.

Le Périgord had a face-lift a while back. The notoriously low ceilings were raised half a foot, the banquettes were reupholstered in tomato-red fabric, and the walls took on a gentle yellowy peach blush. They did not, however, remake the staff. Some nights, the restaurant can seem like a cross between Fawlty Towers and Katz's Delicatessen. The diners do not seem to mind. Inside Le Périgord, they can swaddle themselves in a quietly civilized atmosphere, a million miles from the tumult of the city outside.

Wine list: A fusty, mostly French list dominated by a handful of negociants and in need of an overhaul. **Price range:** Lunch: apps., $8–$15; entrees, $22–$30; desserts, $9; three-course prix-fixe, $32. Dinner: three-course prix-fixe, $57. **Wheelchair access:** Three steps to dining room; restrooms downstairs.

Le Refuge $$$ FRENCH
166 E. 82nd St. (bet. Third & Lexington Aves.) (212) 861-4505
Credit cards: AE Meals: L, D

Small, crowded, hectic and noisy, this perennially popular East Side bistro is surprisingly expensive. But then, the neighborhood doesn't seem to mind the prices.

Price range: Lunch: avg. entree, $17. Dinner: avg. app., $11; entrees, $15–$24; desserts, $8. **Wheelchair access:** Fully accessible. **Features:** Outdoor dining.

Les Halles $$ BRASSERIE/FRENCH
411 Park Ave. S. (bet. 28th & 29th Sts.) (212) 679-4111
Credit cards: All major Meals: Br, L, D, LN

If you're in the mood for good steak frites, you can hardly do better than this butcher shop and restaurant named for the old Paris market district. Small, lively and affordable, it's a satisfying experience.

Price range: Apps., $6–$10; entrees, $15–$29; desserts, $6–$9; prix fixe for two, $50. **Wheelchair access:** Fully accessible. **Features:** Outdoor dining.

Les Halles Downtown   ☆ $$$ FRENCH

15 John St. (near Broadway)   (212) 285-8585
Credit cards: All major   Meals: L, D

The small white floor tiles and the stamped-tin ceiling feel as New York as the Bowery, and a long mahogany bar along one wall, with patrons hunched over their beers and aperitifs, seems more in keeping with the true brasserie spirit than the brilliant but artificial movie sets at Balthazar and Pastis.

The benchmark dishes come through with flying colors. The hanger steak delivers the goods, and so do the fries. The côte de boeuf is the king of meats at Les Halles. It is intended for two, and it may be the most impressively succulent slab of beef on the menu. Mussels are a feature at Les Halles. They come in 10 guises, including the dangerously rich Norman-style mussels, in a sauce of cream, bacon, mushrooms and Calvados. Fish and chips, somewhat surprisingly, score high. The batter is thin, crisp and grease-free. Flawless, in fact.

Wine list: Well-chosen list of 90 wines, mostly French and Californian, and most under $40, with a dozen half-bottles, 22 wines by the glass and 22 beers, half of them on draft. **Price range:** Apps., $6–$10; entrees, $10–$26; desserts, $6. **Wheelchair access:** One flight to restrooms.

Leshko's $25 & Under   DINER/NEW AMERICAN

111 Ave. A (at 7th St.)   (212) 473-9208
Credit cards: AE   Meals: B, L, D, LN

For decades, Leshko's has held down a corner near Tompkins Square Park in what was once called the Pierogi Belt, in deference to the neighborhood's Slavic population. In 1999, new owners changed both the décor and the food. The menu offers a well-prepared selection of New York-American favorites with a few East European touches like pierogi, red cabbage and spätzle thrown in for old time's sake. Leshko's menu of main courses may be predictable, but that doesn't make a dish like juicy slow-roasted chicken, redolent of sage and lemon, less enjoyable, especially with its side of mushroom-and-onion spätzle. Chicken pot pie is first-rate, and the meatloaf sandwich, served on brown bread with sweet-and-tart house-made ketchup, is unbeatable. Desserts are resolutely uninspiring.

Other recommended dishes: Green salad, endive and watercress salad, steamed mussels, shrimp cakes, pork chop. **Price range:** Apps., $5–$8; entrees, $11–$16. **Wheelchair access:** Ramp at entrance; narrow restroom entrance.

Le Singe Vert $$ FRENCH

160 Seventh Ave. (bet. 19th & 20th Sts.)   (212) 366-4100
Credit cards: AE   Meals: Br, L, D, LN

Like its East Village sibling Jules, Le Singe Vert offers decent French bistro fare in an area that is not overrun with it, making it highly popular. The food is neither exciting nor memorable nor cheap, making Le Singe a neighborhood restaurant, but no more.

Price range: Lunch: apps., $7; entrees, $14–$15; desserts, $5. Dinner: apps., $6–$10; entrees, $15–$22; desserts, $7. **Wheelchair access:** Restrooms not accessible. **Features:** Outdoor dining.

Le Tableau $25 & Under   MEDITERRANEAN
511 E. 5th St. (bet. Aves. A & B)   (212) 260-1333
Credit cards: Cash only   Meals: Br, D   Closed Mon.

This simple storefront restaurant turns out superb Mediterranean fare. Unconventional dishes stimulate the mouth with new flavors and textures, like a spicy calamari tagine that incorporates anchovies, hummus and olive purée. Main courses are familiar, yet they are presented in inventive ways, like tender, juicy roast chicken served on a bed of garlicky escarole and white beans, with a thin layer of mashed potatoes poking through. Desserts can be excellent. The dining room is dimly lighted with candles and can become noisy, especially when a jazz trio begins playing in the late evening.

Other recommended dishes: Foie gras terrine with brioche, roasted shrimp, steamed mussels, mesclun salad, pasta with wild mushroom ragout, roasted monkfish, sliced leg of lamb, peppered duck breast, confit. **Alcohol:** Bring your own. **Price range:** Apps., $5–$9; entrees, $10–$15. **Wheelchair access:** All one level. **Features:** Outdoor dining.

Levana $$$ KOSHER/NEW AMERICAN
141 W. 69th St. (bet. Columbus Ave. & Broadway)   (212) 877-8457
Credit cards: All major   Meals: L, D   Closed Sat., Sun.

New York City's most pretentious glatt kosher restaurant serves fancy, expensive fare to Orthodox yuppies. If you're looking for kosher creativity, this is the place.

Price range: Apps., $5–$15; entrees, $17–$40; desserts, $8–$13. Prix fixe: lunch, $20; dinner, $28. Tasting menu, $55. **Wheelchair access:** Three steps down to dining room, staff will assist.

L'Express $ BISTRO
249 Park Ave. S. (bet. 19th & 20th Sts.)   (212) 254-5858
Credit cards: All major   Meals: B, Br, L, D, LN

It's open 24 hours a day, and though you can find better little French restaurants at 8 P.M., you won't find many better at 3 in the morning. L'Express offers a solid bistro menu with unexpectedly earthy surprises like pigs' feet and tripe. The staff is likable and the food has been improving since the restaurant opened.

Price range: Lunch: apps., $5–$7; entrees, $7–$14; desserts, $4–$6. Dinner: apps., $5–$7; entrees, $10–$18; desserts, $4–$6. **Wheelchair access:** Fully accessible.

Le Zie 2000 $25 & Under   ITALIAN

172 Seventh Ave. (at 20th St.)   (212) 206-8686
Credit cards: All major   Meals: L, D

This modest little trattoria offers some terrific Venetian dishes, like
an inspired salad that features pliant octopus and soft potatoes acting in precise textural counterpoint. The chef has a sure hand with
pastas like rigatoni with rosemary, served al dente in a perfectly
proportioned sauce. Risotto with squid is also superbly cooked.
Striped bass fillet with fennel and white beans is moist and wonderfully flavorful. Desserts are a weak point.

Other recommended dishes: Cichetti, bresaola with arugula and
Parmesan. **Alcohol:** Bring your own. **Price range:** Apps., $6–$9;
entrees, $9–$17. **Wheelchair access:** All one level.

Le Zinc   ☆ $$ BISTRO

139 Duane St. (bet. Church St. & W. Broadway)   (212) 513-0001
Credit cards: All major   Meals: Br, L, D, LN

Certain restaurants, agreeable but hardly special, manage to catch
fire. Le Zinc is one of them. In 2000, the owners of Chanterelle took
it over, did some minimal redecorating, put the kitchen in the
hands of Chanterelle's sous-chef. His low-key bistro menu, with an
Asian accent here and a down-home touch there, qualifies as
upmarket Manhattan comfort food, reliable and reasonably priced.
Le Zinc offers a menu-within-a-menu of charcuterie, and there's no
doubt about it, the terrines here are superior. Main courses make
the usual bistro stops, with competently executed dishes like skirt
steak in a red wine reduction, skate with brown butter and capers,
and rib steak and French fries. Maple crème caramel is luscious,
with a seductive smoky-burnt taste. Le Zinc takes no reservations.
After 7:30, prepare to wait.

Wine list: A good French-dominated international list of about 85
wines, many of them modest country wines, with nearly 40 wines
by the glass. **Price range:** Lunch: apps., $4–$11; entrees, $8–$15;
desserts, $5–$7. Dinner: apps., $5–$15; entrees, $12–$19; desserts,
$5–$7. **Wheelchair access:** Separate ramp entrance; restrooms on
dining room level.

Le Zoo $25 & Under   BISTRO/FRENCH

314 W. 11th St. (at Greenwich St.)   (212) 620-0393
Credit cards: All major   Meals: D, LN

This popular little restaurant can get crowded, loud and zoolike,
but the food is good and often creative. Where you might reasonably expect to find steak frites, roast chicken and pâté de cam-
pagne, there are instead such combinations as monkfish with
honey and lime sauce, or wonderfully flavorful sliced scallops
served in puff pastry with a leek-and-chive coulis. The dessert
selection is small and classically French, offering satisfying choices.
The restaurant does not take reservations, but once you are seated,
the atmosphere is relaxed, casual and unrushed, though not quiet.

Alcohol: Beer and wine. **Price range:** Apps., $6–$9; entrees,
$13–$16; desserts, $6–$7. **Wheelchair access:** Fully accessible.

Lil' Frankie's Pizza $25 & Under   PIZZA

19 First Ave. (near 2nd St.)   (212) 420-4900
Credit cards: Cash only   Meals: L, D, LN

Lil' Frankie's oven, which is heated by burning wood, produces not only pizzas but pastas al forno, vegetables and even some desserts. The hive-shaped oven dominates a small but bustling front room of booths and mosaics. In the rear is a larger but equally close-packed room that gets loud when crowded. The pizza toppings here are excellent. But the crust, wafer-thin and crisp, is almost flavorless. While the pizzas show room for improvement, other dishes that emerge from the oven are superb. Service is friendly and there is a nice selection of inexpensive Italian wines, like a raspy, fruity aglianico from Campania.

Other recommended dishes: Whole branzino, roasted chicken, Caprese salad, fava bean and dandelion soup, Nutella focaccino. **Price range:** Apps., $4–$7; pizzas and entrees, $6–$14. **Wheelchair access:** Step at front; restroom is narrow.

L'Impero   ☆ ☆ ☆ $$$ ITALIAN

45 Tudor City Pl. (near 42nd St.)   (212) 599-5045
Credit cards: All major   Meals: L, D   Closed Sun.

L'Impero digs deeply into the robust, generous spirit of the Italian countryside, turning out dishes full of flavors that are joyous and highly refined, served in a dining room that emanates a gracious warmth. Though you can opt for a conventional appetizer-main course approach, L'Impero's $48 tasting menu is a great alternative.

It's hard to imagine a more satisfying appetizer than a pool of creamy polenta, served with a small copper pot of fricasseed mushroom. Flavors grow louder and more assertive in the pastas. Spaghetti with sea urchin is piquant and distinct. Main courses quietly satisfy rather than excite. An exception is roasted capretto, or baby goat, a robust dish with potatoes and artichokes. Venison is tender and luxurious with chestnut spaetzle, while a seared fillet of branzino over rosemary-scented lentils is moist and full of flavor.

If L'Impero has a weak point, it is the desserts. Slender sesame cannoli are decent, and chocolate "soup" is both as awful and delicious as it sounds. *(Eric Asimov)*

Other recommended dishes: Cranberry bean soup, roasted lobster with chickpeas, stewed octopus, roasted quail, black pasta with seafood, farfalle with sweetbreads, duck and foie gras agnolotti, spaghetti with tomato and basil, roasted cod. **Wine list:** Excellent; mostly Italian, but many French and American bottles, too. **Price range:** Apps., $8–$15; pastas, $13–$25; entrees, $19–$29; desserts, $7.50–$9.50. Prix fixe: lunch, $42; dinner, $49. **Wheelchair access:** Wheelchair entrance through lobby.

Little Havana $25 & Under   CUBAN/CARIBBEAN

30 Cornelia St. (bet. Bleecker & W. 4th Sts.)   (212) 255-2212
Credit cards: All major   Meals: D   Closed Mon.

This restaurant combines classic Cuban dishes with an appreciation for organic, healthful ingredients. The result is lighter Cuban food that sacrifices none of the flavor. Ceviche is a sterling appetizer, especially when the flavor of the shrimp is activated by a splash of the hot sauce served in tiny pitchers, and lentil soup is wonderfully subtle. The menu is small, befitting the size of the restaurant, but the main courses include a couple of terrific choices. Sautéed shrimp is superbly shrimpy, and filet mignon is tender and buttery. Roast pork, a Cuban staple, seems dry at first, but it comes to life with tomatillo sauce. The one real disappointment was tamales with an odd flavor and not much pork in the stuffing. Service is solicitous and caring.

Other recommended dishes: Market salad, kale and butternut squash, sautéed boneless chicken breast, cheesecake. **Alcohol:** Beer and wine. **Price range:** Apps., $6–$9; entrees, $10–$15. **Wheelchair access:** Steps in front; restroom is very narrow.

The Little Place $25 & Under MEXICAN

73 W. Broadway (at Warren St.) (212) 528-3175
Credit cards: Cash only. Meals: B, L, D Closed Sat. & Sun.

This is no more than a small counter with another half-dozen stools opposite, serving homespun Mexican dishes and soups, sandwiches and breakfasts. The tamales are especially good: moist chicken encased in a tube of corn dough steamed in a corn husk and painted with either a complex mole sauce or a tangy green salsa made with tomatillos. The Little Place also serves excellent chili made with ground beef and black beans, and terrific soups like savory potato-spinach.

Other recommended dishes: Beef or chicken fajitas. **Wheelchair access:** Not accessible. **Specials:** Take out, delivery.

Locanda Vini & Olii $25 & Under ITALIAN

129 Gates Ave., Clinton Hill, Brooklyn (718) 622-9202
Credit cards: Cash only Meals: D Closed Mon.

This mom-and-pop trattoria was a pharmacy for 130 years. The woodwork has been lovingly restored, and many old features have been left intact, like small wooden apothecary drawers, rolling wood ladders and old counters used for a small bar and to display desserts. Even so, if it were one more trattoria with the same old food, it would provoke yawns. But Locanda's menu is full of surprising dishes.

Superb choices abound among the pastas, especially the maltagliati, fat strands of carrot-colored pasta in a light ricotta sauce with soft fava beans, diced prosciutto and sage. Beyond pasta, Locanda offers a small, changing selection of main courses like tender braised pork ribs, or excellent braised lamb, baked in a small round bread. The small list of wines includes some excellent choices from little-known producers. The best dessert may have been the simplest: small circular biscotti, flavored with anise and barely sweet.

Other recommended dishes: Shrimp with chickpeas, seafood charcuterie, bresaola with pears, venison cacciatorino, lasagna with chickpea and sausage sauce, guitar-string pasta with sardine, dill and raisin sauce, penne with walnut sauce, pappardelle with duck ragú, pici with porcinis, ricotta cheesecake with rose water. **Price range:** Apps., $5–$8; entrees, $6–$16. **Wheelchair access:** Two steps at entrance; restroom is narrow.

Lola $$$ NEW AMERICAN
30 W. 22nd St. (bet. Fifth & Sixth Aves.)   (212) 675-6700
Credit cards: All major   Meals: Br, L, D, LN

This is a festive place that presents American cooking with a touch of soul and a touch of Asia. Lola also offers three seatings for its popular gospel brunch on Sundays. The brunch menu includes caramelized banana hallah french toast, smoked trout with goat cheese and scrambled eggs, and poached eggs with yuca hash. Apple charlotte mousse cake and maple walnut streusel cake are some of the desserts.

Price range: Two-course prix-fixe lunch, $20. Gospel brunch, $30. Dinner: apps., $9–$13; entrees, $23–$35; desserts, $9. **Features:** Outdoor dining.

Lombardi's $25 & Under   PIZZA
32 Spring St. (bet. Mulberry & Mott Sts.)   (212) 941-7994
Credit cards: Cash only   Meals: L, D, LN

The dining room reeks of history at this reincarnation of the original Lombardi's, which is often credited with introducing pizza to New York City. The old-fashioned coal-oven pizza is terrific, with a light, thin, crisp and gloriously smoky crust topped with fine mozzarella and tomatoes. The garlicky clam pizza is exceptional.

Alcohol: Beer and wine. **Price range:** Apps., $8.50; pizzas, $12.50–$20. **Wheelchair access:** Fully accessible. **Features:** Outdoor dining.

Lomzynianka $25 & Under   POLISH
646 Manhattan Ave., Greenpoint, Brooklyn   (718) 389-9439
Credit cards: Cash only.   Meals: L, D

Any number of Polish restaurants line the streets of Greenpoint, and one of the best is Lomzynianka (pronounced Lahm-zhin-YAHN-eh-ka). The small dining room has the look of authenticity that comes only from artificiality: brick wallpaper, plastic tablecloths, fake plants and a stag's head with tinsel-draped antlers.

Salad and soup, supplemented by rye bread, is almost enough for a meal. Main courses, generally rustic dishes, include tender boiled beef that is a perfect vehicle for a mildly sharp horseradish sauce. Try the bigos, a traditional stew for leftovers, here made with sauerkraut, dill and extremely tender chunks of boiled beef. Given the attractive cafes in the neighborhood, it might be tempting to go elsewhere for dessert, but the blintzes are too good for that.

Other recommended dishes: Borschts, potato pancakes, veal meatballs with dill sauce, stuffed cabbage, chicken cutlet. **Price range:** Apps., $1–$4; entrees, $3–$6. **Wheelchair access:** Not accessible.

Long Tan $25 & Under   THAI

196 Fifth Ave., Park Slope, Brooklyn   (718) 622-8444
Credit cards: MC/V   Meals: D, LN

At Long Tan, a team of Thai cooks work the woks in the open
kitchen, stirring and tossing with flames leaping above their heads.
There are a number of wonderful dishes, like the broad noodle with
beef, which is described on the menu as a "Thai Bolognese." The
massaman lamb curry is brothy and creamy with coconut milk. The
yellow curry is like a spiced elixir with cubes of butternut squash
and beads of corn. One dessert stands out: a warm heap of rice flavored with coconut milk, with a mango half sliced and turned
inside out (a technique called the hedgehog; you will see why). It is
a good idea to come thirsty. The litchi martini and a full-bodied and
citrusy plum wine sangria lead a long list of drinks. A thoughtful
wine list follows. *(Amanda Hesser)*

Other recommended dishes: Crab and mango summer roll, shredded duck with frisée and anise. **Price range:** Apps., $4–$8; entrees,
$7–$13. **Wheelchair access:** Step at entrance.

Los Dos Rancheros $25 & Under   MEXICAN

507 Ninth Ave. (at 38th St.)   (212) 868-7780
Credit cards: Cash only   Meals: B, L, D

The dining room may be bare-bones (unpretentious is an under-
statement), but the restaurant serves authentic, delicious Mexican
fare, like pollo con pipián, chicken with a fiery green sauce made of
ground pumpkin seeds, and excellent soft tacos with fillings ranging
from chicken to braised pork to tongue and goat.

Alcohol: Beer and wine. **Price range:** Apps., $1–$2; entrees, $2–$8;
desserts, $2.

Lot 61 $$ NEW AMERICAN

550 W. 21st St. (bet. 10th & 11th Aves.)   (212) 243-6555
Credit cards: All major   Meals: D, LN

Some places just can't decide whether they want to be galleries,
bars or restaurants. Lot 61, a cavernous room filled with low-slung
sofas and cocktail tables, is among them. The huge former garage is
filled with good art that was commissioned for the site. It serves
good food, too, of the upscale snack variety. With everything from
figs and foie gras to french fries, this is bar food with attitude.

Price range: Apps., $6–$15; entrees, $12–$20; desserts, $5–$7. Tasting menu, $35. **Wheelchair access:** Fully accessible.

Lotus   ☆ $$$$ NEW AMERICAN

409 W. 14th St. (near Ninth Ave.)   (212) 243-4420
Credit cards: All major   Meals: D   Closed Sun. & Mon.

Lotus serves New American cuisine with global accents in a coolly
styled dining room that feels more like a bar and lounge than a
restaurant. Lotus in the meatpacking district, has dispensed with
the red carpet out front. It has also replaced its menu with food
inspired by the cooking of several Southeast Asian countries.

Wine list: Medium-size, with pricey Champagnes and offbeat New World selections. **Price range:** Three-course prix fixe, $55; five-course tasting menu, $75, seven-course tasting menu, $100. **Wheelchair access:** One level.

Lozoo ☆ $$ CHINESE
140 W. Houston (near Sullivan St.) (646) 602-8888
Credit cards: All major Meals: D

Lozoo, a coolly contemporary restaurant and lounge that specializes in refined Shanghai cooking, is idiosyncratic, ambitious and nervy. Lozoo, whose name means green tea in Mandarin, presents the kind of dishes that might be served at a banquet in Shanghai. The play of textures is complex and deceptive. Three kinds of baby eggplant, cut into long strips and sautéed, share the plate with identical lengths of firm, chewy rice gluten that impersonate the eggplant. One of the best appetizers is baby escargots in crispy tofu. Also try the poached pork belly with marinated bamboo strips and fat tsai, a fuzzy black tree fungus. No one walks into a Chinese restaurant anticipating a great dessert, but Lozoo confounds expectations with a truly memorable crepe cake.

Other recommended dishes: Poached mushrooms, crab in whipped egg white, tea-smoked chicken. **Wine list:** Workmanlike list of 25 wines. **Price range:** Apps., $5–$11; entrees, $15–$20; desserts, $3–$7. **Wheelchair access:** Wheelchair lift.

Luca $25 & Under ITALIAN
1712 First Ave. (near 89th St.) (212) 987-9260
Credit cards: MC/V Meals: D

This superb neighborhood Italian restaurant is spare but good-looking, with beige walls and rustic floor tiles. The menu offers dishes skillfully cooked to order that emphasize lusty flavors. The antipasto for two is very generous and very good. Pastas, like bigoli with a buttery shrimp-and-radicchio sauce, are terrific, as are main courses like grilled calamari and crisp grilled Cornish hen.

Other recommended dishes: Warm pear and Gorgonzola tart, bigoli al ragu d'agnello, ravioli with pumpkin, risotto with shrimp and asparagus, grilled calamari, Cornish hen, potato-crusted salmon, granita. **Price range:** Apps., $6–$12; entrees, $9–$24. **Wheelchair access:** All one level.

Luca Lounge $25 & Under ITALIAN/PIZZA
220 Ave. B (near 13th St.) (212) 674-9400
Credit cards: Cash only Meals: D, LN Closed Mon.

If further evidence is needed of the encroaching gentrification of Alphabet City, look no farther than Luca Lounge. As busy as the bar area is here, you can still find tranquillity in the big, pretty garden on two levels in the rear and in the narrow, paneled dining room. You can also find a selection of excellent antipasti and salads (especially radicchio with tuna, olives and tomatoes, and spinach with pecorino cheese and sweet green apples), served individually or in family portions, and little pizzas with wafer-thin, very crisp crusts and a small selection of traditional toppings.

Wheelchair access: Step to entrance.

Lucien $25 & Under   BISTRO/FRENCH
14 First Ave. (bet. 1st & 2nd Sts.)   (212) 260-6481
Credit cards: AE   Meals: L, D, LN

This crowded, somewhat disheveled little French place serves old-fashioned homey meals. The menu is familiar, but the prices are modest and, best of all, the cooking is for the most part very well executed. One of the best main courses is lapin moutarde, tasty, tender pieces of rabbit in a creamy mustard sauce over egg noodles. Desserts are superb, especially a fabulous tarte Tatin.

Other recommended dishes: Fish soup, sandwiches, bavette (flank steak), passion fruit tart. **Alcohol:** Beer and wine. **Price range:** Avg. lunch, $8–$9; dinner, $15; dessert, $6. **Wheelchair access:** Fully accessible.

L'Ulivo Focacceria $ ITALIAN/PIZZA
184 Spring St. (bet. Thompson & Sullivan Sts.)   (212) 431-1212
Credit cards: Cash only   Meals: L, D, LN

This is an upscale focacceria serving thin-crust pizza, pasta and the like in an attractively Italian setting. Pizzas come in a dozen varieties; there are also various kinds of carpaccio, vitello tonnato, salads, a few desserts and various wines. And the espresso is excellent. The small room (52 seats) is very attractive and prices are reasonable, making this a fine place to stop for a snack when you are in SoHo.

Alcohol: Beer and wine. **Price range:** Apps., $8–$12; entrees, $12–$16; desserts, $5; pizza, $11–$12. **Wheelchair access:** Fully accessible.

Lunchbox Food Company $25 & Under
DINER/AMERICAN
357 West St. (near Clarkson St.)   (646) 230-9466
Credit cards: All major   Meals: B, Br, L, D, LN

The Lunchbox Food Company is one fine-looking diner, yet this is no humble coffee shop. Lunchbox takes a connoisseur's attitude toward ingredients and preparations, but offers simple, tasty food for reasonable prices. Partisans of the classic tuna sandwich might sneer at the fancy-pants tuna blended with sherry vinaigrette and layered with roasted tomatoes and almond-arugula pesto on grilled olive bread. But what sounds overly complex is pure pleasure in the mouth. Lunchbox doesn't mess around with its burger. It is juicy and full of flavor, and served on a glossy brioche roll. For dinner, try tea-smoked cod hash, served with frisée, bacon, toasts and a poached egg. Desserts are inconsistent. But a thin, fudgy dark chocolate brownie is superb, as is chocolate bread pudding.

Other recommended dishes: French country salad, roasted beet soup, chicken salad sandwich, brussels sprouts, red wine and lavender steak, French toast. **Price range:** Breakfast, $1.75–$5.75. Lunch, $7–$10. Dinner: small dishes, $6–$10; large dishes, $15–$22. **Wheelchair access:** Three steps at entrance, narrow corridor to restrooms. **Features:** Outdoor dining.

Lupa $25 & Under   ITALIAN
170 Thompson St. (at Houston St.)   (212) 982-5089
Credit cards: All major   Meals: L, D

Word has gotten out about the intensely delicious Roman trattoria food, the breadth of the wine list and the warmth of the staff at Lupa, so it can be as crowded and clamorous as a Roman rush hour. Appetizers range from the classic to the bizarre. Prosciutto di Parma arrives in thin, nutty slices, while beet carpaccio is not only amusing, but also delicious. Pastas are simple and tasty, like spicy spaghetti with oil, garlic and hot pepper. Saltimbocca, thin slices of veal layered with prosciutto, is good and juicy, while crisply fried baccala with fennel and mint is unusual and delicious. Lupa's 130-bottle wine list seems to explore every little-known nook of Italy, but the resident wine expert takes great delight in directing you to the perfect choice. The best dessert choice is something from the cheese tray.

Other recommended dishes: Bavette with caciocavallo cheese and pepper, sardines, ricotta with Sardinian honey. **Price range:** Apps., $5–$9; entrees, $9–$15. **Wheelchair access:** Step in front; restrooms are narrow. **Features:** Two tables for outdoor dining.

Lutèce   ☆☆ $$$$ FRENCH
249 E. 50th St.   (212) 752-2225
Credit cards: All major   Meals: L, D

One of the oldest, most celebrated French restaurants in New York, Lutèce was always a byword for refined cuisine and high style. The new Lutèce tries to project a fresher, more contemporary image while retaining an old-fashioned sense of luxury and formality. The chaste, very elegant dining room retains the garden motif.

Chef David Féau brings a youthful touch to a classic French style, with respectful innovations that never violate good taste. Certain dishes convince you that Lutèce has found the right chef to bring it back to the first rank, especially pommes soufflés, and sautéed black bass with a rich vanilla jus. Mr. Féau integrates Asian spices and ingredients with a fine hand. Among the desserts, a superior pistachio soufflé with sour cherries and a tart cherry sorbet stands head and shoulders above its confrères.

The service at Lutèce remains an anachronism. In the restaurant's very limited confines, many captains move about, trying to stay out of the way of white-jacketed members of the lower orders. The captains radiate charm and good humor, but the whole system suggests severe overmanning.

Wine list: An impressive if uneven list of more than 400 wines, mostly French, with about 35 half-bottles and 15 wines by the glass. **Price range:** Lunch: three-course prix fixe, $38. Dinner: three-course prix fixe, $72. **Wheelchair access:** Two steps down to narrow entrance. Restrooms are one flight up.

Luxia $$ CONTINENTAL

315 W. 48th St. (bet. Eighth & Ninth Aves.)   (212) 957-0800
Credit cards: All major   Meals: L, D, LN

A pleasant garden, an inviting tiled bar and solicitous service make Luxia an attractive choice in the theater district. The menu qualifies as continental — European without any distinct ethnicity — and the food is decent though not memorable.

Price range: Apps., $6–$13; entrees, $13–$24. **Wheelchair access:** Fully accessible. **Features:** Outdoor dining.

Luzia's $25 & Under   PORTUGUESE

429 Amsterdam Ave. (bet. 80th & 81st Sts.)   (212) 595-2000
Credit cards: All major   Meals: Br, L, D   Closed Mon.

One of New York's Portuguese restaurants began life as a takeout place. Then the neighborhood fell in love with the small restaurant and started staying for dinner. Larger than it used to be but still cozy, Luzia's serves wonderful Portuguese comfort food, like caldo verde, shrimp pie and cataplana, the soupy stew of pork and clams. It also produces remarkably delicious non-Portuguese dishes, like beef brisket that is tender and peppery. Luzia's has great flan, and a nice list of Portuguese wines.

Other recommended dishes: White bean salad, clams and mussels; shrimp pie, grilled sausage, bacalhau, braised chicken legs, Portuguese steak, chocolate hazelnut cake, fruitcake. **Alcohol:** Beer and wine. **Price range:** $20–$25. **Wheelchair access:** All one level. **Features:** Outdoor dining.

Maeda Sushi $$$ SUSHI

16 E. 41st St. (bet. Fifth & Madison Aves.)   (212) 685-4293
Credit cards: All major   Meals: L, D

Maeda Sushi is absolutely traditional. Although the kitchen makes a few concessions to non-Japanese customers by offering some non-sushi dishes, this is not the place to try tempura. It is, however, a fine sushi bar, the sort of restaurant that would reward the effort of making yourself known to Maeda-san. If you do, you can probably snag those great slices of kanpachi.

Price range: Apps., $6–$14; entrees, $15–$45; desserts, $4–$5. Tasting menu, $80. **Wheelchair access:** Not accessible.

Malaysian Rasa Sayang $$ PAN-ASIAN

75-19 Broadway, Jackson Heights, Queens   (718) 424-9054
Credit cards: Cash only   Meals: L, D   Closed Tue.

A blend of Malay, Chinese and Indian, with dashes of Thai and even Portuguese, Malaysian is one of the great polyglot food cultures and therefore fits right into the complicated ethnic puzzle of Queens. The restaurant presents a modest face. The color and drama are found in the kitchen, where the cooking is fresh, vibrant and fiery. On one visit, the waiter tried to protect a group of diners from the menu. "Too strong flavored for you," he said about the sambal shrimp, a spicy stir-fry of minced chilies, scallions, galangal and shrimp in a potent shrimp-paste stock. Strong flavored was exactly right. He forgot to add sublime. Asam laksa, another stand-out, is Malaysia's meal in a bowl, a spicy sweet-sour fish soup with fat round noodles and crunchy strips of cucumber. Milder dishes are just as impressive.

Price range: Entrees, $5–$20. **Wheelchair access:** Fully accessible.

Maloney & Porcelli ☆ $$$ SEAFOOD/STEAKHOUSE
37 E. 50th St. (bet. Park & Madison Aves.)   (212) 750-2233
Credit cards: All major   Meals: L, D

This is a comfortable, wood-toned, masculine room decorated with eagles and filled with lawyers and investment bankers. This is theme eating for grown-ups, a place where the food is more fun to discuss than consume. Crackling pork shank is an original and delicious dish, a great ball of meat, deep fried until the skin turns into cracklings, then slowly roasted. A hefty grilled rib eye comes with the bone sticking over the edge of the plate, and sirloin steaks are crusty and flavorful. End the meal with drunken doughnuts: warm twists of sugar-dusted dough and three pots of liquor-laced jam. (*Ruth Reichl*)

Wine list: Good and fairly priced, with an innovative list of 40 wines under $40. **Price range:** Apps., $8–$15; entrees, $19–$32; desserts, $8. **Wheelchair access:** Fully accessible. **Features:** Outdoor dining.

Mama's Food Shop $25 & Under   AMERICAN
200 E. 3rd St. (bet. Aves. A & B)   (212) 777-4425
Credit cards: Cash only   Meals: L, D   Closed Sun.

This is a simple takeout shop and restaurant where you point at what you want and they dish it up, but the food is outstanding: grilled salmon, fried chicken and meatloaf. Vegetable side dishes are especially good, like brussels sprouts, carrots, beets and mashed potatoes.

Price range: Entrees, $8–$11; desserts, $3. **Wheelchair access:** Fully accessible.

Mandoo Bar $25 & Under   KOREAN
2 W. 32nd St. (bet. Fifth & Sixth Aves.)   (212) 279-3075
Credit cards: All major   Meals: L, D

Mandoo is the Korean word for dumplings, and as you enter past a glass-enclosed kitchen, you can see the chefs rolling and cutting dough, stuffing and folding it. Start with a platter of baby mandoo, bite-size half-moons stuffed with beef, pork and leeks and notable for a wrapper so sheer that it is almost transparent. Or try crisp, savory pan-fried mandoo, filled with pork and minced cabbage. Dumplings account for half the dishes on the menu, but some of the best selections are not dumplings at all. Fried tofu makes an excellent appetizer (hot pepper sauce gives them a jolt). Bibimbop, a casserole of rice, vegetables and ground beef served in a stone crock, is fresh, light and delicate.

173

The spare, handsome dining room is filled with blond wood tables, which have cushioned benches rather than chairs. Service is swift and courteous, and food arrives quickly.

Other recommended dishes: Casserole with rice cakes, cellophane noodles, fish cakes and hot sauce, pa jun. **Price range:** Apps., $4–$9; entrees, $6–$24. **Wheelchair access:** Steps at entrance and to restrooms.

Manetta's $25 & Under   PIZZA/ITALIAN
10-76 Jackson Ave. (near 50th Ave.), Long Island City, Queens
   (718) 786-6171
Credit cards: All major   Meals: L, D   Closed Sun.

At Manetta's in Long Island City, pizzas are delivered by waiters of the professional diner-staff variety. At night, when the room plays host to families and visitors to the neighborhood's budding art scene, the liquid of choice is the house red, tannic, harsh on the throat, absolutely agreeable. Traditional starters are all believable. There are also pasta entrees, a decent if uninspired collection that runs to penne with smoked salmon and cream and fettuccine with Bolognese sauce. But the best thing about Manetta's is the pizza. From the brick oven by the door come thin-crusted single-portion pies of high quality and low price that would probably rate as the best in any city in the United States save this one. Here, it falls in the upper middle of a crowded top tier: Manetta's sits above, say, Arturo's on Houston Street, but somewhere below Grimaldi's in Brooklyn Heights. *(Sam Sifton)*

Other recommended dishes: Caesar salad, alla diavlo pizza, heros. **Price range:** Apps., $4–$7.50; pastas, $9–$15; sandwiches and pizzas, $5.50–$10. **Wheelchair access:** Fully accessible.

Manhattan Ocean Club   ☆☆ $$$$ SEAFOOD
57 W. 58th St. (bet. Fifth & Sixth Aves.)   (212) 371-7777
Credit cards: All major   Meals: L, D

Tony, comfortable and trim as a luxury yacht, this is the steakhouse of fish restaurants. It has a masculine air, and you sense that the people who come here would rather eat steak, but their doctors won't let them. Eating here is an indulgence; the prices are high, especially if you begin with a shellfish bouquet for which you are charged for each clam, shrimp and oyster. Soups like the creamy clam chowder are less expensive but no less delicious (the fish soup is so intense it is almost a meal in itself). The simple preparations are the most appealing here but one of my favorite dishes is the oysters buried in tiny morels covered with cream and baked in the shell. The dish is an edible definition of luxury. Desserts are almost all big and sweet. *(Ruth Reichl)*

Wine list: White wines from California and France dominate the list, which is good and fairly priced. **Price range:** Lunch: apps., $8–$14; entrees, $20–$27; desserts, $9; summer prix-fixe lunch, $20. Dinner: apps., $9–$31; entrees, $23–$30; desserts, $10. **Wheelchair access:** Not accessible.

Man Ray ☆ $$$

NEW AMERICAN

147 W. 15th St. (bet. Sixth & Seventh Aves.)   (212) 929-5000
Credit cards: All major   Meals: D

Man Ray ought to have the DNA of a velvet-rope restaurant. The
Parisian original is a celebrity magnet. Man Ray is not like that,
though. The welcome at the door is warm. The servers, in contrast
to the layered hipness of the décor, talk like ordinary people and
seem eager to please. Somewhere along the line, Man Ray decided
that a restaurant does not have to sneer to be stylish.

The louche stage-set interior, with its ruby reds and jade greens,
almost demands a little theatricality on the menu. But the sushi
menu plays it perfectly straight. The quality is good, too. Two fish
entrees stand out: turbot with a crust of goat-cheese Gouda, and
Arctic char, slow-baked to a pinkish-orange pearlescence. For a
temple of design, Man Ray has an awfully happy dessert menu. It's
as if Ron Howard seized control of the production. Chocolate-
peanut butter tart, a candy bar in disguise, takes full advantage of
one of the greatest flavor combinations known to the human palate.

Wine list: An international list of about 100 bottles, most organized
by price ($35, $65 and $95), with 15 wines by the glass. **Price
range:** Apps., $7–$15; entrees, $19–$29; sushi and sashimi plates,
$23–$34; sushi rolls, $5–$10; desserts, $9. **Wheelchair access:**
Fully accessible.

March ☆☆☆ $$$$

NEW AMERICAN

405 E. 58th St. (near First Ave.)   (212) 754-6272
Credit cards: All major   Meals: L, D

A romantic gem, March offers its patrons refined American cuisine
in a cozy, antique-filled town house. Its celebrated chef-owner,
Wayne Nish, has created an opportunity for culinary diversion by
replacing the usual three-course restaurant menu — appetizer,
entree and dessert — with one that allows you to choose several
smaller courses.

Extensive renovations have given March a new two-level dining area, with one room downstairs and the other, smaller room
on the mezzanine, both illuminated by a slanting skylight and
decorated with 17th-century Venetian botanical prints. The seats
have increased to 85 from 50. For all the changes, March retains
its intimate feel. On a recent visit Mr. Nish was still turning out
inspired food. The dessert menu includes sophisticated takes on
homey desserts, like butterscotch pot de crème with crème fraîche
and ginger snaps. *(Ruth Reichl, updated by William Grimes)*

Wine list: Excellent, with a wide variety of styles and prices. **Price
range:** Prix fixe lunch, $39. Dinner: four courses, $68 (with specially
selected wines, $108); five courses, $85 (with wines, $135); six
courses, $102 (with wines, $162). **Wheelchair access:** Dining room
up two small steps; restrooms down a steep flight of stairs. **Features:** Outdoor dining (terrace).

Marichu $$
BASQUE/SPANISH

342 E. 46th St. (bet. First & Second Aves.)   (212) 370-1866
Credit cards: All major   Meals: L, D

Unusual Basque dishes in an unusual location, near the United Nations, draw a crowd of diplomats and others interested in selections like clams in a garlic-and-wine sauce and tender baby squid served in a nutty sauce of leeks, onions, tomatoes and ink. Try the crowd-pleasing shrimp in sizzling garlic sauce, the fillet of red snapper in a garlic vinaigrette with scalloped potatoes, or red peppers stuffed with a creamy purée of codfish in an intense sauce made with dried red peppers.

Price range: Tapas, $2–$7; apps., $7–$9; entrees, $14–$24; desserts, $5–$7; prix-fixe, $32. **Wheelchair access:** Dining room is one step up; restrooms are narrow. **Features:** Outdoor dining.

MarkJoseph Steakhouse ☆ $$$ STEAKHOUSE

261 Water St. (Peck Slip)   (212) 277-0020
Credit cards: All major   Meals L, D   Closed Sun.

Situated in the South Street Seaport Historic District, MarkJoseph is a classic unbuttoned steakhouse, bustling, casual and masculine. The sound level is roughly equivalent to a boxing crowd when the dining room is full, especially in a few of the enclosed nooks.

Like Peter Luger, MarkJoseph is a porterhouse specialist, offering huge steaks that serve two, three or four people each. The steak is presliced, and the waiters quickly distribute the meat, spooning the juices over the slices. Here is where the resemblance to Luger ends, for while the porterhouse is remarkably tender, it cannot match the firm, chewy texture of the Luger porterhouse or its funky mineral-laden flavor. Fortunately, MarkJoseph goes beyond the porterhouse. Its rib steak, served unsliced on the bone, has an excellent, subtle dry-aged flavor. Sirloin steak, already sliced, is likewise densely flavored and pleasingly chewy. One worthy alternative to steak is an order of the meaty double lamb chops, massive yet delicately tender. All desserts are "mit schlag", and excellent schlag it is. Thick, rich and creamy, it's a fine accompaniment to a tart, supple Key lime pie. *(Eric Asimov)*

Wine list: Heavy on California cabernets, with a few excellent Spanish and Italian choices, but short on Bordeaux and pinot noirs. **Price range:** Apps., $2–$25; entrees, $19–$38; desserts, $7.50. **Wheelchair access:** Ramp available.

Maroons $25 & Under SOUTHERN/JAMAICAN

244 W. 16 St. (bet. Seventh & Eighth Aves.)   (212) 206-8640
Credit cards: All major   Meals: L, D, LN

Maroons is divided into a small, handsome dining room and a separate homey lounge. The menu, too, is a split proposition, neatly divided between Southern and Jamaican dishes. Appetizers are largely excellent, like meaty, spicy jerk chicken wings, and cod fritters that are tasty, light and puffy. From the South come fine little crab cakes and a generous pile of baby back ribs. Seafood entrees are especially enticing, like Jamaican fried fish and baked catfish, moist and positively beefy. Service is friendly but occasionally spacey.

Other recommended dishes: Yuca puffs, broiled snapper, oxtail ravioli, jerk chicken, carrot cake. **Wine list:** Unfortunately most bottles are $30–$35. **Price range:** Apps., $4–$8; entrees, $12–$19. **Wheelchair access:** One step at entrance.

Marseille ☆☆ $$$ FRENCH/MEDITERRANEAN

630 Ninth Ave. (near 44th St.) (212) 333-3410
Credit cards: All major Meals: D

Marseille is a spacious, confident-feeling brasserie on the western edge of the theater district. The chef likes the Moroccan aspect of Marseille, France's most Arab-influenced city. His enthusiasm is reflected in the look of the dining room, with its blue Moroccan floor tiles and apricot-colored walls, and in a fondness for cous-cous, preserved lemon, dates and lamb.

An ideal way to start a meal at Marseille is to order a meze plate and a glass of rosé. On average, two out of the three bites on the plates score high. The very rich seafood lasagna layered with crab meat, cockles and mussels in a buttery mussel sauce is a kind of seafood sandwich by other means, and it is a hard act to follow. One worthy competitor among the entrees is roasted chicken, marinated in olive oil, garlic and smoked paprika. Any discussion of the desserts must begin with the already renowned, or notorious, crunchy peanut butter tart. It's a play on one of America's most common snacks, a stalk of celery with peanut butter.

Wine list: About 130 modestly priced bottles with a bias toward country wines from the Mediterranean. There are 17 wines by the glass and a dozen half bottles. **Price range:** Apps., $7–$12; entrees, $16–$24; desserts, $7–$8; seven-course tasting menu, $65. **Wheelchair access:** One level.

Marumi $25 & Under JAPANESE/SUSHI

546 La Guardia Pl. (bet. 3rd & Bleecker Sts.) (212) 979-7055
Credit cards: All major Meals: L, D

This versatile, reliable Japanese restaurant near N.Y.U. offers a cross-section of casual Japanese dining. The service is swift, efficient and charming and will even go the extra mile in preventing bad choices. It's rare that you get such an interesting assortment of sushi at an inexpensive restaurant, like mirugai, or geoduck clam. Other worthwhile dishes are broiled eel, noodle soups and the economic bento box meals. The hefty tempura is about the only dish one might skip.

Alcohol: Beer. **Price range:** Apps., $4–$5; entrees, $9–$15; desserts, $3–$4. **Wheelchair access:** Restrooms not accessible.

Master Grill $25 & Under BRAZILIAN

34-09 College Point Blvd., Flushing, Queens (718) 762-0300
Credit cards: All major Meals: L, D

Possibly the most elaborate Brazilian rodizio in the city, Master Grill feels like an enormous banquet hall, with seating for 1,000 people and a samba band playing full tilt. It's all great fun if you're in the mood. The buffet itself is the size of a small restaurant, where you can fortify yourself with all manner of marinated vegetables, fruit, seafood, pasta, rolls, roasted potatoes and fried plantains. While the buffet dishes are nothing special, they are easy to fill up on before the meat starts arriving. The parade of all-you-can-eat grilled meats, from chicken hearts to six kinds of beef, goes on as long as you can hold out.

Price range: All you can eat, $19. **Wheelchair access:** All one level. **Features:** Parking available.

Max $25 & Under   ITALIAN
51 Ave. B (near 4th St.)   (212) 539-0111
Credit cards: Cash only   Meals: L, D, LN

A tiny Italian restaurant wholly without pretensions, it has been packed since it opened. The draw is exactly what has always attracted people to neighborhood restaurants: well-prepared food, served with warmth. Best of all, Max is cheap.

Max's buffalo-milk mozzarella is an excellent place to start. For the most part, Max's pastas are very enjoyable. Fettuccine al sugo Toscano has a wonderfully mellow meat sauce with layers of flavor that unfold in the mouth, while rigatoni Napoletano is served southern Italian style, with meatballs and sausages left intact in the sauce. Max has a brief list of wines under $25 and, oddly given the food prices, a broader selection for $25 to $40. Desserts include a good tiramisu and an excellent caramel panna cotta.

Other recommended dishes: Black linguine with shrimp, rigatoni alla Siciliana, rack of lamb, meatloaf Neopolitan style, osso buco, crème brûlée. **Price range:** Apps., $5–$9; entrees, $9–$15. **Wheelchair access:** Ramp to restroom.

Max SoHa $25 & Under   ITALIAN/AMERICAN
1274 Amsterdam Ave. (at 123rd St.)   (212) 531-2221
Credit cards: Cash only   Meals: L, D

Judging by the crowds waiting for tables outside this small, boxy restaurant near Columbia University, the neighborhood has clearly thirsted for a place like Max SoHa, which offers home-style dishes with few frills and no luxuries, other than a superior list of moderately priced Italian wines. It does not break culinary ground, but what it does, it does very well. Each of its three salads is a good choice. For more substantial appetizers, Max's fresh buffalo mozzarella is superb. It goes beautifully with thin slices of prosciutto or in the classic Caprese, with sweet fresh tomatoes and basil. Pastas are basic and served in the American fashion, under a deluge of sauce. They can be excellent, though. Specials change nightly, and may include sliced skirt steak, deliciously redolent of rosemary, or a breaded pork chop, the flawless equivalent of a crisp and greaseless pork schnitzel, topped with chopped tomatoes and arugula.

Other recommended dishes: Fennel salad, beets with goat cheese, green salad, gnocchi with tomato sauce, rigatoni al ragu Napoletano, fettuccine al sugo Toscano, penne with sausage and broccoli rabe. **Price range:** Apps., $5–$9; entrees, $9–$15. **Wheelchair access:** Not accessible.

Maya ☆☆ $$$ MEXICAN/TEX-MEX

1191 First Ave. (bet. 64th & 65th Sts.) (212) 585-1818
Credit cards: All major Meals: D

Some of New York's most interesting Mexican food is served in this
bright, festive but often noisy room. Although you can stick to margaritas and guacamole, you'll miss the best part if you don't try
some of the more unusual dishes. Rock shrimp ceviche is breath-
taking, the seafood salad simply delicious and I loved the roasted
corn soup with huitlacoche dumpling, the chunky guacamole and
the tacos al pastor, two little tortillas served with marinated pork
and fresh salsa. The most impressive main courses are chicken
mole (the dark sauce is truly complex) and pipian de puerco,
grilled pork marinated in tamarind and served on a bed of puréed
roasted corn. Desserts are not impressive, however; the flan is flat,
the sorbets too sweet. (*Ruth Reichl*)

Wine list: Negligible. Try the house margaritas or a shot of tequila
with a shot of sangrita (a tart mixture of juices). **Price range:**
Apps., $8–$10; entrees, $17–$25; desserts $6–$8. **Wheelchair
access:** All one level.

Meet ☆ $$$ NEW AMERICAN/MEDITERRANEAN

71-73 Gansevoort St. (at Washington St.) (212) 242-0990
Credit cards: All major Meals: D, LN

As its name suggests, Meet wants to be a place where people meet.
Ideally, these would be young, good-looking people. In an effort to
attract this crowd, the owners have fashioned a visually arresting
dining room. The interior designer failed to use a tape measure,
however. Tables are arranged to inflict maximum discomfort on diners, and they pose insurmountable challenges to waiters. Still, in
the meatpacking district, an area plagued with posturing and
underperforming restaurants, Meet shines with a virtuous light. It
wants to do the right thing, more or less.

Diners who keep their attention riveted on the plate will find
honest bistro fare with a contemporary spin. The kitchen is the
conscience of Meet. It seems fitting that the best desserts on the
menu should also be the plainest-sounding. Try the rice pudding
fritters or the juvenile ice cream sandwiches.

If you like to eat, come before 8, when the waiters still control
the operation. If you like to meet, come later.

Wine list: Limited, with a poor selection of wines by the glass.
Price range: Apps., $7–$14; entrees, $16–$24; desserts, $7–$8.
Wheelchair access: One level.

Mekong $25 & Under VIETNAMESE

44 Prince St. (near Mulberry St.) (212) 343-8169
Credit cards: All major Meals: L, D

The atmosphere at Mekong is thoroughly Americanized, with a
relaxed SoHo ambiance, but the food is authentically Vietnamese,
achieving a balance of flavors and textures highlighted by fresh
herbs and pungent fish sauce. Grilled pork with lemongrass over
rice noodles and stewed fish in a fiery caramel sauce are two of the

better dishes. Mekong also offers a well-chosen, moderately priced wine list.

Other recommended dishes: Shredded chicken salad; steamed rice crepes; grilled shrimp with sugar cane; shrimp rolls; hot-and-sour fish soup; beef with black pepper, butter and onions; squid with curry sauce; chicken with green peppers; seitan with green peppers. **Price range:** Entrees, $10–$22. **Wheelchair access:** All one level. **Features:** Outdoor dining.

Meltemi $25 & Under   GREEK/SEAFOOD

905 First Ave. (at 51st St.)   (212) 355-4040
Credit cards: All major   Meals: L, D

This friendly Greek restaurant offers big portions of simply pre-pared seafood, like grilled octopus with oil and lemon, and typical Greek offerings like grilled whole porgy and red mullet. Appetizers are generous, and two portions can easily feed four people. Grilled seafood is the centerpiece here; and the grilled shrimp is served butterflied, full of flavor and so delicate you can even eat the shell. The enthusiastic staff adds to Meltemi's enjoyable atmosphere.

Other recommended dishes: Assortment of cold spreads, loukanika laconias, Greek salad, beets in vinaigrette, swordfish steak, tuna steak, desserts. **Price range:** Lunch: apps., $5–$10; entrees, $11–$15; desserts, $4. Dinner: apps., $6–$10; entrees, $15–$29. **Wheelchair access:** Restrooms not accessible.

Menchanko-Tei $25 & Under   JAPANESE/NOODLES

43 W. 55th St. (bet. Fifth & Sixth Aves.)   (212) 247-1585
131 E. 45th St. (bet. Lexington & Third Aves.)   (212) 986-6805
Credit cards: All major   Meals: B, L, D, LN

Great big bowls of noodles are the thing at Menchanko-Tei, which means House of Mixed Noodles in Japanese. The house special, fat egg noodles in a fragrant chicken broth, is full of shrimp, little rice cakes and ground fish. Japanese business executives seem to have found homes away from home at the Midtown branches of this noodle shop. The food is authentic and inexpensive. It's especially good if you can get someone to translate the specials, written only in Japanese.

Alcohol: Beer and wine. **Price range:** Apps., $3–$8; entrees, $7–$13; desserts, $3. **Wheelchair access:** Fully accessible.

Mercer Kitchen   ☆☆ $$$$ FRENCH

Mercer Hotel, 99 Prince St. (at Mercer St.)   (212) 966-5454
Credit cards: All major   Meals: B, L, D, LN

The SoHo location and Vongerichten connection ensure a steady flow of customers who imagine they are eating at one of Manhat-tan's hipper restaurants. Time, however, has not been particularly kind to the Mercer Kitchen, which is riding on its once cutting-edge reputation. The menu feels dated, and the kitchen does only a pass-able job with dishes like crab fritters in three dipping sauces, grilled squid salad with sweet chili sauce, and a squishy, over-steamed skate flavored with tarragon and unpleasantly crusted with sesame seeds. There's help at hand on the dessert menu, which boasts a terrific caramelized banana cake and glazed ricotta cheesecake with cherries poached in wine. The last two steps down into the murky dining room are absolutely treacherous. *(Review by William Grimes; stars previously awarded by Ruth Reichl.)*

Wine list: Interesting, affordable and very well chosen for the food. **Price range:** Lunch: apps., $8–$14; entrees, $9–$15. Dinner: apps., $9–$15; entrees, $19–$35; desserts, $8. **Wheelchair access:** Restaurant is in a basement, but has an elevator.

Merge $25 & Under   NEW AMERICAN
142 W. 10th St. (near Greenwich Ave.)   (212) 691-7757
Credit cards: AE   Meals: D

The music at Merge is too loud, and the dining area is too close to the bar, but the service is friendly and efficient, and best of all, the food is not only delicious but also a great value. Appetizers are especially good. The notion of sushi fruit salad may not inspire immediate hosannas, but the combination of coconut and mango with Asian coleslaw and thin slices of tuna and salmon is an extraordinary blend of flavors and textures. Hanger steak is juicy and beefy, and the fine pan-roasted cod is worth ordering just for the accompaniments of braised cabbage, bacon and garlic potato chips. The wine list includes a few good choices under $30, but most cost more. Desserts also include some winners, like a sweet potato panna cotta with a caramel sauce. For a truly retro experience, you can make your own s'mores at the table.

Other recommended dishes: Fried oysters, roasted pork chops. **Price range:** Apps., $6–$8; entrees, $15–$20. **Wheelchair access:** Entrance and dining on one level; restrooms are down a flight.

Mermaid Inn $25 & Under   SEAFOOD
96 Second Ave. (near 5th St.)   (212) 674-5870
Credit cards: All major   Meals: D, LN

The Mermaid Inn offers a dead-on rendition of a casual fish shack, where the simple preparations and small, intelligent wine list meet all the style and attitude requirements of the East Village. The front room has maybe two dozen seats and a bar with weathered beams and old marine charts. A larger rear room eases the crowding, but the acoustics in the room, with its high-timbered ceiling and brick walls, are dreadful. To start, clam fritters are puffed up to the size of tennis balls and are delicious with a tangy lemon rémoulade. Fried oysters are simple and satisfying, as is a classic shrimp cocktail. Smartly the main courses are kept simple, while paying close attention to seasoning. Seared scallops benefit merely from being well salted and peppered. Dorade royale, stuffed with herbs and served whole, is moist and flavorful. Mermaid has decided not to offer a dessert menu. Instead, the kitchen sends out a free demitasse of chocolate or butterscotch pudding.

Other recommended dishes: Raw oysters, barbecued shrimp, sardines, crisp skate, Old Bay fries. **Price range:** Apps., $6–$12; entrees, $14–$21. **Wheelchair access:** All one level. **Features:** Outdoor dining.

181

Mesa Grill ☆☆ $$$$ SOUTHWESTERN

102 Fifth Ave. (bet. 15th & 16th Sts.) (212) 807-7400
Credit cards: All major Meals: Br, L, D

An instant hit on opening its doors in 1991, Mesa Grill is still a
downtown favorite, crowded and clamorous at lunch, and even
more crowded and clamorous at night. Despite the cookbooks, the
television shows, and a second restaurant, Bolo, chef-owner Bobby
Flay has somehow managed to keep Mesa Grill alive and kicking.

Mr. Flay goes after big flavors and he knows how to get them.
The thick, reduced bourbon and ancho chili glaze on his pork tenderloins, for example, is a swirl of sweetness, smoke and spice. He
also uses chilies and spices for flavor, not for heat. Sixteen-spice
chicken sounds like a tongue-scorcher. It turns out to be a subtly
handled, tingling orchestration of flavors. Mr. Flay has kept only
one dish from bygone years, a corn tamale stuffed with corn and
firm, flavorful shrimp, in a roasted garlic sauce. It is the house classic — simple, straightforward and irresistible.

Mesa Grill is not the restaurant for a heart-to-heart talk, but it's
ideal for a screaming fight. A good way to get one going is to cruise
the margarita list. It is an inspirational document, and a rebuke to
the appalling inventions that have made the drink synonymous
with everyone's worst cocktail memory.

Wine list: About 90 American wines, 14 by the glass. **Price range:**
Lunch: apps., $7–$11; entrees, $11–$19; desserts, $8–$9. Dinner:
apps., $8–$14; entrees, $19–$33; desserts, $8–$9. **Wheelchair
access:** Restrooms on street level.

Meskerem $25 & Under AFRICAN/ETHIOPIAN

468 W. 47th St. (bet. Ninth & 10th Aves.) (212) 664-0520
Credit cards: All major Meals: L, D, LN

A meal at Meskerem, a plain, almost generic restaurant, demon-
strates how good Ethiopian food can be. The stews, which are
eaten with pieces of a spongy sourdough bread called injera, are
intensely spicy but three-dimensionally so, with flavors that build
and change in the mouth.

Alcohol: Beer and wine. **Price range:** Avg. app., $4; entree, $8–$11;
dessert, $3. **Wheelchair access:** Fully accessible.

Metisse $25 & Under BISTRO/FRENCH

239 W. 105th St. (bet. Amsterdam Ave. & Broadway) (212) 666-8825
Credit cards: All major Meals: D

A true neighborhood restaurant with an owner who prowls his
small dining room relentlessly to make sure all is well. Main
courses seem less consistent than the appetizers, but roast chicken
is superior, flavored with rosemary and served in a vinaigrette with
crisp sliced potatoes and braised carrots. Roast leg of lamb and
pork medallions are also good. Desserts count for something, too,
especially the warm chocolate cake with the runny inside, and the
brioche topped with caramelized apples and caramel sauce.

Other recommended dishes: Oxtail on open-face ravioli, potato
ravioli, tuna tartar, goat cheese terrine, sautéed sweetbreads, lamb

chops. **Price range:** Apps., $5–$8; entrees, $13–$20. **Wheelchair access:** Steps to entrance; restrooms are narrow.

Metrazur $$$ MEDITERRANEAN/NEW AMERICAN

404 East Balcony, Grand Central Terminal   (212) 687-4600
Credit cards: All major   Meals: L, D

In a city with no shortage of stunning views, there are few prospects more impressive than Grand Central Terminal's main concourse. Metrazur (on the east balcony), with its spare, cool décor and low-slung lines, makes the visual swirl and the busy hum of Grand Central part of the meal. There's never any doubt that you are eating in a train station. Once they get over the first flush of excitement, diners will find themselves staring at food so undistinguished it nearly disappears on the plate. At its best, it's easy-listening food.

Wine list: A well-chosen international selection of about 70 wines, with five half-bottles and 11 wines by the glass. **Price range:** Apps., $7–$13; entrees, $22–$27; desserts, $8. Three-course pre-theater dinner, $29. Brunch, $20. **Wheelchair access:** Elevators in Northeast Passage, next to Track 23.

Metsovo $25 & Under GREEK

65 W. 70th St. (near Columbus Ave.)   (212) 873-2300
Credit cards: All major   Meals: D

Metsovo's dim, romantic dining room is a far cry from the usual bright blue and white artifact-bedecked Greek restaurant. Instead of seafood, this restaurant, named after a town in northwestern Greece, specializes in hearty stews, roasts and savory pies from the hills that form a spine through the region. The house specialties form the heart of the menu and are the best choices. Try Epirus mountain pies, which are offered with different fillings each day. They are all delicious. You may never receive the same selection of desserts twice, so hope for the luscious fig compote, or the wonderfully thick and fresh yogurt.

Other recommended dishes: Taramosalata, tzatziki, skordalia, eggplant salad, chopped salad, baby lamb. **Price range:** Apps, $5–$9; entrees, $13–$25. **Wheelchair access:** Steps to entrance; stairs to restrooms.

Mexicana Mama $25 & Under MEXICAN

525 Hudson St. (at W. 10th St.)   (212) 924-4119
Credit cards: Cash only   Meals: L, D   Closed Mon.

While this colorful restaurant's small menu doesn't register high on a scale of authenticity, the food succeeds in a more important measure: it tastes good. Rather than using the traditional mutton or goat, for example, a dish like barbacoa is made with beef, braised and then cooked slowly in a corn husk until it is fall-away tender, like pot roast. Authentic? No. Tasty? Definitely. Other worthy dishes include pollo con mole, a boneless chicken breast that is surprisingly juicy, with a terrific reddish-brown mole that is made with sesame seeds, chocolate and just enough chili heat to balance the sweetness of the chocolate.

Other recommended dishes: Tacos de puerco, flautas triologia, vanilla flan. **Price range:** Apps., $8; entrees, $8–$17; desserts, $5–$7. **Wheelchair access:** Restrooms not accessible.

Mezze $$ MEDITERRANEAN

10 E. 44th St. (bet. Fifth & Madison Aves.)   (212) 697-6644
Credit cards: All major   Meals: B, L   Closed Sat., Sun.

Mezze, one of Matthew Kenney's restaurants, is an attractive, informal, Middle Eastern fantasy with takeout service downstairs and a sit-down cafe upstairs. It is packed at lunchtime, with people lining up to choose from more than a dozen salads and flatbread sandwiches, like roasted vegetables with preserved lemon, Moroccan spiced carrots and spicy chicken salad. There are also flatbread pizzas, a new breakfast menu and main courses like spiced shrimp with tomato jam and a lamb shank with couscous. Mezze is open by day; dinner is delivery only.

Price range: Apps., $5–$8; entrees, $9–$17; desserts, $4–$6. **Wheelchair access:** Not accessible.

Michael Jordan's   ☆☆ $$$$ STEAKHOUSE

23 Vanderbilt Ave. (in Grand Central Terminal)   (212) 655-2300
Credit cards: All major   Meals: L, D

Michael Jordan has retired, but the steakhouse lives on, a little shopworn but still offering one of the most exciting dining locations in Manhattan. Not many restaurants can give customers the sights and sounds of Grand Central along with their shrimp cocktail and grilled ribeye. Take away the station, and you're left with a decent but not extraordinary by-the-book steakhouse. The service ranges from wobbly to downright confused. The steaks, fortunately, are high quality, and the kitchen knows what to do with them, although the house steak sauce, presented in bottles on the table, is far too sweet. The menu does not stray far from the time-honored steakhouse formula, moving from shrimp cocktail to filet mignon to New York cheesecake without skipping a beat. Nothing on the menu quite competes with the sound of the track announcer calling commuters to their trains, unless it's the Michael Jordan chocolate cake, an awesome, 12-layer slice of heaven that four people could easily share. *(Review by William Grimes; stars previously awarded by Ruth Reichl.)*

Wine list: Excellent wines at fair prices; terrible wines by the glass. **Price range:** Apps., $8–$16; entrees, $18–$34; side dishes, $7; desserts, $5–$9. **Wheelchair access:** Elevator to restaurant.

Michael's   ☆☆ $$$ NEW AMERICAN

24 W. 55th St. (bet. Fifth & Sixth Aves.)   (212) 767-0555
Credit cards: All major   Meals: B, L, D   Closed Sun.

Home of the power lunch. All of publishing goes to Michael's because the room is attractive and filled with good art. The menu offers one of the city's finest selections of fancy salads (some large enough to feed a small nation). The best food on the menu is unabashedly American, including grilled chicken, grilled lobster, good steaks and chops, and California cuisine. There are several daily fish selections. For dessert, the classic collection of tarts and cakes is very enticing. (*Ruth Reichl*)

Wine list: Wide-ranging with a fine selection of French and American wines at fair prices. **Price range:** Apps., $12–$18; entrees, $22–$34; desserts, $9. **Wheelchair access:** Steps to dining room.

Mickey Mantle's $$ AMERICAN
42 Central Park S. (bet. Fifth & Sixth Aves.)   (212) 688-7777
Credit cards: All major   Meals: L, D

Televisions everywhere showing great games past and present. As sports bars go, Mantle's is more restaurant than bar, with fine burgers, chicken and desserts. A standing ovation if you're a Mantle fan, otherwise have someone wake you when it's over. A perfect place for children after a day in Central Park.

Price range: Apps., $6–$9; entrees, $12–$25; desserts, $5–$7. **Wheelchair access:** Fully accessible. **Features:** Outdoor dining.

Mi Cocina   ☆☆ $$ MEXICAN
57 Jane St. (at Hudson St.)   (212) 627-8273
Credit cards: All major   Meals: D

After 10 years on the corner of Jane Street and Hudson Street, Mi Cocina has become a white-tablecloth restaurant, with prices to match. The new Mi Cocina makes a visual splash, with apricot walls and coral ceilings, decorated with small, brightly colored paintings with a strong folk-art influence. The acoustics have not been tampered with. The noise level is deafening. But maybe the 60 tequilas have something to do with that.

     Mi Cocina now has foie gras, sautéed with grilled pineapple and tequila, a very strange idea. Sautéed shrimp are served in a truly fiery adobo sauce that can be tamed with some soothing quesadillas filled with shiitake mushrooms and cheese. The dozen or so entrees, not counting specials, include some very traditional dishes like chicken enchiladas with mole poblabo sauce and red snapper. Chile en nogada, one of the more enticing entrees, is a poblano chile stuffed with a pork picadillo flavored with raisins, lemon and almonds. A walnut cream sauce and sprinkling of pomegranate seeds finishes the dish.

Price range: Apps., $7–$18; entrees, $17–$25; desserts, $8–$12. **Wheelchair access:** Fully accessible.

Milan's $25 & Under   EAST EUROPEAN
719 Fifth Ave., Park Slope, Brooklyn   (718) 788-7384
Credit cards: Cash only   Meals: L, D   Closed Mon.

This bright, friendly place is one of the few restaurants in New York to offer genuine Slovakian cooking as well as traditional Eastern European cooking. That means hearty, solid fare heavy on meats, cream, cabbage and potatoes. Bygos, a blend of chopped kielbasa and smoked meats, cabbage and cream sauce, is an unusual turn on the formula, while goulash — chunks of tender beef in a meat, tomato and herb sauce — is terrific, served with slices of steamed white bread.

Other recommended dishes: Potato pancakes, halusky. **Alcohol:** Beer and wine. **Price range:** Apps., $4; entrees, $6–$9; desserts, $2–$4. **Wheelchair access:** Fully accessible.

Mill Korean $25 & Under   KOREAN
2895 Broadway (bet. 112th & 113th Sts.)   (212) 666-7653
Credit cards: All major   Meals: L, D

This place is a reincarnation of the Mill, a greasy spoon luncheonette for generations of Columbia students. It still has lime rickeys and egg creams, but the emphasis is now Korean, with terrific offerings like sweet-and-spicy beef short ribs and huge portions of bibimbap, the egg and rice mixture served with meat or vegetables. A scallion pancake, big as a small pizza, is savory and delicate, as is a similar pancake, with shrimp and squid. Tiny pork dumplings are terrific, and a couple of these dishes can make up an entire meal, especially when supplemented by kim chee and other free hors d'oeuvres.

Alcohol: Beer and wine. **Price range:** Apps., $6–$7; entrees, $7–$11. **Wheelchair access:** Fully accessible.

The Minnow $$ SEAFOOD
442 9th St., Park Slope, Brooklyn   (718) 832-5500
Credit cards: All major   Meals: D   Closed Tue.

As the name might suggest, the Minnow is small, and it specializes in fish. Littleneck clams, in a lime and cucumber salsa, sit cheek by jowl (or fin by gill) on the menu with New England fish cakes, served with paprika aioli. The cod, simply roasted, is plopped atop a thick shellfish chowder. Bluefish, an underrated, overlooked local species, finds gainful employment here. It's a big, meaty, full-flavored fish, served with a roasted red pepper purée, smoked shrimp and steamed cabbage. Lobster shows up twice, in a warm cocktail dressed with fino sherry vinaigrette and in a main course of grilled lobster with mushroom linguine in a port wine reduction. The wine list, a minnow in its own right, tops out at $35.

Price range: Entrees, $14–$18. **Wheelchair access:** Accessible.

Mirchi $25 & Under   INDIAN
29 Seventh Ave. (near Morton St.)   (212) 414-0931
Credit cards: All major   Meals: L, D

Mirchi's clean and simple design, casual service and loud Indian-by-way-of-London techno music suggest other youth-oriented restaurants with bar crowds rather than other Indian restaurants. Yet the food is strictly Indian, with not even a hint of fusion. The focus is street foods and other small plates, a deceiving concept since many portions are quite large. Mirchi's other point of departure is forceful spicing, with occasionally very high heat (the word mirchi means hot, as in chilies). Chicken tak-a-tak, shredded chicken essentially stir-fried, is exceptional, with a peppery bite augmented by garlic, ginger and chili. Among the main courses jaipuri lal maas is a fabulous and subtle lamb dish, made, the menu says, with 30 red chilies. Yet the chunks of lamb are not fiery but hauntingly spicy.

Other recommended dishes: Grilled shrimp in tamarind sauce, hyderabadi baingan, ragda pattice, chicken chat, dhoklas, kicheri. **Price range:** Apps., $4–$9; entrees, $9–$19. **Wheelchair access:** All one level. **Features:** Outdoor dining.

Miss Maude's Spoonbread Too

$25 & Under SOUTHERN
547 Lenox Ave. (near 137th St.) (212) 690-3100
Credit cards: All major Meals: Br, L, D

Miss Maude's practically invites you in for a meal. Its walls are adorned with kitchen tools and black-and-white family photos, while each of its shiny red or yellow tables holds a fat, fresh rose. The generous portions of Southern dishes are not only robust and hearty, but also sometimes subtle, which is no surprise, since Miss Maude's is owned by Norma Jean Darden, the caterer and cookbook author, who also owns Miss Mamie's Spoonbread Too.

Meals are served Southern style, with large portions of two sides. The smothered pork chops are thin but flavorful enough to stand up to the peppery brown gravy. Close behind are the excellent fried shrimp with traces of cornmeal in the delectable crust. Fried chicken is as it should be, with a crisp, oniony crust. Except for banana pudding, produced in all its soft vanilla-wafer glory, the desserts are a disappointment.

Other recommended dishes: Macaroni and cheese, meatloaf, collard greens, candied yams, potato salad, short ribs, pork ribs. **Price range:** Dinners, $10–$13. **Wheelchair access:** One level.

Miss Williamsburg $25 & Under DINER/ITALIAN
206 Kent Ave., Williamsburg, Brooklyn, (718) 963-0802
Credit cards: Cash only Meals: D Closed Mon.

Once the greasiest of spoons, this diner has been scrubbed until gleaming inside and now serves dishes of pasta rather than burgers and fries. Miss Williamsburg offers a small selection of uncomplicated, inexpensive dishes that qualify both as good Italian food and great diner food. Among the pastas, try spaghetti alla chittara, thick shoelaces of house-made spaghetti with a perfectly proportioned sauce of chopped fresh tomatoes, arugula and roasted garlic, or the spinach-and-ricotta ravioli. Two main courses stand out: a thin and moist pork loin, and straccetti alla rugantino, thin, ragged strips of sautéed beef blanched almost beige in a white-wine sauce, all texture and lively flavor. The one absolute winner among desserts is a honey-flavored mousse with pine nuts.

Other recommended dishes: Vegetable salad, octopus salad, mussels, lasagna, skewers of shrimp and squid, roast chicken, grilled pork chop. **Price range:** Apps., $4–$6; entrees, $8–$14. **Wheelchair access:** Steps to entrance; restrooms are narrow.

Miyagi

$25 & Under

JAPANESE/SUSHI

220 W. 13th St. (near Greenwich Ave.)
(212) 620-3830
Credit cards: All major   Meals: L, D   Closed Sun.

Miyagi is a pretty little Japanese restaurant which seats just 45 people. It has the casual, welcoming air of an ideal neighborhood
restaurant, with waitresses who are decorous despite jeans and T-
shirts. Miyagi reserves elegance for what counts, like etched glass
sake carafes and, of course, the freshest ingredients. The menu has
many familiar choices and just enough offbeat selections to keep
things interesting. Consider the fried Alaska: ground salmon,
asparagus and mint wrapped in seaweed like a sushi roll and
expertly deep fried, then served in bite-size pieces with a miso
dressing. It's a perfect melange of flavors and textures. Miyagi's
sushi and sashimi are just what you hope for in a midpriced restaurant: fresh and clean, with the cool distant flavor of the ocean.
Beyond the sushi horizon, the best dish is a simple broiled mackerel, which virtually melts in your mouth.

Other recommended dishes: Negimaki, steamed monkfish liver,
hijiki, spinach with sesame sauce. **Price range:** Apps., $3–$8;
entrees, $10–$15; sushi and sashimi combinations, $14 –$22.
Wheelchair access: Steps at entrance; tiny restroom.

Moda   ☆☆ $$$

ITALIAN

Flatotel, 135 W. 52nd St. (near Sixth Ave.)
(212) 887-9880
Credit cards: All major   Meals: L, D

Moda's coolly stylish dining room has a subtly minimalist look with
warm touches. The effect is unexpectedly ingratiating. Moda's executive chef is much-traveled and it shows in his intelligent rethinking of Italian cuisine. The menu reflects a commitment to prime
ingredients and a quiet determination not to let style overrule substance. It feels fresh and inventive, but it's never silly.

The menu format is flexible, with dishes categorized as small
plates and big plates with side dishes like whipped Parmesan potatoes. Sautéed escarole deserves special attention. A simple roast
chicken, plump and succulent, broke through the boredom barrier,
and grilled quail with polenta, very straightforward, takes off with
the addition of a concentrated jam heated with cracked black pepper. The easy choice for dessert is a modest-looking bittersweet
chocolate cake that's halfway toward being a pudding.

Wine list: A modest list of about 60 wines, about half of them Italian. **Price range:** Lunch: apps., $7–$11; entrees, $14–$25. Dinner,
apps., $8–$16; entrees, $17–$28; desserts, $8–$12. **Wheelchair
access:** One level.

Molyvos   ☆☆ $$$

GREEK

871 Seventh Ave. (near 55th St.)
(212) 582-7500
Credit Cards: All major   Meals: L, D

From the long bar in the front, with booths and a large wooden
communal table, to the airy room in the rear, its walls cluttered
with urns and vases, Molyvos is pleasingly informal and spacious.

Of course, it's hard to resist the old standbys, like the outstanding Greek mezedes. Meaty pastitsio, served in a small ramekin and

deftly touched with cinnamon and nutmeg, may be the best you've ever had. The best main courses tend to be the most straightforward. The kitchen gives special care to the fresh fish grilled simply over wood. Baby lamb chops are perfect with no more than a sprinkling of salt and pepper. Desserts include many of the standards, yet they are executed exceptionally well and served in enormous portions. Best of all was a sensational new dessert, a rough-textured walnut cake, flavored with olive oil, yet pleasingly sweet. Service is efficient and friendly, yet there seemed to be puzzling gaps in knowledge. *(Eric Asimov)*

Wine list: Extensive selection of Greek bottles, supplemented with many other good choices, especially from southern Italy. **Price range:** Lunch entrees, $13–$35. Dinner: apps., $8–$13; entrees, $19–$35; desserts, $7. **Wheelchair access:** Ramp available to entrance.

Mombar $25 & Under   MIDDLE EASTERN
25-22 Steinway St. (bet. 25th & 28th Aves.), Astoria, Queens
(718) 728-9858
Credit cards: Cash only   Meals: D, LN   Closed Mon.

There's no sign for Mombar, just a couple of huge eyes built into the storefront. A door forms a sort of nose between the eyes, and what you see on entering is not so much a restaurant as a work of art. From the elaborate mosaic floor to the windows of stained glass every surface is covered with the creations of Moustafa El Sayed, the owner, chef and resident artist.

Mombar has no menus; someone simply recites the choices. They almost always include the restaurant's namesake, a house-made Egyptian sausage of lamb, beef and rice with dill and garlic, served warm with chickpeas. (A vegetarian version is also served.) With food, too, Mr. Sayed is an artist: he serves personal interpretations of dishes and seems as if he's cooking at home. Chicken tagine is a moist and smoky North African stew with olives and vegetables. Mombar usually has several house-made desserts, like baklava dripping with honey or couscous cake, the grains compressed with prunes and dried apricots, luscious with strawberries and sour cream.

Other recommended dishes: Assorted appetizers, grilled striped bass, roasted duck with molasses, rabbit. **Price range:** Apps., $5–$8; entrees, $18. **Wheelchair access:** Ramp at entrance.

Montrachet   ☆☆☆ $$$$ FRENCH
239 W. Broadway (near White St.)   (212) 219-2777
Credit cards: All major   Meals: L (Fri. only), D   Closed Sun.

After so many years, TriBeCa's first serious restaurant has achieved a pleasant patina of age without losing its casual charm and thoughtful service. Montrachet seems more Gallic than ever with muscular French cooking that seems just right for the small bistro-like dining rooms. Main dishes tend to be straightforward, relying on excellence of execution rather than originality. Try the memorable roast chicken served with a rich potato purée and a robust garlic sauce. When a restaurant is named for a wine region it is difficult to pass up a cheese course. Montrachet offers a small selection of fine, ripe cheeses: each makes a fine prelude to dessert. Try the napoleon. It looks like the classic airy pastry, but mascarpone filling gives this confection an entirely new character. (*Ruth Reichl*)

Wine list: Excellent, with a specialty in Burgundies. **Price range:** Lunch: apps., $9–$20; entrees, $14–$20; desserts, $8; prix fixe, $20 and $28. Dinner: apps., $11–$22; entrees, $26–$29; desserts, $9. Prix fixe, $30, $44, $78 and $90. **Wheelchair access:** Steps to dining rooms.

Morrells ☆ $$ NEW AMERICAN
900 Broadway (near 20th St.) (212) 253-0900
Credit cards: All major Meals: L, D Closed Sun.

Morrells is a greatly expanded version of the little wine bar and cafe next to the Morrells wine store in Rockefeller Center. Diners face a nonstop bombardment of fine wines before, during and after the meal. The choices run into the thousands. If this sounds like a wine-lover's paradise, it is.

The rules of the game require wine to be woven into the texture of virtually every dish, sometimes discreetly, sometimes as pure gimmick. The wine in a reduction sauce casts a spell over the superlative Kobe-style beef from Lobel's. The wine never stops flowing. It is in the sherry vinegar sprinkled over slices of Austrian speck; in rabbit crepes with pinot noir syrup; in coq au riesling; and in Champagne fricassee of lobster. When the wine makes a natural fit, the conceit seems clever. Many of the appetizers are simply too sweet. For dessert, Black Forest napoleon, a transformation of the traditional cake into a pastry format, tastes exactly like a liquid-center, chocolate-covered cherry. At a restaurant that dotes on clever tricks, this may be the cleverest one of all. Not counting the wine list, of course.

Other recommended dishes: Mushroom chowder with smoked bacon, fluke sashimi, short ribs marinated in red wine, sturgeon with sweet pea broth, ribeye steak with cabernet syrup, softshell crabs with aioli, blueberry strudel, fig tart. **Wine list:** A list of 2,000 wines, when the reserve list is included. The main list of about 800, organized by grape variety, concentrates on high quality and moderate price. About 120 wines by the glass. **Price range:** Lunch, apps., $8–$12; entrees, $13–$25; desserts, $6.50–$7. Dinner, apps., $9–$16; entrees, $21–$28; desserts, $6–$8.50. **Wheelchair access:** All one level.

Morrell Wine Bar & Cafe $$$ NEW AMERICAN
1 Rockefeller Plaza (on W. 49th St.) (212) 262-7700
Credit cards: All major Meals: Br, L, D

The cafe may be small, but the wine list is large, about 2,000 bottles supplied by Morrell Wine Shop next door, with about 50 wines available by the glass. And the closet-sized kitchen somehow manages to send out satisfying, well-conceived dishes, with an eye on the wine list. Roast loin of beef with truffled mashed potatoes swims in a cabernet jus. And the dessert list includes wine-inflected dishes like a tawny port flan and a vanilla-bean pound cake topped with dried fruits macerated in muscat, the opulent, apricot-scented white wine from the south of France.

Wine list: 2,000 bottles, ranging in price from $16–$6000. 110 wines by the glass, $5–$49. **Price range:** Apps, $8–$16; entrees, $17–$28. Mon. night wine dinner, $50. **Wheelchair access:** Fully accessible.

Moustache $25 & Under   MIDDLE EASTERN

90 Bedford St. (bet. Grove & Barrow Sts.)   (212) 229-2220
265 E. 10th St. (bet. First Ave. & Ave. A)   (212) 228-2022
Credit cards: Cash only   Meals: L, D, LN

These small, excellent Middle Eastern restaurants specialize in "pitzas," exceptional pizza–like dishes made with pita dough, including lahmajun, the Turkish specialty with a savory layer of ground lamb on crisp crust, and zaatar, a crisp individual pizza topped with a smoky, aromatic combination of olive oil, thyme, sesame seeds and sumac. Falafel is run-of-the-mill, but a sandwich of sliced lamb in pita bread with onion and tomato is brought to life by a minty lemon mayonnaise.

Other recommended dishes: Hummus, baba gannouj, spinach and chickpea salad, foul; zatter bread, loomi. **Alcohol:** Beer and wine. **Price range:** $3–$12. **Wheelchair access:** All one level. **Features:** Outdoor dining (at E. 10th St. location).

Mughlai $25 & Under   INDIAN

320 Columbus Ave. (at 71st St.)   (212) 724-6363
Credit cards: All major   Meals: L, D

Mughlai offers tantalizing glimpses of the pleasures of Indian food. Its menu offers the litany of familiar dishes, but it also invites diners to try uncommon regional dishes. Almost always at Mughlai, the less familiar dishes are better. Dal papri, potatoes and chickpeas blended in a tangy tamarind-and-yogurt sauce and served cool, is a superb appetizer. Pepper chicken, a dish from the southwestern state of Kerala, is another adventure: the pieces of stewed chicken, coated in ground black pepper, seem to dance invitingly across the mouth. Also excellent are baghare baigan, small eggplants in an aromatic sauce of ground peanuts, sesame, tamarind and coconut. But old standbys such as chicken vindaloo or Tandoori dishes are as disappointing as the other dishes are invigorating.

Other recommended dishes: Aloo papri chat, shammi kebabs, achar gosht, lamb pasanda. **Price range:** Apps., $5–$9; entrees, $7–$19. **Wheelchair access:** One step up at entrance; restrooms are narrow.

Muzy $25 & Under   KOREAN

81 St. Marks Pl. (near First Ave.)   (212) 533-6876
Credit cards: All major   Meals: D, LN

Muzy is a bold break from the past, offering a small menu of light appetizers and noodle dishes. Seating about 15 people, Muzy practically disappears into the streetscape. Yet it is pleasingly sleek and minimalist, with contoured walls made from what appear to be silver and gray industrial tiles. Though the emphasis seems to be on light dishes, Muzy's food can't help offering the robust, lusty flavors that characterize Korean cuisine. Noodle dishes occupy central stage, and giant casseroles of curly egg noodles, filled with hot chili-spiked broth, arrive boiling at the table. The small list of beer and wine is perfunctory, but not so the juices. A blend of apple and orange juice is tart and wonderful, while the ginger-limeade manages to be spicy and refreshing at the same time.

Other recommended dishes: Mandoo, sautéed tofu, pa jun, seafood pa jun, bibimbop, spicy sautéed pork, fresh juices. **Alcohol:** Beer and wine. **Price range:** Apps., $5–$12; entrees, $8–$15. **Wheelchair access:** Not accessible.

Nadaman Hakubai ☆ ☆ $$$$ JAPANESE

Kitano Hotel, 66 Park Ave. (at 38th St.)   (212) 885-7111
Credit cards: All major   Meals: B, L, D

New York City's most expensive restaurant serves kaiseki cuisine in private, brightly lighted tatami rooms. Nadaman Hakubai offers serenity and the extraordinary sense of experiencing another culture. A visit to one of this restaurant's tatami rooms is like a quick trip to Japan. Kaiseki cuisine, associated with the tea ceremony, is food for the soul as well as the body, meant to feed the eye with its beauty and the spirit with its meaning. The courses — served by kimono-clad hostesses — follow a strict order and each is intended to introduce the coming season. The way to enjoy this is to abandon yourself to the experience, appreciating the peace, the subtlety of the flavors and the sense that you are being pampered as never before. Unless you are an extremely adventurous eater, you will probably not like every dish you are served. But in spite of the occasional disappointment, each evening at the restaurant has been an immensely rewarding experience. Worth $150? Think of it this way: A trip to Japan would cost considerably more. (*Ruth Reichl*)

Wine list: There is a wine list, but the waitresses tend to be baffled by it. It is best to stick to sake and beer. **Price range:** Kaiseki dinners in private tatami rooms, $100 minimum per person, for a minimum of four people. Traditional Japanese breakfast in the dining room is $25 or $28; mini kaiseki lunch, $60; kaiseki dinners in the main restaurant begin at $80 (and are not particularly recommended). **Wheelchair access:** The restaurant is below street level, but there is an elevator.

Nam $25 & Under VIETNAMESE

110 Reade St. (at W. Broadway)   (212) 267-1777
Credit cards: All major   Meals: L, D

Nam's high ceiling, stylishly draped chairs, candles and cleverly backlighted old pictures of Vietnam make it feel almost Parisian. The menu offers some seldom-seen recipes like banh la, fragile rectangular noodles stuffed with minced shrimp, wrapped in banana leaves and steamed, giving them a deliciously cheeselike richness. Banh xeo, a cross between a crepe and an omelet, is crisp on the bottom and filled not just with the usual mushrooms and bean sprouts, but also with a voluptuous mélange of coconut-flavored rice, shrimp and chicken. More familiar dishes are also well rendered. Goi du du, green papaya salad, is pungent and refreshing, augmented by paper-thin slices of salty dried beef. Ca chien is a transcendent dish, a red snapper made barely crisp on the surface yet wonderfully moist and flavorful within, just right dipped in nuoc cham.

Other recommended dishes: Grilled Asian eggplant, chopped monkfish with rice crackers, jicama, sausage and shrimp rolls, chicken baked with ginger, grilled pork with vermicelli, ginger crème caramel, coconut custard. **Price range:** Apps., $4–$8; entrees, $9–$16. **Wheelchair access:** Not accessible.

Nam Phuong $25 & Under VIETNAMESE
19 Sixth Ave. (at Walker St.) (212) 431-7715
Credit cards: MC/V Meals: L, D

With its dim lights, wall-length mirrors and neon signs, this pleasant Vietnamese restaurant fits well into its TriBeCa neighborhood. Nam Phuong serves delicious soups like pho tai, a traditional northern Vietnamese recipe with a rich, almost velvety cilantro-scented beef stock filled with paper-thin slices of tender steak and rice noodles. The southern version of pho, hu tieu, is equally good, the rice noodle soup full of sliced pork and shrimp. A nice counterpart to the soups is the cool, refreshing shredded chicken salad flavored with mint, lemongrass and lime and spiced with chilies. Iced Vietnamese coffee, made with condensed milk, is like a coffee milkshake, while lemonade is sweet and refreshing, made with green Vietnamese lemons.

Other recommended dishes: Spring rolls, barbecued beef rolls, steamed rice crepes with sausage, chao tom, sautéed seitan, grilled pork on rice noodle, tropical fruit shake. **Price range:** Apps., $4–$9; entrees, $8–$24. **Wheelchair access:** All one level.

National Cafe $25 & Under CUBAN/LATIN AMERICAN
210 First Ave. (near 13th St.) (212) 473-9354
Credit cards: All major Meals: L, D

If you order a roast pork sandwich at this tiny Cuban restaurant, you can watch its construction. The server picks up a leg of pork and carefully carves pieces of the tender meat, piling them high on a hero roll. Then she places a chicharrón (a crisp piece of fried pork skin) on top. The result is delicious and filling, like almost everything else on the menu.

Alcohol: Beer and wine. **Price range:** Apps., $2–$3; entrees, $7–$9; desserts, $2–$3. **Wheelchair access:** Not accessible.

New Green Bo $ CHINESE
66 Bayard St. (bet. Mott & Elizabeth Sts.) (212) 625-2359
Credit cards: Cash only Meals: L, D, LN

This bright, plain restaurant in Chinatown looks like many other bright, plain restaurants in the neighborhood, except that it offers delicious Shanghai specialties like soup dumplings, smoked fish and eel with chives.

Price range: Apps., $2–$7; entrees, $3–$24; desserts, $3.

New Lok Kee

$25 & Under   CHINESE

36-50 Main St. (near 37th Ave.), Flushing, Queens   (718) 762-6048
Credit cards: Cash only   Meals: L, D, LN

After fire destroyed Chinatown's Sun Lok Kee, it reopened as New Lok Kee in Flushing. Its menu is the same, and so, it seems, is the kitchen staff. Only the dining room, now a clean and open space decorated with mirrors, orchids and fish tanks, is truly new. Clams with black-bean sauce is a good place to start. An order of crabs in the Cantonese style is also excellent. Pan-fried flounder, served on the bone in a terrifically delicate sauce that's most redolent of ginger and garlic, is a real showstopper. Ask for the fabulous casserole of white eel flavored with pork belly that's not on the menu but is readily available all the same. New Lok Kee is a triumphant return to form for a fixture of old New York. Its tradition of informal excellence is cooked into every meal. *(Sam Sifton)*

Other recommended dishes: Salt-and-pepper shrimp, ginger-scallion lo mein, fried chicken, fried duck, Peking pork chops, flowering chives. **Price range:** Soup and side dishes, $1–$10; entrees, $3.50–$16. **Wheelchair access:** Incline at door.

New York Kom Tang Kalbi House

$25 & Under   KOREAN

32 W. 32nd St. (bet. Fifth & Sixth Aves.)   (212) 947-8482
Credit cards: All major   Meals: 24 hrs.   Closed Sun.

Tabletop cooking is a Korean tradition, and though most tabletop grills these days are gas-powered, some older Korean restaurants, like the New York Kom Tang Kalbi House, use braziers filled with natural wood charcoal. Meals are served traditionally, beginning with panchan, a half-dozen or so free plates of nibbles to snack on before the meal and to use as condiments. As you nibble, waiters maneuver around the bright dining room, gingerly carrying braziers, coals ablaze. If you've ordered a grilled dish, they'll soon push the panchan aside, remove your table's metallic centerpiece and set up the brazier. The heat covers you like a down jacket. Kalbi, the meat of short ribs sliced off the bones for grilling ease, is the specialty, and it's good, tender, flavorful and mildly sweet from its marinade. Try the jeyook gui, slices of pork bathed in a wonderful sweet and spicy sauce.

Kom Tang means long-simmered soup, and the soups here are especially good. Kori kom tang is oxtails in a milky smooth, supremely comforting meat broth. Mandoo kuk is similar, stuffed with beef and pork-filled dumplings, while tuk kuk is a lighter yet similarly soothing broth with pliant, supple rice cakes.

Price range: Grilled dishes, $15–$19; other dishes, $8–$23. **Wheelchair access:** Not accessible.

Next Door Nobu   ☆ ☆ ☆   **$$$$**   JAPANESE

105 Hudson St. (near Franklin St.)   (212) 334-4445
Credit cards: All major   Meals: D, LN

Slightly more casual than Nobu, Next Door Nobu takes no reservations and does not serve lunch. To dine here, come early: later arrivals may wait up to 90 minutes for a table. But the food is as accomplished (and as expensive) as Nobu's. And while the menu features many of the same dishes, it strives for its own identity, with an emphasis on raw shellfish, whole fish served for an entire table, noodles, and texture.

Black cod with miso makes a fine dish. Noodles range from the portly white udon to the more austere soba with their subtle chewiness. The few meat dishes on the menu are memorable. The sliced Kobe beef tataki comes with little side dishes that add both flavor and texture. Mochi ice cream balls are the most appealing way to end a meal. (*Ruth Reichl*)

Wine list: Interesting, well-chosen, but the special sake, served cold in chilled bamboo glasses, seems perfect for this food. **Price range:** Soup and salad, $4–$13; noodle dishes, $10–$15; hot dishes, $8–$32; sushi and sashimi, $3–$8 a piece; desserts, $8–$13. **Wheelchair access:** Steep steps to dining room.

Nha Trang $25 & Under   CHINESE/VIETNAMESE
87 Baxter St. (bet. White & Walker Sts.)   (212) 233-5948
148 Centre St. (near Walker St.)   (212) 941-9292
Credit cards: Cash only   Meals: L, D

Nothing fancy about Nha Trang. It's just a plain storefront with a bright dining room, but you may have to jostle with hordes of jurors for the excellent Vietnamese food. The owners opened a second, restaurant a block west on Centre Street.

Familiar dishes are flawless here, like chao tom, grilled shrimp paste wrapped around a short stalk of sugar cane. Grilled dishes are also superb, like little cylinders of sweet and savory barbecued beef over rice vermicelli. Vietnamese iced coffee, made with sweetened condensed milk, can be a fine dessert.

Other recommended dishes: Cool beef salad, beef with rice-noodle soup, summer rolls, barbecued pork chop, grilled chicken, soft-shell crabs, chicken curry, water spinach. **Price range:** Apps., $4–$9; entrees, $4–$16. **Wheelchair access:** All one level.

Nice Matin   ☆☆ $$ FRENCH
201 W. 79th St. (at Amsterdam Ave.)   (212) 873-6423
Credit cards: All major   Meals: Br, L, D

Nice Matin, named after the largest daily newspaper in the South of France, gives the Upper West Side a splash of Provençal sunshine and a heady introduction to the cuisine of Nice, home of the pissaladière, pan bagnat and, if we are to believe the menu, a whopping big burger topped with comté cheese, smeared with aioli. It's the best thing to happen to a hamburger since Daniel Boulud worked foie gras and short ribs into an all-beef patty. The menu is anchored in the potent flavors, bright colors and fragrant herbs that define Niçoise cooking, adjusting here and innovating there, always in a way that feels true to the local idiom. The trouchia, a Swiss chard and onion frittata flavored with Parmesan cheese, is a glorious thing. Bitter orange, one of the great Niçoise flavors, shows up in an impressive daube of beef short ribs, a glistening, black monolith of meat whose richness is nicely offset by orange and sage. For dessert try the chocolate ganache.

Do not attempt conversation. The brutal acoustics at Nice Matin preclude it. Diners can either scream at one another or study the décor, which flummoxes nearly everyone.

Other recommended dishes: Soupe au pistou, rosemary-grilled leg of lamb, zucchini stuffed with short ribs, fennel-cured mackerel, daube, lamb ravioli, lemon-chocolate pot de crème. **Wine list:** An even-handed international list of 140 wines that could use more from the South of France. Most wines are under $40, and 20 are sold by the glass. **Price range:** Lunch: apps., $5.50–$9.75; entrees, $8.25–$19.75; desserts, $7. Dinner: apps., $4–$12.50; entrees, $15.75–$24.75; desserts, $7. **Wheelchair access:** Accessible.

Nicholson ☆ $$$ FRENCH

323 E. 58th St. (bet. First & Second Aves.)   (212) 355-6769
Credit cards: All major   Meals: D   Closed Sun.

Nicholson occupies a peculiar spot, perched at the edge of the entrance to the upper roadway of the Queensboro Bridge. It looks like a guardhouse, and it's not much larger. It has a very distinctive dining room, whose décor was once described as Spanish-Portuguese belle époque, and things have become only more complex. Stillness reigns, interrupted only by the gentle creak of the parquet floor, signaling the approach of a waiter, who, in truth, seems less like an employee than a faithful family retainer, just as the restaurant feels a bit like a room in the far west wing of Crotchet Castle.

Like the décor, the food at Nicholson swings wildly between extremes. It can be romantic and elegant, or almost insanely misjudged. Truffle cream, truffles, caviar and mushrooms loom large in Mr. Woodside's cooking vocabulary. After the grand tour, it's a short, sweet trip at dessert time. Nicholson limits itself to a few classic soufflés, led by a superb but breathtakingly alcoholic apple-Calvados souffle, and a poached peach with Champagne sabayon.

Wine list: A not very interesting list of 60 bottles, most of them French and American, but with some real bargains at the low end. **Price range:** Four courses, $64; six courses, $78; eight courses, $98 ($135 with matching wines). **Wheelchair access:** Entrance is five steps down; restrooms on dining room level.

Nick & Toni's ☆☆ $$$ MEDITERRANEAN

100 W. 67th St. (bet. Broadway & Columbus)   (212) 496-4000
Credit cards: All major   Meals: L, D

A great neighborhood restaurant, Nick & Toni's is a lot like the neighborhood it serves: casual, crowded and noisy. But there is one thing that sets it apart from most of the neighborhood's restaurants: the food is really delicious. Nick & Toni's starts with good ingredients and leaves them alone. The menu changes constantly, but there are a few perennials, like the impeccable Caesar salad — crisp, lightly dressed, perfectly pungent. Often there is a fine pasta. Desserts are simple and seasonal. (*Ruth Reichl*)

Wine list: Excellent choices, especially from the lesser-known regions of France; many by the glass. **Price range:** Apps., $6–$11; entrees, $11–$28; desserts, $8. **Wheelchair access:** One step up to dining room.

Nick's Family-Style Restaurant and Pizzeria
$25 & Under   PIZZA/ITALIAN

1814 Second Ave. (near 94th St.)   (212) 987-5700
Credit cards: All major   Meals: L, D

Nick's — a small, pleasant corner spot with brick walls, a pressed tin ceiling and hearty service — adheres to all the Italian family-style macaroni-and-gravy hokum. What separates Nick's from some of the others is a track record of taking food seriously, especially pizza. The crust is beautifully thin and crisp, blackened in spots and smoky. Tomato sauce is well-seasoned, and toppings are excellent. Beyond pizza, try tiny baked clams heaped with bread crumbs, garlic and herbs. Shrimp Zi Pepe are excellent. Pastas are not going to break new ground, yet the simplicity of the familiar preparations is redeeming.

Other recommended dishes: Pizzas, spinach salad, linguine in white clam sauce, orecchiette with broccoli rape and sausage, spaghetti with garlic and oil, cannoli. **Price range:** Apps. (family-style), $5–$17; entrees, $11–$22. **Wheelchair access:** All one level.

Nicole's   ☆☆ $$$ ENGLISH

10 E. 60th St. (bet. Madison & Fifth Aves.)   (212) 223-2288
Credit cards: All major   Meals: Br, L

Nicole's (located in the Nicole Farhi store) hums and buzzes at lunchtime. It's filled with stylish diners, nearly all of them women. At night, the store closes, shadows descend, and Nicole's light and airy downstairs dining room takes on a somber tinge.

The notion of high-style dining in department stores and fancy boutiques is relatively novel here, but Nicole's does a lot to make it go down easy. The bright, appealing menu has a shrewd minimalist touch and just the right English notes. The chef is a precisionist about flavor, and picky when it comes to fresh ingredients. Nicole's does not go in for big, flashy effects. It's happy with clever little touches. The Moroccan cumin and lemon chicken is irresistible. Nicole's wisely steers toward simple, homey sweets like lemon pudding, a fluffy mousse that develops density and texture as the spoon reaches deeper into the white ceramic pot. Nicole's also offers cheeses from Neal's Yard Dairy in London.

Wine list: A modest but well-chosen 60-bottle list with 14 wines by the glass. **Price range:** Apps., $8–$17; entrees, $14–$32; desserts, $8. **Wheelchair access:** Two steps to entrance.

92   ☆ $$ NEW AMERICAN

45 E. 92nd St. (bet. Fifth & Madison Aves.)   (212) 828-5300
Credit cards: All major   Meals: Br, L, D

Ninety-two, named for its location on 92nd Street, is to all intents and purposes a diner. The place has fat leather banquettes that look as if they might have been taken from a 1930's train station, cozy booths and dark wooden tables. One virtue of 92 is that it fulfills the diner role without overthinking it. There's onion soup, along with cheeseburgers, and the fried onion rings have a sweet-hot Thai dipping sauce. The food is hit or miss. Macaroni and cheese deserves applause. The fine-grained meatloaf is dense and flavorful.

The daily specials shine, especially the expertly handled fish and chips, utterly greaseless, and the generous slab of pork ribs. The best of the desserts is the classic chocolate sundae and a firm, unctuous chocolate-pudding cake, the sort of dessert that almost demands that you remove the spoon very slowly from your mouth after each bite.

Wine list: A decent, modestly priced international list of about 40 wines, 14 sold by the glass and 12 by the carafe. **Price range:** Lunch: apps., $8–$9; entrees and sandwiches, $14–$24. Dinner: apps., $8–$12; entrees, $19–$29; desserts, $5–$8.Tuesday, 5 to 10 P.M.; Wednesday through Saturday, 5 P.M. to midnight. **Wheelchair access:** One level.

NL   ☆ $$$ DUTCH/INDONESIAN
169 Sullivan St. (near Houston St.)   (212) 387-8801
Credit cards: All major   Meals: D

A Dutch restaurant seems like an inside joke. But NL, (short for Netherlands) has the last laugh. It serves a clever mix of beloved Dutch standbys, Indonesian dishes that have gained honorary Dutch citizenship and invented dishes that use homey Dutch ingredients like herring, potatoes, cheese and the yogurt cream known as hangop. Dutch food is not fancy, and the chef does not fuss with simple, traditional dishes like mosterdsoep, a tangy, light-bodied mustard soup accented with slivers of scallion. Sauerkraut risotto sounds forbidding; it turns out to be one of the best things on the menu, once you get past the overcooked rice.

One thing the Dutch indisputably do well is cheese, but NL presents an abbreviated plate of Friesland cheese flavored with cumin and clove. The cheese simply cannot compete with the poffertjes, soft, puffy mini-pancakes sprinkled with powdered anise and served with a scoop of vanilla butter. Just as good is the chocolate cake dusted with powdered sugar. On the side is a spoonful of thick cream made with Advoocat, a Dutch liqueur similar to eggnog.

Wine list: A very short but decent list of about 20 wines, with five wines by the glass, six Dutch beers, and a good selection of Dutch spirits and liqueurs. **Price range:** Apps., $8–$14; entrees, $18–$25; desserts, $8–$13. **Wheelchair access:** Restroom on street level.

Nobu   ☆ ☆ ☆ $$$$ JAPANESE
105 Hudson St. (at Franklin St.)   (212) 219-0500
Credit cards: All major   Meals: L, D

Chic, casual and pulsing with energy, Nobu cannot be compared with any other restaurant. The spirit of invention of its chef-owner, Nobuyuki Matsuhisa — incorporating new ingredients into old dishes or retooling traditional recipes — lighted a spark in the kitchen, igniting each chef to new and increasingly daring feats. The result is something that seems like a Japanese dish but is not..

The best time to eat at Nobu is lunchtime. Order an omakase meal and let the chefs choose your meal for you. No kitchen turns out a more spectacular plate of sushi. Desserts include a warm chocolate soufflé cake with siso syrup and green tea ice cream that comes in a bento box.

Popularity may be taking its toll. On a recent visit, the Benihana overtones, a weakness for gaudy gimmicks, and the tourist clientele, added up to a less than deluxe experience. Edwyn Ferrari, the new chef, can both dazzle and dismay with his omakase. The sushi maintains a high level of quality, however, and the black cod with miso is still one of the most luxurious taste experiences in New York. (*Ruth Reichl, updated by William Grimes*)

Wine list: A lovely choice of wines that go well with the food. But the cold Hokusetsu sake shows this food off to best advantage. **Price range:** Lunch: avg. $40 per person; prix-fixe, $20. Dinner: avg. $60–$75 per person; tasting menus, $80 and up. **Wheelchair access:** Ramp to dining room at back door.

Noche ☆ $$$ LATIN AMERICAN
1604 Broadway (near 49th St.)   (212) 541-7070
Credit cards: All major   Meals: L, D   Closed Sun.

Broadway could use more places like Noche, a multilevel pan-Latin restaurant with a striking design, a spirited atmosphere and excellent value. The background music is loud, and some nights, live mambo music starts around 9. Good appetizers include anticuchos, skewered bites of tender steak, savory chorizo and head-on shrimp; a platter of three tamales; fajitas, almost enough for a meal; and a calamari salad. Main courses are a carnivore's delight, especially the pork dishes. Apart from shrimp, the seafood dishes don't stand up to the meat selections. Noche's desserts are a surprising highlight. Try the almond-chocolate tamales, tres leches cake or coconut flan. (*Eric Asimov*)

Other recommended dishes: Roast suckling pig, braised pork shank, braised short ribs, shrimp in peanut-plantain sauce, Cubano sandwich. **Wine list:** Small and well chosen, with a nice selection of tropical cocktails. **Price range:** Lunch: apps., $6–$9; sandwiches and entrees, $9–$15; desserts, $7. Dinner: apps., $7–$12; entrees, $15–$22; desserts, $8. **Wheelchair access:** Elevator to dining room and restrooms.

Noche Mexicana $25 & Under MEXICAN
852 Amsterdam Ave. (near 102nd St.)   (212) 662-6900
Credit cards: Cash only   Meals: L, D

Noche Mexicana, a new taqueria on Amsterdam, serves a largely Mexican clientele. The trim little dining room is bright and pleasant, though a jukebox blares impossibly loud music. The welcome is warm, and the menu is translated.

Language does not matter when you're served a dish as delicious as the sautéed shrimp with chipotle salsa. Alongside are herbed rice, creamy puréed beans and fragrant corn tortillas, all of which come with main courses. Noche Mexicana offers a full range of tacos and other antijitos, or street snacks. The tacos are made the authentic way, with two soft corn tortillas providing a gripping surface for the filling, augmented by lettuce, tomatoes, onions and cilantro. Highlights include tacos al pastor, which are filled with the traditional blend of pork chunks and pineapple, and tacos cesina, made with a salty preserved beef.

Other recommended dishes: Pipian de pollo, chicken enchiladas, tamales. **Alcohol:** Bring your own. **Price range:** Small dishes, $2–$6; entrees, $6–$10. **Wheelchair access:** Not accessible.

Nostalgias · $25 & Under · BOLIVIAN
85-09 Northern Blvd., Jackson Heights, Queens · (718) 533-9120
Credit cards: All major · Meals: L, D · Closed Mon.

This big, glossy restaurant is an excellent introduction to Bolivian food, which resembles Peruvian but with its own distinctive stamp. Papas a la huancaina looks almost identical to the Peruvian specialty of cold boiled potatoes served in a spicy cheese sauce, but the Bolivian dish is made with ground peanuts, yellow peppers, hard-cooked eggs and olives. Look for dishes like chicharrón de puerco, delicious pieces of subtly-spiced pork served on the bone with white corn and boiled purple potatoes. Another pork dish, lechòn, is powerfully suffused with garlic and served with both white and sweet potatoes. Saltenas, or empanadas, and soups are generally delicious.

Other recommended dishes: Khallo cochabambino, humintas, orejon, batidos, chairo paceño, pollo dorado, chola. **Alcohol:** Beer. **Price range:** Apps., $2–$5; entrees, $6–$10. **Wheelchair access:** All one level.

Novitá · ☆ · $$ · ITALIAN
102 E. 22nd St. (bet. Park & Lexington Aves.) · (212) 677-2222
Credit cards: All major · Meals: L, D

The small room has been completely redecorated to give it the clean, elegant lines of a Milanese restaurant. Despite the elegance of the décor, the family-run restaurant has all the warmth of a mom-and-pop place. If you begin the meal with the ravioli of the day, you will not be disappointed. Or try the roast duck, which is served in a rich Barolo sauce. And grilled slices of steak, bathed in a pungent balsamic vinegar sauce on a fine warm bean salad, are deeply satisfying. Try the nouvelle ricotta cheesecake, a sort of cookies-and-cream confection with tuiles and berries.

Wine list: The all-Italian list is small but well chosen and reasonably priced. **Price range:** Apps., $8–$11; pastas, $14–$16; entrees, $19–$22; desserts, $7; prix-fixe lunch, $20. **Wheelchair access:** Not accessible. **Features:** Outdoor dining (sidewalk).

NYC · $$ · NEW AMERICAN
75 Greenwich Ave. (at Seventh Ave. S.) · (212) 366-6004
Credit cards: All major · Meals: D

NYC is, at heart, a glorified cafe. Slatted wooden window blinds cast film noir shadows across the interior. The menu has an easygoing, high-low feeling, with appetizers like crab pancake given a deluxe makeover with smoked salmon, crème fraîche and salmon roe, and steamed cockles in a potent broth thick with collard greens, roasted tomatoes and smoked bacon. The salad list is long, with occasional small, inventive touches.

There are five vegetarian entrees, none of them throwaways, including an open-faced ravioli with okra, baby zucchini and sage; BS goat cheese agnolotti with dried tomatoes, artichokes and Parmesan broth.

Price range: Entrees, $11–$29. **Wheelchair access:** Fully accessible.

Oceana   ☆☆☆ $$$$ SEAFOOD
55 E. 54th St. (bet. Park & Madison Aves.)   (212) 759-5941
Credit cards: All major   Meals: L, D   Closed Sun.

The good ship Oceana — a two-story town house decorated to resemble a yacht — has found a new surge of energy. Oysters on the half shell, each topped with a dollop of sturgeon caviar, are perfection. But the more complicated appetizers show what the kitchen can do. It brings a light touch to sweet lobster with lovage dressing. It uses fragrant pea leaves to send out a fresh green scent in a well-executed risotto that's plumped out with hen-of-the-woods mushrooms and chubby rock shrimp. Perhaps the most impressive entree is loup de mer, topped with a thin golden crouton and poised on a bed of coconut-flavored basmati rice. The desserts, although they often have a homey or even rustic touch, are presented elegantly, a prime example being pistachio semifreddo and chocolate crumb chiffon.

In restaurant years Oceana, which opened over a decade ago, is entering late middle age, but it shows no sign of faltering.

Other recommended dishes: Gnocchi with bacon cream, cinnamon-apple doughnut with Calvados ice cream. **Wine list:** An outstanding international list of more than 1,000 wines. **Price range:** Lunch, three courses, $45. Dinner, three courses, $68 ($100 with matching wines); six-course tasting menu, $110 ($180 with matching wines). **Wheelchair access:** Two steps up to dining room. Restrooms are downstairs.

Ocean Grill   ☆ $$ SEAFOOD
384 Columbus Ave. (bet. 78th & 79th Sts.)   (212) 579-2300
Credit cards: All major   Meals: Br, L, D, LN

The room is big and attractively understated, with a raw bar in the front and a boisterous clientele. Crab cakes are crisp and plump and served with a fine roasted corn salsa. The grilled fish are all nicely handled, and the french fries are excellent. Cold poached salmon is very pleasant, and even the hamburger is good. The sundae, an intense combination of brownies, hot fudge and ice cream, would make any child happy. (*Ruth Reichl*)

Wine list: Decent and fairly priced. **Price range:** Lunch: apps., $5–$9; entrees, $8–$18; three-course prix fixe, $18. Dinner: apps., $5–$11; entrees $15–$22; desserts $5–$7; pre-theater prix fixe, $20. **Wheelchair access:** Not accessible. **Features:** Outdoor dining (sidewalk).

Odeon ☆ ☆ $$

BISTRO/NEW AMERICAN

145 W. Broadway (at Thomas St.)
(212) 233-0507

Credit cards: All major
Meals: Br, L, D, LN

The Odeon, a beacon for Manhattan night crawlers since the early 1980's, may be the most consistent restaurant ever to put down roots south of 14th Street. It has always delivered solid bistro cuisine in an attitude-free atmosphere, even when it was the very definition of hip. It makes a strong first impression when the waiter greets diners with a hunk of chewy, rustic French bread and a small dish of black olives seasoned with lemon and lime zest. The menu is simple, with appetizers like a classic American shrimp cocktail rubbing shoulders with frisee aux lardons and onion soup. You expect to find a hangar steak with french fries, and there it is, along with trout amandine and a somewhat unusual grilled pork tenderloin with broccoli rabe, faro and bourbon sauce. Desserts run to homey American classics, like chocolate pudding, or bistro standbys like profiteroles. It may well be that in its 20 years of existence, the Odeon has never served a bad meal, and that's saying something. *(Review by William Grimes; stars previously awarded by Ruth Reichl.)*

Price range: Apps., $7.50–$11; entrees,$16–$26; desserts, $6–$8.
Wheelchair access: Fully accessible. **Features:** Outdoor dining (patio).

Ola ☆ $$

NUEVO LATINO

304 E. 48th St. (near Second Ave.)
(212) 759-0590

Credit cards: All major   Meals: L, D
Closed Sun.

At Ola, a narrow set of steps decorated in Spanish tile leads to a small, crowded bar, and onward to a long, booth-lined room that feels like a superdiner. If you can manage to land one of the secluded booths at the very back of the restaurant, there's a slim chance you might be able to hear the conversation at the table. Ola stands for "of Latin America." This vague affiliation allows the chef to do whatever on earth he wants, as long it has a Latin flavor. The tapas menu makes plenty of room for novelty items. The juicy "killer" dates are wrapped in bacon, stuffed with almonds and smothered in Cabrales cheese sauce. Two dates plus one of the "mystery" meatballs, a lump of velvety Kobe beef in a mushroom cream sauce, could make a meal. Like so many dishes on the menu, these are shameless and irresistible. Don't miss all-out flavor assaults like his whole grilled dorado in a spicy shrimp, scallop and calamari sauce, or lamb chops arranged on a heap of crisp shreds of lamb shank in a sauce made from feta cheese and huacatay, a Peruvian marigold. For dessert, the guava goat cheese cake is a chaste pillar of sweet, silky cheese topped with a bright slick of guava. Or try bright-orange roulade wrapped in flubber-like passion fruit gelatin.

Other recommended dishes: Oyster ceviche, scallop ceviche, chicken with Manchego fondue. **Wine list:** A workmanlike list of 100 wines, modestly priced, with the emphasis on Spain and South America. A dozen wines are offered by the glass. **Price range:**

Lunch: apps., $4–$13; entrees, $10–$22; desserts, $8. Dinner: apps., $4–$15; entrees, $22–$29; desserts, $8. **Wheelchair access:** Steps up to bar level and again to dining room level.

Old Devil Moon $25 & Under   SOUTHERN

511 E. 12th St. (bet. Aves. A & B)   (212) 475-4357
Credit cards: All major   Meals: Br, D   Closed Mon.

With mismatched chairs and tables, and walls covered with land-scapes, animals and old postcards, Old Devil Moon looks like the product of a thousand flea markets. Southern cuisine is the specialty, with huge helpings of pork chops and chicken, sometimes with Asian touches. Breakfasts are terrific, especially when country ham is served. The desserts are generous, full flavored and very rich, like dense peanut butter pie, powerful devil's-food cake and fine seasonal fruit pies.

Other recommended dishes: Ham and eggs, biscuits and gravy, frittata, greens with white beans, johnny cakes, sweet potato scallion hash, gnocchi, spice-crusted chicken, pork chops, chocolate pecan pie. **Alcohol:** Beer and wine. **Price range:** Apps., $5–$8; entrees, $8–$22; desserts, $4. **Wheelchair access:** Everything is on one level, but the restrooms are narrow.

Old Homestead $$$$ STEAKHOUSE

56 Ninth Ave. (bet. 14th & 15th Sts.)   (212) 242-9040
Credit cards: All major   Meals: L, D

The Old Homestead has been sitting in the middle of Manhattan's meatpacking district since 1868. For sheer quantity, nothing can beat the Homestead. When you order a porterhouse for two, a prodigious steak arrives, as thick as a fat book and twice as heavy. Other significant cuts include chateaubriand for two, the heavy-cut sirloin and prime ribs served on the bone. If you want to spend more than $100 a pound for Japanese Kobe beef, the Old Homestead happily accommodates you (although the meat is pretty disappointing). Just call in advance.

Price range: Apps., $5–$11; entrees, $25–$32; desserts, $4–$10. **Wheelchair access:** Fully accessible.

Old San Juan $25 & Under   PUERTO RICAN

765 Ninth Ave. (bet. 51st & 52nd Sts.)   (212) 262-6761
462 Second Ave. (at 26th St.)   (212) 779-9360
Credit: All major   Meals: L, D

One of New York's few Puerto Rican restaurants, Old San Juan serves unusual dishes like pasteles, similar to tamales except they are made with green bananas rather than corn; richly flavorful asopao, the soupy rice stew, and mild, tender stewed goat. It's not much for atmosphere, but service is friendly.

Price range: Entrees, $15; desserts, $3; lunch special, $7. **Wheelchair access:** Fully accessible. **Features:** Outdoor dining.

Olica ☆☆☆ $$$ FRENCH/NEW AMERICAN

145 E. 50th St. (bet. Lexington & Third Aves.)　　　(212) 583-0001
Credit cards: All major　　　Meals: B, L, D　　　Closed Sun.

Olica, formerly L'Actuel, is an even better restaurant than its prede-
cessor. The new restaurant has gotten a style upgrade that includes
Oriental rugs for the dark-wood floor and velvet upholstery for the
banquettes. In the center of the room there's a lush green lawn of
wheat grass that diners cannot resist combing with their fingers.

Chef Jean-Yves Schillinger cooks with the kind of easy confidence that bespeaks years of classic training. His best dishes have
the simplicity and clarity that only a complex culinary tradition can
produce. Three dishes are holdovers from L'Actuel: a classic Alsat-
ian tarte flambée; the delicious tuna-wasabi tarte flambée; and
scrambled eggs with caviar, a quiet, understated indulgence.

The dessert menu is dominated by a three-act chocolate drama.
The molten chocolate cake turned out to be a pleasant surprise.
Chocolate mille-feuille, diamond-shaped sheets of chocolate that
sandwich blobs of chocolate mousse flavored with bitter orange,
ran a close second. Just as good was a dome of bittersweet chocolate mousse that concealed a surprise in the center, chunks of apple
marmalade.

Wine list: A mostly French list of about 250 bottles, with both bargains and splurge wines, and many Champagnes. **Price range:**
Apps., $7–$16; entrees, $18–$25; dessert, $8–$9. **Wheelchair
access:** One level. **Features:** Outdoor dining.

Olives ☆ $$$ MEDITERRANEAN

W Union Square Hotel, 281 Park Ave. S. (at 17th St.) (212) 353-8345
Credit cards: All major　　　Meals: B, Br, L, D

Chef Todd English seduced Boston with his first Olives, and his
exuberant brand of cooking, which he calls "interpretive Mediterranean," made him a culinary star. Olives begat more Olives, in
Washington, Aspen and Las Vegas. And there are the television
shows and the cookbooks.

The W Union Square has been a magnet for young fun-seekers
since the day it opened. They have slouched all over its lounge,
packed the little bar at Olives and now populate Underbar, a floor
down, in great numbers. The dining-room crowd is fairly sedate,
and certainly older, but Olives is a hot ticket. Why? The food is easy
to like but hard to respect. Mr. English is the Thomas Wolfe of
chefs: no sooner is a thought in his head than it's on the plate. But
at least half the time the food at Olives really delivers. Do not look
for light, because you won't find it, but it's hard to beat Mr. English
for sheer palate-engulfing flavor. Rack of venison, wrapped in sliced
pears and roasted on rosemary branches, ranks as one of the best
venison dishes in New York. Desserts are the kind that make diners
feel pleasantly guilty. The napoleon seems halfway between a
French pastry and a banana split.

Wine list: A widely international list of 370 wines, reasonably
priced, with many Champagnes and 25 wines by the glass. **Price
range:** Lunch, apps., $9–$15; entrees, $13–$30; desserts, $8–$11.
Dinner, apps., $10 –$15; entrees, $18–$30; desserts, $8–$11. **Wheelchair access:** An elevator in the hotel lobby services the restrooms.

O Mai
$25 & Under   VIETNAMESE

158 Ninth Ave. (near 20th St.)   (212) 633-0550
Credit cards: All major   Meals: D

The restaurant has no sign out front, only potted bamboo plants
that wave in the cool Chelsea breeze. Behind them, bathed in soft,
amber light, sits a crowded storefront. The din is incredible and the
mood bright, everyone laughing. It is a heavily stylized place that
serves traditional, delicate Vietnamese fare, little of it blunted for
the Western palate. Start with the bewitching steamed clams with
kaffir leaves and lemon grass or the exceedingly good shrimp
dumplings called banh la. Main courses are less uniform in their
quality. The best available are a roasted duck with lime-ginger dipping sauce and that bird's less expensive cousin, a roasted chicken,
served with the same sauce. They are simple meals, beautifully
cooked. For dessert, it's the dark chocolate mousse with
caramelized orange sauce that everyone clamors for. *(Sam Sifton)*

Other recommended dishes: Spring rolls, papaya salad, grilled
calamari, sirloin tips, barbecue pork. **Price range:** Apps., $5–$9;
soups, noodles and entrees, $6–$17. **Wheelchair access:** Narrow
entrance; crowded dining room.

ONEc.p.s.
Satisfactory   **$**   BRASSERIE

Plaza Hotel, 1 Central Park S. (at Fifth Ave.)   (212) 583-1111
Credit cards: All major   Meals: Br, L, D

ONEc.p.s., whose little initials refer to Central Park South, does not
manage to pull off the difficult trick of transforming the former
Edwardian Room at the Plaza Hotel into a fresh-feeling brasserie.
The signs of struggle are everywhere. To arrest the eye, the designer
Adam Tihany has covered the ancient, massive chandeliers with
cartoonish red lampshades. Installing a bar near the entrance lends
some hum and buzz, but the place still wrestles with an identity
crisis. Is ONEc.p.s. a fine-dining experience or a breezy, slap-on-
the-back sort of place?

    Good food tends to silence awkward questions. Unfortunately,
there's not a lot of it here. Simpler is better at ONEc.p.s. The shellfish "bouquet" for two or more diner is a respectable seafood platter and rack of lamb with shepherd's pie gets the job done. For
dessert, try the tarte Tatin with a robust apple flavor or an excellent
little pecan tart.

Wine list: An international, eclectic list of about 180 wines, with
very slim pickings under $40. Eight wines are available in half bot-
tles. **Price range:** Apps., $9–$28; entrees, $18–$29; desserts,
$9–$13. **Wheelchair access:** Ramp at hotel entrance; accessible
restrooms are available by elevator in the lobby.

One If By Land, Two If By Sea
☆   **$$$$**
CONTINENTAL

17 Barrow St. (near Seventh Ave. S.)   (212) 255-8649
Credit cards: All major   Meals: D

Considered by many to be the most romantic restaurant in New York,
it is almost always booked. The lights are low, the gas fireplaces burn
even in the summer and a pianist serenades you with music. Known

mainly for the 1950's specialty Beef Wellington, the food has grown
more ambitious of late. Wild field greens with Champagne vinaigrette
and quenelles of Roquefort mousse is a perfectly fine salad. The
seared tuna is fresh and rosy, and the lightly smoked and roasted
rack of lamb is a fine piece of meat. Even poached peaches with pistachio ice cream are good. *(Ruth Reichl)*

Wine list: No bargains; generally better on American wines than
European ones. **Price range:** Three courses, $64; seven courses,
$75. **Wheelchair access:** Restrooms not accessible.

Onieal's Grand Street ☆ $$$ NEW AMERICAN

174 Grand St. (bet. Centre & Mulberry Sts.)   (212) 941-9119
Credit cards: All major   Meals: Br, L, D, LN

This is a beautiful, cozy restaurant with warm wood, a carved ceiling and fabric-covered banquettes. This small, clubby restaurant is
dripping with history: ask about the tunnel in the basement. Many
of the adventurous dishes are excellent, and seemingly simple
dishes are often more interesting than they sound. *(Ruth Reichl)*

Wine list: Not nearly so inventive as the menu; prices are fair.
Price range: Apps., $6–$11; entrees, $17–$24; desserts, $8. **Wheel-
chair access:** Step to dining room.

Ony $25 & Under JAPANESE/NOODLES

357 Sixth Ave. (near W. 4th St.)   (212) 414-8429
Credit cards: All major   Meals: L, D, LN

Like most Japanese restaurants in New York, Ony's menu includes
a full selection of sushi rolls. But its reason for being is noodles,
which is why the angled counter in the front of the bright and stylish dining room is for noodles, not sushi. In fact, the word Ony is
an acronym for Original Noodles for You.

    Slender lanterns hang over sleek blond wood tables, supple-
mented by little candles, while a second counter in the rear accom-
modates slurpers in a hurry. Simple noodle dishes include the
superb ramen noodles with pork chops. The central portion of the
menu is occupied by more complex noodle dishes, which are
served in miniature cauldrons. The oyster Menchanko, a miso broth
with ramen noodles, is thick with fat, tender oysters, chunks of
tofu, vegetables and billowy sheets of soy-milk skin. You can also
design your own Menchankos, selecting broth, noodles and perhaps fewer fillings.

Price range: Apps., $4–$9; entrees, $8–$18. **Wheelchair access:**
One level.

Orologio $ ITALIAN

162 Ave. A (bet. 10th & 11th Sts.)   (212) 228-6900
Credit cards: Cash only   Meals: D, LN

The most remarkable thing about this low-priced pasta restaurant
in the East Village is the seating, long tables that run around the
perimeter of the blocky room. Good luck if you need to get up in
the middle of a meal. You, and everybody around you, are in for an
ordeal. The food is decent and a good value.

Price range: Apps., $6–$8; pastas, $8–$9; entrees, $13–$15; desserts, $5. **Wheelchair access:** Restrooms not accessible. **Features:** Outdoor dining.

Orsay ☆☆ $$$

BISTRO/BRASSERIE

1057 Lexington Ave. (at 75th St.) (212) 517-6400
Credit cards: All major Meals: Br, L, D, LN

The restaurant looks as if it was ordered from a kit, with a lot of shiny brass, pristine leather banquettes and authentic French waiter costumes. But the cuisine does not follow the script. It has a fresh, wayward bent and an international style that saves Orsay from being yet one more exercise in French nostalgia.

One area of the menu worth lingering over showcases Orsay's hickory-chip smoker, which gives a dark, woodsy bite to salmon and to a dense, deeply flavored duck sausage. Oddly enough in this traditional setting, it's the traditional brasserie and bistro dishes that disappoint. Hanger steak is ordinary and rather tough. The T-bone is a better bet, and filet mignon, buttery-textured and enrobed in a thick pink-peppercorn sauce, hits it just right. The pastry chef limits his flights of fancy to small embellishments. His restrained raspberry napoleon is a perfectly executed classic, and the warm apple tart is flawless.

Wine list: A thoughtfully chosen list of about 150 wines, mostly French and tilted toward Bordeaux and Burgundy, but with a decent showing of wines from Italy, Spain and Austria. A dozen half bottles. **Price range:** Apps., $8–$14; entrees, $15–$26; desserts, $10. **Wheelchair access:** A restroom on the first floor. **Features:** Outdoor dining (terrace).

Orso $$$

ITALIAN

322 W. 46th St. (bet. Eighth & Ninth Aves.) (212) 489-7212
Credit cards: All major Meals: L, D

Pretty and pricey. Italian food in the theater district that is most fun late at night, when theater people come around for dinner after they have removed their makeup. The menu changes constantly, but the food is reliable.

Price range: Apps., $7–$9; entrees, $18–$22; desserts, $6–$7. **Wheelchair access:** Not accessible.

Osso Buco $25 & Under

ITALIAN

1662 Third Ave. (at 93rd St.) (212) 426-5422
88 University Pl. (bet. 11th & 12th Sts.) (212) 645-4525
Credit cards: All major Meals: L, D

Osso Buco is a family-style Italian-American restaurant that manages to remove the meal from the mythology. The menu includes nothing surprising or unusual, but much of the food is tasty and satisfying, with far more high points than lows. And it's a good value: the family-style portions, described as double size, are closer to triple. Even so, Osso Buco is much more of a casual neighborhood place than a destination for big groups. It's hard to imagine better fried calamari; linguine in a garlicky white clam sauce is also good. The veal dishes shine, particularly saltimbocca, a Friday night special, and the restaurant's namesake, osso buco, a bright and hearty veal shank stew, are also good. Service at Osso Buco is efficient and professional, blissfully free of singing waiters and overly gregarious types.

Other recommended dishes: Tricolore salad, Caesar salad, baked clams, ravioli with meat sauce. **Price range:** Apps., $10–$16; entrees, $15–$48 (prices are for family-style portions). **Wheelchair access:** Steps in dining room and to restrooms.

Osteria del Circo ☆ $$$ ITALIAN
120 W. 55th St. (near Sixth Ave.) (212) 265-3636
Credit cards: All major Meals: L, D

Osteria del Circo is a younger, more casual offshoot of the very grand Le Cirque 2000, a kind of one-ring circus to Sirio Maccioni's three-ring, Monte Carlo version. The freshened Osteria del Circo has new harlequin-pattern fabric on the chairs, circus-theme midnight-blue banquettes, lots of trapezes hung from the ceiling, and a big metal lion draped over the coat-check concession.

The restaurant has lots of visual pizazz, and enough Italian warmth to fire the ovens. It's easy enough to settle in, enjoy the show and not worry too much about the undeniable fact that the food is nothing special. Simple is best. Appetizers and pastas, on balance, outperform the entrees. The risotto is packed with button-size bay scallops, the rice firm but dissolving into creaminess at the edges. Main courses mostly fall apart, but roasted rabbit loin stuffed with fennel sausage acquits itself with honor, and cacciucco del Circo, a rustic fish stew, helps redeem the fish category.

The pastry chef, comes through with very pleasing desserts. The zuccotto al cioccolato is a suave, velvety dessert, intensely chocolaty without being cloying.

Wine list: A moderate-size list very strong on Tuscan and Piedmont wines. **Price range:** Lunch, apps., $8–$18; entrees, $12–$28. Dinner, apps., $9–$18; entrees, $14–$30; desserts, $6–$10; three-course prix-fixe, $39. **Wheelchair access:** One level.

Osteria del Sole $25 & Under ITALIAN
267 W. 4th Street (near Perry St.) (212) 620-6840
Credit cards: All major Meals: L, D

Never before have I been to a restaurant where the food was so good and the service so abysmal. While the waiter one night could not remember the beers on tap or the selection of ice creams, the beef carpaccio was thin and silky, and the pappardelle tossed with braised duck and porcini mushrooms pulsated with aroma.

On another night the waiter brought the wrong pasta, but also a delicious suckling pig roasted with myrtle. Simple things like cantaloupe draped with prosciutto and fried shrimp, calamari and strips of eggplant are flawless. On the dessert menu, there is a fluffy tiramisù and bananas, lightly fried and coated in sugar.

So Osteria del Sole is not a bad restaurant, and this is just why you may leave frustrated. (*Amanda Hesser*)

Other recommended dishes: Polenta with porcini mushrooms, fried shrimp and calamari, pappardelle with braised duck, trenette with sardines and Sicilian oranges, limoncello tartuffo. **Price range:** Apps., $6–$13; entrees, $10–$20. **Wheelchair access:** Steps to entrance.

Otabe ☆☆ $$$ JAPANESE
68 E. 56th St. (bet. Park & Madison Aves.) (212) 223-7575
Credit cards: All major Meals: L, D

Two separate dining rooms offer two different dining experiences. In the teppan room in the back it is a very upscale Benihana (with Kobe beef for those willing to pay the price). The elegant front dining room serves kaiseki-like cuisine. The kaiseki dinner is a lovely and accessible introduction to the most poetic food of Japan. Kaiseki is a ceremonial cuisine that is traditionally served in many small courses meant to reflect the season. Less ambitious eaters might want to sample fewer dishes. Soft-shell crab, fried and topped with a mixture of grated turnip and red peppers, is appealing. Desserts are the big surprise at Otabe; more French than Japanese, they are original, beautiful and very delicious. The teppan room has a separate menu, and each course is cooked before your eyes by your personal chef. (*Ruth Reichl*)

Wine list: The small list seems like an afterthought. **Price range:** Apps., $4–$12; entrees, $15–$65; desserts, $6–$10. **Wheelchair access:** Ramp to dining room.

Otto ☆☆ $ ITALIAN
1 Fifth Ave. (at 8th St.) (212) 995-9559
Credit cards: All major Meals: L, D

Otto is advertised as an enoteca and pizzeria, which is more and less than the truth. There is a serious all-Italian list. There are also a lot of pizzas, some traditional, others unique to Otto, and all cooked on top of the griddle rather than in an oven. But Otto may be the only pizzeria in New York where it's possible to skip the pizza entirely. The menu is devised, ingeniously, to stave off boredom, with separate categories devoted to antipasti, bruschettas, pizzas, fried appetizers, cheeses and desserts.

Otto has average pizzas, good pizzas, excellent pizzas and odd pizzas, like the one topped with ricotta, sliced potato and marinated anchovies. The pizza topped with lardo, or cured salt pork, is terrific. The fritto category is rewarding. Whitebait, fried to the crackling point, are perfection. For dessert, the gelati come plain and fancy, including the stunning sour ricotta gelato with crunchy glazed walnuts and dried figs.

Other recommended dishes: Pizza bianca, fennel and bottarga pizza, cauliflower with lemon and olives, chickpea fritters, marinated anchovies. **Wine list:** An impressive moderately priced list of nearly 500 wines covering all regions of Italy. **Price range:** Antipasti, bruschettas and fritti, $4–$8; pizzas, $7–$14; cheeses and desserts, $3–$10. **Wheelchair access:** All one level.

Ouest ☆☆ $$$ NEW AMERICAN/BISTRO

2315 Broadway (at 84th St.) (212) 580-8700
Credit cards: All major Meals: D

Long before the food arrives, Ouest (pronounced WEST), has most
diners eating out of the palm of its hand. It may have solved the
longest-running problem in restaurantland. How do you create a
lively atmosphere without obliterating the possibility of an intimate
meal? Thickly padded round booths with tall sides do the trick.
(Pray for a booth; the balcony seating is dark, cramped and loud.)

The cooking has a sane, rooted quality that makes it appropriate
for what is, when all is said and done, a neighborhood restaurant.
Main courses drift toward the comfort zone, with purées and soft
polenta to swaddle homey ingredients in a cushiony layer. Nuggets
of pork tenderloin wrapped in bacon are nicely set off by a thick,
garlicky white-bean purée and peppercorn sauce. Roast halibut has
a solid, uncomplicated appeal, and the same can be said of the special section of the menu devoted to simple grilled meats. Those in
an uncompromising meat mood should head straight for the short
ribs. For dessert try the rhubarb crisp with strawberry juice, classic
and all-American.

Wine list: A budget-priced bistro list of about 100 wines, mostly
French, Italian and Californian, with 10 wines by the glass. **Price
range:** Apps., $7–$12; entrees, $16–$27; desserts, $6–$8. **Wheelchair access:** Restrooms on street level.

Our Place Shanghai Tea Garden
$25 & Under CHINESE

141 E. 55th St. (bet. Lexington & Third Aves.) (212) 753-3900
Credit cards: All major Meals: L, D

With its elevated service and thick linens, Our Place has the feel of
a fine yet informal banquet. The Shanghai dishes are rich and satisfying, beautifully rendered, yet accessible to Americans, who make
up most of the clientele. The waiters are supremely attentive, dividing portions onto plates, putting umbrellas into drinks for young
children and generally offering to do anything short of feeding you.
Silver-dollar-size steamed soup dumplings are well-seasoned and
nicely textured. The kitchen excels at tofu dishes, like rich and delicious braised bean curd with crab meat and spinach, and knots of
bean curd skin tossed with fresh soybeans and chopped mustard
greens. Noodle dishes are also superb.

Other recommended dishes: Turnip pastries, cold vegetable duck,
fresh bacon and bean curd skin, lion's head, fried yellowfish. **Price
range:** Apps., $3–$9; entrees, $10–$25. **Wheelchair access:** One
level; restrooms are narrow.

Oyster Bar and Restaurant $$$ SEAFOOD

Grand Central Terminal (Lexington Ave. at 42nd St.) (212) 490-6650
Credit cards: All major Meals: L, D Closed Sun.

Today, there is really only one restaurant in the city where diners
can experience the oyster in its full glory, and that's the Oyster Bar

in Grand Central Terminal. The Oyster Bar, in business since 1913, may be the most infuriating restaurant in New York. For a certain kind of dining, nothing can beat it. Everything about the experience — the din and the tumult, the oyster shuckers working double-time, the vaulted tile ceilings — is almost transcendentally New York. Step away from the lunch counter, however, and a different Oyster Bar looms, a horribly overpriced, mediocre fish restaurant with poor service. The oyster list, with more than 30 varieties offered daily, shines as brightly as ever. The problems start if you leave the oyster trail. The bouillabaisse is a crime against nature. It's almost a rule that any dish with a sauce fails. The service can be charmingly inept or uncharmingly inept.

Other recommended dishes: Oysters on the half shell, broiled oysters with anchovy butter, oyster pan roast, cheesecake. **Wine list:** A 300-bottle list, mostly French and American, with bargains galore. **Price range:** Apps., $6.25–$15.50; entrees, $19.95–$29.95; desserts, $4.75–$6.50. **Wheelchair access:** There are no steps from street level to the entrance a floor below; restrooms are on dining level.

Oznot's Dish $25 & Under   MEDITERRANEAN
79 Berry St., Williamsburg, Brooklyn   (718) 599-6596
Credit cards: MC/V   Meals: Br, L, D, LN

In a neighborhood like Williamsburg, restaurants are routinely called quirky and offbeat. But Oznot's is truly unusual, a veritable flea market of mosaics, mismatched furniture and artwork set on a rickety, uneven wood floor. The blend of Mediterranean food is just as interesting.

Price range: Lunch: apps., $4–$6; entrees, $5–$9. Dinner: apps., $5–$9; entrees, $10–$22; desserts, $6. **Wheelchair access:** Not accessible.

Pachas $25 & Under   LATIN AMERICAN
93-21 37th Ave., Flushing, Queens   (718) 397-0729
Credit cards: All major   Meals: B, L, D, LN

The Colombian-Venezuelan menu at Pachas presents problems. For one thing, the cuisines of Venezuela and Colombia have many dishes in common, yet items on the Venezuelan menu seem to lack sparkle. Order from the much bigger Colombian menu and the difference will be clear. Try the sublime arepa buche, a blend of tender tripe, tomato and onion, boiled down to a soulful essence. On one visit, the waitress watched with a knowing look. "Colombian food can't be beat," she said. Among the best dishes is the muchacho relleno, pork loin stuffed with chopped peppers, tomatoes, onions and peas and covered with a peppery Creole sauce. Pachas has no liquor license but makes excellent batidos, or fruit shakes, in tropical flavors like lulo, a sweet and tart citrus.

Other recommended dishes: Arepas Colombian style with chicken and avocado, shredded beef, cheese or tripe stew; calentando. **Price range:** Apps., $1–$7; entrees, $6–$13. **Wheelchair access:** All one level.

Palacinka $25 & Under   CAFE/CREPES

28 Grand St. (at Sixth Ave.)   (212) 625-0362
Credit cards: Cash only   Meals: B, Br, L, D

This little restaurant, decorated with the sort of 1930's travel para-
phernalia romanticized in J. Peterman catalogues, specializes in
crepes. The cylindrical buckwheat-flour crepes are terrific and come
with Gruyere and egg, or with roasted chicken, goat cheese and
roasted peppers. Dessert crepes are also great, particularly the lime,
which is made with white flour, dusted with sugar and drizzled
with fresh lime juice.

Price range: Sandwiches and salads, $7–$9; savory crepes, $7–$8;
sweet crepes, $4–$6. **Wheelchair access:** All on All one level.

Paladar $25 & Under   CARIBBEAN/MEXICAN

161 Ludlow St. (near Stanton St.)   (212) 473-3535
Credit cards: Cash only   Meals: D, LN

A long bar is the centerpiece of Paladar's narrow pastel-colored
front dining room. A better choice when weather permits is the
wider garden area. The menu hews closely to Mexican and
Caribbean dishes. Standout appetizers include sopes,thick but delicate corn tortillas covered in avocado salsa and a fragrant sauce of
fermented black beans, and a savory quesadilla with chorizo and
roasted tomatoes. Seafood is a highlight, with excellent choices like
roasted mahi-mahi in an orange-chili vinaigrette over coconut-flavored rice. Seafood guisado, a sort of bouillabaisse, has a complex
coconut broth that is simultaneously smoky and spicy.

Other recommended dishes: Ceviche, fried calamari, watercress
salad, stuffed pork chop, sautéed shrimp, tres leches cake, coconut
flan. **Price range:** Apps., $4–$8; entrees, $9–$14. **Wheelchair
access:** Not accessible.

Palm $$$ STEAKHOUSE

837 Second Ave. (bet. 44th & 45th Sts.)   (212) 687-2953
840 Second Ave. (bet. 44th & 45th Sts.)   (212) 697-5198
250 W. 50th St. (bet. Broadway & Eighth Ave.)   (212) 333-7256
Credit cards: All major   Meals: L, D

Great steak, rude waiters and the world's best hash brown potatoes. The walls are covered with caricatures, the floor is covered
with sawdust and if you want to experience the real New York rush,
this is the place for you. If you can't get into the Palm, you may
want to settle for second best, **Palm Too** (the 840 Second Ave. location). Then again, probably not. It is NEVER as good as the place
across the street.

The newest addition (on 50th St.) doesn't have the original
Palm's venerable gritty patina, built up over 73 years of charring
steaks and meat-eating smokers. And the celebrity cartoons on the
walls, many of them reproductions of the originals at the Palm on
Second Avenue, do not have that baked-on aura. But it is pretty and
spacious, with a big bar area with piano music, and several private
rooms. A number of light lunch items like crab cakes and Cobb
salad have been added.

Price range: Lunch: apps., $7–$14; entrees, $11–$35; desserts, $8. Dinner, apps., $10–$16; entrees, $16–$38; desserts, $8. **Wheelchair access:** Fully accessible.

Pamir $25 & Under   AFGHANI

1437 Second Ave. (at 75th St.)   (212) 734-3791
Credit cards: MC/V   Meals: L, D

Pamir is a friendly, attractive little restaurant festooned with rugs and artifacts that glow in the candlelight. Afghan cuisine is something of a patchwork quilt, joining bits and pieces of the cuisines of the surrounding Middle Eastern and South Asian cultures. Bulanee, crisp, almost flat stuffed turnovers, for example, are reminiscent of samosas, yet they seem more delicate and refined. Aushak, lacy, flat scallion-stuffed dumplings that resemble wontons, are topped with the contrasting flavors of cooling fresh mint and a savory yogurt and meat sauce. The list of main courses seems extensive, but a small range of ingredients are simply packaged in different ways. More interesting variations include norange palaw, a mound of rice dotted with almonds, pistachios, carrots and little strips of orange peel, covering tender chunks of stewed lamb. The main courses come with a green salad and a round of puffy Afghan bread.

Other recommended dishes: Sliced potatoes with chickpeas, yogurt and cucumbers; kebabs; lamb with spinach; sautéed pumpkin; baklava. **Price range:** Apps., $3.25 to $4.95; entrees, $11.95 to $16.50. **Wheelchair access:** Steps to restrooms.

Pampa $25 & Under   ARGENTINE

768 Amsterdam Ave. (bet. 97th & 98th Sts.)   (212) 865-2929
Credit cards: Cash or check only   Meals: D

The restaurant pickings are slim on Amsterdam Avenue in the 90's, where this rustic but pleasant and inexpensive Argentine meatery stands out for its lean, flavorful steaks. Grilled steaks, skirt steaks and filet mignon are all outstanding, as is the rotisserie-cooked Peruvian chicken. Vegetables? Worry about them some other time.

Alcohol: Beer and wine. **Price range:** Apps., $2–$8; entrees, $8–$15; desserts, $4–$6. **Wheelchair access:** Fully accessible. **Features:** Outdoor dining.

Pampano   ☆☆ $$$ MEXICAN

209 E. 49th St. (near Third Ave.)   (212) 751-4545
Credit cards: All major   Meals: L, D

Plácido Domingo turned to Richard Sandoval, the chef and owner of Maya, to work some magic into a restaurant that seemed to have only one thing going for it, Mr. Domingo's name. Mr. Sandoval rose to the challenge. Wiping the slate clean, he created a Mexican seafood menu, fresh and contemporary, that brings spice, color and excitement to a formerly listless dining room that has been redecorated in a startling white-on-white beach style. Chiles de árbol apply mild heat to what may be Pampano's signature dish, an appetizer of three miniature lobster tacos on soft tortillas. Raw bar appetizers like cherrystone clams with a spicy vinaigrette deflect attention, unwisely, from ceviches like shrimp in a spicy chipotle sauce with avocado and jicama. The menu does include a few meat dishes, notably a flavorful if messy rib-eye steak heaped with yellow-tomato salsa, guacamole and a long list of adornments.

For dessert try pastel de elote, slices of warm, pudding-like corn cake served with rich coconut ice cream and hibiscus sauce.

When restaurants begin revising their formulas and rewriting their menus, the end is usually near. Pampano, against the odds, has finally found a way to get started.

Other recommended dishes: Black-bean soup with seafood sausage, smoked swordfish dip, shrimp empanadas, pan-fried snapper with cactus salad, shrimp with anaheim peppers stuffed with goat cheese, lamb in banana leaf. **Wine list:** An adventurous list of about 150 wines, with an emphasis on California. **Price range:** Lunch: apps., $7–$9.50; entrees, $17.50–$20; three-course prix fixe, $20. Dinner: apps., $9.50–$14; entrees, $20.50–$26; desserts, $5.50–7.95 **Wheelchair access:** Several steps to dining room.

Pam Real Thai Food $25 & Under   THAI
404 W. 49th St. (at 9th Ave.)   (212) 333-7500
Credit cards: Cash only   Meals: L, D

Most Thai restaurants in New York must appeal to a largely American clientele, which leads many of them to compromise by adding sweetness and toning down the long, slow buildup of chili heat that is a Thai characteristic. At this sweet little restaurant, the compromises are not always obvious. The owner says the restaurant tones down the heat for the supposedly tender American palate, but your palate will revel in the kitchen's sure-handed spicing. Pam's curries are superb. Try chu chee curry with pork, with its underlying flavor of coconut milk laced with chili heat and a pungent but refreshing dimension added by lime leaves. Also try pad kra prow with beef, which has plenty of basil flavor, balanced by garlic and chilies.

Pam is a resolutely plain place. The boxy dining room offers some travel posters to take your mind off the industrial ceiling tile.

Other recommended dishes: Crisp duck salad, green papaya salad, panang curry, duck with green beans. **Price range:** Apps., $3–$6; entrees, $7–$14. **Wheelchair access:** One level.

Panino'teca 275 $25 & Under   SANDWICHES/ITALIAN
275 Smith St. (near Sackett St.), Carroll Gardens, Brooklyn
                                                  (718) 237-2728
Credit cards: Cash only   Meals: L, D   Closed Mon.

The Italian sandwich and wine bar is an equivalent of the Spanish tapas bar, a relaxed place to drop in for a snack and a drink, with the option of moving on or making a night of it. Panino'teca is a small, boxy room, which seems plain until you look more closely and find unexpected details, like the series of reclining nudes laminated onto the bar.

The sandwich portion of the menu is divided into four sections: bruschetta; toasts, which, like the bruschetta, are served open-faced; tramezzini, triangular, crustless white-bread sandwiches; and panini, pressed sandwiches made with small hero rolls. For sheer freshness, the bruschetta are highlights. They include a tomato and basil, and a tramezzini with prosciutto and fig jam. For dessert, you can't go wrong with a panini slathered with Nutella, the chocolate and hazelnut spread, and a sweet caramel-apple shortcake is creamy and luscious.

Other recommended dishes: Figs stuffed with prosciutto; arugula salad with pancetta, potato, artichoke and tuna; tuna and roasted pepper tramezzini; panini with bresaola. **Price range:** Apps., $5–$9; bruschetta and sandwiches, $3–$7. **Wheelchair access:** One step at entrance; restrooms are narrow.

Pan Pan Restaurant $ SOUTHERN

500 Lenox Ave. (at Malcolm X. Blvd.) (212) 926-4900
Credit cards: Cash only Meals: B, L, D

This simple luncheonette in Harlem offers excellent waffles, served alone or in that classic combination of fried chicken and waffles, as well as other Southern breakfast specialties like salmon croquettes with grits and buttery biscuits.

Alcohol: Beer. **Price range:** Dishes from $2–$10. **Wheelchair access:** Restrooms not accessible.

Pão $25 & Under PORTUGUESE

322 Spring St. (at Greenwich St.) (212) 334-5464
Credit cards: All major Meals: L, D, LN

The small menu in this small (34 seats) restaurant offers traditional Portuguese cuisine with a contemporary touch. To begin, try roasted quail on cabbage braised with linguica — the mild Portuguese sausage — and black grapes; baked octopus in garlic-cilantro vinaigrette, and an excellent potato broth with shredded kale, chunks of potato and slices of sausage. Main dishes include pork and clams in a roasted-red-pepper sauce; grilled shrimp served with a clam-and-shrimp-studded lemony bread pudding, and sautéed salt cod with egg, onion and straw potatoes. Desserts are not to be missed, particularly the pudding with port-and-prune sauce and the rice pudding with citrus, nutmeg and cinnamon.

Price range: Lunch: apps., $4–$7; entrees, $9–$13; desserts, $4. Dinner: apps., $6–$9; entrees, $14–$17; desserts, $5–$6. **Wheelchair access:** All one level. **Features:** Outdoor dining.

Paola's ☆☆ $$$ ITALIAN

245 E. 84th St. (bet. Second & Third Aves.) (212) 794-1890
Credit cards: All major Meals: L, D

Everybody in New York seems to be looking for the perfect neighborhood restaurant. This may be it. Paola's is one of New York City's best and least-known Italian restaurants. Paola makes some of the city's finest pasta, and the wine list is wonderful. No regular would even consider starting a meal here without an order of carciofi alla giudea, as fine a version of baby artichokes fried in the style of the Roman ghetto as you will find in this country. But pastas are the soul of the menu. Filled pastas such as cazunzei and pansotti are wonderful. Entrees are a different matter, and the preparations can be inconsistent. The safe choice here is the veal scaloppine. Desserts, with the exception of a fine, light ricotta cake, seem like an afterthought. (*Ruth Reichl*)

Wine list: Many good and unusual Italian wines at reasonable prices. **Price range:** Apps., $6–$14; pastas, $14–$19; entrees, $17–$29; desserts, $8. **Wheelchair access:** Step to dining room. **Features:** Outdoor dining.

Paradou $25 & Under   FRENCH/SANDWICHES
8 Little W. 12th St. (near Ninth Ave.)   (212) 463-8345
Credit cards: D/MC/V   Meals: D, LN

Paradou is a panini shop born of a different Mediterranean coast where the specialty is "sandwichs grillés," as they would say in Provence. The little high-ceilinged dining room is imbued with the sunny white and yellow colors of Provence. Tables and the bar are constructed of shellacked wine crates. The room is comfortable if at times loud. But while Paradou strives for a relaxed Mediterranean atmosphere, waiters at times strike haughty Parisian poses.

Paradou excels where it counts, with a delicious range of sand-wiches, some distinctly French, and some — well, we'll just call them Mediterranean. The sampler of five tartines for $10 is the best deal. The larger grilled sandwiches, served on pressed, toasted baguettes with a small salad, make surprisingly substantial meals.

Other recommended dishes: Sausages and lentils, chocolates, cheeses, Nutella and banana crepe, citrus crepe. **Price range:** Tartines, salads and sandwiches, $5–$15; larger plates, $12–$20. **Wheelchair access:** One level.

Paris Commune $ FRENCH
411 Bleecker St. (bet. W. 11th & Bank Sts.)   (212) 929-0509
Credit cards: All major   Meals: Br, D

The dim candlelight, the brick walls with dusty portraits, the floor as level as a wavy ocean all combine to epitomize the Greenwich Village grotto. Paris Commune is a friendly local hangout with a simple, appealing French-inspired menu.

Price range: Apps., $5–$8; entrees, $11–$20; desserts, $5. **Wheelchair access:** Restrooms not accessible.

Parish & Company   ☆ $$ NEW AMERICAN
202 Ninth Ave. (at 22nd St.)   (212) 414-4988
Credit cards: All major   Meals: L, D, LN

Parish & Company's very eclectic mix-and-match menu roams far and wide but never seems to lose its way. It is a model neighbor-hood restaurant for tough times. The tables are covered in brown paper, and the restaurant will win no beauty contests. But Parish & Company, modest and overachieving, pays attention to detail. The menu offers most dishes in appetizer and entree sizes, making it possible to create a meal consisting of many small bites. The small plates include some good ceviches, especially scallops marinated in white miso. Cured sardines, fat and happy, are arranged simply with a scattering of bitter greens. The kitchen can stumble badly. But steamed halibut responds wonderfully to a piquant, nearly transparent broth flavored with ginger and fennel. Chilean sea bass, a richer, oilier fish, is coated with soy, sherry, lime and galangal. Desserts can be lackluster. The audacious avocado-chocolate experiment, despite its sadistic overtones, may be the way to go.

Other recommended dishes: Potato gnocchi with ghee, wild yam pierogi, scallop dumpling, sardines with tomato confit. **Wine list:** Small, serviceable, moderately priced. **Price range:** Lunch: apps., $3–$9; entrees, $13–$19; desserts, $5–$6. Dinner: apps., $4–$13; entrees, $13–$23; desserts, $5–$7. **Wheelchair access:** Restrooms on dining level.

Park Avalon $$ NEW AMERICAN

225 Park Ave. S. (bet. 18th & 19th Sts.)   (212) 533-2500
Credit cards: All major   Meals: Br, L, D

It's young, exuberant and very noisy. It is also reasonably priced and the American food is good. No wonder there are almost always lines. Especially good for the Sunday jazz brunch.

Price range: Lunch: apps., $5–$7; entrees, $9–$11; desserts, $5–$7. Dinner: apps., $6–$8; entrees, $14; desserts, $5–$7. **Wheelchair access:** Fully accessible.

Park Avenue Cafe   ☆ ☆ $$$$ NEW AMERICAN

100 E. 63rd St. (near Park Ave.)   (212) 644-1900
Credit cards: All major   Meals: L, D

Park Avenue Cafe, which opened to great fanfare in 1992, is still a good restaurant, but it feels a little past its prime. This does not seem to bother the Upper East Siders who treat it as a beloved neighborhood fixture where they can relax and eat sanely reinterpreted, high-spirited American food. The restaurant looks like a Cracker Barrel made over by Martha Stewart. And the hapless waiters wear silly ties with a hideous American flag pattern. It's an impressive display of nerdsmanship.

Pastas are among the best dishes on the menu, but the most sinfully indulgent experience is the formidable terrine of foie gras, served folksy style in a glass jar with fig jam smeared on the hinged lid. This is the whole hog, so to speak. The signature "swordchop" still holds its place on the menu, a mighty slab of swordfish attached to the collarbone. The restaurant's signature dessert, the admittedly ridiculous Park Avenue Park Bench, really does succeed as theater. With its chocolate slatted bench and leaning lamppost topped by a white chocolate globe, it exudes a strange, twilight melancholy.

Wine list: A reasonably priced if not terribly adventurous list of more than 200 wines with emphasis on California. **Price range:** Lunch, apps., $9–$17; entrees, $20–$29; desserts, $5–$9. Dinner, apps., $12–$16; entrees, $20–$42; desserts, $9–$12. Three-course prix- fixe, $65. **Wheelchair access:** One step up at entrance, six steps to restrooms.

Park Bistro ☆☆☆ $$$ Bistro/French

414 Park Ave. S. (bet. 28th & 29th Sts.)   (212) 689-1360
Credit cards: All major   Meals: L, D

A classic French bistro, from the décor (photos of Paris in the
1950's) to the menu (magret, onglet and so forth). It offers seductive Gallic fare, good wines at reasonable prices and a cozy setting.
After languishing in recent years, it looks as though the restaurant
is on the upswing again with the arrival of Philippe Roussel, who
has put some verve and style back in the kitchen. It's still one of
the most atmospheric bistros in town, with one of the warmest wel-
comes. There is a daily selection of imported cheeses, and to top off
the meal, thin warm apple tart with Armagnac and vanilla ice
cream; fresh roasted fig tart, or the ubiquitous crème brûlée. There
is a large and interesting selection of tea in addition to several cof-
fees. (*Ruth Reichl, updated by William Grimes*)

Price range: Apps., $9–$12.50; entrees, $19–$24; dessert, $7.
Wheelchair access: Fully accessible.

Park View at the Boathouse ☆☆ $$$
New American

Loeb Boathouse, Central Park, E. 72nd St. entrance   (212) 517-2233
Credit cards: All major   Meals: Br, L, D

Is this Manhattan's most romantic spot? Very possibly. Situated in
the Loeb Boathouse next to Central Park's prettiest lake, it combines the country charm with views of skyscrapers peeking over the
trees. The conversion from the Boathouse Cafe has added interesting, eclectic food and a good wine list. Even when you are eating
one of the less fortunate entrees, the setting is so swell that you feel
lucky to be there. The live jazz at the adjacent cafe, which is still
called the Boathouse Cafe, is a real bonus. (*Ruth Reichl*)

Wine list: Interesting and filled with unusual choices and hard-to-
find bottles. **Price range:** Brunch: apps., $8–$12; entrees, $14–$23.
Lunch: apps., $10–$14; entrees, $18–$26. Dinner: apps., $8–$14;
entrees, $18–$30; desserts, $7–$8. **Wheelchair access:** Indoor dining room at street level; ramp down to dock. **Features:** Good view,
outdoor dining.

Pascalou $25 & Under   Bistro/French

1308 Madison Ave. (near 93rd St.)   (212) 534-7522
Credit cards: MC/V   Meals: Br, L, D

This likable neighborhood restaurant, which looks like a well-worn
family restaurant in southwestern France, offers well-prepared
French and Italian dishes, occasionally with Asian touches. There
are a half-dozen pastas available, including seafood capellini and
polenta with mozzarella, basil, pesto and grilled shrimp. Entrees
include roasted chicken with rosemary, calf's liver, shrimp curry
with basmati rice, a fish of the day, and a wok-sautéed vegetable
platter.

Other recommended dishes: Duck confit, bowtie pasta with mushrooms and truffle oil, lamb chops. **Alcohol:** Beer and wine. **Price
range:** Apps., $7–$14; entrees, $13–$22; desserts, $7–$10. Prix-fixe

dinner (5-6:45 P.M.), $18.45. **Wheelchair access:** Restrooms not accessible.

Pastis ☆ $$$

9 Ninth Ave. (at Little W. 12th)
Credit cards: All major

BRASSERIE/FRENCH
(212) 929-4844
Meals: L, D, LN

New Yorkers tolerate the most cramped and overcrowded living conditions in the United States, so they naturally gravitate to places of entertainment that are even more cramped and overcrowded. This instinct partly explains the overpowering allure of Pastis, a restaurant named after a drink that most Americans would not touch with a 10-foot pole. What do diners get for their suffering? A meal that's as good as it needs to be, but no better.

The menu is so traditional that virtually every dish could qualify for protection by the French Ministry of Culture. It's a deliberate invitation to simple pleasures. A frisée aux lardons is, as the French say, correct. There are a few American-style concessions, like hamburgers. But the point of the exercise lies in dishes like braised beef with glazed carrots, a rich, savory and unabashedly declassé hunk of meat. If steak frites is the acid test of a dependable bistro, however, then Pastis needs to work a little harder. Its béarnaise sauce — dense and creamy, with a sharp vinegar note — is fine, and the fries are too, but the steak is a little tough and stringy. The dessert menu is a minefield, but the crêpes suzette rise up in glory, and the floating island floats, a cloud with just enough substance to support its light custardy sauce.

Wine list: About 40 wines by the bottle, most from Bordeaux and Burgundy, with about 25 more modest bistro wines by the glass, half carafe, and carafe. **Price range:** Apps., $6–$11, entrees, $14–$17; desserts, $7. **Wheelchair access:** All one level.

Patio Dining $25 & Under

31 Second Ave. (near 1st St.)
Credit cards: All major   Meals: D

NEW AMERICAN
(212) 460-9171
Closed Sun. & Mon.

The 30-seat Patio has all the signs of a dreamy fantasy of an East Village restaurant. The narrow dining room, a mélange of flea-market décor, is more atmospheric than comfortable. Candles offer dim moody lighting, and the tiny tables are graced with daisies poking out of milk bottles.

The chef, Sara Jenkins, creates a new menu every night, according to what looks good in the market. She is an inspired matchmaker, pairing, for example, meltingly tender pork belly with mildly bitter braised endive, supported by crisp little roasted potatoes and caramelized garlic cloves.

It's hard to make a case that a cramped little East Village restaurant, with a friendly but barely trained staff, ought to offer a wine list with more bottles over $100 — four — than under $30 — zero. The real value of Patio is to see what Ms. Jenkins is up to each evening. She never falls back on easy choices, so occasional misses are forgivable.

Price range: Apps., $7–$12; entrees, $12–$22. **Wheelchair access:** One level. Features: Outdoor dining (patio).

Patois $25 & Under   BISTRO/FRENCH

255 Smith St., Carroll Gardens, Brooklyn   (718) 855-1535
Credit cards: All major   Meals: Br, D   Closed Mon.

This small storefront restaurant offers rich, gutsy bistro fare that
can range from authentically French tripe stew — a mellow, wonderful dish, if not destined for popularity — to juicy pork chops and
satisfying casseroles. Dishes don't always work, but it's nice that
Patois is trying.

Other recommended dishes: Lamb and white bean casserole;
warm leek, Roquefort and potato tart; grilled Provençal vegetables;
steamed mussels; split-pea soup; chocolate cake; tarte Tatin. **Alcohol:** Beer and wine. **Price range:** Apps., $5–$8; entrees, $10–$17.
Wheelchair access: One step at entrance; entrance to restroom is
narrow. **Features:** Outdoor dining.

Patria   ☆☆☆ $$$$ NUEVO LATINO

250 Park Ave. S. (20th St.)   (212) 777-6211
Credit cards: All major   Meals: L, D

When Andrew DiCataldo succeeded the hugely popular Douglas
Rodriguez as executive chef at Patria, he must have felt like a may-
oral candidate running in the shadow of Rudolph W. Giuliani. Mr.
DiCataldo has settled in, found his footing and hit his stride. Patria
is his show now, and you can sense it. The tone is a little quieter, a
little less like a big, nonstop party. The service is more dignified.
Even the busboys are suave. And the food is superb.

Mr. DiCataldo can splash color and flavor all over the plate —
what's the point of nuevo Latino if you don't — but he has a fine,
disciplined hand. He understands subtleties. His menu is fun, high
flying and inventive, but the ideas never spin out of control. One
simple entree stands out: roast chicken in a smoky chipotle sauce
flavored with huitlacoche, or corn fungus.

For dessert, the honors go to three little flans, vanilla, corn and
pineapple, and to a disarmingly spare-looking plate dotted with
bombones, or frozen buttons of dulce de leche covered in shaved
chocolate and accompanied by cherry marmalade.

Wine list: Nearly 500 wines, emphasizing Spain, Chile and
Argentina. There are 18 wines by the glass, 32 half bottles and 23
magnum and larger bottles. **Price range:** Lunch entrees, $10–$20;
three-course prix-fixe, $20. Dinner: apps., $9–$16; entrees, $24–$32;
desserts, $8; three-course vegetarian tasting menu, $45; five
courses, $59; five-course nonvegetarian tasting menu, $69; seven
courses, $79. **Wheelchair access:** One level.

Patroon   ☆ $$$$ STEAKHOUSE/NEW AMERICAN

160 E. 46th St. (bet. Third & Lexington Aves.)   (212) 883-7373
Credit cards: All major   Meals: L, D

The new Patroon, done up in contrasting shades of brown and
beige, looks more like the dining room of an airport hotel than an
up-to-date "21" Club. This is not to suggest that Patroon has
become inexpensive. It's a steakhouse with steakhouse prices, but
the menu has been pruned of almost all excess and, for that matter,
individuality. Simplicity now rules. The small selection of oysters

on the half shell are superb. A jumbo crab cake is practically all meat, a thoroughly satisfying mouthful of pure flavor. As far as beef goes, though, little things tend to go wrong. Steaks, for example, were consistently overcooked. Where the steaks are wanting, fish dishes are excellent. Dover sole was supremely elegant.

Desserts are straightforward in the typical steakhouse way — hefty wedges of creamy cheesecake, chocolate cake with an interior that has the consistency of chocolate pudding and hearty hot fudge sundaes. *(Eric Asimov)*

Wine list: Extensive, with many rare and expensive bottles but excellent moderately priced choices as well. **Price range:** Lunch entrees, $17–$33. Dinner: apps., $9–$19; entrees, $20–$42; desserts, $8.50. **Wheelchair access:** Restrooms are narrow.

Patsy's Italian $$ ITALIAN

236 W. 56th St. (bet. Broadway & Eighth Ave.)   (212) 247-3491
Credit cards: All major   Meals: L, D

Rao's for the rest of us. If Damon Runyon were still around, this is where he'd eat. The menu features seriously old-fashioned New York Italian dishes like mozzarella in carozza served in enormous portions. Good hot appetizers like clams posillipo, chopped salads and lots of stuffed dishes with red sauce.

Price range: Apps., $10–$12; entrees, $16–$31; desserts, $6–$7.
Wheelchair access: Restrooms not accessible.

Patsy's Pizzeria $25 & Under PIZZA

509 Third Ave. (at 34th St.)   (212) 689-7500
67 University Pl. (bet. 10th & 11th Sts.)   (212) 533-3500
61 W. 74th St. (at Columbus Ave.)   (212) 579-3000
1312 Second Ave. (at 69th St.)   (212) 639-1000
2287 First Ave. (bet. 117th & 118th Sts.)   (212) 534-9783
Credit cards: Cash only   Meals: L, D

Patsy's Pizzerias are turning up all over town, as this chain continues to expand. As chains go, Patsy's is a good thing since the ambition is to make classic New York pizza. On the whole, they all do a pretty good job, with smooth, thin crusts and superb toppings.

Price range: Apps., $6–$10; entrees, $8–$15; desserts, $5–$6.
Wheelchair access: Fully accessible.

Payard Pâtisserie ☆ ☆ $$$ BISTRO/FRENCH

1032 Lexington Ave. (at 73rd St.)   (212) 717-5252
Credit cards: All major   Meals: L, D   Closed Sun.

This is the ultimate Upper East Side bistro, a whimsical belle epoque cafe and pastry shop, complete with mirrors, mahogany and hand-blown lamps. Just about everything here is extraordinary, from the inventive bistro menu to the amazing pastries sold in the bakery. A recent visit showed that chef Philippe Bertineau is still going strong, with inventive, impeccably executed dishes like a twice baked cheese soufflé with Parmesan cream sauce, sardines stuffed with quince chutney, and a simple sirloin steak with four-peppercorn sauce. The terrine of foie gras is the real thing, and irresistible. And then there is dessert: clear, true flavors, beautifully presented. (*Ruth Reichl, updated by William Grimes*)

Wine list: Beautifully chosen and reasonably priced. **Price range:** Apps., $6–$15; sandwiches, $10–$12; entrees, $17–$25; desserts, $7–$15; tea, $14–$20. **Wheelchair access:** Main dining room and restrooms at street level.

Pearl Oyster Bar $25 & Under   SEAFOOD

18 Cornelia St. (bet. Bleecker & W. 4th St.)   (212) 691-8211
Credit cards: MC/V   Meals: L, D   Closed Sun.

It's just a marble counter with a few small tables, but Pearl has won over its neighborhood with its casual charm and Maine-inspired seafood. The restaurant is modeled on the Swan Oyster Depot in San Francisco, and when packed exudes a Barbary Coast rakishness. The menu changes seasonally, but grilled pompano was sweet and delicious, while scallop chowder was unusual and satisfying. Lobster rolls are big and delicious, and blueberry pie is sensational. Don't forget the oysters.

Other recommended dishes: Green salad, seared sea scallops. **Alcohol:** Beer and wine. **Price range:** Apps., $7–$9; entrees, $17–$26; desserts, $5. **Wheelchair access:** One step up at entrance; aisle to restroom is narrow.

Pearson's Texas Barbecue $25 & Under
BARBECUE

71-04 35th Ave., Jackson Heights, Queens   (718) 779-7715
Credit cards: Cash only   Meals: L, D   Closed Mon. & Tue.

The only pit barbecue restaurant in New York City has a new home, and the barbecue is better than ever. The smoke outside may be gone, but once you enter Legends, a pleasant-enough brick-and-panel bar, you know you're in the right place. In the rear, burnished slabs of pork ribs glisten behind a counter next to piles of plump sausages and chickens turned almost chestnut by smoke. Even so, the glory of Pearson's is its brisket, superb, tender and fully imbued with smoke from the rosy-brown, almost crisp exterior through to the pink center. It is so good that it needs none of the tomato-based barbecue sauce, which is offered in mild, medium and hot gradations. Pork ribs are excellent, meaty, smoky and well-flavored.

Other recommended dishes: North Carolina-style pork, chicken, sausages, ribs. **Price range:** Sandwiches, $6; barbecue by the pound, $4–$14. **Wheelchair access:** One level; restroom is narrow. **Features:** Outdoor dining.

Peasant   ☆ $$$ ITALIAN

194 Elizabeth St. (bet. Prince & Spring Sts.)   (212) 965-9511
Credit cards: All major   Meals: D   Closed Mon.

The concrete floor and the brushed-aluminum chairs send off warning signals. Is Peasant, despite the name, going to be an exercise in deprivation chic? But closer inspection suggests that all is not as it seems. At the far end of the room, a brick pizza oven radiates heat. Even the forbidding chairs are form-fitting and inexplicably comfortable, and the black-clad waiters are full of gee-whiz enthusiasm.

Peasant has built a following by sticking to some very simple premises. Keep the food simple, rustic and Italian. Cook it over a wood fire. Serve big portions. Be nice. That's about it. When the formula works, Peasant sends out highly satisfying food, fresh and flavorful, with the rich tanginess that wood smoke imparts. The wood fire adds a sublime crunch to the excellent crust of Peasant's little pizzas. The pasta is good, not great. Among the desserts, the best choices are vanilla-soaked bread pudding, served with a caramel-swathed scoop of white chocolate gelato, and a heroically proportioned peach pie with a rough lattice crust.

Wine list: Fifty Italian wines, half of them $40 or under, with an emphasis on lesser-known regions like Calabria, Emilia-Romagna and Puglia. **Price range:** Apps., $8–$12; entrees, $19–$24; desserts, $8. **Wheelchair access:** All one level.

Penang $$ MALAYSIAN

109 Spring St. (bet. Mercer & Greene Sts.)	(212) 274-8883
240 Columbus Ave. (at 71st St.)	(212) 769-3988
1596 Second Ave. (at 83rd St.)	(212) 585-3838
64 Third Ave. (at 11th St.)	(212) 228-7888
38-04 Prince St., Flushing, Queens	(718) 321-2078
Credit cards: All major	Meals: L, D, LN

What started as a small Malaysian storefront in Flushing has turned into an institution. The SoHo outpost is, as you might expect, the most exciting of the lot, if only for the people watching. But all of the branches offer surprisingly authentic Malaysian flavors. The dish not to miss is the roti canai, a seductive, savory crepe served with coconut milk sauce.

Other recommended dishes: Roti tellur, fried calamari, won ton soup, chicken or beef satay, Penang noodles, mee goreng, beef rendang, kari ayam kering, clams with black bean sauce, grilled baby eggplant, kangkung, peanut pancake. **Price range:** Lunch: avg. app., $4; entree, $6; dessert, $7. Dinner: avg. app., $7; entree, $14; dessert, $7. **Wheelchair access:** Not accessible.

Pepolino $25 & Under ITALIAN

281 W. Broadway (near Lispenard St.)	(212) 966-9983
Credit cards: AE	Meals: L, D, LN

There's a lot to like about Pepolino. The small, cheerful dining room seems to glow with warmth, the greeting is friendly, and the service is good-natured. The gnocchi at Pepolino are ethereal, as light as miniature clouds, making up with intense flavor what they lack in mass. The chef also makes a glorious pappa al pomodoro, the Tuscan specialty of ripe tomatoes, shreds of stale bread and fragrant olive oil, cooked into a delicious mush. Pastas are marvelous, like spaghetti with braised leeks and Parmesan, and sturdy rigatoni with sausage and arugula. One dessert stands out clearly: a wonderfully dense chocolate cake, intensely flavored with coffee.

Other recommended dishes: Spinach soufflé, yellow pepper soup, salmon steamed with fennel and cannellini beans, snapper with leeks and beans. **Price range:** Apps., $5–$9; entrees, $11–$19. **Wheelchair access:** Long flight of steps to entrance.

223

Persepolis $25 & Under PERSIAN

1423 Second Ave. (near 75th St.) (212) 535-1100
Credit cards: All major Meals: L, D

A friendly restaurant that specializes in simpler Persian dishes, like
refreshing salads and gently spiced grilled meats. A dish of yogurt
and cucumber, blended with a little mint, is the ideal cool complement to Persepolis's tiny rounds of fresh pita bread and rectangles
of flat bread. Kebabs seem pleasantly light.

Other recommended dishes: Hummus; sherazi salad; tabbouleh;
kebabs of salmon, filet mignon, chicken or chopped steak. **Price
range:** Apps., $4–$5; entrees, $10–$26; desserts, $4. **Wheelchair
access:** All one level. **Features:** Outdoor dining.

Peter Luger ☆☆☆ $$$$ STEAKHOUSE

178 Broadway, Williamsburg, Brooklyn (718) 387-7400
Credit cards: Cash only Meals: L, D

Peter Luger serves no lobsters, takes no major credit cards and
lacks a great wine list. Service, though professional and often
humorous, can sometimes be brusque. With its bare wooden tables,
the place looks like a beer hall that has not changed since it opened
in 1887. So why is it packed night and day, seven days a week?
Simple: Peter Luger has the best steak in New York City. The family
that runs the restaurant buys fresh shortloins and dry-ages them on
the premises. An occasional diner will choose the thick and powerfully delicious lamb chops, or the fine salmon. French fries are terrific — hot and crisp with a powerful potato flavor.

The restaurant does well by desserts, serving a fine, rich
cheesecake and a fluffy chocolate mousse cake. A little whipped
cream? Why not? What's a little more cholesterol at this point?
(*Ruth Reichl*)

Wine list: A limited wine list, but they do pour big, powerful cocktails. **Price range:** Lunch: Avg. price for two courses: $40. Dinner:
avg. price for three courses, $60. **Wheelchair access:** Fully accessi-
ble. **Features:** Parking available.

Petrosino $25 & Under ITALIAN

190 Norfolk St. (near E. Houston St.) (212) 673-3773
Credit cards: Cash only (A.T.M. on premises) Meals: Br, D, LN

Petrosino presents a cross section of Italian regional dishes and a
modest but excellent list of southern Italian wines. But what really
stands out are the bold flavors in lively, forthright dishes that are
unmarred by fussiness or pretension. Service is warm and responsive. Petrosino's open spirit is reflected in the dining room, which
achieves a well-calibrated dimness that makes everybody look
good. The prices don't look so good. Some careful limbo dancing is
required to qualify as $25 & Under.

Duck low if you must, but don't miss the inzimino di seppie, a
superb and generous Tuscan stew of squid, spinach and chick peas.
If price is an issue, stick with a pasta as a main course, like farrotto
with crumbled fennel sausage and smoked mozzarella. You should-
n't overlook Petrosino's desserts, which, in a sloppy, tiramisù world

show rare precision. Nutella-laced ricotta cheesecake is both terrifically flavored and textured.

Other recommended dishes: Tagliatelle al pomodor, gnocchi al pesto trapanese, calamari with watermelon and cucumber, hanger steak, budino, chocolate sformato with organge. **Price range:** Apps., $6–$14; pastas and entrees, $12–$22; desserts, $7. **Wheelchair access:** All one level.

Petrossian ☆☆ $$$$ NEW AMERICAN/RUSSIAN
182 W. 58th St. (at Seventh Ave.)   (212) 245-2214
Credit cards: All major   Meals: Br, L, D

Nobody in New York City serves better caviar, and nobody does it with more style. The dark room is covered with Art Deco splendor, the waiters wear blue blazers and an obsequious air, and the caviar arrives with warm toast, blini and beautiful little spoons. Vodka is served in icy little flutes that make it taste somehow better. Should you desire something else, the restaurant has introduced a fanciful menu with each entree accompanied by a reinvented blin, traditionally a buckwheat pancake. Brochette of lamb, for example, comes with an okra blin, seared bonito with a basil and sardine blin. This splash of creativity is, alas, not very successful. (*Ruth Reichl, updated by William Grimes*)

Price range: Prix-fixe brunch, $28. Prix-fixe lunch, $22 or $39. Dinner: apps., $8-14; entrees, $24–$34; desserts, $9; prix fixe, $38. **Wheelchair access:** Restrooms not accessible.

Philip Marie $25 & Under NEW AMERICAN
569 Hudson St. (at W. 11th St.)   (212) 242-6200
Credit cards: All major   Meals: D   Closed Mon.

This warm, welcoming husband-and-wife operation is the kind of place where you can smell the comforting aroma of a wood-burning fire, even though there's no fireplace. Service is efficient but casual, and the food — hearty American fare with some creative twists — inspires good feelings. Among the best dishes are a great lamb shank, braised in sour mash whisky and served with dirty rice, pine nuts and currants, and a delicious salad of smoked trout, pink grapefruit, radicchio and walnuts.

Other recommended dishes: Parsley salad with country ham, dried tomatoes and Wisconsin Asiago cheese; pumpkin fritters; chocolate hazelnut torte. **Price range:** Apps., $5–$9; entrees, $14–$18. **Wheelchair access:** Ramp at entrance; restrooms downstairs.

Pho Grand $25 & Under VIETNAMESE
277C Grand St. (near Forsyth St.)   (212) 965-5366
Credit cards: All major   Meals: L, D

When you go to Pho Grand, begin by ordering the avocado juice. It is a phenomenal treat, thick and creamy but not heavy and only a bit sweet. Timing is not Pho Grand's specialty. Appetizers and entrees may arrive all at once. Amid the avalanche are some fabulous combinations. Grilled beef sesame, plump little rolls of beef served on a flat rice noodle cake, was fatty and tender. A chicken curry exhibited perfect pitch: a warm heat flush with ginger and a creamy broth. There are 17 phos (noodle soups) available, mostly differentiated by the cut of meat in the broth.

Caramel custard is the only dessert on the menu. But many of the drinks would work well for dessert, including a yellow bean purée topped with red beans, green gummy candies, shaved ice and coconut milk. Try it. (*Amanda Hesser*)

Other recommended dishes: Steamed rice crepes with pork, caramel fish, grilled pork chop. **Price range:** Apps., $3–$12; entrees, $4–$15. **Wheelchair access:** Entrance is up one step.

Piadina $25 & Under   ITALIAN
57 W. 10th St. (bet. Fifth & Sixth Aves.)   (212) 460-8017
Credit cards: Cash only   Meals: D, LN

This subterranean grotto is another classic Greenwich Village restaurant designed like a rustic Italian farmhouse. The menu offers simple Italian dishes and piadinas, the round, unleavened griddled bread that has been eaten for centuries in the Romagna region. A piadina is a wonderful appetizer for two, particularly with stuffings like prosciutto or cheese and arugula.

Other recommended dishes: Passatelli, mussels, polenta, green bean salad, fennel salad, chicken alla cacciatora, pork loin, red snapper, seared tuna, wild mushroom risotto. **Alcohol:** Beer and wine. **Price range:** Apps., $6; entrees, $11–$14; desserts, $6. **Wheelchair access:** Two steps down to dining room; restrooms are narrow.

Picholine   ☆☆☆ $$$$ MEDITERRANEAN/FRENCH
35 W. 64th St. (bet. Broadway & Central Pk. W.)   (212) 724-8585
Credit cards: All major   Meals: L, D

After 10 years, Picholine is beginning to feel like an institution. One key to its longevity is a ferocious commitment to quality and the restless inventiveness of its chef-owner, Terrance Brennan, who constantly finds ways to freshen the menu or introduce attractive promotions, like an all-cheese menu with wine pairings. Picholine has the look of a classic, always the same but always new. A recent menu featured a creamy, briny sea urchin panna cotta with a chilled saline consomme and caviar. It was pure essence of ocean. White gazpacho with a red gazpacho granité made an ideal mid-summer appetizer, a perfect combination of fire and ice. Refinement and originality animate the entire menu, from squab in a licorice glaze to halibut poached in a truffle-scented broth and served with a pea mousseline. Desserts are exquisite but not precious. The best may be a very simple baba au rhum with cherry marmelade. Picholine's cheese cart needs no introduction. It set new standards for the entire city. (*Review by William Grimes; stars previously awarded by Ruth Reichl.*)

Wine list: An expanded list with more French selections and nice choices among the smaller French wines as well as some good American pinot noirs. Knowledgeable, helpful staff. **Price range:**

Apps., $13.50–$25; entrees, $29–$38; desserts, $9–$15. **Wheelchair access:** Two steps up to dining room.

Pietro's $$$ ITALIAN/STEAKHOUSE
232 E. 43rd St. (bet. Second & Third Aves.)   (212) 682-9760
Credit cards: All major   Meals: L, D   Closed Sun.

One of New York's great old steakhouses has been serving terrific meat since 1932 along with standard Italian-American fare. Although it has never regained the character it had before it moved to its current home in 1984, the restaurant continues to be extremely reliable, with great Caesar salads and excellent service.

Price range: Apps., from $9; entrees, $19–$32; desserts, from $6. **Wheelchair access:** Restrooms not accessible.

Pig Heaven $25 & Under   CHINESE
1540 Second Ave. (near 80th St.)   (212) 744-4333
Credit cards: All major   Meals: L, D

Pig Heaven has a sleekly modern look, with a handsome bar, almond-shaped hanging lamps and a table of ceramic and carved decorative pigs. Its terrific Chinese-American food is spiced and presented in ways that please westerners, yet it is fresh and prepared with finesse. The best place to start is the pork selection, particularly roasted Cantonese dishes like suckling pig, strips of juicy meat under a layer of moist fat and wafer-thin, deliciously crisp skin. Dumplings are excellent. Desserts are a bizarre selection, including frozen praline mousse.

Other recommended dishes: Hacked chicken, scallion pancakes, white-cooked pork, pork soong, shredded pork with pickled Sichuan vegetables, beef with broccoli, Peking snowball. **Price range:** Apps., $3–$10; entrees, $8–$19. **Wheelchair access:** Step at entrance.

Ping's   ☆☆ $$ CHINESE
83-02 Queens Blvd., Elmhurst, Queens   (718) 396-1238
Credit cards: AE   Meals: B, Br, L, D, LN

Ping's looks like hundreds of other Chinese restaurants in New York City. The big square room is casual and brightly lighted, with a bank of aquariums near the back. Not until I approached the fish tanks did I appreciate how extraordinary the food was likely to be: in addition to the usual lobsters and sea bass, there were two types of live shrimp, three kinds of crab, both fresh- and salt-water eels and a number of fish rarely seen swimming around in restaurants. Fried giant prawns filled with roe and served with little sweet-potato dumplings were superb. Dungeness crab, topped with fried garlic, was irresistible, as was a home-style dish of greens with bits of pork and eggs. A perfect ending to the meal is steamed papayas wrapped in paper. For the best options, ask for the translation of the Chinese menu. (*Ruth Reichl*)

Alcohol: Wine and beer. **Price range:** Apps., $2–$7; entrees, from $8 (live seafood is market-priced). **Wheelchair access:** One level.

Ping's Seafood   ☆☆ $$ CHINESE
22 Mott St. (bet. Worth & Mosco Sts.)   (212) 602-9988
Credit cards: All major   Meals: L, D

Anyone who misses the gaudy sign outside gets the message a few
steps inside the restaurant. Near the door, a high-rise of stacked fish
tanks offers the menu headliners, a stellar cast that includes but is
by no means limited to lobsters, eels, scallops, sea bass and shrimp.
The seafood in the tanks ends up on your plate, pretty much short-
cutting the freshness issue. The preparations are minimal — a gin-
ger-garlic sauce for the lobster, for example, or black bean sauce for
the eel — and the results are maximal. Scallops, quickly steamed,
come in three choices of sauce: garlic, black bean or XO, a Hong
Kong innovation that's sweet and sour, hot and salty. Ping's XO is
superlative, dense with tiny bits of dried shrimp and chilies.

One of the more appealing rituals at Ping's is winter melon
soup. You must call a day ahead, since the melon, which flourishes
in the summer despite its name, has to steam for six hours. It
comes as a bulging green bowl brimming with what initially seems
to be nothing more than a mild-flavored chicken stock. As the ladle
dips deeper into the gourd, interesting things begin to emerge —
bits of fresh scallop and dried scallop, ham, dried white fungus,
shrimp, frog and crab. This seems like the perfect emblem for
Ping's, an exotic package with thrilling secrets inside.

Wine list: Minimal. **Price range**: Apps., $2–$6; entrees, $7–$30;
live seafood market-priced. **Wheelchair access**: Dining room up
one flight of stairs; restroom down one flight.

Pintaile's Pizza $25 & Under   PIZZA
26 E. 91st St. (bet. Fifth & Madison Aves.)   (212) 722-1967
1443 York Ave. (bet. 76th & 77th Sts.)   (212) 717-4990
1577 York Ave. (bet. 83rd & 84th Sts.)   (212) 396-3479
Credit cards: MC/V   Meals: L, D

Pintaile's, which has several branches scattered around Manhattan, specializes in pizzas with crisp, paper-thin crusts that are
light in calories and heft yet full of flavor. The classic pie is the
best, made with sliced plum tomatoes rather than sauce, with
mozzarella, Parmesan and herbs. Vegans can order it without the
cheese. Other nonmeat choices include wild mushrooms; goat
cheese, eggplant, pine nuts and olives, and Greek pizza, made
with feta cheese, olives and artichoke hearts.

Price range: $1.35–$14.

Pintxos $25 & Under   BASQUE/SPANISH
510 Greenwich St. (at Spring St.)   (212) 343-9923
Credit cards: AE   Meals: L, D   Closed Sun.

Pintxos is one of only a few Basque restaurants in Manhattan, but it
is also worth knowing about because it's such a sweet, charming
place. The food is hearty yet subtle, with delicate flavorings that are
surprising in food that seems so straightforward. Basque dishes
earn the spotlight, like baby squid served over rice in a sauce of its
own ink, or gambas a la plancha, a half dozen big prawns, grilled

and served in their shells with heads intact. The all-Spanish wine list is very small but offers perfect choices for this fare.

Other recommended dishes: Grilled prawns, sautéed peppers, peppers stuffed with puréed cod, marinated anchovies, grilled lamb chops, sea bass in green sauce, octopus, chorizo. **Alcohol:** Beer and wine. **Price range:** Tapas, $2–$3; apps., $3–$7; entrees, $8–$16. **Wheelchair access:** Steps at entrance and at restroom.

P.J. Clarke's $25 & Under AMERICAN
915 Third Ave. (at 55th St.) (212) 317-1616
Credit cards: All major Meals: L, D, LN

When the family that had owned P.J. Clarke's since 1949 sold the place, it was hard not to believe that an era had ended. After a lengthy renovation, the first, comforting impression is that absolutely nothing has changed. The big bar in front is still a riot of noise with bartenders in white aprons sending out perfectly pulled pints of Guinness to jovial customers, half of whom look like Brian Dennehy. The beveled glass behind the bar, the worn wood floor, the red-and-white checked tablecloths, even the men's room with its massive ice-filled urinals, are all still there. On closer examination, differences emerge. But the saloon spirit is certainly intact.

Nobody ever went to P. J. Clarke's for the food. The burger is tolerable, juicy and flavorful, although the flavor comes more from the charring than the beef and the bun is flimsy. The Caesar has a good dose of anchovy mixed into the dressing. New England clam chowder is packed with clams, and the raw oysters are terrific. Desserts include great rice pudding and a tall wedge of coconut-lemon cake that looks as if it arrived straight from a church picnic. At Clarke's, the flavor of the place counts far more than the food. The old vibe that made Clarke's such a hangout lives on, and diners seem to be enjoying themselves regardless of how they feel about the burger.

Other recommended dishes: Spinach salad, fish and chips, roast chicken. **Price range:** Apps., $4–$10; entrees, $8–$33. **Wheelchair access:** Step at entrance, restrooms are narrow.

Plan Eat Thailand $25 & Under THAI
133 N. 7th St., Williamsburg, Brooklyn (718) 599-0516
Credit cards: Cash only Meals: L, D, LN

This unusual, much-applauded Thai restaurant has its ups and downs, but more often than not serves spicy, meticulously prepared dishes like ground pork salad, sautéed bean curd and striped bass with crunchy greens. Plan Eat Thailand is often crowded and loud.

Price range: Apps., $3–$5; entrees, $5–$13. **Wheelchair access:** Fully accessible.

Po $25 & Under ITALIAN
31 Cornelia St. (near Bleecker St.) (212) 645-2189
Credit cards: AE Meals: L (Wed.–Sun.), D

Years ago, before Mario Batali was a celebrity chef, he opened this small, vivacious trattoria. Mr. Batali has officially cut his ties to Po, and his departure is the best thing that could have happened. Now, Po must stand on its own, and the food is as good as it was years ago. What's more, Po's prices have stayed remarkably reasonable.

Appetizers are a strong point. Salads, too, are exceptional, like roasted beets as rich as chocolate, served with artichoke leaves and melted taleggio cheese. Pasta standouts include spaghetti carbonara, just right, with no intrusion on the flavors of butter, cheese and pancetta. A paillard of lamb, as long as a skirt steak, is almost beefy, daubed with aioli and served over sweet grape tomatoes.

Desserts include both a sublimely dense terrine of dark chocolate with a core of rich marzipan and a strangely artless chilled cappuccino with a scoop of coffee gelato tossed in.

Other recommended dishes: Marinated anchovies, steamed clams and mussels, cucumber salad, linguine with clams, grilled pork, quail. **Price range:** Apps., $7–$8; entrees, $13–$18. **Wheelchair access:** Step at entrance. **Features:** Two tables for outdoor dining.

Pongal $25 & Under   INDIAN/KOSHER/VEGETARIAN
110 Lexington Ave. (near 27th St.)   (212) 696-9458
Credit cards: All major   Meals: L, D

With its brick wall, spare design and halogen lighting, Pongal looks like a generic neighborhood restaurant. Only the spicy aromas wafting in from the kitchen and the music playing in the background give it away. The delectable vegetarian cuisine of South India is the specialty at Pongal, where the food is kosher as well. The centerpiece dishes are the daunting dosai, huge crepes made of various fermented batters that are stuffed and rolled into cylinders that can stretch two-and-a-half feet. But they are light and delicious, filled with spiced mixtures of potatoes and onions. Pongal also serves a wonderful shrikhand, a dessert made of yogurt custard flavored with nutmeg, cardamom and saffron.

Other recommended dishes: Iddly rasam, iddly sambar, vada rasam, vada sambar, dahi vada, spinach pakoda, paper crepe masala, onion rava masala, mysore masala, utthappam, Pongal special, raita. **Alcohol:** Beer and wine. **Price range:** Apps., $4–$9; entrees, $8–$15; desserts, $4–$7. **Wheelchair access:** Entrance and dining room are on one level; restrooms are narrow.

Pop   ☆ $$$ PAN-ASIAN/BISTRO
127 Fourth Ave. (near 12th St.)   (212) 767-1800
Credit cards: All major   Meals: D

Pop is a bright, happy place with a noncommittal, nonemotive décor and a crowd-pleasing menu that hips and hops from one culinary source to another. The result is toe-tapping food. The plates are sprinkled with little surprises — fun, palate-pleasing footnotes like the ingenious slaw of fine-shaved brussels sprouts that comes with a thick, juicy veal chop in quince and pomegranate sauce. The dishes seem to hit the mark about half the time. A perfectly straightforward wild mushroom soup is earthy and deeply flavored. Whole broiled baby lobster is an all-stops-out production, coated with ginger, scallion and coriander, then doused in a kind of hot and sour soup made of lobster stock infused with seaweed and bonito flakes. For dessert, try the caramel bread pudding, which is simple and winning, and the strawberry cream cake, an all-out assault on the pleasure zones.

Wine list: A short, eclectic list, reasonably priced except the Champagnes, with 19 wines by the glass. **Price range:** Apps., $9–$15 ($85 for one ounce of beluga caviar on toast); entrees, $24–$36; desserts, $8–$10. Five-course tasting menu, $75; six courses, $95. **Wheelchair access:** Restroom on dining level.

Post House $$$$ STEAKHOUSE
28 E. 63rd St. (bet. Park & Madison Aves.)   (212) 935-2888
Credit cards: All major   Meals: L, D

Possibly New York City's most civilized steakhouse. This is the place for people who want their porterhouse with pomp and ceremony. They get it, along with good seafood, good service, high prices and a very good wine list.

Price range: Lunch: apps., $7–$14; entrees, $19–$34; desserts, $8. Dinner: apps., $8–$15; entrees, $23–$34; desserts, $8. **Wheelchair access:** Not accessible.

Pravda $$ RUSSIAN
281 Lafayette St. (bet. Prince & Houston Sts.)   (212) 226-4944
Credit cards: All major   Meals: D, LN   Closed Sun.

A subterranean room with interesting décor, comfortable chairs and good air circulation, Pravda is frequented by trendy, good-looking patrons who seem to wear a lot of black. Four main dishes are on the menu — chicken Kiev, beef stroganoff, skewered grilled lamb and a fish of the day — but the most interesting items are the Russian snacks, the several dozen vodkas, eight kinds of martinis (served in individual mini-shakers) and the mainstay: caviar. Spinach and cheese piroshki wrapped in rich, flaky pastry are terrific, as is the borscht: sweet, sour and filled with flavor. The blinis are superb: thin, tangy and worth the splurge on Scottish smoked salmon or sevruga, osetra or beluga caviar. Desserts include pear crepe, warm apple tart with spiced red wine sauce, and strawberry vodka sorbet.

Price range: Apps., $8; entrees, $12–$18; desserts, $6. **Wheelchair access:** Fully accessible.

Primavera   ☆ $$$$ ITALIAN
1578 First Ave. (at 82nd St.)   (212) 861-8608
Credit cards: All major   Meals: D, LN

The wood-paneled room has the patrician air of a private club, but the tables are very close together and the noise sometimes drowns out conversation. The restaurant serves Italian food for people who don't care how high the bill is. Regular customers know that the truffles will be grated with a lavish hand and the bill will be enormous. If you have to ask the price of the specials, you probably don't belong here. And the waiters will certainly let you know it. Still, all the pastas were never less than superb (fettucine was feather-light and fabulous) and some specials were excellent. The ricotta cheesecake was rich, light and buttery. (*Ruth Reichl*)

Wine list: Big names at big prices; the lesser wines are so sloppily listed that they often lack vintage years. **Price range:** Apps., $13–$25; pastas and risottos, $20–$25; entrees, $27–$40; desserts, $10–$13. **Wheelchair access:** Restrooms are down a flight of stairs.

Prime Burger $ HAMBURGERS

5 E. 51st St. (bet. Fifth & Madison Aves.) (212) 759-4729
Credit cards: Cash only Meals: B, L, D

You feel as if you're entering a time warp when you enter Prime Burger. The décor is strictly 1950's and early 60's, and the seating system is quaint: Trays attached to the arms of chairs swing out to allow you to sit down. The burgers are terrific, and the seating makes eating them even more fun. Pies and cakes are first-rate.

Price range: Entrees, $3–$5; desserts, $2–$3. **Wheelchair access:** Not accessible.

Provence   ☆ $$$ FRENCH

38 Macdougal St. (near Prince St.) (212) 475-7500
Credit cards: AE, V Meals: L, D

A charmingly crowded French cafe straight out of the French countryside. But while the atmosphere is charming and romantic, the food feels tired. The wine list, however, is interesting. A few dishes still work well. Mussels gratinées, baked on the half shell and sprinkled with almonds and garlic, were very tasty. Bourride, a pale fish soup, is thickened with aioli; don't miss it. Pot au feu is also a fine example of hearty country cooking, and the bouillabaisse, served only on Fridays, was superb. (*Ruth Reichl, updated by Eric Asimov*)

Wine list: Good, with an emphasis on out-of-the-ordinary French wines from small vineyards. **Price range:** Lunch: apps., $5–$9; entrees, $13–$22. Dinner: apps., $5–$9; entrees, $16–$26; desserts, $6–$8. Brunch prix-fixe, $20. **Wheelchair access:** All one level. **Features:** Outdoor dining.

Prune $25 & Under AMERICAN/CONTINENTAL

54 E. 1st St. (near First Ave.) (212) 677-6221
Credit cards: Major Meals: Br, D

The idiosyncratic name (the chef and owner's childhood nickname) is perfect for this unconventional little place. The menu isn't even divided into conventional categories, though price indicates whether a dish is small, midsize or a main course. The food is excellent and unusual, fascinating and even funny, as with the slices of duck breast that taste of smoke, vinegar and pepper, like pastrami, and are served with an omelet flavored with rye. Voilá! Pastrami on rye. The braised lamb shoulder is a perfect stew with tomatoes and vegetables in an assertive broth. Desserts are terrific, like cornmeal poundcake drenched in sweet rosemary syrup.

Other recommended dishes: Grilled bacon chop, fried oysters, grilled shrimp with anchovy butter, roasted marrow bones, deviled dark-meat chicken, cod with cinnamon and thyme, pistachio pithivier. **Price range:** Apps., $4–$7; midsize dishes, $8–$14; entrees, $16–$30. **Wheelchair access:** One step at entrance; restroom is narrow.

Puttanesca $25 & Under   ITALIAN
859 Ninth Ave. (at 56th St.)   (212) 581-4177
Credit cards: AE   Meals: L, D

At Puttanesca, a popular neighborhood trattoria that has expanded, the rule is, the simpler the better. Uncomplicated dishes, made with exceedingly fresh ingredients, include an excellent Caesar salad (I have not found the Caesar salad of my dreams, but Puttanesca's comes close), perfectly grilled vegetables and mussels steamed in white wine and garlic.

Other recommended dishes: Polenta with onions and zucchini, green salad, spaghetti with garlic and olive oil, spinach linguine with shrimp, mushroom fettuccine with seafood, sautéed rabbit, veal piccata, tiramisu, chocolate almond tart. **Price range:** Apps., $4–$8; entrees, $7–$17; desserts, $5. **Wheelchair access:** Fully accessible. **Features:** Outdoor dining.

Q Café $$ PAN-LATIN
244 E. 79th St. (bet. Second & Third Aves.)   (212) 717-6500
Credit cards: All major   Meals: Br, D

The surroundings are cool and pleasant. Warm ochre walls and plain wooden tables seem about right for the low-key, engaging menu. Vibrant color, strong flavors and spice are the three requirements for the menu. Where they come from is less important.

The food is Latin in the mildest way. The Venezuelan chef draws on the flavors and ingredients of South America and the Caribbean to establish tone and color, without committing herself to anything in particular. Roasted lobster tail with green risotto, one of the best entrees, picks up a slight tropical tang from grilled mango sauce. Desserts are messy and toothachingly sweet. The chaste option is a large phyllo basket filled with fresh fruit.

Price range: Entrees, $12–$22. **Wheelchair access:** Fully accessible.

Quatorze Bis $$$ BISTRO/FRENCH
323 E. 79th St. (bet. First & Second Aves.)   (212) 535-1414
Credit cards: All major   Meals: Br, L, D

Although it has not been as funky and appealing since it moved uptown from 14th Street, this remains one of New York City's quintessential bistros, from the zinc bar and pure Parisian looks to the menu of steak frites and fruits de mer.

Price range: Lunch: apps., $8–$10; entrees, $9.95–$29; desserts, $6.50–$8; prix fixe, $16. Dinner: apps., $8–$10; entrees, $18.95–$29; desserts, $6–$8. **Wheelchair access:** Restrooms not accessible.

Queen of Sheba

$25 & Under   ETHIOPIAN

650 10th Ave. (at W. 46th St.)   (212) 397-0610
Credit cards: V, MC   Meals: L, D

With its brick-and-ocher walls and good-looking crowd, Queen of
Sheba is one of the more inviting Ethiopian restaurants in New
York. And the food is pretty good, too: beef and lamb stews flavored with a rousing dark-red hot sauce, and wonderful vegetarian
dishes seasoned with complex spice blends, all eaten with pieces of
injera, a spongy flat bread with the enticing flavor of sourdough.

Price Range: Apps., $3.25–$5.50; entrees, $8.50–$16. **Wheelchair
access:** Fully accessible.

Rafina

$25 & Under   GREEK/SEAFOOD

1481 York Ave. (near 78th St.)   (212) 327-0950
Credit cards: All major   Meals: D

At this elemental Greek restaurant specializing in seafood, you know
exactly what you'll get: simple ingredients, simply prepared. Charcoal-grilled octopus is crunchy outside, tender within, while grilled
whole fish like porgy, red snapper and striped bass are enhanced by
their simple marinade of olive oil, lemon juice, oregano and garlic,
and they arrive moist and delicious. The pleasant, bright room is decorated in blue and white and bedecked in Greek seafood décor.

Other recommended dishes: Assortment of cold spreads, beets
with skordalia, loukanika laconias, grilled octopus, swordfish steak,
baby lamb chops, beef patties. **Price range:** Apps., $4–$9; entrees,
$13–$25. **Wheelchair access:** Restrooms are narrow.

Raga

$25 & Under   FRENCH/INDIAN

433 E. 6th St. (bet. Ave. A & First Ave.)   (212) 388-0957
Credit cards: All major   Meals: D

A gulf separates this small, great-looking restaurant from the block
of Indian restaurants on the other side of First Avenue. Raga is one
of the first Indian fusion restaurants, combining Indian spicing and
ingredients with European ingredients and presentation. The result
is largely successful, with dishes like terrific curried shrimp and
filet mignon rubbed with garam masala, but with occasional clink-
ers, too.

Other recommended dishes: Seared sea scallops, samosas, prawns,
crab cakes, grilled mahi-mahi, lamb stew, ginger crème brûlée.
Alcohol: Beer and wine. **Price range:** Apps., $5–$9; entrees,
$12–$17. **Wheelchair access:** Fully accessible.

Rain

$25 & Under   PAN-ASIAN

100 W. 82nd St. (near Columbus Ave.)   (212) 501-0776
1059 Third Ave. (bet. 62nd & 63rd Sts.)   (212) 223-3669
Credit cards: All major   Meals: L, D

Rain is one of the most compelling of the growing crop of restaurants specializing in Southeast Asian cuisines. The dining rooms
seem perpetually busy, service is pleasant and helpful, and much of
the food is quite good. Cold vegetarian summer rolls are wonder-

234

fully cooling, while green papaya salad is fiery yet refreshing. Vietnamese charred beef salad, a spicy, beautifully presented composition that balances cool herbal and citrus flavors with spicy heat, is top-notch, as is Thai chicken-and-coconut soup. The best main courses are stir-fried beef in peanut sauce and stir-fried Chinese eggplant with an excellent yellow bean sauce.

Other recommended dishes: Grilled salmon, bananas steamed in coconut milk, chocolate cake. **Price range:** Apps., $7–$10; entrees, $12–$23; desserts, $6. **Wheelchair access:** Fully accessible.

Rainbow Grill $$$$ ITALIAN

30 Rockefeller Plaza (49thSt. bet. Sixth & Seventh Aves.)
    (212) 632-5100
Credit cards: All major   Meals: Br, L, D

Dinner at the Rainbow Grill is not so much a meal as a real estate transaction. You want to occupy 16 square feet in Midtown with an unsurpassed view? Prepare to pay. The old Promenade Bar atop 30 Rockefeller Center is gone, and so is the elegance and romance. The Cipriani family have whittled down the bar operation and expanded the dining area, installing double rows of tables to make the Rainbow Grill. It's a little like an airplane. Diners with window seats get the view. The rest get to watch their fellow diners. Under the new regime, the Rainbow Room is used primarily for private parties. The public can dine and dance on either Friday or Saturday night, depending on the room's irregular schedule. The grill is open for lunch and dinner seven days a week.

The food at the Rainbow Grill is Italian, very simple and perfectly acceptable at half the price. The prices are brazen, especially in light of the cheap tables, cafeteria silverware and drip-dry tablecloths. Like the waiters in their white dinner jackets, the menu strikes a traditional note, with straightforward appetizers like prosciutto with melon, and buffalo mozzarella with tomatoes. Main courses, too, stick to the middle of the road, with dishes like veal Milanese, red snapper with tomatoes and capers, and veal Marsala. Perhaps after the sticker shock, management decided that the customers should not be further agitated by the food. The view, by the way, is still spectacular.

Price range: Lunch: prix-fixe, $30 and $50; apps., $14–$25; entrees, $34–$44; desserts, $11–$12. Dinner: prix-fixe, $60; apps, $15–$25; entrees, $36–$48; desserts, $12–$13. **Wheelchair access:** Fully accessible. **Features:** Good view.

Rao's $$$$ ITALIAN

455 E. 114th St. (at Pleasant Ave.)   (212) 722-6709
Credit cards: Cash only   Meals: D   Closed Sat., Sun.

You'd think that after more than a century of eating at Rao's, people would get tired of the place, but no. This simple little Italian restaurant, one of the few remnants of a once bustling Italian neighborhood, continues to be one of the hardest tables to get in New York. You can't get in unless you know somebody or you are very persistent. If you do manage to get a seat, you'll find old New York Italian food and characters straight out of Damon Runyon. The truth is, the atmosphere is better than the food. Most people will not have the opportunity to taste Rao's lemon chicken, veal chop or linguine with garlic and oil, but Rao's has made it easier for people to live vicariously. You can now purchase the Rao's cookbook and bottles of Rao's sauce, visit the Web site (www.raos.com) and even buy the Rao's CD of music to dine by.

Price range: Avg. meal, $65 per person. **Wheelchair access:** Three steps to dining room.

Raoul's $$$ Bistro/French
180 Prince St. (bet. Sullivan & Thompson Sts.)   (212) 966-3518
Credit cards: All major   Meals: D

This perpetually trendy spot has a genuine neighborhood feel and a hospitable staff serving decent French food. Although the booths are cramped and the prices are high, there is almost always some-one famous in the room.

Price range: Apps., $5–$22; entrees, $16–$30; desserts, $6–$10. **Wheelchair access:** Restrooms not accessible. **Features:** Outdoor dining.

Red Bar Restaurant ☆ $$$ American/Bistro
339 E. 75th St.   (212) 472-7577
Credit cards: All major   Meals: D

Red Bar offers warmth, style and good, unpretentious food. Dark hardwood floors, red wainscoting and white skirting boards give a country-house feel. It has limited aims, and a menu that refuses to strain for effect. Much of the menu is devoted to bistro standards, some presented very straightforwardly, others with a grace note or two. Sweet peppers are added to sautéed skate with lemon and capers, for example, but there's no fussing at all with the pan-roasted chicken with black olive mashed potatoes.

The chef has a bit of a sweet tooth, and it detracts from some otherwise exemplary entrees. And while dessert should be the part of the menu dedicated to sin and indulgence, he makes polite desserts, although a dense frozen parfait made with three choco-lates scores an unexpected bull's-eye.

Wine list: A well-priced but rather predictable international list of about 90 wines, with nine wines by the glass. **Price range:** Apps., $7–$14; entrees, $19–$29; desserts, $7–$8. **Wheelchair access:** Two steps up to the entrance; the restrooms are down one flight.

The Red Cat ☆ $$ Bistro/American
227 10th Ave. (near 23rd St.)   (212) 242-1122
Credit cards: All major   Meals: D, LN

A lot of restaurants make a big noise about being warm, welcoming and accessible. The Red Cat, with little ado, manages to be all three. It is stylish, but not snooty, cool but relaxed. The menu reflects the spirit of the place with a lineup of solid, well-executed American bistro dishes, with a little trick or twist on each plate. The obligatory steak dish comes with a ragout of roasted shallots, tomatoes and cracked olives. The short dessert list does not disap-point. The carmelized banana tart cannot be improved upon, but it is — by a scoop of praline ice cream. Unfortunately, when the kitchen slips, the food can be dull and ordinary, and the service can drift from casual to spaced out.

Wine list: Plenty of $30 bottles, and 16 wines by the glass. **Price range:** Dinner: apps., $7–$14; entrees, $18–$28; desserts, $8. **Wheelchair access:** Not accessible.

Redeye Grill ☆ $$$ NEW AMERICAN
890 Seventh Ave. (at 56th St.)   (212) 541-9000
Credit cards: All major   Meals: Br, L, D, LN

The boisterous room seems as big as Grand Central Terminal and is lively at almost any hour. There's something for everyone on the vast menu, from smoked fish to raw clams, Chinese chicken, pasta, even a hamburger — late into the night. The small grilled lobster, served with a little potato cake and pristine haricots verts, was lovely. The steak of choice here would be the hanger steak, tender slices piled onto a biscuit. The plain Jane cream-cheese bundt cake looks so modest you know it has to be the best of the desserts. Usually it is. (*Ruth Reichl*)

Wine list: Well chosen, interesting and well priced. **Price range:** Apps., $7–$19; entrees, $18–$35; desserts, $7–$8. **Wheelchair access:** Ramp at side entrance.

Relish $25 & Under AMERICAN/DINER
225 Wythe Ave., Williamsburg, Brooklyn   (718) 963-4546
Credit cards: All major   Meals: L, D, LN

Relish is a diner of gleaming, embossed stainless steel. One curious appetizer is both a nod to the neighborhood's older Polish population and the most daring item on the menu, if only because a cast-iron constitution may be necessary to withstand it: garlicky breaded kielbasa corn dogs, as cute as four little blimps surrounding a pile of greens. Among the main courses, roast chicken with pecan waffles is a great version of this Harlem classic. Hanger steak comes with a fine smoked tomato sauce that works well with the meat.

The desserts could use a little work. Thin beignets concealing a well of chocolate sauce in the middle are the best bet. Relish offers a wine list that, with few bottles under $25, seems a little expensive. Oddly, and perhaps presaging a revival, Relish also serves a pretty good egg cream.

Other recommended dishes: Artichoke, fried clams, pork chop, fried catfish. **Price range:** Apps., $6–$11; entrees, $11–$17. **Wheelchair access:** Steps at entrance, steps to restrooms.

Remi ☆☆ $$$ ITALIAN
145 W. 53rd St. (bet. Sixth & Seventh Aves.)   (212) 581-4242
Credit cards: All major   Meals: L, D

Remi's stunning Gothic interior — a 25-foot-high ceiling, medieval arches and a room-length mural of Venice — and the kitchen's enticing and inventive Northern Italian fare make it easy to understand its continued popularity. The diverse menu includes enticing pastas and main courses like garganelli blended with Coho salmon in balsamic sauce; veal-and-spinach-filled cannelloni in rosemary sauce; baked red snapper in a seafood broth, and salmon in a horseradish crust, finished with red wine sauce. (*Ruth Reichl*)

Price range: Apps., $9–$14; entrees, $16–$28; desserts, $8. **Wheelchair access:** Fully accessible. **Features:** Outdoor dining.

René Pujol $$$ FRENCH

321 W. 51st St. (bet. Eighth & Ninth Aves.) (212) 246-3023
Credit cards: All major   Meals: L, D   Closed Sun.

Walk in the door and you know instantly that you are in a restaurant run by pros. The classic French restaurant has been feeding the theater district for a very long time and it's still going strong. Unlike its neighbors, which serve bistro food, René Pujol proudly turns out high-end French fare in a civilized atmosphere.

Price range: Lunch: entrees, $17–$27; three-course prix fixe, $27. Dinner: apps., $7–$12; entrees, $20–$30; desserts, $7–$9; three-course prix fixe, $38. **Wheelchair access:** Not accessible.

Republic $25 & Under ASIAN/NOODLES

37 Union Sq. W. (near 17th St.) (212) 627-7172
Credit cards: All major   Meals: L, D, LN

This original, stylishly modern restaurant specializes in Asian noodles. Republic makes no claims to authenticity, but the food is fresh and well conceived, and the ethnic antecedents of most dishes are clear. Among the best noodle choices are slices of grilled beef marinated with galanga and mint and served on rice noodles, thin slices of pork marinated in garlic and soy and served on cold vermicelli, and strips of spicy chicken served in a rich Thai-style broth laced with coconut milk. Food is served quickly, and the backless benches, comfortable enough for a fast meal, don't encourage lingering.

Other recommended dishes: Chicken salad, grilled Japanese eggplant, sashimi salad, seaweed salad, seafood salad, barbecued pork, coconut chicken, vegetables with rice noodles. **Price range:** Apps., $4–$5; entrees, $6–$9; desserts, $3–$4. **Wheelchair access:** All one level. **Features:** Outdoor dining.

Republi'K $25 & Under PAN-LATIN

114 Dyckman St. (near Nagle Ave.) (212) 304-1717
Credit cards: All major   Meals: D

Republi'K, a pan-Latino restaurant in Inwood, is one of the new standouts far uptown, where the level of comfort rarely goes beyond fluorescent lights and plastic tablecloths. From outside, it looks almost like a bunker, but inside it opens into a sleek dining room with an adjacent bar and a lounge upstairs. The less expensive end of the menu can be superb. A grilled half chicken is juicy and full of flavor beneath its crisp skin. Grilled skirt steak, too, is richly flavored, served with mashed yautia, a sweet tarolike root vegetable, and three chimichurri sauces. Best of all is roasted pork shank, a fist-size hunk of meat encased in crisp skin served with fabulous yuca fries.

A main course with side dishes makes for a significant meal, but appetizers are offered. Try the exceptionally light and crisp fried baby shrimp and calamari, and spicy grilled prawns served on sticks. The best desserts are an empanada filled with guava paste and a flanlike corn custard as sweet as can be.

Price range: Apps., $7–$12; entrees, $14–$34. **Wheelchair access:** All one level.

Rhone $$$ BISTRO/FRENCH
63 Gansevoort St. (bet. Greenwich & Washington Sts.)

(212) 367-8440

Credit cards: All major   Meals: D   Closed Sun.

In the French pecking order, the wines of Bordeaux and Burgundy are king and queen. The Rhone runs a distant third, but this wine bar and restaurant reverses the hierarchy. The region's big, spicy reds and succulent whites get top billing, from marquee names like Chateauneuf-du-Pape and Hermitage to lesser fry like Vacqueyras and Lirac. The wine list offers about 150 choices by the bottle and more than 30 by the glass, starting at $6 or $7.

The food sticks to very simple bistro basics, for the most part, although the lobster truffle salad with smoked bacon and Yukon gold potatoes puts on the dog. Pork belly salad with artichokes and fava beans is more like it, and braised lamb shank with vegetables is a plateful of flavor.

Wine list: All wines from the Rhone Valley. **Price range:** Apps, $8–$90; entrees, $24–$28. **Wheelchair access:** Fully accessible.

Rice $25 & Under   ECLECTIC
227 Mott St. (bet. Spring & Prince Sts.)   (212) 226-5775
Credit cards: Cash only   Meals: L, D, LN

This small 25-seat restaurant and takeout shop serves only rice dishes. The brick-and-metal dining room is as simple and no-frills as the food. Six kinds of rice are served, and you choose toppings to match the rice from a selection that might include sensational black beans in tomato sauce, cool Vietnamese chicken salad and Thai beef salad. Rice has a small selection of beers and an intriguing wine list that specializes in rieslings.

Other recommended dishes: Chicken curry, chicken satay, rice pudding, banana-leaf pastry. **Alcohol:** Beer and wine. **Price range:** Apps., $4–$6; entrees, $5–$11; desserts, $2–$3. **Wheelchair access:** Not accessible.

Rice 'n' Beans $25 & Under   BRAZILIAN
744 Ninth Ave. (bet. 50th & 51st Sts.)   (212) 265-4444
Credit cards: AE/D   Meals: L, D

Brazilian home cooking is the hearty specialty of this friendly little restaurant, which serves steaming bowls of caldo verde, the wonderfully rich, smoky soup, and huge portions of such dishes as feijoada, a black bean stew heaped with pork, sausage, bacon and beef. Rice 'n' Beans is small and drafty, but the welcome is warm.

Alcohol: Beer and wine. **Price range:** Lunch: apps., $3; entrees, $5–$9; desserts, $4. Dinner: apps., $3; entrees, $9–$17; desserts, $4. **Wheelchair access:** Not accessible.

Rinconcito Mexicano $ MEXICAN/TEX-MEX
307 W. 39th St. (bet. Eighth & Ninth Aves.) (212) 268-1704
Credit cards: All major Meals: L, D Closed Sat., Sun.

This tiny restaurant is little more than an aisle in the garment center. English is barely spoken, but the food needs no translation: soft tacos with the freshest and most authentic ingredients, like sautéed pork, calf's tongue, goat, chorizo and pork skin. The aroma of corn rises from the steamed tacos, and the refried beans are still pleasantly grainy.

Alcohol: Beer. **Price range:** Avg. entree, $8; dessert, $4. **Wheelchair access:** Not accessible.

Rinconcito Peruano $25 & Under PERUVIAN
803 Ninth Ave. (at 53rd St.) (212) 333-5685
Credit cards: Cash only Meals: L, D

Don't be deceived by appearances at this humble Peruvian storefront. Dishes like papas a la huancaina, sliced potatoes that are all but invisible under a blanket of cheese sauce, may lack visual appeal, but the combination of the mellow potatoes, served cold, and the unexpectedly spicy sauce is delicious. Lomito al jugo con arroz is a wonderful combination of stir-fried beef served over rice with pickled onions and tomatoes, which add just the right amount of sweetness to offset the spicy brown sauce.

Price range: Apps., $2–$6; entrees, $7–$10; desserts, $2–$4. **Wheelchair access:** Not accessible.

Rio Mar Restaurant $ SPANISH
7 Ninth Ave. (at W. 12th St.) (212) 242-1623
Credit cards: AE Meals: L, D, LN

A lively old Spanish restaurant with a menu of favorites like sautéed chorizo, shrimp in garlic sauce and seafood in a thick parsley sauce. There is often live Spanish music; if the musicians aren't there, the jukebox is sure to be playing.

Price range: Lunch, $6–$7. Dinner: apps., $6; entrees, $13–$14; desserts, $2–$3. **Wheelchair access:** Restrooms not accessible.

Risa $25 & Under PIZZA/ITALIAN
47 E. Houston St. (near Mulberry St.) (212) 625-1712
Credit cards: All major Meals: L, D, LN

The best pizzas are quick works of simple art, delicate and carefully composed, with the best ingredients. Risa's pies taste as good as they look. The crust is thin and light, with a gentle, crisp snap.

The cheese and tomato pie is impeccably fresh, and other toppings only enhance. Designer pies, like one made with speck (a smoked ham), arugula and mascarpone, are notable for their subtlety.

Beyond pizzas, Risa offers pastas that are fine if not especially unusual. The waffled flat bread, baked in the pizza oven and flavored with herbs, salt and pepper, is absolutely delicious. The dining room is low-key, with couples and the occasional family at the widely spaced tables with their comfortable leather banquettes.

Other recommended dishes: Arugula and fennel salad, gemelli di salsicca, Tagliolini al pesto, ravioli with bottarga, pappardelle with beef and sausage. **Price range:** Apps., $6–$9; pizzas, $9–$12; entrees, $9–$20. **Wheelchair access:** Dining room is one flight up.

The River Café ☆☆ $$$$ NEW AMERICAN
1 Water St. Brooklyn Heights (718) 522-5200
Credit cards: All major Meals: Br, L, D

Most diners come to the River Café to gaze at the twinkling lights of Lower Manhattan, celebrate a promotion or impress a date. It's a special-occasion restaurant, Tavern on the Green with a river attached, and its patrons, many of them out-of-towners, do not book a table in search of culinary adventure. The kitchen aims to please but not to shock, and executive chef Brad Steelman shows a gift for making fairly simple food seem a lot more elegant than it really is. It says something about the River Café that you can order its most touristy dessert, the Brooklyn Bridge rendered in chocolate, without shame. Don't let it overshadow the excellent baklava.

Enchanted by the sight of moonlight on the East River, it is easy to ignore a few uncomfortable facts. The luxury is mostly show. Waiters in tuxedos and the restaurant's strict jackets-only rule do establish a certain tone, but the tuxedo shirts look permanent-press, the flatware could have come from a cafeteria and the insistent piano belongs in the lounge of a small-town hotel.

The River Café abounds in such oddities and anachronisms, but in the end it manages to be, if not all things to all people, then certainly a lot of things to all sorts of people.

Wine list: A classic list of about 300 wines, mostly French and Californian, with 20 half bottles and about 30 wines in larger sizes. **Price range:** Lunch: apps., $10–$16; entrees, $19–$26; desserts, $12–$16. Dinner: three-course prix fixe, $70; six-course tasting menu, $90. **Wheelchair access:** One level.

RM ☆☆☆ $$$$ SEAFOOD
33 E. 60th St. (bet. Fifth & Madison Aves.) (212) 319-3800
Credit cards: All major Meals: L, D Closed Sun.

After eight years as chef at Oceana, Rick Moonen left to open his own restaurant in 2002. He is that rare chef whose creations are both gutsy and academic. Each dish is a carefully controlled, reasoned construction. Sweet roasted scallops are perched on a disk of breaded oxtail, an earthy, brilliant combination. Lemon-cured arctic char is simple and luxuriously pure.

Not everything succeeds, but the few clunkers are the exceptions. Good entree choices include poached halibut with fennel cream, walleyed pike wrapped in potato slices, skate encrusted with pistachio and crisp-skinned loup de mer.

The dessert selections are more flamboyant, often matching sweets and cheeses on a single plate. A bittersweet chocolate mousse served with oozy goat cheese was a perfect match. *(Eric Asimov)*

Other recommended dishes: Yellowtail tataki, garlic "velouté" with cod and pancetta, spaghettini with lobster Bolognese, walnut torte with St.-Nectaire. **Wine list:** A bit sparse, though with some good bottles under $40. **Price range:** Three-course prix fixe, $58. Six-course tasting menu, $100. **Wheelchair access:** Ramps available for steps to entrance and dining room.

Rocco's on 22nd $$ ITALIAN

12 E. 22nd St. (near Broadway) (212) 353-0500
Credit cards: All major Meals: D Closed Sun.

Rocco's on 22nd, the subject of the NBC series "The Restaurant," may be the most famous restaurant in Manhattan. Not many viewers will shake off the image of a fire breaking out in the kitchen, setting off sprinklers upstairs and sending clouds of smoke into the dining room.

Things are quieter now. What remains is the humble vision of Rocco DiSpirito, who conceived of Rocco's as a shrine to the Italian-American cooking that he grew up with. The menu runs through the Italian-American hit parade with feeling. Spaghetti with Mama's meatballs competes with Uncle Joe's sausage and peppers, lasagna Bolognese, linguine with red or white clam sauce, veal Parmesan and orecchiette with broccoli rabe and sausage. Olive oil and garlic loom large. It's all very straightforward, two-fisted and uncomplicated. So why on earth did they have all that trouble on opening night?

Price range: Pastas and entrees, $13–$28; side dishes, $5–$12. **Features:** Outdoor dining.

Rocking Horse Café $25 & Under MEXICAN

182 Eighth Ave. (near 19th Street) (212) 463-9511
Credit cards: All major Meals: Br, L, D

In the mid-1990's, Rocking Horse was one of the most exciting Mexican restaurants in New York. Happily, it has regained its footing. The small, bright bar and dining room exude energy and liveliness without descending to the tequila-fueled rowdiness typical of many Mexican restaurants. Starters are a high point. Little tamales imbued with subtly earthy huitlacoche, a funky corn fungus, are a wonderful counterpoint to a spicy poblano chili sauce. A salad of crisp cornmeal-swathed calamari, with frisée, tart orange sections and cubes of chorizo is a superb combination of flavors. Main courses are more mellow than striking. Layers of flavors sneak up without overwhelming, offering quiet pleasures. Mixiote, a slow-roasted pork stew, practically falls apart with the touch of a fork. Birria de pollo, another traditional stew, is made with chicken thighs, which stay moist through prolonged marinating and braising. Not all the desserts work, but Rocking Horse gets points for creativity.

Other recommended dishes: Pork skewers with tomato-jalapeño salsa, lobster turnovers, duck confit crepes, chicken with pipian sauce, shrimp with papaya and poblano chilies, chicken enchiladas, buñuelos, coconut flan. **Price range:** Dinner: apps., $6.95–$9.95; entrees, $14.95–$22.95. **Wheelchair access:** Restrooms downstairs. **Features:** Outdoor dining.

Rosa Mexicano   Satisfactory $$ MEXICAN

61 Columbus Ave. (at 62nd St.)
Credit cards: All major

(212) 977-7700
Meals: Br, L, D

Overall, the cooking at Rosa Mexicano is pallid and dull. It's Latin without passion or flair, but with enough bright spots along the way to offer hope. The best comes first. When a guacamole cart comes rolling by, hail it. The cart superintendent will construct a superlative avocado experience, mashing ingredients in the traditional lava-stone molcajete. The kitchen seems most successful with deep, earthy flavors, as in a small appetizer casserole of sautéed mushrooms, tomatoes and onions. Main courses from the grill are unexceptional, and the nongrilled entrees make, at most, a mildly pleasing impression. Desserts are very sweet and very forgettable, except for the delicia de chocolate, a tall column of velvety mousse resting on a crunchy chocolate and peanut butter disk.

David Rockwell's design for the restaurant has a splashy exuberance that's missing from the food. The colors tingle and vibrate, and he outdoes himself in the restaurant's most memorable feature, a glittering blue tile wall with a thin sheet of water running over its two-story surface.

Wine list: A nice list of about 50 wines, mostly American and Spanish, with one Mexican cabernet-merlot. There are more than 20 tequilas. **Price range:** Lunch: apps., $6–$11; entrees, $13–$20; desserts, $7. Dinner: apps., $8–$18; entrees, $18–$28; desserts, $7. **Wheelchair access:** Elevator to second-floor dining room and restrooms.

Rose Water $25 & Under   NEW AMERICAN

787 Union St., Park Slope, Brooklyn
Credit cards: All major

(718) 783-3800
Meals: L, D

Rose Water offers innovative cooking, moderate prices and a relaxed ambience. Even the basket of house-made bread is unusual, with corn bread flavored with bittersweet fenugreek; a flat, unleavened bread stuffed with cheese like an Italian piadina; and pita dusted on the inside with paprika and powdered cherry pits. Lovers of esoterica will find much to ponder. Tatsoi, a delicate Asian green, appears in a fine frisee salad with fingerling potatoes and grapes. A brik is a crisp North African turnover filled with ground lamb, caraway and mint and surrounded with a pungent parsley sauce. Rose Water offers a pork chop with a fabulous flavor, and a fine thin-sliced rump steak, served over roasted hot and sweet peppers. The brief wine list includes some intelligent, moderately priced choices, but desserts need work.

Other recommended dishes: Fattoush with chanterelles; striped bass with charmoula; salad with beets, feta and shallots; yogurt with rose hip preserves; cheese plate. **Price range:** Apps., $5–$7; entrees, $13–$17. **Wheelchair access:** All one level.

Royal Kebab and Curry House $ Indian

2701 Broadway (at 103rd St.)   (212) 665-4700
Credit cards: MC/V   Meals: L, D, LN

An unprepossessing corner spot that does a lot of takeout business, Royal is one of the better neighborhood Indian restaurants around. The menu includes the usual tandoori dishes and a few vegetarian specialties as well, but they are all well prepared.

Alcohol: Beer and wine. **Price range:** Apps., $2–$6; entrees, $6–$10; desserts, $2–$3. **Wheelchair access:** Not accessible.

Royal Siam $25 & Under   Thai

240 Eighth Ave. (bet. 22nd & 23rd Sts.)   (212) 741-1732
Credit cards: All major   Meals: L, D

Royal Siam's generic décor of mirrored walls, Thai posters and glass-topped tables belie some of the most flavorful and attractively prepared Thai cooking around. Dishes to look for include tom yum koong, or shrimp and mushroom soup in a lemony seafood broth; tod mun pla, fish cakes paired with a bright peanut sauce; and nuur yunk namtok, or grilled steak served sliced on a bed of mixed greens with cucumber and tomato. You can't go wrong with dishes of sautéed squid in a sauce enriched with onion, chili pepper, basil and garlic; shrimp in a spicy sauce of curry and coconut milk, and barbecued chicken in an aromatic blend of herbs and spices.

Other recommended dishes: Steamed dumplings, tofu tod, yum pla muk, soft-shell crabs with basil and chili, koong pad bai kraprow, pad Thai, gluay buach chee. **Alcohol:** Beer and wine. **Price range:** Lunch: apps., $3–$5; entrees, $6–$9; desserts, $3. Dinner: apps., $4–$6; entrees, $9–$15; desserts, $3–$5. **Wheelchair access:** One step up to dining room; restrooms are narrow.

Ruben's Empanadas $25 & Under

Latin American

64 Fulton St. (bet. Gold & Cliff Sts.)   (212) 962-5330
15 Bridge St. (at White & Hall Sts.)   (212) 509-3825
Credit cards: Cash or check only   Meals: L   Closed Sat., Sun.

From Cornish pasties to Jamaican meat patties, meat-filled pastries are found the world over. Empanadas are the South American version. Ruben's, a trim, clean storefront, is just right for grabbing a quick meal. A couple of empanadas, perfectly turned crusts that are crisp around the edges and plump with spicy chicken, savory Argentine sausage or other fillings, make a fine fast lunch.

Price range: Apps., $3–$9; entrees, $7–$11; desserts, $2–$4. **Wheelchair access:** Fully accessible.

Ruby Foo's ☆☆ $$ PAN-ASIAN

2182 Broadway (at 77th St.)
1626 Broadway (at 49th St.)
Credit cards: All major
(212) 724-6700

Meals: Br, L, D, LN

The glitziest restaurant on the Upper West Side has everything it takes to make the neighborhood happy: fabulous décor, interesting pan-Asian food and the sort of atmosphere that appeals to families with children as well as singles on the prowl. Not to mention affordable prices. The menu offers everything from dim sum to sushi with side trips through Thailand, tailored to American tastes. With the exception of dim sum, the weakest link in the menu, the Chinese food is seductive. A memorable Japanese dish is the miso-glazed black cod. But it is the Southeast Asian dishes that really sing. The green curry chicken has a fiery coconut-based sauce that is irresistible. Desserts are purely American and purely wonderful, especially the raspberry-passion fruit parfait. (*Ruth Reichl*)

Wine list: Well chosen and reasonably priced. **Price range:** Apps., $5–$9; entrees, $10–$20; desserts, $5–$7. **Wheelchair access:** Fully accessible.

Rue des Crepes $25 & Under CREPES

104 Eighth Ave. (near 15th St.)
Credit cards: All major
(212) 242-9900

Meals: B, Br, L, D

The little dining room resembles a cobblestone Left Bank street by way of Disney World, complete with street signs and other con-trived cues. But it matters little, because the crepes are very good. Savory combinations, wrapped in soft buckwheat crepes, include merguez sausage with white beans and garlic and chewy flank steak with caramelized onions. Especially good are sweet fillings, like Nutella and banana, and the simple lemon and butter wrapped in white-flour crepes.

Alcohol: Beer and wine. **Price range:** Brunch: prix fixe, $12. **Other meals:** entrees, $4–$9. **Wheelchair access:** Step to entrance.

Ruth's Chris Steak House $$$$ STEAKHOUSE

148 W. 51st St. (bet. Sixth & Seventh Aves.)
Credit cards: All major
(212) 245-9600

Meals: L, D, LN

The New York City branch of this national chain looks so bland you could be in Iowa. The steaks are big and decent, but why would you want to eat in a New Orleans steakhouse when you're in the middle of Manhattan?

Price range: Lunch entrees, $11–$34. Dinner: apps., $6–$12; entrees, $19–$34; desserts, $4–$7. **Wheelchair access:** Not accessible.

Sabor $25 & Under TAPAS/PAN-LATIN

462 Amsterdam Ave. (near 82nd St.)
Credit cards: All major
(212) 579-2929

Meals: L (weekends), D

The menu here has enough subdivisions to keep a law student busy for hours. Beyond tapas, other sections are devoted, in Spanish and

English, to ceviches, empanadas, cheeses, charcuterie, skewers, salads, a raw bar, side dishes and tapas grandes, mercifully translated as "main courses."

Certain things stand out among the main courses, like a fine, beefy grilled skirt steak served with ajilimujili, a purée of fresh pepper, garlic and lime juice, over coarse, nutty mashed malanga and a braised lamb shank. Sabor's paella takes liberties but is delicious and beautifully presented. Also try the delightful tapas. The small wine list includes some good inexpensive choices. The small dessert selection has one standout, a creamy dulce de leche cheesecake that tastes like pure caramel.

Other recommended dishes: Sirloin steak, grilled tuna, boquerones, grilled lamb sausages, tuna ceviche, Andalusian Caesar salad. **Price range:** Tapas, $5–$10; entrees, $11–$16. **Wheelchair access:** Big step at entrance; dining room and restrooms on All one level.

Saigon Grill $25 & Under   VIETNAMESE
1700 Second Ave. (at 88th St.)   (212) 996-4600
Credit cards: All major   Meals: L, D

While Saigon Grill's business is mostly takeout, it is also a pleasant place to stay and eat, with some of the best Vietnamese food on the Upper East Side. Noodle dishes and soups like pho bo, the North Vietnamese standard of oxtail broth with paper-thin slices of beef, are excellent, as is chao tom, the snack of grilled shrimp paste wrapped around sugar cane that is so often a throwaway at Vietnamese restaurants

Alcohol: Beer. **Price range:** Apps., $4–$6; entrees, $7–$14; desserts, $2. **Wheelchair access:** Not accessible.

Salaam Bombay   ☆ ☆ $$ INDIAN
317 Greenwich St. (near Duane St.)   (212) 226-9400
Credit cards: All major   Meals: L, D

This pleasant Indian restaurant doesn't have the flash and excitement of some of Tribeca's more well-known restaurants, but what it lacks in style it more than makes up for in food. Its menu ranges through the north and mid-section of the Indian subcontinent, offering fresh, fragrant, precisely seasoned regional dishes. Jingha bagharela, an appetizer of sautéed shrimp is perfumed with garlic, curry leaves and mustard seeds, while more familiar dishes like lamb vindaloo are expertly rendered. Service is formal but pleasant, and if you go on a weekend, a sitar player often performs. *(Review by Eric Asimov; stars previously awarded by Ruth Reichl.)*

Price range: Lunch buffet, $12. Lunch and dinner: apps., $5–$11; entrees, $10–$20; desserts, $5–$8. **Wheelchair access:** Dining area is up a few small stairs. **Features:** Outdoor dining.

Salam Cafe $25 & Under   MIDDLE EASTERN
104 W. 13th St. (bet. Sixth & Seventh Aves.)   (212) 741-0277
Credit cards: All major   Meals: D

Syrian dishes are the specialty, but the menu ranges as far as
Morocco and India. Top-notch appetizers include foule, the Egyptian bean salad, fragrant with cumin and garlic. While you could
make a meal of the appetizers, you would miss excellent main
courses. Salam's short wine list surprisingly includes some fine values in first-growth Bordeaux.

Other recommended dishes: Baba gannouj, hummus, yogurt with
mint and cucumber, Palestinian air-dried beef, meat pie, Syrian
sausages, Moroccan chicken, lamb kebabs, chicken ouzi, baklava.
Price range: Apps., $4–$8; entrees, $12–$20; desserts, $4–$6.
Wheelchair access: Two steps at entrance narrow passage to
restrooms. **Features:** Outdoor dining.

Salón México   ☆ $$$ MEXICAN
134-136 E. 26th St. (near Lexington Ave.)   (212) 685-9400
Credit cards: All major   Meals: L, D

Salón México, a dim, starkly decorated restaurant, is a highly personal, quirky homage to the foods and pleasures of Mexico. Certain
dishes, like chilaquiles, a loosely organized casserole based on day-
old tortillas, do not veer very far from their traditional sources.
Other dishes, like carne al tequila — a shell steak smothered in a
tequila and Cognac sauce and served with cremini, shiitake and
portobello mushrooms — strike out for new territory. Most of the
modernized dishes are handled with restraint and good taste. But
the heart and soul of the menu lies in the more orthodox dishes like
a poblano chili stuffed with shrimp and scallops, then covered in a
thick layer of Manchego cheese and chipotle sauce, or duck breast
in a pumpkin-seed sauce sharpened with serrano chilies and tart
tomatillos. For dessert, try the apple tart or tequila cake.

Other recommended dishes: Sopa Azteca, duck empanadas. **Wine
list:** About 40 modest wines, with an emphasis on Spain, supplemented by a very big tequila and margarita list. **Price range:** Apps.,
$6–$14; entrees, $15–$26; desserts, $8. **Wheelchair access:** Three
steps down to dining room.

Sal's and Carmine's Pizza $ PIZZA
2671 Broadway (bet. 101st & 102nd Sts.)   (212) 663-7651
Credit cards: Cash only   Meals: L, D

Unlike so many other neighborhood pizzerias, you know who is
making the pizza at Sal's and Carmine's. One of the two is always
there shaping the pies and spreading the sauce. They use the freshest mozzarella, and the difference is apparent when you taste the
creaminess, so different from the rubbery sensation of so many pizzas. Sausage is also excellent. Sal's and Carmine's refuses to let a
pie out of their sight until you take possession of it. Delivery is out
of the question.

Price range: Pizzas, $11–$14 (plus $3 for additional toppings).
Wheelchair access: Not accessible.

Salt $25 & Under   NEW AMERICAN

58 Macdougal St. (near Houston St.)
Credit cards: All major

(212) 674-4968
Meals: Br, D

Salt, a small American bistro in SoHo, soothes rather than challenges and is drawing in youthful crowds nightly. The menu offers two main-course options: conventional entrees or Protein Plus 2 plates where diners select a simple main course and two side dishes. Protein Plus 2 is the way to go, whether pairing a whole dorade royale with buttery Yukon Gold potatoes and roasted brussels sprouts, or smoky slices of roasted duck breast with puréed butternut squash and braised beets and carrots. The chef-composed main courses were less successful. For dessert, stick with chocolate, like a moist, airy devil's food cake or a chocolate bread pudding.

Other recommended dishes: Mushroom bread pudding, honey glaze dates wrapped in bacon, lamb shank with merguez, roasted chicken breast, steak, tagliatelle with mushrooms and pancetta, flourless chocolate cake. **Price range:** Apps., $7.50–$9.50; entrees, $13.50–$20.50. **Wheelchair access:** Ramp at entrance; aisles and restroom are narrow.

Sammy's Roumanian $$$ STEAKHOUSE/JEWISH

157 Chrystie St. (bet. Delancey & Houston Sts.)
Credit cards: All major

(212) 673-0330
Meals: D

The kitschy Borscht Belt party atmosphere, the enormous garlic-rubbed beef tenderloins and the bowls of schmaltz — rendered chicken fat — on every table make Sammy's a nostalgic paean to the days before cholesterol consciousness. The fluorescent lights and the rec room décor have a certain charm, but Sammy's real appeal is in the impossibly heavy food laden with schmaltz, and gribeness, the cracklings left over from making schmaltz, often mixed with caramelized onions. Beyond the tenderloin, Sammy's specializes in fried kreplach and stuffed cabbage. Vodka may be the only beverage powerful enough to wash this food down.

Price range: Apps., $6–$12; entrees, $13–$29; desserts, $4–$5. **Wheelchair access:** Dining room is three steps down.

Sandobe Sushi $$ SUSHI

330 E. 11th St. (bet. First & Second Aves.)
Credit cards: Cash only

(212) 780-0328
Meals: D, LN

The East Village is thick with sushi restaurants and Sandobe is one of the more unusual ones. Sushi rolls are the specialty, with all sorts of creative combinations that sound like overkill but are quite good. Try the Justin roll — salmon, shrimp, eel and crabmeat — or the Erik roll — yellowtail, tuna, salmon and crabmeat. Ordinary sushi and sashimi are not as good. Be prepared to wait. Sandobe is usually crowded.

Alcohol: Beer and wine. **Price range:** Apps., $3–$4; sushi dinner, $20–$50. **Wheelchair access:** Not accessible.

San Domenico   ☆ ☆ $$$$ ITALIAN

240 Central Park S. (near Broadway)   (212) 265-5959
Credit cards: All major   Meals: L (mon.-Fri.), D

With its high visibility, high prices and general air of luxury, San Domenico has served as a flagship for serious Italian cuisine since it opened in 1988. So is San Domenico New York's finest Italian restaurant? Yes and no. The kitchen continues to perform marvels. Since 1996, Odette Fada has been in charge, and her talent is indisputable. She has a sure Italian hand, a refined palate and a sense of adventure. Ms. Fada does not overwork her food. She knows just how to add a touch of distinction and then, just as important, she knows when to stop. The pastas at San Domenico simply shock the competition. They are incomparable. Some seem almost unfair, like the giant dome-shaped ravioli stuffed with a soft egg yolk and drowned in truffle butter. With Italian chefs, there is usually a fall-off when the entrees arrive. At San Domenico, there is a leveling off, but no dip, with dishes like saddle of roasted rabbit in a beautifully restrained garlic and pecorino sauce. The desserts, led by the house tiramisù, are excellent.

While the kitchen is sending out three-star food, the dining room is working from a different script. The restaurant, by virtue of its location, caters to many tourists, and the waiters respond accordingly with aggressive salesmanship or sometimes outright bullying. And the kitchen, for all its virtues, can be uneven, sending out food at very strangely timed intervals. In Ms. Fada, San Domenico has a more than worthy successor to a long list of distinguished chefs. She doesn't need to live up to the restaurant. The restaurant needs to live up to her.

Other recommended dishes: Bottarga with oranges and tomatoes, scafata, baby octopus with rosemary olive oil, sea urchin ravioli, risotto with zucchini and mint, veal fillet in mushroom broth. **Wine list:** Expensive, with a strong commitment to Italian wines, especially by high-powered and high-priced producers, with not enough representation from newer regions. **Price range:** Lunch: apps. and pastas, $9.50–$13.50; entrees, $17.50–$19.50. Dinner: apps., $9–$15; pastas, $17.50–$21; entrees, $26.50–$29.50; desserts, $12.50–$16.50; three-course prix fixe, $50. **Wheelchair access:** Not accessible.

San Pietro $$$ ITALIAN

18 E. 54th St. (bet. Fifth & Madison Aves.)   (212) 753-9015
Credit cards: All major   Meals: L, D   Closed Sun.

Expensive and uneven Italian food for well-heeled businessmen. San Pietro clearly can produce good food: the many regular customers seem to know how to navigate the menu and each time I've been at the restaurant the food on all the other tables has looked better than mine. The fish are usually excellent and there are some very fine pastas. Nobody bothers to pretend that new customers are favored patrons, and the service is often perfunctory.

Wine list: The Italian and American wines include many excellent bottles at fair prices. **Price range:** Lunch: apps., $10–$15; entrees, $18–$26; desserts, $9. Dinner: apps., $12–$18; entrees, $19–$32;

desserts, $9. **Wheelchair access:** Fully accessible. **Features:** Outdoor dining.

Sapori d'Ischia $25 & Under   ITALIAN

55-15 37th Ave., Woodside, Queens   (718) 446-1500
Credit cards: Cash only   Meals: D

By day, Sapori d'Ischia is a bright and thriving Italian specialty market. But a transformation occurs around 5 P.M. The trays of hot food are put away, along with the display of pizza by the slice. Candles are lighted, soft music begins to play and a waiter takes over, welcoming guests, handing out menus and offering wine. Almost every table has a "reserved" sign on it. If the transformation seems unlikely, so is the site, an industrial block where the restaurant is barely discernible among the garages and auto glass shops that line this part of 37th Avenue.

The kitchen turns out fine individual pizzas, but the small menu has other excellent choices, like budino di carciofi, or artichoke puree, an Ischian specialty that is soft as flan and set atop a luscious combination of grilled pancetta and peppers, and fettuccine al'Antonio, an extraordinarily rich dish of fresh pasta with cream and prosciutto prepared at the table in a bowl carved out of a wheel of Parmesan. Sapori offers only a few wines, including a pedestrian Chianti and an inky negroamaro.

Other recommended dishes: Polenta with mushrooms and robiola, rigatoni with eggplant and ricotta, steak. **Price range:** Apps., $8; entrees, $8–$14. **Wheelchair access:** All one level.

Sapphire $$ INDIAN

1845 Broadway (at 63rd St.)   (212) 245-4444
Credit cards: All major   Meals: L, D

Sapphire may not be the last word in Indian cuisine, but it is good enough and good-looking enough to advance the cause. The extensive menu includes the usual hit parade of samosas, curries, tandoori treats and even mulligatawny soup. But it also includes some sleepers like chutney idli, a small cake of steamed lentil and rice flour topped with a coconut curry. Spicier and just as good is kadhi pakoda, another appetizer. Chicken is unfailingly moist, tender and flavorful, especially the chicken Nizami, a masala dish with cashews, coconut and sesame seeds. Two breads deserve special mention, the nan stuffed with garlic and kulcha, and a soft flatbread baked in the tandoori oven, this one stuffed with crab meat.

Sapphire has a pleasingly understated opulence, with ornately carved Mogul-period wooden doors and windows, brought over from Rajasthan, and embroidered panels of Jodhpur silk hung from the ceiling like small banners.

Wine list: Wines from Morocco, Argentina, Australia, France and Italy, starting at $28. **Price range:** Lunch buffet, $12. Dinner: apps., $5–11; entrees, $12–$20. **Wheelchair access:** Fully accessible.

Sarabeth's $$ AMERICAN

945 Madison Ave. (at 75th St.) (212) 570-3670
1295 Madison Ave. (at 92nd St.) (212) 410-7335
423 Amsterdam Ave. (at 80th St.) (212) 496-6280
Credit cards: All major Meals: B, Br, L, D

These nostalgic, floral sanctuaries from modern life have their good days and their bad days. At brunch, for example, you are almost as likely to receive an undercooked waffle or pancakes that are still batter in the center as you are a fully cooked meal. Too bad, because the grainy cornmeal waffles, served with warm syrup and compote, are delicious, as are the desserts. Pastries are excellent. Don't forget to buy some jam.

Price range: Avg. meal, $17. **Wheelchair access:** Fully accessible.

Saul $25 & Under NEW AMERICAN

140 Smith St., Boerum Hill, Brooklyn (718) 935-9844
Credit cards: MC/V Meals: Br, D

The small menu in this sweet little brick storefront offers strong, clear flavors, bolstered by background harmonies that augment without overshadowing. Duck confit is expertly made, framed by earthy black lentils, and big enough for a main course, justifying a splurge on the sumptuous sautéed foie gras. The main courses seem familiar—salmon, chicken, pork loin—but they are beautifully handled and surprisingly good. Desserts are wonderful, like lush baked Alaska with a chocolate cookie crust.

Other recommended dishes: Bacon and onion tart, roast chicken, sautéed salmon, roast pork loin, seared scallops, lemon custard cake, black plum tart. **Price range:** Apps., $5–$11; main courses, $15–$20. **Wheelchair access:** One step at entrance.

Savore $$ ITALIAN

200 Spring St. (at Sullivan St.) (212) 431-1212
Credit cards: All major Meals: L, D, LN

The room is wonderful, with the cool elegance of a real Tuscan trattoria. The food is mostly authentic Tuscan fare, and mostly very good. Antipasti include smoked goose carpaccio, a shrimp dish of the day and a plate of Tuscan charcuterie with bruschetta. The pastas are particularly recommended. Among the main dishes are breast of duck in pomegranate sauce; imported fish from the Mediterranean, and wild boar in the style of the Maremma marshlands, which are famous for game.

Price range: Lunch: apps., $8–$12; entrees, $14–$18; desserts, $6. Dinner: apps., $8–$14; entrees, $14–$22; desserts, $6. **Wheelchair access:** Fully accessible. **Features:** Outdoor dining.

Savoy $$$ NEW AMERICAN

70 Prince St. (bet. Crosby & Lafayette Sts.) (212) 219-8570
Credit cards: All major Meals: L, D

After nearly 13 years the Savoy has shed its Garbo-like image of secrecy, transforming the ground floor into a modern-looking cafe with diner overtones. The huge windows now make the Savoy's interior almost shockingly visible to the outside world. The upstairs remains old-fashioned and intimate. The brick fireplace survives intact. Peter Hoffman, the Savoy's chef and owner, sticks with the same cooking philosophy that has won a loyal following over the years, shopping the greenmarkets for local produce and pushing organic foods whenever possible. The makeover now gives him two formats: an all-day cafe menu and a more formal menu upstairs. Downstairs, pastas and sandwiches outnumber main courses. The shifting dinner menu sticks with one of Savoy's signatures, duck breast baked in salt crust. Savoy always put a premium on fresh ingredients, but the restaurant itself always looked old. The new-model Savoy retains the charm that has made it a perennial favorite, but it now looks a lot more like the food it serves.

Price range: Lunch: entrees, $10–$16; desserts, $6. Dinner: apps., $8–$12; entrees, $24–$26; desserts, $8. 4-course prix-fixe, $48. **Wheelchair access:** Fully accessible.

Scalini Fedeli ☆ $$ ITALIAN
165 Duane St. (at Hudson St.)   (212) 528-0400
Credit cards: All major   Meals: L, D

Scalini Fedeli means "steps of faith," and in this case, it's a leap. The original Scalini Fedeli is one of New Jersey's most highly regarded and popular dining spots. This new location has no edge. What it has, instead, is old-fashioned grace. The dining room, with its well-spaced tables and conservative country-Italian décor, is as soothing as a massage. The food is pleasing, for the most part, but it rarely takes flight, and when it does, the dish is likely to be disarmingly simple. The main courses are satisfying, decorous and rather unassuming. For dessert, the panna cotta takes a back seat to the dense chocolate tart, and to the clever miniature cannoli, painted with chocolate and filled with espresso-flavored mascarpone cream.

Food isn't everything. That may sound dismissive, but it isn't. There are dozens of intangibles that go into a meal and contribute to a diner's sense of satisfaction. Scalini Fedeli rates very high on most of these.

Wine list: Some 225 French, Italian and American wines; 22 half bottles. **Price range:** Lunch: apps., $7–$10; entrees, $17–$23; desserts, $7. Dinner: three courses, $60. **Wheelchair access:** Two steps up to entrance; restrooms are downstairs.

Sciuscià ☆ $$$ ITALIAN/MEDITERRANEAN
Hotel Giraffe, 365 Park Ave. S. (near 26th St.)   (212) 213-4008
Credit cards: All major   Meals: L, D

A slightly mad cheeriness pervades Sciuscià, an eccentric subterranean restaurant that can seem like an Italian version of Alice's tea party. With its truly hideous surroundings, it manages to please the palate, if not the eye. The great strength of the chef's Italian-accented Mediterranean menu is pasta. Paccheri served with a wonderful sweet sauce of stewed pork belly and onions. Cavatelli come with mussels in a spicy tomato sauce with a real zip. The appetizers, on the whole, put in a stronger showing than the main courses.

Two Spanish appetizers are among the best: sliced, grilled chorizo with thin slices of potatoes and onion, and steamed clams and mussels. Among the more successful entrees is a pan-seared striped bass heaped with spicy chorizo, caramelized onions, green beans and cherry tomatoes.

Other recommended dishes: Paccheri with genovese lobster ravioli in Champagne sauce, rack of lamb with couscous and merguez sauce, molten chocolate cake, apple tart. **Wine list:** A bistro-size, mostly Italian list of about 90 bottles, with an emphasis on lesser regions. **Price range:** Lunch: multicourse "piatto unico," $22.50. Dinner: apps., $7–$12; entrees, $14 –$28; desserts, $7. **Wheelchair access:** Elevator in hotel lobby.

Screening Room ☆ ☆ $$$ NEW AMERICAN
54 Varick St. (below Canal St.)   (212) 334-2100
Credit cards: All major   Meals: Br, L, D

It's a bar. It's a restaurant. It's a movie theater. It is also dark, casual and slightly scruffy. The slightly funky bar serves appealing snacks like lobster rolls, onion rings and Philadelphia cheese steaks. The restaurant offers serious American food on the order of grilled duck and spectacular desserts. The best appetizer is the pan-fried artichokes, served on lemony greens topped with shavings of Parmesan cheese. The simplest dishes are the most impressive: roast chicken; a fine piece of grilled tuna; cedar-planked salmon with chard. For dessert try the lemon icebox cake, a riff on lemon meringue pie. (*Ruth Reichl*)

Wine list: Appealingly wide range of prices and styles, though none below $20. **Price range:** Lounge menu, $5–$13. Brunch, $5–$17. Dinner: apps., $7–$10; entrees, $13–$22; desserts, $6–$8. **Wheelchair access:** All one level.

Sea Grill ☆ ☆ $$$ SEAFOOD
19 W. 49th St., Rockefeller Center.   (212) 332-7610
Credit cards: All major   Meals: L, D   Closed Sun.

A refiguring of the Rockefeller Center concourse has made the Sea Grill smaller, and a redesign by Adam Tihany has given it a cooler, cleaner and snappier appearance. But the main draw remains unchanged. Look out the windows at night and you see the golden figure of Prometheus, splashed by colored jets of water. In winter, skaters circle the ice. In warm weather, the skating rink becomes an outdoor extension of the restaurant, with canvas umbrellas.

Like the new design, the Sea Grill's menu aims at a new target: casual luxury. Much of the menu, with trimmed-back prices, has a brasserie feel to it, with heaping, almost alarmingly abundant shellfish platters, and a changing daily menu of day-boat fish that are simply grilled, sautéed or seared. The renowned crab cake from the old Sea Grill remains, displaying the rough-hewn virtues that distinguish a real crab cake from a thousand prettified pretenders. For dessert, a "palette of sorbets" comes on a shiny silver platter shaped like a painter's palette. As a tourist pleaser, this one is hard to beat, but it gets serious competition from the mile-high chocolate parfait, served on a giant plate with a silhouette of the New York skyline executed in powdered cocoa.

Wine list: About 115 mostly French and American wines, organized by taste characteristics; 18 wines are available by the half-bottle, 14 by the glass. **Price range:** Apps., $8–$16, entrees, $21–$32; desserts, $9–$14. **Wheelchair access:** Elevator on 49th Street. Restrooms are on dining room level.

71 Clinton Fresh Food ☆☆ $$

BISTRO/NEW AMERICAN

71 Clinton St. (near Rivington St.)　　　　(212) 614-6960
Credit cards: All major　　Meals: D　　　　Closed Sun.

Well-known chef Wylie Dufresne left this popular resaurant to open his own place making room for a new talented chef, Matt Reguin. He has wisely chosen not to venture far from the sort of elegantly composed contemporary American dishes that won Mr. Dufresne so much applause. A fat square of Arctic char, for example, is lacquered with a glaze just sweet enough to bring out the sweetness of the fish itself, which is offset by salty, spicy rounds of chorizo and slivers of green onion, a graceful and delicious combination of flavors and textures. Mr. Reguin likes to add fruit to the mix, serving a sour cherry chutney with wonderfully tender slices of venison. A sweet strawberry relish added just the right fresh note to slices of buttery Wagyu sirloin.

The restaurant remains as crowded as ever, literally the elbow-to-elbow seating requires just about everybody along a banquette to engage in oblique flanking movements for one person to get up to use the restroom. Of course, this has always been part of 71 Clinton's charm — the casual spot with serious cuisine in an unlikely neighborhood. The appeal is undimmed.

Wine list: An original and distinctive list of about 30 wines, half of them available by the glass. **Price range:** Apps., $7–$10; entrees, $15–$22; desserts, $6. **Wheelchair access:** All one level.

Sevilla $25 & Under SPANISH

62 Charles St. (at W. 4th St.)　　　　(212) 243-9513
Credit cards: All major　　　　Meals: L, D, LN

This old-style Spanish restaurant is a relic from the 1950's, or maybe even before. The yellowed menus indicate a kitchen that hasn't changed in decades, and who can argue with Sevilla's philosophy, which seems to be, the more garlic the better. Wash it all down with sangría.

Price range: Apps., $7–$10; entrees, $12–$33; desserts, $4. **Wheelchair access:** Fully accessible. **Features:** Outdoor dining.

Shaan of India ☆☆ $$ INDIAN

57 W. 48th St. (bet. Fifth & Sixth Aves.)　　　(212) 977-8400
Credit cards: All major　　　　Meals: L, D

Most of the food at Shaan is delicious, but the big menu can be a minefield. Sometimes different dishes turn out to taste more or less the same. But order right, and the food can be a complete delight. Dahi batata poori, tiny puffs of the great Indian bread stuffed with a searingly spicy mixture of minced potatoes, chickpeas and bean sprouts, are a great beginning, as is tawa chicken, moist, boneless pieces of white meat cooked with onions, peppers and lots of spices. Vegetable dishes like methi palak corn, baby corn in a sumptuous spinach sauce shot through with the strong taste of fenugreek, are a joy. (*Ruth Reichl*)

Price range: Lunch buffet, $14. Dinner: apps., $9–$11; entrees, $11-16; desserts, $5; pre-theater prix fixe, $22. **Wheelchair access:** Fully accessible.

Shabu-Tatsu $25 & Under JAPANESE
1414 York Ave. (at 75th St.) (212) 472-3322
216 E. 10th St. (bet. First & Second Aves.) (212) 477-2972
Credit cards: All major Meals: Br, D

These two bright, festive and informal restaurants specialize in sukiyaki and shabu shabu, dishes that are cooked on circular metal grills set over burners in the center of each table. Whichever you choose, the food is great fun to make and it's delicious.

Other recommended dishes: Yook hwe, kimchi, boiled soybeans, yakiniku, ice cream. **Alcohol:** Beer and wine. **Price range:** Brunch, $8–$9. Dinner: apps., $4–$6; avg. entree, $20; desserts, $4. **Wheelchair access:** Fully accessible.

Shaffer City Oyster Bar $$ SEAFOOD
5 W. 21st St. (bet. Fifth & Sixth Aves.) (212) 255-9827
Credit cards: All major Meals: L, D Closed Sun.

An old-time New York City oyster saloon, updated for the 21st century. The atmosphere may be casual, but given the price of seafood, this is not the all-you-can-eat affair of the past. The menu offers everything from caviar to seafood risotto with tarragon and basil essence. Try the roasted halibut on a very spicy turnip purée and, for dessert, the strawberry napoleon. But the best things really are the oysters: raw, poached or deliciously fried.

Price range: Lunch: apps., $7–$10; entrees, $10–$15. Dinner: apps., $7–$12; entrees, $16–$27; desserts, $7. **Wheelchair access:** Fully accessible. **Features:** Outdoor dining.

Shanghai Cuisine $ CHINESE
89 Bayard St. (at Mulberry St.) (212) 732-8988
Credit cards: All major Meals: L, D

This popular and crowded Chinatown restaurant offers the usual enormous menu. The Shanghai dishes are clearly a cut above the others, with terrific appetizers like smoked fish, soup dumplings with pork or crab and mock duck. Look for crisp baby yellow fish, fish head casserole and stewed pork among the main courses.

Alcohol: Beer and wine. **Price range:** Apps., $2–$6; avg. entree, $10–$11; desserts, $5. **Wheelchair access:** Fully accessible.

Shanghai Tide $25 & Under CHINESE

135-20 40th Rd., Flushing, Queens (718) 661-4234
77 W. Houston St. (at Wooster St.) (212) 614-9550
Credit cards: MC/V Meals: L, D

The bright, handsome Flushing branch, one of the best Chinese
places in the area, serves many excellent Shanghai specialties. You
know you're in for an unusual meal when you enter and see fish
tanks full of lively eels. Service is unusually friendly and helpful.
The newer SoHo branch doesn't achieve the same high level.

Recommended dishes: Crab-meat-and-pork juicy buns, wined crabs,
jellyfish with celery, smoked fish, fried juicy buns, fried yellow fish
with seaweed, deep-fried bamboo shoots, lion's head with cabbage,
pork shoulder with greens, eel in brown sauce, Shanghai-style pan-
fried noodles. **Price range:** Apps., $4–$6; entrees, $7–$14 (specials to
$25). **Wheelchair access:** Restrooms not accessible.

Sharz Cafe & Wine Bar $25 & Under ITALIAN

177 E. 90th St. (bet. Third & Lexington Aves.) (212) 369-1010
Credit cards: D/DC/MC/V Meals: L, D

A legion of regulars appears nightly in this small cafe, attracted by
the warm, homey feeling and the good food. The biggest part of the
menu is devoted to pastas, like terrific spaghetti bolognese and a
fine penne with chunks of fennel sausage in a tomato-and-cream
sauce. The wine list is improving, with about 50 wines available by
the glass.

Other recommended dishes: Blackberry-peach cobbler, chocolate
custard, cheesecake. **Price range:** Apps., $5–$9; entrees, $10–$24;
desserts, $5–$7. **Wheelchair access:** Fully accessible.

Shinbashi $$$ JAPANESE

280 Park Ave. (at 48th St.) (212) 661-3915
Credit cards: All major Meals: L, D Closed Sun.

A venerable Japanese restaurant where the waitresses wear traditional Japanese dress and the traditional food is fine. The room is
starting to show its age a bit, but that only adds to the charm.

Price range: Lunch: avg. app., $10; entree, $20. Dinner: avg. app.,
$15; entree, $25; dessert, $5. **Wheelchair access:** Fully accessible.

Shun Lee Palace ☆☆ $$$ CHINESE

155 E. 55th St. (bet. Lexington & Third Aves.) (212) 371-8844
Credit cards: All major Meals: L, D

Shun Lee is a New York institution, with a cool opulence that is
almost a caricature of a Chinese-American palace. Regular customers are so pampered that first-timers look on enviously as they
are shunted off to a table in the far less luxurious bar area. It is a
restaurant in which you need to invest a little time for the staff to
figure out what you like. The chefs do impressive things with whole
fish, and the restaurant's owner likes to appear at the table with

live fish swimming around in basins and suggest various ways the kitchen might prepare them.

A recent visit served as a reminder that no one quite matches Shun Lee for its blend of showmanship and culinary quality. The menu ranges too far and wide (why chicken satay?), but dishes like prawns on banana leaf with curry sauce; sliced duckling with young ginger root and hot pepper; and clams in an unctuous, sweet and garlicky black bean sauce could hardly be better. The carved fruits and vegetables are show stoppers, especially the orange carp, with scales, fashioned from fresh melon. (*Ruth Reichl, updated by William Grimes*)

Wine list: There are a few wines that go well with the food. **Price range:** Lunch prix fixe, $20. Dinner: apps., $4–$14; entrees, $9–$30; desserts, $5–$7. **Wheelchair access:** Fully accessible.

Shun Lee West $$$ CHINESE
43 W. 65th St. (at Columbus)   (212) 595-8895
Credit cards: All major   Meals: Br, L, D, LN

A cavernous Chinese restaurant near Lincoln Center that is always packed. The kitchen can do great things, but they are rarely produced for a clientele that sticks mostly to the familiar. If you want the best food, call ahead and discuss the menu. Good Peking duck.

Price range: Lunch: avg. app., $9; entree, $15. Dinner: avg. app., $12; entree, $19; dessert, $6. **Wheelchair access:** Not accessible.

Silver Swan $25 & Under   GERMAN
41 E. 20th St. (bet. Broadway & Park Ave. S.)   (212) 254-3611
Credit cards: All major   Meals: L, D, LN

The excellent selection of more than 75 beers and ales is reason enough to enjoy Silver Swan's solid German fare in a friendly atmosphere. Rauchbier, or smoked beer, made with smoked malt, goes perfectly with kassler rippchen, smoked pork chops served with vinegary sauerkraut, while any of more than a dozen Bavarian wheat beers are just right with weisswurst, mild veal sausage, or bratwurst, juicy pork sausage. This is not the place to eat if you are longing for vegetables, which run the gamut from cabbage to potatoes, cooked until soft. Meat is another matter, however, starting with five varieties of schnitzel and ending with a satisfying sauerbraten.

Price range: Apps., $5–$9; entrees, $14–$27; desserts, $5. **Wheelchair access:** One level; hall to restrooms is narrow. **Features:** Outdoor dining.

66   ☆ ☆ $$$$ CHINESE
241 Church St. (near Leonard St.)   (212) 925-0202
Credit cards: All major   Meals: L, D

Over the last 12 years, Jean-Georges Vongerichten has displayed a knack for developing an appealing, innovative culinary idea, packaging it attractively and putting it in the right spot. Mr. Vongerichten's most polished production yet may be 66. It is an elegantly understated room subdivided into discrete dining areas by frosted glass panels. The design is flawless. The food is hit and miss. It's hard to imagine, in principle, a more appealing menu. Diners can wander at will among noodles, soups, dim sum, small vegetable plates, clever appetizers, and larger entree-like dishes, ordering entirely by whim. Make the right choices, and you'll have the meal of your life.

Appetizers, like lacquered pork belly and two-flavored shrimp, can be inspired. Vegetables are serviceable. The beef short ribs and the steamed cod in a fragrant, smoky broth are excellent. Peking duck earns a gentleman's C. Desserts are quirky, ingenious and hugely entertaining. The dim sum redux — an assortment of sweet treats served in steamer baskets — is irresistible.

Other recommended dishes: Shrimp toast with water chestnuts, potato noodles, pea shoot and tofu dumpling, shrimp and foie gras dumpling, frozen mandarin orange segments. **Wine list:** A small but sensible list. **Price range:** Apps., $4.50–$18; entrees, $18–$40; desserts, $8–$12. **Wheelchair access:** Fully accessible.

Smith & Wollensky   ☆☆ $$$$ STEAKHOUSE
797 Third Ave. (at 49th St.)   (212) 753-1530
Credit cards: All major   Meals: L, D, LN

If you were trying to design a classic steakhouse, this is what it would look like — big, plain, comfortable and manly. It is also one of the few steakhouses that never lets you down: the service is swell, the steaks are consistently very, very good (if rarely great) and the portions are huge. Beyond that, if you have noncarnivores to feed, the restaurant knows how to do it. The lobsters are perfect specimens, and the chicken is cooked by people who actually seem to like chicken. Desserts, unfortunately, leave a great deal to be desired. Smith & Wollensky may not have the eccentric ugliness of Palm or the Damon Runyon airs of other New York steakhouses, but it has a no-nonsense down-to-earth plainness. This is a place for two-fisted eating. (*Ruth Reichl*)

Wine list: Big, deep and filled with impressive and expensive wines; for less expensive bottles, ask for the Wollensky's Grill list. **Price range:** Lunch: apps., $6–$15; entrees, $15–$28. Dinner: apps. $6–$15; entrees, $19–$65; desserts, $7–$9. **Wheelchair access:** Not accessible.

Snack $25 & Under   GREEK
105 Thompson St. (at Prince St.)   (212) 925-1040
Credit cards: All major   Meals: L, D

At 380 square feet, kitchen included, and with seating for 10, barely, Snack is one of Manhattan's smallest restaurants. But taste Snack's stifado, a wonderful stew of braised lamb, delicately spiced with cinnamon and oregano and touched with the sweet juices of a currant, apricot and almond pilaf, and you know right away that Snack is worth squeezing into.

Chicken boureki, a triangle of puff pastry layered with sesame seeds and stuffed with chicken, feta, mushrooms and herbs, is a close-your-eyes-and-sigh kind of dish.

Other recommended dishes: Skordalia, tzatziki, olive boureki, roast chicken, yogurt with honey, "halvah." **Alcohol:** Beer and wine. **Price range:** Apps., $4–$8; entrees, $8–$13. **Wheelchair access:** Steps at entrance; narrow way to restroom.

Snackbar $25 & Under   SEAFOOD/NEW AMERICAN
111 W. 17th St. (near Sixth Ave.)   (212) 627-3700
Credit cards: All major   Meals: L, D

Snackbar is the sort of restaurant that you might be inclined to hate: loud and cynically fashionable, with distracted waiters and fake martinis by the pitcher. But open your mouth and start eating, and annoyance gives way to pleasure. Food so good retouches the experience.

Snackbar is sleek and narrow with cool, clean lines and the menu is stripped down and à la carte. You construct your own main course, selecting a centerpiece ingredient, adding a sauce and sides. The quality of the ingredients is superb, and seafood makes up a significant part of the menu. One reason the prices seem so reasonable are those sides you do not get. If you want anything more, it will cost you.

Other recommended dishes: Rouget, scallops, mahi-mahi, seared foie gras, big-eye tuna, flank steak, sweetbreads, poussin, tomato terrine, steamed littleneck clams, clams casino. **Price range:** Apps., $6.50–$15.50; entrees, $13.50–$24. **Wheelchair access:** Not accessible.

Soba Nippon $25 & Under   JAPANESE
19 W. 52nd St. (bet. Fifth & Sixth Aves.)   (212) 489-2525
Credit cards: All major   Meals: L, D

The long dining room is airy and comfortable if somewhat plain, though pretty bamboo sprays arch over the plain wood tables. Soba Nippon serves sushi, as well as teriyaki and donburi dishes, but soba is the specialty. Few places make better noodles.

Try the cold soba noodles served plain, which sounds spartan but really is not. The pale brown noodles arrive on a flat basket with a dipping sauce of fish stock and soy. You can add scallions and wasabi, or simply dip the noodles and slurp them home, the better to appreciate their smooth texture and the hint of resistance as you chew. Eventually, a small, simmering pot of liquid is placed on the table. This is the broth in which the noodles were boiled, and it is said to be full of nutrients. Pour the broth into the dipping sauce — now add the scallions and wasabi — and drink. It's marvelous. The cold soba is offered in half a dozen variations. One fine alternative to soba is cold inaniwa udon noodles, as thin as spaghetti, with a pure, clean flavor. Soba Nippon's hot soba soups are excellent as well, especially soba with agedashi tofu.

Other recommended dishes: Watercress in sesame sauce, sautéed burdock. **Price range:** Apps., $4–$13.80; entrees, $8–$17. **Wheelchair access:** All one level.

Soba-Ya $25 & Under   JAPANESE/NOODLES

229 E. 9th St. (bet. Second & Third Aves.)   (212) 533-6966
Credit cards: All major   Meals: L, D

Noodles are the focus at this bright, handsome little Japanese restaurant, one of several nearby owned by the same group. The soba noodles — buckwheat, pale tan and smooth — are served hot in soups or cold, a better bet for appreciating their lightness and clear flavors. Appetizers are excellent, differing night to night but sometimes including cooked marinated spinach, rice with shreds of marinated sardines and fried squares of marvelously fresh tofu.

Alcohol: Beer, wine and sake. **Price range:** Apps., $3–$8; noodles and rice bowls, $7–$14. **Wheelchair access:** All one level.

SoHo Kitchen & Bar $$ NEW AMERICAN

103 Greene St. (bet. Spring & Prince Sts.)   (212) 925-1866
Credit cards: All major   Meals: Br, L, D, LN

Food is an afterthought at this dim, cavernous wine bar with high ceilings and brick walls. It serves dozens of wines by the glass, by the half-size tasting glass and even by smaller tastes for comparing and contrasting a series of wines.

Price range: Apps., $5–$8; entrees, $10–$15; desserts, $5. Avg. Sunday brunch, $8. **Wheelchair access:** Fully accessible.

Soho Steak $25 & Under   BISTRO/FRENCH

90 Thompson St. (near Spring St.)   (212) 226-0602
Credit cards: Cash only   Meals: Br, D

This thoroughly French little restaurant, drawing a young, good-looking crowd, emphasizes meat but is no simple steakhouse. It is a cleverly conceived, bustling bistro that serves creative dishes for lower prices than you might imagine. Steak frites, of course, is top-notch. Few places offer this much value for this kind of money.

Other recommended dishes: Grilled foie gras, braised oxtail ravioli, lamb shank, filet mignon carpaccio, sautéed squab, grilled sirloin, seared filet mignon, roasted pheasant, venison, pear tart, cheese plate. **Alcohol:** Beer and wine. **Price range:** Brunch, $5–$12. Dinner: apps., $7–$9; entrees, $14–$16; desserts, $5–$7. **Wheelchair access:** Fully accessible.

Solera   ☆ ☆ $$$ SPANISH

216 E. 53rd St. (bet. Second & Third Aves.)   (212) 644-1166
Credit cards: All major   Meals: L, D, LN   Closed Sun.

Solera, one of Manhattan's first serious Spanish restaurants, has always taken for granted what other restaurants advertise as innovations. It has had a tapas bar, with a stellar array of sherries to match, ever since it opened. The wine list, constantly renewed, showed a commitment to Spanish wines before they became the next thing. When food writers and diners first awakened to regional Spanish cooking, they found that Solera had arrived ahead of them. The restaurant continues to deliver quality Spanish food, backed up by a terrific wine list, in a charming, rustic dining room. Classic tapas like chorizo or stuffed piquillo peppers provide a convenient excuse for getting at the sherries. The more substantial appetizers include a generous plate of fried seafood, a lobster-mushroom crepe, and a salpicon of seafood in watermelon gazpacho. Main courses can be quite adventurous, like the rabbit crepinette with snail and leek escabeche, or cod confit with smoked manchego and pil-pil soup. Some new-wave desserts have been added to the menu, including an improbable-sounding but delicious picatostes, three chocolate drops on toast points with olive oil. Solera, admirably, has a style, as opposed to a formula. And it still feels fresh. *(Review by William Grimes; stars previously awarded by Ruth Reichl.)*

Wine list: The all-Spanish list is excellent and the staff knows it well. **Price range:** Prix-fixe lunch, $32. Dinner: apps., $9–$12; entrees, $25–$35; desserts, $9; tapas, $3–$10. **Wheelchair access:** All one level.

Sosa Borella $25 & Under   AMERICAN/ARGENTINE

460 Greenwich St. (near Desbrosses St.)
Credit cards: All major
(212) 431-5093
Meals: B, Br, L, D

This quiet spot is all you could seek in a neighborhood restaurant. From the enticing pastries in the morning to the extensive list of delicious sandwiches at midday to the Argentine menu that comes out at night, Sosa does well by its food. It's friendly, handsome and reasonably priced to boot.

Other recommended dishes: Sandwiches, including bresaola, smoked turkey with roasted peppers and brie, and prosciutto with mozzarella and roasted peppers; French toast; oatmeal fruit brûlée; strip steak; beef short ribs; empanada; apple tart. **Alcohol:** Beer and wine. **Price range:** Avg. breakfast, $8. Avg. lunch, $15. Dinner: avg. app., $8; entree, $18; dessert, $6. **Wheelchair access:** Fully accessible.

Soul Cafe $$ SOUTHERN/CARIBBEAN

444 W. 42nd St. (bet. Ninth & 10th Aves.)
Credit cards: All major
(212) 244-7685
Meals: D, LN

A late-night scene, complete with big portions of soul food and live music. The plush, L-shaped supper club promises "Afro-centered cuisine with Southern flair and a touch of the Caribbean." By that it means largely Southern and Caribbean food that has been updated, often for diet-conscious customers. The menu includes appetizers like Maryland she-crab soup and grilled lamb ribs, and main courses like jerk duck, braised short ribs and red snapper crusted with sweet potatoes and plantains. Side dishes are traditionally Southern, like macaroni and cheese, candied yams and string beans.

Price range: Apps., $6–$12; entrees, $10–$23; desserts, $6. **Wheelchair access:** Fully accessible.

Soul Fixins' $25 & Under   SOUTHERN

371 W. 34th St. (bet. Eighth & Ninth Aves.)   (212) 736-1345
Credit cards: All major   Meals: L, D   Closed Sun.

You can pull up one of the dozen or so seats at this small storefront, but Soul Fixins' Southern food travels well, and it's nice to be
able to spread out in comfort with dishes like meaty spareribs
bathed in gloriously smoky sauce and crisp fried chicken. Side
dishes (two came with each main course) were uniformly good.

Other recommended dishes: Collards, green beans, candied yams.
Price range: Avg. app., $6; entree, $10; dessert, $3. **Wheelchair
access:** Fully accessible.

Sparks   ☆ $$$$ STEAKHOUSE

210 E. 46th St. (bet. Second & Third Aves.)   (212) 687-4855
Credit cards: All major   Meals: L, D   Closed Sun.

Even within the two-fisted genre of New York steakhouses, few
places are as decidedly masculine as Sparks. Yet, even though a
dinner at Sparks brings out the raucous bond trader in even the
mildest-mannered diner, it all feels exactly right. The bar is
crowded with people waiting for tables, and there always seems to
be a wait. The kitchen has been inconsistent in the past, but when
things are right, the thick, salt-crusted prime sirloins and lamb
chops are superb. Stick with the steak house classics and take time
to explore the superb wine list. Service is friendly but at times care-
less. *(Review by Eric Asimov; stars previously awarded by Ruth
Reichl.)*

Wine list: Large, impressive, extremely reasonable. **Price range:**
Apps., $7–$16; entrees, $20–$90 (for a five-and-a-half-pound lobster). **Wheelchair access:** All one level.

Sripraphai $25 & Under   THAI

64-13 39th Ave., Woodside, Queens   (718) 899-9599
Credit cards: All major   Meals: L, D

Sripraphai is not much to look at. It's a small restaurant with a big
television monitor and, for some reason, it's closed on Wednesdays.
But what it offers is some of the best, sharpest and clearest Thai
cooking in the city. The menu is enormous, arriving in a bound volume with occasional photographs and cryptic English descriptions.
Meat dishes are excellent, particularly beef and roast duck yums, or
salads, which are simultaneously searingly spicy yet cooling, made
with chili, fish sauce, lime juice and mint. The highly unusual catfish salad is also very good. Curries tend to be extremely spicy, too,
Other worthy options include chicken soup with coconut milk and
galanga, and many of the noodle dishes.

Price range: Entrees, $6–$11. **Wheelchair access:** Not accessible.

Stage Deli $$ DELI

834 Seventh Ave. (bet. 53rd & 54th Sts.)   (212) 245-7850
Credit cards: All major   Meals: B, L, D, LN

A classic New York deli with giant sandwiches, giant crowds, giant prices. It hasn't been the same since Max Asnes left.

Price range: Avg. breakfast, $7–$8. Avg. lunch, $10–$12. Avg. dinner, $15–$20. **Wheelchair access:** Fully accessible. **Features:** Outdoor dining.

Strip House ☆ $$$ STEAKHOUSE

13 E. 12th St. (bet. Fifth Ave. & University Pl.)   (212) 328-0000
Credit cards: All major   Meals: D

As the name suggests, there's a burlesque theme hard at work here. The walls are lined with lust-red flocked wallpaper and the banquettes are upholstered in quilted red leather. Vintage photographs of old-time strippers cover the walls. It all makes for a cheery, comfortable atmosphere, with none of the backslapping locker-room style of the old-line steakhouses. The meat is respectable, but not much more than that. The rib chop is awfully fatty, but the swaggering porterhouse comes through in a big way. The filet mignon and New York strip steaks are perfectly acceptable. The rest of the menu, however, shows a more playful side. Lamb comes in a three-way dish listed on the menu as Ménage à Trois, consisting of a first-rate chop, a loin and a braised flank.

Desserts bring mixed results, but the fruit savarin is excellent and the caramelized apple tart with mascarpone ice cream and brown sugar hard sauce is as good as it sounds.

Wine list: An attractively international list of more than 200 wines, with 26 half bottles and 13 wines by the glass. **Price range:** Apps., $9–$14; entrees, $22–$32; desserts, $8. **Wheelchair access:** All one level.

Suba ☆ $$ SPANISH/ECLECTIC

109 Ludlow St. (near Delancey St.)   (212) 982-5714
Credit cards: All major   Meals: D

The descent to the dining room at Suba is a plunge into the netherworld, a series of twists and turns along a staircase made from industrial grating. In this twilight environment, diners will encounter food as lurid as the setting. It is borderline hysterical. The chef takes Spain as a departure point but quickly speeds off to points unknown. Some of this is wildly misconceived. Some of it is wonderful. None of it is boring.

Goat cheese is everywhere on the menu, most successfully, or at least intriguingly, in a kind of napoleon consisting of thin black-pepper tuiles, serrano ham, quince paste and cheese. Grilled skirt steak with ginger green beans sounds plain, but an ocher-colored dab of ginger mustard makes all the difference. Hot, fruity and tantalizingly complex, it sends out shock waves of flavor. Try the flourless chocolate cake served with a coffee-avocado shake. It's a minor triumph, and the right kind of weird. Suba pulls off just enough of these little inside jokes to keep your mind off the sound system.

Wine list: A sensible, moderate-price list of about 30 wines, emphasizing Spain. **Price range:** Apps., $7–$12; entrees, $18–$25; desserts, $7. **Wheelchair access:** Restrooms and lounge accessible.

Sueños $$ MEXICAN

311 W. 17th St. (bet. First & Second Aves.)   (212) 243-1333
Credit cards: All major   Meals: D

Sueños (the name is Spanish for dreams) does have an air of enchantment about it. The tiny dining room is decorated in hot tropical colors, with glass-enclosed displays of folk art substituting for windows on one wall. On the other, an open-air desert rock garden occupies the space between the restaurant and the building next door. Sue Torres, formerly the chef at the Rocking Horse Cafe in Chelsea, specializes in what might be called new Mexican cuisine. Her updated takes on traditional Mexican dishes include a a steamed pork tamale stuffed with shrimp in a beurre blanc flavored with ancho chiles, and desserts like sponge cake with Crema de Mezcal whipped cream. The room may be small, but the kitchen has big ideas. Adventurous palates will jump for innovations like plantain and goat cheese pancakes, the side dish that comes with tamarind-glazed sirloin steak, or chicken and squash blossom enchiladas in pumpkin-seed sauce.

Price range: Apps., $7–$10; entrees, $17–$23, desserts, $7–$8.
Wheelchair access: Not accessible.

The Sultan $25 & Under   TURKISH

1435 Second Ave. (near 74th St.)   (212) 861-2828
Credit cards: All major   Meals: L, D

This friendly storefront restaurant offers mainstream Turkish dishes that are notable for their fresh, lively flavors. Meals begin with a basket of puffy house-made bread studded with tiny black sesame seeds, and a dish of tahini blended with pekmez, a thick grape syrup. Kebabs are universally good here, especially the lamb yogurt kebab, and whole trout is grilled perfectly, then filleted at the table. The dessert menu is predictable yet well prepared.

Price range: Apps., $5; entrees, $12–$17; desserts, $5. **Wheelchair access:** Fully accessible.

Sunrise 27 $25 & Under   CHINESE

27 Division St. (bet. Market & Catherine Sts.)   (212) 219-8498
Credit cards: All major   Meals: B, L, D, LN

At Sunrise 27, a glossy Cantonese seafood house east of the Bowery in Chinatown, almost all the seafood is excellent. Shrimp in their shells are served two ways, perfectly steamed just enough to allow the subtle shrimpy flavor to emerge, and salt-and-pepper style, barely crisp and deliciously savory.

    Apart from seafood, highlights include crisp little sparerib tips, and squab minced with vegetables and served wrapped in a big leaf of iceberg lettuce. Peking duck is served two ways, its crisp skin lathered with hoisin and embraced in doily-like pancakes, or its savory meat shredded and served with vegetables.

Service is efficient, more brusque than friendly. An auxiliary dining room downstairs is a little more stark than the street-level room, and, when crowded, waiters may try to hustle you along.

Other recommended dishes: Oysters with black bean sauce, scallops with XO sauce, clams with flowering chives, steamed striped bass, pan-fried noodles with seafood, sautéed snow-pea shoots. **Price range:** Apps., $6–$11; entrees, $9–$20 (specialty items are more). **Wheelchair access:** One level.

Supper $25 & Under   ITALIAN
156 E. 2nd St. (near Ave. A)   212) 477-7600
Credit cards: Cash only   Meals: Br, D, LN

Decorated in standard-issue mismatched tables and chairs with brick walls, tile flooring and antique chandeliers, Supper is divided into three sections: a sidewalk area that would be awfully pleasant on warm evenings if those waiting for seats weren't staring at you like dogs waiting for table scraps; a rear dining room bounded by a mirrored wall and a windowed wine cellar; and a front dining room centered on an open kitchen.

It's an entertaining view of house-made pastas being cooked to order, but it also displays Supper struggling at busy hours to serve food at a proper pace and sequence. At quieter times, though, Supper's simple yet quirky appeal is easy to fathom. Consider sharing a pasta as an appetizer, especially tajarin d'ortice, the Piedmontese name for tagliatelle prepared simply with mint and butter. On weekends, Supper serves bollito misto, the Northern Italian feast of boiled meats.

Other recommended dishes: Mozzarella with tomatoes, panzanella, fennel salad, roasted beet salad, tagliatelle Bolognese, "priest stranglers," veal tortelloni al sugo d'arrosto, risotto, hazelnut panna cotta. **Price range:** Apps., $4– $9; entrees, $8–$19. **Wheelchair access:** Not accessible. **Features:** Outdoor dining.

Supreme Macaroni Co. $ ITALIAN
511 Ninth Ave. (bet. 38th & 39th Sts.)   (212) 564-8074
Credit cards: All major   Meals: L, D   Closed Sun.

Behind the grocery store is the gloriously old-fashioned Italian restaurant, from the days when pasta was macaroni, sauce was called gravy and wine was served in juice glasses. It all comes alive again here, where tomatoes, peppers and sausages rule. Isn't it nice that some things don't change?

Alcohol: Beer and wine. **Price range:** Avg. lunch, $11–$12. Avg. dinner, $18–$19. **Wheelchair access:** Fully accessible.

Sur $25 & Under   ARGENTINE
232 Smith St., Carroll Gardens, Brooklyn   (718) 875-1716
Credit cards: All major   Meals: Br, D

This brick-walled, candlelit Argentine restaurant is warm and inviting without any of the usual gaucho clichés. The focus, naturally, is on beef, with top choices including the lean, almost grassy Argentine sirloin, served with a mound of crisp, salty french fries.

Alternatives to beef include juicy and flavorful roast chicken and several pasta dishes. For dessert, try the crepes filled with dulce de leche, a sublime caramel-like confection of cream and sugar.

Price range: Apps., $4–$7; entrees, $12–$19. **Wheelchair access:** All one level.

Surya ☆☆ $$ INDIAN

302 Bleecker St. (bet. Seventh Ave. S. & Grove St.)　(212) 807-7770
Credit cards: All major　Meals: Br, D

The restaurant named for the sun (in Tamil) actually has a small garden in the back along with a sleek interior. Its menu features mostly south Indian dishes, often filtered through the technique of France. The main courses have a bold freshness. Rack of lamb is particularly impressive. But what is most splendid about Surya is the entirely meatless side of the menu. (*Ruth Reichl*)

Wine list: Small and unimaginative. **Price range:** Apps., $7–$10; entrees, $11–$24; desserts, $6–$9. **Wheelchair access:** One level.

Sushiden $$$ JAPANESE/SUSHI

123 W. 49th St. (bet. Sixth & Seventh Aves.)　(212) 398-2800
Credit cards: All major　Meals: L, D　Closed Sun.

Always reliable sushi from a sushi bar that is as welcoming to non-Japanese customers as it is to the Japanese. One of the few places that almost always has good toro.

Alcohol: Beer and wine. **Price range:** Avg. lunch, $20. Avg. dinner, $25–$30. **Wheelchair access:** Restrooms not accessible.

Sushi Masa $25 & Under JAPANESE/SUSHI

141 E. 47th St. (bet. Lexington & Third Aves.)　(212) 715-0837
Credit cards: All major　Meals: L, D　Closed Sun.

The small bright dining room here is extremely inviting, the service warm and pleasant. But what makes this restaurant special is the combination of high quality ingredients and the reasonable prices. At lunch order the specialty of the house, Sushi Masa gozen, an assortment of dishes that is like a small banquet (salad, dobin soup, sashimi, broiled tuna and pickled vegetables). At dinner try chirashi sushi (which many Japanese customers were eating), raw fish on top of vinegared rice. The sushi and sashimi assortments are all fresh and attractively presented.

Other recommended dishes: Edamame, eel-don, oysters with ponzu sauce. **Wine list:** Has the usual selection of sakes, plum wines and light-bodied, inoffensive Japanese beers, but there is one more, a malty dark beer from Asahi. **Price range:** Lunch, $8–$25. Dinner, $12–$25. **Wheelchair access:** Steps at entrance; corridor to restrooms is narrow.

Sushi of Gari $$ JAPANESE/SUSHI
402 E. 78th St. (at First Ave.)   (212) 517-5340
Credit cards: All major   Meals: D

This simple little Japanese restaurant on the East Side offers
a nice selection of sushi along with a range of other Japanese specialties like tempura, noodles and fried dishes. Sushi, though, is
the best bet, along with delicious appetizers like boiled spinach
with sesame sauce and delicate little dumplings.

Alcohol: Beer and wine. **Price range:** Avg. $25–$30 per person.
Wheelchair access: Fully accessible.

Sushi Rose $$ JAPANESE/SUSHI
248 E. 52nd St. (bet. Second & Third Aves.)   (212) 813-1800
Credit cards: All major   Meals: L, D   Closed Sun.

This tiny, attractive second-floor restaurant looks traditional and
expensive, but it is neither. The chef works amazingly fast, slicing
extremely large pieces of sashimi for which the restaurant charges
rather moderate prices.

Alcohol: Beer and wine. **Price range:** Avg. lunch, $12. Avg. dinner,
$20. **Wheelchair access:** Fully accessible.

Sushisay $$$ JAPANESE/SUSHI
38 E. 51st St. (bet. Park & Madison Aves.)   (212) 755-1780
Credit cards: All major   Meals: L, D   Closed Sun.

Classic enough to please a Japanese clientele; friendly enough to
please an American one. Small and attractively spare, Sushisay
saves its best fish for the sushi bar and its very best fish for the
regular customers, the ones who get the special chopsticks.

Alcohol: Beer and wine. **Price range:** Avg. lunch, $30. Avg. dinner,
$50. **Wheelchair access:** Not accessible.

Sushi Seki   ☆☆ $$$ JAPANESE/SUSHI
1143 First Ave. (near 62nd St.)   (212) 371-0238
Credit cards: All major   Meals: D, LN   Closed Sun.

Sushi Seki will produce traditional sushi if you wish, but its specialty is a modern style in which each piece is topped with a little
sauce. It is a respectful adaptation that stays true to the essentials
without being bound by the approved methods. Yellowtail comes
with garlic sauce and also a sliver of jalapeño. Fluke, its flavor clear
and clean, comes with a dab of sweet plum sauce. Young snapper
arrives glistening with tangy citrus juice and Okinawa salt. There
are a few more-traditional preparations, like thin white slices of
fresh octopus. The rear dining room is quiet and feels slightly
removed from the action at the sushi bar, where sushi is prepared
with artistry, dedication and panache. *(Eric Asimov)*

Other recommended dishes: Sashimi, edamame. **Wine list:** Nice
selection of sakes; modest list of wines and beers. **Price range:**
Apps., $4–$7; entrees, $8–$20; sushi, $18–$35; chef selection,
$40–$100 or more. **Wheelchair access:** One step at entrance;
entrance to restroom is narrow.

Sushi Yasuda ☆☆☆ $$$ JAPANESE/SUSHI

204 E. 43rd St. (bet. Second & Third Aves.)   (212) 972-1001
Credit cards: All major   Meals: L, D   Closed Sun.

Sushi Yasuda looks like it was headed for TriBeCa and took a wrong
turn. In one of the city's dreariest restaurant neighborhoods, it
glows like a strange mineral, with a cool, celery-green facade.
Inside, the dining room is bathed in light. Floors, walls and ceiling
are lined in blond wood. The mood is quiet, contemplative, austere.
But Sushi Yasuda has a lot of downtown in its soul. The manager
and the waitresses are young. The exemplary service has an open,
friendly quality to it. At the same time, the menu is dead serious, a
purist's paradise of multiple choices among fish species — nearly
30, a startling number for a small restaurant — and elegantly presented appetizers and side dishes.

But sushi is only half the story. The daily menu includes a
small, transparent sheet of special appetizers, and they are worth
jumping for. It is often said that the test of a real sushi restaurant is
its omelet; Sushi Yasuda's is excellent — dozens of compressed, tis-
sue-thin layers of egg with a crisp edge. Dessert is not usually an
exciting moment in a sushi restaurant. Mochi rice makes the difference here: Japan's answer to flubber, mochi is a highly glutinous
rice that can be rolled out into a sticky, pasta-like wrapper ready for
filling with home-made red-bean ice cream and green-tea ice cream.

Alcohol: No wines, but four Japanese beers, and a half-dozen
sakes. **Price range:** Apps., $6–$10.50; sushi, $3–$9 a piece;
desserts, $4–$6. **Wheelchair access:** Restrooms on street level.

Sushi Zen $$$ JAPANESE/SUSHI

57 W. 46th St. (bet. Fifth & Sixth Aves.)   (212) 302-0707
Credit cards: All major   Meals: L, D   Closed Sun.

Exotic, inventive sushi that spans the range from exciting and wonderful to just plain weird.

Price range: Lunch, $20–$40. Dinner, $30–$50. **Wheelchair
access:** Restrooms not accessible. **Features:** Outdoor dining.

Svenningsen's $25 & Under   SEAFOOD

292 Fifth Ave. (near 30th St.)   (212) 465-1888
Credit cards: Meals: L, D

Svenignsen's owner, Ron Svenningsen, was Marble Collegiate
church's head chef for 16 year. The congregants have followed him
here. He should begin by firing his decorator, but rewards await.
Mr. Svenningsen buys excellent seafood and puts it to righteous
use. A half-dozen mighty-size cherrystones arrive on the half shell
accompanied by a sly cilantro cocktail sauce. They taste as if they
were pulled from the sea only minutes before. Or try a dark, buttery
lobster stew, or a lighter, saltier, but no less attractive seafood
chowder. Among the entree options, crab cakes are perhaps the
best. Pan-seared sea scallops are fine as well, plump and sweet.
Baked haddock stuffed with crab meat in a lobster sauce is remarkable, very tender and rich. Finish with a rice pudding, have a cup

of coffee and look at the gentle interaction between those serving and those eating. No, it's not a pretty room. But it is a kind one. *(Sam Sifton)*

Other recommended dishes: Clams on the half shell, stuffed clams, chowder, lobster stew, lobster roll, sea scallops, crab cakes. **Price range:** Starters, $3.50–$13.50; entrees, $14.50–$21.50. **Wheelchair access:** Fully accessible.

Sweet 'n' Tart Cafe $25 & Under   CHINESE
76 Mott St. (south of Canal St.)   (212) 334-8088
20 Mott St. (bet. Chatham Sq. & Pell St.)   (212) 964-0380
136-11 38th Ave., Flushing, Queens   (718) 661-3380
Credit cards: Cash only   Meals: B, L, D, LN

The specialty here is tong shui, a range of sweet tonics intended to benefit specific parts of the body or to balance one's yin and yang. But Sweet 'n' Tart's more typical dishes are terrific as well, like Chinese sausage and taro with rice, served in a tall bamboo steamer, and congee with beef, pork and squid. Little English is spoken here, but waitresses describe dishes as well as they can.

Other recommended dishes: Noodles, dumplings, home-style rice dishes. **Price range:** $5–$14. **Wheelchair access:** All one level.

Sylvia's $ SOUTHERN
328 Lenox Ave. (bet. 126th & 127th Sts.)   (212) 996-0660
Credit cards: All major   Meals: Br, L, D

Tour buses pull up in front for a sanitized taste of Harlem. The food's not fabulous, but it offers everything you expect: fried chicken, collard greens and sweet potato pie. Best for the gospel brunch on Sunday.

Price range: Avg. breakfast, $3. Avg. lunch, $7. Dinner: apps., $5; entrees, $9–$13; desserts, $3. Gospel brunch, $16. **Wheelchair access:** Fully accessible.

Szechuan Gourmet $25 & Under   CHINESE
135-15 37th Ave., Flushing, Queens   (718) 888-9388
Credit cards: Cash only   Meals: L, D, LN

Szechuan Gourmet serves food grounded in the regional flavor principles, using plenty of chili and hot oil to achieve the spiciness known as "la," and lots of Sichuan peppercorns to produce the flowery, tingly sensation called "ma." The pale yellow dining room is bright and pleasant. Food arrives fast and furiously without regard to the Western-style order of courses. If you are unfamiliar with the combination of ma and la, there may be no better dish to sample than sliced beef tendon in hot sauce. The spiciness has dimension and flavor. The dumplings and wontons were doughy, but dan dan noodles, called noodles in meat sauce on the menu, were fresh and forceful. Dry sautéed green beans are superb. Enchanted pork is first-rate with curls of sautéed pork belly paired with scallions and greens in a tangy, peppery sauce.

Other recommended dishes: Pickled vegetables, eggplant in garlic sauce, fried duck. **Price range:** Apps., $2–$8; entrees, $6–$15. **Wheelchair access:** Steps at entrance; way to restroom is narrow.

Tabla ☆ ☆ ☆ $$$$ AMERICAN/INDIAN
11 Madison Ave. (near 25th St.)   (212) 889-0667
Credit cards: All major   Meals: L, D

Tabla made a big noise when it first opened. Floyd Cardoz's imaginative weaving of Indian spices and ingredients into French-based cuisine felt thoroughly original, a new step forward in the fusion concept. With time, Tabla has become a little complacent. It's an uncomfortable restaurant to be in, with closely spaced tables and horrible acoustics, and the kitchen often performs in lackluster fashion, muddling flavors that should be precisely defined. The pea and potato samosas come in a thick, tough wrapper, and the house onion rings are greasy. When the kitchen is on its game, dishes like chicken with flaked rice and toasted cashews or tandoori roasted rabbit with mustard greens and sweet onions still tingle the taste buds. But it's getting harder to remember what all the fuss was about at Tabla. *(Review by William Grimes; stars previously awarded by Ruth Reichl.)*

Price range: Lunch entrees, $17–$23. Dinner: apps., $9–$18; entrees, $25–$35; desserts, $9. **Wheelchair access:** Restrooms at street level; dining room upstairs. **Features:** Outdoor dining.

Taco Taco $ MEXICAN/TEX-MEX
1726 Second Ave. (bet. 89th & 90th Sts.)   (212) 289-8226
Credit cards: Cash only   Meals: L, D

Every neighborhood should have a Mexican restaurant like this where the atmosphere is casual and pleasant but the food is serious. Tacos, naturally, are the mainstay, with fillings like pork with sautéed cabbage, tongue and crumbled chorizo. More ambitious dishes include tender pork marinated with smoky chipotle chilies and grilled. Even nachos are made with unusual care.

Alcohol: Beer and wine. **Price range:** Lunch entrees, $4.85–$8. Dinner: apps., $3–$6; entrees, $9–$12; desserts, $3. **Wheelchair access:** Not accessible.

Tagine $25 & Under MOROCCAN
537 Ninth Ave. (near 40th St.)   (212) 564-7292
Credit cards: All major   Meals: L, D, LN

Though Tagine is self-conscious enough to call itself a "dining gallery," it is a low-budget operation. The dim, alluring dining room seems a blizzard of colors and styles. In the front is a small stage, where jazz bands play nightly after 9:30; downstairs is a lounge area for other performances. The languorous service may lead you to believe that food is not the focus here, but you'll relax when appetizers arrive. The restaurant's signature tagines, fragrant stews served in traditional earthenware vessels with conical lids, are the least satisfying of the main courses, though the chicken tagine and lamb shank are quite good. Tagine offers a full bar and a brief wine list, including a grapey Moroccan red. Desserts can be excellent, like semolina cake soaked in orange blossom water.

Other recommended dishes: Roasted pepper salad, sautéed collard green, spinach andkale, zaalouk, couscous, pastilla, merguez sausage, cookies. **Price range:** Apps., $5–$10; entrees, $13–$20. **Wheelchair access:** All one level.

Tai Hong Lau $$ CHINESE
70 Mott St. (bet. Bayard & Canal Sts.)   (212) 219-1431
Credit cards: All major   Meals: B, Br, L, D

A Chinatown favorite, especially among non-Chinese. The Cantonese food is very good and slightly more expensive than that of its neighbors.

Price range: Lunch: apps., $2–$5; entrees, $5–$12; desserts, $2–$5. Dinner: apps., $3–$12; entrees, $9–$17; desserts, $2–$5. **Features:** Outdoor dining.

Taka $$ JAPANESE/SUSHI
61 Grove St. (at Seventh Ave. S.)   (212) 242-3699
Credit cards: All major   Meals: D   Closed Mon.

Three things distinguish this sushi bar from other Japanese restaurants in New York City. One is that the sushi chef is a woman, Taka Yoneyama, who is a joy to watch as she swoops and cuts. The second is her unusual presentation. Leave the choice to the chef and you will get tuna decorated with leaves of edible gold, or squid stuffed with spiced cod roe and shiso, cut into pinwheels and stacked like sculpture. The salmon roe scattered across the top glitters like jewels. The plates are handmade and the restaurant is tiny. With its few tables and miniature sushi bar, Taka has the intimate scale found in Tokyo.

Alcohol: Beer and wine. **Price range:** Apps., $4–$8; entrees, $10–$27; desserts, $3–$7. **Wheelchair access:** Not accessible.

Tamarind   ☆☆ $$$ INDIAN
41-43 E. 22nd St. (bet. Broadway & Park Ave. S.)   (212) 674-7400
Credit cards: All major   Meals: L, D

Tamarind, named for the sweet-and-sour fruit, looks and feels fresh. The menu treats Indian cuisine as a genuine culinary language, like French, able to assimilate nontraditional ingredients and techniques. It's a clear-cut victory for the cause of Indian food. The setting helps. Tamarind is stylishly decorated, with a cool ivory and white color scheme. The raised, wrap-around banquettes make diners seem aloof and regal.

Many dishes are executed with great delicacy, like the Calcutta specialty known as raj kachori, a lightly spiced chickpea croquette with a paper-thin crisp skin. For whatever reason, anything involving shrimp succeeds wildly, like shrimp balchau, an exotic shrimp cocktail with a smoothly fiery chili-masala sauce containing tiny chunks of firm tomato. Vegetarian dishes also seem to bring out the best at Tamarind. The tandoor does not perform flawlessly, though some dishes emerge moist and succulent from the oven, like

271

noorani kebab, chunks of spiced chicken flavored with saffron. The lunch menu at Tamarind is ingenious, with five set menus, each representing a coherent Indian meal.

Wine list: About 200 wines, with 11 by the glass, and five Indian beers. **Price range:** Lunch: prix fixe, $20. Dinner: apps., $5–$16; entrees, $13–$35; desserts, $5. **Wheelchair access:** All one level.

Tanti Baci Caffe $25 & Under   ITALIAN
163 W. 10th St. (bet. Seventh Ave. S. & Waverly Pl.)   (212) 647-9651
Credit cards: MC/V   Meals: L, D

Tanti Baci (Italian for many kisses) is wonderfully cavelike in the cellar of a small building. The menu is appropriately basic, simply salads and a selection of pastas, you choose the sauce. There are many time-honored preparations in which the freshness of the ingredients shines through.

Recommended dishes: Potato and egg salad, white beans, insalate Caprese, pastas, tiramisu, chocolate mousse cake, sorbets. **Alcohol:** Beer and wine. **Price range:** Lunch: avg. app., $4; entree, $7; dessert, $4. Dinner: avg. app., $5; entree, $8; dessert, $5. **Wheelchair access:** One flight down from the street; the restroom is very narrow. **Features:** Outdoor dining.

Tapería Madrid $25 & Under   SPANISH/TAPAS
1471 Second Ave. (near 77th St.)   (212) 794-2923
Credit cards: All major   Meals: D, LN

From the low timbered ceiling to the wood plank floor and the long family-style tables with wide benches, Tapería Madrid has every appearance of a credible Spanish tapas bar. Add in the exuberant crowds, the dark room and the pitchers of sangria on almost every table, and you have the real thing, primarily a bar with a selection of tapas, small portions to go with a few glasses of wine or sherry. A glass of the dry and enticingly tangy fino sherry goes beautifully with olives, or with boquerónes, fresh anchovies marinated in olive oil and garlic. In fact, the sherries go with almost everything. Desserts include a fine caramel flan, and there is a nice selection of Spanish cheeses.

Other recommended dishes: Marinated olives, scallops in white wine and lemon sauce, grilled sardines, Spanish sausage. **Wine list:** There is an excellent selection here. **Price range:** Tapas, $5–$10. **Wheelchair access:** All one level.

Tappo   ☆ $$$ MEDITERRANEAN
403 E. 12th St. (at First Ave.)   (212) 505-0001
Credit cards: All major   Meals: D, LN

A really good neighborhood restaurant can be hard to find, but Tappo, in the East Village, hits the mark. The food is simple and fresh; the setting feels like a farmhouse kitchen, dark and cool, with heavy ceiling beams and long wooden tables.

The menu has a long, unchanging list of appetizers that mixes traditional Italian starters with less predictable Spanish and Middle Eastern dishes, but the best of them, regardless of origin, have the sparkle that can only come from fresh ingredients. Entrees, which change nightly, are deliberately plain. Baby chicken sautéed in herbs and white wine is just the sort of unpretentious dish that a place like Tappo should serve, and the kitchen turns out a superior roasted branzino. The pastas can be excellent. Best of all is a big bowl of very firm rigatoncini lightly sauced with prosciutto, arugula and radicchio. The standout dessert is a dense panna cotta drizzled with sweetly pungent 25-year-old balsamic vinegar.

Wine list: An adventurous 130-bottle list, mostly Italian and French, with an emphasis on country wines, and 21 wines by the glass. **Price range:** Dinner, appetizers, $7–$14; entrees, $15–$26; desserts, $7. **Wheelchair access:** One step up at entrance; restrooms on dining room level.

Taprobane $

SRI LANKAN

234 W. 56th St. (bet. Eighth Ave. & Broadway)   (212) 333-4203
Credit cards: All major   Meals: Br, L, D

This is the second-best Sri Lankan restaurant in New York City, after Lakruwana. Unfortunately, these may be the only two Sri Lankan restaurants in New York. Still, the food has improved since Taprobane opened, and it's worth tasting the spicy, unusual fare. It is similar to Indian food but with different spicing in the curries, and different dishes, like hoppers, delicate pancakes made of rice flour and coconut milk.

Price range: Lunch: apps., $5–$6; entrees, $6–$8. Dinner: apps., $5–$9; entrees, $10–$16. **Wheelchair access:** Not accessible.

Taquería de Mexico $25 & Under

MEXICAN/TEX-MEX

93 Greenwich Ave. (bet. W. 12th & Bank Sts.)   (212) 255-5212
Credit cards: Cash only   Meals: B, Br, L, D, LN

This handsome taquería has the same owners as Mi Cocina, one of the city's top Mexican restaurants, and their meticulous care is evident in Mexican street food like tacos and taquitos al pastor. The restaurant has enlarged its menu and serves more complex dishes, like sautéed shrimp with cactus pads and roast chicken glazed with ancho adobo sauce. The stylish little dining room, with turquoise tables and colorful paintings and masks, looks at if it had been plucked out of Cuernavaca.

Other recommended dishes: Taquitos, tacos, tamales, guacamole, burritos, fajitas, tortas, Mexican beverages. **Alcohol:** Beer and wine. **Price range:** Lunch: apps., $3–$5; entrees, $7–$12; desserts, $2. Dinner: apps., $5–$8; entrees, $10–$17; desserts, $4; three-course prix fixe, $20. **Wheelchair access:** All one level.

The Tasting Room ☆ $$$ NEW AMERICAN

72 E. 1st St. (at First Avenue)   (212) 358-7831
Credit cards: All major   Meals: D   Closed Sun.

The Tasting Room follows the new downtown paradigm in almost every respect. The room is spartan and cramped. The menu has been edited down to a handful of dishes, and the restaurant radiates a sense of mission, with earnest service. The formula seems to work. Diners pack the place night after night. When the restaurant is not caught up in its own spell, it does the honorable work of serving good food at a moderate price in a pleasant atmosphere, with a clever format. The menu allows diners to combine several tasting portions into a meal or to order the usual appetizer and main course. What sets the Tasting Room apart is its ferociously ambitious wine list, a nicely priced, all-American roster that ventures well off the beaten track. In comparison, the menu is a mere footnote. Half of it makes an impression, half seems like easy-listening music, pleasant but bland.

For dessert, however, Renée's Mother's Cheesecake is a cheesecake to die for, lighter than air, with a barely-there crust and a restrained sweetness level. And when it's not runny, the dark chocolate tart cannot be resisted.

Wine list: An all-American list of more than 350 wines, with unusual varietals like melon, pinot meunier and lemberger; a dozen wines by the glass. **Price range:** Apps,. $7–$15; entrees, $13–$29; desserts, $6. **Wheelchair access:** Step to dining room.

Tavern on Jane $25 & Under   AMERICAN
31 Eighth Ave. (at Jane St.)   (212) 675-2526
Credit cards: All major   Meals: L, D, LN

Tavern on Jane is a convivial, unpretentious neighborhood bar and grill. Like other old-fashioned taverns, it is a refuge. Regulars have their usual at the bar, and neighborhood residents grab a table and are ready to order. The standard menu is a reliable step above pub grub. Of more interest are the daily specials, like excellent, crab cakes with a mango salsa, and meaty pork chops in an applejack sauce, big enough to cover the plate. Otherwise, the simplest dishes are preferable, like a hanger steak, and a good, honest hamburger. There is a perfunctory wine list with a few decent bottles under $25, but it's more of a beer place. Skip dessert.

Other recommended dishes: Chicken wings, mussels, grilled shrimp, gazpacho, lamb shank. **Price range:** Apps., $3–$9; entrees, $10–19. **Wheelchair access:** Step in front; restrooms not accessible.

Tavern on the Green ☆ $$$$ NEW AMERICAN
Central Park W. (at 67th St.)   (212) 873-3200
Credit cards: All major   Meals: Br, L, D

This is America's largest-grossing restaurant, a wonderland of lights, flowers, chandeliers and balloons that can make a child out of the most cynical adult. Patrick Clark, who died in February 1998, was a terrific chef, and he's left a culinary legacy for his successors to follow. But even he was not able to overcome the tavern's unaccountably rude and lax service. Even so, the people keep coming, for the glittery setting and for dishes like mustard-and-herb-crusted rack of pork, served with braised red cabbage and potatoes mashed with horseradish. The trick is simply getting the food. (*Ruth Reichl*)

Wine list: Large and wide-ranging with a few bargains among the high-end wines. **Price range:** Apps., $8–$65 (Beluga caviar); entrees, $18–$37. Prix-fixe lunch, Mon.–Fri., $20–$25. Prix-fixe dinner, Mon.-Fri, 5-6:30 P.M., $33–$42. **Wheelchair access:** Fully accessible. **Features:** Good view, outdoor dining.

Tea & Sympathy $25 & Under   ENGLISH

108 Greenwich Ave. (bet. 12th & 13th Sts.)   (212) 807-8329
Credit cards: Cash only   Meals: Br, L, D

In cold weather, the windows of this little English restaurant are frosted over, and a blast of cold air cuts through every time the door opens. It's the perfect atmosphere for the old-fashioned but delicious food, like shepherd's pie, Sussex chicken, bangers and mash, and the full English breakfasts. Afternoon tea, served with finger sandwiches and delicate scones, is wonderful, and service is always charming.

Price range: Lunch: apps. $4; entrees, $7–$15; desserts, $6. Dinner: apps., $5; entrees, $7–$15; desserts, $6. **Wheelchair access:** Not accessible.

Tea Box Cafe $$ JAPANESE

693 Fifth Ave. (bet. 54th & 55th Sts.)   (212) 350-0180
Credit cards: All major   Meals: L   Closed Sun.

Beautiful food in a serene setting, hardly what you expect to find in a department store. The exquisite East-West tea, served in the basement of the Takashimaya department store, is a nice way to while away an afternoon hour, and the Zen-like dining room attracts a crowd as stylish as the cafe's minimalist serving trays. Tea can include three open-face "sandwiches" like marinated cucumber on pressed rice; chicken and wasabi on Japanese bread, and a delicate spring roll, served with fried sweet potato and slivers of grapefruit. For dessert, slender butter cookies and two of the most luxurious chocolates imaginable.

Price range: Avg. entree, $15. **Wheelchair access:** Fully accessible.

Teodora   ☆ $$$ ITALIAN

141 E. 57th St. (near Lexington Ave.)   (212) 826-7101
Credit cards: All major   Meals: L, D

With its beige walls, slightly dulled by the residue of nights of dining, and its worn terrazzo and wood floors that slope this way and that, Teodora feels as if it's been around forever. In a bilevel dining room, the restaurant offers specialties from the Emilia-Romagna region. Lasagna, cooked ever so slowly until the béchamel and Bolognese sauces meld into a creamy whole, is a model of painstaking preparation. Pastas break little new ground and are served American-style, heaped with sauce, but some are very good nonetheless. Filet mignon, also sliced thin, is fanned around a heap of bitter broccoli rabe. On the heavier end of the scale, meltingly tender osso buco, full of herbs, arrives with a tiny fork sticking up from the center of a shin bone, for digging out the deliciously gelatinous marrow. Seafood dishes were lackluster.

Desserts are a familiar lot, with some fine choices. But the best is ciambelle, a traditional cake of Emilia-Romagna. *(Eric Asimov)*

Wine list: Ranges over Italy's many wine regions, with concentrations in Piedmont and Tuscany, but also a good selection from southern Italy, with worthy choices in the $35 to $75 range. **Price range:** Apps., $7–$13; pastas, $14–$19; entrees, $18–$28; desserts, $7. **Wheelchair access:** Narrow entrance; first-floor dining room is on street level but restrooms are on second floor.

Tequilita's $25 & Under   MEXICAN

5213 Fourth Ave., Sunset Park, Brooklyn   (718) 492-4303
Credit cards: Cash only   Meals: L, D

Sunset Park has a growing Mexican population, and Tequilita's, a cheerful little storefront, is one of the better taquerías that dot the neighborhood. Pozole is terrific, thick with hominy and pork, and the tacos are superb, with several unusual choices like chewy pig's ears and blood sausage. Chicken enchiladas are served with a spicy, subtle mole sauce.

Price range: Apps., $4; entrees, $6–$8. **Wheelchair access:** Not accessible.

Terrance Brennan's Seafood and Chophouse   ☆ ☆ $$$$ SEAFOOD/STEAKHOUSE

Benjamin Hotel, 565 Lexington Ave.(near 50th St.)   (212) 715-2400
Credit cards: All major   B, Br, L, D

Terrance Brennan's Seafood and Chophouse is a throwback to the time when fine dining meant big, juicy steaks and four-pound lobsters, followed by baked Alaska and crèpes suzette. The menu features unadorned ingredients that come into their own with sauces or flavored butters selected by the diner. The two great categories are steaks and seafood. The execution rarely falters. You can count on your steak's making it to the table with a thick, black crust and a tender, pink interior. The fish, too, is seared perfectly. The porterhouse steak, a fearsome thing meant for two, has good depth of flavor and a luscious mouth feel, as does the chateaubriand for two. The fish is high quality, especially plump bay scallops. For dessert, try the cheesecake, sweetened with chunks of pecan praline and a gooey caramel sauce, or the baked Alaska.

Other recommended dishes: Deviled egg trifle with caviar; potato, cheese and bacon tart; rib roast; apple pot pie. **Wine list:** A mostly French and American list of about 220 bottles, moderately priced, with an emphasis on American reds. **Price range:** Lunch: entrees, $15.50–$36.95; prix fixe, $29.95. Dinner: apps., $11.50–$20.50; entrees, $19.95–$36.95; desserts, $12; pretheater prix fixe, $32.95. **Wheelchair access:** All one level.

Thali $25 & Under   INDIAN/VEGETARIAN

28 Greenwich Ave. (near W. 10th St.)   (212) 367-7411
Credit cards: Cash only   Meals: L, D

Tiny Thali is strictly minimalist; you don't even get a menu. What you do get is fascinating vegetarian Indian fare served on the traditional thali, a circular metal tray that holds all the components of a meal. The ingredients change every night but can include an appetizer like khapoli potato wadas, flash-fried balls of potato and spices, or steamed cakes made with rice or chickpea flour. Main courses may feature ingredients as unusual as karela, a bitter gourd; toori, or Chinese okra, and tinda, a small green squash.

Price range: Avg. lunch, $6. Avg. dinner, $10. Avg. brunch, $8.
Wheelchair access: Narrow entrance and restroom.

Thias $$$ GREEK/SEAFOOD
103 W. 77th St. (bet. Columbus & Amsterdam Aves.) (212) 721-6603
Credit cards: All major   Meals: D

This is a no-frills, respectable estiatorio (Greek fish joint), the kind of place that diners can slip into like a comfortable shoe. A meal starts with small tastes, like the fish-roe mayonnaise known as taramosalata, spread on chunks of pita bread. Two of the less commonly encountered spreads are among the best, a spicy blend of feta cheese, hot peppers and olive oil (ktipiti), and a roasted beets one marinated with olive oil and garlic (patzaria skordalia).

The main drama centers on the fresh fish, displayed on a heap of shaved ice. The menu lists about 15 species, the waiter expresses enthusiasm about two or three of them, and then it's simply a matter of letting the chef grill your daurade, porgy, bream or rouget. A drizzle of oil, a squirt of lemon and, perhaps, a light dusting of herbs finish the job.

Price range: Entrees, $18–$29. **Wheelchair access:** Fully accessible.

38th Street Restaurant and Bakery
$25 & Under   CHINESE
273 W. 38th St. (bet. Seventh & Eighth Aves.)   (212) 575-6978
Credit cards: Cash only   Meals: B, L   Closed Sun.

This Chinese hole in the wall, is indeed something special. A counter-service restaurant in the Garment District, it is packed daily at lunch with an almost entirely Chinese clientele, which lines up out on the sidewalk from noon to 1:30. Service is fast. The food is already cooked and it's astoundingly cheap: two main dishes and rice — a truly filling portion — for $3.75. For steam-table fare, it's surprisingly delicious. No one pays attention to the menu. Simply gesture at the dozen or so dishes on the counter, which, along with the barbecued meats, make up the selection, and move toward the register. Somehow, you end up with the right meal, served whether you're staying or leaving in a foam container with a plastic fork — no chopsticks here. Tables are communal, and groups will probably have to split up. Tea is self-serve, from an urn in the middle of the bright, fluorescent room. The hard part is over. Now you can eat.

Other recommended dishes: Barbecued pork, barbecued duck, barbecued chicken, pork and tofu, scrambled eggs with shrimp, sautéed greens, bok choy, green beans, roast pork buns. **Price range:** Lunch, two courses with rice for $3.75. Menu prices higher.
Wheelchair access: Not accessible

36 Bar and Barbecue ☆ $$ KOREAN

5 W. 36th St. (near Fifth Ave.) (212) 563-3737
Credit cards: All major Meals: L, D, LN

The aroma of wood smoke, sweet and penetrating, makes a powerful first impression at 36 Bar and Barbecue, a tiny, enormously
appealing Korean barbecue restaurant. It is shooting for a younger,
hipper and more mixed clientele than the often forbidding Korean
restaurants clustered along the side streets east of Macy's. The
food, and the manners, remain traditional. A small menu sticks
with classic Korean dishes, but the kitchen distinguishes itself in
selecting prime ingredients. The marinated beef short ribs destined
for the grill are exceptionally tender, a far cry from the tough, mus-
cly strips offered at a hundred other Korean restaurants. Sashimi-
grade tuna cut into blocks have a gemlike luminescence.

The waiters at 36, who speak English well, work hard to make
the menu accessible. They explain, they offer suggestions, they
demonstrate how things are done. They remind you that at heart
Korean food is homey. It has rituals, but is not rule-bound.

Other recommended dishes: Scallion pancake with calamari and
shrimp, beef tartare in sesame marinade, chilled tofu salad, spicy
tofu stew with kimchi, bibimbap with barbecued beef, barbecued
tuna. **Wine list:** None. Sakes and Asian beers. **Price range:** Apps.,
$7–$8; entrees, $8–$19; desserts, $3. **Wheelchair access:**
Restrooms on dining level.

Thom ☆ $$$ FUSION/NEW AMERICAN

Thompson Hotel, 60 Thompson St. (near Broome St.)
  (212) 219-2000
Credit cards: All major Meals: D

It may be that Thom was intended to be a people-watching experience first and a dining experience second. As an exercise in style,
it's hard to criticize. In a stylishly designed boutique hotel, Thom is
the place. Thom looks good.

The chef, Jonathan Eismann, a model in his spare time, cooks
with undeniable panache, but the idiom he has chosen, heavily
reliant on pure Asian flavors and subtle effects, demands more clarity and definition than he delivers. The menu is certainly not boring, although Mr. Eismann seems to have a weakness for sweets.
Pan-broiled beef fillet, with short ribs braised in cabernet, meets the
sweetness challenge and emerges triumphant. When Mr. Eismann
hits it, the results can be exciting. Fermented chilies added a subtle
fire to shrimp in a thick curry sauce.

The pastry chef comes up with a few winning combinations,
like toasted almond anglaise served with a warm plum cake, which
is rich and light at the same time.

Wine list: About 135 wines, mostly French and American, with
some wild cards, and a dozen wines by the glass. **Price range:**
Apps., $8–$19; entrees, $19–$29; desserts, $7–$9. **Wheelchair
access:** No steps to restaurant or restrooms.

Tibetan Yak $25 & Under   TIBETAN

72-20 Roosevelt Ave., Jackson Heights, Queens   (718) 779-1119
Credit cards: All major   Meals: L, D

Though it is almost directly under the Roosevelt Avenue train
tracks, Tibetan Yak feels like a respite from the urban crush. The
decoration is minimal, simply Tibetan symbols of luck painted on
the walls, along with a painting of a yak so lifelike you can almost
feel its hot breath and wet nose. The service could not be sweeter,
though the language barrier is strong.

Many dishes show a direct influence of China or India. Momo,
or Tibetan dumplings, look exactly like Chinese potstickers. The
Yak's momo are served steamed or fried, stuffed with meat or vegetables. The steamed vegetable momo are ethereal. The best dishes
are direct and true, with clear flavors enhanced with gentle and
occasionally gutsy seasonings. Pork chili offers the clear taste sensation of chilies without the heat. For dessert try dey-see. It is
essentially rice, lightly sweetened, served with golden raisins and a
dollop of yogurt over the top, and that's it.

Other recommended dishes: Noodles in barley and sugar, fried
rice, noodles in broth with beef and spinach, bean thread noodles
with vegetables, curry with chicken or lamb. **Price range:** Soups
and salads, $3–$4; larger plates, $6–$10. **Wheelchair access:** Sharp
angle at entrance; narrow hall to restrooms.

Tierras Colombianas $25 & Under   COLOMBIAN

82-18 Roosevelt Ave., Jackson Heights, Queens   (718) 426-8868
33-01 Broadway (at 33rd St.), Astoria, Queens   (718) 956-3012
Credit cards: Cash only   Meals: L, D

Excess is the way at this Colombian restaurant, one of the more polished spots in Jackson Heights. The ultimate dish is the mountain
plate, which includes a tender steak that has been pounded thin,
immersed in lime juice and garlic and then grilled; chicharrón,
which is fried pork skin; a mountain of yellow rice with a sea of
wonderfully plump pinto beans; fried plantains; a thick wedge of
avocado, and a small, circular arepa, or corn cake, and sitting on top
of all this food, a single fried egg.

Other recommended dishes: Grilled loin of pork, fried whole red
snapper, grilled top round steak, breaded fried chicken cutlets.
Price range: Complete meals, $5–$17. **Wheelchair access:**
Entrance, aisles and restrooms are narrow.

Time Cafe $ NEW AMERICAN

380 Lafayette St. (bet. Third & Fourth Aves.)   (212) 533-7000
2330 Broadway (at 85th St.)   (212) 579-5100
87 Seventh Ave. S. (at Barrow St.)   (212) 220-9100
Credit cards: All major   Meals: B, Br, L, D

With its big, airy dining room, and Fez, an adjacent bar and performance space at the East Village location, Time Cafe has always
drawn a young, trendy crowd. The contemporary American food is
such that, an hour later, you may not remember what you ate. Still,
it's popular enough to have given rise to offspring in the West Village and on the Upper West Side.

Price range: Lunch: sandwiches, $7–$10; entrees, $9–$14. Dinner: apps., $5–$8; entrees, $12–$20; desserts, $5–$6. **Wheelchair access:** Fully accessible. **Features:** Outdoor dining.

Tin Room Cafe $ ITALIAN

1 Front St., Brooklyn Heights (718) 246-0310
Credit cards: All major Meals: L, D

This quaintly pretty little restaurant under the Brooklyn Bridge features live opera singers, a garden and an inexpensive menu. The food does not surprise or impress; go for the atmosphere.

Alcohol: Beer and wine. **Price range:** Lunch: apps., $4–$6; entrees, $5–$16; two-course prix fixe, $8. Dinner: apps., $5–$7; entrees, $8–$24; desserts, $6; three-course prix fixe, $14. **Wheelchair access:** Step at entrance. **Features:** Free parking.

Tocqueville ☆☆ $$$$ FRENCH

15 E. 15th St. (bet. Fifth Ave. & Union Sq. W.) (212) 647-1515
Credit cards: All major Meals: L, D Closed Sun.

In a small, trapezoidal room off Union Square, Tocqueville is a quiet haven of good taste, good food and good service. The menu is limited. The décor is done with a very light touch, suggesting luxury without overburdening the room. Although tiny, Tocqueville never feels cramped.

The restaurant is the late-arriving offspring of Marco Polo, the catering place next door; owner Marco Moreira, with his supply lines already well established, had access to good raw materials, putting him ahead of the game before he started. Mr. Moreira takes a robust approach to most entrees. His roasted rack of lamb, for example, is surrounded by braised artichokes, mushrooms and fava beans in a red-wine reduction.

Desserts do honor to the menu. Warm chocolate cake comes with a scoop of green ice cream. Upside-down banana tart is a little marvel, dripping with caramel, it's teamed up with a ball of brown-sugar ice cream.

Wine list: About 150 wines on an international list, about one-third of them priced at less than $40. There are 17 wines by the glass. **Price range:** Lunch: apps., $8–$14; entrees, $14–$26; desserts, $8. Three-course prix-fixe, $20. Dinner: apps., $9–$22; entrees, $24–$31; desserts $8. **Wheelchair access:** All one level.

Tomoe Sushi $25 & Under JAPANESE/SUSHI

172 Thompson St. (near Houston St.) (212) 777-9436
Credit cards: All major Meals: L, D Closed Sun., Tue.

Long lines of people seem perpetually planted in front of this small, plain restaurant, waiting to order the terrific, inexpensive sushi. The large assortment can include clean, clear-flavored mackerel; yellowtail as soft as whipped butter; sweet shrimp, and glazed eel. The nonsushi menu includes excellent cold soba noodles and delicate shumai (shrimp dumplings).

Price range: Apps., $4–$6; entrees, $6–$31; desserts, $3. Dinner: apps., $4–$12; entrees, $12–$25; desserts, $3. **Wheelchair access:** Fully accessible.

Topaz Thai $25 & Under   THAI

127 W. 56th St. (bet. Sixth & Seventh Aves.)   (212) 957-8020
Credit cards: All major   Meals: L, D

This Thai restaurant offers fine Thai cooking in a convenient Midtown location. Soups, like the delicious tom kha gai, made with chicken stock, coconut milk, chili peppers and lime, are particularly good, as are spicy dishes like the soupy jungle curry made with scallops and green beans. The restaurant has a peculiar nautical theme courtesy of a previous tenant — Art Deco paneling, triangular sconces and wooden captain's chairs.

Other recommended dishes: Mee krob, curry puffs, yum woonsen, gai yang, spareribs. **Price range:** Apps., $4–$9; entrees, $8–$18; desserts, $5. **Wheelchair access:** Not accessible.

Toraya $ JAPANESE

17 E. 71st St. (bet. Fifth & Madison Aves.)   (212) 861-1700
Credit cards: All major   Meals: L   Closed Sun.

Entering Toraya is like stepping into a hushed and peaceful Japanese temple. This tea salon has a menu of unusual Japanese dishes, but the highlights are the beautiful, meticulously fashioned pastries like zangetsu, a soft ginger-flavored pancake folded over a filling of sweetened azuki bean paste, etched with a pattern of chrysanthemum petals. They are delicate, delicious and unforgettable.

Price range: Lunch items from $5; desserts, $2.30–$10. **Wheelchair access:** Not accessible.

Totonno Pizzeria $25 & Under   PIZZA

1524 Neptune Ave., Coney Island, Brooklyn   (718) 372-8606
1544 Second Ave. (bet. 80th & 81st Sts.)   (212) 327-2800
Credit cards: Cash only at Coney Island   Meals: L, D
Closed Mon., Tue. (Coney Island)

The original Totonno's, one of the early giants of New York City coal-oven pizza, is legendary both for its irregular hours and its devotion to artisanal pies served in humble surroundings. With its site in a small Italian bastion near Coney Island, Totonno's almost feels as if it's in another city, but the pressed tin walls are covered with testimonials from the glory days. Measured against the vast sea of pizzas, Totonno is still near the top, but measured against its past, Totonno doesn't keep up. Unlike the humble Coney Island pizzeria, the Uptown branch is duded up for the neighborhood.

Alcohol: Beer and wine. **Price range:** Pizzas, $14–$16. **Wheelchair access:** Not accessible.

Tournesol
$25 & Under
50-12 Vernon Blvd., Long Island City, Queens
Credit cards: Cash only

BISTRO/FRENCH
(718) 472-4355
Meals: L, D

Like a flower poking through the gritty concrete near the mouth of the Queens-Midtown Tunnel, Tournesol, a new French bistro in Long Island City, is a spray of brightness on a field of gray. The dining room is pleasant, with textured beige walls, a handsome bar and mirrors, while the chef displays a sure hand with Tournesol's small selection of bistro dishes.

Many inexpensive French restaurants don't make their own pâtés and terrines, but Tournesol does, as is evident in the lively, creamy terrine of foie gras. Roasted cod with rosemary is perfectly cooked and wonderfully restrained. If it's meat you prefer, hangar steak with béarnaise has more flavor than most. Tournesol's short wine list is a starting place, with some decent inexpensive selections but nothing exciting.

Other recommended dishes: Rabbit terrine, soups, frisée salad, seared scallops, grilled skate, monkfish wrapped in bacon, duck breast with poached pear. **Price range:** Apps., $5–$8; entrees, $12–$17. **Wheelchair access:** Step in front; restrooms narrow.

Tout Va Bien
$$
311 W. 51st St. (bet. Eighth & Ninth Aves.)
Credit cards: All major

BISTRO/FRENCH
(212) 974-9051
Meals: L, D

A classic New York City bistro in the theater district that has been around for 50 years serving just what you would expect in a rustic atmosphere. Even the soundtrack is predictable.

Price range: Apps., $6–$10; entrees, $14–$22; desserts, $6. **Wheelchair access:** Not accessible.

Town
☆☆☆ **$$$**
Chambers Hotel, 15 W. 56th St. (bet. Fifth & Sixth Ave.)

NEW AMERICAN
(212) 582-4445
Meals: B, L, D

Credit cards: All major

There's nothing flashy about Town, but it has an unmistakable sense of style that starts with the dining room, one floor down from the lobby in the Chambers Hotel. David Rockwell, who designed the hotel as well as the restaurant, has brought in lightness and air by lining the room in translucent sheets of blond wood.

It's a civilized, adult setting that suits Geoffrey Zakarian's elegant, clean cooking, which seems almost effortlessly assured. With no visible signs of strain, he manages to enliven his dishes with just the half twist that makes them distinctive, as in a simple roasted skate served with three sorbet-shaped quenelles: pea-peppermint, apple-miso, and eggplant with hazelnut oil and quatre-épices. The foie gras terrine is a work of art — tempting layers of solid meat suspended in mousse and topped by a thick, fearless layer of yellow fat. The execution at Town rarely falters. Slabs of spice-crusted duck, deeply flavored, need no knife, and Mr. Zakarian does wonderful things to them. He adds a hearty buckwheat pilaf and caramelized endive stuffed with thin slices of apple.

The dessert list is strong, and one is a showstopper with a strong New Orleans accent. It starts with a basket of sugar-powdered beignets filled with molten chocolate. Then comes a perfect frozen dome with a matte-brown cocoa surface. It's a chilled version of café brûlot, a flaming liqueur-laced coffee. The ingredients are solidified into a thick layer of coffee ice cream flavored with rum, orange and lemon zest, and Grand Marnier.

Wine list: A solid list, mostly American, of about 200 bottles, with 18 half bottles and 10 wines by the glass. **Price range:** Lunch: apps., $9–$18; entrees, $19–$36; desserts, $9–$10. Dinner: three course prix fixe, $69. **Wheelchair access:** Elevator in hotel lobby.

Trailer Park Lounge and Grill $ AMERICAN

271 W. 23rd St. (bet. Seventh & Eighth Aves.) (212) 463-8000
Credit cards: All major Meals: L, D, LN

Trailer Park is not so much a restaurant as a walk-in diorama: it has an actual trailer, a chubby turquoise and white 1959 Spartanette, with a fake coconut tree and some lawn chairs. A small metal frame on the wall encloses a can of Spam. In one corner there is a tribute to Tonya Harding. The trick here is to serve food that qualifies as trashy but that diners might really want to order. It's a fine line between popular American classics, like the immortal cheese burger, and inside jokes like Moon Pie, the only dessert served at Trailer Park. The appetite for kitsch dies quickly when the time comes to chew it. The good news is that Trailer Park makes a better-than-average chili, best consumed on top of its extreme nachos. Trailer Park does one thing amazingly well: its sweet potato fries, served with all entrees. Anyone tempted to linger at the tables will think twice when the diabolically bad country music kicks in. This place rates half a hoot.

Price range: Entrees, $6–$9. **Wheelchair access:** Fully accessible.

Trattoria L'incontro $25 & Under ITALIAN

21-76 31st St. (near Ditmars Blvd.), Astoria, Queens (718) 721-3532
Credit cards: All major Meals: L, D Closed Mon.

The restaurant looks like an impersonal, assembly-line place. Yet L'Incontro has all the warmth of a corner mom-and-pop — or more accurately, mom-and-son. The owner and chef, Rocco Sacramone, is aided by his mother, Tina Sacramone, who oversees the pasta-making operation.

Pastas are excellent, particularly the fresh ones made by Mrs. Sacramone and, like the appetizers, enhanced by their simplicity. Cavatelli, a short, ribbed pasta, is well matched with crumbled sausage, cabbage and just a touch of truffle oil. Even spaghetti and meatballs shine, thanks to a lively tomato sauce. L'Incontro has a nice selection of wines under $25, as well as a few worthy splurges.

Other recommended dishes: Grilled escarole and beans, cacciatorino, grilled octopus, pizza, breaded sole and shrimp, rabbit, osso buco. **Price range:** Apps., $5–$9; pizzas, $6–$9; entrees, $9–$25. **Wheelchair access:** All one level.

Tribeca Grill ☆☆ $$$ NEW AMERICAN

375 Greenwich St. (at Franklin St.)
(212) 941-3900
Credit cards: All major
Meals: Br, L, D

Robert De Niro's first venture into the restaurant business in what the neighbors sometimes call Bob Row is a cool, casual outpost of modern American cuisine with an almost constant flow of celebrity guests. And the food's good. The big, airy space with exposed bricks, colorful banquettes and comfortable tables centers on a massive handsome mahogany bar many may remember as the original bar of Maxwell's Plum. The beguiling fare remains a steady lure. (*Ruth Reichl*)

Price range: Apps., $8–$11; entrees, $12–$32. Brunch, $11–$18. Lunch prix-fixe, $20. **Wheelchair access:** Fully accessible. **Features:** Outdoor dining.

Triomphe ☆☆ $ FRENCH/NEW AMERICAN

Iroquois Hotel, 49 W. 44th St. (bet. Fifth & Sixth Aves.)
(212) 453-4233
Credit cards: All major
Meals: B, L, D

In a city with flash to spare, this restaurant has a rare commodity: charm. The setting is subdued and adult, with pristine white walls, dark walnut floors and a dome ceiling with precise, crenelated moldings. It is an awkwardly proportioned room, but clever decorating has smoothed out the worst of the problems. The food is appropriately simple and understated.

The small menu abounds in small pleasures supported by big flavors, like the chewy brioche croutons that shore up a rich, vermouth-scented stew of Malpeque oysters, packed with potatoes and leeks. Again and again, Triomphe quietly strikes the right note. When the main ingredient calls for more, the chef opens up the flavors. A hefty rib-eye steak comes with fat grilled cèpes and a muscular brandy demi-glace, and a thick slab of salmon gets the works: a caviar-dotted beurre blanc, a scattering of grilled shrimp and parsnip whipped potatoes.

Wine list: A short, rather mundane list of 65 wines, mostly French and Californian, at budget prices, with 10 by the glass. **Price range:** Lunch entrees, $14–$22. Dinner: apps., $9–$14; entrees, $25–$31; desserts, $8. **Wheelchair access:** Four steps up to hotel and restaurant. Restrooms are in hotel lobby, on same level as dining room.

Trionfo $$$ ITALIAN

224 W. 51st St. (bet. Eighth Ave. & Broadway)
(212) 262-6660
Credit cards: All major
Meals: L, D

Small and modestly decorated with good northern Italian food and surprisingly high prices for the neighborhood. Regulars are treated with great affection, but no one will feel slighted.

Price range: Avg. app., $10; pasta, $14; entree, $19; dessert, $6. **Wheelchair access:** Restrooms not accessible. **Features:** Outdoor dining.

Triple Eight Palace $$ CHINESE

88 E. Broadway (bet. Division & Market Sts.)   (212) 941-8886
Credit cards: All major   Meals: L, D

Eight, in case you hadn't guessed, is a lucky number in China. And
you'll be lucky to eat the fine dim sum in this large, dim restaurant
just beneath the Manhattan Bridge.

Price range: Lunch, $7–$9. Dinner, $10–$15. **Wheelchair access:**
Not accessible.

Trois Canards $$ BISTRO/FRENCH

184 Eighth Ave. (bet. 19th & 20th Sts.)   (212) 929-4320
Credit cards: All major   Meals: Br, L, D

Ducks are everywhere in this pleasant if slightly too cute Chelsea
bistro. The food is primarily bistro French with modern touches.
And yet, in the hip new art world that Chelsea has become, this
seems more like the old Chelsea than the new.

Price range: Lunch: apps., $6–$8; entrees, $10–$13. Dinner: apps.,
$7–$9; entrees, $15–$22; desserts, $6–$7. **Wheelchair access:**
Restrooms not accessible. **Features:** Outdoor dining.

Tsampa $25 & Under   TIBETAN

212 E. 9th St. (bet. Second & Third Aves.)   (212) 614-3226
Credit cards: All major   Meals: L, D, LN

Tsampa is peaceful and contemplative, as one might imagine of a
Tibetan restaurant, except when the juicer goes off with a horrible
mechanical whine. But Tsampa stands out from other Tibetan
restaurants because the food is unusually well spiced. Steamed
momos — light, delicate crescent-shaped dumplings — come with
a fiery dipping sauce that ignites the flavors. The earthy phing sha
— chicken and collard greens blended with mung bean noodles —
is a lively main course.

Other recommended dishes: Lentil soup; spicy udon noodles;
grilled whole trout; grilled salmon; yam and pumpkin pie; rice with
yogurt, raisins and pine nuts. **Alcohol:** Beer and wine. **Price range:**
Apps., $5; entrees, $9–$13; desserts, $4. **Wheelchair access:** All
one level.

Tsuki $25 & Under   SUSHI/JAPANESE

1410 First Ave. (near 75th St.)   (212) 517-6860
Credit cards: AE   Meals: D

Tsuki is a modest storefront that has a warm family feeling. As at
many sushi bars, non-sushi items are available. Try a bowl of the
house-made tofu, served warm with ginger and soy. Sushi, though,
is the thing, and for a neighborhood restaurant, Tsuki has an extensive list of fish. Those include fine, delicately flavored red snapper,
and the richer, slightly oily horse mackerel. Little crabs, fried until
they just turn red, and eaten shell and all are daunting. Baby eels
are another unusual offering. They are tender and subtle. Tsuki
offers a dozen sakes, mostly moderately priced, served in masus,
square wooden vessels that regulars can inscribe and store behind
the bar.

Price range: Assorted sushi and sashimi, $10.50–$24.50; à la carte, $3–$6.50; chef's selection, $36 and up. **Wheelchair access:** Ramp at entrance, restroom is narrow.

Tuk Tuk $25 & Under THAI

204 Smith St., Boerum Hill, Brooklyn (718) 222-5598
Credit cards: Cash only Meals: L, D

While the kitchen here is aiming for more authentic flavors than the usual tamed and sweetened New York versions, the narrow, minimalist dining room, with its long brick wall, handsome hanging lights and bleached wood floor, fits right into the Smith Street lineup of casually appealing restaurants. On weekend evenings a band offers a quiet blend of jazz and bossa nova.

Unless you enjoy spicy food, Tuk Tuk's robust curries will test your endurance. The chili presence is pronounced, yet subtly woven in with other flavors so that it does not simply overpower. Two frequent specials are among the best dishes: shreds of crisp duck, as rich as confit, served with onions and bell peppers; and a deep-fried red snapper, each delicately crisp piece simultaneously spicy, sweet and sour.

Other recommended dishes: Hot pot dumplings, mussel pancake, chicken soup with coconut broth, curries, stir-fried rice noodles, chicken with garlic and pepper sauce. **Alcohol:** Beer and wine. **Price range:** Apps., $4–$6; entrees, $6–$16. **Wheelchair access:** One level.

Tupelo Grill $$$ STEAKHOUSE

1 Penn Plaza (bet. Seventh & Eighth Aves. at 33rd St.)
(212) 760-2700
Credit cards: All major Meals: L, D

A manly sort of place with a menu that reads like an ode to protein and waiters who look like they work out in a serious way. The porterhouses for two, three or four come with plenty of butter spooned over the top, the sirloin is good and the lamb chops are small, soft and smooth as velvet. There are a couple of sissy dishes, including the most bizarre chopped salad you can imagine. Skip dessert.

Price range: Apps., $6–$18; entrees, $17–$34; desserts, $6.

Turkish Kitchen $$ TURKISH

386 Third Ave. (bet. 27th & 28th Sts.) (212) 679-1810
Credit cards: All major Meals: L, D

Wonderful Turkish food in a dimly romantic setting. The food will remind you of the culinary links between Greece and Turkey. Appetizers are the star of this large, trim, red-walled dining room. Phyllo dough is rolled parchment thin, tucked around sharp, house-made feta cheese and fried to make the crisp sigara boregi, while mint, cucumber and garlic are folded into thick yogurt to make cacik. Reliable main courses include a succulent kasarli kofte, a spicy blend of ground lamb and beef; grilled lamb chops, and hunkar begendi, lamb stewed with tomatoes and served over a smoky egg-plant purée.

Price range: Four-course prix-fixe lunch, $14. Dinner: apps., $6–$9; entrees, $14–$19; desserts, $6. **Wheelchair access:** Three steps to entrance; restrooms not accessible.

Turkuaz $25 & Under TURKISH/MIDDLE EASTERN
2637 Broadway (at 100th St.)   (212) 665-9541
Credit cards: All major   Meals: D

Turkuaz differs from other restaurants not only because the food is good, but also because it has a clear identity. The dining room is draped in billowy fabric so that it resembles an Ottoman tent. Seat covers give chairs a lush appearance, and the staff is adorned in tra-ditional Turkish costumes.

There is also an extensive menu featuring excellent cold appetiz-ers. The lineup includes the usual Middle Eastern complement, like creamy hummus and smoky baba ghanouj, along with Turkish spe-cialties like patlican salatasi, a tangy, garlic-enhanced eggplant purée. Main courses tend to be simple and elementally satisfying, like beyti kebab, spicy chopped lamb charcoal-grilled with herbs and garlic, and tender, well-flavored lamb chops. For added com-plexity, adana yogurtlu, a blend of beef and lamb layered with yogurt and tomato sauce over crisp bread, is well put together. Desserts include the usual baklava and kadayif, as well as a neat variation on rice pudding, served with the top caramelized like crème brûlée.

Other recommended dishes: Cacik, haydari, shepherd's salad, lah-macun, pides, acili ezme, Turkish soft drinks. **Price range:** Apps., $4–$8; entrees, $12–$24. **Wheelchair access:** Restrooms down a flight of stairs.

Tuscan ☆ ☆ $$$$ ITALIAN
622 Third Ave. (at 40th St.)   (212) 404-1700
Credit cards: All major   Meals: Br, L, D   Closed Sun.

The former Tuscan Steak, now simply called Tuscan, is a much bet-ter restaurant. Tuscan retains the party atmosphere and the throb-bing bar scene on the mezzanine level. But the large, stylish dining room now emphasizes variety rather than abundance.

Nearly half the menu is devoted to an assortment of well-made antipasti. The steaks, marinated and grilled with herbs over wood chips, remain a feature of the menu, but they compete for attention with a rotating list of daily specials, daily risottos and main courses, like boiled veal with spicy fruits, that offer an imaginative escape from the standard Italian tour of duty. The restaurant's signature dish is bocconcini, miniature footballs of buttery polenta dough, reeking of truffle, that are deep-fried until they achieve a dark-brown crust. They are completely seductive.

Other recommended dishes: Meatballs, linguine with pancetta and clams, marinated langoustines, trout with walnut pesto. **Wine list:** About 300 wines, with some imaginative choices from Tuscany and Piedmont. **Price range:** Apps., $6- $18; entrees, $19–$44; desserts,

$9–$15. **Wheelchair access:** Elevator behind coat check serves all levels.

Tuscan Square $$$ ITALIAN
16 W. 51st St. (bet. Fifth & Sixth Aves.)   (212) 977-7777
Credit cards: All major   Meals: B, L, D

Pino Luongo has opened his first theme park restaurant in Rocke-feller Center. The theme here is Tuscany, complete with plates, linens, clothing and, of course, food. The food can be very good, from interesting antipasto plates to fine, spare plates of pasta, but you never forget you're eating in a store.

Price range: Lunch: apps., $6–$10; pastas, $12–$17; entrees, $18–$22; desserts, $7. Dinner: apps., $9–$12; pastas, $15–$18; entrees, $20–$32; desserts, $9. **Wheelchair access:** Fully accessible.

"21" Club   ☆☆ $$$$ AMERICAN
21 W. 52nd St. (bet. Fifth & Sixth Aves.)   (212) 582-7200
Credit cards: All major   Meals: L, D   Closed Sun.

Of all the restaurants in New York City, none has a richer history. American royalty has been entertaining at "21" for most of this cen-tury. The restaurant continues to be operated like a club where unknowns are inexorably led to the farthest dining room where they can watch from a distance as the more favored clients are pampered and petted. Nothing much else has changed either. The menu has been modernized but with mixed results. The basics are still superb, however. Great steak, rack of lamb, Dover sole, and the "21" burger, and several traditional desserts such as rice pudding and crème brûlée are all worthwhile. (*Ruth Reichl*)

Wine list: Huge with surprisingly fair prices. **Price range:** Lunch: apps., $14–$24; entrees, $25–$42; desserts, $11; three-course prix-fixe lunch, $29. Dinner: apps., $14–$25; entrees, $25–$42; desserts, $11; prix-fixe dinner, $33. **Wheelchair access:** Ramp at service entrance.

26 Seats $25 & Under   FRENCH
168 Ave. B (at 11th St.)   (212) 677-4787
Credit cards: AE   Meals: D   Closed Mon.

The name 26 Seats says a lot about this sweet little French restau-rant near Tompkins Square Park. The narrow dining room is what real estate people call intimate, yet it's relatively comfortable and the waitresses are friendly and kind to children (who take up less room, of course).

    The menu's French country offerings, hitting familiar regional notes, are both satisfying and a good value. From Provence comes a pissaladière, and from Lyon, fat rounds of savory garlic sausage. The main courses, too, are well-executed versions of familiar recipes, with the occasional pleasing twist. A coating of mustard and ginger gives life to a grilled chicken breast. The modest wine list includes several appropriately priced choices, like a sprightly muscadet, an Alsatian riesling from Pierre Sparr and a decent pinot noir from the South of France. For dessert, a wedge of apple tart is the best choice.

Other recommended dishes: Snails in garlic sauce, butternut squash soup, mesclun salad, endive salad, salmon, steak au poivre, magret de canard. **Price range:** Apps., $6–$9; entrees, $11–$17. **Wheelchair access:** Not accessible.

2 West $$$$ NEW AMERICAN
Ritz-Carlton Hotel, 2 West St. (near Battery Pl.)   (917) 790-2525
Credit cards: All major   Meals: L, D

The restaurant 2 West, in the new Ritz-Carlton Hotel in Battery Park City, has barely a toehold on the island of Manhattan. One step back, and it would be bathing in the Hudson. By any measure, it qualifies as a restaurant off the beaten track. Persistence, though, will be rewarded with food of decent quality served in shiny, anonymous surroundings. At lunch, a heaping salad of arugula topped with big shavings of Manchego cheese was impeccable and braised oxtail and short ribs on broad Asian noodles was an inspired chill-chaser. At dinner, the better entrees include roasted lobster with papardelle and artichokes in lobster sauce, seared skate on a mound of mashed potatoes with citrus jus, and veal chop and roasted sweetbreads with potato gnocchi.

For dessert try the gingersnap napoleon with caramel mousse, and even better than the napoleon itself is the crunchy peanut butter ice cream that comes with it.

Price range: Entrees, $22–$42. **Wheelchair access:** Accessible.

Ubol's Kitchen $25 & Under   THAI
24-42 Steinway St., Astoria, Queens   (718) 545-2874
Credit cards: All major   Meals: L, D

This simply decorated but authentic (there's a Buddhist shrine in the rear) Thai restaurant does not stint on its spicing or seasoning. Dishes marked on the menu as hot and spicy can be counted on to be searing, while dishes traditionally rich in fish sauce are suitably pungent. Top dishes include spicy salads and curries. Bamboo salad is one of the more unusual Thai dishes, made with strands of fermented bamboo shoots, chilies and lime juice. (Ubol's is pronounced YEW-bahnz.)

Other recommended dishes: Spicy ground pork salad, spicy squid salad, green papaya salad, chicken with coconut milk soup, tamarind fish, green curry with fish balls, jungle curry with chicken, Panang curry with chicken. **Alcohol:** Beer and wine. **Price range:** Apps., $4–$10; entrees, $6–$15; desserts, $3. **Wheelchair access:** Fully accessible.

Ulrika's $$ SWEDISH
115 E. 60th St. (bet Lexington & Park Aves.)   (212) 355-7069
Credit cards: All major   Meals: Br, L, D

This small, rustic restaurant showcases the homey food of Hyltebruk, a tiny town in southern Sweden. The place is filled with Swedish furniture, swanky Swedish flatware and the work of local

Swedish artists on the wall. There is herring, of course. Mustard herring, pickled herring and matjes herring come on big appetizer plates with chunks of firm, sharpish Vasterbotten cheese. The excellent salmon gravlax go down beautifully with the restaurant's own pilsner, a clean, medium-bodied brew with a crisp, hoppy bite to it. Swedish cuisine is not refined, but it is earthy, flavorful and satisfying, like beef á la Rydberg, tender cubes of tenderloin in a mustard gravy served with sautéed potatoes and an optional raw egg yolk, which Swedes pour over the meat and potatoes, letting the heat partially cook it.

Two desserts deserve special mention. The pannkaks Tarta could not be cuter: a stack of miniature pancakes oozing bright-yellow cloudberry jam and festively decorated with blueberries speared on a long toothpick. But there's one dessert that goes straight to the heart, a little basket of assorted Swedish cookies. For Americans it will feel like an early Christmas present.

Wine list: Varied, but mostly Americans. $24–$42. By the glass: $6–$10. **Price range:** Brunch: $7–$21. Lunch: apps, $6–$12; entrees, $14–$20; prix fixe, $22. Dinner: apps, $6–$15; entrees, $15–$23. **Wheelchair access:** Steps down from sidewalk.

Uncle George's $25 & Under GREEK

33-19 Broadway, Astoria, Queens (718) 626-0593
Credit cards: Cash only   Meals: B, L, D   Open 24 Hours

A cross between a giant diner that's always open and a boisterous family restaurant, Uncle George's is an Astoria Greek classic. Portions are big, service is speedy and the menu offers every kind of Greek dish, from great grilled fish to the ubiquitous spanakopita (spinach pie) and pastitsio (macaroni, meat sauce and cream sauce). You won't leave hungry. With bright lights, plastic table covers and seats crowded into every spot, it's fair to say that Uncle George's doesn't attract people for the décor.

Other recommended dishes: Tzatziki, yogurt and fish-egg dip, mashed potato and garlic dip, sautéed octopus, stewed rabbit, baked eggplant, barbecued pork, lamb burgers. **Alcohol:** Beer and wine. **Price range:** Apps., $2–$5; entrees, $6–$12. **Wheelchair access:** Fully accessible. **Features:** Outdoor dining.

Uncle Nick's $25 & Under GREEK/SEAFOOD

747 Ninth Ave. (bet. 50th & 51st Sts.) (212) 245-7992
Credit cards: All major   Meals: L, D, LN

Once a little hole in the wall, Uncle Nick's developed a loyal following and expanded into a handsome Greek seafood taverna in Clinton. The fresh, pristine fish and other Greek specialties have won it a devoted following. Appetizers are terrific. While the fish is always fresh, too often it is overcooked and arrives dry. Make clear to the staff how you want it cooked.

Other recommended dishes: Three-spread combination, dandelion salad, sautéed Greek sausage, saganakityri, swordfish kebab, salmon steak, souvlaki, chicken souvlaki, baklava. **Price range:** Apps., from $5; entrees, from $8; desserts, from $3. **Wheelchair access:** Fully accessible.

Union Pacific ☆☆☆ $$$$ FRENCH/ASIAN

111 E. 22nd St. (near Park Ave. S.) (212) 995-8500
Credit cards: All major   Meals: L, D   Closed Sun.

Television audiences may not know it, but Rocco DiSpirito made his name with sophisticated Asian fusion cooking at Union Pacific, now all of six years old. It might be a good idea for patrons of Rocco's on 22nd, the chef's downscale Italian-American venture, to see just what made Mr. DiSpirito a star in the first place. It's the intelligent grafting of Asian ingredients onto Western dishes that makes Union Pacific a standout. The cooking is imaginative but unforced, a quality immediately apparent in a carpaccio of squash blossom with pickled onion and sansho peppercorns, or fragrant fennel soup with sake-poached oysters. Miso and lavender combine to make a lovely, aromatic vinaigrette for a simple salad of baby lettuces. Likewise, hot and sour XO sauce, a Hong Kong specialty, brings out the sweetness in soft-shell crabs. Sauteed skate in brown butter, a bistro standby, is served here not with capers but a lime pickle swiss chard, an ingenious way of cutting the richness of the butter. Desserts can seem almost Californian, like the peach and goat cheese tart with lavender-raspberry sorbet. *(Review by William Grimes; stars previously awarded by Ruth Reichl.)*

Wine list: Unusual and interesting, with many Austrian wines.
Price range: Lunch: apps., $12–$17; entrees, $18–$29; desserts, $8–$10; three-course prix fixe, $20.04. Dinner: three-course prix fixe, $68 with supplements; five-course prix fixe, $85. **Wheelchair access:** Fully accessible.

Union Square Café ☆☆ $$$ NEW AMERICAN

21 E. 16th St. (near Union Sq. W.) (212) 243-4020
Credit cards: All major   Meals: L, D

There's a reason why Union Square Café has become one of the city's most beloved dining spots, and a top destination for tourists. The restaurant treats its guests very well. It makes them feel welcome by catering to their every whim in an openhanded, Midwestern manner that disguises a disciplined, highly professional understanding of service that broke the mold in New York.

It's not the food that's setting off the stampede, however. Union Square has not changed, but the world has changed around it. Michael Romano, the executive chef and part owner, does what he has always done, and done very well, which is to turn out jazzed-up bistro and trattoria fare with utter consistency. The signature fried calamari, a dull cliché elsewhere in town, deserve their star billing. Although there are several foreign accents heard on the menu, Italian dominates, especially in the pasta dishes, which put many Italian restaurants to shame. In general, Union Square has mastered the art of pleasing without challenging. The spice-braised lamb, one of the restaurant's recurring specials, strikes a mildly exotic Mediterranean-Indian note, but it is the equivalent of an ethnic crossover hit, just sweet enough to be mainstream.

Desserts aim for an artful blend of homey and exotic, most memorably in the banana tart with a caramel shellac.

Wine list: A serious, carefully chosen list of about 300 bottles, mostly French, Italian and Californian. Many wines under $40, and

15 wines by the glass. **Price range:** Lunch entrees, $13–$18. Dinner: apps., $8–$15; entrees, $21–$29; desserts, $8. **Wheelchair access:** Not accessible.

United Noodles $25 & Under   PAN-ASIAN

349 E. 12th St. (near First Ave.)   (212) 614-0155
Credit cards: Meals: D

United Noodles is a simple, narrow storefront that radiates a happy warmth as it plays host, nightly, to an incredible mix of people. They all enter its stylish interior on the strength of its inexpensive and interesting menu of deconstructed Asian food. Try the forest mushroom rolls. The texture of the mushrooms in the mouth, played off the silky wrapping and sweet peanut sauce, is terrific. For your main course try the apple-cider glazed cod with sweet-potato purée. It is a triumph. And the cold soba sashimi — which amounts to a plate of sashimi thrown into a blender, dressings and all, with cold soba noodles — is a brilliant fusion dish: Honmura An meets Nobu. For dessert, there's a convincing warm chocolate cake with ice cream, and a delicious poached pear. *(Sam Sifton)*

Other recommended dishes: Spiced tofu, shrimp wonton, calamari, sashimi, broccoli pea soup, pad thai. **Price range:** Apps., $6–$8; entrees, $9–$15. **Wheelchair access:** Step to entrance.

The Upstairs at "21"   ☆ ☆ $$$$

NEW AMERICAN

21 W. 52nd St. (bet. Fifth & Sixth Aves.)   (212) 265-1900
Credit cards: All major   Meals: D   Closed Sun., Mon.

The new upstairs dining room at the "21" Club is a club within a club, a small, windowless room ruled by its own peculiar rituals, meant to suggest a vanished world of privilege and high style. It gives the chef the opportunity to cut loose and cook the kind of food that could never fly in the deeply conservative dining room downstairs. The evening begins with a long, narrow plate containing three amuse-bouches for each diner. Meals come in two formats, a four-course à la carte dinner and a six-course tasting menu.

The chef makes every effort to dazzle, whether with odd flavor pairings, bright splashes of color or odd ingredients. It's successful about half the time. One sparkling instance is sea scallops, done sashimi style, with a creamy mussel dressing and a layer of osetra caviar. The standout on the dessert menu is chocolate-hazelnut mousse on a base of crumbled chocolate cookie, served with chocolate sorbet.

Other recommended dishes: Venison with huckleberry syrup and crushed-wheat risotto, spicy lobster gratin. **Wine list:** Extensive list, mostly French and Californian, drawn from the "21" cellar. **Price range:** Four-course prix fixe, $85; six-course tasting menu, $125 ($185 with matching wines). **Wheelchair access:** Ramp at entrance; elevator to dining room.

Uskudar
$25 & Under   TURKISH

1405 Second Ave. (near 73rd St.)   (212) 988-2641
Credit cards: All major   Meals: L, D

This sliver of a Turkish restaurant is the very model of a successful neighborhood institution. On any given night, the inviting dining room, which seats no more than 24, is crowded with families, couples and the occasional lone diner. The selection of appetizers includes excellent spreads.

Uskudar's kebabs are uncommonly juicy, particularly the shish kebab, with tender cubes of marinated lamb. But the best dishes are the stews. There's etli bamya, lamb with baby okra, and Hunkar begendi, another hearty lamb stew, made with tomatoes and herbs and served over pureed eggplant, an enticing combination. Uskudar makes its own desserts, and though they are familiar, they are excellent, especially kadayif, shredded wheat with ground walnuts and drenched in honey.

Other recommended dishes: Patlican, ezme, chicken with garlic, imam bayildi, grilled quail, apricots stuffed with almonds. **Price range:** Apps., $5–$7; entrees, $13–$16. **Wheelchair access:** Not accessible.

Vanderbilt Station
$$$ NEW AMERICAN

4 Park Ave. (at 33rd St.)   (212) 889-3369
Credit cards: All major   Meals: Br, L, D

The first thing you notice on entering Vanderbilt Station is the vaulted tile ceiling. Because the ceiling is practically low enough to touch, all the colorful, intricately three-dimensional details of Rafael Guastavino's elaborate design are fresh to the eye, right before you. The chef and owner, Kieran Brew, prowls the small dining room pushing a silver trolley, carving slices of prime rib priced by the inch ($21 for the first inch, $7 for each additional half inch). The prime rib is top notch: tender, rare and primarily thrilling, served with an exceptional, eggy Yorkshire pudding. The menu also offers a Diamond Jim Brady Shellfish Indulgence Platter that includes lobster, shrimp, oysters, mussels, clams and caviar, a mere snack for Diamond Jim, but, in deference to modern appetites, intended for two to four people. Service is friendly, direct and open, with zero attitude, not what you would expect from the Vanderbilts, perhaps, but as honest and innocent as America fancied itself to be in that bygone era. *(Eric Asimov)*

Price range: Apps., $5–$16; entrees, $17–$34. **Wheelchair access:** Fully accessible.

Vatan
$25 & Under   INDIAN/VEGETARIAN

409 Third Ave. (at 29th St.)   (212) 689-5666
Credit cards: All major   Meals: D   Closed Mon.

This astounding Indian restaurant transports you to a bright, animated Indian village with thatched roofs and artificial banyan trees. Vatan specializes in the rich, spicy yet subtle vegetarian cuisine of Gujarat. For one price, a parade of little dishes is served, which might include khaman, a delicious fluffy steamed cake of lentil flour with black mustard seeds; delicate little samosas; patrel, taro leaves layered with spicy chickpea paste and steamed, and more.

Price range: $22. **Wheelchair access:** All one level.

Va Tutto! $25 & Under   ITALIAN

23 Cleveland Pl. (near Kenmare St.)   (212) 941-0286
Credit cards: All major   Meals: L, D   Closed Mon.

Va Tutto!, Italian for "Anything Goes," is a warm and welcoming Tuscan-oriented restaurant with a lovely garden. For lunch try the panini povero, a sumptuous sandwich of scrambled eggs, mozzarella, tomato sauce and herbs that somehow holds together on crusty grilled bread. The best main courses are the pastas al forno, baked dishes like a thin wedge of lasagna with fennel sausage, roasted peppers and plum tomatoes, and sumptuous cannelloni stuffed with spinach, mushrooms and Parmesan. Also wonderful are ribbons of pasta with speck (an excellent ham from the Alto Adige). For dessert, try the house-made focaccia lathered with Nutella, that European chocolate-hazelnut spread, and a scoop of rich fig-flavored gelato. And Va Tutto! offers the rare panna cotta in which flavor triumphs over texture.

Other recommended dishes: Grilled calamari, rigatoni amatriciana, roasted chicken, quail, insalata di funghi. **Price range:** Apps., $7–$10; entrees, $13–$23. **Wheelchair access:** Steps to garden.

Verbena   ☆ $$$ NEW AMERICAN

54 Irving Pl. (near 17th St.)   (212) 260-5454
Credit cards: All major   Meals: Br, D

After a face-lift and expansion, Verbena looks attractive. The tight dining room retains its very adult sense of calm and style, and a cool, breezy and secluded courtyard garden has been created in the back, with white canvas overhead. Now the bad news.

The new place seems more like a comfortable compromise than an exciting new departure. The menu has a plainness to it now and a simplicity that can be boring. Roast chicken with green beans, herbed plum tomatoes and escarole, for example, is perfectly respectable, but not much more than that. The bolder dishes sometimes hit and sometimes miss. The sirloin steak is a remarkably rich, tender cut, beautifully charred outside. Desserts are polite, but at the start of the meal, your waiter will ask if you are interested in the Bing cherry upside-down cake. It is baked to order and needs extra time. Say yes. The cake is better than Mom ever made.

Wine list: An imaginative list of about 150 wines, half of them French, half American and Australian, with 35 half bottles and eight to 12 wines by the glass. **Price range:** Apps., $8–$13; entrees, $15–$28; desserts, $6–$12. Four-course tasting menu, $58; four-course vegetarian tasting menu, $52. **Wheelchair access:** Steps to entrance and garden.

Veritas ☆☆☆ $$$$ NEW AMERICAN

43 E. 20th St. (near Park Ave. S.)
Credit cards: All major

(212) 353-3700
Meals: D

When you think of Veritas, you think first and foremost of the wine list. Its extraordinary length and breadth can make a visit to Veritas begin days before you get there, as you consult and agonize over the wine list on the restaurant's web site (*www.veritas-nyc.com*). The wines (and the wine prices) are the hard part. Almost overlooked, and much easier to navigate, is Scott Bryan's small menu, which, though constructed to go beautifully with wine, would be wonderful with water as well. It's full of strong and simple flavors, like a sweet corn and black truffle ravioli that purrs, "Butter," and crisp, earthy sweetbreads. Seared duck breast melts in the mouth, and roast saddle of lamb cries out for a well-aged Pauillac (or perhaps a well-aged Barolo), which come to think of it is the idea, anyway. *(Review by Eric Asimov; stars previously awarded by Ruth Reichl.)*

Wine list: Enormous, memorable and well priced. **Price range:** Three course prix-fixe dinner, $68. **Wheelchair access:** Fully accessible.

Vernon's New Jerk House $25 & Under
JAMAICAN

987 233rd St., Eastchester, the Bronx
Credit cards: Cash only

(718) 655-8348
Meals: L, D

Vernon's, which opened 20 years ago, serves better jerk than ever. It's not the most comfortable restaurant; you place your order at a counter and take a seat in the small dining room, or just take the food home. Much of the food is kept warm on a steam table, including the main course accompaniments: earthy rice and peas, excellent steamed carrots and cabbage and sweet plantains, as well as stews like tender curried goat in a rich brown sauce — full of thyme and ginger and mellow until a little spice begins to kick in.

Jerk, though, is not left to simmer. It's kept back in the kitchen. Finally, it appears on the table, practically overflowing on the plate. Whether chicken or pork, the meat seems infused with a bright, tangy sensation that creeps into and finally engulfs the mouth, filling it with the flavors of ginger, allspice, thyme, vinegar and soy, all underscored with the moderate but escalating heat of Scotch bonnet peppers.

Price range: Complete meals, $6–$8. **Wheelchair access:** Not accessible.

Veselka $25 & Under EAST EUROPEAN

144 Second Ave. (at 9th St.)
Credit cards: All major   Meals: B, Br, L, D

(212) 228-9682
Open 24 hours

At this renovated Eastern European luncheonette, bohemian angst meets Slavic charm over kasha and blintzes. Great breakfasts can include hearty buckwheat pancakes, thick potato pancakes or delightful cheese blintzes. Soups are also very good, especially the excellent Ukrainian borscht, rich with just a touch of sweetness.

Alcohol: Beer. **Price range:** Apps., $3–$5; entrees, $6–$9; desserts, $3–$5. **Wheelchair access:** Fully accessible. **Features:** Outdoor dining.

Vespa Cibobuono $ ITALIAN
1625 Second Ave. (bet. 84th & 85th Sts.)   (212) 472-2050
Credit cards: All major   Meals: D

Simple pastas served in a pleasant nook of a dining room make Vespa a good choice for a decent meal if you're in the area, especially in warm weather when you can enjoy the garden.

Alcohol: Beer and wine. **Price range:** Apps., $7–$12; entrees, $11–$25; desserts, $6. **Wheelchair access:** Fully accessible. **Features:** Outdoor dining.

Via Emilia $25 & Under   ITALIAN
240 Park Ave. S. (near 20th St.)   (212) 505-3072
Credit cards: Cash only   Meals: L, D   Closed Sun.

There is one thing that will always bring diners to a restaurant's doorstep: good food. Via Emilia doesn't have much else to go on. The restaurant has all the physical charm of a bus station. It has brick walls and wood banquettes.

The real reason to dine at Via Emilia, though, is for the tortellini and tortelloni, which are made at the restaurant. Chicken and wild mushroom tortelloni were large and pillowy. The lasagne is a perfect model, and shouldn't be missed.

The desserts could humble some of the finest pastry chefs. The crème brûlée was one of the best. And the tiramisù may explain why the clichéd dessert was popularized in the first place.

There is yet one more treat. The restaurant has an exceptional list of inexpensive Lambrusco, sparkling red wines from Modena, served chilled. (*Amanda Hesser*)

Other recommended dishes: Cotechino, pork chop, tartuffo. **Price range:** Apps., $5–$8; entrees, $8–$15. **Wheelchair access:** Not accessible.

Via Quadronno $25 & Under   ITALIAN/SANDWICHES
25 E. 73rd St. (near Madison Ave.)   (212) 650-9880
Credit cards: All major   Meals: B, L, D, LN

Via Quadronno reflects both the requirements of the neighborhood and its own ties to Milan. The cafe stretches past a selection of gelati to a timbered rear room with a mural featuring a flying boar. It's not exactly comfortable seating; some tables come with backless stools, others with rickety folding chairs, perhaps in an effort to keep the shopping and tourist crowd moving in and out. Prices are also higher, especially for wine, which is served by the bottle. Sandwich prices are more reasonable, and the servings are generous, like the single-ingredient panini semplici, served on small, warm ciabatta. The open-faced tartufata is not quite the blend of minced porcini mushrooms, olive oil and truffles as billed on the menu, but it is earthy and pleasing. The best part of the menu is the desserts, especially crisp, buttery and beautiful pear and plum tarts.

Other recommended dishes: Ham and fontina cheese, chocolate and hazelnut gelati. **Alcohol:** Beer and wine only. **Price range:** Entrees, $13–$22. **Wheelchair access:** One step at entrance; four steps to dining room.

Vicala $25 & Under   FUSION
111 Avenue C. (near 7th St.)   (212) 254-2229
Credit cards: All major   Meals: D

With good food and friendly, unpretentious service, Vicala gets things right. The minimalist dining room, done in shades of gray and black with sleek wood banquettes, is a stylish suit on an avenue full of ragged jeans. The cooking is likewise sleek, fusing French techniques with Asian flavorings, resulting in exalted dishes with Vietnamese roots. You won't find carpaccio at any Vietnamese restaurant, for example, but here the paper-thin layer of beef is flavored with lemongrass and a peppery citrus sauce. An appetizer of minced shrimp on toasted baguette is blended with chili, garlic and peanut sauce. Voilá nouveau shrimp toast! Cubes of tender filet mignon are extraordinarily flavorful, bathed in a tangy marinade and served with caramelized cloves of garlic, onions and tomatoes.

Other recommended dishes: Tuna tartar, fried crab, five-spice quail, squid stuffed with shrimp, grilled pork, lamb chops, scallops in coconut curry, duck breast, sweet soup. **Price range:** Apps., $5–$9; entrees, $9–$20. Not accessible.

Viceversa ☆ $$ ITALIAN
325 W. 51st St. (bet. Eighth & Ninth Aves.)   (212) 399-9265
Credit cards: All major   Meals: L, D

With its crisp earth-colored awnings and gleaming facade, Viceversa (pronounced VEE-chey-VAIR-suh) stands out on one of Manhattan's grungier blocks like a Versace suit. Inside, the décor is so minimal that it seems to disappear in the course of an evening, a blur of light beige walls, dark hardwood floors and antique terra cotta vases. Managers and wait staff project an unmistakable Italian warmth, and the menu is honest and unpretentious, a solid lineup of mostly northern Italian dishes.

Casoncelli alla bergamasca deserves star billing in Viceversa's strong ensemble cast of pastas. It is a ravioli filled with chopped veal, crushed amaretti, raisins and Parmesan, then topped with butter, crisped sage leaves and fried pancetta — a salty, herbal sauce that offsets the sweetness of the stuffing. For flavorful simplicity, it would be hard to top the tender slices of beef loin, coated in a rich, vibrant sauce of balsamic vinegar and shallots.

Wine list: A limited, uninspiring, mostly Italian list, with nine wines by the glass. **Price range:** Lunch, apps., $6–$12; entrees, $13–$19; desserts, $5; three-course prix-fixe, $20. Dinner, apps., $8–$13; entrees, $17–$23; desserts, $6. **Wheelchair access:** Steps to entrance. **Features:** Outdoor dining (garden).

Victor's Cafe 52 $$$ CUBAN

236 W. 52nd St. (bet. Broadway & Eighth Ave.)   (212) 586-7714
Credit cards: All major   Meals: L, D, LN

Asia de Cuba does a better job of capturing the halcyon glamour of Havana in the 1950's, but this old theater district standby treats the food of Cuba with more respect. If you want to taste ropa vieja (literally "old clothes," but it's a meat stew) in an upscale atmosphere, this is a good place to do it.

Price range: Lunch entrees, $9–$19. Dinner: apps., $7–$22; entrees, $12–$30; desserts, $5–$8. **Wheelchair access:** Not accessible.

Villa Berulia $$ ITALIAN

107 E. 34th St. (bet. Lexington & Park Aves.)   (212) 689-1970
Credit cards: All major   Meals: L, D   Closed Sun.

A pleasant, unassuming neighborhood Italian restaurant in a neighborhood with very few restaurants. The ceilings look like cottage cheese, the wine list is not memorable and the menu is filled with dishes you have seen before. But the welcome is warm, and if you're looking for someplace to eat on East 34th Street, this will do.

Price range: Apps., $6–$10; entrees, $14–$27; desserts, $6. **Wheelchair access:** Fully accessible.

Village   ☆ $$ BISTRO/FRENCH

62 W. 9th St. (at Fifth Ave.)   (212) 505-3355
Credit cards: All major   Meals: D, LN

Village is simple and sleek. The plain red canvas awning out front strikes the right note; inside it is cool and soothing, with wood floors, maroon leather upholstery and hanging lights that look like grooved melons. A long bar in solid mahogany dominates the front room, which is lined with cozy booths. The main dining room, with tables and banquettes, gets a sense of air and light from an enormous domed skylight.

The food is good, not great. But every once in a while, pure inspiration flickers and you get a glimpse of the superbistro that Village might have been, or might yet become. For the most part, the chef sticks to bistro and café classics, like herring with cucumber and potato salad. Both steak au poivre and steak with béarnaise sauce are correct, as the French say. The star dessert is an ice cream sundae stuffed with miniature brownies and cherries and buried under a thick chocolate sauce.

Wine list: A modest and modestly priced bistro list of 36 French and American wines, with seven wines by the glass or carafe. **Price range:** Apps., $5–$11; entrees, $17–$23; desserts, $5–$8; prix-fixe, $25. Café menu: most dishes under $10. **Wheelchair access:** Steps to entrance; restrooms upstairs.

Villa Mosconi $$ ITALIAN

69 Macdougal St. (bet. Bleecker & Houston Sts.) (212) 673-0390
Credit cards: All major   Meals: L, D   Closed Sunday

A good old red-sauce restaurant that has been in the Village for
years. If you're longing for a taste of old-time Italian-American cuisine, you could do worse than this pleasant restaurant with its
pleasant garden.

Price range: Apps., $7–$13; entrees, $10–$22; desserts, $3–$6.
Wheelchair access: Fully accessible.

Vince & Eddie's $$ AMERICAN

70 W. 68th St. (bet. Columbus Ave. & Central Park W.)
(212) 721-0068
Credit cards: All major   Meals: Br, L, D

Never great, never terrible. Fairly standard American food in a
fairly standard rustic setting. The small garden is attractive, and
it's a fine place for a bite after a concert at Lincoln Center.

Price range: Apps., $7–$11; entrees, $16–$22; desserts, $7. **Wheel-
chair access:** Fully accessible. **Features:** Outdoor dining.

Vine ☆ $$$ NEW AMERICAN

25 Broad St. (at Exchange Pl.)   (212) 344-8463
Credit cards: All major   Meals: L, D   Closed Sun.

Vine is pleasant, airy and woody, with views of the New York Stock
Exchange out the tall front windows. The food is quite decent, in a
middle-of-the-road, easy-listening sort of way. The food plows fairly
familiar ground, usually described as new American with international accents. But when it's good, it's very good.

One entree is a real eyeful: slices of sashimi-grade tuna, served
rare, and surrounded by tall, sculptured obelisks of roasted parsnip
and carrot, with paintlike spatterings of beet sauce, a carrot-ginger
reduction and parsley water. It's a party on a plate — fun to look at,
but ordinary to eat. On the dessert menu, the chocolate soufflé,
adrift in a flood of chocolate soup, is serenely voluptuous. Top honors, however, go to the peanut butter mousse, balanced on a raft of
caramelized bananas soaked in buttered rum. The dessert is almost
too darling to eat.

Wine list: A fairly predictable list of about 150 mostly French and
American wines, with 16 wines by the glass. **Price range:** Lunch
entrees, $19–$28. Dinner: apps., $9–$16; entrees, $23–$29; desserts
$10. **Wheelchair access:** Enter through Vine Market next door.

Virgil's Real BBQ $25 & Under BARBECUE

152 W. 44th St. (bet. Broadway & Sixth Ave.)   (212) 921-9494
Credit cards: All major   Meals: L, D, LN

With its framed photographs of restaurants, cattle and pigs, aprons
and other artifacts covering the walls, Virgil's is a wildly popular
shrine to barbecue joints around the country. If the food isn't quite
authentic, the formula comes close enough and it works. And the
place smells great, as any barbecue place should. Highlights on the

menu include hush puppies served with a maple syrup butter; smoked Texas links with mustard slaw; crab cakes; barbecued shrimp and Texas red chili with corn bread. For main fare, big barbecue platters carry enticing selections of Owensboro lamb, Maryland ham, Carolina pork shoulder, Texas beef brisket and more.

Price range: Apps., $5–$9; entrees, $11–$19; desserts, $5–$6. **Wheelchair access:** Fully accessible.

Vong $$$$

THAI/FRENCH
200 E. 54th St. (at Third Ave.)   (212) 486-9592
Credit cards: All major   Meals: L, D

Jean-Georges Vongerichten does Thai in this sensuous spot. If the food is not quite up to the standard of his other restaurants (Jo Jo and Jean Georges), it is still extremely satisfying. The food combines Thai ingredients with mostly French techniques, and it is very good. So are the desserts, especially the white pepper ice cream. After more than a decade in business, Vong has every right to slow down, but a recent visit suggested that it's rolling right along at a good clip, with crisp service and fusion food that still feels fresh and exciting. The only place in town for roasted sweetbreads on licorice satay.

Price range: Prix-fixe lunch, $28. Dinner: apps., $12–$25; entrees, $20–$36; desserts, $8–$10; pre-theater prix fixe, $38; six-course tasting menu, $68 per person (whole table must order). **Wheelchair access:** Fully accessible. **Features:** Outdoor dining.

Voyage   ☆ $$$

BISTRO
117 Perry St. (near Greenwich St.)   (212) 255-9191
Credit cards: All major   Meals: D

The menu at Voyage is a culinary tour that wanders from Africa to South America to the American South. It offers global down-home cooking, in which A-list ingredients are combined with more marginal ones. Truffled scallops, almost ludicrously classy in Voyage's simple surroundings, find themselves face to face with creamy grits and red-eye gravy, a high-low match-up that works brilliantly. Some of Voyage's less successful creations qualify as highfalutin diner food. Bourbon glazed squab with dirty rice sounds appealing, but bourbon glaze, it turns out, does not marry all that well with squab. Like many other downtown restaurants, Voyage has not quite decided whether it's a lounge or not. The service, as a result, can be casual to a fault.

Other recommended dishes: Fried oysters, spoon bread with shrimp and crayfish ragout, pork tenderloin with ham-hock-stuffed plantains, oxtail croquettes, cappuccino tapioca. **Wine list:** A small, modestly priced international list. **Price range:** Apps., $6–$14; entrees, $14–$28; desserts, $7. **Wheelchair access:** All one level.

Vox   ☆ $$

BISTRO/PAN-LATIN

165 Eighth Ave. (bet. 17th & 18th Sts.)   (646) 486-3188
Credit cards: All major   Meals: L, D

At Vox (short for "vox populi"), the voice of the people has appar-
ently cried out for a modern-feeling bistro with Asian and nonclas-
sical Latin accents. If Vox has a signature, it is probably "paella
(646)." The numerals refer to Vox's area code, which is Manhattan's newest and therefore appropriate for this jazzed-up Spanish
classic. It's a garlicky, assertive paella. For dessert, Mexican chocolate soufflé cake has the off-sweet quality that moves chocolate into
the adult-dessert category. And the banana-peanut financier seems
more like an ethereal muffin, but among muffins, it is a god.

Vox seems to get a more diverse crowd than many other Chelsea
restaurants. Gay diners feel welcome enough to be affectionate with
each other, and elderly diners can be spotted here and there, at ease
even though their shoes do not have four-inch soles.

Wine list: An eclectic, even scrambled, 42-bottle list, with most
wines under $40. **Price range:** Apps., $6–$12; entrees, $18–$23;
desserts, $5–$7. **Wheelchair access:** Restrooms are downstairs.

Walker's $

BAR SNACKS

16 N. Moore St. (at Varick St.)   (212) 941-0142
Credit cards: All major   Meals: Br, L, D, LN

This handsome old bar draws a legion of regulars and temporary
regulars (jurors, that is) for a menu of burgers, salads and other
simple dishes. The atmosphere is thick with history.

Price range: Apps., $3–$8; entrees, $9–$15; desserts, $5–$6.
Wheelchair access: Fully accessible. **Features:** Outdoor dining.

Wallsé   ☆ ☆ $$$

AUSTRIAN

344 W. 11th St. (at Washington St.)   (212) 352-2300
Credit cards: All major   Meals: D, LN

The name comes from Wallsee, chef and owner Kurt Gutenbrun-
ner's hometown. The décor is chaste, with white walls, black banquettes and black chairs that have a jolt of unexpected color on
their neon-yellow and red seats. The menu and the wine list seem
perfectly suited to what is, in effect, a glorified neighborhood
restaurant. The rather short list of dishes is relatively simple, but
within the chef's self-imposed limits, he achieves splendid results.
A light touch with horseradish cream makes a salad of smoked
trout and eel a highlight on the menu. Again and again, Mr. Guten-
brunner hits on a happy idea that elevates his down-home Austrian
sources. The result is a highly personal style that qualifies as high
bistro. Wiener schnitzel at Wallsé is nothing more than Wiener
schnitzel, but it comes with butter-coated, waxy-textured parsley
potatoes. The best dessert is the quark dumplings. The combination
of quark and flour translates into a feather-light sphere, not too
sweet, that melts on the tongue like manna.

New York never knew it needed Austrian cooking. Now it may
not be able to live without it.

Wine list: An imaginative, well-chosen list of 55 mostly Austrian and French wines, with nine wines by the glass. **Price range:** Apps., $8–$16; entrees, $19–$25; desserts, $8. **Wheelchair access:** Sstep to dining room; restrooms downstairs.

Washington Park ☆ ☆ $$$ NEW AMERICAN
24 Fifth Ave. (at 9th St.)   (212) 529-4400
Credit cards: All major   Meals: D

Washington Park, with its pale lemon walls, straw-seat bistro chairs and waiters in Thomas Pink checked shirts, takes its casualness very seriously. In California, casual is not just the opposite of formal. It's a rigorous style code. It demands commitment, and when it's done right, as it is at Washington Park, it can effortlessly split the difference between a cafe and a top-flight French dining room.

The sunny, airy surroundings seem perfectly suited to the simple market-inspired cooking chef Jonathan Waxman serves. The seasons and the Greenmarket dictate his menu, which changes almost nightly. Mr. Waxman, who gained fame in the mid-1980's at Jams, has kept a couple of his signature dishes on the menu, first and most celebrated, his chicken with french fries, a dish whose fame is mystifying. Generally speaking, Mr. Waxman has chosen to work in a spare style. When things click, they achieve the small-scale perfection that can make minor art seem more satisfying than major art. When the equation doesn't quite work out, the food can seem unremarkable. The dessert menu changes frequently. The traditional strawberry shortcake delivers as promised. But brioche pudding with lemon curd and blueberries sails right off the charts.

Wine list: A well-chosen bistro list of about 75 international wines, with 20 by the glass. There is also a serious 1,000-bottle reserve list. **Price range:** Apps., $12–$16; entrees, $24–$32; desserts, $9 $11; five-course tasting menu, $59. **Wheelchair access:** Enter on 9th St.

Water Club ☆ ☆ $$$$ NEW AMERICAN
500 E. 30th St. (at the East River)   (212) 683-3333
Credit cards: All major   Meals: Br, L, D

Compared with the views from River Café and Water's Edge in Queens, the East River view from the Water Club lacks drama. Nonetheless, it's a wonderful feeling to sit close to the water, even in the Water Club's somewhat stodgy yacht club atmosphere. The food, unfortunately, doesn't live up to expectations. Classics like Dover sole and prime sirloin simply do not shine through, while more complicated preparations like coriander-scented tuna with sautéed watercress seem like trendy hodgepodges. Straightforward desserts like strawberry shortcake are worth waiting for. *(Ruth Reichl, updated by Eric Asimov)*

Wine list: The mostly French and American selection is fairly priced. **Price range:** Lunch: apps., $8–$13; entrees, $16–$22; desserts, $7; prix fixe, $20 or $28. Dinner: apps., $9–$15; entrees, $26–$35; desserts, $7; prix fixe, $38. **Wheelchair access:** There is a ramp to enter the restaurant and an accessible restroom on the main floor. **Features:** Good view, outdoor dining.

WD-50 ☆☆ $$$ NEW AMERICAN

50 Clinton St. (Rivington St.) (212) 477-2900
Credit cards: All major   Meals: D   Closed Sun.

At WD-50, Wylie Dufresne seems to have decided that the simple, elegant style that seduced diners and critics at his first restaurant, 71 Clinton Fresh Food, was too easy to like. This time, he challenges his customers, provoking them with risky flavor combinations and ingredients in unfamiliar roles. Mr. Dufresne, one of the most distinctive culinary talents in New York, takes risks at WD-50. He has a restless artistic temperament, and a total lack of fear. Opinions will split right down the middle about his latest project, but not about him. It would be nice to see a little more pleasure and a little less intellect at WD-50, but in the end, Mr. Dufresne should listen to his muse and ignore everyone else.

Mr. Dufresne's new digs, carved out of what used to be a bodega, isn't particularly comfortable or attractive. The view on the plate is much more appealing. Two appetizers stand out from the pack, visually and conceptually: Stellar Bay oysters puréed and flattened into a thin sheet that looks like a slice of polished marble with a scattering of dried olives and tiny diced Granny Smith apple; and WD-50's famous terrine, a neat rectangle of firm, creamy chilled foie gras topped with anchovy fillets, like some satanic pastry. A smooth, insinuating cauliflower-almond purée, spread on the plate in a thin layer, makes a creamy off-sweet frosting for sea bass. For dessert try the absolutely brilliant parsnip cake, a sly reinterpretation of carrot cake.

Other recommended dishes: Squid "linguine," pork belly with black soybeans and turnips, cherry clafoutis. **Wine list:** A carefully chosen international selection of about 50 wines, with 25 sold by the glass. **Price range:** Apps., $12–$16; entrees, $22–$28; desserts, $10. Wheelchair access: One flight down to restrooms.

'Wichcraft $25 & Under SANDWICHES

49 E. 19th St. (bet. Broadway & Park Ave. S.) (212) 780-0577
Credit cards: All major   Meals: B, L (to 7 P.M.)   Closed Sun.

When 'Wichcraft opened in mid-May, it was immediately the hottest sandwich shop in town. Unlike Craft and Craftbar, Tom Colicchio's high-end and midrange operations, the two-level 'Wichcraft seems an exercise in entrepreneurship, unstylish except for its bewitching name. For the most part, Mr. Colicchio, who preaches the gospel of top-flight ingredients, simply handled, sticks to his philosophy. The sandwiches are careful constructions that offer just enough contrasting flavors and textures to keep things interesting, while avoiding extraneous piled-on curlicues or clichés.

Each dessert is a clear, pure example of the Colicchio philosophy at its most basic, whether a tart and tangy strawberry-rhubarb cobbler, thin peanut butter cookies sandwiching sweet peanut butter cream or a moist, racy lemon tart.

Other recommended dishes: Anchovies with egg on country bread; pork loin, coppa and fontina; tuna with fennel and black olives; pork loin with red cabbage and jalepeño; chicken with roasted red pepper, mozzarella and pesto. **Price range:** Sandwiches, $5–$9.50; desserts, $1.50–$3. **Wheelchair access:** Upstairs dining; restrooms next door at Craftbar.

Wollensky's Grill $$$ NEW AMERICAN/STEAKHOUSE

201 E. 49th St. (at Third Ave.)
Credit cards: All major

(212) 753-0444
Meals: L, D, LN

An after-work crowd, usually of beefy men, packs this free-wheeling, casual, less-expensive annex to the well-known steakhouse Smith & Wollensky. It's cramped and noisy, but you can get good steaks, of course, excellent burgers and a nice variety of wines by the glass. A few sidewalk tables are available in warm weather if you don't mind the incessant traffic.

Price range: Apps., $10–$15; entrees, $10–$30; desserts, $3–$8. **Wheelchair access:** Fully accessible.

Wondee Siam II $25 & Under THAI

813 Ninth Ave. (near 54th St.)
Credit cards: MC/V

(917) 286-1726
Meals: L, D

The evolution of Wondee Siam II is a mystery. The original Wondee Siam, a cramped place just a block south on Ninth Avenue, offers a strictly Thai menu with excellent curries and terrific salads. The new, pleasantly spacious restaurant has supplemented those Thai dishes with an unexpected host of hoary pan-Asian dishes that wouldn't be out of place in a lantern-lighted Tiki lounge, with names like two buddies (sautéed shrimp and scallops), squid in love (fried squid with green beans and chili paste), raspberry duck and jumbo shrimp on fire (shrimp literally on fire).

And yet, along with these Americanized dishes is a set of Thai standards that are as fresh and delicious as those at the old place. Green papaya salad, with peanuts for crunch, dried shrimp for pungency and lime juice for refreshment, was as spicy as the shrimp dish was not, while yum woon sen, spicy bean-thread noodles tossed with ground chicken, squid and shrimp, performed a dazzling balancing act between chili heat and citrus zing. Curry dishes don't live up to the standards of the original Wondee.

Other recommended dishes: Tom yum goong; fried tofu; basil rolls; duck salad with cashews, apples and pineapple; crisp duck with basil-chili sauce. **Price range:** Apps., $4–$10; entrees, $8–$14. **Wheelchair access:** Step at entrance.

Woo Chon $$$ KOREAN

8 W. 36th St. (bet. Fifth & Sixth Aves.)
41-19 Kissena Blvd., Flushing, Queens
Credit cards: All major

(212) 695-0676
(718) 463-0803
Meals: B, Br, L, D, LN

Two locations, each in the heart of a Koreatown, offer an all-purpose Korean menu 24 hours a day. Good kalbi (marinated short ribs) to barbecue right at the table, a fine version of the Korean seafood pancake haemul pajun, and all the kimchi you can eat.

Price range: Apps., $5–$9; entrees, $9–$22; desserts, $3–$6. **Wheelchair access:** Fully accessible.

Wu Liang Ye

$25 & Under   CHINESE

338 Lexington Ave. (bet. 39th & 40th Sts.)   (212) 370-9647
36 W. 48th St. (bet. Fifth & Sixth Aves.)   (212) 398-2308
215 E. 86th St. (bet. Second & Third Aves.)   (212) 534-8899
Credit cards: All major   Meals: L, D, LN

Though each of these branches of a Chinese restaurant chain differs slightly in menu and atmosphere, they all specialize in lively, robust Sichuan dishes, notable for their meticulous preparation. Sliced conch is one of their more unusual dishes, firm, chewy and nutty, served with spicy red oil. Four kinds of dumplings are all delicate and flavorful.

Other recommended dishes: Cold noodles with sesame sauce, soup with fish fillets and cabbage, dumplings, tea-smoked duck, double-cooked bacon with chili sauce, chef's bean curd with spicy sauce. **Price range:** $8–$20. **Wheelchair access:** Steps at entrance.

Xunta

$25 & Under   SPANISH/TAPAS

174 First Ave. (near 11th St.)   (212) 614-0620
Credit cards: All major   Meals: D, LN

Xunta (pronounced SHOON-tuh) has the authentic feeling of a Spanish tapas bar. It's informal, crowded and loud, with dozens of tapas. The selection of Spanish wines and sherries is just right.

Recommended dishes: Tortilla espanola, grilled sardines, octopus salad, pork with potatoes and peppers, little clams in a marinade of wine and garlic. **Price range:** Tapas, $3–$16. **Wheelchair access:** Steps to restrooms.

Ya Bowl

$25 & Under   JAPANESE

125 W. 45th St. (bet. Sixth & Seventh Aves.)   (212) 764-3017
Credit cards: All major   Meals: L, D, LN   Closed Sun.

This sweet little Japanese restaurant on the fringe of Times Square looks like a New York living room. The raison d'être is the bowl meals: one-pot meals in which hot food is served over rice in a bowl. Salmon teriyaki is typical, a well-cooked salmon steak brushed with sweet teriyaki sauce, which drips into the rice below. Even better is the unusual sukiyaki, the beef-and-vegetable stew which is simmered in a sweet soy sauce and served with egg over rice. Skip the mundane selection of sushi.

Other recommended dishes: Chicken cutlet, chicken cutlet curry, soba noodles, edamame, boiled spinach, gyoza, chocolate-espresso cake. **Alcohol:** Beer and wine. **Price range:** Lunch, $7–$15. Dinner: apps., $5–$10; entrees, $11–$15. **Wheelchair access:** Fully accessible. **Features:** Outdoor dining.

Yakiniku JuJu

$25 & Under   JAPANESE

157 E. 28th St. (bet. Madison & Park Aves.)   (212) 684-7830
Credit cards: All major   Meals: D

This small and friendly restaurant specializes in cook-it-yourself shabu-shabu, sukiyaki and Japanese barbecue. To get in, you descend steps to a subterranean doorway. Then you pass through a low, narrow hallway, up a spiral staircase and, finally, into a small dining room of booths, each outfitted with a gas-powered grill (and a fire extinguisher). It is a tableau that cries out for an appetizer of "salted squid guts," which arrive in a pretty little dish immersed in a pasty liquid. Another unusual appetizer is takoyaki, croquettes the size of golf balls stuffed with pieces of octopus and flavored with dried seaweed, ginger and a fruity sauce. Barely crisp on the surface, they collapse into a delicious porridge in the mouth.

Main courses are big and come with soup and salad. The choices include yakiniku, in which you cook pieces of meat and vegetables directly on the grill; shabu-shabu, in which you swish the meat and vegetables through boiling broth; and sukiyaki, the traditional Japanese stew, in which you simmer meat and vegetables in a slightly sweet soy-based sauce.

Price range: Dinner for two, $30–$46; for four, up to $80. A la carte, $10–$20. **Wheelchair access:** Stairs to the dining room.

Yang Pyung Seoul $25 & Under   KOREAN
43 W. 33rd St. (bet. Fifth Ave. & Broadway)   (212) 629-5599
Credit cards: All major   Open 24 hrs. (except Sun. after 10:30 P.M.)

With a reputation for smoothing the head and soothing the stomach — specifically for hangovers — hae jang gook is a specialty at Yang Pyung Seoul, a bright, friendly 24-hour restaurant. It is a wonderful soup. The broth is deep and flavorful, full of ultra-tender tripe and earthy house-made blood sausage. Luckily you don't need a headache to love the food at Yang Pyung. The menu offers some rarely seen North Korean dishes. One of these, kimchi with seafood, is cool, bright and refreshing. Nokdu bin dae thuk, mung bean pancakes are as savory as latkes. Jap chae, smooth stir-fried yam noodles with vegetables and beef, is almost irresistible.

Each meal ends with tiny containers of yogurt. Sweet and liquid, it tastes almost like a tropical Life Saver, and you down it like a shot of whiskey. It's a delightful finish, and best of all, no hangover.

Other recommended dishes: Bone marrow soup, beef and noodle broth, squid and vegetable stir-fry, pa jun. **Alcohol:** Beer and wine. **Price range:** $8–$30. **Wheelchair access:** All one level.

Yujin ☆ $$$ JAPANESE
24 E. 12th St. (near University Pl.)   (212) 924-4286
Credit cards: All major   Meals: L (Mon.–Fri.), D

Does Japan need truffle oil? Where you stand on the question will probably determine how much you like Yujin, a bold, fitfully successful experiment in modernizing traditional Japanese food by using French techniques and non-Asian ingredients. Yujin puts a youthful spin on Japanese cuisine without doing anything foolish. A large part of the menu is devoted to thoroughly traditional sushi and sashimi. Then comes the truffle oil.

It turns up in an entree of sautéed striped bass with shimeji mushrooms — delicious, but in the end, a little strange. The menu at Yujin lurches and wobbles. It can be inspired, ordinary or just plain wrongheaded, in a fascinating way. Yujin is serious about sushi. The selection of fish, of consistently high quality, is broad.

Yujin stakes its reputation, though, on innovative dishes. On a menu filled with surprises, pear strudel may be the biggest.

The restaurant's design, like the menu, achieves some brilliant effects before going off the rails. It's a fantasy landscape that visually complements the adventurous menu.

Other recommended dishes: Seared scallops with string beans and asparagus, seared yellowfin tuna with satsumaimo potatoes, soft-shell crab with soy butter sauce, lime sake parfait. **Wine list:** A better than average bistro list of 45 wines, with 11 by the glass, supplemented by 20 sakes. **Price range:** Lunch: three-course prix fixe, $22. Dinner: apps., $6–$14; sushi by the piece, $3–$8; entrees, $20–$29; desserts, $7–$9. **Wheelchair access:** All one level.

Zarela ☆☆ $$ MEXICAN/TEX-MEX

953 Second Ave. (bet. 50th & 51st Sts.) (212) 644-6740
Credit cards: All major Meals: L, D

As one of the first restaurants in New York to treat Mexican food as a cuisine rather than as an adjunct to frozen margaritas, Zarela will always occupy a special place in the hearts of Mexican food lovers. The question now is, as other Mexican restaurants catch up to and even overtake it, how will Zarela hold its own? After diverting her attention to some other unsuccessful restaurant projects, Zarela Martinez, the chef and owner, seems to be refocusing on her flagship. Old favorites like spicy snapper hash, Yucan pork shoulder in sour orange sauce and shrimp in smoky chipotle sauce are still enticing, and the crowded dining room can often be as noisy as a rollicking party, but Ms. Martinez will have to redouble her efforts to whip everything into shape. Guacamole that arrives too cold, as if it's been refrigerated, cannot compete with the tableside preparation at other Mexican restaurants, and too often the staff does not seem to have a good grasp of the menu. *(Review by Eric Asimov; stars previously awarded by Ruth Reichl.)*

Price range: Lunch: avg. entree, $14. Dinner: avg. app., $8; entree, $22; dessert, $8. **Wheelchair access:** Restrooms not accessible.

Zaytoons $25 & Under MIDDLE EASTERN

283 Smith St., Cobble Hill, Brooklyn (718) 875-1880
Credit cards: All major Meals: D, LN

Of the many moderately priced Middle Eastern restaurants around, few offer the combination of genial, relaxed surroundings and simple but meticulously prepared food that Zaytoons does. If you have had only the sort of hardened disks of pita bread that come in plastic bags, tasting the baked-to-order pitas at this little corner cafe may be a revelation. The soft, pillowy bread is perfect for scooping up cool salads and dips like tangy hummus; and excellent cucumber-and-yogurt salad with crumbled feta and plenty of refreshing mint. The pitas also form the basis of savory Middle Eastern pizzas and the terrific zatter bread, baked just to the brink of crispness and served glistening with olive oil and fragrant with thyme, salt and toasted sesame seeds. Kebabs are moist and succulent, while basbousa, a light semolina cake with honey and almonds, makes a pleasing dessert.

Other recommended dishes: Mujadarra, potato salad, grape leaves, shawarma, mint iced tea. **Price range:** Apps., $3–$6; entrees, $5–$9. **Wheelchair access:** One step at entrance.

Zen Palate $$ ASIAN/VEGETARIAN
663 Ninth Ave. (at 46th St.) (212) 582-1669
34 Union Sq. E. (at 16th St.) (212) 614-9291
2170 Broadway (bet. 76th & 77th Sts.) (212) 501-7768
Credit cards: All major Meals: L, D

Who would have expected a restaurant serving the austere food of Buddhist monks to be so successful? There are now three Zen Palates, each architecturally serene and beautiful, each offering dishes like "Jewel of Happiness" (mini-mushroom steaks with endive) and "Beauty Quest" (sautéed wheat gluten). If you like meatless Asian cuisine, this is for you.

Price range: Apps., $6–$7; entrees, $9–$10; desserts, $4. **Wheelchair access:** Fully accessible.

Zerza $25 & Under MOROCCAN
304 E. 6th St. (near Second Ave.) (212) 529-8250
Credit cards: All major Meals: L, D, LN

At Zerza, the menu and the décor are distinctively Moroccan. As you enter — up steps strewn with rose petals to the dining room decorated with punctured-brass hanging lanterns — you feel as if you've crossed a border. The North African pop music in the background, the little dishes of olives and the list of Moroccan and Algerian wines certainly convey a sense of a different place. Zerza's strongest dishes are among the mezze, or small plates. Harira, an earthy vegetable soup, is superb. The best main courses are the tagines, stews served in earthenware pots, but they can sometimes be painfully cloying. Couscous, was disappointingly dry. A meal would not be complete without intensely sweet mint tea. It's the final, distinctively Moroccan touch.

Other recommended dishes: Roasted peppers, roasted eggplant, merguez, briouats, pissaladière, maakuda, duck tagine, chicken tagine, seafood bastilla. **Price range:** Apps., $3.25–$8.95; entrees, $9.95–$15.95. **Wheelchair access:** Not accessible.

Zipangu ☆ $$$ JAPANESE
71 University Pl. (bet. 10th & 11th Sts.) (212) 673-0634
Credit cards: All major Meals: D Closed Sun.

This is an idiosyncratic, even eccentric, modern Japanese restaurant. It has an otherworldly ring to it that suits the restaurant, which has a bar on the street level and two weirdly decorated dining rooms down a steep, narrow flight of stairs. The menu also straddles at least two styles. It is bold, inventive and, in some cases, quite strange. It demands attention, and it gets it with a startling appetizer, monkfish liver worked into a kind of dense custard with tofu, then pressed into a martini glass. The chef has a light touch, lightened even further in a section of the menu devoted to spa dishes. These include salmon tartare with crunchy red dots of tobiko, wasabi and a cool note provided by purée of green apples. Wasabi adds Japanese heat to a light guacamole sauce, a simple and ingenious dressing for shrimp and squid. The rib-eye steak, fork-tender, is outfitted in a robe of onion purée.

Japanese cuisine barely recognizes the idea of dessert. But Zipangu does. There's the expected, a small cake of sweet bean ice cream wrapped in a chewy casing of mochi rice, and the unexpected, a bracing, ice-cold gelée of ruby red grapefruit and cranberry with a swirl of brandy cream sauce. Coffee is made at the table in what looks like a giant beaker and test tube.

Wine list: A minimal list, with a good selection of sakes by the glass and bottle. **Price range:** Apps., $7–$13; entrees, $14–$22; desserts, $4–$8; five-course tasting menu, $40; six-course tasting menu, $50. **Wheelchair access:** Not accessible.

Zito's East $25 & Under PIZZA
211 First Ave. (bet. 12th & 13th Sts.) (212) 473-3400
Credit cards: All major Meals: Br, L, D

Bread-making, not pizza-making, is the tradition at this pizzeria. In the back of the long, narrow dining room are twin brick coal-fired ovens, which produce superb pizzas with smooth, flawless crusts. Sausage is excellent, and the mozzarella is freshly made, outshining the rather ordinary tomato sauce.

Alcohol: Beer and wine. **Price range:** Apps., $4–$7; large pizza, $11 and up; entrees, $5–$15; desserts, $3–$4. **Wheelchair access:** Fully accessible.

Zitoune ☆ $$ MOROCCAN
46 Gansevoort St. (at Greenwich St.) (212) 675-5224
Credit cards: All major Meals: L, D

Zitoune, which is Arabic for olive, is a lively bistro serving updated Moroccan cuisine. The chef may be English, but you'd never guess from the subtle touch he brings to traditional Moroccan tagines, briks, briwats and bsteeyas. He orchestrates his spices deftly, and he modernizes with quiet good taste.

The lamb carpaccio, for example, a Moroccan-inflected innovation, is an attractively presented plate of small, leaf-thin circles of meat lightly seasoned with raz al hanout. Crab briwats, tubes of flaky phyllo stuffed with a creamy, lemony mixture of crab and mung bean vermicelli, come with a thick, concentrated puddle of tomato chutney and spiced orange dressing. The phyllo casing is ethereal. Lamb tagine, one of those dishes that simply must be done right at a restaurant like this, is excellent, complexly spiced and cooked nearly to the melting point.

Zitoune's best dessert, a made-to-order bsteeya packed with dried fruit and nuts that's worth the extra 20 minutes it requires.

Wine list: A modest and modestly priced bistro list with about 50 wines, mostly French and American. **Price range:** Lunch: apps., $5–$8; entrees, $8–$13. Dinner: apps., $6–$10; entrees, $16–$20.50; desserts, $6.50. **Wheelchair access:** One level.

Zócalo ☆ $$$ MEXICAN

174 E. 82nd St. (bet Third & Lexington Aves.) (212) 717-7772
Credit cards: All major Meals: D

Most of the action at Zócalo is at the colorful, convivial bar in the
front of the restaurant. But in a rear sky-lighted room filled with
colorful folk art, it is possible to enjoy Mexican food that is often
interesting, though rarely challenging or unusual, in relative tranquillity. Though the chef, Ivy Stark, has left, it remains a popular
neighborhood destination. Her best dishes included the flautas de
carnitas, slender flutes filled with smoky chunks of pork, or the
huge portion of sautéed squid with cubes of chorizo and piquillo
peppers. Familiar dishes are well rendered, like chunky guacamole
and chicken quesadillas and enchiladas. Good entrees include
chicken en mole negro, mahi-mahi tacos and pork ribs with barbecue sauce wrapped in banana leaves. *(Eric Asimov)*

Other recommended dishes: Plantain empanadas, hanger steak,
seared tuna. **Wine list:** Small but well chosen; the tequila selection
is extensive. **Price range:** Apps., $7.50–$10; entrees, $17.50–$24;
desserts, $6.50. **Wheelchair access:** Two steps at entrance.

Zum Schneider $25 & Under GERMAN

107 Ave. C (at 7th St.) (212) 598-1098
Credit cards: Cash only Meals: L, D

Essentially an indoor beer garden, Zum Schneider sets no new culinary standards; the simple menu hews closely to the Bavarian formula of wurst, pork and cabbage. But it has accomplished the
unlikely feat of making a German place cool. With its cement floor,
lively bar, timbered walls and ceiling, and hip-hop playing in the
background, it's easy to imagine Zum Schneider in an equally hip
neighborhood in Munich. Tables (with benches) are occupied family style, and while food is delivered to the table, you generally
must order at the bar. The bar offers a dozen excellent seasonal
draft beers, all German, and 10 more in bottles. Zum takes great
care to serve each beer in the correct glassware.

Other recommended dishes: Schneider gröstl, pancake soup,
smoked pork chop, three sausage platter. **Price range:** $7–$12.
Wheelchair access: All one level.

Zuni $25 & Under SOUTHWESTERN

598 Ninth Ave. (at 43rd St.) (212) 765-7626
Credit cards: All major Meals: Br, L, D, LN

The original focus at this appealing little restaurant was Southwestern, and the atmosphere still reflects this, but the current menu is
all over the map, with Southwestern dishes like chili-rubbed rib-eye
steak, New Orleans specialties like jambalaya and geographically
indecipherable offerings like sesame-crusted salmon with mango-
and-black-bean salsa and basmati rice. If it's too confusing, settle
for meatloaf and garlic mashed potatoes. It's all pretty good.

Price range: Apps., $7; entrees, $8–$15; desserts, $6. **Wheelchair
access:** Step to dining room; restroom downstairs.

A Guide to Restaurants by Neighborhood

THE WEST SIDE

West 100's

		On/Near
Amy Ruth's	Southern	116 St/Lenox Av
Bayou	Cajun/Southern	Lenox Av/125 St
Charles' Southern-Style	*Southern*	*F. Douglass/151 St*
Copeland's	Southern	145 St/Amstdm
Carne	Steakhouse	Bway/105 St
Dalia's	Tapas	Amstdm/109 St
El Presidente	Caribbean	Bway/164 St
Max SoHa	Italian/American	Amstdm/123 St
Metisse	Bistro/French	105 St/Amstdm
Mill Korean	Korean	Bway/112 St
Miss Maude's Spoonbread	Southern	Lenox Av/137th St
Noche Mexicana	Mexican	Amstdm/102 St
Pan Pan	Southern	Lenox/Malcolm X
Republi'K	Pan-Latin	Dyckman/Nagle
Royal Kebab	Indian	Bway/103 St
Sal's and Carmine's	Pizza	Bway/101 St
Sylvia's	Southern	Lenox Av/126 St
Turkuaz	*Turkish/Middle Eastern*	*Bway/100 St*

West 90's

		On/Near
Alouette	Bistro/French	Bway/97 St
Café Con Leche	Latin American	Amstdm/95 St
Carmine's	Italian	Bway/90 St
Cooke's Corner	*European/American*	*Amstdm/90 St*
Gabriela's	Mexican	Amstdm/93 St
Gennaro	Italian	Amstdm/93 St
Pampa	Latin American	Amstdm/97 St

West 80's

		On/Near
Aix ☆☆	French	Bway/88 St
Artie's New York Deli	Deli	Bway/82 St
Avenue	Bistro/French	Columbus/85 St
Barney Greengrass	Deli	Amstdm/86 St
Café Con Leche	Latin American	Amstdm/80 St
Cafe La Grolla	Italian	Amstdm/80 St
Calle Ocho ☆	Pan-Latin	Columbus/81 St
Celeste	*Pizza/Italian*	*Amstdm/85 St*
Dock's Oyster Bar ☆	Seafood	Bway/89 St
E J's Luncheonette	Diner	Amstdm/81 St
Fred's	New American	Amstdm/83 St
Isola	Italian	Columbus/83 Stt
Jean-Luc ☆	Bistro/French	Columbus/84 St
La Grolla ☆	Italian	Amstdm/80 St
Luzia's	Portuguese	Amstdm/80 St
Ouest	New American/Bistro	Bway/84 St
Rain	Pan Asian	82 St/Columbus
Sabor	Tapas/Pan-Latin	Amstdm/82 St
Saigon Grill	Vietnamese	Bway/87 St
Sarabeth's	New American	Amstdm/80 St
Time Cafe	New American	Bway/85 St

West 70's

		On/Near
Alice's Tea Cup	American	73 St/Columbus
Café Frida	Mexican	Columbus/77 St
Cafe Luxembourg	Bistro	70 St/Amstdm

Note: Restaurants in **boldface italics** are Eric Asimov's choices for the best inexpensive restaurants in New York

West 70's *(continued)*

		On/Near
China Fun	Chinese	Columbus/71 St
Compass ☆☆	New American	70 St/Amstdm
Diwan's Curry House	Indian	Columbus/74 St
Josie's	New American	Amstdm/74 St
Metsovo	Greek	70 St/Columbus
Mughlai	Indian	Columbus/71 St
Nice Matin ☆☆	French	79 St/Amstdm
Ocean Grill ☆	Seafood	Columbus/78 St
Patsy's	Pizza	74 St/Columbus
Penang	Malaysian	Columbus/71 St
Ruby Foo's ☆☆	Pan-Asian	Bway/77 St
Thias	Greek/Seafood	77 St/Columbus
Zen Palate	Vegetarian	Bway/76 St

LINCOLN CENTER
West 60's

		On/Near
Café des Artistes	Continental	67 St/Cntrl Pk W
Gabriel's ☆☆	Italian	60 St/Bway
Jean Georges ☆☆☆☆	New American	Cntrl Pk W/60 St
John's	Italian/Pizza	65 St/Bway
Levana	Kosher/American	69 St/Columbus
Nick and Toni's ☆☆	Mediterranean	67 St/Bway
Picholine ☆☆☆	Mediterranean/French	64 St/Bway
Rosa Mexicano	Mexican	Columbus/62 St
Sapphire	Indian	Bway/63 St
Shun Lee West	Chinese	65 St/Columbus
Tavern on the Green ☆	New American	Cntrl Pk W/67 St
Vince & Eddie's	New American	68 St/Columbus

THEATER DISTRICT — WEST 50's
West 55th–59th

		On/Near
Alain Ducasse ☆☆☆☆	French	58 St/6 Av
Atelier ☆☆☆	French	Cntrl Pk S/6 Av
Brasserie 8 $^1/_2$ ☆	Brasserie/French	57 St/5 Av
Bricco Ristorante	Italian	56 St/8 Av
Carnegie Deli	Deli	7 Av/55 St
Estiatorio Milos ☆☆	Greek/Seafood	55 St/6 Av
Joe's Shanghai ☆☆	Chinese	56 St/5 Av
La Caravelle ☆☆☆	French	55 St/6 Av
La Côte Basque ☆☆☆	French	55 St/6 Av
La Vineria	Italian	55 St/5 Av
Manhattan Ocean Club ☆☆	Seafood	58 St/6 Av
Menchanko-Tei	Japanese	55 St/6 Av
Michael's ☆☆	New American	55 St/5 Av
Mickey Mantle's	American	Cntrl Pk S/6 Av
Molyvos ☆☆	Greek	7 Av/55 St
Patsy's	Italian	56 St/Bway
Petrossian ☆☆	Russian	58 St/7 Av
Puttanesca	Italian	9 Av/56 St
Redeye Grill ☆	New American	7 Av/56 St
San Domenico ☆☆	Italian	Cntrl Pk S/Bway
Taprobane	Sri Lankan	56 St/8 Av
Topaz Thai	Thai	56 St/6 Av
Town ☆☆☆	New American	56 St/6 Av

West 50th–54th

		On/Near
Aquavit ☆☆☆	Scandinavian	54 St/6 Av
Ben Benson's ☆	Steakhouse	52 St/6 Av
China Fun	Chinese	Bway/51 St
Cité	Steakhouse	51 St/6 Av
Gallagher's	Steakhouse	52 St/Bway

Hallo Berlin	German	51 St/9 Av
Il Gattopardo ☆☆	Italian	54 St/5 Av
Island Burgers	Hamburgers	9 Av/51 St
Judson Grill ☆☆☆	New American	52 St/6 Av
Kabul Cafe	Afghani	54 St/8 Av
La Locanda	Italian	9 Av/50 St
Le Bernardin ☆☆☆☆	French/Seafood	51 St/6 Av
Moda ☆☆	Italian	52 St/6 Av
Old San Juan	Puerto Rican	9 Av/51 St
Osteria del Circo ☆	Italian	55 St/6 Av
Remi ☆☆	Italian	53 St/6 Av
René Pujol	French	51 St/8 Av
Rice 'n' Beans	Brazilian	9 Av/50 St
Rinconcito Peruano	Peruvian	9 Av/53 St
Ruth's Chris	Steakhouse	51 St/6 Av
Stage Deli	Deli	7 Av/53 St
Tout Va Bien	French	51 St/8 Av
Trionfo	Italian	51 St/8 Av
Tuscan Square	Italian	51 St/6 Av
"21" Club ☆☆	New American	52 St/6 Av
Uncle Nick's	Greek	9 Av/50 St
Upstairs at "21" ☆☆	New American	52 St/5 Av
Viceversa ☆	Italian	51 St/8 Av
Victor's Cafe 52	Latin American	52 St/Bway
Wondee Siam II	Thai	9 Av/54 St

THEATER DISTRICT — WEST 40's

West 45th–49th   On/Near

Amarone	Italian	9 Av/47 St
Baldoria ☆	Italian	49 St/7 Av
Bali Nusa Indah	Indonesian	9 Av/45 St
Barbetta	Italian	46 St/8 Av
Becco	Italian	46 St/8 Av
Blue Fin ☆☆	Seafood	Bway/47 St
Churrascaria Plataforma ☆☆	Brazilian	49 St/8 Av
Citarella the Restaurant ☆☆	Seafood/Fusion	6 Av/49 St
District ☆	New American	46 St/6 Av
Edison Cafe	Diner	47 St/Bway
Firebird ☆☆	Russian	46 St/8 Av
Hell's Kitchen	Mexican	9 Av/47 St
Ipanema	Latin American	46 St/6 Av
Jack Rose	New American/Steak	8 Av/47 St
Joe Allen	New American	46 St/8 Av
Luxia	Italian	48 St/8 Av
Meskerem	African	47 St/9 Av
Morrell Wine Bar & Cafe	New American	Rockefeller Plz
Noche ☆	Latin American	Bway/49 St
Orso	Italian	46 St/8 Av
Pam Real Thai Food	*Thai*	*49 St/9 Av*
Queen of Sheba	Ethiopian	10 Av/46 St
Rainbow Grill	Italian	Rockefeller Plz
Sea Grill ☆☆	Seafood	Rockefeller Plz
Shaan Of India	Indian	48 St/6 Av
Sushiden	Japanese/Sushi	49 St/6 Av
Sushi Zen	Japanese/Sushi	46 St/6 Av
Wu Liang Ye	*Chinese*	*48 St/6 Av*
Ya Bowl	Japanese	45 St/6 Av
Zen Palate	Vegetarian	9 Av/46 St

West 40th–44th   On/Near

Algonquin	American	44 St/6 Av
Carmine's	Italian	44 St/7 Av
Caribbean Spice	Caribbean	44 St/9 Av

Note: Restaurants in ***boldface italics*** are Eric Asimov's choices for the best inexpensive restaurants in New York

West 40th–44th *(continued)* {On/Near}

		On/Near
Chez Josephine ☆☆	Bistro/French	42 St/9 Av
Chimichurri Grill	Latin American	9 Av/43 St
Esca ☆☆	Italian/Seafood	43 St/9 Av
Hallo Berlin	German	10 Av/44 St
Ilo ☆☆☆	New American	40 St/5 Av
John's Pizzeria	Italian/Pizza	44 St/7 Av
Lakruwana	Sri Lankan	44 St/8 Av
Le Madeleine	French	43 St/9 Av
Marseille ☆☆	Mediterranean/French	9 Av/44 St
Soul Cafe	Southern	42 St/9 Av
Tagine	Moroccan	9 Av/40 St
Triomphe ☆☆	French/New American	44 St/6 Av
Virgil's Real BBQ	Barbecue	44 St/Bway
Zuni	Southwestern	9 Av/43 St

GARMENT CENTER / MADISON SQ. GARDEN
West 30's

		On/Near
Cho Dang Gol ☆☆	Korean	35 St/6 Av
Djerdan Burek	Balkan	38 St/7 Av
Han Bat	Korean	35 St/6 Av
Havana NY	Latin American/Cuban	36 St/5 Av
Ida Mae Kitchen ☆	New American/Southern	38 St/Bway
Keens	Steakhouse	36 St/6 Av
Larry Forgione's	New American	5 Av/39 St
Los Dos Rancheros	Mexican	9 Av/38 St
Mandoo Bar	Korean	32 St/5 Av
New York Kom Tang Kalbi	Korean	32 St./5 Av
Rinconcito Mexicano	Peruvian	39 St/8 Av
Soul Fixins'	Southern	34 St/8 Av
Supreme Macaroni Co.	Italian	9 Av/38 St
Svenningsen's	Seafood	5 Av/30 St
38th Street Restaurant	Chinese	38 St/7 Av
36 Bar and Barbecue ☆	Korean	36 St/5 Av
Tupelo Grill	Steakhouse	33 St/7 Av
Woo Chon	Korean	36 St/6 Av
Yang Pyung Seoul	*Korean*	*33 St/5 Av*

CHELSEA & ENVIRONS
West 20's

		On/Near
Arezzo ☆	Italian	22 St/5 Av
The Basil ☆	Thai	23 St/7 Av
Biricchino	Italian	29 St/8 Av
Bongo	Seafood	10 Av/28 St
Bottino	Italian	10 Av/24 St
Bright Food Shop	New American	8 Av/21 St
Cabo Rojo	Puerto Rican	10 Av/25 St
Cal's	Continental	21 St/6 Av
Chelsea Bistro & Bar ☆☆	Bistro/French	23 St/8 Av
Empire Diner	Diner	10 Av/22 St
Gus's Figs	Mediterranean	27 St/7 Av
F&B	Hot Dogs/Sausage	23 St/7 Av
Fresco Tortilla	Mexican/Tex-Mex	8 Av/22 St
Fresco Tortilla	Mexican/Tex-Mex	6 Av/25 St
Grand Sichuan	*Chinese*	*9 Av/24 St*
The Half King	Pub/American	23 St/10 Av
Le Gamin	French	9 Av/21 St
Le Zie 2000	*Italian*	*7 Av/20 St*
Lola	New American	22 St/5 Av
Lot 61	New American	21 St/10 Av
O Mai	*Vietnamese*	*9 Av/20 St*
Parish & Company ☆	New American	9 Av/22 St

The Red Cat ☆	New American	10 Av/23 St
Royal Siam	Thai	8 Av/22 St
Shaffer City Oyster Bar	Seafood	21 St/6 Av
Trailer Park	American	23 St/7 Av

West 14th–19th   On/Near

Amuse ☆☆	New American	87 St/6 Av
AZ ☆☆☆	Fusion	17 St/5 Av
Blue Water Grill ☆	Seafood	Union Sq W/16 St
Cafe Riazor	Spanish	16 St/7 Av
Coffee Shop	Diner	Union Sq W/16 St
El Cid	Spanish	15 St/8 Av
Frank's ☆	Steakhouse	10 Av/15 St
Fresco Tortilla Grill	Mexican/Tex-Mex	14 St/7 Av
Green Table	New American	9 Av/15 St
L'Acajou	French	19 St/6 Av
La Taza De Oro	Latin American	8 Av/14 St
Le Madri ☆☆	Italian	18 St/6 Av
Le Singe Vert	French	7 Av/19 St
Lotus ☆	New American	14 St/9 Av
Maroons	Southern/Jamaican	16 St/7 Av
Man Ray	New American	15 St/6 Av
Old Homestead	Steakhouse	9 Av/14 St
Republic	Pan-Asian	Union Sq W/17 St
Rocking Horse Cafe	*Mexican/Tex-Mex*	*8 Av/19 St*
Rue des Crepes	Crepes	8 Av/15 St
Snackbar	Seafood/New American	17 St/6 Av
Trois Canards	French	8 Av/19 St
Vox ☆	Bistro/Pan-Latin	8 Av/17 St

THE EAST SIDE

East 100's   On/Near

El Paso Taqueria	Mexican	Lex/104 St
El Rincón Boricua	*Puerto Rican*	*119 St/Lex*
Emily's	Southern	5 Av/111 St
Rao's	Italian	114 St/Pleasant
La Fonda Boricua	Latin American	106 St/3 Av
Patsy's	Pizza	1 Av/117 St

East 90's   On/Near

Barking Dog	Diner	3 Av/94 St
Brother Jimmy's	Barbecue	3 Av/92 St
Nick's Family-Style	Pizza/Italian	2 Av/94 St
92 ☆	New American	92 St/Madison
Osso Buco	Italian	3 Av/93 St
Pascalou	Bistro/French	Madison/93 St
Pintaile's	Pizza	91 St/5 Av
Sarabeth's	New American	Madison/92 St
Sharz	Mediterranean	90 St/3 Av

East 80's   On/Near

Beyoglu	Turkish	3 Av/81 St
Caffe Bella Sera	Pizza	1 Av/84 St
Café Sabarsky ☆☆	Austro-Hungarian	5 Av/86 St
Centolire ☆☆	Italian	Madison/86 St
Dakshin	*Indian*	*1 Av/89 St*
Elaine's	Italian	2 Av/88 St
Emo's	Korean	2 Av/81 St
Etats-Unis ☆☆	New American	81 St/2 Av
Heidelberg	German	2 Av/85 St
Le Refuge	French	82 St/3 Av
Luca	*Italian*	*1 Av/89 St*

Note: Restaurants in **boldface italics** are Eric Asimov's choices for the best inexpensive restaurants in New York

East 80's *(continued)*

		On/Near
Paola's ☆☆	Italian	85 St/2 Av
Penang	Malaysian	2 Av/83 St
Pig Heaven	Chinese	2 Av/80 St
Pintaile's Pizza	Pizza	York/83 St
Primavera ☆	Italian	1 Av/82 St
Saigon Grill	Vietnamese	2 Av/88 St
Taco Taco	*Mexican/Tex-Mex*	*2 Av/89 St*
Totonno Pizzeria	Pizza	2 Av/80 St
Vespa Cibobuono	Italian	2 Av/84 St
Wu Liang Ye	*Chinese*	*86 St/3 Av*
Zócalo ☆	Mexican	82 St/3 Av

East 70's

		On/Near
Ajisai	*Japanese/Sushi*	*1 Av/76 St*
Bandol	French	78 St/Lex
Bistro Le Steak	Bistro/Steak	3 Av/75 St
Brother Jimmy's	Barbecue	1 Av/76 St
Café Boulud ☆☆☆	French	76 St/Madison
Candle Cafe	Vegetarian	3 Av/74 St
Dumonet at the Carlyle ☆☆	French	76 St/Madison
E J's Luncheonette	Diner	3 Av/73 St
Hacienda de Argentina ☆	Argentine	75 St/1 Av
Henry's Evergreen	Chinese	1 Av/70 St
Orsay	Bistro/Brasserie	Lex/75 St
Park View ☆☆	New American	Central Pk/72 St
Payard Pâtisserie ☆☆	Bistro/French	Lex/73 St
Persepolis	Mediterranean	2 Av/75 St
Pintaile's Pizza	Pizza	York/76 St
Q Café	Pan-Latin	79 St/2 Av
Quatorze Bis	Bistro/French	79 St/1 Av
Rafina	Greek/Seafood	York/78 St
Red Bar Restaurant	American/Bistro	75 St/2 Av
Sarabeth's	New American	Madison/75 St
Shabu-Tatsu	Japanese	York/75 St
The Sultan	Turkish	2 Av/74 St
Sushi of Gari	Japanese/Sushi	78 St/1 Av
Toraya	Japanese	71 St/5 Av
Tsuki	*Sushi/Japanese*	*1 Av/75 St*
Usküdar	Turkish	2 Av/73 St
Via Quadronno	Italian/Sandwiches	73 St./Madison

East 60's

		On/Near
Aureole ☆☆	New American	61 St/Madison
Arabelle ☆	French	64 St/Lex
Barbalùc ☆	Italian	65 St/Park
Brasserie 360 ☆☆	French/Sushi	60 St/3 Av
Circus ☆☆	Brazilian	Lex/62 St
Daniel ☆☆☆☆	French	65 St/Park
Gino	Italian	Lex/60 St
John's Pizzeria	Italian/Pizza	64 St/1 Av
Jo Jo ☆☆☆	New American	64 St/Lex
Maya ☆☆	Mexican/Tex-Mex	1 Av/64 St
Nicole's ☆☆	English	60 St/Madison
Park Avenue Cafe	New American	63 St/Park
Patsy's	Pizza	2 Av/69 St
Post House	Steakhouse	63 St/Park
Rain	Pan-Asian	3 Av/62 St
RM ☆☆☆	Seafood	60 St/5 Av
Sushi Seki ☆☆	Japanese/Sushi	1 Av/62 St
Ulrika's	Swedish	60 St/Lex

East 55th–59th

		On/Near
Ada ☆☆	Indian	58 St/2 Av

Bouterin ☆	French	59 St/1 Av
Caviarteria	East European	Park Av/59 St
Da Antonio	Italian	55 St/3 Av
Dawat ☆	Indian	58 St/3 Av
Felidia ☆☆☆	Northern Italian	58 St/2 Av
Fifty Seven Fifty Seven ☆☆☆	American	57 St/Park
Grand Sichuan Eastern	*Chinese*	*2 Av/56 St*
Guastavino's ☆☆	Brasserie/French	59 St/1 Av
Il Valentino ☆☆	Italian	56 St/1 Av
Jimmy's Downtown	Pan-Latin	57 St/1 Av
Le Colonial ☆☆	Vietnamese	57 St/Lex
March ☆☆☆	New American	58 St/1 Av
Nicholson ☆	French	58 St/2 Av
Otabe ☆☆	Japanese	56 St/Park
Our Place Shanghai	*Chinese*	*55 St/3 Av*
P.J. Clarke's	American	3 Av/55 St
Shun Lee Palace ☆☆	Chinese	55 St/Lex
Teodora	Italian	57 St/Lex

East 50th–54th — On/Near

Bice ☆☆	Italian	54 St/5 Av
Billy's	American	1 Av/52 St
Brasserie ☆☆	Brasserie/French	53 St/Lex
Bukhara Grill	*Indian*	*58 St/2 Av*
Caviar Russe	Russian	Madison/54 St
Four Seasons ☆☆☆	New American	52 St/Park
Jubilee	French	54 St/1 Av
La Grenouille ☆☆☆	French	52 St/5 Av
Le Bateau Ivre	Bistro/French	51 St/2 Av
Le Cirque 2000 ☆☆☆	New American	Madison/50 St
Le Perigord ☆☆	French	52 St/1 Av
Lutèce ☆☆	French	50 St/2 Av
Maloney & Porcelli ☆	Steak/Seafood	50 St/Park
Meltemi	Greek/Seafood	1 Av/51 St
Oceana ☆☆	Seafood	54 St/Park
Olica ☆☆☆	French/New American	50 St/Lex
Prime Burger	Hamburgers	51 St/5 Av
San Pietro	Italian	54 St/5 Av
Solera ☆☆	Spanish	53 St/2 Av
Sushi Rose	Japanese/Sushi	52 St/2 Av
Sushisay	Japanese/Sushi	51 St/Park
Tea Box Café	Japanese	5 Av/54 St
Terrance Brennan's ☆☆	Seafood/Steakhouse	Lex/50 St
Vong	Thai/French	54 St/3 Av
Zarela ☆☆	Mexican/Tex-Mex	2 Av/50 St

East 45th–49th — On/Near

Avra ☆	Seafood/Greek	48 St/Lex
Bobby Van's ☆	Steakhouse	Park Av/46 St
Bukhara Grill	*Indian*	*49 St/2 Av*
Cafe Centro ☆☆	Mediterranean	Park Av/45 St
Comfort Diner	Diner	45 St/2 Av
Da Mario	Italian	1 Av/49 St
D'Artagnan ☆☆	French	46 St/Lex
Diwan ☆☆	Indian	48 St/Lex
Django ☆	Bistro/French	Lex/46 St
Heartbeat ☆☆	New American	49 St/Lex
Il Postino	Italian	49 St/1 Av
Katsu-Hama	*Japanese*	*47 St/Madison*
Kurumazushi ☆☆☆	Japanese	47 St/5 Av
Marichu	Spanish	46 St/1 Av
Menchanko-Tei	Japanese/Noodles	45 St/Lex
Ola ☆	Latin American	48 St/2 Av

Note: Restaurants in **boldface italics** are Eric Asimov's choices for the best inexpensive restaurants in New York

East 45th–49th *(continued)*

Pampano ☆☆	Mexican	49 St/3 Av
Patroon ☆	New American	46 St/Lex
Shinbashi	Japanese	Park Av/48 St
Smith & Wollensky ☆☆	Steakhouse	3 Av/49 St
Sparks ☆	Steakhouse	46 St/3 Av
Sushi Masa	Japanese/Sushi	47 St/Lex
Wollensky's Grill	New American	49 St/3 Av

East 40th–44th

On/Near

Branzini ☆	Italian	Madison/41 St
Caviarteria	East European	Grand Central
Dock's ☆	Seafood	3 Av/40 St
Knodel	Scandinavian/Sausages	Grand Central
L'Impero ☆☆☆	Italian	Tudor City/42 St
Maeda	Japanese/Sushi	41 St/5 Av
Metrazur	Mediterranean	Grand Central
Mezze	Mediterranean	44 St/5 Av
Michael Jordan's ☆☆	Steakhouse	Grand Central
Oyster Bar	Seafood	Grand Central
Palm	Steakhouse	2 Av/44 St
Pietro's	Italian/Steakhouse	43 St/2 Av
Sushi Yasuda ☆☆☆	Japanese/Sushi	43 St/3 Av
Tuscan ☆☆	Italian	3 Av/40 St

East 30's

On/Near

Artisanal ☆☆	Bistro	Park/32 St
Asia de Cuba ☆	Asian/Latin	Madison/37 St
Da Ciro	Italian	Lex/33 St
Hangawi ☆☆	Korean/Vegetarian	32 St/5 Av
Icon ☆☆	New American	39 St/Lex
Nadaman Hakubai ☆☆	Japanese	Park/38 St
Patsy's	Pizza	3 Av/34 St
Vanderbilt Station	New American	Park/33 St
Villa Berulia	Italian	34 St/Lex
Water Club ☆☆	New American	30 St/East River
Wu Liang Ye	*Chinese*	*Lex/39 St*

East 20's

On/Near

Anh	*Vietnamese*	*3 Av/27 St*
Beppe	Italian	22 St/Park
Bolo ☆☆☆	Spanish	22 St/Park
Blue Smoke ☆	Barbecue	27 St/Park
Bread Bar at Tabla	*New American/Fusion*	*Madison/25 St*
Dos Caminos	Mexican	Park/26 St
Eleven Madison Park ☆☆	New American	Madison/24 St
Fleur de Sel ☆☆	French	20 St/5 Av
Fresco Tortilla	Mexican/Tex-Mex	Lex/23 St
Gramercy Tavern ☆☆☆	New American	20 St/Bway
I Trulli ☆☆	Italian	27 St/Lex
Les Halles	French	Park/28 St
Morrells ☆	New American	Bway/20 St
Novitá ☆	Italian	22 St/Park
Park Bistro ☆☆☆	Bistro/French	Park/28 St
Patria ☆☆☆	Latin American	Park/20 St
Pongal	*Indian/Veg.*	*Lex/27 St*
Rocco's on 22nd	Italian	22 St/Bway
Salón México ☆	Mexican	26 St/Lex
Sciuscia ☆	Italian/Mediterranean	Park/26 St
Silver Swan	German	20 St/Bway
Tabla ☆☆☆	Pan Asian	Madison/25 St
Tamarind	Indian	22 St/Bway
Turkish Kitchen	Turkish	3 Av/27 St

Union Pacific ☆☆☆	French/Asian	22 St/Park
Vatan ☆☆☆	*Indian*	*3 Av/29 St*
Veritas ☆☆☆	New American	20 St/Park
Via Emilia	Italian	Park/20 St
Yakiniku JuJu	Japanese	28 St/Madison

East 14th–19th

		On/Near
Angelo & Maxie's ☆	Steakhouse	Park Av S/19 St
Blue Velvet 1929	Vietnamese	1 Av/14 St
Candela ☆	New American	16 St/Union Sq
Chat 'n Chew	New American	16 St/5 Av
Craft ☆☆☆	New American	19 St/Bway
Craftbar	*New American*	*19 St/Bway*
Havana Central	Cuban/Pan-Latin	17 St/5 Av
Irving on Irving	New American	Irving/17 St
Lady Mendl's	English	Irving/17 St
Lamu ☆	Global/Mediterranean	19 St/Bway
L'Express	Bistro/French	Park Av S/19 St
Mesa Grill ☆☆	Southwestern	5 Av/15 St
Olives ☆	Mediterranean	Park Av S/17 St
Park Avalon	New American	Park Av S/18 St
Steak Frites	Bistro	16 St/5 Av
Sueños	Mexican	17 St/1 Av
Tocqueville ☆☆	French	15 St/Union Sq W
Union Square Cafe	New American	16 St/5 Av
Verbena ☆☆	New American	Irving/17 St
'Wichcraft	Sandwiches	19 St/Bway
Zen Palate	Vegetarian	Union Sq E/16 St

EAST VILLAGE (BELOW 14TH ST.)

		On/Near
Acquario	Mediterranean	Bleecker/Bowery
Assenzio	Italian	4 St/Av A
Bambou ☆☆	Caribbean	14 St/2 Av
Bar Veloce	Italian/Sandwiches	2 Av/11 St
Boca Chica	Pan-Latin	1 Av/1 St
Brick Lane Curry House	Indian	6 St/1 Av
Bulgin' Waffles	Waffles	1 Av/3 St
Butter ☆	New American	Lafayette/Astor
Caracas Arepa Bar	Venezuelan	7 St/1 Av
Caravan of Dreams	Kosher/Vegetarian	6 St/1 Av
Casa Adela	Caribbean	Av C/5 St
Casimir	Bistro/French	Av B/6 St
Cocina Cuzco	Peruvian	Av A/4 St
Col Legno	Italian	9 St/2 Av
Coup ☆	New American	6 St/Av A
Cyclo	Vietnamese	1 Av/12 St
Daily Chow	Pan-Asian	2 St/Bowery
Danal	New American	10 St/3 Av
Dok Suni	Korean	1 Av/7 St
Elvie's Turo-Turo	Filipino	1 Av/12 St
Esashi	Sushi	Av A/2 St
Esperanto	Pan-Latin	Av C/9 St
Euzkadi	Basque	4 St/1 Av
First	New American	1 Av/5 St
Fish	Seafood	Bleecker/Jones
Flor's Kitchen	Latin American	1 Av/9 St
Frank	Italian	2 Av/5 St
Habib's Place	Middle Eastern	St. Marks/Av A
Holy Basil	*Thai*	*2 Av/9 St*
Il Bagatto	Italian	2 St/Av A
Il Covo dell'Est	Italian	Av A/13 St
Il Posto Accanto	Italian/Sandwiches	2 St/Av B

Note: Restaurants in **boldface italics** are Eric Asimov's choices for the best inexpensive restaurants in New York

East Village *(continued)*

		On/Near
industry(food) ☆	New American	6 St/Av A
Jewel Bako	Sushi	5 St/2 Av
La Paella	Spanish	9 St/2 Av
Lavagna	Mediterranean	5 St/Av B
Leshko's	Diner	Av A/7 St
Le Tableau	Mediterranean	5 St/Av A
Lil' Frankie's Pizza	Pizza	1 Av/2 St
Luca	*Italian*	*Av B/13 St*
Lucien	Bistro/French	1 Av/1 St
Max	Italian	Av B/4 St
Mama's Food Shop	*American*	*3 St/Av A*
Mermaid Inn	*Seafood*	*2 Av/5 St*
Moustache	*Middle Eastern*	*10 St/1 Av*
Muzy	Korean	St. Marks/1 Av
National Cafe	*Spanish*	*1 Av/13 St*
Old Devil Moon	Southern	12 St/Av A
Orologio	Italian	Av A/10 St
Otto ☆☆	Italian	5 Av/8 St
Penang	Malaysian	3 Av/11 St
Pisces	Seafood	Av A/6 St
Pop ☆	New American	4 Av/12 St
Prune	*American/Continental*	*1 St/1 Av*
Raga	French/Indian	6 St/Av A
Sandobe Sushi	Japanese/Sushi	11 St/1 Av
Shabu-Tatsu	Japanese	10 St/1 Av
Soba-Ya	*Japanese/Noodles*	*9 St/2 Av*
Stepmama	Sandwiches	3 St/Av B
Supper	*Italian*	*2 St/Av A*
Tappo ☆	Mediterranean	12 St/1 Av
The Tasting Room ☆	New American	1 St/1 Av
Time Cafe	New American	Lafayette/3 St
Tsampa	Tibetan	9 St/2 Av
26 Seats	French	Av B/11 St
United Noodles	Pan-Asian	12 St/1 Av
Veselka	East European	2 Av/9 St
Vicala	Fusion	Av C/7 St
Xunta	Spanish/Tapas	1 Av/11 St
Yujin ☆	Japanese	12 St/University
Zito's East	Pizza	1 Av/12 St
Zerza	Moroccan	6 St/2 Av
Zum Schneider	German	Av C/7 St

LOWER EAST SIDE

		On/Near
aKa Café	*Fusion*	*Clinton/Rivington*
Alias	*New American*	*Clinton/Rivington*
Capitale ☆☆	New American	Bowery/Grand
Congee Village	*Chinese*	*Orchard/Delancey*
Crudo	Spanish	Clinton/Rivington
Good World Bar & Grill	Scandinavian	Orchard/Division
Katz's Deli	*Deli*	*Houston/Ludlow*
Paladar	Caribbean/Mexican	Ludlow/Stanton
Petrosino	*Italian*	*Norfolk/Houston*
Pho Grand	Vietnamese	Grand/Forsyth
Sammy's Roumanian	Steakhouse	Chrystie/Delancey
Suba ☆	Spanish/Eclectic	Ludlow/Delancey
71 Clinton Fresh Food ☆☆	Bistro/New American	Clinton/Rivington
WD-50 ☆☆	New American	Clinton/Rivington

GREENWICH VILLAGE / WEST VILLAGE

		On/Near
Agave ☆	Southwestern	7 Av/Charles
Alfama ☆	Portuguese	Hudson/Perry

Annissa	New American	Barrow/7 Av
A.O.C. Bedford	Spanish	Bedford/Downing
Babbo ☆☆☆	Italian	Waverly/Macdougal
Bar Pitti	*Italian*	*6 Av/Houston*
Blue Hill ☆☆	French	Washington/6 Av
Blue Ribbon Bakery	New American	Downing/Bedford
Boughalem	New American	Bedford/Halston
Cafe Asean	Southeast Asian	10 St/Greenwich
Cafe de Bruxelles	Belgian	Greenwich/7 Av
Café Topsy	English	Hudson/Bank
Corner Bistro	Bar Snacks	4 St/Jane
Crispo	Italian	14 St/7 Av
Da Andrea	*Italian*	*Hudson/Perry*
Da Silvano	Italian	6 Av/Houston
Deborah	New American	Carmine/Bleecker
E J's	Diner	6 Av/9 St
Florent	French	Gansevoort/ Washington
Gonzo	Pizza/Italian	13 St/7 Av
Good	Pan-Latin	Greenwich/Bank
Gotham Bar and Grill ☆☆☆	New American	12 St/Univ Pl
Gradisca	Italian	13 St/6 Av
Il Mulino	Italian	3 St/Sullivan
'ino	*Italian/Sandwiches*	*Bedford/6 Av*
Inside	New American	Jones/Bleecker
Japonica	Japanese/Sushi	University/12 St
Jarnac ☆	French	12 St/Greenwich
Jefferson ☆☆	New American/Asian	10 St/Greenwich
John's Pizzeria	Italian/Pizza	Bleecker/6 Av
Junno's	Japanese/Korean	Downing/Bedford
Knickerbocker Bar & Grill	Steakhouse	University/9 St
La Metairie	French	10 St/4 St
La Nonna ☆	Italian	13 St/6 Av Greenwich
La Palapa	*Mexican*	*St. Marks/Greene*
La Sandwicherie	Sandwiches/Moroccan	Greenwich/ Gansevoort
Le Gigot	French	Cornelia/4 St
Le Zoo	Bistro/French	11 St/Greenwich
Little Havana	Caribbean	Cornelia/Bleecker
Lupa	*Italian*	*Thompson/Bleecker*
Marumi	Japanese/Sushi	LaGuardia/3 St
Meet ☆	New American	Gansevoort/ Washington
Merge	New American	10 St/Waverly
Mexicana Mama	*Mexican/Tex-Mex*	*Hudson/10 St*
Mi Cocina ☆☆	Mexican/Tex-Mex	Jane/Hudson
Mirchi	*Indian*	*7 Av/Morton*
Moustache	*Middle Eastern*	*Bedford/Grove*
One If By Land, Two If ☆	French	Barrow/4 St
Ony	Japanese/Noodles	6 Av/4 St
Osteria del Sole	Italian	4 St/Perry
Paradou	French/Sandwiches	12 St/9 Av
Paris Commune	French	Bleecker/11 St
Pastis ☆	Bistro/French	9 Av/Little W 12 St
Patsy's Pizzeria	Pizza	University Pl./10 St
Pearl Oyster Bar	*Seafood*	*Cornelia/Bleecker*
Pepe Verde	Italian	Hudson/Perry
Philip Marie	New American	Hudson/11 St
Piadina	Italian	10 St/5 Av
Po	*Italian*	*Cornelia/Bleecker*
Rhone	Bistro/French	Gansevoort/ Greenwich

Note: Restaurants in ***boldface italics*** are Eric Asimov's choices for the best inexpensive restaurants in New York

Greenwich/West Village *(continued)*

		On/Near
Rio Mar	Spanish	9 Av/12
Salam Café	Middle Eastern	13 St/6 Av
Salt	New American	Macdougal/Houston
Sevilla	Spanish	Charles/4 St
Strip House	Steakhouse	12 St/5 Av
Surya ☆☆	Indian	Bleecker/7 Av S
Taka	Japanese/Sushi	Grove/7 Av S
Tanti Baci Caffe	Italian	10 St/7 Av S
Taqueria de Mexico	Mexican/Tex-Mex	Greenwich/12 St
Tea & Sympathy	English	Greenwich/12 St
Thali	Vegetarian	Greenwich/10 St
Time Cafe	New American	7 Av S./Barrow
Tomoe Sushi	Japanese/Sushi	Thompson/Bleecker
Tortilla Flats	Mexican/Tex-Mex	Washington/12 St
Village	9 St/5 Av	Bistro/French
Villa Mosconi	Italian	Macdougal/Bleecker
Voyage	Bistro	Perry/Greenwich
Washington Park ☆☆	New American	5 Av/9 St
Zipangu ☆	Japanese	University/10 St
Zitoune ☆	Moroccan	Gansevoort/ Greenwich

CHINATOWN

Congee	*Chinese*	*Bowery/Grand*
Dim Sum Go Go	Chinese	E. Bway/Chatham
Excellent Dumpling House	Chinese	Lafayette/Canal
Funky Broome	*Chinese*	*Mott/Broome*
Goody's ☆	Chinese	E. Bway/Chatham
Grand Sichuan ☆	Chinese	Canal/Bowery
Jing Fong	Chinese	Elizabeth/Bayard
Joe's Shanghai ☆☆	Chinese	Pell/Bowery
New Green Bo	Chinese	Bayard/Mott
Nha Trang	*Vietnamese*	*Baxter/White*
Nha Trang	*Vietnamese*	*Centre/Walker*
Onieal's Grand Street ☆	New American	Grand/Centre
Ping's Seafood	Chinese/Seafood	Mott/Worth
Sunrise 27	Chinese	Division/Market
Sweet 'n' Tart Cafe	Chinese	Mott/Canal
Triple Eight Palace	Chinese	E. Bway/Division
Shanghai Cuisine	Chinese	Bayard/Mulberry
Tai Hong Lau	Chinese	Mott/Canal

SOHO/TRIBECA

		On/Near
Aquagrill ☆☆	Seafood	Spring/6 Av
Arqua ☆☆	Italian	Warren/ W. Broadway
Azafron ☆	Spanish/Tapas	Spring/Lafayette
Balthazar ☆☆	Brasserie/French	Spring/Lafayette
Baluchi's	Indian	Spring/Sullivan
Bistrot Margot	Bistro/French	Prince/Mott
Blue Ribbon	New American	Sullivan/Prince
Blue Ribbon Sushi ☆☆	Japanese/Sushi	Sullivan/Prince
Bouley ☆☆☆☆	French	W. Broadway/Duane
Bread	Sandwiches	Spring/Elizabeth
Cafe Colonial	New American	Houston/Elizabeth
Cafe Habana	Latin American	Prince/Elizabeth
Cafe Juniper	New American	Duane/Greenwich
Café Lebowitz	New American	Spring/Elizabeth
Canteen	New American	Mercer/Prince
Caviarteria	East European	W. Broadway/Canal

Restaurant	Cuisine	Location
Chanterelle ☆☆☆	French	Harrison/Hudson
City Hall ☆☆	New American	Duane/Church
Cupping Room	New American	W. Bway/Broome
Danube ☆☆☆	Viennese/German	Hudson/Duane
Downtown ☆	Italian	W. Bway/Broome
Ear Inn	Bar Snacks	Spring/Greenwich
Eight Mile Creek ☆☆	Australian	Mulberry/Prince
El Teddy's	Mexican/Tex-Mex	W. Bway/White
F.illi Ponte	Italian	Desbrosses/West
Franklin Station	Southeast Asian	W. Bway/Franklin
Fresh ☆☆	Seafood	Reade/W. Bway
Ghenet	African	Mulberry/Houston
Grace	New American	Franklin/Church
The Harrison ☆☆	New American	Greenwich/Harrison
Herban Kitchen	Vegetarian	Hudson/Spring
Honmura An ☆☆☆	Japanese/Noodles	Mercer/Houston
Isla	Pan-Latin/Cuban	Downing/Bedford
Island Grill	Caribbean	Lafayette/Centre
Jane ☆	New American/Bistro	Houston/Thompson
Jean Claude	Bistro/French	Sullivan/Prince
Kana	Spanish	Spring/Greenwich
Kelley & Ping	Noodles/Thai	Greene/Houston
Kitchen Club	French/Japanese	Prince/Mott
Kitchenette	New American	W. Bway/Warren
Kori	*Korean*	*Church/Leonard*
Layla ☆☆	Middle Eastern/Mediterranean	W. Bway/Franklin
L'ecole	French	Bway/Grand
Le Gamin	French	Macdougal/Houston
Le Zinc	Bistro	Duane/Church
The Little Place	Mexican	W. Bway/Warren
Lombardi's	*Pizza*	*Spring/Mulberry*
Lozoo ☆	Chinese	Houston/Sullivan
L'ulivo Focacceria	Italian/Pizza	Spring/Thompson
Lunchbox Food Company	*Diner/American*	*West/Clarkson*
Mekong	Vietnamese	Prince/Mulberry
Mercer Kitchen ☆☆	French	Prince/Mercer
Montrachet ☆☆☆	French	W. Broadway/White
Nam	*Vietnamese*	*Reade/W. Bway*
Nam Phuong	Vietnamese	Sixth Av/Walker
Next Door Nobu ☆☆☆	Japanese	Hudson/Franklin
NL	Dutch/Indonesian	Sullivan/Houston
Nobu ☆☆☆	Japanese	Hudson/Franklin
Odeon ☆☆	French/American	W. Bway/Thomas
Palacinka	Crepes	Grand/6 Av
Pão	Portuguese	Spring/Greenwich
Peasant ☆	Italian	Elizabeth/Prince
Penang	Malaysian	Spring/Mercer
Pepolino	Italian	W. Bway/Lispenard
Pintxos	Spanish	Greenwich/Spring
Pravda	Russian	Lafayette/Prince
Provence ☆	French	MacDougal/Prince
Raoul's	Bistro/French	Prince/Sullivan
Rice	PanAsian	Mott/Spring
Risa	Pizza/Italian	Houston/Mulberry
Ruben's Empanadas	Latin American	Bridge/White
Salaam Bombay ☆☆	Indian	Greenwich/Duane
Savore	Italian	Spring/Sullivan
Savoy	New American	Prince/Crosby
Scalini Fedeli ☆	Italian	Duane/Hudson
Screening Room ☆☆	New American	Varick/Canal
66 ☆☆	Chinese	Church/Leonard
Snack	*Greek*	*Thompson/Prince*

Note: Restaurants in *boldface italics* are Eric Asimov's choices for the best inexpensive restaurants in New York

SoHo/TriBeCa *(continued)*

		On/Near
SoHo Kitchen & Bar	New American	Greene/Spring
Soho Steak	Bistro/Steak	Thompson/Spring
Sosa Borella	Latin American	Greenwich/ Desbrosses
Thom ☆	Fusion/New American	Thompson/Broome
Tribeca Grill ☆☆	New American	Greenwich/Franklin
Va Tutto!	Italian	Cleveland/Kenmare
Walker's	Bar Snacks	N. Moore/Varick

FINANCIAL DISTRICT

		On/Near
American Park ☆	New American	Battery Park/State
Bayard's ☆☆	New American	Hanover Sq/Pearl
Bennie's Thai Café	Thai	Fulton/Gold
Delmonico's ☆	New American	Beaver/Williams
14 Wall Street ☆	French/New American	Wall/Bway
Harry's	Continental	Hanover Sq/Stone
Les Halles Downtown ☆	French	John St/Bway
MarkJoseph Steakhouse ☆	Steakhouse	Water/Peck Slip
Ruben's Empanadas	Latin American	Fulton/Gold
2 West	New American	West/Battery Pl
Vine ☆	New American	Broad/Exchange

THE BRONX

The Feeding Tree	Caribbean
Vernon's New Jerk House	Jamaican

BROOKLYN

Bay Ridge
Lento's	Italian

Boerum Hill
Saul	New American
Tuk Tuk	Thai

Brooklyn Heights
Gage & Tollner	Seafood
Kapadokya	Turkish
River Café ☆☆	New American
Tin Room Cafe	Italian

Carroll Gardens
Alma	Mexican
Banania Cafe	Bistro/French
Ferdinando's Focacceria	*Italian*
Patois	French
Sur	Latin American

Clinton Hill
Locanda Vini & Olii	*Italian*

Coney Island
Totonno Pizzeria	Pizza

Fort Greene
Cambodian Cuisine	Southeast Asian

Greenpoint
Lomzynianka	Polish

Midwood
DiFara Pizza — *Pizza*

Park Slope
Al Di La — *Italian*
Bistro St. Mark's — *Bistro*
Blue Ribbon Brooklyn — American/Seafood
Blue Ribbon Sushi (Brooklyn) ☆ — Japanese/Sushi
Coco Roco — Latin American
Cocotte — French/Bistro
Cucina ☆ — Italian
Lento's — Italian
Long Tan — Thai
Milan's — East European
Rose Water — New American/Mediterranean

Prospect Heights
Biscuit — Southern/Barbecue
Garden Café — *New American*

Red Hook
Hope & Anchor — Diner/American

Sunset Park
Tequilita's — Mexican/Tex-Mex

Williamsburg
Bahia — Salvadoran
Chickenbone Café — *New American*
Diner — *Diner/Steakhouse*
DuMont — New American
Fernicola Osteria — Italian
Khao Sarn — Thai
Miss Williamsburg — Diner
Oznot's Dish — Mediterranean
Peter Luger ☆☆☆ — Steakhouse
Plan-Eat Thailand — Thai

QUEENS
Astoria
Arharn Thai — Thai
Balkh Shish Kebab House — Middle Eastern
Cavo — Italian
Christos Hasapo-Taverna — Greek/Steakhouse
Churrascaria Girassol — *Brazilian*
Demetris — Greek
Elias Corner — Greek
Mombar — Middle Eastern
Ubol's Kitchen — Thai
Uncle George's — Greek

Corona
Bajo el Puente — Peruvian
El Gauchito — Latin American
Green Field — Latin American
La Esquina Criolla — *South American*

Elmhurst
Joe's Shanghai — Chinese

Note: Restaurants in ***boldface italics*** are Eric Asimov's choices for the best inexpensive restaurants in New York

Flushing

East Buffet & Restaurant	*Chinese*
Joe's Shanghai	Chinese
K.B. Garden	Chinese
Master Grill	Brazilian
New Lok Kee	Chinese
Pachas	South American/Latin American
Penang	Malaysian
Shanghai Tang	Chinese
Sweet 'n'Tart Cafe	Chinese
Szechuan Gourmet	Chinese
Woo Chon	Korean

Jackson Heights

Delhi Palace	Indian
Jackson Diner	Indian
Kabab King Diner	*Pakistani*
Malaysian Rasa Sayang	Malaysian
Nostalgias	Latin American
Pearson's Texas Barbecue	*Barbecue*
Tibetan Yak	Tibetan
Tierras Colombianas	Latin American

Long Island City

Bella Via	Italian
Tournesol	*Bistro/French*
Manetta's	Pizza/Italian

Rego Park

Goody's	Chinese
Kazan Turkish Cuisine	Turkish

Sunnyside

Chipper	English
La Lupe	Mexican/Tex-Mex

Woodside

La Flor	Eclectic
Sapori d'Ischia	Italian
Sripraphai	*Thai*

STATEN ISLAND

Aesop's Tables	French/New American

A Guide to Restaurants by Cuisine

Afghani
Balkh Shish Kebab
Kabul Cafe

African
Meskerem
Queen of Sheba
Tagine

American
The Algonquin
Alice's Tea Cup
Billy's
Fifty Seven Fifty Seven
☆☆☆
The Half King
Hope & Anchor
Knickerbocker
*Lunchbox Food
        Company*
Mama's Food Shop
Max SoHa
Mickey Mantle's
P.J. Clarke's
Prune
Red Bar Restaurant
Trailer Park

*See also: Barbecue, Bar
Snacks, Diner, Ham-
burgers, New American,
Southern, Southwestern,
and Steakhouse*

Argentine
Chimichurri Grill
Cooke's Corner
El Gauchito
Hacienda de
        Argentina ☆
Pampa
Sosa Borella
Sur

Australian
Eight Mile Creek ☆☆

Austro-Hungarian
Café Sabarsky ☆☆

Balkan
Djerdan Burek

Bar Snacks
Corner Bistro
Ear Inn
Walker's

Barbecue
Biscuit
Blue Smoke ☆

Brother Jimmy's BBQ
Pearson's
Virgil's Real BBQ

Basque
Euzkadi

Belgian
Cafe de Bruxelles

Bistro
Artisanal ☆☆
Banania Cafe
Barrio ☆
Bistro St. Mark's
Cocotte
Django ☆
Jean-Luc ☆
Le Zinc ☆
Orsay ☆☆
Pop ☆
Rhone
71 Clinton ☆☆
Tournesol
Village
Vox ☆
Voyage ☆

Brasserie
Balthazar ☆☆
Brasserie ☆☆
Brasserie 8 $1/2$ ☆
Guastavino's ☆☆
Les Halles
Pastis ☆

Brazilian
Churrascaria
        Plataforma
Churrascaria Girassol
Master Grill
Rice 'n' Beans

Cajun/Creole
Bayou

Caribbean
Bambou ☆☆
Caribbean Spice
Casa Adela
El Presidente
The Feeding Tree
Island Grill
Little Havana
Maroons
Paladar
Vernon's

Chinese
China Fun
Congee
Congee Village

Dim Sum Go Go ☆
East Buffet
Excellent Dumpling
        House
Funky Broome
Grand Sichuan
Grand Sichuan Eastern
Henry's Evergreen
Jing Fong
Joe's Shanghai ☆☆
K.B. Garden
Lozoo ☆
New Green Bo
New Lok Kee
Nha Trang
Our Place
Pig Heaven
Ping's ☆☆
Ping's Seafood
Shanghai Cuisine
Shanghai Tide
Shun Lee Palace ☆☆
Shun Lee West
66 ☆☆
Sunrise 27
Sweet 'n' Tart Cafe
Szechuan Gourmet
Tai Hong Lau
38th Street Restaurant
Triple Eight Palace
Wu Liang Ye

Continental
Cafe des Artistes
Cal's
Prune

Crepes
Palacinka
Rue des Crepes

Deli
Artie's
Barney Greengrass
Carnegie Deli
Katz's Deli
Stage Deli

Diner
Barking Dog
Coffee Shop
Diner
E J's
Edison Cafe
Empire Diner
Hope & Anchor
Leshko's
*Lunchbox Food
        Company*
Miss Williamsburg

Note: Restaurants in **boldface italics** are Eric Asimov's choices for the best
inexpensive restaurants in New York

East European
Caviarteria
Milan's
Veselka

English
Chipper
Chip Shop
Café Topsy
Lady Mendl's
Nicole's ☆☆
Tea & Sympathy

Fast Food
F&B
Knodel

French
Aix ☆☆
Alain Ducasse ☆☆☆☆
Alouette
Arabelle ☆
Avenue
Atelier ☆☆☆
Balthazar ☆☆
Banania Cafe
Bandol
Bayard's ☆☆
Bistro Le Steak
Bistrot Margot
Blue Hill ☆☆
Bouley Bakery ☆☆☆☆
Bouterin ☆
Brasserie ☆☆
Brasserie 8 ¹/₂ ☆
Brasserie 360 ☆☆
Café Boulud ☆☆☆
Cafe Centro ☆☆
Casimir
Chanterelle ☆☆☆
Chelsea Bistro ☆☆
Chez Josephine ☆☆
Cocotte
Daniel ☆☆☆☆
D'Artagnan ☆
Django ☆
Dumonet ☆☆
Florent
Fleur de Sel ☆☆
14 Wall Street ☆
Guastavino's ☆☆
Jarnac ☆
Jean Claude
Jean Georges ☆☆☆☆
Jean-Luc ☆
Jubilee
Kitchen Club
L'Acajou
La Caravelle ☆☆☆
La Côte Basque ☆☆☆
La Grenouille ☆☆☆
La Metairie
La Tour
Le Bateau Ivre
Le Bernardin ☆☆☆☆
Cirque 2000 ☆☆☆
L'ecole

Le Gamin
Le Gigot
Le Madeleine
Le Perigord ☆☆
Le Refuge
Les Halles
Les Halles Downtown ☆
Le Singe Vert
Le Tableau
L'Express
Le Zoo
Lucien
Lutèce ☆☆
Marseille ☆☆
Mercer Kitchen ☆☆
Metisse
Montrachet ☆☆☆
Nice Matin ☆☆
Nicholson ☆
Odeon ☆☆
Olica ☆☆☆
One If By Land ☆
Paradou
Paris Commune
Park Bistro ☆☆☆
Pascalou
Pastis ☆
Patois
Payard Pâtisserie ☆☆
Picholine ☆☆☆
Provence ☆
Quatorze Bis
Raoul's
René Pujol
Rhone
Tocqueville ☆☆
Tournesol
Tout Va Bien
Triomphe ☆☆
Trois Canards
26 Seats
Union Pacific ☆☆☆
Village

Fusion
aKa Café
AZ ☆☆☆
Bread Bar at Tabla
Citarella ☆☆
Thali
Thom ☆
Verbena ☆
Vicala

German
Hallo Berlin
Heidelberg
Roetelle A.G.
Silver Swan
Zum Schneider

Greek
Avra ☆
Christos Hasapo
Demetris
Elias Corner
Estiatorio Milos ☆☆

Meltemi
Metsovo
Molyvos ☆☆
Rafina
Snack
Thias
Uncle George's
Uncle Nick's

Hamburgers
Island Burgers
Mickey Mantle's
Prime Burger

Indian
Ada ☆☆
Brick Lane
Bukhara Grill
Dakshin
Dawat ☆
Delhi Palace
Diwan's
Diwan ☆☆
Jackson Diner
Mirchi
Mughlai
Pongal
Raga
Royal Kebab
Salaam Bombay ☆☆
Sapphire
Shaan
Surya ☆☆
Tamarind ☆☆
Taprobane
Vatan

Indonesian
Bali Nusa Indah
NL

Italian
Al Di La
Amarone
Arqua ☆☆
Arezzo ☆
Assenzio
Babbo ☆☆☆
Baldoria
Barbalùc ☆
Bar Pitti
Bar Veloce
Barbetta
Becco
Bella Via
Beppe ☆☆
Bice ☆☆
Biricchino
Bottino
Branzini ☆
Bricco
Cafe La Grolla
Carmine's
Cavo
Celeste
Centolire ☆☆
Ciao Europa

Col Legno
Crispo
Cucina ☆
Da Andrea
Da Antonio
Da Ciro
Da Mario
Da Nico
Da Silvano
Delmonico's
Don Peppe's
Elaine's
Esca ☆☆
Felidia ☆☆☆
Ferdinando's
Fernicola Osteria ☆
F.Illi Ponte
Frank
Gennaro
Gino
Gonzo
Gradisca
Il Bagatto
Il Covo dell'Est
Il Gattopardo ☆☆
Il Mulino
Il Postino
Il Posto Accanto
Il Valentino ☆☆
'ino
I Trulli ☆☆
Isola
La Grolla ☆
La Locanda
La Nonna ☆
La Vineria
Le Madri ☆☆
Lento's
Le Zie 2000
L'Impero ☆☆☆
Locanda Vini & Olii
Luca
L'ulivo
Lupa
Luxia
Manetta's
Max
Max SoHa
Miss Williamsburg
Moda ☆☆
Nick's
Novitá ☆
Orologio
Orso
Osso Buco
Osteria del Circo ☆
Osteria del Sole
Otto ☆☆
Paola's ☆☆
Patsy's
Peasant ☆
Pepe Verde
Pepolino
Petrosino

Piadina
Pietro's
Po
Primavera ☆
Puttanesca
Rainbow Grill
Rao's
Remi ☆☆
Rocco's on 22nd
San Domenico ☆☆
San Pietro
Sapori d'Ischia
Savore
Scalini Fedeli ☆
Sciuscia ☆
Supreme Macaroni Co.
Tanti Baci
Teodora
Tin Room Cafe
Trionfo Ristorante
Tuscan
Tuscan Square
Va Tutto!
Vespa Cibobuono
Via Emilia
Viceversa
Via Quadronno
Villa Berulia
Villa Mosconi
Vivolo

Japanese
Ajisai
Blue Ribbon Sushi ☆☆
Blue Ribbon Sushi
  (Brooklyn) ☆
Esashi
Honmura An ☆☆☆
Japonica
Junno's
Katsu-Hama
Kitchen Club
Kurumazushi ☆☆☆
Maeda Sushi
Marumi
Menchanko-Tei
Nadaman Hakubai ☆☆
Next Door Nobu ☆☆☆
Nobu ☆☆☆
Otabe ☆☆
Ony
Sandobe Sushi
Shabu-Tatsu
Shinbashi
Soba Nippon
Soba-Ya
Supper
Sushiden
Sushi Masa
Sushi of Gari
Sushi Rose
Sushisay
Sushi Seki ☆☆
Sushi Yasuda ☆☆☆

Sushi Zen
Taka
Teodora ☆
Tomoe
Toraya
Tsuki
Ya Bowl
Yakiniku JuJu
Yujin ☆
Zipangu ☆

Korean
Cho Dang Gol ☆☆
Do Hwa
Dok Suni
Emo's
Han Bat
Hangawi ☆☆
Junno's
Kori
Mill Korean
Mandoo Bar
Muzy
New York Kom Tang
Kalbi House
36 Bar and Barbecue ☆
Woo Chon
Yang Pyung Seoul

Kosher
Caravan of Dreams
Levana
Pongal
Sammy's

Latin American
Asia de Cuba ☆
Bahia
Boca Chica
Cabo Rojo
Cafe Con Leche
Cafe Habana
Caracas Arepa Bar
Chimichurri Grill
Churrascaria
Plataforma ☆☆
Circus ☆☆
Cocina Cuzco
Coco Roco
El Gauchito
El Presidente
El Rincón Boricua
Flor's Kitchen
Hacienda de
        Argentina ☆
Havana NY
Ipanema
La Esquina Criolla
La Fonda Boricua
La Taza De Oro
National Cafe
Nostalgias
Ola
Old San Juan
Pachas

Note: Restaurants in ***boldface italics*** are Eric Asimov's choices for the best inexpensive restaurants in New York

Pampa
Patria ☆☆☆
Rinconcito Peruano
Ruben's Empanadas
Sosa Borella
Sur
Tierras Colombianas
Victor's Cafe 52

Malaysian
Malaysian Rasa Sayang
Penang

Mediterranean
Acquario
Gus's Figs
Lavagna
Layla ☆☆
Le Tableau
Lamu ☆
Marseille ☆☆
Metrazur
Mezze
Nick and Toni's ☆☆
Olives ☆
Ouest ☆☆
Oznot's Dish
Persepolis
Picholine ☆☆☆
Sciuscia ☆
Sharz Cafe & Wine Bar
Tappo ☆

Mexican/
Tex-Mex
Alma
Café Frida
Dos Caminos
El Teddy's
El Paso Taqueria
Fresco Tortilla Grill
Gabriela's
Hell's Kitchen
La Lupe
La Palapa
The Little Place
Los Dos Rancheros
Maya ☆☆
Mexicana Mama
Mi Cocina ☆☆
Noche ☆
Noche Mexicana
Paladar
Pampano ☆☆
Q Café
Rinconcito Mexicano
Rocking Horse
Rosa Mexicano
Salón México ☆
Sueños
Taco Taco
Taqueria de Mexico
Tequila's
Tortilla Flats
Zarela ☆☆
Zócalo ☆

Middle Eastern
Balkh
Habib's Place
Hoomoos Asli
Layla ☆☆
Mombar
Moustache
Salam Café
Turkuaz
Zerza

New American
Aesop's Tables
Alias
American Park ☆
Amuse ☆☆
Annissa
Aureole ☆☆
Bayard's ☆☆
Blue Ribbon
Blue Ribbon Brooklyn
Bread Bar at Tabla
Bright Food Shop
Butter ☆
Café Lebowitz
Candela Restaurant ☆
Canteen
Chickenbone Café
Capitale ☆☆
Chat 'n Chew
City Hall ☆☆
Compass ☆☆
Coup ☆
Craft ☆☆☆
Craftbar
Cupping Room
Danal
Deborah
Delmonico's ☆
District ☆
DuMont
11 Madison Pk ☆☆
Etats-Unis ☆☆
First
Four Seasons ☆☆☆
14 Wall Street ☆
Fred's
Good
Gotham ☆☆☆
Grace
Gramercy Tavern ☆☆☆
Green Table
The Grocery
The Harrison ☆☆
Heartbeat ☆☆
Herban Kitchen
Icon ☆☆
Ida Mae Kitchen ☆
Ilo ☆☆☆
industry(food) ☆
Inside
Jack Rose
Jane ☆
Jefferson ☆☆
Joe Allen
Jo Jo ☆☆☆
Josie's

Judson Grill ☆☆☆
Kitchenette
Le Cirque 2000 ☆☆☆
Levana
Larry Forgione's
       Signature Cafe
Lotus ☆
Lola
Lot 61
Man Ray ☆
March ☆☆☆
Meet ☆
Merge
Metrazur
Michael's ☆☆
Morrell
Morrells ☆
92 ☆
Odeon ☆☆
Onieal's Grand Street ☆
Olica ☆☆☆
Panorama Cafe
Parish & Company ☆
Park Avalon
Park Avenue Cafe ☆☆
Park View ☆☆
Patroon ☆
Philip Marie
Pop ☆
The Red Cat ☆
Redeye Grill ☆
River Café ☆☆
Rose Water
Sarabeth's
Salt
Saul
Savoy
Screening Room ☆☆
71 Clinton ☆☆
Snackbar
SoHo Kitchen & Bar
The Tasting Room ☆
Tavern on the Green ☆
Thom ☆
Time Cafe
The Tonic ☆☆
Town ☆☆☆
Tribeca Grill ☆☆
"21" Club ☆☆
2 West
Union Square Cafe
       ☆☆☆
Upstairs at "21" ☆☆
Vanderbilt Station
Verbena ☆☆
Veritas ☆☆☆
Vince & Eddie's
Vine ☆
Washington Park ☆☆
Water Club ☆☆
WD-50 ☆☆
Wollensky's Grill

Noodles
Honmura An ☆☆☆
Kelley & Ping
Menchanko-Tei

Ony
Republic
Soba-Ya

Pakistani
Kabab King Diner

Pan-Asian
Asia de Cuba ☆
AZ
Cafe Asean
Daily Chow
Pop ☆
Rain
Republic
Rice
Ruby Foo's ☆☆
Tabla ☆☆☆
United Noodles

Pan-Latin
Boca Chica
Calle Ocho ☆
Esperanto
Good
Havana Central
Isla
Jimmy's Downtown
Patria ☆☆☆
Republi'K
Vox ☆

Peruvian
Bajo el Puente

Pizza
Caffe Bella Sera
Celeste
DiFara Pizza
Gonzo
John's
Lil' Frankie's Pizza
Lombardi's
L'ulivo
Manetta's
Nick's
Patsy's
Pintaile's
Risa
Sal's and Carmine's
Totonno

Polish
Lomzynianka

Portuguese
Alfama ☆
Pão

Russian
Caviar Russe
Firebird ☆☆
Petrossian ☆☆
Pravda

Sandwiches
Bread
La Sandwicherie

Paradou
'Wichcraft

Scandinavian
Aquavit ☆☆☆
Good World
Knodel
Ulrika's

Seafood
Aquagrill ☆☆
Avra ☆
Blue Water Grill ☆
Blue Fin ☆☆
Bongo
Citarella ☆☆
Dock's ☆
Elias Corner
Esca ☆☆
Estiatorio Milos ☆☆
Fish
Fresh ☆☆
Gage & Tollner
Le Bernardin ☆☆☆☆
Manhattan Ocean Club
☆☆
Meltemi
Mermaid Inn
Ocean Grill ☆
Oceana ☆☆
Oyster Bar
Pearl Oyster Bar
Pisces
Rafina
RM ☆☆☆
Sea Grill ☆☆
Shaffer City Oyster Bar
Snackbar
Svenningsen's
Terrance Brennan's ☆☆
Thias

Southeast Asian
Cafe Asean
Cambodian Cuisine
Elvie's Turo-Turo
Franklin Station Cafe
Penang

Southern
Amy Ruth's
Bayou
Biscuit
Charles'
Copeland's
Emily's
Ida Mae Kitchen ☆
Maroons
Miss Maude's
Old Devil Moon
Pan Pan
Soul Cafe
Soul Fixins'
Sylvia's

Southwestern
Agave ☆

Mesa Grill ☆☆

Spanish
A.O.C. Bedford
Azafron ☆
Bolo ☆☆☆
Crudo
Cafe Riazor
El Cid
Kāna
La Paella
Marichu
National Cafe
Pintxos
Rio Mar
Sevilla
Solera ☆☆
Suba ☆
Xunta

Sri Lankan
Lakruwana
Taprobane

Steakhouse
Angelo & Maxie's ☆
Ben Benson's ☆
Bistro Le Steak
Bobby Van's ☆
Carne
Christos Hasapo
Churrascaria
Plataforma ☆☆
Cité
Frank's ☆
Jack Rose
Keens
Knickerbocker Bar
Maloney & Porcelli ☆
MarkJoseph ☆
Michael Jordan's ☆☆
Old Homestead
Palm
Peter Luger ☆☆☆
Pietro's
Post House
Ruth's Chris
Sammy's Roumanian
Smith & Wollensky ☆☆
Soho Steak
Sparks ☆
Strip House ☆
Terrance Brennan's ☆☆
Tupelo Grill
Wollensky's Grill

Sushi
Ajisai
Blue Ribbon Sushi ☆☆
Blue Ribbon Sushi
(Brooklyn) ☆
Brasserie 360 ☆☆
Esashi
Japonica
Jewel Bako
Kurumazushi
Maeda

331

Marumi
Sandobe Sushi
Sushiden
Sushi Masa
Sushi of Gari
Sushi Rose
Sushisay
Sushi Seki ☆☆
Sushi Yasuda ☆☆☆
Sushi Zen
Taka
Tomoe Sushi
Tsuki

Tapas
Azafron ☆
Dalia's
Sabor
Solera ☆☆
Xunta

Thai
Arharn Thai
The Basil ☆
Bennie's Thai Café
Holy Basil

Kelley & Ping
Khao Sarn
Long Tan
Pam Real Thai Food
Plan Eat Thailand
Royal Siam
Sripraphai
Topaz Thai
Tuk Tuk
Ubol's Kitchen
Vong
Wondee Siam II

Tibetan
Tibetan Yak
Tsampa

Turkish
Beyoglu
Hoomoos Asli
Kapadokya
Kazan Turkish Cuisine
The Sultan
Turkish Kitchen
Turkuaz
Uskudar

Vegetarian
Candle Cafe
Caravan of Dreams
Hangawi ☆☆
Herban Kitchen
Pongal
Zen Palate

Vietnamese
Anh
Blue Velvet 1929
Cyclo
Le Colonial ☆☆
Mekong
Nam
Nam Phuong
Nha Trang
O Mai
Pho Grand
Saigon Grill

Viennese
Danube ☆☆☆
Wallsé ☆☆

KITTICHAI GO THOMPSON
THAI 12.2.07

Note: Restaurants in **boldface italics** are Eric Asimov's choices for the best inexpensive restaurants in New York